DEAL WITH THE DEVIL

DEAL WITH THE DEVIL

THE FBI'S SECRET THIRTY-YEAR RELATIONSHIP WITH A MAFIA KILLER

PETER LANCE

wm
WILLIAM MORROW
An Imprint of HarperCollins*Publishers*

HarperCollins books may be purchased for educational, business, or sales promotional use. For information please write: Special Markets Department, HarperCollins Publishers, 10 East 53rd Street, New York, NY 10022.

FIRST EDITION

Library of Congress Cataloging-in-Publication Data has been applied for.

ISBN 978-0-06-145534-6

13 14 15 16 17 NMSG/RRD 10 9 8 7 6 5 4 3 2 1

To the families of Mary Bari, Patrick Porco, and the dozens
of other murder victims who were killed by Gregory Scarpa Sr.,
or killed on his orders, during the three decades he was
protected by the FBI as a Top Echelon informant

If I don't have my money by Thursday, I'll put him right in the fucking hospital. . . . I wanna break his mother's face and break his fuckin' legs and arms.
—Greg Scarpa Sr., recorded on a series of FBI wiretaps[1]

He told me he stopped counting at fifty [murders].
—Larry Mazza, Scarpa's protégé and co-conspirator[2]

In my heart, as Scarpa's handler, of course I knew he was doing hits. . . .[3]
A defense lawyer asked me on the stand if I admired Scarpa. I said I admired the way the man was able to conduct himself in such a treacherous environment and survive all the years he had survived without getting killed. That takes a special talent.[4]
—Former FBI Supervisory Special Agent R. Lindley DeVecchio,
Greg Scarpa Sr.'s contacting agent

A line had been blurred. . . . He was compromised. He had lost track of who he was.
—FBI Special Agent Chris Favo, DeVecchio's number two in the FBI's
Colombo Squad, on DeVecchio's relationship with Scarpa[5]

This is the most stunning example of official corruption that I have ever seen.
—Brooklyn DA Charles Hynes after indicting DeVecchio on four counts
of murder in 2006 relating to his alleged leaks to Scarpa[6]

I will never forgive the Brooklyn DA for irresponsibly pursuing this case.
—Lin DeVecchio after the dismissal of
murder charges against him in 2007[7]

What is undeniable was that in the face of the obvious menace posed by organized crime, the FBI was willing . . . to make their own deal with the devil. They gave Scarpa virtual criminal immunity . . . in return for the information, true and false, he willingly supplied. . . . Not only did the FBI shield Scarpa from prosecution for his own crimes, they also actively recruited him to participate in crimes under their direction. That a thug like Scarpa would be employed by the federal government . . . is a shocking demonstration of the government's unacceptable willingness to employ criminality to fight crime.
—Judge Gustin Reichbach after the DeVecchio
murder case was dismissed[8]

CONTENTS

PART III

PART IV

PART V

INTRODUCTION

Gregory Scarpa Sr. was a study in complication. A peacock dresser, he carried a wad of $5,000 in cash at all times.[1] He wore a seven-carat pinky ring and a diamond-studded watch.[2] He made millions from drug dealing, hijackings, loan sharking, high-end jewelry scores, bank heists, and stolen securities. He owned homes in Las Vegas, Brooklyn, Florida, and Staten Island, and a co-op apartment on Manhattan's exclusive Sutton Place. He was the biggest trafficker in stolen credit cards in New York and ran an international auto theft ring.[3] A single bank robbery by his notorious Bypass crew on the July 4 weekend in 1974 netted $15 million in thirteen duffel bags full of cash and jewels.[4] His sports betting operation made $2.5 million a year. His crew grossed $70,000 weekly in drug sales.[5] And yet, fifteen years after becoming a "made" member of the Colombo crime family, when he was a senior capo, Scarpa was arrested for "pilfering" coins from a pay phone.[6] He simply couldn't resist a chance to steal—even a handful of change from the phone company.

Five foot ten, two hundred and twenty pounds,[7] Scarpa was described by one of his FBI contacting agents as "an ox of a man; like a short piano mover [with a] thick neck and huge biceps."[8] For more than forty-two years, as a made member of the Colombo family (borgata), he roamed the streets of Brooklyn like a feudal lord, earning the nicknames "the Grim Reaper,"[9] "the Mad Hatter,"[10] "Hannibal Lecter,"[11] and "the Killing Machine."[12] He even signed personal letters with the initials "KM."[13]

**Greg Scarpa Sr., a.k.a.
"the Grim Reaper"**

But Scarpa was also a homebody with three separate families. In 1949 he married Connie Forrest. They had four children, including Gregory Jr.,[14] who started doing crimes for his father at the age of sixteen.[15] Then, while still married to Connie, whom he shipped off to New Jersey, Scarpa moved in with Linda Diana, a gorgeous brunette nineteen years younger, who had been dating wiseguys since her mid-teens.[16] Scarpa had two children with Linda, but in an effort to hide the fact that they were Greg's, she married a man named Schiro, who believed the kids were his own. Then, in 1975 while still married to Forrest and living as Linda's common-law husband, Scarpa ran off to Las Vegas and married Lili Dajani, a thirty-five-year-old[17] former Miss Israel.[18] Years later, Dajani's lover, an ex–abortion doctor named Eli Shkolnik, was murdered on Scarpa's orders.[19] Yet in 1979 Scarpa agreed to let Linda carry on a torrid sexual relationship with Larry Mazza, a handsome eighteen-year-old delivery boy—and later made Mazza his protégé, schooling him in the crimes of loan sharking, bank robbery, and homicide.[20]

"I started out one way and ended up with the devil," Mazza later said.[21] The former grocery worker expressed shock when Scarpa once suggested to him that they kill the mother of a mob turncoat in order to demonstrate "what happens to rats."[22]

Still, Scarpa, who bragged that he "loved the smell of gunpowder,"[23] had no compunctions about killing women. When he heard that Mary Bari, the beautiful mistress of the family underboss, might talk to authorities, he had her lured to a club, then shot her in the head point-blank and dumped her body in a rolled-up canvas two miles away. Later, when the dog of one of his crew members' wives found a piece of the dead woman's ear, Scarpa joked about it over dinner.[24] "He was just a vicious, violent animal," said Mazza. "Unscrupulous and treacherous . . . just a horrible human being."[25]

And yet Scarpa's daughter, "Little Linda" Schiro, described him as "incredibly loving—the kind of dad who was there for us every night for dinner at five o'clock. Whatever he was on the outside, he was really gentle at home."[26] Like a true sociopath, Scarpa was apparently capable of shifting at will from brutal murderer to loyal dad. After one bloody rubout, when Mazza and Scarpa shot a rival in the head, they went home to play with Greg's infant grandson, drink wine, and watch *Seinfeld* on TV.[27]

"He could transform himself," said Little Linda. "He could go kill someone and five minutes later he'd be home watching *Wheel of Fortune* with my brother and me."[28]

The Grim Reaper ruled Thirteenth Avenue in Bensonhurst with an iron fist. He was responsible for more than twenty-five separate homicides between 1980 and 1992. With Mazza's help, Scarpa killed three people in one four-week period. He shot one of his victims with a rifle while the man was stringing Christmas lights with his wife.[29] He killed a seventy-eight-year-old member of the Genovese family because the old man happened to be in the wrong place at the wrong time.[30] Then, a few weeks later, after FBI and NYPD surveillance had been pulled away from a Mafia social club, he rolled up next to Colombo capo Nicholas Grancio, and when his own rifle jammed,[31] he ordered Grancio shot.[32] Grancio's nose was blown off and one of his teeth was later found in a nearby building. At another point, tipped that Cosmo Catanzano, one of his crew members, might talk to the Feds, Scarpa ordered Catanzano's grave dug in advance of the murder, but Catanzano escaped when DEA agents arrested him before the execution could take place.[33]

"The man was the master of the unpredictable and he knew absolutely no bounds of fear," said Joseph Benfante, one of Scarpa's former lawyers.[34] "If he'd lived four hundred years ago, he would have been a pirate."[35] The brazen Scarpa even gave himself a reason to wear an eye patch. In 1992, after being diagnosed with HIV and given only months to live, he broke house arrest and went after a pair of local drug dealers who had threatened his younger son.[36] In the ensuing gun battle, Scarpa got his right eye shot out, but he walked home and downed a glass of scotch before Larry Mazza was summoned and drove him to the hospital.[37]

"Scarpa had an action jones," one former assistant district attorney recalled.[38] Another investigator described the killer's need to stay on the edge: "Capos ain't supposed to be out on the street hijacking trucks, doing drug deals," he said. "I mean, that's why you have a crew. But Greg was there. He always had to walk point."[39]

And yet, even as he openly disparaged "rats," Scarpa devoted more than three decades off and on to betraying his larger "family," the Colombos.

The Secret Files

The 1,153 pages of files uncovered in this investigation reveal that more than two years before celebrated Mafia turncoat Joseph Valachi "sang" to the McClellan rackets committee in a historic series of hearings televised from coast to coast, Scarpa was already coughing up the family's most intimate secrets to the FBI.

The detailed multipage memos called airtels (later designated as FBI 209 reports) show that Scarpa, whose code designation was NY 3461-C-TE, met two or three times a month with agents from the FBI's New York Office. During these secret sessions, conducted in hotel rooms, automobiles, and Scarpa's various homes in Brooklyn, he fed them the kind of inside-the-family dirt that J. Edgar Hoover craved. Every one of those airtels went straight to the Director himself, and as we'll see, while many of the debriefings contained detailed intelligence on the organizational structure of the Mafia,[40] "34," as Scarpa was known, also gave the Bureau reams of disinformation.[41]

A brilliant Machiavellian strategist, Scarpa not only stayed on the street for forty-two years, avoiding prison after twenty separate arrests or indictments for his crimes,* but he repeatedly "ratted out" his competition in the family—literally eliminating many of the capos above him along with the two family bosses: Joseph Colombo[42] and Carmine Persico.[43] He also succeeded in fomenting a series of internal conflicts or wars that tore the borgata apart.

It was Scarpa whose duplicity paved the way for the notorious assassination attempt on Joseph Colombo at an Italian-American Civil Rights

---

* See Appendix C.

League rally in front of fifty thousand people in 1971.[44] It was Scarpa whose backdoor machinations ignited the second Colombo war between wiseguys loyal to Persico and the violent Gallo brothers in the early 1970s, and it was Scarpa who fueled the battle that led to the infamous rubout of Crazy Joe Gallo in 1972.[45] Most important to the Feds, it was Scarpa who provided the probable cause that led to the Title III wiretaps in the historic Mafia Commission case in the mid-1980s, sending Persico and two other New York bosses to prison for life.[46]

In 1989, Everett Hatcher, a decorated DEA agent, was gunned down by Scarpa's nephew Gus Farace, who was a member of Greg's Wimpy Boys crew.[47] That cold-blooded shooting led to the formation of a five-hundred-man FBI/DEA task force and an international manhunt that lasted more than nine months. New evidence now suggests that it was Scarpa who later set up his own nephew's murder to take the heat off the other New York families.[48]

Scarpa was such a master chess player that he used his position as a Top Echelon informant to earn hundreds of thousands of dollars, beyond the millions he made from racketeering. Not only did the FBI pay him more than $158,000 in fees and bonuses for his services,[49] but his control agent from the mid-1960s to the early '70s, Anthony Villano, brokered kickbacks from insurance companies for some of the high-end hijackings Scarpa was executing.[50] Those "rewards," amounting to tens of thousands of dollars, went back to Scarpa for his own thefts of "swag" ranging from liquor to negotiable stocks to gold bullion, jewelry, and mercury. Scarpa even got a cut of a reward for the return of the famous Regina Pacis jewels after a gang of junkies stole the coveted items from a Brooklyn church. That led to national headlines for the Bureau after Villano negotiated the recovery.[51]

The Killing Machine also worked for the government in a series of "black bag jobs" that he performed off the books. The first was his well-known trip to Mississippi in the summer of 1964, when he tortured a Ku Klux Klan member in order to solve the mystery of the MISSBURN case—locating the bodies of slain civil rights workers Goodman, Schwerner, and Chaney when FBI agents assigned to the probe came up empty.[52]

After breaking a second civil rights murder in 1966 as an FBI "special" asset,[53] Scarpa traveled to Costa Rica in the early 1980s to extradite fugitive

Colombo capo Anthony Peraino, the notorious porn king who had made millions from the production of the film *Deep Throat*.[54]

In return for his assistance to the Feds, Scarpa collected in spades, using his influence with the FBI to avoid prosecution on three separate indictments by organized crime strike forces over the years. Not only did he beat a 1974 indictment for stealing $520,000 in securities and conspiring to counterfeit, transport, and sell $4 million in IBM stock,[55] but when Secret Service agents arrested him in 1986 for credit card fraud, on charges that could have led to seven years in prison and a $250,000 fine, the FBI intervened and helped him get his sentence reduced to probation and a $10,000 fine.[56]

By that time, Scarpa had been infected with HIV after a tainted blood transfusion and was given only months to live.[57] At least that's what the government told the sentencing judge. If he'd gone to prison then, Scarpa would never have been on the street to foment his last great conspiracy: the third Colombo war. But he lived for another six years.

The man who vouched for him at the time was Roy Lindley DeVecchio, known in the Bureau as "Mr. Organized Crime" for his purported success putting wiseguys away. After officially reopening Scarpa in 1980 after a five-year hiatus, Lin, as he was known, quickly rose through the Bureau ranks, commanding two organized crime squads. He also taught informant development at the FBI Academy and became supervising case agent on the Mafia Commission case, due in large part to his "management" of Informant NY 3461-C-TE, a.k.a. "34."

But defense attorneys would later allege that Lin's relationship with Scarpa was an "unholy alliance." In 1994, the FBI opened an Office of Professional Responsibility internal affairs investigation after four agents under DeVecchio effectively accused him of leaking key intelligence to the Mafia killer.[58] DeVecchio, who refused to take a polygraph test, was nevertheless granted immunity during the probe, making it virtually impossible for the Justice Department to indict him. In 1996, he retired with a full pension. Later, he was granted immunity a second time, but he answered, "I don't recall," or words to that effect, more than fifty times at a 1997 hearing as defense lawyers tried to peel back the layers obscuring his clandestine dealings with Scarpa.[59]

In March 2006, the Brooklyn district attorney unsealed an indictment charging Lin DeVecchio with four counts of murder stemming from his twelve-year relationship with Gregory Scarpa Sr.[60] The following year, after an aborted two-week trial, those charges were dismissed. But not before Scarpa's protégé Larry Mazza testified that his homicidal mentor had "stopped counting" after fifty executions.[61] Said Scarpa's own daughter, Little Linda Schiro, "It was like growing up with a serial killer."[62]

The Killing Machine's most violent period came during that third Colombo war, which he incited. The death toll during that conflict was fourteen, and the evidence demonstrates that Scarpa was personally responsible for at least six of the hits. Each time he executed a significant rubout, Scarpa would punch the satanic digits 6-6-6 into the pager of his consigliere to let him know that the job was done.[63]

A final murder he committed four days after Christmas in 1992 brought the number of homicides he'd ordered or executed on Lin DeVecchio's watch to twenty-six. That figure amounted to more than half the murders Mazza says Scarpa committed before he quit keeping track.[64] (Mazza later reaffirmed the number in a 2012 interview with the *New York Post*.[65]) Those fifty homicides made the Grim Reaper perhaps the most prolific hit man in the history of organized crime and put him in the ranks of the world's top serial killers.[66] The fact that most of those deaths occurred while he was being paid as a virtual agent provocateur by the Feds is a testament to the FBI's willingness to make "a deal with the devil," as DeVecchio's trial judge put it.[67]

A Month in Jail over More Than Four Decades

In more than forty-two years as a hyper-violent gangster, Gregory Scarpa Sr. served only thirty days in jail—and that was during the years when he was "closed" as an FBI source. The rest of that time, a series of FBI agents intervened to keep the so-called Mad Hatter on the street. But that wasn't the most disturbing aspect of Scarpa's relationship with the government. In light of the 1,150-plus pages of FBI files on Scarpa we've now accessed, it can be fairly argued that the FBI's very *playbook* against "La Cosa Nostra" was defined and shaped by what Scarpa fed them—particularly in the years from 1961 to 1972, when J. Edgar Hoover himself was on the receiving end of "34's" airtels. Given the Bureau's relationship with Scarpa, it's no surprise that a senior federal judge sentenced one minor Colombo capo convicted in 1992 to multiple life terms for crimes far less repugnant than Scarpa's.[68]

Even as he was being ravaged by HIV—shrinking from 220 pounds to an emaciated 116 toward the end of his life—Scarpa beat the real grim reaper by many years, staying alive to commit multiple homicides as he schemed to take over the family in the phony war he'd engineered. Few figures in the annals of organized crime have operated with such tenacity, deviousness, and reckless disregard for human life. The fact that he served as the FBI's secret weapon, against what Lin DeVecchio calls "the Mafia enemy," only underscores the moral ambiguity that runs through this story.

Drawing on secret FBI airtels never before seen outside the Bureau, in the pages ahead we'll reveal how Gregory Scarpa Sr., then a young capo for the Profaci crime family, led J. Edgar Hoover himself into the inner sanctum of the underworld. Once that alliance began, there seemed to be no turning back for the Bureau. "They enlisted a violent killer to stop much less capable murderers," says defense lawyer Ellen Resnick, whose work helped expose this "unholy alliance."[69] "It was the ultimate ends-justify-the-means relationship."

As you turn the pages of this book, there are two crucial questions to keep in mind. Who was in charge: the special agents like Tony Villano and Lin DeVecchio, who were responsible for "controlling" Scarpa, or the killer himself? And who got the most out of this deal with the devil: the FBI or the very "Mafia enemy" they sought to defeat?

PART I

Chapter 1

THE KISS OF DEATH

The day before his testimony before the Senate Permanent Subcommittee on Investigations, Joseph Michael Valachi, a Mafia killer, was escorted out of the District of Columbia jail by a protection detail worthy of a chief of state. A dozen U.S. marshals surrounded him. Ten DC police officers prowled the corridors outside the third-floor caucus room where he was prepped for his groundbreaking confession.[1]

For months, Valachi, who was being held in special protective custody, had shocked his FBI handlers with stunning revelations about the inner workings of the secret national criminal organization he called Cosa Nostra, or "Our Thing."[2] Now, for the first time, he would rip back the curtain and confess not just to the McClellan rackets committee, but to a national television and radio audience of millions.

The security detail was not misplaced. Valachi, or "Joe Cargo," as he was known in the Genovese crime family,[3] had a $100,000 contract on his head. It was issued by Vito Genovese himself. At that moment, although he was doing life in an Atlanta penitentiary on a narcotics conviction, Don Vito was regarded among New York's Five Families as the *capo di tutti capi,* the "boss of bosses." Valachi had been a loyal soldier who had killed for his borgata multiple times. But sixteen months earlier, Genovese had pushed him to the brink of betrayal after grabbing him with both hands and kissing him on the lips.

It was the *bacio della morte,* a Mafia fatwa.

The kiss of death.[4]

Now, in Washington on the morning of September 26, 1963, before five hundred people jammed into the Senate Caucus Room, Valachi, dressed in a black suit, white shirt, and silver tie, chain-smoked and rubbed his palms to wipe off the sweat from the hot TV lights. Speaking in a hollow, guttural voice, he proceeded to lay bare the criminal organization he'd joined back in 1930.[5]

Over the days that followed, using a series of massive flowcharts created by the government, Valachi unmasked the heads of the New York families. For the first time in public he revealed that the Genovese and Gambino families each had four hundred and fifty members devoted to extortion, loan sharking, gambling, narcotics trafficking, and murder. He detailed the structure of each borgata, starting with the boss, or representante, on top; then an underboss; then a consigliere, or counsel; and then a series of caporegimes, or captains, with soldati, or soldiers, on the bottom.

Valachi testifying before the McClellan Committee and a national TV audience

These terms would become part of the American lexicon six years later with the publication of Mario Puzo's iconic novel *The Godfather.*

In fact, Valachi himself is believed to have been the inspiration for the character of Frank Pentangeli in the film *The Godfather: Part II,* who appears before a Senate committee and then commits suicide.[6] Valachi would later try to kill himself in federal custody after the Justice Department blocked his plans to publish an 1,180-page manuscript[7] he'd written with the FBI's encouragement.[8] A third-party version of his story, written by author Peter Maas, who had originally been retained by the Justice Department to edit the memoirs, was later published as *The Valachi Papers*. The book went on to become an international bestseller that was adapted into a motion picture with Charles Bronson in the title role.[9]

By September 1963, Valachi had been in the Bureau's exclusive custody for a year.[10] Now, insisting that his goal was to "destroy the Cosa Nostra bosses and leaders," he betrayed the oath he'd taken upon his induction into the family back in 1930, when it was headed by Salvatore Maranzano.[11]

Living by the Gun and the Knife

As his voice echoed off the marble walls of the Caucus Room, Valachi told of being driven "ninety miles upstate" from Manhattan to a private residence. There he was taken into a large room where thirty-five men were seated around a long table.

"There was a gun and a knife on the table," Valachi testified. "I sat at the edge. They sat me down next to Maranzano. I repeated some words in Sicilian after him."

Senator McClellan then asked, "What did the words mean?"

" 'You live by the gun and the knife and die by the gun and the knife,' " Valachi replied. At that point, he said, Maranzano gave him a small "Mass card" with a picture of a saint and set it ablaze in his cupped hands. "I repeated in Sicilian," said Valachi, showing how he passed the burning paper from hand to hand, " 'This is the way I burn if I betray the organization.' "

Valachi then testified that the other men around the table "threw out a number," each one holding up from one to five fingers. Adding up the total and beginning with Maranzano, counting down from the man on his left, the number was deducted around the table until the man with the last number was designated as Valachi's "godfather." In his case it was Joseph Bonanno, who would go on to head his own family after Maranzano's death in 1931.

At that point, said Valachi, staring into the TV cameras, they asked him what finger he shot with. He then identified his trigger finger and it was pricked with a pin. Bonanno did the same and pressed *his* finger against Valachi's, symbolizing that they "were united in blood." Valachi then told the Senate panel he was given two "rules of Cosa Nostra." One was "a promise" not to covet another member's wife, sister, or daughter.

"And the second?" asked one of the senators.

At that point Valachi grew grim, knowing he had already broken it. "This is the worst thing I can do, to tell about the ceremony," he said. "This here, what I'm telling you, what I'm exposing to you and the press and everybody . . . this is my doom."

Defying Hoover's Statements on the Mafia

In virtually every published reference to Valachi's appearance before the McClellan Committee, he is credited with being the first Mafia figure in history to reveal the secrets of Cosa Nostra.[12] Attorney General Robert Kennedy himself made that point. In a piece for the *New York Times Magazine* published shortly after Valachi's testimony, Kennedy wrote, "For the first time an insider, a knowledgeable member of the racketeering hierarchy, has broken the underworld's code of silence."[13]

William Hundley, then head of the Justice Department's Organized Crime and Racketeering Section, who sat behind Valachi at the hearing, went even further. "What he did is beyond measure," he said afterward. "Before Valachi came along, we had no concrete evidence that anything like this actually existed. . . . But Valachi named names. He revealed what the structure was and how it operated. In a word, he showed us the face of the enemy."[14]

On the surface, Valachi's coast-to-coast televised confession was seen as an embarrassment to J. Edgar Hoover, the iron-fisted FBI director who for years was famous for denying the very existence of the Mafia. "No single individual or coalition of racketeers dominates organized crime across the country," Hoover said at one point.[15] As Sanford J. Unger wrote in his exhaustively researched history of the Bureau, "Neither the investigation of Murder Incorporated in Brooklyn in the early 1940s, nor the work in the 1950s of New York District Attorney Frank S. Hogan and the Federal Bureau of Narcotics, nor the inquiry conducted by Senator Estes Kefauver of Tennessee could persuade the Director to say otherwise."[16]

There were several purported reasons for Hoover's apparent blindness to what Valachi called "Our Thing." First, the statistics-driven Hoover preferred the case-clearance rates of easy-to-solve crimes like bank robbery and interstate auto theft to the much more time-consuming prosecution of organized crime. Second, given that the starting salary at the Bureau in the mid-1950s was $5,500, Hoover was terrified that his incorruptible agents would be tempted by the lure of mob money.[17]

Many also believed that there were more personal motives behind the Director's unwillingness to acknowledge the existence of the Sicilian-dominated national crime syndicate. There was the lingering allegation that the Mafia had material on Hoover (purported to be a homosexual) that might have been used to blackmail him.[18]

Further, the Director maintained an abiding hatred for Harry J. Anslinger, the former assistant commissioner in the Bureau of Prohibition, who fought bootleggers in the 1920s only to become head of the Treasury Department's Federal Bureau of Narcotics (FBN) in 1930.

As far back as the early 1950s, Anslinger's FBN agents had been compiling dossiers on Mafiosi from coast to coast. Anslinger even sent a list to the Bureau of more than three hundred crime family members.[19] Former agent Neil J. Welch remembers "burning shiny grayish reproductions" of the FBN list "on primitive office copiers and passing [them] secretly from agent to agent like some heretical religious creed—which it was."[20] Later, when he became the special agent in charge (SAC) of the FBI's Detroit office, Welch remembered finding a copy of the list. "It had the answers," he wrote. "But no one would listen . . . every LCN [La Cosa Nostra] member we have is on the list without exception."

"So," as *Boston Globe* reporter Ralph Ranalli writes in his book *Deadly Alliance,* "while Eliot Ness and his agents from the U.S. Treasury Prohibition Bureau went after Capone in the 1930s, and Anslinger's FBN targeted the Mafia . . . which poured tons of cheap heroin in the inner cities in the forties and fifties, Hoover stayed out of the fight."[21]

It wasn't until after November 14, 1957, when more than a hundred Mafiosi from coast to coast were discovered at a secret meeting in Apalachin, New York, that Hoover finally took the blinders off.

The First Mafia Summit

A month before that meeting, Lucky Luciano, the first official boss of Valachi's family, who had been deported from the United States in 1946, convened an international summit of Mafiosi at the Hotel des Palmes in Palermo, Sicily.[22] The details of that secret conclave were reported for the first time by investigative reporter Claire Sterling in her extraordinary 1990 study of the Sicilian Mafia, known in Italy as La Piovra, "the Octopus."[23]

Joseph Valachi had actually described Luciano as "the boss of all bosses under the table,"[24] and that fall in Palermo he summoned representatives from all the major U.S. borgatas to the hotel to lay out his plan for what would soon become a deadly $1.6 billion narcotics pipeline known as the "French Connection." Morphine base harvested in the "Golden Triangle" of Laos, Cambodia, and Vietnam would be smuggled into Marseilles, France, where it would be refined into what was later marketed on the streets of America as No. 4 China White heroin.[25] The distribution network would actually include a series of pizzerias, giving rise to what the media called the "Pizza Connection." After that network was broken by the Feds, the mass indictments that followed led to the longest-running trial in the history of the Southern District of New York.[26]

As Sterling noted, the Apalachin meeting, attended by Mafia bosses from Los Angeles, Miami, Chicago, Cleveland, Dallas, Detroit, Kansas City, and Philadelphia,[27] was principally designed by Luciano to get the American cugines (cousins) to accept his narcotics import plan. They would agree to take a percentage from the Sicilian-based operation while maintaining deniability with the Feds.[28]

But the meeting was compromised when a New York State trooper named Edgar D. Croswell stumbled onto the line of black limos parked at the fifty-three-acre estate of mobster Joseph Barbara. After a roadblock was set up, the attendees scattered, many of them into the neighboring woods and farmlands in their silk suits and wingtip shoes, tossing away guns and cash as they ran. Up to fifty Mafiosi escaped, but fifty-eight were arrested.[29] One of the escapees was Valachi's "godfather," Joseph "Joe Bananas" Bonanno.[30]

The Top Hoodlum Program

Two weeks after the Apalachin arrests, Hoover set up what he called the "Top Hoodlum Program," in which each FBI SAC was expected to compile a list of ten organized crime, or "OC," figures within his jurisdiction.[31]

Anthony Villano, the veteran New York agent who "ran" Gregory Scarpa Sr. for six years, wrote in his memoir, *Brick Agent,* that his supervisor warned him that Top Hoodlum "might very well be only a temporary operation designed to satisfy criticism and would be disbanded after the heat died down."[32] As *Boston Globe* reporter Ralph Ranalli reports, however, the defection of Joseph Valachi "was the second major event (after Apalachin) that forced the FBI into the war on the Mafia for good." Ranalli notes that "by the early 1980s attacking organized crime had become not only the FBI's, but the Justice Department's, first priority.[33] It was a far cry from the 'Mafia doesn't exist' days of Hoover."

The Director even went so far as to embrace Valachi's name for the organization—but he added an unnecessary article, labeling it "La Cosa Nostra," which literally translated as "The Our Thing."[34] That allowed Hoover, who loved abbreviations, to identify the mob in all future Bureau communiqués as LCN.

For years, the Director had authorized electronic surveillance, or ELSUR, against suspected members of the Communist Party USA. The tactics included illegal wiretaps, break-ins, and searches,[35] all done without warrants. As veteran Chicago agent William Roemer recalled in his memoir, *Man Against the Mob,* Hoover "believed he had the authority to install bugs since more than one attorney general had authorized him to use wiretaps to preserve the national security."[36] On that basis, Hoover permitted agents to engage in what Roemer calls "black bag jobs," conducting break-ins to install bugs at mob locations in cities across the country.

By 1958, within months of the Apalachin incident, Hoover had ordered hundreds of these illegal wiretaps, describing them in memos as "highly confidential sources." But the tactic soon began yielding some embarrassing revelations. One bug in a Mafia-controlled Chicago tailor shop linked two members of Congress to the mob.[37] Another, in a Washington, DC, hotel, ignited an influence-peddling "party-girl" scandal involving President Lyndon Johnson's former top aide Bobby Baker.[38] In the mid-1960s, legendary Washington lawyer Edward Bennett Williams successfully sued the FBI over ELSUR in Las Vegas.[39]

So President Johnson demanded that the FBI cease and desist all illegal surveillance—not just shutting off the tape recorders, but physically removing every bug the special agents had installed. When the Bureau's listening devices went dark on July 11, 1965, veteran agent Ralph Hill said, "it was like being in a cave and cutting off the lights."[40] Mob-busting Chicago agent Roemer described it as "one of the worst days of [his] life."[41]

Top Echelon

As the CIA had known for years, the best intelligence often comes from human sources, known in tradecraft as HUMINT. But the house that Hoover built had avoided the Mafia elephant in the room for so long that the FBI was slow to develop informants. At least that was the conventional wisdom. However, the research uncovered in this investigation tells a different story. As early as November 1961, nearly two years before Valachi's appearance before the McClellan Committee, Hoover instructed all SACs to "develop particularly qualified live sources within the upper echelon of the organized hoodlum element who will be capable of furnishing the quality information needed to attack organized crime."[42]

The Director's designation for the program was "Top Echelon." In the years to come, the FBI would develop up to four hundred of these highly placed sources[43] whose identities were so closely guarded that they were known to only three agents in a given Bureau office and only by a code number.[44]

As time passed the covers on these Top Echelon Criminal Informants (TECIs) were occasionally blown, causing shockwaves. In 1985, for instance, it was disclosed that former Teamsters president Jackie Presser was a TECI with Bureau permission to commit "ordinary crimes."[45] Frank "Lefty" Rosenthal, the Las Vegas odds maker chronicled in Nicholas Pileggi's book and screenplay *Casino*,[46] was also later outed as a TE Bureau source.[47] Rosenthal survived a car bomb, but another TECI in Cleveland wasn't so lucky: After escaping multiple attempts on his life, Danny "the Irishman" Greene, a former union official and racketeer engaged in a long-running battle with local Mafiosi, was killed when a remote-controlled bomb went off in a car parked next to his.[48]

Federal protection could only go so far.

Until the Gregory Scarpa scandal, the biggest blowup over a Top Echelon informant came with the revelation that Boston FBI agent John

Connolly had leaked critical intelligence to James "Whitey" Bulger, boss of the murderous Winter Hill Gang.[49] Giving Bulger a pass in return for his purported cooperation against LCN, Connolly was ultimately convicted of racketeering and obstruction of justice. Later charged in nineteen murders, Bulger spent sixteen years on the lam before being captured in California in June 2011.[50] *Boston Globe* reporter Ralph Ranalli filed more than four hundred articles on the Bulger-Connolly scandal, and in *Deadly Alliance* he writes, "The first reference to something called the 'Top Echelon Criminal Informant Program' in FBI memos began appearing during the period between Valachi's conversion in 1963 and Johnson's shutdown of the illegal bugs in 1965."

New Evidence on Top Echelon

Ranalli's conclusion is accurate and based on what was known outside of the Bureau in the historical record until now. But hundreds of pages of newly released secret FBI airtel memos from the New York Office sent directly to "the Director" now reveal that twenty-two months before Joseph Valachi shocked the nation with his revelations, Hoover was receiving direct intelligence from the regular secret debriefings of Greg Scarpa Sr.[51]

The extraordinary details in those documents, which we'll begin to disclose in the next chapter, are proof positive that, even as the McClellan Committee was presenting Valachi as the first insider to reveal the workings of organized crime in America, Hoover himself knew every secret detail that "Cargo Joe" was about to confess. In fact, there's a compelling case to be made that the FBI actually *fed* Valachi some of the most damaging details in his testimony long before he took his seat in the Senate Caucus Room.

The source of that intel wasn't a wiretap or some low-level Mafia snitch, but the Brooklyn capo who would later be known as the Killing Machine: Gregory Scarpa.

Chapter 2

A TRUE MACHIAVELLI

Undercutting Bobby Kennedy's assertion that Joe Valachi's confession represented "the first time" a Mafia member had "broken the . . . code of silence," twelve days before Valachi's televised testimony, *Parade* magazine published an article under J. Edgar Hoover's byline. In the piece, entitled "The Inside Story on Organized Crime," Hoover used the term "La Cosa Nostra" for the first time.[1] Further, in the September 1963 issue of the *Law Enforcement Bulletin,* Hoover wrote that Valachi's revelations "corroborated and embellished the facts developed by the FBI as early as 1961."[2] On October 3, during the second week of hearings, Senator McClellan himself was quoted in a UPI story admitting that much of Valachi's testimony, heralded by some as groundbreaking, was "not especially new."[3]

As former *New York Times* organized crime reporter Selwyn Raab writes in his encyclopedic Mafia history, *Five Families,* "Valachi's information was limited to his experiences in the New York area as a lowly soldier in the trenches."[4] Ernest Volkman, author of *Gangbusters,* was more unkind. "Joe Valachi was a low-scale knuckle-dragging hood who was never going to be more than a soldier," he said in a 2009 documentary.[5] In that same program William Hundley, Valachi's government lawyer during the hearings, admitted that "Valachi had a sixth-grade education" and attributed the witness's performance before the subcommittee to his "street smarts" and the "adrenaline [that] started to flow" once Valachi "got in front of those klieg lights."[6]

Were those factors sufficient to lend authority to Valachi's expansive account of the Mafia's national network? Thomas L. Jones, who files organized crime reports for TruTV.com, thinks not.

"In many ways, [getting] Valachi's viewpoint was like asking a gas jockey at a Shell station about the strategy of the board of directors," he writes. "A barely literate, low-ranking member of the Mafia, Valachi was often obviously talking beyond his personal experience."[7]

Raab notes that "before his public appearance, Valachi had been coached by agents, spoon-fed information about other families that the Bureau had picked up." But he suggests that this intelligence had come from electronic surveillance. "Hoover had used [Valachi] as a transmitter," Raab writes, "to publicize facts the FBI wanted Congress and the public to know about the Mob without revealing that the data had been obtained through unconstitutional methods."[8]

Valachi at the hearing, with flow charts prepared by the FBI

It's true that, for a bottom-rung "soldato," Valachi was something of a social climber. He had married the daughter of Gaetano Reina, the former boss of his family, and Vito Genovese himself had been the best man at his wedding.[9] That status gave Valachi access beyond his official standing in the borgata. In *The Valachi Papers,* his biographer, Peter Maas, claimed that the former driver and "button man" had "nearly total recall."[10] But Valachi's experience, which was limited to the New York families, could never have given him the inside knowledge necessary to fill in the detailed charts displayed at the hearings. In fact, as Raab points out, Valachi was "even unaware that Chicago's Mob called itself 'the Outfit,' New England's was 'the Office,' and Buffalo's was 'the Arm.'"[11]

So, if Valachi was coached by the FBI, then where did their knowledge come from? Was Hoover's network of illegal wiretaps the source, as Raab suggests? Or did the FBI acquire the knowledge they fed him in a different way? The files discovered in this investigation prove that Hoover's awareness of the Mafia's inner secrets came from at least one human source: confidential informant NY 3461-C-TE.

A Betrayal "Punishable by Death"

Gregory Scarpa Sr. was first officially "opened" as a criminal informant in the FBI's New York Office (NYO) on August 25, 1960, more than three years before Valachi's public testimony. His original file number was FBI #584217A. But his recruitment came only after he was arrested and charged in connection with the attempted armed hijacking of an Akers Motor Lines tractor trailer in New York City on December 11, 1959.[12] At the time of Scarpa's arrest on March 7, 1960, the authorities found eighty-four cases of liquor at his home on Staten Island—the haul from an earlier truck hijacking of a Marcell's Motor Express truck on February 27. The Akers hijacking charges were dismissed[13] and the files suggest that Scarpa agreed to cooperate with the Feds at that time. But he refused to talk when agents tried to press him on the whereabouts of his older brother, Salvatore "Sal" Scarpa, and a short time later he was closed.[14]

By August 1961, however, the first of three wars for control of the Profaci-Colombo crime family had broken out between forces loyal to Joseph Profaci, Scarpa's boss, and the violent Gallo brothers, Larry, Albert (a.k.a. "Kid Blast"), and Joseph (a.k.a. "Crazy Joe").[15] Concerned about the violence, and eager to reconnect with a live source inside the family, Bureau agents paid three separate visits to Scarpa's social club. But he repeatedly spurned them, insisting that "people were beginning to ask questions concerning why the [FBI] was contacting him."[16] The agents told Scarpa they'd leave him alone but gave him a number to call if he ever changed his mind.[17]

We don't know for sure what ultimately caused him to pick up the phone, but at that point Scarpa was still under indictment in connection with the Marcell's liquor hijacking. In October 1961, he finally made contact and was formally "reopened." A 1966 FBI letter describing his re-recruitment states that the "informant . . . indicated that he desired to furnish information . . . only because he had a personal liking for the agents [and] faith in [their] discretion"—an early indication of Scarpa's talent at manipulating and stroking his handlers.[18]

By March 20, 1962, Scarpa was upgraded to the special status of Top Echelon Criminal Informant (TECI).[19] By June, the FBI memos indicate that he was supplying information on a "continuous basis regarding the feud between the Profaci and Gallo groups."[20] At that point, the Bureau started paying him on a regular basis. The Marcell's Motor Express hijacking case also went away: It was dismissed on March 28, 1963.[21]

On November 21, 1961, J. Edgar Hoover himself received the first of dozens of multipage briefings from the special agent in charge (SAC) of the FBI's New York Office. This four-page report identifies the source as "GREGORY SCARPA . . . a current member of the JOSEPH PROFACI group" and calls him "an individual worthy of concentration and attention."[22]

The memo gives Scarpa's address on Staten Island, his height, weight, and date of birth, and his police record, showing five arrests between 1950 and 1960 on gun possession, menacing, and hijacking charges. It lists his various aliases as "Gregory Scarba" and "Gregory Scarbo," and cites his "criminal associates," which included his brother Sal, Profaci consigliere Charles LoCicero, and Carmine J. Persico Jr., who went on to become boss of the family. More than twenty years later, Scarpa would furnish the FBI with probable cause to secure Title III wiretaps that helped send Persico away for life in the landmark "Mafia Commission" case.[23] He also spent years undermining LoCicero and may have played a role in his murder.* In the mid-1990s, one of Greg Sr.'s lawyers would underscore that duplicity by calling him "a true Machiavelli."[24]

Though he'd reached the level of caporegime, or captain, by 1961, in talking to the Feds Scarpa routinely downplayed his own importance within the family. One FBI memo listed him as having "an interest in a ravioli business in Brooklyn."[25] Another stated that he "has never really had any legitimate occupation, but has been a silent partner in various restaurants and bars."[26] It would have been impossible, however, for Scarpa to have furnished Hoover with the detailed intelligence he did without having access to meetings at the highest tier of the family. It was access that no mere soldier in the insulated,

---

* See Chapter 8.

need-to-know structure of the Mafia could have had. Five years after Scarpa became a TE informant, the FBI's assistant director called him "the most valuable Top Echelon informant of the New York Office."[27]

And just as Gregory Scarpa delivered for the FBI, the Bureau reciprocated. There's little doubt that his association with the FBI for more than thirty years was the principal reason that Scarpa avoided prison—beating multiple felony charges and serving only that single month in jail before his final conviction.* In the meantime, as Scarpa "ratted out" his competition, the evidence suggests that he became privy to the kind of intelligence only the Feds could provide. And that access to information, in turn, helped earn him a senior position in the Profaci-Colombo hierarchy. The airtels reflect that he was able to collect intelligence at the boss level through all three administrations, from Joseph Profaci to Joseph Colombo to Carmine Persico. By Scarpa's own admission, his revelations would have been "punishable by death" if his cover had been blown. But in a criminal enterprise where the life of an informant can be dangerously short, he played both sides of the street with lethal skill—a game of double-cross equaled by few in the annals of organized crime.

Intelligence Surpassing Valachi's

Seven months after Gregory Scarpa became a federal informant, the Bureau's New York SAC sent Hoover an eleven-page airtel with revelations that made Valachi's testimony appear superficial in comparison. Dozens of other airtels can be accessed via my website, www.peterlance.com, but we're producing this June 18, 1962, memo in its entirety† for two reasons. First, it's an important benchmark to help us measure Hoover's true knowledge of the Mafia at this point in the early 1960s. Second, though many of the early memos can be corroborated as truthful, the dozens of later airtels and 209 memos also demonstrate Scarpa's capacity to lie and manipulate his Bureau handlers. As such, they put Lin DeVecchio's public comments

---

* See Appendix C for Scarpa's arrests and the disposition of the cases.
† See Appendix D.

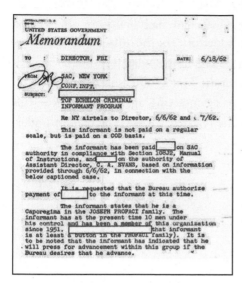

about "34," the confidential informant he "admired," in stark new perspective.

For example, according to this 1962 airtel, Scarpa had become a made member of LCN in 1950 at the young age of twenty-four. Eleven years later, he had risen to the position of caporegime, or captain, in what was then the Profaci family.[28] Yet in his 2011 book *We're Going to Win This Thing*, DeVecchio states with confidence that Scarpa was "never a capo."[29]

Who was right? The G-man or the hit man?[30] Later in this book we'll quote from DeVecchio's memoir in order to answer that question.

Apart from a few depositions from a 1988 civil suit, and the transcripts of his sentencing hearing in 1993, Greg Scarpa Sr. left very little direct testimony on the historical record. He never testified in any of the Colombo War trials, where DeVecchio took the stand as an expert witness.[31] Yet these airtels offer a penetrating new look into the mind of a highly gifted criminal who successfully manipulated his fellow Mafiosi while outflanking the best and the brightest in the FBI. Though written by his FBI handlers, the memos resonate with Scarpa's voice. They show him to be a master chess player, complaining of money trouble as his justification for approaching the Feds, expressing his willingness to be used by them, even flattering them with reassurances that the FBI was "the only police agency" he trusted.

Still, woven throughout his factual accounts of the structure of LCN are a series of half-truths and lies intended to placate his contacting agents. With some redactions (white boxes blocking out certain names and dates) the airtel looks pretty much as it did when it hit J. Edgar Hoover's desk in 1962.

Scarpa's first extended statement to the Feds was expansive, covering everything from the history of the Mafia (dating back to the days of Sicily's Black Hand) to the structure of the Commission and each family within it, specifically identifying each rank: representante (boss), underboss, consigliere (counselor), caporegime (captain), and "Good Fellow" or "button man" (soldier). He also confirmed the identities of the bosses of all five New York families and the officials of the Profaci borgata down through the rank of capo, not to mention every detail of the Mafia induction ceremony.

On page 11 of the airtel, Scarpa's contacting agent noted, "The full potential of this informant is yet to be realized." It was the biggest understatement in the entire document.

Chapter 3

HITTING THE BOSS

There's little doubt, from what we know of Gregory Scarpa Sr.'s trajectory in the Colombo family, that by 1962 his "full potential" was yet to be realized. In return for betraying LCN, he was able to con his FBI handlers into paying off a $3,000 debt he claimed he owed. They also agreed to furnish him with future payments.[1] Within a year he was getting a regular stipend of $125 a month, the equivalent of $940.45 in 2013 dollars.[2] But his criminal activity in the decades to come proved that his pledge on page 3 of the June 18, 1962, airtel—that he would cease "all [but necessary] activities relating to the organization" was a bold-faced lie. As was his suggestion that he could "more or less retire." As Valachi said during the hearings, "Once you're in you can't get out. You try, but they hunt you down."[3]

The same could be said of a "Good Fellow" who attempted to slough off or dial back on his contributions as an "earner." Just as sharks have to keep swimming or die, a Mafioso doesn't have the privilege of downtime. As a capo who had been "straightened out" for more than a decade, Scarpa knew that once he'd taken the oath, he was in the family for life. Thus, his suggestion that he might "cease all activities" was clearly designed to curry favor with the agents and play down his criminal behavior.

Further, in light of his murderous track record, the conclusion on page 4 that Scarpa wasn't just "reliable" but "emotionally stable" underscores the mask Scarpa presented to his Bureau handlers—and their willingness to believe him.

Retired veteran DEA Special Agent Mike Levine, who dealt with multiple criminal informants (CIs) in his career, warns about the dangers of federal agents getting misled by their informants. "When it comes to CIs," he says, "you have to be extremely careful that they are not feeding you information that will lead you the wrong way, or that they're not using you to eliminate their competitors or further their own agenda. This problem is particularly acute when you are dealing with an intelligent CI, and Scarpa was as smart as they come. While he gave the FBI LCN intel at a very high level, he also lied to them, and if his handlers weren't extremely careful they easily could have been duped."[4]

Between November 21, 1961, and December 6, 1963, the New York SAC sent forty-six separate airtels to the Director with information furnished by Scarpa. Many of them were duplicative. The details on the Commission, its rules, and the induction ceremony were repeated verbatim in multiple memos. Scarpa was always paid "COD." But he supplied enough tantalizing information over the years to more than justify the cash flow. Hundreds of additional airtels and 209 informant memos would be produced and sent to FBI headquarters from New York, and they continued off and on for twenty years after Hoover's death in 1972. The airtels stopped only in 1975, when Scarpa was closed for five years, before resuming after he was officially reopened by Lin DeVecchio in the summer of 1980 and continuing until 1992.

Until Scarpa's 1975 closure, memos like the one below were regularly interspersed with his detailed debriefings. They served to reassure the DC brass by reiterating the mantra that the man later described

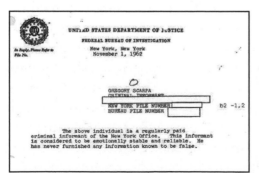

as "the Mad Hatter" was truthful, "emotionally stable and reliable" and "has never furnished any information known to be false."

Many of these airtels are available at www.peterlance .com. But in the pages ahead we'll include some of the highlights. They begin in November 1961 and offer extraordinary insight into the activities of Joseph Profaci, the family boss at the time. Known as "the Olive Oil King of New York," Profaci was described by Attorney General Robert Kennedy as "one of the most powerful underworld figures in the United States." He ran his family from what was described as "a cluttered office" at the Mamma Mia Importing Company at 1414 Sixty-Fifth Street in Brooklyn.[5]

Profaci was a complicated boss. He'd served a year in prison in Sicily for theft before emigrating to the United States in 1921.[6] Yet he was deeply devout, and despite the murderous racketeering of his underworld family, he harbored dreams of one day returning to Italy to be decorated by the Pope with a Vatican knighthood.[7]

Virtually everything the FBI learned about Profaci in the early 1960s came from the debriefings of Gregory Scarpa Sr., whose principal "padrone" in the borgata was Charles LoCicero. In the following excerpt from an air-tel, Scarpa, identified as "the informant," is described as a "leader" in the crime family.

> June 25, 1962: The informant is a leader in the Profaci gang of the New York underworld organization whose leadership comprises the "Commission." He is closely allied with CHARLES LOCICERO . . . who has been identified as an advisor to the Profaci organization. The informant is currently active as an operator of a numbers racket in Brooklyn.[8]

Known as "Charlie the Sidge," LoCicero was consigliere during the first of three wars within the family. The initial Profaci-Gallo conflict was waged from 1961 to 1964.[9] At least seven members of the family were murdered and three others went missing and were presumed dead.[10] The dispute arose because a crew of hotheaded young soldiers, who had reportedly carried out a legendary contract killing, felt cheated. The gang included Carmine Persico, known as "Junior," and the three violent Gallo brothers, Crazy Joe, Larry, and their younger brother Kid Blast.[11] Their claim to fame derived from their alleged participation in the most celebrated Mafia rubout of the 1950s: the barbershop slaying of Umberto "Albert" Anastasia, the boss of what is now the Gambino family.

The Barbershop Quintet

Nicknamed "the Lord High Executioner," Anastasia was one of the principals behind the Brooklyn-based "kill-for-hire" organization known as Murder Incorporated. Named by Harry Feeney, a reporter for the *New York World-Telegram,* Murder Inc. was responsible for hundreds of homicides nationwide from 1931 to 1940.[12]

On October 25, 1957, Anastasia was getting a haircut at the Park Sheraton Hotel in midtown Manhattan when, shortly after ten fifteen A.M.,

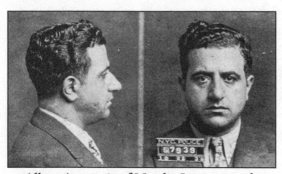

Albert Anastasia of Murder Incorporated, dubbed "the Lord High Executioner"

two gunmen came in wearing fedoras and hiding their faces behind sunglasses and scarves. One of them told the shop owner, "Keep your mouth shut if you don't want your head blown off." Then, while Anastasia sat with his eyes closed, they quickly moved to chair number four in the thirty-five-by-twenty-eight-foot shop and opened fire.[13] Ten shots rang out. The first two blew Anastasia from the chair, forcing him against the mirrored glass wall. Struck in the left hand and wrist and right hip, he ricocheted off a glass cabinet as the shooters kept firing. They hit him one more time in the

The Anastasia crime scene

back and finished him with a bullet to the back of the head.

The gunmen coolly departed, dropping one .38 Colt in a hotel corridor as they headed toward West Fifty-Fifth Street and the second (a .32 pistol) on the steps leading down to the BMT subway.

The murder was never solved, but almost thirty years later, a witness at a federal trial testified that Carmine Persico took credit for the hit.[14] Crazy Joe Gallo also boasted of his own involvement. Claiming that a five-man crew had pulled off the hit, Gallo joked that Anastasia had been dispatched by "a barbershop quintet."[15]

Having made their bones with the Anastasia murder, Persico and the Gallo brothers waited patiently for Profaci to take care of them. Then, in 1959, they saw a chance for advancement. Frank "Frankie Shots" Abbatemarco was a fifty-nine-year-old Profaci captain who raked in $2.5 million a year—almost $7,000 daily—from a lucrative numbers and loan-sharking operation. On November 4, as he left Cardiello's bar near Park Slope, two men in fedoras and topcoats started firing.[16] They chased Abbatemarco back into the tavern and finished him off with six shots. Joe Gallo was later identified as one of the shooters.[17]

Expecting Profaci to reward them with Abbatemarco's action, Persico and the Gallos were outraged when the boss distributed the capo's operations to upper-tier family cronies. On February 27, 1961, nine months before Scarpa started fully cooperating with the Feds, the Gallos kidnapped four of Profaci's top men, including his brother Frank, his brother-in-law Joseph Magliocco, and Joseph Colombo, a top Profaci killer who would one day rule the family. Charles LoCicero, who was highly regarded in the family, negotiated their release, and Profaci put out the word that he wanted to make peace with the rebel faction. But soon enough, the boss would renege and use Carmine Persico to sell out the Gallo brothers.

Tempted by the Snake

Gregory Scarpa, the FBI's new eyes and ears inside the family, provided the Bureau with the intimate details of what followed. Around this time, Profaci learned that he was dying of cancer. We don't know to what degree his failing health contributed to his subornation of Persico, but after the betrayal, Carmine was forever branded "the Snake" by other members of the family. Nonetheless, in a debriefing from the fall of 1961, Scarpa recounted how Persico had first asked him to throw in with the Gallo side.

> November 13, 1961: Informant stated that when the GALLOS first left the organization . . . CARMINE PERSICO originally went with the GALLOS and approach[ed] the Informant in an effort to persuade him to join. The informant stated that he knew the GALLOS were crazy . . . all of the men who originally went with them are either dead or have returned to the organization. . . . After the [GALLOS] were "made" they began to run wild and pushed for more and more authority in the organization. As a result of this, the decision was made to dispose of them.[18]

Scarpa explained that a "peace" meeting was proposed to Larry Gallo, who was asked to come to the Sahara Lounge in Brooklyn with two crew members on Sunday, August 20, 1961. Persico apparently guaranteed their safety. But when they arrived, Carmine and another Profaci killer, Joseph Scimone, threw a rope around Larry's neck and started to strangle him.[19] The murder was interrupted when a police officer happened by.*

In the airtels, Scarpa offered new details on the attempted hit, insisting that a garrote, not a gun, was the weapon of choice because of the "heat" then coming down on the Mafia.

> March 20, 1962: Informant advised that it would [not] be a good idea to gun them down and leave bodies lying all over the streets in Brooklyn. He stated that the plan was to just have them disappear and never be seen again. Informant stated that on Sunday when the attempt was made on LARRY GALLO, three of the men in the Sahara Lounge were to disappear. If the plans had worked and these three had been successfully taken care of, a call would have been made to JOE GALLO . . . to come down for a pow-wow, that his brother was there and that JOE GALLO would have been disposed of when he came in.[20]

Persico and Scimone were later indicted in the garroting, but the charges were dismissed.[21] That same year Joe Gallo was convicted of extortion and an attempt was made to poison him as he awaited transport to Sing Sing prison.[22]

---

* This incident was depicted in the film *The Godfather: Part II,* with the character of Frank Pentangeli representing Larry Gallo.

A Plot to Kill the Boss

By May 1962, Scarpa told the FBI that his padrone, Charles LoCicero, the family consigliere, was "endeavoring to get JOSEPH PROFACI to step down as head of the Brooklyn organization."[23] As Profaci lay dying, Charlie "the Sidge" made his own plans to take over as godfather, but he was thwarted when "Joe Malayak" Magliocco, the three-hundred-pound underboss, was anointed godfather by the Commission.

> July 2, 1962: Informant advised that on seven one sixty two, AMBROSE MAGLIOCCO advised that his brother JOSEPH MAGLIOCCO had been selected as boss . . . and SALVATORE MUSSACCHIO, also known as SALLY THE SHEIK [was selected] CONSIGLIERE.

At that point, Scarpa confirmed that LoCicero was demoted from consigliere—the number three position in the family—to capo. Angered, the Sidge decided to retaliate, and this report was flashed as a teletype from New York to Headquarters.

> September 13, 1962: Informant advised that CHARLES LOCICERO had assigned informant to kill JOSEPH MAGLIOCCO. LOCICERO assigned ███████████ to drive for informant on [the] hit. Informant and ███████████ cased Long Island estate of MAGLIOCCO on September 11 last.*

The prospect of Gregory Scarpa, their principal confidential informant, being contracted to hit the new family boss caused immediate alarm within the FBI. That teletype was quickly followed by another, sixteen hours later:

> September 13, 1962: Informant has been instructed that under no circumstances can he participate in the murder of JOSEPH MAGLIOCCO.

---

* Henceforth all redactions in the airtels and 209s will be marked in black: ███████████.

Given the swift negative reaction, four days later Scarpa attempted to placate the Bureau brass:

> September 19, 1962: LOCICERO did not get Commission approval for the assassination of MAGLIOCCO, but did not want to admit that to Informant. From the conversation with LOCICERO the Informant does not feel there will be any action against MAGLIOCCO in the immediate future.

We don't know whether Scarpa had told the FBI the truth about LoCicero's alleged takeover plan or whether he concocted the proposed rubout to enhance his own status with the Bureau, but one of the most revealing memos in the newly released files was sent to Hoover on November 15, 1962. It came from the SAC of the FBI's New York Office, who suggested that, depending on who survived the internecine warfare, Scarpa could end up in a senior leadership position.

> November 15, 1962: This source is furnishing excellent information from a position within the Italian criminal organization. . . . It is of particular interest that LOCICERO is attempting to undermine MAGLIOCCO in hopes of taking over the "family" himself. It would appear that such a move, if successful, would place this source [Scarpa] in the inner circle at the top operational level of one of the most important "families" in the . . . organization. As such, this situation should be followed very closely.

Nearly three decades later, after the third war within the family (1991–1993), defense lawyers would argue that the FBI had protected Scarpa at all costs over the years because they wanted their own informant at the top of one of the Five Families.[24]

The position of boss would have given Scarpa a seat on the ruling Mafia Commission—an unprecedented achievement for the Bureau if such a goal had been realized. We now have confirmation from the FBI's own files that the New York SAC recognized that potential as far back as 1962.

Joseph Magliocco's reign as family boss was short-lived. After he succumbed to a heart attack in late December 1963, control of the family went to Joseph Colombo, the son of a Cosa Nostra soldier who had served as a top enforcer for Profaci during the first conflict with the Gallo brothers.

Colombo was anointed as Don after he followed Carmine the Snake's path and betrayed a plot he'd been contracted to execute against the heads of the Gambino and Lucchese families. As it turned out, Joe Malayak was closely aligned with Joseph Bonanno, Valachi's godfather, who came up with a scheme to murder Thomas Lucchese and Carlo Gambino, two other Commission members. Colombo was given the contract, but rather than carry it out, he came clean. Magliocco was then stripped of his title, Bonanno was exiled, and Colombo was awarded the position of boss by a grateful Carlo Gambino, the most powerful Commission member at the time.[25]

Chapter 4

THE SPECIAL
GOES SOUTH

Seven months later, J. Edgar Hoover finally found a way to make some affirmative use of the Brooklyn hit man who had been on his payroll for three years. "Whatever else he may have passed along in the way of intelligence," says Fredric Dannen of the *New Yorker,* who wrote a definitive profile of Scarpa in 1996, "we know from the work he did in Mississippi that he became a clandestine asset for Hoover."[1]

In that hot summer of 1964, the biggest crisis facing the U.S. Justice Department was the disappearance of three young civil rights workers, Andrew Goodman, Michael Schwerner, and James Chaney. Working for the Congress of Racial Equality (CORE), they had traveled to Philadelphia, Mississippi, on June 21 to look into the Klan's role in burning the Mount Zion United Methodist Church and disappeared that same night. When their empty, fire-charred Ford station wagon was recovered a short time later, the FBI was called in to work the case.

Evidence later presented at trial would prove that the local KKK kleagle, or recruiter, Edgar Ray Killen, had conspired with a deputy sheriff to stop the young men for speeding as they left town.[2] After a chase, they were forced off the road, driven thirty-four miles to a remote location, and shot to death in cold blood.[3] Their bodies were thrown back in the station wagon and driven to a nearby farm, where they were buried under fifteen feet of red clay in an earthen dam. The Ford was then set ablaze and dumped in a swamp.

As detailed in my second book, *Cover Up*, the disappearance immediately became a national news story and ignited a firestorm at the Justice Department. Dozens of special agents were rushed to Neshoba County to comb the fields, in what Hoover dubbed the MISSBURN case.[4] The 1988 film *Mississippi Burning* dramatized how the agents located the station wagon. But weeks passed without any significant leads as to the fate of the three young men, and the investigation stopped dead.[5]

"Back then, a lot of local people feared the FBI as much as the Klan and nobody was talking," says Judge W. O. Chet Dillard, who was a state's

FBI missing poster for Goodman, Chaney, and Schwerner

attorney at the time. "Old J. Edgar figured that if he was gonna break that [case]—and he was hurtin' to break it— he was gonna have to go to some extreme measures, and he did."[6]

Sometime in early August, the Bureau enlisted Gregory Scarpa, the FBI's Top Echelon informant—who had earlier been contracted to murder the boss of his own crime family—to go to Mississippi to accomplish what the agents could not.

"Hoover was getting a lot of pressure about the bodies not being found," Scarpa's common-law wife, Linda Schiro, testified in 2007. "They approached Greg to go down to find the bodies."[7]

Schiro, who was seventeen when she and Greg were flown to Mississippi, testified that they went to a hotel and found "eight or nine FBI agents" waiting. Scarpa winked at the agents, Schiro testified; then one of them knocked on the door of their room and gave him a gun.

"Greg changed his clothes," she recalled, "and then he . . . left some money on the dresser. He told me that if he didn't come back to . . . go back home."

An account of the story by Tom Robbins and Jerry Capeci, which ran in the New York *Daily News* in 1994, alleged that "Scarpa, according to sources, kidnapped [a] klansman" who had knowledge of the burial site.[8] "Armed with an FBI-supplied pistol," they wrote, Scarpa "put the gun in his mouth and threatened to 'blow his f——ing brains out' if he didn't spill the beans."

But Judge Dillard, who interviewed a number of sources close to the incident, has a different account—one that suggests that Scarpa became even more violent during the interrogation. "The man who knew where Goodman, Schwerner, and Chaney were buried was the mayor of a local town," says Dillard.[9] "After Scarpa grabbed him, they took him to an undisclosed location, and while the agents waited outside, Scarpa started working on the guy."

Dillard says that Scarpa first "put a pistol to [the mayor's] head, demanding to know where those boys were. But [he] told him a phony story." It was only after Scarpa checked with FBI agents to confirm the lie that he "put the barrel of the gun in the man's mouth and cocked it."

Then, says Dillard, fearing reprisals from the Klan, the mayor lied *a second time* and the agents outside confirmed it. "It was at that point," says Dillard, "that Scarpa took more drastic steps." Taking out a straight razor, he proceeded to unzip the man's fly.

"He was threatenin' to emasculate him," says the judge. And that's when the terrified Klansman "blurted out the location of the dam."[10] Years later, a lawyer who represented Scarpa disclosed that Scarpa, the so-called Mad Hatter, had admitted to the interrogation by razor blade.[11]

On August 4, 1964, the three bodies were recovered six miles southwest of Philadelphia. Goodman and Schwerner had each been shot once in the head. Chaney, the black man in the group, was shot three times and beaten savagely.[12]

Schiro testified that Scarpa later returned to the hotel and told her "they found the bodies." She said that an FBI agent came by to retrieve the gun and handed Greg an envelope with cash "an inch thick" in a rubber band.[13] After that, Schiro and Scarpa vacationed at the Fontainebleau Hotel in Miami Beach.

Scarpa's Next Mission

Eighteen months later, Hoover used Scarpa in a second mission to Mississippi to extract a confession from another KKK member. In early 1966, Vernon F. Dahmer, an African American farmer and shopkeeper who had allowed his store to be used for voter registration, was targeted by the Klan. On January 10, in the dead of night, two carloads of hooded Klansmen, brandishing shotguns and carrying twelve gallons of gasoline, showed up at Dahmer's house and set it on fire.[14] In the blaze that followed, the fifty-eight-year-old Dahmer held the attackers at bay while his family escaped. But he later died in his wife's arms.

As an indication of how seriously Washington reacted to the murder, President Lyndon Johnson sent a telegram of condolence to the Dahmer family and Attorney General Nicholas Katzenbach issued a statement vowing to devote "the full resources of the Justice Department to catching the perpetrators."[15]

"Once again, there were no leads," says Judge Dillard.[16] Eleven days after the firebombing, the FBI's Criminal Investigative Division contacted the New York Office and dispatched Scarpa to Jackson, Mississippi, for what was referred to in an airtel as "a special."[17]

Again he abducted a Klan member and used violent means to extract a confession. But this time, according to Judge Dillard, he was directly "aided and abetted" in the kidnapping by an FBI agent. The Bureau memo to the assistant director requesting Scarpa's help also asked for "enough money to cover [informant's] expenses for hotel room and transportation for the SA, plus two individuals," indicating that Scarpa and Schiro were accompanied by an agent from New York.[18]

The FBI's preliminary investigation led to a Klan captain named Lawrence Byrd, who owned an appliance store called Byrd's Radio and TV Service in nearby Laurel, Mississippi. As Judge Dillard recounts in his book *Clear Burning: Civil Rights, Civil Wrongs*, Scarpa and another man, "wearing wigs," arrived at the appliance store just before closing on January 26, 1966.[19]

"Scarpa and this agent bought a TV set from Lawrence," says Dillard. "They said they were going to pull around back and asked if he could bring it out to their car. When he came out they grabbed him, threw a blanket over him, and shoved him in the vehicle."[20] At that point, says Dillard, they drove to Camp Shelby, a military base in nearby Hattiesburg, where the interrogation took place. There, according to Dillard, who later interviewed Byrd in the Jones County Hospital, Scarpa proceeded to "beat him within an inch of his life. . . . They threatened to string him up and leave him out there naked in the winter, where the animals could get at him," says the judge.[21]

"Lawrence was a tough guy—a big, raw-boned country boy—but he was beat up so bad he was never the same after that," Dillard told writer Fredric Dannen.[22] In fact, an FBI 302 memo dated February 2, 1966, suggests that Byrd was so terrified that he refused to reveal the details to the FBI agents who later questioned him, stating only that he had been the victim of "an armed robbery by unknown persons." The memo insisted that Byrd was "still in a state of semi-shock."[23]

On March 2, 1966, Byrd signed a twenty-two-page confession to his participation in the Dahmer firebombing, implicating himself and seven other Klansmen.[24] Linda Schiro later testified that Greg "got the guy from the Ku Klux Klan . . . to admit that he was [the] one who burnt that house down."[25]

Men from Two Secret Societies

In 1998, Samuel K. Bowers, the imperial wizard of a Mississippi KKK faction, was found guilty in the Dahmer firebombing murder.[26] The FBI later attributed nine murders and three hundred beatings, arsons, and bombings to Bowers's klavern, or local unit, of the Ku Klux Klan's White Knights. He had previously served six years for the Goodman, Schwerner, and Chaney killings, which were executed by the same Klan cell. Edgar Ray Killen, who was the actual ringleader in the MISSBURN murders, escaped conviction in 1967 after an all-white jury deadlocked. But in 2005, when new evidence was developed,[27] he was found guilty of manslaughter. At the age of eighty,[28] Killen was sentenced to sixty years in prison.[29]

Then, in February 2009, Killen filed suit against the FBI, arguing that *his* civil rights had been violated—because of the Bureau's use of Gregory

Scarpa Sr., a Mafia killer, in solving the Goodman, Schwerner, and Chaney kidnap-murders.[30]

"The information that Scarpa obtained by use of torture violates Killen's civil rights . . . [his] right to due process [and] the right to confront witnesses," his lawyer said.

One former DEA special agent, Mike Levine, was astonished by Hoover's decision to enlist a known Mafia strongman to further the cause of justice. "Here the FBI uses a member of a violent secret society—La Cosa Nostra—to travel down to Mississippi on multiple missions to torture confessions out of two guys who were also members of a violent secret society—the Klan. Since when does the federal government have to stoop to levels like that to make cases? This was during the same era when the CIA was trying to get mob guys to kill Castro." As Levine notes, such behavior on the Feds' part was roundly denounced during congressional hearings in the 1970s,[31] and the popular assumption was that it stopped. "But the fact that the Bureau continued to use a multiple murderer like Scarpa right up into the early 1990s," says Levine, "just proves that it didn't."[32]

Anthony Villano, Scarpa's control agent from 1967 to 1973, also disapproved. In his 1977 memoir, *Brick Agent,* Villano wrote, "When I heard the story [about Mississippi] and confirmed it was [Scarpa] I was ashamed that the people I worked for had to go outside the Bureau to find someone to perform their dirty work. An agent could have done what [Scarpa] did, but using him, of course, reduced the potential for scandal about the behavior of agents on the job."[33]

Conflicting Accounts

At least three published descriptions of Scarpa's work for the FBI in Mississippi commingle the 1964 MISSBURN and 1966 Dahmer interrogations into one mission. In *Mafia Son,* a 2009 biography of Scarpa's son Gregory Jr., author Sandra Harmon writes that in 1964, after receiving the gun from the FBI agent in the Mississippi hotel, "Greg Sr. drove a rented car to a small appliance store owned by a Klansman named Byrd."[34] In Harmon's account, Scarpa drove "south for several hours" tailed by "a second car filled with federal agents"; rather than Camp Shelby, she gives the location of

Byrd's interrogation as "a lonely country cabin tucked deep in the Mississippi woods."

Supplying what purports to be actual dialogue from the incident, Harmon then mixes details from Scarpa's interrogation of the KKK mayor from the MISSBURN case and appliance store owner Byrd from the Dahmer case. She even furnishes details, purportedly from Byrd's mouth, about the abduction of Goodman, Schwerner, and Chaney—an incident that took place eighteen months earlier.

Jerry Capeci, a respected reporter on organized crime whose "Gang Land" column appeared for many years in the New York *Daily News* and the *New York Sun,* is credited with being the first reporter to break the Scarpa connection to the MISSBURN story in that June 21, 1994, *Daily News* article he wrote with Tom Robbins.[35] But in a subsequent column published in the *Sun* on January 12, 2006, Capeci also combines details of Scarpa's involvement in the Goodman, Schwerner, and Chaney investigation with the mobster's subsequent role in the Vernon Dahmer murder.[36]

In that *Sun* column, Capeci writes that Scarpa was flown to Miami in the 1964 MISSBURN case *before* he went to Mississippi, then cites details that could only have occurred in 1966 in connection with the Dahmer firebombing investigation, which involved TV and appliance dealer Lawrence Byrd: "Scarpa stopped at his store," writes Capeci, "said he was new in town, and put down a deposit on a television set. He promised to pick it up by closing time. When he returned, he got the merchant to help him carry the TV to his car, slapped him over the head with a pipe, tied him up, and threw him in the trunk of the car. He drove to a prearranged location, a shanty deep among tall loblolly pines where FBI agents were hidden outside."

Like Sandra Harmon in *Mafia Son,* Capeci includes verbatim dialogue that purports to be from Scarpa's interrogation of Byrd: "What happened to the three kids?" he has Scarpa saying, adding the line he included in his 1994 story with Robbins: "Tell me the f——ing truth or I'll blow your f——ing brains out."

Similarly, in a January 17, 2006, piece for the *Village Voice,* where he worked after leaving the *Daily News,* Robbins writes in reference to the MISSBURN incident that Scarpa "walked into a Philadelphia appliance shop owned by a Klan-tied merchant whom the FBI believed knew the fate of the missing civil rights workers. Scarpa convinced the man he had just come to town and wanted a new TV set. But when he returned to pick it up that evening, he slugged the merchant, tossed him in the trunk of a car, and drove him to a remote spot where bureau agents were standing guard."[37]

What makes Robbins's combination of the 1964 and 1966 Scarpa missions interesting is the fact that in his *Village Voice* piece he actually cites the January 21, 1966, FBI memo on Scarpa's recruitment in the Dahmer case. "An agent is seeking permission to use Scarpa 'on a special' again in Mississippi," writes Robbins—proof that he knew of *two missions,* not just the one he and Capeci reported on in 1994—the MISSBURN initiative that they confused with the Dahmer case.

These mistakes by Robbins and Capeci are worth noting because it was an interview they did with Linda Schiro in 1997 that led to the dramatic dismissal of murder charges against Scarpa's fourth major FBI contacting agent, Lin DeVecchio, in 2007. We'll examine the details of that case later.

But whatever conflicts may exist in published accounts of Scarpa's story, one thing is clear: He was a ruthless gangster with little regard for human life and we can now say with certainty that J. Edgar Hoover himself understood that. Nonetheless, the Director continued to encourage the Bureau's use of "34" as an informant.

Testifying in 1986 before the President's Commission on Organized Crime, Marty Light, one of Scarpa's former lawyers, reflected: "Greg was the type of guy who would arrange to have dinner with you. He would laugh, make jokes, ask about your family and then when dessert came, he would just whack you right on the spot."[38] Years later, Scarpa crew member Joseph Ambrosino was asked at trial why they called his boss the Grim Reaper. "He was crazy," Ambrosino replied. "He killed a lot. He was nuts."[39]

Chapter 5

SINATRA, CAPOTE, AND THE ANIMAL

As Greg Scarpa continued receiving those cash payments of $125 a month from the FBI, the special agents who debriefed him continually emphasized his unique benefit and future potential in their airtels to Hoover.

> June 6, 1963: CI has furnished information of great value to the Criminal Intelligence Program and possesses a tremendous potential to fully penetrate the NY Italian underworld.[1]

By September 1964, Scarpa was regularly informing Hoover on the movements of Joe Colombo, the boss of his crime family, who operated out of Cantalupo Realty on Eighty-Sixth Street in Bensonhurst, Brooklyn.[2] On September 21, Scarpa told a story that must have intrigued Hoover, who had made frequent use of illegal electronic surveillance over the years:

> September 21, 1964: On 9/17 informant advised that he had gone to Cantalupo Realty to see JOE COLOMBO and that . . . upon entering the office he observed a telephone repairman and two police officers. He stated that he subsequently ascertained that in the early morning hours,

a neighbor had observed individuals running wires from the office . . . and reported this to COLOMBO. . . . COLOMBO ▬▬▬▬▬ followed the wire to the telephone poles and down the street to a tool shed on the Dyker Beach Golf Course where they located an unmanned tape recorder.

The airtel makes no mention of whether the ELSUR was supplied by the Bureau, but at that point President Johnson's ban on wiretaps was still in effect, and the jerry-rigged nature of the job suggests it was too unsophisticated for Hoover. Besides, with Scarpa on the inside of the family, Hoover had a source capable of giving him much more than any tape recorder in a shed. And, as time passed, the informant did.

In November 1965, Scarpa reported on a kind of mini-Mafia summit involving the heads of two of New York's families, Joe Colombo and Carlo Gambino, along with Raymond Patriarca, who controlled the underworld in New England. Scarpa's presence at the dinner, held at the Bonaparte Restaurant in Brooklyn, underscored his own standing in the family.

> November 3, 1965: Informant . . . advised that on 9/22/65 he met with RAYMOND PATRIARCA, JOSEPH COLOMBO, CARLO GAMBINO and COLOMBO "family" members CHARLE S. MINEO, VINCENT ALOI [and] JOHN FRANZESE.[3]

Playing Hard to Get

By the fall of 1966, the FBI had paid Gregory Scarpa nearly $17,000 since he'd been reopened in 1961, the equivalent of more than $121,000 in 2013 dollars.[4] Up to that point he had dealt with only two contacting agents working out of the FBI's New York Office. The names of the agents are unknown outside the Bureau, redacted even in the newly released airtels chronicling the New York SAC's reports to Hoover.

In March 1965, one of those agents was transferred. By April, when the other agent was sent to Chicago, Scarpa refused to meet with anyone else.[5]

After the second agent left, the Bureau attempted to contact Scarpa seven times through a secret prearranged method, but he never responded. In a memo to Hoover on July 29, 1967, the New York SAC noted that "after the transfer of the original agents who developed informant, he strongly endeavored to discontinue his relationship with the Bureau."

> July 29, 1967: Informant point[ed] out the fact that he had lived in constant fear of discovery and considers himself extremely lucky in escaping detection. He said that if he were "found out" not only would he himself have been killed, but more importantly his relatives and family would have had to endure the resulting shame.[6]

The NYO went so far as to call back one of the two prior contacting agents[7] to reach out to the reluctant CI. At that point, realizing that the Bureau was desperate to get him back, Scarpa played for sympathy, complaining that he owed the IRS $1,400 and New York State another $400, in back taxes.[8] For a gangster who carried $5,000 in his pocket while executing jewelry, bullion, and securities thefts worth hundreds of thousands of dollars, Scarpa was clearly guilty of tax evasion. But the Bureau, hungry to reestablish him as source, seemed uninterested in informing the IRS.

"It would have taken one phone call back in 1967 for his contacting agents to pull his tax returns and determine if he really did owe that $1,800," says former agent Dan Vogel. "But that might have produced confirmation that he was lying to them."[9]

In any case, characterizing Scarpa as "invaluable to [the FBI's] intelligence operation in New York," James H. Gale, the Bureau's assistant director, made a direct appeal to Cartha DeLoach, the deputy director, then the number three man under Hoover.[10] In a memo from August 4, 1967, Scarpa is described as having "identified over 200 members of the LCN in [the] New York and New Jersey area."

> August 4, 1967: His services cannot be duplicated by any other source currently furnishing information to the New York Office. It is believed [to be] in the Bureau's best interests to make every effort to insure that the informant is an active and productive source regarding LCN activity. Approval of the request of the NYO should enable the Bureau to receive

maximum benefit from the services of this source. ACTION: It is recommended that the attached teletype be forwarded to the NYO authorizing the lump-sum payment of ████████████.

Gale's appeal was sent just after Scarpa was reinstated as a Top Echelon informant. By late July 1967, the Bureau decided that his new contacting agent would be Anthony Villano, also known as Tony or Nino.[11]

Villano, a Brooklyn-born Italian American,[12] claimed to have "developed more members of organized crime as sources of information than anyone else in the FBI."[13] In his 1977 memoir, *Brick Agent,* he would describe his relationship with Scarpa as a "marriage." From 1967 until his retirement in 1973, Villano went to extraordinary lengths to protect Scarpa from arrest or prosecution. But he was constantly aware that interacting with the Mafia killer was like playing with explosives.

"I had to reassure myself," he wrote, "that our relationship was not the ultimate perversion of the whole law enforcement idea."[14]

Scarpa had met with his previous handlers once or twice a month, but in an August 25, 1967, airtel, Villano noted, "Arrangements have now been perfected whereby informant will be contacted at a discreet location in various hotels in the NY area on a weekly basis."[15]

Using a kind of carrot-and-stick incentive with the FBI, Scarpa suggested (per the memo) that "if adequately compensated, he would subtly express interest in being elevated to the position of 'caporegima' [*sic*] within the COLOMBO 'family.'"[16] (Apparently Villano hadn't read the airtels of Scarpa's initial briefings, which listed him as a capo five years earlier.) But to frost the cake with a little name-dropping, the airtel, quoting Scarpa, noted, "He continues to be well liked by JOSEPH COLOMBO, especially inasmuch as they are presently partners in informant's numbers operation."

"That line right there should have been a warning to Villano," says former DEA Special Agent Mike Levine. "A wiseguy who's a mere soldier below the captain level is not going to be in partnership with the boss or even talking to him. Scarpa clearly had access to Joe Colombo, but he was jacking up the Bureau for more funds and they were so glad to have him back that nobody was asking any hard questions at the time."[17]

In Villano's memoir, he claims that the real reason Scarpa withdrew from the Bureau was over a debt the killer felt the Bureau owed him.[18]

Using two composite characters ("Julio" and "Nick Biletti") to repre-sent Scarpa,[19] Villano writes that when he first approached Scarpa, the for-mer CI was miffed that the FBI had welched on paying his expenses for the Lawrence Byrd–Vernon Dahmer mission.[20]

"My expenses came to about twenty-three hundred," said Scarpa to Villano, "and that covers . . . the car rentals, motels and meals for the four days I took off. I beat that creep [Byrd] out of eight hundred, so all I want is the rest of what I laid out, fifteen hundred." When Villano made that clear to the SAC, Washington was immediately contacted and "a lump sum pay-ment of $1,500" was quickly approved.[21]

By January 1968, the Bureau had upped Scarpa's monthly cash pay-ments to $600—the equivalent of nearly $4,000 in current dollars[22]—and the airtels started flowing again.[23] Right away, he began showing results:

> January 18, 1968: Based on information furnished by informant . . . approximately 50 individuals have been arrested by the NYCPD* and charged with gambling.[24]

"Of course, you have to keep in mind," says Levine, "that this kind of thing could have served Scarpa's interests. It's entirely possible that some of those fifty guys were competitors of Greg's. If he had a problem with another wiseguy in the family, or he wanted to move in on another guy's action, all he had to do was drop a dime on him with the Bureau. . . . The FBI was eating out of his hand."[25]

Retired FBI Special Agent Dan Vogel adds, "It would be a perfect way to get rid of his competition and, at the same time, stay protected."[26]

Reaching Out to Sinatra

J. Edgar Hoover's thirst for gossip was legendary. One of his closest friends was columnist Walter Winchell, who convinced gangster Louis "Lepke" Buchalter, a partner with Albert Anastasia in Murder Incorporated, to sur-

---

* "NYCPD" was the FBI's designation for the NYPD in its communiqués.

render to Hoover in 1939.[27] Greg Scarpa, who was a brilliant judge of character, understood that. When he revealed the details behind a secret meeting between Joseph Colombo and the man later known as the Chairman of the Board, the account of his debriefing didn't just go out in a traditional airtel; it was flashed to Hoover by teletype from the New York Office.

Barboza before the House Crime Committee, May 25, 1972

In this case the gossip involved not only Frank Sinatra but arguably the most flamboyant and celebrity-conscious writer in the nation at that time, Truman Capote. The story began in Boston, when Joseph "the Animal" Barboza, a vicious killer in the family of New England crime czar Raymond Patriarca, "flipped" and started talking to the Feds.

According to Scarpa, Barboza and his attorney John Fitzgerald, who had lost his leg to a mob car bomb,[28] decided that the Animal would publish his memoirs, as Valachi had done through writer Peter Maas. The initial teletype, written in the bold, clipped style of a telegram, never mentioned Capote, but it was provocative nonetheless.

> February 15th, 1968: Informant advised Joseph Colombo, NY LCN Commission member, recently returned from trip to Miami. Colombo confided to informant, trip was not a vacation but a favor for Raymond Patriarca, New England LCN "Boss." Patriarca aware that Colombo, a close friend of singer Frank Sinatra, requested that Colombo get Sinatra to intercede with Author, known to Sinatra, who is presently writing book based on information from stool pigeon which would be damaging to Patriarca. Colombo said he "sat" with Sinatra in Miami and characterized Author as "bad" and "ruthless" individual. Sinatra said he "would do anything" for Colombo, but that this author might even tell of Sinatra's efforts to muzzle him, and therefore "begged off."[29]

Another teletype, sent from the Boston SAC the next day, clarified what was clearly just a rumor, noting that "the name of Truman Capote had arisen as a possible author for the book, however, no definite agreement has been reached."[30]

Why Raymond Patriarca would suspect that Old Blue Eyes might have any influence over Capote, whose chilling 1965 account of the Clutter family murders, *In Cold Blood,* had become an international bestseller, is anybody's guess. Capote was never known as a Mafia aficionado. Apart from his bestselling books, however, by 1968 Capote was famous for something else: the celebrated Black and White Ball he'd thrown at the Plaza Hotel in 1966 to honor Katharine Graham, owner of the *Washington Post.* Among the masked guests at the affair, later dubbed the "Party of the Century,"[31] were Frank Sinatra and his diminutive then wife, Mia Farrow.[32]

Mia Farrow and Frank Sinatra at the Black and White Ball

Sinatra and Farrow were even mentioned in the second paragraph of society writer Charlotte Curtis's coverage of the event in the *New York Times;* a piece headlined "Capote's Black and White Ball: 'The Most Exquisite of Spectator Sports.'"[33]

We don't know whether Raymond Patriarca was a regular reader of the *Times,* but a later airtel, on March 13, 1968, attempted to explain why Colombo had been dispatched to Miami:

> March 13, 1968: In the recent murder trial of JERRY ANGIULO and others in connection with the gangland slaying of ROCCO DE SEGLIO, questions by the defense attorneys concerning this book [by Barboza] were asked and the name TRUMAN CAPOTE came up during this interrogation.

The airtel concluded with a note saying that, "according to JOSEPH BARBOZA, all discussions relative to this book have ceased. ██████████ has stated that he is no longer interested in same, fearing physical harm." It's impossible to say who the man known as the Animal was more afraid of—Cosa Nostra or the "ruthless" Truman Capote—but this series of entries by Greg Scarpa Sr. was sure to keep Hoover begging for more.

"We Turned Enough Cheeks"

In 1966, Scarpa reported that "an organization is being formed called AID,"* whose purpose was "to combat the anti-Italian sentiment now in the U.S."[34] Three years later, Joseph Colombo had morphed it into the Italian-American Civil Rights League (IACRL), defying the traditional rule that Mafia business be conducted in secret.[35] As far as Colombo was concerned, the FBI's investigation of the mob was nothing more than "harassment." As unrealistic as that may have been, the boss began to identify with minority groups and antiwar protestors, who had also become targets of the Bureau. In one airtel, Scarpa related that the boss had told him, "We turned enough cheeks. We got to take steps. Enough is enough."

On April 30, 1970, after Colombo's son Joe Jr. was arrested, about thirty "members" of the new group picketed the FBI's New York Office, at Third Avenue and Sixty-Ninth Street on Manhattan's Upper East Side.[36] Scarpa not only carried a picket sign, he also acted as an occasional public spokesman for the group, denouncing the government—even as he was secretly betraying the Mafiosi with whom he was picketing. Within weeks, the small cadre of protesters grew to five thousand. By midyear, Colombo boasted that the Civil Rights League had forty-five thousand dues-paying members. The mainstream media didn't take him seriously until the IACRL held its first Unity Day rally at Columbus Circle that June and fifty thousand people showed up.

In November 1970, Frank Sinatra did a benefit concert for the group. Soon its political clout grew exponentially. Later, at Colombo's urging, the ABC television network announced that it would excise the words "Mafia" and "Cosa Nostra" from its popular series *The FBI*.[37] Al Ruddy, who was producing the film adaptation of Mario Puzo's novel *The Godfather,* made the same pledge.[38] Even U.S. Attorney General John Mitchell promised to remove the term "Mafia" from all Justice Department press releases.[39]

In May 1971, Rabbi Meir Kahane, the founder of the Jewish Defense League, announced he was joining forces with the IACRL to fight what he

---

* American-Italian Anti-Defamation (Council).

called harassment by the federal government.[40] As Nicholas Pileggi wrote in the *New York Times,* "After 48 years of hiding behind his lapels, Colombo had emerged as a formidable public figure. He posed for pictures, kissed children, signed autographs, talked to Dick Cavett and Walter Cronkite' and generally comported himself more like a political candidate than a Mafia boss."[41] Colombo even made the cover of *Time,* pointing his finger defiantly at the camera. But while Carlo Gambino was initially supportive, Colombo's high profile soon began to anger the other Commission bosses.

Joseph Colombo, *Time,*
July 12, 1971

On June 28, 1971, Colombo was walking near a stage in Columbus Circle, about to address tens of thousands of supporters at the second Unity Day rally, when a twenty-five-year-old black man named Jerome Johnson, posing as a cameraman, lunged forward and shot him twice in the head. Johnson was killed almost instantly by an unknown shooter and Colombo, critically injured, was rushed to nearby Roosevelt Hospital.[42]

Although the police reported that Johnson had links to the Gambino crime family, another prime suspect was Crazy Joe Gallo, who had been paroled from prison on April 11.[43] Gallo was immediately questioned by police but soon released for lack of evidence. Colombo lay in a coma for years and never recovered, leaving a vacuum for control of the family that touched off a second war for succession.[44]

As the bodies fell, the bloodshed only enhanced Greg Scarpa's value to the FBI—and the airtels to come reveal how he brilliantly exploited the struggle for family dominance between his chief rival, Carmine Persico, and the unpredictable Joey Gallo.

Chapter 6

AGENT PROVOCATEUR

The term "agent provocateur," from the nineteenth-century French, literally means "provocative agent," but it has come to represent a person employed by a law enforcement agency to entice another person to commit an illegal act.[1] Although the FBI paid Gregory Scarpa for his services on a COD basis and insisted in one of its memos that "he [was] not an employee of the Bureau,"[2] the newly released secret files prove beyond a reasonable doubt that Scarpa wasn't just supplying inside intelligence to the Bureau. Rather, he was acting with the apparent consent of top FBI officials to commit crimes and induce other members of the Mafia to break the law.[3]

The Bureau's strategy was clearly to facilitate Scarpa so that he could move higher and higher in the family hierarchy, and thus be positioned to provide J. Edgar Hoover with the kind of top-shelf intelligence on the Mafia he coveted. In the course of Scarpa's two long runs as a Top Echelon informant, from 1962 to 1975 and 1980 to 1992, he officially earned $158,400 in monthly and lump sum payments from the FBI.[4] At the same time, with the help of his FBI contacting agent in the late 1960s, Scarpa pocketed some $52,000 in reward money from insurance companies anxious to recover a portion of the millions of dollars he stole in precious gems, gold, furs, liquor, cigarettes, antiques, negotiable securities, and bonds.[5]

Adjusted for 2013 dollars, the combined total paid to "34" by the FBI and insurance companies was an astonishing $1,077,668.50.[6]

Thus, as a double agent, Scarpa betrayed both of his paymasters: the Bureau and the "family" to which he'd sworn a blood oath back in 1950. With the lethal precision of a deep-cover mole, he supplied federal prosecutors with enough probable cause to secure the Title III wiretaps that led to the virtual dismantling of one of the most powerful and dangerous New York families.[7] Yet the intel he gained from his dealings with the Bureau gave him the edge he needed to eliminate virtually every made member who stood above him in the family or posed a threat to his own criminal interests.

Based on the intel or probable cause he furnished, the Feds eventually indicted the godfathers Joseph Colombo and Carmine Persico; Colombo's son Joseph, whose arrest triggered the Italian-American Civil Rights League picketing at the FBI; Carmine's son Little Allie Boy Persico; underbosses Alphonse Persico and Gennaro "Jerry Lang" Langella; and dozens of capos, including John "Jackie Zambooka" De Ross and Dominick "Donnie Shacks" Montemarano. Finally, Scarpa's plotting also helped him to inflame the conflict with the Gallo brothers, leading to their violent demise and ending their threat to his advancement.

The Scarpa airtels dating from October 1967 through October 1984 offer a fascinating chronicle of the mobster's deliberate undermining of three separate family factions: the Colombos, the Gallos, and the Persicos, culminating in Carmine the Snake's 139-year sentence. Persico's imprisonment paved the way for the third war for the takeover of the family in the early 1990s—the bloody conflict in the streets of Brooklyn that Scarpa instigated and waged while he was under the purported "control" of FBI Supervisory Special Agent Lin DeVecchio.

In the end, Gregory Scarpa Sr. never reached the top of the family. But that was entirely the result of his infection with HIV in 1986, which weakened him and led to his death at the age of sixty-six in 1994. Had Scarpa remained in good health, given his cold-blooded willingness to wipe out all enemies in his path—and the extraordinary protection and intelligence he received from the FBI—there is every likelihood that he would have ascended eventually to the position of boss.

Taking Out Colombo

Scarpa's drive to take control of the family began in earnest in the early 1970s, when he first targeted the very godfather who trusted him. Though Joseph Colombo eventually died in 1978 from the wounds he received during the assassination attempt in Columbus Circle, it's clear from the airtels that he was marked for removal years earlier by Scarpa, the very capo described in those FBI memos as Colombo's "choice lieutenant."[8]

In May 1971, the *New York Times* ran a profile on Colombo, who was then, at forty-eight, the youngest Mafia leader in the country. Noting that "Colombo [put] a high premium on loyalty," the piece reported that the boss had recently been arrested along with thirty others on an interstate gambling charge, for an operation that grossed between $50,000 and $100,000 a week. The article was written by Nicholas Gage, the dean of organized crime reporters at that time and one of the most thorough journalists ever to cover Cosa Nostra. But what Gage could not have known at the time was that the precise intelligence that led to Colombo's arrest had come from Gregory Scarpa. Moreover, it was Scarpa who actually estimated the amount of the protection money, or "pad," that Colombo was using to pay off the NYPD.

> November 3, 1970: Informant advised that . . . JOSEPH COLOMBO is in partnership with approximately ten individuals who each control a numbers operation in the New York area. Informant estimated the weekly gross is between $50,000 and $100,000 and having a weekly payoff to the NYCPD on a divisional and borough level of approximately $2,500–$5,000.[9]

In that same airtel, Scarpa also identified the bagman who made the purported payoffs, though the identity of the courier is redacted in the files as released by the Bureau.

Still, the full significance of Scarpa's duplicity can be measured by examining his FBI debriefing memos in the months leading up to the attempted slaying of Colombo and in the years that followed as the boss wasted away in a coma.

On October 11, 1967, Scarpa informed his contacting agent, Anthony Villano, that Colombo's son, Joseph Anthony Jr., would be married on December 9 at the Queens Terrace Restaurant. The event was guaranteed to bring out the New York LCN hierarchy, giving the Bureau a major surveillance opportunity.

> October 11, 1967: COLOMBO has been taking great pains and precautions to screen the waiters and other employees at the restaurant to make sure no information concerning the affair is "leaked." Informant also learned that there will be no other affair in progress that night and that the entire premises will be used exclusively for ANTHONY's wedding party.[10]

A year later, it was Scarpa Sr. who tipped the Bureau to an alleged scam by the young newlywed Anthony Jr. to melt down up to half a million dollars in U.S. silver coins for sale at a higher price.[11] But that same memo underscored Scarpa's capacity for deceit, because in the months following Anthony's arrest, while publicly protesting it and working actively on behalf of the Italian-American Civil Rights League, Scarpa was secretly telling his FBI handlers he was "disgusted" at Colombo's actions.

> November 9, 1970: Immediately subsequent to COLOMBO JR.'s arrest, COLOMBO SR. became enraged and organized picketing of the NYO of the FBI, alleging harassment. It is interesting to note that this picketing lasted for approximately 2 months, culminating in a march from Columbus Circle. Throughout this entire period the informant participated on a regular basis in all activities and was able to keep the Bureau advised on a current basis as to exactly what COLOMBO's intentions were.

For the first Unity Day rally in 1970, Scarpa even boasted to the Bureau that he had "personally supervised the unloading of about 100 chartered buses from his area alone," noting that the event had the "complete blessing of CARLO GAMBINO," then the boss of bosses in New York.[12] Another memo in November reported that "Informant has the full confidence and a close working relationship with JOSEPH COLOMBO."[13]

But by the spring of 1971, Scarpa was grousing to his contacting agents that Colombo was a "bloodthirsty, vindictive man" who might "be going prematurely senile." In that same airtel, as an example of how Greg Sr. often gave the Bureau conflicting intelligence, he reported that "COLOMBO anticipates no problems with 'CRAZY JOE' [Gallo], who is being released from prison this week." Yet after Colombo was shot Gallo became one of the NYPD's lead suspects, and just days before that second Unity Day rally on June 28, Scarpa reported that Colombo had done a 180-degree turn in assessing the threat:

> June 16, 1971: COLOMBO continued that in the event GALLO hit one of his "crew," informant should be ready, because at that time they would take swift and decisive action and wipe out the entire GALLO mob in one fell swoop.[14]

Without any suspicion that Scarpa was informing on him to the Bureau, Joe Colombo had so much faith in Greg that he was willing to dispatch him to help exterminate an entire faction of the family.

On the Brink of Upheaval

At that point, just before the attack on Colombo, Scarpa painted a vivid portrait for the FBI of a family under siege, noting that Joe Gallo was hunkering down and blocking off streets in his Brooklyn neighborhood.

> June 16, 1971: GALLO has been barricading President Street and will not allow cars in the neighborhood. GALLO had beaten up some "hangers on" and had allegedly hurt his hand while choking the mother of one of his own crew. In addition, GALLO had removed all of the Unity Day posters from shop windows and sent his crew up to scrape any Civil Rights stickers off cars in the neighborhood.

Scarpa used the simmering conflict to his full advantage, making it clear to Bureau officials that his intel was indispensable at a critical time. In fact, that same June 16 airtel confirmed that Bureau officials saw Scarpa as their own "agent provocateur." At that point, they weren't simply content to arrest Mafiosi for breaking the law. The FBI now had an affirmative plan to *destroy* the Colombo family.

June 16, 1971: It is noted the NYO requested a sizeable increase in informant's monthly payments. It is felt that the consistently high quality of information furnished by the source and the risks he is subjected to in his role as a member, are commensurate with the requested increase. JOSEPH "Crazy Joe" GALLO is planning to begin hostilities against COLOMBO. It is therefore of utmost importance that . . . the informant be nurtured and maintained to insure that the ultimate destruction of this "crime" family can be effected.

A Role in Colombo's Shooting?

Given Scarpa's capacity for betrayal, the question of whether he played a role in the attempted assassination in Columbus Circle is worth considering—especially in light of what the airtels now reveal. Twelve days *before* Colombo was gunned down by Jerome Johnson, an African American, Scarpa was laying the groundwork for a scenario that would later support the theory that Joe Gallo was behind the hit.

On 6/10/71: Informant advised that he had recently met with JOE COLOMBO at which time COLOMBO confided that during the previous week he had been told that a car containing a number of Negro individuals was observed circling his block many times in the early AM hours. It is well know[n] that GALLO became friendly with Negro hoodlums while incarcerated and . . . it is possible that GALLO has enlisted their aid at the present time.

Joe Colombo after the shooting

Considering his hatred for Colombo, the reckless Crazy Joe Gallo would certainly have been at the top of any suspect list—reason enough for Scarpa to use Gallo's association with blacks to mask any role that he himself may have played in the assassination attempt. Further, in an airtel documenting his debriefing the day after the Unity Day shooting, Scarpa seemed to know a great deal about Johnson, who was a virtual enigma to the NYPD at that point.

> June 29, 1971: Informant has learned that JOHNSON was a "would-be Black wise guy" and hung out in Greenwich Village . . . and that JOHNSON had often visited social clubs and after hours joints in Brooklyn . . . this is the kind of person who if approached correctly, would "do anything" for a price.[15]

On July 7, Scarpa took a different tack, confirming via Joseph Yacovelli, the consigliere, that Persico would be named underboss in the event of Colombo's death. Now he shifted any potential blame away from himself by suggesting to the FBI that Carmine the Snake was responsible for the aborted hit, and that he'd used Johnson to make it look like Joe Gallo was involved.

> July 7, 1971. Informant advised that as soon as COLOMBO was dead that [Joseph] YACOVELLI [consigliere] would name CARMINE PERSICO as underboss . . . and that perhaps this could have been one of the factors which would have given PERSICO a motive to set up a hit on COLOMBO as well as the fact that JOE GALLO would logically be assumed to be the person who "gave the contract."[16]

At that point, though, Persico was already facing a federal conviction that would eventually lead to a fourteen-year sentence. It was the mercurial Joe Gallo, not Persico, who was Scarpa's immediate threat.[17] If the other family members believed it was Gallo who hired Johnson, Scarpa knew that Crazy Joe would also be marked for death—thus removing him, as well as Persico, as barriers to Scarpa's advancement. This was treachery on an almost Shakespearean level—the kind of machination that would lead Scarpa's own attorney, Lou Diamond, to describe him as a "puppeteer."

"He lived to manipulate people against people," Diamond said in an interview with Fred Dannen for the *New Yorker*. "Greg was probably one of the better gin rummy players. He had an excellent mind. An ability to focus, plan. You had to understand the brilliance of the man."[18] A cunning strategic mind, access to FBI intelligence, and a willingness to commit murder: that was Scarpa's deadly triad of assets, and he used them to his full advantage in the days after Colombo's shooting.

Two weeks after the bloodshed in Columbus Circle, this airtel went to Hoover:

> July 15, 1971. Informant advised that it appears that CARMINE PER-SICO is "on the move" in attempting to gain control of the Colombo family as well as the vast resources of the IACRL. PERSICO had advanced $30,000 to the League to continue present operating expenses.

In the same memo, Scarpa said he'd learned that one of Colombo's brothers-in-law had come to visit the boss at Roosevelt Hospital, and that this unnamed relative had advised Colombo capo Mimi Scialo that he knew "where Joey Gallo would be that night and it might present the excellent opportunity to 'hit him.'" According to Scarpa, however, Scialo told this individual that "because of all the police protection on Gallo it would be a 'kamikaze mission' and that some time should elapse before the hit was attempted."

In keeping with the tradition that revenge is a dish best served cold, the forces within the family waited nine months, until Joe Gallo's birthday, to start the next Colombo war.

Joe Gallo taking the Fifth at a McClellan hearing, February 17, 1959

The Death of Crazy Joe

In a criminal organization that traces its roots back to Sicily, symbols are revered. From the Mass-card pictures of saints burned in the palms of inductees during the initiation ceremony to the pricking of inductees' trigger fingers, the rituals of the mob are rife with meaning. One of the most famous scenes in *The Godfather* was inspired by an incident during the first Colombo war in which Profaci gunmen killed a Gallo loyalist, Joseph "Joe Jelly" Gioiello, and tossed his clothing—filled with fish—in front of a restaurant the Gallo brothers frequented. The image inspired Mario Puzo's immortal line "Luca Brasi sleeps with the fishes."[19]

I had the good fortune to interview Puzo just months before his death in 1999 and he told me that the legendary horse's head scene in his fictional chronicle of the Corleone family was inspired by a real-life Sicilian practice. "If one farmer had a dispute with another farmer," he told me, "the aggrieved party would grab his neighbor's prize piece of livestock. Maybe it was a cow or a sheep or a goat. The animal would be killed and the severed head would be nailed to the door of the rival's home as a warning."[20]

When it came to cruelty, the Mafia had few rivals. So the date chosen to close the books on Crazy Joe was his forty-third birthday. As if to send another message in the bargain, the bloody shootout took place in a restaurant just a block away from police headquarters.

On the last night of his life, Joseph Gregory Gallo, dressed in a pinstriped suit, laughed and drank champagne at the Copacabana nightclub in a party that included his sister Carmella Fiorello; his wife of three weeks, a striking Italian American beauty named Sina Essary; Essary's ten-year-old daughter; and Gallo's burly forty-three-year-old bodyguard, Peter Diapoulas, who was accompanied by a date, Edith Russo of Brooklyn. At four A.M., they took a black 1971 Cadillac downtown to Little Italy for dessert at Umberto's Clam House, a new restaurant on Mulberry Street that had recently been opened by Matty "the Horse" Ianiello, a reputed member of the Genovese family.[21] In a cruel bit of Cosa Nostra irony, the location of the second-most-celebrated murder in recent Mafia history bore the name of Gallo's target in the first: Umberto "Albert" Anastasia.

While sitting at a pair of butcher-block tables near the bar, the party drank soda and ordered Italian delicacies.[22] Gallo, who witnesses said was "jolly and relaxed," was facing the wall when suddenly a pair of assailants came in and opened fire. The lead shooter, described as five foot eight with thinning black hair, carried a .38.[23] As the guns went off and the women screamed, Diapoulas was struck twice and went down.

Joe Gallo, shot in the left elbow and buttock, got up and ran to the street while the other restaurant patrons hit the floor. A volley of shots was fired—twenty in all—as Crazy Joe staggered out onto Hester Street, where one of the shooters finished him with a shot to the back. The killers then fled through a back door and jumped into a pair of getaway cars. Carmella rushed outside and stood over her brother's body, wailing.

A week later, the police reported that they were seeking two associates of Colombo consigliere Joseph Yacovelli who had been on the lam. By early May, Joseph Luparelli, a close Yacovelli associate who had set the Gallo murder plot in motion, had turned himself in.

Umberto's Clam House the morning of the Gallo murder

A detailed investigation by *New York Times* reporter Nick Gage revealed that Luparelli had been at the bar in Umberto's that night when he saw Gallo come in with his party. Yacovelli had been waiting months for an opportunity to strike at Gallo, and as soon as he was contacted, he dispatched the hit team, which included Luparelli; Carmine DiBiase, a Colombo racketeer who had once been charged with murder; and two brothers identified simply as Sisco and Benny.

According to Luparelli, it was DiBiase who opened fire as Gallo and his bodyguard sat with their backs to the door.[24] Four guns were used in the shooting. After fleeing the scene, the hit team drove to Nyack, New York, where they hid out in an apartment Yacovelli had rented months earlier as he plotted Gallo's death.

The bloody public execution of Joe Gallo in front of his family touched off another wave of gangland murders. Within three weeks, ten Mafia figures were rubbed out. The newly released files suggest that one of those homicides was the work of Gregory Scarpa—a hit that came at the same time he was schooling the FBI on this latest outbreak in Colombo hostilities.

Death of a Codefendant

In an airtel recounting a briefing on the day of Gallo's murder, Scarpa not only ID'd Carmine Persico as the man who was ultimately responsible for the plot, but he claimed that two of the five rubouts surrounding the murder involved government informants.

> July 25, 1972: On 4/7/72 Source advised that the murder of GALLO was engineered by the Persico crew as a retaliation for shooting JOE COLOMBO and incidents created by GALLOS. Source said he learned that the PERSICO people met with representatives of other LCN families the previous week and conclusions reached were that 5 people had to be killed including two or three informants. It is noted that JERRY CIPRIO as well as RICHARD GROSSMAN were both murdered and were suspected of being Federal informants.[25]

What that airtel doesn't reveal, but has since been discovered in the course of this investigation, is that Gennaro "Jerry" Ciprio was a close associate of Joseph Colombo, who had been indicted with Greg Scarpa in November 1971 in a plot to steal $450,000 in securities from the U.S. mail.[26] On April 10, three days after Gallo's murder, Ciprio was standing outside of Gennaro's Italian Feast Specialties, a restaurant he owned on Eighty-Sixth Street in the Bath Beach section of Brooklyn, when he was instantly killed by a shotgun blast to the head.[27]

The original securities case was brought in Chicago, where the bonds were taken. Ciprio was listed as the number two defendant behind Scarpa, who was named as the top co-conspirator among a list of eleven charged. But by July 1972, with Ciprio out of the picture, Scarpa's attorney successfully convinced a federal judge to transfer the case to the Eastern District of New York (EDNY) in Brooklyn—Greg's home turf.[28]

On April 6, 1973, for unexplained reasons, the EDNY U.S. attorney appeared in open court and asked that the case be dismissed. The dismissal order made no reference to the other surviving codefendants originally charged with Scarpa.[29]

Meanwhile, the day after Ciprio's murder, a federal agent hastened to tell the *New York Times* that the shotgun-blast victim "was a dangerous man who could have done a lot of damage in any war unless he was hit first."[30] So much for the presumption of innocence. The agent's quote was a New York variation on the old Texas phrase "he needed killing"—not the kind of sentiment one would expect to hear from a government agent, unless he had some reason to excuse the shotgun murder.

The Ciprio murder is more than forty years old; any ancillary evidence was likely destroyed long ago. But the implications in this airtel are potentially staggering. If Ciprio was in fact a "Federal informant," as Scarpa attested, he might have been talking to prosecutors in Chicago, and word that he'd flipped could easily have reached New York. Even if one of "34's" handlers had unwittingly mentioned to him that Ciprio was a cooperating witness (CW), once Scarpa pulled the trigger on Ciprio, whoever had leaked word of Ciprio's status as a CW could have effectively become a co-conspirator to homicide.

There are several "might"s and "maybe"s in that proposition, but it's clear from an examination of the fourteen-page indictment in the securities case that the Feds in Chicago had done a thorough job. With Ciprio as a co-conspirator, Scarpa would have been vulnerable to conviction. But with Ciprio dead, the case would have been far more difficult to prove.

If that was the only evidence, associating Greg Scarpa with the murder might be considered a stretch. But when Carmine Sessa, a longtime Scarpa crew member, started talking to FBI agents, he told them a story that contained remarkable parallels to the securities case from which Ciprio was violently removed.

According to an FBI 302 memo dated April 18, 1994, Sessa told agents that "somebody got killed" during the course of a crime involving "bonds." As Supervisory Special Agents David H. Parker and Robert J. O'Brien related Sessa's debriefing, the case involved a "change in venue in [the] prosecution and the charges were subsequently dropped." Sessa recalled that "Scarpa Sr. and Joseph DeDomenico, a.k.a. Joe Brewster, killed somebody, whose name Sessa didn't know."[31]

Was Jerry Ciprio that victim? We can't say for sure, but without him the case was dismissed—and Greg Scarpa had a habit of eliminating witnesses who threatened him. Further, this wouldn't be the only time that charges were dropped against the FBI's TE informant.

As we'll see, another huge stock fraud case against Scarpa ended up dismissed for unexplained reasons. That one was developed by the Newark Strike Force in 1974.

Can we say definitively that Scarpa killed Ciprio? No. Does he look good for it, as detectives say? Absolutely.

"In the years the FBI ran Scarpa Senior, he was given a virtual hunting license," says defense attorney Flora Edwards, who represented Scarpa's chief rival for control of the family in the 1990s. "Looking at this case, it's clear to me that as soon as Ciprio's name showed up under Greg's in that indictment, he was a dead man."[32]

Chapter 7

GOD, THE MOB,
AND THE FBI

Considering his skill as a "chess player," one has to ask, what was Greg Scarpa's motive in claiming to the Feds that Joey Gallo was behind the Colombo attack? The airtels reveal that Scarpa would have been in jeopardy if Crazy Joe had been successful in reviving his crew. Peter Diapoulas, Gallo's bodyguard, later told reporter Nick Gage that before his death Gallo "planned to establish his gang as the sixth Mafia family in New York."[1]

Whether or not that was a realistic goal, Gallo was determined to get his share of the Colombo family spoils he felt he'd been denied since the hit on Anastasia. In a borgata, where there are only so many slices of the pie, a powerful capo like Scarpa, who had refused to throw in with the Gallo crew, would have been a serious obstacle to Crazy Joe's resurgence. So it's no surprise that, on July 25, a week after the Chicago securities case was moved to Brooklyn, J. Edgar Hoover received an airtel quoting Charlie "Moose" Panarella, a Persico loyalist, as saying that "GREGORY SCARPA is on top of the GALLO hit parade."[2]

In just two and a half years, by acting as the FBI's sole oracle on the Colombo crime family, Scarpa had made a series of brilliant moves.

Whether or not he himself played a role in Colombo's shooting, Scarpa had already taken steps to legally neutralize the boss and his son. He then identified his principal competition in the family, Carmine Persico, as the source of the Gallo murder, and with the death of Crazy Joe he insulated himself from a dangerous rival. At the same time, the rubout of Jerry Ciprio helped him beat a stock-theft charge that could have sent him to prison for years. Given his relationship with the Justice Department, Scarpa had little reason to fear the federal government. That explains why he was willing to take the witness chair before the same Senate subcommittee that had grilled Joe Valachi. His testimony came just three weeks after Colombo was shot.

Defying McClellan

On July 21, 1971, in keeping with the double life he was leading, a defiant Greg Scarpa appeared before the McClellan subcommittee, grinning and dressed to the nines in white loafers, camel-colored slacks, a diamond-studded watch, and a bright blue blazer sporting a gold, red, green, and white lapel pin with the logo of the Italian-American Civil Rights League—the same group he'd privately denigrated to his FBI contact agents.[3] When questioned by the senators about his links to a $100 million theft ring, Scarpa took the Fifth Amendment *sixty times*. This was one exchange involving McClellan, Scarpa, and Florida senator Edward J. Gurney:

> **McClellan:** Do you want to deny whether you met with Colombo?
> **Scarpa:** I respectfully decline to answer the question, Senator, on the ground it may tend to incriminate me.
> **Gurney:** I did notice that you were laughing uproariously at the exchange I had on [dumping mob counterfeit money at] the church bazaar. Were you listening at that time?
> **Scarpa:** I respectfully decline to answer the question, Senator, on the ground that it may tend to incriminate me.[4]

Scarpa wouldn't even say whether he'd ever met Joseph Colombo, even though an FBI airtel to Hoover three days earlier confirmed that Scarpa had spoken to the boss just thirty minutes before Jerome Johnson gunned him down.[5]

Greg Scarpa takes the Fifth at the McClellan hearing, July 21, 1971

Another witness at the hearing—a professional thief serving a five-year prison sentence—testified that the theft ring he worked with had stopped using Scarpa as a fence because they considered him "dangerous."

"Do you consider yourself as dangerous?" McClellan asked Scarpa.

"Do *you,* sir?" Scarpa shot back with a smile.

Defying the chairman of one of the most powerful subcommittees on the Hill is some indication of the kind of power Scarpa believed he had as a result of his direct pipeline to Hoover—and with good reason. Bureau agents routinely intervened to keep Scarpa out of jail so that he could continue feeding Hoover's appetite for inside intelligence on the Mafia. But in that secret quid pro quo, Scarpa stayed on the street to steal a fortune through bank robberies, high-end jewelry heists, auto thefts, cocaine trafficking, and securities fraud. Along the way, he left a trail of dead bodies. Were the secrets he was furnishing to Hoover enough to justify this get-out-of-jail-free card? The Feds seemed to think so.

The Olympic Airways Robberies

By August 1968, the relationship between the streetwise Villano and Scarpa was so productive that the informant earned a $4,000 FBI bonus. The money was a reward for Scarpa's help in solving two thefts relating to Olympic Airways, which was owned at that time by Greek shipping magnate Aristotle Onassis. The airtel memorializing the bonus sounded like the kind of citation for meritorious service handed down to a special agent who had performed above and beyond the call of duty:

January 18, 1968: This payment is in recognition of [Scarpa's] valuable services in connection with the theft from Interstate Shipment cases . . . of gold jewelry stolen from Olympic Airlines* in January 1968 and the armed robbery of Olympic Airlines on July 28th. It is noted that the theft of the jewelry led to the recovery of a substantial amount of jewelry stolen in other robberies elsewhere in the country.[6]

Over the next five years, Scarpa regularly informed the FBI about a series of hijackings and robberies, involving stolen merchandise worth millions of dollars. At the same time, he continued to "put down scores" himself. Now the evidence uncovered in this investigation suggests that Scarpa was double-dipping—working a brilliant con in which he would steal the goods, then tip off Villano to the whereabouts of some or all of the swag so that he could collect bonuses and insurance rewards. Consider these airtels:

September 8, 1967: Informant advised that Sally Buzzo . . . had in his garage the proceeds of a rare coin theft, which took place approximately 4 months ago at JFK airport. . . . These coins included ancient Roman coins . . . they were attempting to sell for $30,000.00.[7]

September 11, 1967: Informant advised that ███████████ had . . . in his physical possession at least $50,000 worth of AMERICAN EXPRESS CHECKS [stolen from] Pier 62, U.S. lines on 4/13/67. Value $620,000.[8]

October 16, 1967: Informant advised that RICHARD FUSCO'S regime (crew) had become deeply involved in UNTAXED CIGARETTES. The above information was furnished to the NYCPD and they subsequently advised that they had arrested 3 persons . . . and had seized 1,500 cartons having a value of $6,000.[9]

November 27, 1968: Informant advised that he had been offered a trailer load of CIGARETTES which had been hijacked [and] a trailer containing KODAK PHOTO EQUIPMENT. A resulting search disclosed an additional 550 cases of stolen CIGARETTES [making a recovery

---

* While the official name of Onassis's airline was Olympic Airways, this FBI memo authorizing payment to Scarpa Sr. mistakenly described it as Olympic Airlines.

of $65,000] and KODAK EQUIPMENT with a wholesale value of $56,000.[10]

July 7, 1969: Informant was able to furnish details of ▓▓▓▓▓▓▓ hangouts [that led to the discovery of] $60,000 worth of stolen MAXWELL HOUSE COFFEE, which had been traveling in interstate commerce.

February 24, 1969: Informant was offered a load of CUTTY SARK WHISKEY in fifths . . . a 1,000 case load at $40.00 per case. As a result of information furnished by Informant . . . approximately $360,000 worth of stolen merchandise was recovered and . . . ten individuals arrested.[11]

March 28, 1970: Informant advised he had heard rumors that ▓▓ ▓▓▓▓▓▓ and possibly two other Chicago hoods had been to NYC . . . seeking to purchase stolen securities to bring back to Chicago. Informant heard that a list of STOLEN MUNICIPALS valued at $550,000 was circulating in Brooklyn, NY and this list included . . . CITY OF COLUMBUS BEARER BONDS in $5,000 [denominations]; [and] CITY OF CLEVELAND BEARER BONDS in $5,000 [denominations].[12]

November 9, 1970: Informant advised of an armed hijacking he knew to involve 400 cylinders of MERCURY from Mongam-Kester Transfer Corp at Staten Island. This vital information permitted Bureau Agents to initiate an extremely discreet surveillance [and effect] the recovery of 324 cylinders valued at $200,000.[13]

As a result of the thefts and hijackings Scarpa reported following the Olympic Airways heists, the Bureau approved six more lump sum payments to him from 1969 to 1973 ranging in amounts from $4,000 to $5,000. Throughout the course of these bonus payments, Scarpa continually complained to Villano that he was strapped for cash and insisted that more income from the FBI would help him to improve his standing in the family and gain greater access to useful intelligence.

In a November 16, 1970, airtel from Assistant Director J. H. Gale to William C. Sullivan, the head of the Bureau's intelligence operation, Gale cited the mercury and Maxwell House coffee seizures and reminded

Sullivan that Scarpa had informed them of the "vociferous smear campaign against the FBI represented by the Italian-American Civil Rights League picketing." The memo also cited Scarpa's help in busting Joseph Colombo's gambling operation and the payoffs to the NYPD, opining that "the informant at extreme personal danger, has enabled the Bureau to penetrate top level LCN activity in New York." Gale closed the memo with a reminder, prompted by Scarpa's requests to Villano, that the informant was "currently in dire need of financial assistance."

As defense attorney Ellen Resnick observes, these airtels leave "no doubt that Gregory Scarpa Sr. had advocates at the highest levels of the FBI in Washington."[14]

Scarpa's "Finder's Fees"

Villano was apparently so snookered by Scarpa's claim of money problems that he devised an even greater source of income for him—one that made the monthly $600 COD payments and bonuses pale in comparison.

In *Brick Agent* Villano writes proudly:

I once figured that Nick Biletti [Scarpa] actually earned $65,000 over an eighteen-month period through our relationship. The Bureau salary accounted for only about twenty percent of his take. The rest came from varyingly grateful insurance companies and others whose valuables were retrieved through Nick's help.

Negotiations for reward money required fancy choreography. Bureau policy officially forbade agents like myself from serving as the middleman between the insurer or trucker and an informant. But no alternative was feasible. The informants could not afford to disclose their identity to the outfits willing to compensate them. The routine was for a source to tell me where a $200,000 load of imported perfume could be found.

The informant would ask for a $20,000 "finder's fee." I would reach the people who were liable for the loss and tell them we had a chance to get back their stuff, but it would cost $20,000. Very often they tried to knock down the price. I'd say that I would check with my informant and see if he'd go for it. A half hour later, without even making an attempt to reach Biletti I would go back to the company and say that $15,000 was the absolute minimum. The terms would be accepted.[15]

In describing Tony Villano, former FBI agent Dan Vogel notes, "you've got an agent who is more or less acting as Scarpa's broker in the deal. What's to prevent the CI from doing hijackings and then leaking back the details on some of them, knowing he's going to get the reward money anyway? This is a classic case of an informant using an agent, versus the way it's supposed to be."[16]

Anthony Villano from the back cover of *Brick Agent*

In *Brick Agent* Villano writes, "I resisted the temptation of some easy cash as a kick-back from my sources after they collected their rewards. I admit to having accepted a bottle of whiskey occasionally." But Scarpa's son later insisted that Villano's relationship with his father amounted to more than that. In a sworn deposition in 2002, Greg Scarpa Jr. stated, "I met my father's first handler, FBI agent Anthony Villano, when I was 16–17 years old . . . at a PAL [Police Athletic League] Center where I was train-ing for the Golden Gloves. My father intro-duced Villano to me as 'the man he reports to.' Villano told me that I was a good fighter but that there were easier ways to make money and that I should work with my father for the FBI. I later learned that my father paid Villano for information and for insulation from prosecution for his criminal activities."[17]

As we'll see later, in 2004 a federal judge found Greg Jr. "not credible" when he made those allegations at a hearing.[18] But the younger Scarpa's reli-ability was demonstrated in 1996 and 2005 when he provided the FBI with highly valuable information on two separate convicted terrorists.[19] We'll examine those details in Chapters 38 and 39. But Villano's own admissions in *Brick Agent* make one element of his relationship with Greg Scarpa Sr. undeniable: He went to extraordinary lengths to insulate his Top Echelon source from prosecution.

The Miami Kidnapping Scam

"Protecting Nick [Scarpa] while making use of his information was a major piece of work for me," Villano writes. He goes on to describe an incident involving Herman "Hy" Gordon, "a notorious Miami fence" famous for his links to Jack "Murph the Surf" Murphy,[20] who was arrested in the 1964 Star of India robbery, the biggest jewel theft in U.S. history.[21]

According to Villano, Scarpa tipped him that Gordon had arrived in New York to inspect a "load of jewelry" stolen by members of the Colombo family. Villano, who fictionalized many details in *Brick Agent,* writes that the score included "a very valuable and distinctive necklace." But the airtels reveal that the "necklace" was actually a pair of "jewel encrusted cups" that were part of the Olympic Airways theft on January 12, 1968.[22] After Gordon agreed to buy the stolen merchandise, Villano writes, the fence paid out $32,000 and headed back to Miami with "$100,000 worth of gems." At that point, Villano says, he contacted Miami Special Agent Joseph Yablonsky, known in the FBI as "the King of Sting."[23] Villano writes that he convinced Yablonsky to "legally get into Gordon's home" in an effort to look for the jewelry.

On the pretext of interviewing Gordon regarding his flights to the Caribbean, Yablonsky then reportedly entered the house and spotted the jewel-encrusted cups in plain sight. According to Villano, that led to a search warrant and Gordon's impending arrest by the FBI for possession of stolen gems. This airtel gives additional details:

> May 3, 1968: As a result of the . . . warrant the Miami office seized 24 pieces of jewelry contained in the Greek shipment and numerous other items of jewelry, loose diamonds and coins. As of this writing, based upon an appraisal by two gemologists, a value of $305,000 was placed on just jewelry items alone.[24]

But at that point in the recovery Scarpa grew concerned. He called Villano to tell him that his past relations with Gordon "could bury him" if he was ever linked back to the case. So Villano came up with an extraordinary plan. "I rushed back to the office," he writes, "to send a teletype to both Miami and the Bureau in Washington informing them that the higher-ups in the LCN were very fearful of Gordon's rolling over [and] had decided to kidnap Gordon's only child, a young daughter." As soon as the bogus teletype was received, Villano contends, the FBI sprang into action and Gordon's daughter was "hustled off to be placed in hiding."

"To help Biletti [Scarpa] retain his good standing with LCN," writes Villano, "I created a phony charge against him."

If Villano was willing to go that far to protect his informant, how far would he go when Scarpa faced criminal charges? The evidence uncovered in this investigation raises compelling questions about the part Anthony Villano and other FBI officials played in keeping Greg Scarpa out of jail. In fact, a comparison of the newly released airtels against an indictment filed by the U.S. attorney in Chicago in 1971, with a superseding indictment the next year, proves that, even as senior FBI officials were *rewarding* Scarpa for giving up stolen securities valued at $550,000, another arm of Justice was *charging* him with stealing municipal bonds, which appear to have come from the same theft.[25]

One hand at Justice didn't seem to know what the other hand was doing, and in the end Greg Scarpa beat the case—with the Bureau's help. We'll examine that story more closely in Chapter 8. Meanwhile, the quintessential example of how Greg Scarpa used his position in the Profaci-Colombo family to please the FBI while enhancing his own rep in the borgata came from his role in the recovery of the Regina Pacis stones.

The Crown Jewels

One of the most famous stories in Brooklyn Mafia lore is Joseph Profaci's involvement in the recovery of two jewel-encrusted crowns stolen from the Regina Pacis (Queen of Peace) Church in Borough Park, the home parish of the devoutly religious boss.

The church was a lavish Renaissance edifice, funded in part by parishioners to the tune of $1 million. Construction began on the building in 1948, and over the next four years more than two thousand tons of Italian marble were used on its interior walls.[26] The church featured sixteen stained-glass windows honoring the Virgin Mother, and behind the altar hung a huge painting of Mary holding the infant Jesus.

Hundreds of parishioners donated family jewelry—including war widows, many of whose donated wedding rings were melted down to create two eighteen-karat-gold crowns, which were hung over the images of the mother and child on the painting. The crowns, decorated with six hundred diamonds, sapphires, and rubies, were valued at the time at $100,000—a sum equal to nearly $870,000 today.[27]

The crowns were normally locked behind a reinforced bronze grillwork and displayed only during important functions. But in January 1952, a week after Pope Pius XII blessed the crowns in Rome, they were stolen from the shrine.[28] Thieves had sawed open a section of the gated grille that protected them. The story made national headlines.[29]

Then, eight days after the theft, the crowns were returned. The thieves were reportedly a pair of brothers, and after the recovery they were found dead, their bodies mutilated, reportedly strangled with rosary beads.[30]

Ten years later, in an airtel to Hoover, Scarpa identified one of the thieves. He told Villano that "a good fellow by the name of BUCKY stole the crown jewels from . . . the church attended by JOSEPH PROFACI [who] had the jewels returned and then ordered BUCKY killed." Scarpa even speculated that "the work" had been done by his mentor Charles LoCicero, because "Bucky" was running numbers for the Sidge at the time.[31] In *Brick Agent*, Villano adds a grisly postscript to the story: In demanding the return of the crowns, he writes, Profaci had insisted on having "one ball from each of those guys" brought to him.

But that wasn't the end of the Regina Pacis story. Twenty-one years after the theft, on January 10, 1973, the crowns were stolen again—this time by "a pair of junkies," as Villano notes in his book.[32] He goes on to write that the thieves happened to visit a gin mill frequented by Scarpa, who overheard them trying to sell the jewels to Charlie "Moose" Panarella, a capo with close ties to Alphonse Persico. Known as "Allie Boy," Persico, who was Carmine's brother, would one day become family underboss. Villano suggests a marginal connection on Scarpa's part, but the newly released airtels reveal that he was much more involved with the jewels than Villano admits.

April 5, 1973: Informant advised that on 1/11/73 CHARLES "MOOSE" PANARELLA, a capo in the COLOMBO LCN family met with him and indicated to source that two young individuals had stolen the Regina

Pacis jewels and that he [source] was to "handle the disposition of the jewels." He said that both are hopheads [addicted to pills]. He said that he felt the thieves did not know the significance of the theft and had voluntarily surrendered the jewels to PANARELLA. On 1/14/73 PANARELLA contacted him and gave him the jewelry. PANARELLA instructed the source to determine the "breakdown" value of the jewelry since he . . . was considering turning them into cash.[33]

Scarpa, the master strategist, understood that the crowns had a value far beyond anything they could bring from a fence. But there was a chance that in brokering the return of the crowns, Scarpa might jeopardize his informant status. As Villano noted in the airtel, "Informant was in no position to 'give up' the jewels without appearing to be cooperating with the FBI." He also suggested that "there was a remote chance that the informant's trustworthiness and judgment in a delicate matter was being tested by certain elements in the PERSICO crew with whom there had been little love lost in the past."

According to Villano, Scarpa arranged for a meeting with Allie Boy Persico and let him know that John Malone, the FBI's assistant director in charge of the New York Office and a "friend of the archbishop," would be immensely grateful if the Persicos would follow Profaci's example from two decades earlier and help recover the stones. If the gems were returned, Villano promised that they wouldn't be dusted for prints and that no one in the Colombo hierarchy would be arrested.

A short time later, "a gruff speaking individual" called the FBI switchboard with word that the missing jewels could be found in a locker at the East Side Airlines Terminal. After Villano and another agent recovered them, Tony writes that "John Malone went berserk with joy." The two agents and their supervisor were nominated by Malone for "incentive awards." Even the FBI operator who took the call got a letter of commendation.

The headline on the story that ran on the national AP wire was "Jewelry Recovered by FBI for Church."[34] It was a stunning public relations success for the Bureau. What Villano leaves out of his book, but the airtel confirms, is that Scarpa received yet another payment of several thousand dollars for his role in the recovery. And in a commendation-like entry, Villano wrote:

January 21, 1973: [SCARPA] demonstrated a sustained coolness and ability to follow Bureau instructions precisely, even while maintaining a difficult posture. The concomitants of this case could hardly have been greater inasmuch as (1) the Bureau received extensive favorable publicity; (2) the recovery of $350,000 of gems with great religious significance was achieved; and (3) the informant's timely suggestions and action under pressure enhanced his position with the PERSICO faction of the COLOMBO family.[35]

But Scarpa's involvement was even more important in retrospect for what it said about his tactical skill. That single tip about Panarella not only reinforced his relationship with Villano, who was regularly kicking back reward money to him; it also endeared Scarpa to Malone, the powerful assistant director in charge of the New York Office.

It also made Carmine Persico and his brother look good. The Snake, who had assumed control of the family after Joseph Colombo's shooting, was now cementing his position as boss. "This was one of those incidents," says James Whalen, a retired special agent from the New York Office, "where Scarpa ended up making everybody happy: God, the mob, and the FBI. It was a triple play."[36]

Chapter 8

THIRTY DAYS IN
FORTY-TWO YEARS

Asked about Gregory Scarpa Sr.'s motivation for cooperating with the Feds, one official told former *New York Times* reporter Selwyn Raab, "It was his insurance policy"—an allusion, wrote Raab, to "Scarpa's hope that he could obtain leniency if he were confronted with a long prison sentence."[1] If that was the Mafia killer's intent, the evidence unearthed in this investigation demonstrates that he was remarkably successful.

From 1950 to 1992, Scarpa was arrested twenty times on charges ranging from gun possession, assault, and hijacking to trafficking in fake securities worth millions. Yet before his final arrest for murder in 1992 he served only thirty days in jail, after pleading guilty in 1978 to the attempted bribery of two police officers.[2]*

In the early 1970s, before the bribery charge,[3] Scarpa was running what an assistant U.S. attorney described as "a sophisticated auto theft ring which stole hundreds of new cars from the streets of New York and had them sent to locations around the world."[4] In the late 1970s Scarpa safeguarded the

---

* A detailed list of his arrests and their dispositions can be found in Appendix C.

proceeds of two substantial crimes: the hijacking of a silver shipment stolen from John F. Kennedy International Airport and the theft of approximately

$2 million in diamonds.[5] In 1986 he was identified as "one of the biggest distributors of counterfeit credit cards in the New York Metropolitan area."[6] After his arrest by undercover Secret Service agents, Scarpa faced a $250,000 fine and up to seven and a half years in prison.[7] But he ended up with a $10,000 fine and five years' probation after Lin DeVecchio intervened on his behalf with the judge.[8]

A lawyer who represented Scarpa put it bluntly: "No one with a track record like that could be so lucky."[9] In a 1992 murder trial under oath, DeVecchio denied that he'd given that kind of help to a confidential informant like Scarpa,[10] but he finally admitted to it in his recent book.[11]

And yet, while Greg Scarpa was getting special protection from the Bureau, other branches of the Justice Department were going to extreme lengths to lock him up.

"Caution Should Be Exercised"

On November 4, 1971, Scarpa was charged with the interstate possession, transport, and sale of $450,000 in securities stolen from the U.S mail, in that case where his named co-conspirator was Gennaro "Jerry" Ciprio, who was killed three days after Joey Gallo.[12]

Though Scarpa slightly overstated the amount of the heist, informing the FBI that the securities were worth $550,000, this was clearly the same theft cited in the March 28, 1970, airtel to Hoover, which identified the securities as stolen Cleveland and Columbus, Ohio, bearer bonds. During his debriefing on that heist, Scarpa pretended he had no personal involvement and was disclosing the theft to the FBI in exchange for a bonus.[13]

As the Chicago Feds were working the case, they were unaware that their principal target in the theft was a Top Echelon Criminal Informant working with the FBI's New York Office. To them, Scarpa was just another wiseguy looking at serious jail time. But in July 1972,[14] after Ciprio's death, the case was transferred to the Justice Department's Eastern District in Brooklyn where it was ultimately dismissed.[15]

The ink on that dismissal was barely dry before Scarpa was facing stolen-securities charges again—this time from the Organized Crime Strike Force in Newark, New Jersey. Prosecutors across the Hudson River were seeking a grand jury indictment of Scarpa for using counterfeit IBM stock certificates that had been printed in New York, sold in New Jersey, and transported to Philadelphia.[16] The estimated face value of the stocks was $4 million—not the kind of number you'd expect to be associated with an FBI informant who was in "dire need of financial assistance."

Throughout the spring and summer of 1973, a flurry of airtels was sent from Newark to Washington keeping Bureau officials in the loop on the progress of the fingerprint analysis tying Scarpa to the fake stock certificates. At the bottom of each airtel was inscribed a warning in bold:

CAUTION SHOULD BE EXERCISED IN THE EVENT ANY CONTACT IS MADE WITH SUBJECT SCARPA . . . IN VIEW OF PREVIOUS ARREST FOR POSSESSION OF A DANGEROUS WEAPON.[17]

"Clearly the Newark Strike Force wanted to nail this guy," says retired FBI agent James Whalen, a veteran of the New York Office.[18] But when word of Scarpa's impending indictment was leaked to a newspaper, the Mad Hatter erupted. He called the Bureau's Newark Office and berated the SAC, insisting that "what appeared in the paper pertaining to the FBI would be nothing compared to what [he was] going to do to embarrass the Bureau."[19] According to an airtel from the Newark SAC to then FBI Director Clarence M. Kelley:

> SCARPA said he is going to reveal every thing, scheme and technique, imaginable pertaining to the FBI because of what is being done to him. SCARPA was asked who he is and the purpose of his call and he replied that "I damn well know who he is."

This was extreme behavior, to say the least, from a CI who was repeatedly described in FBI memos as "emotionally stable and reliable." When the SAC "specifically asked" if Scarpa was "trying to intimidate him," Scarpa replied with profanities, ending the call after insisting that "the New York Office . . . be contacted."[20]

On June 7, 1974, Greg Scarpa Sr. was finally arrested. He was released on a $25,000 bond.[21] With this multimillion-dollar bogus stock case, Scarpa had come a long way from the minor gun-possession and hijacking charges outlined in that first airtel to Hoover in 1961. Now forces within the Justice Department were earnestly trying to send him to prison. But over the next two and a half years—again, for unknown reasons—the IBM stock case experienced a series of delays.

FBI headquarters continued to stay in the loop. On March 13, 1976, Director Kelley got a special-delivery package relating to the case, indicating that the pending prosecution in New Jersey was being monitored at the highest levels of the Bureau.[22] On December 6, the SAC in Newark sent a memo to the Brooklyn Strike Force informing them that the case was set for trial on January 3, 1977.[23]

It's unknown what sort of behind-the-scenes communications, if any, took place at that point among Newark, Washington, and the FBI's New York Office. But on March 30, 1977, the same Newark SAC sent Kelley a memo stating that "the case [was] being placed in a pending inactive status by the Newark Division."[24]

A portion of another memo dated September 9, 1977, stated, "The Bureau will be kept advised of pertinent developments."[25] Both the March and the September memos were heavily redacted before their recent release.

The last record in the newly released files relating to the prosecution of Gregory Scarpa for that $4 million counterfeit-securities sale is dated December 19, 1977. Also heavily redacted, it refers to an "ENCLOSURE TO THE BUREAU" and is labeled "final disposition sheet."[26] In short, the case was effectively dead.

But the mystery of what happened to the indictment didn't become clear until almost eight years later. In a July 22, 1986, memo relating to the closure of Scarpa's credit card case, a prosecutor from the EDNY Organized Crime Strike Force acknowledged that the 1974 securities case had been "dismissed."[27]

"We now know," says defense attorney Flora Edwards, "that for decades Greg Scarpa Sr. was being protected by the Bureau time and time again. The special protection went so far that it literally pitted officials of the Justice Department against each other. But all of those multimillion-dollar white-collar crimes Greg committed pale in comparison to his murders."[28]

"Somebody Got to the Witness"

Scarpa's street reputation as a voracious killer also worked to his advantage when it came to inducing amnesia in witnesses. There are two cases that prove that point, both from the 1960s. In November 1965, Scarpa was at a diner in Lawrence Township, New Jersey, with Nick Bianco, a wiseguy who had transferred into the Colombo borgata from the Patriarca family in Providence, Rhode Island.

A witness saw the two of them, with a third party—unnamed, but identified as "connected"—"pilfering" coins from a phone booth. An airtel dated January 20, 1966, indicates that the three of them were facing fines totaling $6,000, which Joe Colombo himself pledged to pay to make the petty charges go away.[29] But the airtel goes on to say:

> January 20, 1966: Informant has ascertained through his attorney that the individual who initially reported the pilfering of the telephone booth cannot identify any of the 3 defendants and only saw a car leaving from the diner immediately after the pilfering was noted.[30]

The airtel then reports that the failure to ID the suspects based on the witness's sudden memory loss would "invalidate the arrest and search warrant of Bianco's car which was obtained on the basis of this individual's statements."[31]

"This was a case in which some prosecutor put the time in to get a warrant on Bianco's vehicle, which means that initially the witness was certain," says a former agent who worked organized crime in New York and asked not to be identified. "But it feels like somebody got to the witness, and whoever wrote the airtel almost seems to take pleasure in that—that the case against Scarpa might get tossed."[32]

It wasn't the only time Scarpa went free because a witness had a memory lapse. Four years later, in October 1969, Scarpa, his son Greg Jr., and five others were caught unloading a container truck they had driven from a pier in Port Elizabeth, New Jersey. They were arrested for hijacking 870 cases of J&B scotch, worth $70,000, from a Brooklyn warehouse.[33] The Brooklyn DA took the case seriously enough to obtain a six-count indictment, which listed one Robert Dubin as the owner of the hijacked truck.[34] But the case was later dismissed after Dubin reportedly refused to testify at trial.[35]

As another indication of how audacious Scarpa was in manipulating Villano and the FBI officials above him in New York and DC, it should be noted that the J&B hijacking came just six months after Greg had tipped off the Feds to a thousand-case Cutty Sark whiskey heist.[36] That meant that Scarpa was continuing to commit the same types of crimes he was reporting to Villano. The obvious question is whether he had a role in the Cutty Sark theft.

The airtel on that hijacking reports that after some surveillance, "100 cases of Cutty Sark was [*sic*] observed to be unloaded." According to the memo "the stolen scotch was [later] recovered," but we don't know if that reference was to the *entire* thousand-case load, or if it was nine hundred cases short. Scarpa himself told the Feds that he'd "back[ed] off" buying the load "because he did not have a location large enough to handle such a quantity." But if the November 1970 theft of mercury is any indication, he might have kept a few cases for himself. In the mercury hijacking, while Scarpa reported 400 cylinders stolen, the Feds recovered only 324.

"Greg was a scotch drinker," says the former agent from the New York Office who was familiar with Scarpa's habits. "In terms of that Cutty load, I'm betting he grabbed a few cases before reporting the theft. And if Villano was true to form, Greg got a reward to boot."[37]

Charlie the Sidge

One measure of the cold blood that ran through Scarpa's veins was the trajectory of his relationship with Calogero LoCicero, known in the Profaci-Colombo borgata as Charlie the Sidge. Over the years, the Sidge had been arrested eight times on charges ranging from vagrancy to murder. But only two of the arrests resulted in convictions—both times for weapons possession.[38] During the first Colombo war, LoCicero, then acting as family consigliere, had brokered the deal that freed Joseph Colombo and other top Profaci family members who had been kidnapped by the Gallo brothers.

In an airtel to Hoover on March 20, 1962, Scarpa (per his FBI handler) detailed LoCicero's efforts at keeping the peace.[39] But a subsequent memo emphasized the Sidge's up-and-down relationship within the family.

> June 11, 1962: LOCICERO has been reprimanded on many occasions and at one time the order was out to have LOCICERO executed. . . . [But] LOCICERO has always been able to clear himself and come back in the org. LOCICERO is the only official in the PROFACI family who would talk back to PROFACI or argue with PROFACI. LOCICERO hates and is hated by the MAGLIOCCO brothers. LOCICERO holds the permanent rank of captain, but on occasions has acted as boss, underboss and is presently acting as consigliere.

LoCicero's antipathy for "Joe Malayak" led to his aborted attempt to enlist Scarpa to murder Magliocco, as detailed in Chapter 3, and although the hit never materialized, it underscored LoCicero's trust in Greg, who managed a numbers operation for Charlie.[40] Scarpa described LoCicero, who always signed his name with a big "X," as a "top hoodlum in Brooklyn." He insisted that he was "completely loyal to LoCicero and would be willing to accept any orders or requests" that the Sidge might make.[41]

LoCicero's standing in the borgata was so high in 1964 that a *New York Times* piece declared that the "reins of the [Profaci] organization are now reported to be in the hands of Charles LoCicero, known as The Sidge."[42] To emphasize his padrone's power in the family, Scarpa told his FBI handlers a story about how LoCicero had viciously dealt with an "outlaw gang" associated with Ralph "Whitey" Tropiano, an associate of the New England LCN who operated predominantly out of New Haven.[43]

> March 12, 1964: Informant stated that LOCICERO was actually able to penetrate the gang and win their confidence while making them believe he was in with them. LOCICERO decided that all members with the exception of TROPIANO should be killed. LOCICERO's recommenda-

tion was accepted and the job of killing the other gang members was handled primarily by TROPIANO and ███████████. Informant related that they were successful in killing all the other members in a short period of time with the exception of one who was picked up and sentenced to a term in prison. He stated that this member while in prison made statements to the effect that he would get PROFACI, LOCICERO, and others. . . . Within three or four days after this individual was released from prison he was killed and his body dumped in a field.[44]

This airtel demonstrated LoCicero's capacity for brutality and deception when it served the interests of *la famiglia*. But as a sign of just how two-faced Scarpa himself could be, after pledging his loyalty to the Sidge, he also made it clear to the Bureau that "if as a result of LoCicero's efforts to mediate the dispute between the Gallo and Profaci groups, Profaci retaliated against LoCicero, [Scarpa] would then favor the Gallo group."[45] In short, family loyalty or not, Greg Scarpa was a survivor—one who regularly "ratted out" his padrone LoCicero to the FBI.

Cheating His Own Son

Just two months after professing his fealty to the Sidge, Scarpa told his handlers a story about Charlie that seemed to underscore LoCicero's greed. It's a tale that helps to explain the role Scarpa may have ultimately played in his mentor's death.

June 11, 1962: LOCICERO's only love in life is money. To illustrate that Informant told the following story:

It is customary when the child of a member of the family is getting married for invitations to be sent to all members of the family. In response to this invitation, everyone is expected to make a cash gift to the groom to give him a start in life. When LOCICERO's son, FRANK, went to get married, he did not have any money, so LOCICERO told him that he would finance the wedding and FRANK could repay him from the money he received as wedding gifts.

On the day of the wedding when all the members of the PROFACI family had left their envelopes with the cash wedding gifts, LOCICERO took the envelopes from his son, FRANK, and told him that he would count the money and deduct the cost of the wedding.

The following morning, LOCICERO gave FRANK $500.00 and stated that this is a gift from him. The wedding presents did not even cover the cost of the wedding. As a result of such treatment, all of LOCICERO's sons hate him.

In 1964, Charles LoCicero was indicted by a federal grand jury for failing to pay taxes on $53,000 in undisclosed income from 1957 to 1960.[46] Tax evasion was the crime that ultimately brought down Al Capone, and LoCicero was vulnerable to the same strategy. Apparently worried about the potential for an IRS charge, LoCicero reportedly set fire to the Florentine Furniture Corporation, one of his legitimate businesses on Avenue U in Bensonhurst. Not long after that, Scarpa was ready to "burn" him with the Bureau.

> July 9, 1962: . . . according to stories [Informant] heard [Florentine Furniture] was burned in order to destroy LOCICERO's books and records so that they could not be subpoenaed by the IRS.[47]

As a sign that LoCicero was beginning to lose his grip on reality, he reportedly boasted to Scarpa that he'd been elected *boss* of the Profacis by the Commission and went so far as to "express . . . appreciation to Carlo Gambino." But the Sidge, who was sixty years old at the time, reportedly stated that he "felt . . . control of the 'family' should be turned over to younger individuals."[48] That prompted this snide reply from Scarpa:

> October 15, 1963: Informant is of the opinion that LOCICERO was lying and that he was not elected "boss" but was only trying to give the impression he was important.[49]

After Joseph Colombo took the reins, Scarpa made it clear that LoCicero was on a downward slide. By November 1964, Scarpa leaked word that "LoCicero no longer [had] any status whatsoever in the family and [was] constantly being degraded by other members."[50] By 1965, despite his destruction of the books, the former consigliere was convicted on the IRS charges and sentenced to eighteen months in prison.[51] That summer he was held in what was then known as the Federal House of Detention in Manhattan,[52] while the Immigration and Naturalization Service prepared to deport him to Italy.

Colombo, by now the boss of the family, became concerned that Charlie would talk, so he told Scarpa that he would arrange to pay the money necessary to "fix" the case.[53] Eight months later, LoCicero emerged from jail, but Scarpa informed the FBI that the Sidge was "causing trouble within the family." After rumors surfaced that the INS case had been dismissed, Colombo—who had never come through with the "fix" money he'd pledged to pay—became suspicious that the Sidge might have cut a deal with the Feds.[54]

By September 1965, Scarpa told his handlers that "LoCicero [was] completely down and out as far as 'La Cosa Nostra' is concerned" and that he was now "despised and detested" by the other members of LCN.[55]

The situation had apparently grown so dire that LoCicero, once the third-highest-ranking man in the borgata, was getting by on $50 a week.

One Last Big Score?

In addition to his son Frank, the Sidge, who seemed to favor all variations on the name "Charles," had two other sons—Carlo and Charles Jr. He also had a grandson[56] named Richard, who had been arrested for felonious assault at the age of seventeen.[57] The younger LoCicero was locked up again a year later on the same charge, and in 1966 he was indicted for rape. In the Mafia tradition, though, he somehow escaped conviction on all three charges, and he curiously managed to get himself a job as a courier for the brokerage house of Paine, Webber, Jackson & Curtis. Astonishingly, considering his "rap sheet," young Richard was trusted with carrying hundreds of thousands of dollars in securities throughout the Wall Street district.

On August 16, 1966, just as his grandfather Charlie was hitting rock bottom, Richard LoCicero was asked to deliver $370,862 in negotiable stocks from Paine Webber's office at 25 Broad Street to the Grace National Bank two blocks away at Hanover Square. But the young mob-connected courier never made it. Richard later claimed that a man forced him into a building, tied him to a door handle, and escaped with the securities.

Apparently Richard had taken a detour, because the building where he said he'd been accosted was two blocks south and one block east of the bank.

Gregory Scarpa seemed to know every detail of the Paine Webber heist. In fact, according to an airtel memorializing the incident, he told his contacting agent that "it was not actually a theft but a 'give away.' "[58] As Scarpa explained it:

> July 29, 1967: The securities were in "Fat Tony's bar" [at] Fourth Avenue and 20th Street Brooklyn, in the basement [where] they were attempting to sell [them] at 35 cents on the dollar.[59]

It's unclear whether Scarpa received any reward money in exchange for that information, but the airtel states that "the NYCPD subsequently recovered some of the securities involved and made a number of arrests."[60] The airtel notes that the recovery was apparently "based" on intelligence that Scarpa had furnished. Two of the six people arrested were Richard's uncles, the Sidge's sons Carlo, twenty-eight, and Charles, nicknamed "Ditty," twenty-six.

Richard was later called to testify before a Kings County (Brooklyn) grand jury, and even though Scarpa told his contacting agent that the Sidge's grandson had been "uncooperative," the young courier's very appearance on the witness stand sealed his fate.[61]

At three thirty A.M. on April 5, 1967, Richard LoCicero's body was found in the driveway near a row of houses between Sixty-Seventh and Sixty-Eighth Streets in Brooklyn. His corpse was riddled with up to one hundred stab wounds[62] and his stomach had been ripped open.[63] According to the police, after spending the evening bowling in the neighborhood, the younger LoCicero was driven by a friend to his grandmother's house, where he occasionally slept. His mother and stepfather lived a few blocks away in an apartment over a pool room on Eleventh Avenue. The witnesses who found him lying on his back refused to comment to the press. "We don't talk about such things," one middle-aged man told a reporter.[64]

Whether or not Richard had actually confessed to the grand jury was unknown, but in the ways of Cosa Nostra, it didn't matter. The risk was too great that he'd "flipped"—particularly since he had three prior felony arrests on his record and he'd been fingered as a co-conspirator by Scarpa.

After the murder hit the papers, Brooklyn's chief assistant district attorney, Elliott Golden, referred to Richard LoCicero as a "star witness." He then stated emphatically, "We serve notice on the underworld that we will not tolerate such intimidation."[65]

In July, Greg Scarpa Sr. told his contacting agent that Charlie the Sidge had had a "nervous breakdown" and had been hospitalized.[66] The slain courier's grandfather had deteriorated to the point where he was living off a card game run by one of his sons. We may never know whether the bogus securities robbery was a last-ditch ploy to help raise some cash for him. But less than a year after Richard was brutally murdered, Charlie the Sidge himself, onetime consigliere of the Profaci family, was shot to death just blocks from where his grandson had been stabbed.[67]

Live by the Gun, Die by the Gun

LoCicero, then sixty-four, was sitting on the third stool from the door at Calisi's luncheonette at Eleventh Avenue and Sixty-Sixth Street, sipping a malted. On the counter before him was a pack of Lucky Strikes. Suddenly, a gunman with his face obscured fired from the doorway and fled through the busy streets. The weapon was described by terrified witnesses as either "a carbine" or a shotgun.[68] The assailant was never caught, but it's not far-fetched to speculate that Greg Scarpa Sr. may have been the shooter.

First of all, the rifle and shotgun were his weapons of choice.[69] Second, as his former bookmaking partner and sponsor in the family for years, LoCicero had enough evidence on Scarpa to put him away for multiple life terms. Not only had Scarpa made no effort to save his plummeting mentor, but for years he'd been passing on the kind of negative intel that degraded LoCicero to the FBI. Further, Scarpa's actions had put LoCicero's grandson at great risk. Scarpa's debriefing on the Paine Webber "give away" had led to the arrests of Richard's uncles—a chess move that effectively forced the younger LoCicero before the Brooklyn grand jury. After that, his rubout was a foregone conclusion.

As consigliere, Charlie the Sidge had once been within striking distance of a seat on the Mafia Commission. He was a hardened gangster with a criminal record dating back to 1925,[70] a man who had once ordered the wholesale murder of an outlaw gang.[71] But he was no match for the Killing Machine, who used his position of influence with the Bureau to diminish LoCicero's importance in the family.

If Scarpa did pull the trigger on LoCicero, there was little chance the hit would be linked back to him. The luncheonette rubout wasn't exactly a murder the NYPD or the Bureau would rush to solve. As Valachi told the McClellan subcommittee, "you live by the gun and the knife and die by the gun and the knife." Both weapons had been used on the LoCiceros. And there was another prophetic lesson that LoCicero should have learned from Valachi: No one "retires" from the Mafia.

Given his position in the borgata, LoCicero's murder rated a long two-column story in the *New York Times*.[72] But Gregory Scarpa, the treacherous TE informant, had long since written the Sidge's obituary with the Bureau.

Chapter 9

THE OCTOPUS

When Greg Scarpa Sr. first became J. Edgar Hoover's inside source on Cosa Nostra, he described the old-school Sicilian Mafia as the Black Hand or the Comarada. But he left out the name the criminal network was best known by in Italy: La Piovra, or the Octopus. Over the decades, the multiple arms of the Mafia had reached into every institution of Italian society, from the church to parliament to the three principal police agencies that maintained law and order: the Carabinieri, the Polizia di Stato, and the Guardia di Finanza.

In *Octopus,* her exposé on the Mafia's control of the heroin business, Claire Sterling noted that the eight-armed marine mollusk "has the most highly developed brain of all invertebrates. . . . Some kinds inject a poison that paralyzes their prey. The octopus can also squirt a black fluid, forming a dark cloud that hides the animal so it can escape."[1] The more you read the secret memos from "34" sent year after year to the Director from the FBI's New York Office, the more you get a sense of just how far Scarpa's tentacles reached.

He had become the ultimate political gangster. If knowledge is power, then his influence was profound. There's little doubt that the Federal Bureau of Investigation shaped its seminal view of the Mafia from Scarpa's point of view. And, as he manipulated top officials including Hoover into paying off his gambling debts while currying favor with New York officials like Assistant Director in Charge (ADIC) John Malone, Scarpa ensured that in the agent-informant relationship, *he* was the one who called the plays.

In his unique position TECI 3461 supplied the kind of nuance and analysis that a hundred wiretaps could never yield. But since Scarpa controlled the flow of information, he also used his status as a snitch to target others, creating doubt in the minds of his FBI handlers about who could be trusted and who couldn't. A prime example relates to the homicide of Charles LoCicero's grandson Richard.

According to Scarpa, Elliott Golden, the same assistant DA who issued that stern warning to the mob about intimidating witnesses, had himself been compromised by the boss of the Colombo family. In an airtel to Hoover on January 3, 1966—just fifteen months before Richard LoCicero's bloody corpse was discovered—Scarpa made this assertion:

> January 3, 1966: Informant advised that in December, 1965 JOSEPH COLOMBO was engaged in selling benefit tickets for ELLIOT [*sic*] GOLDEN, an Assistant District Attorney in the King's County Office. The tickets cost $3.50 each, but were sold at $20.00 with the balance of $16.50 going to GOLDEN. Informant stated that he sold 20 tickets himself at the request of Colombo.[2]

In a family with a hundred made members at that time and hundreds more associates, the aggregate "kickback" to the assistant DA could have been substantial if Scarpa was telling the truth. Golden, who died in 2008, may never have known that a Top Echelon FBI informant had made such an accusation against him. Indeed, he went on to become a New York State Supreme Court judge.[3] So if the FBI believed the allegation, it didn't hurt the assistant DA's career.

But Golden's public identification of Richard LoCicero as a "star witness" implied that Richard had cooperated. So after Richard's murder, Golden's warning to the Mafia to avoid tampering with the grand jury only served to reinforce their reputation for vengeance against "rats." By speculating that the stabbing might have been linked to Richard's testimony, intentionally or not, Golden was furthering the belief on the streets of Brooklyn that if you informed on the mob you didn't just die, you died badly.

A more intriguing question raised by the airtels is whether Scarpa himself had any role in the initial theft of the Paine Webber securities or in Richard LoCicero's grisly rubout. The evidence is circumstantial but intriguing. First, consider the fact that in relating the story of how the Sidge had pocketed his son's wedding money, Scarpa had already set the stage for a theory he floated *after* Richard's death—that the younger LoCicero might have been killed by his own.

> August 11, 1967: Informant advised concerning the murder of RICH-ARD LOCICERO that . . . the whole LOCICERO family are very poorly regarded and were never "close." He stated that they were constantly fight-ing among themselves and it was the informant's personal unsupported belief RICHARD LOCICERO was killed by ▮▮▮▮▮▮▮▮▮ because they suspected [he] was giving information to the Brooklyn DA's office concerning his involvement in the theft of securities from the brokerage firm of Paine, Webber, Jackson and Curtis.[4]

The airtels also revealed that Scarpa himself had more than a distant knowl-edge of the theft. In fact, two months after that memo went to Hoover, Scarpa came right out and admitted that the Sidge's youngest son had approached him about buying the hot stocks.

> October 6, 1967: Informant telephonically advised that CHARLES LOCICERO, the youngest son of CHARLIE THE SIDGE had approached [him] with an offer to purchase the remaining securities which were obtained in the captioned theft.

Five days later, Scarpa made this report to Anthony Villano by phone:

> October 11, 1967: Informant advised that he had again been contacted by CHARLES LOCICERO aka "DITTY" at which time "DITTY" assured Informant that he personally had possession of between $190,000 and $195,000 worth of securities, which included negotiable bonds from cap-tioned [Paine Webber] theft and would be willing to sell same for 15% of their face value.

So via Ditty LoCicero, Scarpa had access to some of the stolen securities. We know, from his 1971 indictment in Chicago and his 1974 indictment in Newark, that Scarpa specialized in high-end stock thefts. We know how close he was to the LoCicero family. We know the control he might have exercised over Assistant DA Elliott Golden, given his knowledge of the alleged kickbacks on the raffle tickets. We know that Scarpa was adept at tying off any loose ends that might put him in legal jeopardy. And, most of all, we can now appreciate how Scarpa himself was focusing the lens through which the New York Office of the FBI and J. Edgar Hoover viewed the Colombo crime family.

Scarpa had already alleged that the LoCicero sons hated their father, and after the Sidge was rubbed out, a pair of airtels underscored just how disloyal both Scarpa and the family boss were to the man who had once been consigliere:

April 19, 1968: Informant was . . . contacted by [JOSEPH] COLOMBO on 4/22/68 when they attended LOCICERO'S wake. At that time COLOMBO confided that LOCICERO's murder was "no problem . . ." COLOMBO advised that the LOCICERO murder was a "family affair" not having anything to do with "their family"—the COLOMBO LCN family.[5]

April 26, 1968: COLOMBO asked what Informant felt he lost [in LoCicero's death] to which COLOMBO was assured by Informant that although LOCICERO had at one time been his "captain," he never had any "love for him."[6]

In that same memo, Scarpa made an extraordinary statement, which suggested to the FBI that Joseph Colombo himself knew who committed the Sidge's murder.

April 26, 1968: COLOMBO advised that it was inevitable that LOCICERO would be killed by his own "family," since he was responsible for the murder of his grandson RICHARD and COLOMBO was surprised that FRANK had "worked so fast."

There it was in black and white: Greg Scarpa was blaming the Sidge's hit on LoCicero's own son Frank. With that single debriefing, "34" tied off all the loose ends that might have implicated him in the Paine Webber theft, Richard LoCicero's death, or the luncheonette murder of Richard's grandfather. Tony Villano had it from the boss's own lips to Greg's: It had been a family affair, in the traditional sense of the word. The son, who had felt cheated by his old man from the time of his wedding, had reportedly finished him off after the Sidge induced his grandson to steal $370,000 in securities.

Now consider another scenario: Did the down-and-out sixty-four-year-old Sidge, who signed his name with an "X" and was living on $50 a week, have the contacts to fence high-end paper from the Paine Webber heist? That was Scarpa's specialty. Who had the dirt necessary to induce an assistant DA to spill grand jury secrets and put Richard LoCicero in jeopardy in the first place? Who had a motive for silencing the grandson? Who had been offered $195,000 of the stolen stocks? Who had a motive for killing the grandfather, who went back years with him in the family—an impoverished old gangster who might have been persuaded by the Feds to flip? Finally, who was in the best position to explain the theft and the two murders that followed to the FBI, diverting attention away from himself?

The answer is clear: Gregory Scarpa Sr.

The last item in another airtel said it all:

> May 3, 1968: Concerning COLOMBO's above reference to FRANK, this is unquestionably FRANK LOCICERO, son of subject who was arrested 7/27/66 based on information furnished by NY TE Informant and charged with violation of parole.[7]

Not only had Scarpa made sure that the FBI believed Frank LoCicero had killed his own father, but he furnished enough probable cause to ensure Frank's arrest. Curiously, however, Frank was never arrested, indicted, or prosecuted for his father's murder.

Closing Scarpa a Second Time

In 1968, the same year that the Sidge was rubbed out, Gregory Scarpa was arrested for assault after he beat a victim on the head with a pipe. That case too was dismissed. Years later, the FBI would adopt strict guidelines forc-ing the closure of CIs who committed such acts of violence,[8] but as long as J. Edgar Hoover was alive, "34" was protected.

When Hoover died in 1972, however, Scarpa lost his principal "rabbi" in the Bureau. Villano retired a year later. In that summer of 1973 as the Watergate break-in enveloped Hoover's successor L. Patrick Grey, the Bureau's obsession with organized crime seemed to take a backseat to the potential "high crimes and misdemeanors" of the executive branch.

From the day after Villano's retirement through Greg's closing in 1975, Scarpa never gave the FBI a single lead to another high-end theft or hijack-ing. The best he could offer, in February 1974, was a report that a load of hair dryers had been stolen and that his crew had paid $5 apiece for them.[9] With his "broker" Villano gone and no prospect of further reward money, Scarpa had apparently lost his incentive.

In mid-March 1974, Scarpa made another report to the Feds that could hardly be considered Top Echelon intelligence. The "Persico faction," he noted, was now in control of the carting contract for the Brooklyn Navy Yard, which had been turned over to the City of New York.[10] Scarpa didn't supply any details, perhaps because hundreds of thousands of dollars were being stolen from the shipyard via a scheme for which his brother Sal and Charles LoCicero Jr. were later indicted. More on that later, but one thing is clear: By 1975, Hoover's onetime star informant was reduced to passing along what amounted to low-level Mafia gossip:

> March 1, 1975: Source stated that ALLIE BOY PERSICO spends quiet drinking evenings in the Regis Room of the St. Regis Hotel in Manhat-tan where SOURCE claims no one knows him.

That memo wasn't even addressed to the Director, or to any official at Headquarters.[11] It apparently stayed in the New York Office. On May 5, the Director did get a two-line airtel. With no explanation, it simply said: "Above captioned source is presently being closed by the New York Office."[12]

For the next five years, Gregory Scarpa Sr., the most important Mafia informant in the history of the FBI's New York Office, went dark. It was during this period, in 1976, when Scarpa, lacking the "insurance" he'd enjoyed with the Bureau, was first arrested for gambling. Two years later he was arrested again, after offering seven hundred dollars to two NYPD cops to protect his numbers racket. That's the crime that led to his thirty-day jail term.[13]

As Fred Dannen reported in the *New Yorker,* though, Greg Scarpa "hated doing time."[14] So when Lin DeVecchio officially reopened him in 1980, after five years "in the cold," Scarpa was ready to reassume his Top Echelon status.

Taking Years to Reopen Scarpa

R. Lindley DeVecchio, mid-1980s

After joining the Bureau in 1966, DeVecchio was first assigned to the Albany Office. The following year, at the age of twenty-seven, he made it to New York City. There he became, in his words, the "youngest guy ever assigned to Organized Crime."[15] Curiously, 1967 was the same year Tony Villano took over as Scarpa's contacting agent after Greg had withdrawn for several months following the transfer of his original handlers. Villano continued to use him as a source until he retired in 1973.

In his memoir, *We're Going to Win This Thing,* DeVecchio writes that he learned of "34" on his first day in the Organized Crime Section, and that he was later informed of Scarpa's actual identity by a supervisor. If DeVecchio ever needed any information, he was told, he should "go to Tony."[16] In a 1996 interview with Dannen, DeVecchio insisted that he'd "learned a lot of things by watching Tony."[17] But he didn't say what he learned about Scarpa or why he didn't seek to run him himself in 1973 when Villano left the Bureau.

One of the enduring mysteries that DeVecchio never resolves in his book is why he didn't try to reopen Scarpa for five years after his closing in 1975. In fact, thirteen years went by from the time DeVecchio first learned about Scarpa in 1967 to the day in 1980 when he says he finally contacted him.[18]

As DeVecchio tells it, that turned out to be an auspicious meeting for both of them. "From the day of our first sit-down," he writes, "and for the ensuing twelve years, Scarpa furnished incredibly valuable information that led to countless RICO convictions and life sentences."[19] It was Scarpa's "singular" intelligence that gave the government the probable cause it needed to obtain seventeen key Title III wiretaps and fifty reauthorizations that brought down the bosses of three of the Five Families in the Mafia Commission case.[20] The inside intel he got from "34" made DeVecchio a rising star in the New York Office, where he was eventually promoted to supervisory special agent in charge of not one but two family squads. Meanwhile, Scarpa remained free to steal millions through murder, drug dealing, hijacking, larceny, and racketeering. By 1991, he felt confident enough to trigger the third and bloodiest war for control of the Colombo crime family.

The relationship between Greg Scarpa and Lin DeVecchio proved to be double-edged. It was that third conflict fed by FBI intelligence that almost cost DeVecchio his job and later came close to landing him in prison. Was the relationship between the killer and the agent the kind of "ultimate perversion" Tony Villano had worried about? Was it, as Brooklyn DA Charles Hynes once contended, "the most stunning example of official corruption" his office had prosecuted?[21] Or, as DeVecchio argues in his book, was he "framed" by ambitious agents and incompetent prosecutors?

And there are other questions that beg to be answered. Why did *People v. DeVecchio*—the biggest organized crime case in the New York Supreme Court in recent memory—fall apart two weeks into trial? Was it because of the perjury of Linda Schiro, as alleged, or were there other reasons? Was there any link between the state murder charges leveled against DeVecchio and the federal prosecution of the notorious "Mafia Cops"? And if there was, how might that have affected either case? The answers to those questions lie buried in more than ten thousand pages of court pleadings, wiretap transcripts, and FBI memos, which we've examined during the research for this book.

New Revelations from "Gaspipe"

Another key to the story may come from the one Mafia boss still alive and in prison who not only committed crimes with Gregory Scarpa, but who insists that he stayed out of jail and furthered his racketeering career by tapping into the same "law enforcement" source as Scarpa. Despite efforts by federal prosecutors and prison officials to silence him, Anthony "Gaspipe" Casso, who broke the law with Greg Scarpa Sr. from the early days of their youth, has come forward to make some surprising allegations that are sure to challenge the conventional media assumptions about the G-man and the hit man.

Veteran organized crime reporter Jerry Capeci, to whom DeVecchio was accused of leaking intelligence back in 1994, once wrote that Greg Scarpa "regarded himself as a James Bond figure." *Mission: Impossible,* wrote Capeci, was his "favorite television show."[22] Clearly, the so-called Grim Reaper saw himself as having a license to kill. The question is, how much help, if any, did he get from Lin DeVecchio in furthering his 007 persona? We'll endeavor to answer that.

This is a story about homicide, duplicity, and government misconduct, where the rigid line between right and wrong grew tenuous and sometimes broke; where the lofty goal of eradicating organized crime forced federal agents to compromise their integrity in a system that suborned the very criminal behavior they were sworn to stop.

It's a system in which different federal judges in the same courthouse sent some Mafiosi to jail for life while releasing others who had committed even more vicious crimes. In the "deal with the devil" made by the FBI in protecting Gregory Scarpa Sr., there are lessons to be learned about the price some FBI agents were willing to pay to defeat "the Mafia enemy." We'll explore all of that in the chapters ahead.

Chapter 10

GUNS AND RABBIS

In a chapter of his memoir entitled "The Grim Reaper," Lin DeVecchio gives a detailed account of his reopening of Greg Scarpa, which he says occurred on "a beautiful day in June in 1980" when he drove a beat-up Bureau-issued 1975 Plymouth over to 216 Avenue J, in the Midwood section of Brooklyn, and parked across from the house Scarpa shared with his common-law wife, Linda Schiro, and their two children, "Little Linda" and Joey.

In the book, DeVecchio says he waited for about half an hour until Scarpa walked out of the house and got into "a big black Lincoln." DeVecchio pulled in behind him, he writes, blocking his exit. After Scarpa got out, with what DeVecchio describes as a "who-the-fuck-are-you?" look on his face, Lin says he showed his Bureau credentials and told Scarpa that Tony Villano suggested he "look him up someday if [he] needed help."[1]

DeVecchio writes that after he reminded Scarpa what a "great help" he had been to the Bureau in the past and gave him his phone number, Scarpa called him two weeks later and told him to "come alone" to a meeting at the Avenue J house.

It was at that meeting, according to his book, that DeVecchio first met Schiro, whom he describes as an "attractive woman . . . provocatively dressed" and wearing "a little too much makeup." Sitting down with Scarpa in their living room, DeVecchio writes, *he* did most of the talking, "speaking the language used by wiseguys, with a lot of four letter words thrown in." It was a style that did not come to him naturally.

Roy Lindley DeVecchio, born in Fresno, California, was the son of a senior army officer. He was well educated, having earned a BA and a master's degree; his brother Jay was a partner in the Washington office of Jenner & Block, one of the nation's most distinguished law firms.[2] The name Lindley came from his blond, blue-eyed mother's side of the family.[3] When he was growing up, his father was posted to a series of exotic locations, from Bermuda to Tokyo to Rome, where Lin learned to speak fluent Italian while the family lived in what he describes as "a beautiful apartment."[4] During his childhood his parents frequently took him to the opera. He asked to take violin lessons and became an avid stamp collector. In short, he was the antithesis of tough-talking, streetwise "Nino" Villano, the Brooklyn-born son of an Italian immigrant.

In recruiting a dangerous capo like Scarpa, then, Lin DeVecchio had to assume another personality. After their initial meeting, whenever DeVecchio met with Scarpa, he writes that he "always wore" the "costume of a Brooklyn wiseguy." That included gold chains and a pinky ring to "emulate" the Mafia style.[5] Throughout the book he repeatedly uses profanities to describe his interaction with Scarpa and other informants. "Over time I learned to speak their language, to use their vocabulary, and that made me more effective," he writes.[6]

In one sequence he recalls watching one of his CIs in the Meatpacking District "beat the daylights" out of a robber who had just mugged a gay prostitute. "Gimme the fuckin' knife," he quotes the informant as saying. "This cocksucker's solicitin' these fags, then he's grabbin' their fuckin' money, the cocksucker. Gimme the fuckin' knife. I'm gonna cut his nuts off."

When he lectured at the FBI Academy, DeVecchio writes, he told the agent trainees, some of whom were Catholic or Mormon, that "even with a post-graduate degree, my speech has been reduced to gutter language. And if that bothers you, go fuck yourselves."

In his book, DeVecchio admits that he admired Scarpa, "a man even the wiseguys feared." To make his point, he describes how Scarpa once "had a beef with two capos" over whether they "were entitled to a split on a certain score."

They knew they needed muscle and confronted him, even though Scarpa was merely a soldier. They took about fifty guys with them. Scarpa stood alone, shouting at the capos and telling them to go fuck themselves and get out. He didn't budge an inch and the capos retreated.

That reference to Scarpa as "merely a soldier," when he is repeatedly identified in the FBI airtels as a "caporegime" or "capo," raises the question of whether DeVecchio had actually read Scarpa's extensive file in any depth before reopening him.

In his memoir, DeVecchio writes that he "went through the 209 files of closed informants" and picked "the thickest file," which turned out to be Scarpa's.[7] DeVecchio testified under oath at a 1997 hearing that he "looked at" Scarpa's closed files.[8] In an interview for a documentary on Greg Scarpa Sr. for the Biography Channel in September 2012, the former supervisory special agent said, "I opened the [Scarpa Sr.] file, read everything I could find out about this man."[9] But there are many conflicts between his account in *We're Going to Win This Thing* and the facts as stated in the newly released airtels and memos.

Valachi vs. Scarpa

For one thing, DeVecchio refers only to "209 files" in his book, describing them as "usually three or four sentences of pertinent inside information."[10] As we've documented, however, some of the airtels run up to thirteen single-spaced pages, revealing volumes of material from Scarpa's debriefings between 1961 and 1973.

As noted, seventy-four of DeVecchio's relatively brief and cryptic 209s were released in the mid-1990s, but those were separate from the hundreds of pages of airtels we've used to document Scarpa's secret relationship with the FBI dating back to 1961.[11] One indication that DeVecchio may not have examined that material is his assertion that "Valachi gave us the term Cosa Nostra. . . . He also gave us the names we still use today to identify the Mafia families . . . Colombo, Bonanno, Genovese, Gambino, and Lucchese."[12] No one who had studied the Scarpa airtels from two years before Valachi first started "singing" could overlook the fact that those revelations were first made by *Greg Scarpa Sr.* in briefings sent directly to Hoover from the NYO. Is it possible that Lin DeVecchio reopened "34" without fully appreciating the mobster's skill as a cold-blooded manipulator? Did he underestimate Scarpa's capacity to lie to Bureau agents and use his position as a TE informant for personal gain?

There is one section in DeVecchio's book that sheds light on that question and points to a certain lack of precision on his part. In citing Tony Villano's memoir, *Brick Agent,* Lin writes that Villano "described an informant to whom he gave the name Rico Conte."

> Tony wrote that in 1952 Conte had described the secret structure and inner workings of the American Mafia to his then handlers. But they thought it was Conte's imagination running wild and dismissed it as a tall tale. Tony died a few years ago, so I can't ask him now, but I always suspected that the character of Rico Conte was based on Greg Scarpa.[13]

That statement suggests that DeVecchio, or his collaborator, Charles Brandt, may have paid only cursory attention to the details of *Brick Agent,* because the composite Villano uses for Greg Scarpa Sr. is not Rico Conte—a mobster who had served considerable prison time—but the aforementioned characters of Julio and Nick Biletti. If Lin had read any of the initial airtels sent to Hoover at the time of Scarpa's recruitment in 1961, he would have known that Greg's detailed reports on "the secret structure and inner workings" of the LCN were genuine and certainly didn't amount to a "tall tale."

DeVecchio, who worked in the New York Office in close proximity to Villano for six years, writes that he "learned a lot just by watching" him. So that raises several questions. Did he ask Villano about his star informant back then? If, as Lin writes, he became aware of "34" on his first day on the job, did he familiarize himself with Villano's Scarpa airtels so that he could judge whether the newly reopened TE informant was lying to him? Or is it possible that Lin DeVecchio, who rose to the rank of supervisory special agent running two squads, didn't do the homework necessary to educate himself about a dangerous killer before formalizing relations with him?

He describes Senior's file as "thick," but the 902 pages of airtels from 1961 to Greg's closing in 1975 rival the size of a Manhattan phone directory. Did DeVecchio, whom a defense lawyer once called "Mr. Organized Crime,"[14] actually overlook the files that we're now describing in this book? Or was he being disingenuous and somehow covering for Scarpa?

One reason to question DeVecchio is his description of how he recruited Scarpa. His account in the book, which mirrors what he said in a *60 Minutes* interview after its release,[15] conflicts with the very first airtel sent to Washington from the NYO after Scarpa's formal reopening in 1980. While Lin now claims that his "initial meeting" with Scarpa took place outside the mobster's house on that June day[16] and he formally connected with him "about two weeks later," the newly disclosed files suggest that it actually took him half a year to "persuade" Scarpa to start informing on the Colombo family once again.

JULY 1, 1980: SOURCE WAS CLOSED BY COMMUNICATION DATED MAY 5TH, 1975. IT IS NOTED THAT APPROXIMATELY SIX MONTHS HAVE BEEN REQUIRED TO DISCREETLY RE-CONTACT THE SOURCE AND TO PERSUADE [*sic*] HIM TO RESUME FURNISHING INFORMATION WHICH IS OF EXTREMELY HIGH QUALITY AND UNOBTAINABLE FROM ANY OTHER CURRENT NYO SOURCE.[17]

**FBI teletype to the Director saying "six months"
required to reopen "source" (Scarpa Sr.)**

So was it two weeks or six months? The discrepancy is significant when one considers DeVecchio's sworn testimony during the trial of Scarpa's son Greg Jr. What follows is an exchange he had under oath with Junior's attorney Larry Silverman on October 14, 1998.

Silverman: There came a time that you went out then and met with Mr. Scarpa Sr.?
DeVecchio: That's correct.

Silverman: Do you recall what year it was?

DeVecchio: I believe it was 1980.

Silverman: Where did you meet with him, sir?

DeVecchio: My initial contact was outside his home at the time.

Silverman: About how long after the first meeting did you get together with him?

DeVecchio: I would say within a few weeks but I can't be certain of the precise time, certain.[18]

Was DeVecchio's "initial contact" with Scarpa outside the house on Avenue J, as he testified under oath, or sometime in the previous half year, as he indicated in his 209 to Washington? Or could it have been much earlier? As we'll see at the end of this book, in a recent interview from federal prison Greg Scarpa Jr. insisted his father made contact with DeVecchio *years* before his formal reopening in the summer of 1980.

And the date when Greg Sr. returned to the FBI fold isn't the only conflict between DeVecchio's trial testimony and what he wrote in his book. In the pages ahead we'll cite multiple discrepancies between what we now know of Scarpa's activities and the seventy-four FBI 209s seemingly written by DeVecchio between December 1980 and August 1993.[19]

Whenever it was that Lin re-recruited Scarpa, and whatever the cultural differences between them, the agent and the wiseguy had two important things in common: Each of them had a passionate interest in guns, and each of them had "rabbis," or protectors in the Justice Department who intervened to support them. In Scarpa's case it was the New York SAC and senior FBI officials, who repeatedly approved his cash payments and kept him on the Bureau's payroll. In DeVecchio's case it was Rudolph Giuliani, then the top aide to the deputy attorney general of the United States.

The German Luger Bust

Gregory Scarpa Sr. was an expert marksman. He not only loved guns, he also sold them. One investigator told writer Bob Drury that Scarpa personally tested the illegal weapons, mostly rifles, that he and his crew sold "to make sure anybody that bought a gun from him wasn't getting a raw deal."[20] Later, during the third Colombo war, Scarpa rigged a vehicle with compartments concealing shotguns, rifles, and pistols. He cruised the streets in this "death car," using it to knock off his rivals.[21]

In his book, Lin DeVecchio reveals a similar affinity for firearms. "From the first time I fired a pistol, I loved shooting and I loved guns," he writes. He claims to be a "crack shot," indeed "one of the better shots in the Bureau."[22] And, again like Scarpa, DeVecchio didn't just use guns, he sold them.

In early 1976, at a time when his FBI salary was likely under $40,000,[23] DeVecchio was arrested by undercover agents of the Bureau of Alcohol, Tobacco and Firearms (ATF) for selling two German Lugers valued at $60,000.[24] According to a story published thirty years later by *New York Times* reporter Alan Feuer, the arrest occurred "when Mr. DeVecchio traveled from New York to King of Prussia, Pa., to sell a Nazi-era Luger at the Valley Forge Gun Show."[25]

In testimony under oath at a 1997 federal court hearing, DeVecchio admitted that while working as an active-duty agent he regularly attended gun shows "in different parts of the United States" with a gun dealer who was a friend of his.[26] Asked by defense lawyer Gerald Shargel if he had "told people, including undercover agents," that he was a "silent partner" with the dealer, DeVecchio said, "No. Nothing like that."

In his book, DeVecchio insists that he sold only one Luger to an ATF agent and that he did it on behalf of the "grieving wife" of a thirty-six-year-old medical doctor killed in a car crash. "All the proceeds went to her," he writes.

In court, DeVecchio admitted that he made the sale in the parking lot of the gun show, without filing the requisite paperwork, and that he asked "to be paid in cash or to have checks made out to cash."[27] When confronted by Shargel at the hearing with documents from the case in which the ATF agents reportedly accused him of making "incomplete or false statements," DeVecchio testified that he "couldn't recall" that. In fact, in the course of the two-day hearing, he responded, "I don't recall," or words to that effect, more than fifty times.[28]

Admitting that he sold two guns (which would have been in violation of federal firearms statutes), DeVecchio was asked by Shargel whether the widow's entire collection wasn't worth closer to $250,000.

He replied, "That was handled by the gun dealer."

Shargel: With you, wasn't that right?

DeVecchio: Not all the time. I was not always present with him.

Shargel: Didn't you tell the agents that you were in for a commission?

DeVecchio: I don't recall what I said to them.

Shargel: You don't recall?

DeVecchio: No it was twenty-two years ago. I don't recall that.

Shargel: Well how many different checks did you cash. Do you recall?

DeVecchio: I have no idea.

By statute it's a felony, punishable by up to five years in prison on each count, for "any person except a . . . licensed dealer to engage in the business of . . . dealing in firearms."[29]

As Alan Feuer reported in the *Times*, "Without a license, [DeVecchio] moved through the stalls of the firearms bazaar, and was soon approached by Michael Flax, an undercover agent with [ATF]." Flax told Feuer that his job was to troll the shows in plainclothes looking for illicit deals and that in 1976 "several people he caught similarly selling guns without paperwork went to prison."

Flax, who is now retired, told Feuer that his modus operandi for undercover buys was to approach prospective unlicensed sellers and say, "Gee I'd like to get this gun. . . . Do we have to go through all the paperwork?" According to Feuer, Flax said that he bought one Luger from DeVecchio in the parking lot, and after a multiweek investigation "a second agent secretly recorded the F.B.I. man selling another gun." Flax told Feuer that at one point DeVecchio "gave him a phone number at which he might be reached. It was, he said, an office of the New York F.B.I."

As Feuer reported, "a few weeks later, Mr. Flax brought the case to [Daniel M.] Clements, then a young federal prosecutor in Baltimore."

"Flax comes to me saying, 'You're not going to believe this,'" Clements told Feuer, "'I have an F.B.I. agent selling guns illegally.'"

But as he moved forward to prosecute, Clements recalled, he was thwarted by Rudolph W. Giuliani, then a thirty-two-year-old aide to Judge Harold Tyler, the deputy attorney general in Washington. After being asked by Giuliani to prepare a pair of memoranda on the case, Clements told

Feuer that he met with the aide twice. At both meetings, "Mr. Giuliani repeated his desire not to prosecute the case, saying the guns were old and the sale of them without paperwork did not warrant prosecution."

So ultimately, just as with the series of Justice Department indictments of Gregory Scarpa, the illegal gun sale case against Lin DeVecchio (in Flax's words) "went away."

In his memoir, DeVecchio writes off the incident as a kind of technicality.

> I sold one to an undercover agent who was scouting the gun shows trying to buy from people who didn't file the appropriate paperwork. It was like shooting fish in a barrel because so many of the collectors didn't want to be on record in case their guns were later restricted by new gun control statutes to the point where they couldn't resell them. And some of these people had tens of thousands of dollars tied up in their collections. Well, I was one of the fish that got shot in the barrel.[30]

But his claim that he sold just one Luger is inconsistent with his testimony in 1997, when he admitted to selling two.[31] Further, in another section of that testimony, referring back to the Luger arrest, DeVecchio claimed ignorance of the law:

Shargel: You know that was a violation and it was found by the investigating authorities that you had violated section 922 of Title 18. You know that, right?

DeVecchio: I know that now. . . . I didn't know it at that time. I wouldn't have violated it.

Shargel: You didn't know you were breaking the law at the time you were doing it?

DeVecchio: That's correct.

Shargel: Did you know at the time that knowledge wasn't an element under the subsection of 922?

DeVecchio: I don't know what the Act reads or all the paragraphs in them.

Shargel: Are you aware as you sit here now, Judge Harold Tyler[,] then with the United States Department of Justice, concluded that you had clearly violated the law; and only as a matter of discretion you would not be indicted.

DeVecchio: I had no knowledge of that.

We can only speculate about how Lin DeVecchio might have treated a Mafioso who claimed he wasn't aware of a law he'd broken. But the important
point here is that early on, Rudy Giuliani decided that Lin DeVecchio was
an agent worth protecting, just as top FBI officials found Greg Scarpa worthy of special treatment.

In the mid-1980s, when Giuliani, then the U.S. Attorney for the
Southern District of New York, declared war on the Mafia, DeVecchio
returned the favor by using Greg Scarpa to provide the probable cause that
legalized most of the wiretaps used to convict three family bosses in the
Commission case.[32] That prosecution helped solidify Giuliani's reputation
as a crime buster and advanced his political career exponentially.

Years later, in 2007, when DeVecchio faced four counts of murder following his indictment by the Brooklyn DA, the Justice Department delivered for him again by paying for part of his legal bill, which was estimated at
the time to be $450,000.[33] For those fees to be approved, the U.S. attorney
general himself, or his designee, had to conclude that DeVecchio's actions
were within the "scope" of his employment at the Bureau and that the payment of the fees was "in the interest of the United States."[34]

"With Scarpa and DeVecchio," says attorney Gerald Shargel, "the law
was being selectively enforced. In protecting Greg from his many crimes,
the Bureau was shielding a Mafia killer. In allowing DeVecchio to escape
prosecution for the illegal gun sales, the Justice Department was protecting
an FBI agent. In both instances the intervention was legally and morally
wrong."[35]

Giuliani's help to DeVecchio in the German Luger case was a variation
on the mysterious quid pro quo that had insulated Greg Scarpa Sr. So as
the Grim Reaper began his twelve-year association with "Mr. Organized
Crime," the two men shared much more than a love for guns.

PART II

Chapter 11

THE ROYAL MARRIAGE

The FBI's *Manual of Investigative and Operational Guidelines* (MIOG), the rule book governing the conduct of all special agents, requires that when a confidential informant is opened he must interface with two contacting agents.[1] "This is an ironclad rule to make sure a single agent doesn't get too cozy with their informant," says retired Special Agent Jim Whalen, who worked in the New York Office.[2]

From the moment Lin DeVecchio reopened Greg Scarpa, however, he dealt with him one-on-one. According to a report later issued by the Department of Justice inspector general, that particular relationship ran counter to "FBI protocol."[3] But it was formally sanctioned in an FBI memo on March 11, 1981, which not only granted DeVecchio permission to meet Scarpa alone but also waived the rule that Scarpa must sign for "monies paid."[4]

As DeVecchio writes in his book, "The CI is required to sign a receipt, but no truly effective TE will ever sign anything, so you're careful not to look foolish when you ask. You're required to have a backup agent to witness the handling of cash. Again, no Top Echelon worthy of the term will ever agree to meet with two of you. Top Echelon is a royal marriage and three is a crowd. You seek a waiver from the brass."[5]

A federal judge later concluded that the agent-informant guidelines were waived in this instance "on account of Scarpa's distrust of anyone else."[6]

Another FBI guideline DeVecchio managed to avoid in dealing with Scarpa was the recommendation that supervisors shouldn't run CIs themselves. When DeVecchio reached the rank of supervisory special agent (SSA) in 1983,[7] former agent Whalen argues, he should have passed off TECI "34" to agents under him in his squad.

"It was carved in stone," says Whalen, "that no supervisor shall handle an informant. But the New York SAC made an exception for DeVecchio."[8] The question is, in the cost-benefit analysis, whether that special treatment was worth it.

In his book, the former SSA lavishes praise on Scarpa. "From the day of our first sit-down and for the ensuing twelve years," he writes, "Scarpa furnished incredibly valuable information that led to countless RICO convictions and life sentences; Title III bugs and taps; solutions of murders and other serious crimes; and the Mafia Commission Case that, along with the individual family hierarchy cases, was a big part of the undoing of the Mafia's power in New York."[9] A November 10, 1980, airtel stated that Scarpa provided the FBI with an organizational chart of the Colombo family,[10] and continued to pass on intelligence on other soldiers and capos.[11]

There's also little doubt that tying his star to Scarpa helped DeVecchio's career take off. He was eventually given the Bonanno and Colombo squads to oversee, and he became the supervising agent on the Mafia Commission case.[12] "The guys who had TE's were the king shits of the office," said one Organized Crime Strike Force prosecutor in Boston who talked to *Boston Globe* reporter Ralph Ranalli.[13] But at what price?

As the newly released airtels demonstrate, in the early weeks of their relationship, Scarpa was already furnishing DeVecchio with false information about a homicide.

The aforementioned airtel included a comment Scarpa had made a few months earlier about a recent homicide:

> ON AUGUST 26, 1980, SOURCE ADVISED THAT DOMINIC [*sic*] SOMMA, A COLOMBO FAMILY MEMBER, WAS RECENTLY HIT ON A CONTRACT APPROVED BY CARMINE PERSICO.

But what Scarpa doesn't say is that he killed Somma *himself*—in a spectacular shooting in front of six other members of his crew at the Wimpy Boys social club. His role in the murder was later confirmed in a May 1993 FBI

302 memo covering the debriefing of Carmine Sessa, a former Colombo consigliere who was Scarpa's chief asset during the third Colombo war, from 1991 to 1993.

The story behind Somma's rubout begins with the attempted burglary by Scarpa's crew of the Dime Savings Bank in Queens in late August 1980. Working inside the bank during the off-hours break-in were Sessa, Robert  "Bobby Zam" Zambardi, Dominic Cataldo, Joseph Figueroa, Joseph "Joe Brewster" DeDomenico, and Costabile "Gus" Farace, who was Scarpa's nephew. Their specialty was looting safe-deposit boxes after gaining entry by bypassing alarm systems. The so-called Bypass crew often broke into banks over weekends, when they'd have extended access to the vaults.[14]

On this particular job, according to Sessa, Somma was working outside as a lookout with Scarpa's son Greg Jr. Their assignment was "to radio the men inside, if there were any problems." But as Sessa told Special Agents Jeffrey W. Tomlinson and Howard Leadbetter II, "SCARPA JR. was neglectful and a security guard walked in on the burglars."

Wimpy Boys club, 7506 Thirteenth Avenue, Brooklyn

Thinking fast, Joe Brewster told the guard that they were a cleaning crew and while the guard was calling in to confirm their story, the Bypass crew escaped. Later, Somma complained to the crew's nominal boss, capo Anthony "Scappi" Scarpati, about Junior's performance.[15]

In an earlier interview, Sessa had said that the shooting of "Big Donny" Somma had initially been sanctioned by Allie Boy Persico, who had learned that Somma was dealing drugs. But that contract was about to be withdrawn. Now, apparently furious that his son had been criticized, Scarpa told Sessa that he wanted to "hit" Donny "before the orders for his murder were cancelled."[16] So the Grim Reaper summoned Somma to the ironically named Wimpy Boys club, where he did business.

Later that day, as Big Donny walked in unaware of the danger he faced, he passed John and Joseph Saponaro, two brothers who were playing cards in an outer room. He then went straight to Scarpa's office in back. Inside, Scarpa was waiting, along with Joe Brewster, Farace, Zambardi, and Sessa. As soon as Somma came through the door, Scarpa pulled "a revolver with a long barrel from a desk drawer" and killed him instantly.

"We're all talking and joking and out of nowhere Greg whips out a piece and shoots the guy in the head," Sessa said. "Christ almighty, the guy's brains were all over me! My ears were ringing from the gunshot. Calm as he can be, he told us to roll the body in the rug and get rid of it."[17] Sessa later told the Feds that he, Zambardi, and Greg Jr. dumped the body near the Arthur Kill landfill on Staten Island.

The fact that Dominick Somma would have the effrontery to complain about Scarpa's son was all it took to set Scarpa off. He would continue to smolder over the incident, later telling Sessa, "I'd like to dig him up and shoot him again."[18] Still, in the very same 209 in which he reported Somma's death, DeVecchio assured Bureau officials that:

> This informant has not exhibited any tendencies toward emotional instability and has furnished no information known to be false.

Did Lin DeVecchio know that Scarpa was lying to him about the Somma hit? We can't say for sure, but we can get some insight from DeVecchio's own book. In his memoir, rather than describing the murder as a contract hit "approved by Carmine Persico," as he did in that August 26, 1980, airtel, DeVecchio uses Big Donny's murder to make the point that Scarpa "was indeed a fearless individual who enjoyed killing."

> Once a member of Scarpa's crew complained about his son's lackluster performance during a bypass bank burglary and Scarpa responded to the complaint by drilling the man on the spot and having him buried.[19]

Clearly, at the time when he was writing his book in 2010 Lin DeVecchio knew the truth about Dominick Somma's execution and burial. The question is, did he know it when he sent that airtel to Headquarters thirty years before? If so, he was passing on false information to his superiors in DC— and, worse, facilitating Scarpa's lies.

Thus, in assessing the agent's twelve-year relationship with Greg Scarpa Sr., the central question is as old as the Watergate scandal: What did DeVecchio know and when did he know it?

Scarpa and the Beauty Queen

The guidelines on how FBI agents should react to knowledge of criminal activity by an informant were revised by Attorney General Benjamin Civiletti on December 4, 1980, five months after the Bureau reopened Scarpa. They provided that "if necessary and appropriate, informants may be authorized to participate in two different types of otherwise criminal activity" at the behest of the FBI: "ordinary" and "extraordinary."

"Ordinary" criminal activity (effectively misdemeanors) could be authorized by an FBI field office supervisor or higher FBI official. "Extraordinary" criminal activity was defined as any activity involving "a significant risk of violence, corrupt actions by high public officials, or severe financial loss to a victim." Only SACs could authorize extraordinary criminal activity, and only with the approval of the pertinent U.S. attorney.[20] And in no case was homicide ever sanctioned or envisioned as a crime the Justice Department would permit.

Two days before the Civiletti guidelines were issued, DeVecchio filed a short 209 memo involving routine intelligence from Scarpa on low-level Colombo family matters:

> Source advised that JACKIE DI ROSS and JOHN PATE are currently shylocking JUNIOR PERSICO's money in the Staten Island area. The source advised that DI ROSS has been meeting frequently with CARMINE PERSICO, and more recently has been used by PERSICO to contact members of other LCN families on PERSICO's behalf.[21]

But the very next day, December 3, 1980, Gregory Scarpa committed his second murder since DeVecchio had reopened him that past summer.

There was no mention of the homicide in any of the recently released 209 memos or airtels sent to FBI Headquarters.

As we've seen, on February 2, 1975, while he was still married to Connie

Forrest and living with Linda Schiro, Scarpa flew to Las Vegas for a quickie marriage to Lili Dajani, who was Miss Israel 1960.[22] According to a series of articles in the Long Beach *Press-Telegram*, Dajani was the daughter of Dr. Isa Dajani, an Arab dentist "who trace[d] his lineage to the time of the Crusades" and Mrs. Chava Rechtman-Dajani of Santa Monica, California, "a descendant of six generations of Jewish settlers who founded the town of Rehovot, Israel."[23]

But the former beauty queen's marriage to Scarpa wasn't her first trip to the altar in Las Vegas. As reported in the *Press-Telegram* in March 1961, after contacting the California Highway Patrol and reporting her daughter "missing,"[24] Mrs. Rechtman-Dajani notified the police that Lili had eloped to Nevada with a twenty-four-year-old man named Martin Geller and that she had sent her mother a telegram that read "Are Married."[25] The couple then reportedly traveled to New York for their honeymoon.

Lili Dajani, 1960

The five-foot-seven beauty queen, who was one of fifteen semifinalists in the 1960 Miss International Beauty Congress,[26] reportedly spoke five languages, including English, French, Italian, Arabic, and Hebrew.[27]

Fourteen years later, when she made her second wedding trip to Las Vegas with Greg Scarpa, Ms. Dajani initially gave her address on the marriage certificate as Los Angeles. But her new address as Scarpa's third wife was typed in at the top of the certificate: 36 Sutton Place South, Apartment 8G, a posh co-op Scarpa owned in one of Manhattan's most exclusive neighborhoods. A copy of the marriage certificate is reproduced in Appendix B.

In 1980, Dajani, then forty years old, was working as a nurse-receptionist at the Central Women's Center, a facility run by Eliezer Shkolnik, a fifty-two-year-old doctor whose medical license had reportedly been revoked in 1976 due to conditions at the clinic, where he performed abortions.

In 2006, quoting unnamed sources, veteran Mafia columnist Jerry Capeci reported in the *New York Sun* that "during the period that Dajani worked for the married Dr. Shkolnik they became lovers . . . a relationship that contributed to his messy divorce that ended with the ex-doctor changing the name of the women's center, placing it in Ms. Dajani's name, and remaining on as the center's administrator."[28]

Capeci also reported that "sources said Ms. Dajani and Scarpa Sr. also had a business relationship. She had invested money with Scarpa . . . an investigative source said, adding that Ms. Dajani was 'upset with Scarpa' about her losses."

Later, Shkolnik reportedly moved in with his parents in their Forest Hills, Queens, apartment, telling his son, "I'm finally going to get the business back."[29] He also reportedly started talking to the IRS about Dajani and her relationship with Scarpa.

Then, according to Capeci, at seven thirty A.M. on December 3, 1980, Scarpa, Joe Brewster DeDomenico, and a third unnamed cohort entered the lobby of the Forest Hills building and shot Shkolnik in the head. The former abortion doctor was reportedly found with $1,500 in cash and expensive gold jewelry on his body, ruling out robbery as a motive for the crime.

In the 2006 "Gang Land" column that broke the Shkolnik story, Capeci quoted unnamed sources as stating that "shortly after he signed up Scarpa, Mr. DeVecchio allegedly alerted his murderous informer that Shkolnik . . . was cooperating with an Internal Revenue Service probe into Scarpa's activities." Capeci also interviewed Shkolnik's son Hunter, a Manhattan attorney, and quoted him as saying that the day *after* the murder he got a phone call from an anonymous source informing him that an "FBI agent . . . had something to do" with his father's death.

In 2007, just before Lin DeVecchio's homicide trial, Capeci reported that Gregory Scarpa Jr. was prepared to testify that he was the unnamed third co-conspirator in the Shkolnik hit team. He reportedly told prosecutors that his participation in the hit came after a special request from his father, who was proud of the work he did.[30]

According to Capeci, "Prosecutors say the slaying of Shkolnik . . . was set in motion by Mr. DeVecchio in the fall of 1980, when he allegedly alerted Colombo mobster Gregory Scarpa Sr. that the ex-doctor was cooperating in a tax probe of the gangster, with whom he shared a mistress."[31]

But later, when the Brooklyn district attorney tried to include the Shkolnik homicide in a list of "prior bad acts" that might be used to impeach

DeVecchio during his murder trial,[32] Judge Gustin Reichbach rejected the motion, holding that proof of this homicide, "made very late in the proceedings, long after the . . . indictment was returned," would be "highly prejudicial."[33]

DeVecchio never mentions the Shkolnik murder or Scarpa's relationship with Dajani in his book. Nor was there a hint of the homicide in his next memorandum, which he filed on March 1, 1981—a detailed four-page FBI letterhead memo on his debriefings of "34" during the period when the violent Forest Hills slaying took place.[34]

As we'll soon see, one of the members of the Shkolnik hit team, Joe Brewster, was later murdered on Scarpa's orders. That homicide became one of the four counts in the Brooklyn DA's prosecution of DeVecchio.[35] But the key point to keep in mind at this juncture, even putting aside DeVecchio's possible involvement in the Shkolnik rubout, was that less than half a year into Scarpa's new stint as a paid Top Echelon informant for the Bureau, the Grim Reaper was continuing to commit murders.

In the *60 Minutes* piece on DeVecchio's book, Ellen Corcella, the former Eastern District of New York (EDNY) assistant U.S. attorney who prosecuted a Colombo war case in 1995, underscored the implications of having an FBI informant, who is known to be violent, killing people while he's an official Bureau CI.

"You are absolutely not supposed to keep an informant on the street that is killing people," she told correspondent Anderson Cooper.

"Even if that person is giving you valuable information which may have other arrests as a result of it?" Cooper asked.

"The question I would put to your question," Corcella replied, "is, when is it valuable enough information that you let people continue to kill other people on the street?"[36]

"I Knew He Was Doing Hits"

In his memoir, *Brick Agent,* Anthony Villano wrote that "Bureau instructions specifically state that if an agent becomes aware of a conspiracy to commit a criminal act wherein an innocent person might get hurt, it must be prevented from taking place."[37] As we'll see, during the third Colombo war, which was incited and principally waged by Greg Scarpa, at least half a dozen innocent bystanders were wounded and two were killed.[38] That happened more than a decade into Lin DeVecchio's tenure as Scarpa's "control" agent.

Was DeVecchio aware back in the early 1980s that Greg was continuing to commit murders? Without commenting on the time frame, DeVecchio answers that question himself in his book. "In my heart, as Scarpa's handler, of course I knew he was doing hits," he writes.[39]

But how much did DeVecchio know of the details?

In his 1993 debriefing, former Scarpa crew member Carmine Sessa confessed to knowledge of another early 1980s Scarpa homicide. During a session with FBI agents Tomlinson and Leadbetter II on May 10, 1993, Sessa recalled that the unknown male, referred to in that FBI 302 as "the victim," owed a loan-shark debt to Colombo captain Anthony Scarpati. So Scarpa enticed the man to meet him at Occasions, a club Sessa owned at 6908 Thirteenth Avenue in Brooklyn.

Most of the same crew who were witnesses to the murder and disposal of Dominick Somma, including the Saponaro brothers, Joe Brewster DeDomenico, Bobby Zambardi, and Greg Jr., all reportedly hid out on the first floor of the club. According to Sessa, as soon as the victim walked in, he was tackled to the floor and then shot point-blank by Greg Sr.[40]

Sessa reported that the body was then wrapped in canvas and driven by Zambardi to a collision shop on Sixty-Third Street between Fifteenth and Sixteenth Avenues. It was then moved to a van and reportedly parked by a member of Dominick "Donny Shacks" Montemarano's crew at a location not far from Scarpa's Wimpy Boys social club. There it sat all day—for so long that Scarpa actually started to complain about it, since the original "plan had called for the van to be picked up right away."

This was the third Scarpa murder since DeVecchio began running him, and there is nothing in the 209s or memos from that period that even hints at the rubout. This killing would take on added significance later, because Occasions, Sessa's club, was the site of another infamous killing by the Grim Reaper—one of those cited in the Brooklyn DA's indictment against DeVecchio. We'll describe the details of that grisly hit in the next chapter.[41]

The Limo Rubouts

Greg Scarpa Sr. was responsible for at least two more murders in the early 1980s. Both of them involved limo drivers and the motive in both hits was personal.

Alfred Longobardi was a limo driver who was "married to the mob," in that he'd been the first husband of Scarpa crew member Carmine Imbriale's wife. According to Carmine Sessa, Greg was "upset" with Imbriale when he married her.[42]

By July 1982, in partnership with his father and "Scappi" Scarpati, Scarpa's son Greg Jr. was running a nightclub on Staten Island called On the Rocks. One night, Longobardi reportedly came in and got drunk, firing off an insult at Junior. As with Dominick Somma, that slight to Scarpa's son merited a death sentence in the elder Scarpa's mind. But according to John Kroger, a former assistant U.S. attorney in Brooklyn, Junior himself initially attempted to do the "work."[43] He reportedly used a knife to flatten one of Longobardi's tires as his limo sat parked outside his house. The alleged plan was for Greg Jr. to hit him from behind as he changed the tire.

But when Longobardi got out of the car, he was carrying his infant son. Since Mafia rules forbid the involvement of families in hits, Junior backed away.

The reprieve didn't last long.

As Carmine Sessa told it to FBI agents, Greg Sr. ordered his son and the same crew that had taken care of the victim in Sessa's club to "participate in Longobardi's murder."

Joe Brewster DeDomenico, Greg Sr.'s. most trusted crew member, was ordered to hire Longobardi's stretch. The driver was to pick up DeDomenico and Greg Sr. at the airport for a trip to Staten Island, where they would execute him once they arrived. The body would then be left in the stretch, and three other cars from Scarpa's crew would be waiting to provide backup and a getaway.

Sessa met them back at the Wimpy Boys club, where Greg Sr. told Sessa that he'd shot Longobardi as the driver parked the stretch. To send a message about "respect," Scarpa had shot away Longobardi's face,[44] forcing his family to identify him from his tattoos when they came to claim the body. Such was the price that Gregory Scarpa Sr., the FBI's star informant, exacted from anyone who would dare insult his firstborn son.

But there was a hitch. As it turned out, when Joe Brewster ordered the limo, he'd placed the call from a pay phone at Mike's Candy, a convenience store Scarpa Sr. owned a few doors down from the social club.[45] When the police traced the limo order back to the store, they started looking for DeDomenico, who was forced to hide out for some time in a Long Island hotel until the heat was off.[46]

The death of the second limo driver came after a much more serious offense against one of Greg Sr.'s children.

Confessing a Murder to Lin

"Little Linda" Schiro, Gregory's daughter with Linda Schiro, traveled back and forth to school with her brother Joey via a Brooklyn car service that her father had hired. In an interview she gave for a Discovery Channel documentary that aired in December 2011, Little Linda said that one day, after her brother stayed home sick, instead of taking her to school, their regular driver took her into Prospect Park. "At that time he tried to rape me," she said. "I didn't even know if I was going to make it out of the park."[47] Using her "instincts," Schiro said, she convinced the driver that if he met her after school they could "go somewhere."

The driver then took her to school, where she ran into a bathroom, her shirt ripped from the struggle, and called her mother.

In a subsequent *New York Post* story reported by Brad Hamilton in 2012, Little Linda identified the driver as one Jose Guzman and gave additional details about the alleged attack.[48] "He ripped the buttons on my shirt," she said, "and started licking my hand. . . . It was disgusting." In the *Post* account, Schiro said that she was "hysterical, crying," and that later, her mother, Big Linda, "went to the car service with a knife and threatened the dispatcher."

According to Carmine Sessa, when an enraged Greg Sr. went to the car service, he learned that the driver had quit that particular company. Eventually, though, Scarpa discovered Guzman's home address and located Little Linda's alleged attacker near a park, where he was severely beaten.

But that apparently wasn't enough for the Mad Hatter. Sessa told the FBI agents debriefing him that the very thought of the violation continued to prey on Scarpa's mind—so much so that he eventually ordered the driver's execution.

Using the same MO he'd employed with Longobardi, Scarpa had Joe Brewster and Bobby Zam rent the driver's own Cadillac Seville. They directed him to stop at Sixty-Fourth Street in Brooklyn, where, Sessa confessed, he and Scarpa Jr. "shot and killed the victim." In his book, however, Lin DeVecchio attributes the murder to *his own informant,* Greg Scarpa Sr., adding that the driver was "a Puerto Rican not involved in the life."

According to DeVecchio's version, Greg Sr. first got a cane and limped into the limo driver's office, where he "whipped him with it." But then, unable to live with himself, Scarpa confessed to Lin that he "went back and killed him."[49]

According to the *Post* story, Guzman was "shot dead, pleading for his life . . . in broad daylight." Reporter Hamilton puts the location two blocks away from where Sessa described it, "in the middle of 62nd Street in Bensonhurst."[50]

"The next thing I knew, the car service driver was killed," said Little Linda in the documentary. "I can only assume that he didn't know who my father was."

It's significant that in his own book, Lin DeVecchio admitted that Scarpa had confessed this murder to him, but does not say when he knew about it. If "34" had done it while he was DeVecchio's informant, under Justice Department guidelines such a confession should have triggered not just Scarpa's immediate closing as an informant, but a report to both Lin's FBI supervisor and the U.S. attorney for the EDNY.

In 2007, after DeVecchio was indicted by the Brooklyn DA on four counts of murder conspiracy, his attorneys moved to have the sensational case switched to federal court. But in rejecting that motion, Judge Frederic Block cited the AG's Guidelines "circumscribing authorization for confidential informants to commit crimes."

Under the Guidelines in effect during the period covered by the 2007 indictment, a CI could not be authorized to commit a crime of violence unless a special agent in charge, after consulting with the appropriate United States attorney, determined in writing that (1) "the conduct [was] necessary to obtain information or evidence for paramount prosecutive purposes, to establish or maintain credibility or cover with persons associated with criminal activity under investigation, or to prevent or avoid the danger of death or serious bodily injury," and (2) such necessity "outweigh[ed] the seriousness of the conduct involved."[51]

The current guidelines are even more restrictive: "A [Department of Justice law enforcement agency] is *never* permitted to authorize a CI to participate in an act of violence."[52]

But as the 1980s unfolded there was much more violence to come. According to Assistant U.S. Attorney Kroger, Greg Scarpa Sr. committed another murder within three years of being reopened by Lin DeVecchio. Once again, his accomplice was Carmine Sessa.

By early January 1983, among his other criminal activities, Greg Sr. was running an international auto-theft ring that stole high-end vehicles and shipped them overseas. At one point, Scarpa came to believe that Sal "the Hammerhead" Cardaci was about to inform on Billy Meli, one of "34's" crew members, who was close to Greg Jr. Cardaci was then lured to Mike's Candy, where Sessa shot him in the head with a .357 Magnum.

As Kroger described it, the body was then "stripped, covered with lime and buried down in the candy store basement."[53] But there isn't a word about that murder in any of the 209s that continued to flow to FBI Headquarters in Washington. Not a word on the murders of Longobardi and Guzman, the car service driver who allegedly molested Little Linda. Similarly, there was no mention in the FBI airtels or 209s of Greg Scarpa Sr.'s next vicious homicide. This time the victim was Mary Bari, the ravishing mistress of Allie Boy Persico.

Chapter 12

GOING TO HELL
FOR THIS

In 1969, Mary Bari was on the verge of her sixteenth birthday. She was a student at New Utrecht High School in Brooklyn and the daughter of a candy store owner. One day, she was standing on a street corner near school when the man who would later rise to the rank of underboss of the Colombo crime family[1] rolled up next to her.[2] Twenty-four years older and married, Alphonse Persico was the brother of Carmine "the Snake." They called him "Allie Boy," but there was nothing boyish about him. He dressed in thousand-dollar suits, drove a white Rolls-Royce, and never went out without an armed bodyguard. To the drop-dead-gorgeous Mary, he was like no one she'd ever met.

"Once they started dating, he started showering her with gifts," said one of her relatives. "He took her to Vegas, to Hawaii, to Florida. He gave her a fox fur coat. He gave her diamond rings."[3] Even though her mother, Louise, tried to warn her that the Persicos were "bad people," the headstrong Mary wouldn't listen. "She had a real crush on him," the relative said. With her looks and figure, the petite five-foot-two brunette[4] had always been sought after by the neighborhood boys, but now they stayed away. Even knowing that Allie Boy would never leave his wife, Dora, Mary pretended he was a normal boyfriend; she introduced him to her family and invited him to her sister's wedding. To please him, she even got a tattoo of a peach (a pet name) on her derriere. And for eleven years, as the dangerous roller coaster she was riding stayed on its tracks, she lived a life many girls from Bensonhurst only dreamed of.

But the Feds were closing in on the Persico brothers. In May 1980, Allie Boy was convicted of extortion for attempting to collect on a $10,000 loan-sharking debt. With a vigorish (or "vig") of two points, or two hundred dollars, a week, it was a relatively minor loan, considering that by the mid-1980s Greg Scarpa Sr. had a "bank" with several million dollars "out on the street."[5] But Persico was facing a sentence of sixty years.[6] So in June 1980, just before he was to appear before Judge Jack B. Weinstein in Eastern District federal court, Allie Boy disappeared.[7] He was so terrified of prison that he forfeited a $250,000 bond and went on the lam, staying out of sight for the next seven years.

Mary discovered how right her mother had been when Persico's men came to her house and demanded back all the gifts that he'd given her—

Mary Bari

including diamonds and other jewelry.[8] She was out of work for a year before she got a call from Carmine Sessa. He was looking for a cocktail waitress for his club Occasions in Bay Ridge.[9]

Being close to "the life" with Allie Boy, and knowing what it meant when the mob turned against you, Mary should have heard the alarm bells. Carmine Sessa would later plead guilty to his involvement in thirteen homicides, most of them committed jointly with Greg Scarpa Sr.[10] But by 1984 Mary was desperate for a job. So on the night of September 25, 1984, she got herself dolled up in a black tank top and white stiletto heels with a lizard belt over designer jeans. They sent a car for her driven by Anthony Frezza, a heavyset Colombo associate known as "Tony Muscles."[11]

As they headed to the club at 6908 Thirteenth Avenue, Mary had no way of knowing that this was the same location where Greg Scarpa Sr. had murdered that loan-sharking victim a few years earlier. She had no way of knowing that around that time Scarpa had told his protégé Larry Mazza that Mary "was going to give up Allie Boy's location. She was going to rat on him."[12] She had no way of knowing that earlier that morning Scarpa had called Carmine Sessa and told him he needed to use his club again for a murder.[13] Scarpa had said that Bari was dating somebody in "law enforcement"[14] and that she "may have [had] information" on Allie Boy's hideout, which she could let slip.

Considering the way he'd abandoned her, it was unlikely that Mary knew *anything* about Persico's whereabouts. But Greg Sr., whom Sessa later admitted was "treacherous,"[15] really didn't need to justify himself to Carmine. He wasn't even going to bother to clear this hit with anyone above him in the family. He'd committed other homicides on the FBI's watch and he had reason to be confident that he could get away with this one.

Linda Schiro, Scarpa's common-law wife, later testified that Bari had been marked for death after Lin DeVecchio came to their house on Avenue J that morning. She said that Lin walked into the kitchen, his usual meeting place with Scarpa, and said, "We have a problem with . . . Mary Bari."[16] Testifying under oath at DeVecchio's murder trial in 2007, Schiro insisted that DeVecchio had told his informant that Bari was "looking to rat out Allie Boy."

"You have to take care of this," Schiro testified that DeVecchio told Scarpa. "She's going to be a problem." As he spoke, she said, DeVecchio had "a smirk" on his face.[17]

Dumping Her on the Street

At that same trial, in which DeVecchio was charged in three other homicides, Carmine Sessa testified that Anthony Frezza showed up at his club with Bari later that night. As they walked in, Scarpa was waiting there with Greg Jr., Joe Brewster DeDomenico, and Bobby Zambardi—the same crew that had reportedly done "the work" in the loan-shark murder.

"Junior put his arm around her," said Sessa. "She thought it was a friendly gesture." Then he pushed her to the ground. At that point, "Greg

Senior walked over and shot her in the head."[18] After that, Sessa testified that they "wrapped up the body . . . in a blanket or tarp" and put it in the trunk of Senior's car. Sessa followed in his car. Scarpa stopped near Washington Cemetery around Twentieth Avenue, a few miles away. But at that point Sessa spotted an NYPD squad car and flashed his high beams as a signal for Senior to keep going.

They ended up dropping Mary's body on McDonald Avenue, under the elevated train a few blocks from Scarpa Sr.'s own house. Sessa lived upstairs from his club at the time, and he testified that later that night he heard a knock at the door. When he opened up, there were six NYPD detectives outside. Apparently Mary had told someone about the location of the job interview, and when she never returned her family got worried. But Sessa insisted that he kept his mouth shut with the cops.

The next day, Sessa cleaned the club with bleach and hosed down the floor. At that point he found what he described as "a piece of flesh" and a shell casing. When he told Greg Sr. about the visit from the police, Scarpa told him, "Don't worry about it."[19] Schiro testified that after the murder Lin DeVecchio came to the house and joked with Scarpa about where he'd dumped Mary's corpse. "Lin says, 'Why didn't you just bring the body right in front of the house?'" she testified. "And Greg started laughing."[20]

Two days later Linda Schiro's testimony was discredited when the case was dismissed.[21] The abrupt end in the trial, after only two weeks, came when Jerry Capeci and Tom Robbins came forward with tapes of a 1997 interview they'd done with Schiro.[22] The recordings directly contradicted Schiro's sworn testimony in one of the four homicides. But there was no mention of DeVecchio's role, if he had any, in the murder of Mary Bari.[23]

Schiro later insisted that she had cleared DeVecchio during her interviews with Capeci and Robbins in order to "protect Lin," who was still helping her, and because she was "nervous and afraid" of possible reprisals from the FBI.[24] But she insisted that she was telling the truth at the trial. In 2008, after a special district attorney was appointed to determine whether she had committed perjury, Schiro was not charged.[25]

At that same 2007 trial, Larry Mazza, who was Scarpa's self-described "right-hand man,"[26] testified under oath that Greg Sr. had told him he'd shot Bari himself because she was a woman and "he was the only one that . . . had the stomach for it."[27]

Mazza then went on to recount the details of a dinner that took place not long after the murder at Romano's, an Italian restaurant on Thirteenth Avenue that Senior frequented. On that night, Mazza testified, Greg Sr. was there with Linda, Carmine Sessa, and Sessa's wife, Annie. "We were sitting, pretty much joking," said Mazza. It was a "festive-type of atmosphere." During the dinner, said Mazza, Scarpa recalled that when he shot Mary in the head one of her ears "went flying."[28] Annie Sessa then told them that her dog had later found the ear in the club. Everybody at the table "laughed," said Mazza. "It was a joke."

DeVecchio's attorneys vehemently denied his possible link to the Bari homicide, along with the other three murder-conspiracy charges brought by the Brooklyn DA. With the dismissal of the case, he can never be tried again for the crime. Later in this book, we'll examine Linda Schiro's credibility in depth. But Tommy Dades, a veteran NYPD detective who helped make the case against DeVecchio, has insisted that Schiro was telling the truth.[29]

At a pretrial hearing in August 2007, Dades testified that Greg Scarpa Jr. had told him that he'd learned of DeVecchio's alleged connection to the Bari homicide from his father.[30] A veteran of the NYPD's Intelligence Division, which focused on organized crime cases, Dades went to work in the DA's office after he retired in 2004.[31] He had multiple meetings with Greg Scarpa Jr., whom the Brooklyn DA had flown to New York from the Supermax prison in Colorado in anticipation of his testimony against DeVecchio.[32]

Jerry Capeci reported in the months before the trial, "Sources say prosecutors plan to use [the] long-imprisoned mobster, son of the late Scarpa, Gregory Scarpa Jr., to back up their key prosecution witness—Scarpa's longtime lover, Linda Schiro—regarding two mob rubouts the son was involved in before he was incarcerated in 1988."

One of those murders was the killing of Mary Bari. But when the case was dismissed, Greg Scarpa Jr. was returned to finish out a forty-year sentence without ever getting a chance to take the stand. One factor in assessing Scarpa Jr.'s credibility would have been his willingness to admit to his alleged participation in the Bari murder.

So in a pretrial hearing, under oath, retired detective Dades described several meetings he had with the younger Scarpa. In one debriefing, said

Dades, Junior admitted to his role in Mary's killing and corroborated Schiro's contention that DeVecchio had "relayed the information" to his father about Bari's being "an informant."[33] According to Dades, Greg Jr. told him that when his father demanded the Bari execution, Colombo capo "Scappi" Scarpati warned, "We're probably going to go to hell for this."[34]

"Greg Sr. told Greg Jr. that he was informed by 'D' that Mary Bari was being targeted to cooperate," Dades testified, explaining that "D" stood for DeVecchio. "Greg Sr. told Greg Jr., 'She's gotta go,'" said Dades, adding, "Greg Jr. said he was very shocked at that because Mary Bari was a stand-up girl. There was no way she was going to cooperate."[35]

For Dades, the killing of Mary Bari was personal. He testified at the hearing that he "kind of grew up with Mary. Her father was Pat, who owned Pat's Candy Store across the street from my house and I remember how devastated [he] was when she was murdered."[36]

According to an account in the *New York Post* by reporters Jennifer Fermino and Todd Venezia, Bari's face was so badly disfigured that when her body was recovered, her sister was able to identify her only from the peach tattoo she'd gotten to please Allie Boy Persico. Fermino and Venezia also reported that Bari's brother became "so obsessed with finding the real killer, that he wound up killing himself with a drug overdose" three years later, in 1987.[37] That was the same year that U.S. marshals finally located Persico, who had been hiding under an alias in West Hartford, Connecticut.[38] He was ultimately sentenced to twenty-five years and died of cancer at a prison hospital two years later.[39]

The Job Interview

Even absent any link between Lin DeVecchio and the Bari homicide, the death of this young woman represents another shocking example of how Greg Scarpa Sr. operated with murderous impunity during his tenure as a star informant for the FBI.

At the same time, DeVecchio's treatment of Bari's murder in his own memoir is worthy of note. In a kind of introduction to the book entitled "The Job Interview," DeVecchio and coauthor Charles Brandt deliver what reads like a fictional account of the murder from Bari's own point of view.

It begins with her putting on makeup at her home before getting picked up for the trip to Occasions and includes detailed dialogue between Bari, the unnamed driver of the car, and the murder crew at Sessa's club. The account even references Bari's inner thoughts. In this sequence, she compares herself to Allie Boy's wife:

> I look the youngest of anybody out there. Her and me both gave Allie Boy the best years of our lives. But no way she's ending up with him. I'll raise holy hell, Mary thought. You know what? You can push me only so far. It's about time these people did something for me. They can afford it.

Later, on the ride to the club, DeVecchio and Brandt have Bari talking to the driver about "how Hollywood discriminates against Italian-American women." In fact they quote Bari word for word expressing displeasure that "they didn't even use an Italian girl to play the Italian girl in *Saturday Night Fever*." After stating—incorrectly—that "the driver dropped Mary Bari off in front of Carmine Sessa's club and drove off," DeVecchio and Brandt then describe her murder in explicit detail, complete with statements purportedly made at the time by Greg Sr. and his son.

"Don't you look foxy?" Greg Jr. says in the account. The coauthors note that "Junior did not have his father's strong good looks, but he did get respect."[40]

Then, moments before Junior's father shoots Mary in the head, DeVecchio and Brandt describe her inner thoughts: "Greg Scarpa was some sexy-looking man," they have her thinking, describing Senior as "solid, powerful, dressed sharp, nice mustache, a born leader." They end the section with a verbatim quotation of the FBI 209 that DeVecchio filed on November 21, 1984, two months after the murder. Not surprisingly, it contains nothing about the homicide.

As to the source, if any, that DeVecchio and Brandt used for this account, one thing seems certain: It wasn't Greg Jr. The younger Scarpa was willing to testify against Lin DeVecchio, and in his interviews with me he categorically denied that he described the Bari hit for Lin. Nor does the source seem to have been Carmine Sessa, whose only account of the killing is a one-page FBI 302 memo that contains no dialogue. No other FBI files have surfaced of any account by Robert Zambardi. And the other two witnesses to the murder are dead: Anthony Frezza was reportedly killed in October 1985,[41] and Joseph "Joe Brewster" DeDomenico, the godfather of Junior's daughter, was killed in 1987.[42] (We'll take an in-depth look at that rubout—one of the four murders in the Brooklyn DA's indictment of Lin DeVecchio—in Chapter 16.)

In the fall of 2011, as I was finishing the research on this book, I e-mailed Charles Brandt asking him to document his source for the detailed account of Mary Bari's homicide. He never responded. I also e-mailed Douglas Grover, Lin DeVecchio's attorney, requesting an interview with him and his client.

A year later, I sent an Express Mail letter directly to DeVecchio at his address in Sarasota, Florida. U.S. Postal Service records show that he signed for it. But I never received a response from him.

Chapter 13

LOVE COLLISION

Of the many complex relationships in this epic underworld story, few are more complicated than the strange triangle that joined Gregory Scarpa Sr. to his common-law wife, Linda Schiro, and to Larry Mazza, the handsome delivery boy who first became her lover and later became a killer. While he was never formally made, Mazza, who eventually pled guilty to participation in four murders and served nine years in prison,[1] racked up a homicide record that would rival the "work" of most hardened wiseguys.

While many of the most violent mob leaders, such as Carmine Persico and Sammy "the Bull" Gravano, started out in Brooklyn street gangs,[2] Mazza was a product of the solid middle class. In an interview with me in 2013 he said that he'd been a Roman Catholic altar boy.[3] His father was a lieutenant in the New York City Fire Department. Larry aspired at first to be an insurance broker and had a year of college under his belt before his relationship with Greg Scarpa Sr. finally drew him into a web of loan shark- ing, extortion, robbery, and murder.[4] The story of his seduction into "the life," which began with a sexual encounter and exploded into a murderous rampage, is a cautionary tale that's never been fully told.

In 2007, when I interviewed Linda Schiro, her answer to my first ques- tion sounded like the opening line from Nicholas Pileggi's screen adaptation of his book *Wiseguy,* which became the Martin Scorsese film *GoodFellas.*

"As far back as I can remember, I always wanted to be a gangster," exclaims the character played by Ray Liotta, based on the late real-life Lucchese family associate Henry Hill.

When I asked Linda what had so impressed her about the mob she said, "Since I was a kid, I grew up with gangsters in the neighborhood, having card games, having crap games, hanging out in the pool room next door to my grandmother's, and I was impressed with them, the way they pulled up in their new cars. The way they dressed. I just grew up with them."[5]

In her two days of testimony during the DeVecchio trial, Schiro described her early life in Bensonhurst, Brooklyn. Like Mary Bari, she did a year at New Utrecht High before dropping out for a secretarial job on Wall Street. But she'd been dating wiseguys from the age of fifteen.[6] Two years later, in 1962, she was at the bar of the Flamingo Lounge, a mob hangout on Seventy-Second Street and Thirteenth Avenue, when Greg Scarpa Sr. walked in.[7]

Once he spotted her, Linda said, Scarpa walked over and asked to be introduced. Then they danced. "He told me how beautiful I was and asked for my number. I told him no. I would call him." Scarpa was thirty-six at the time, nineteen years older than Linda, and he was married.

Linda Diana Schiro with Greg Scarpa Sr.

Within a matter of weeks, she learned that Scarpa was a "gangster" with "the Colombo crime family." But that didn't put her off. If anything, she was intrigued—particularly one night when she saw the bartender get "nasty" with a friend of Scarpa's. "Greg told him to walk out from behind the bar," she testified. Then "he took him into the bathroom and . . . flushed his head in the toilet bowl."[8]

Linda soon learned that Scarpa was doing burglaries and hijackings. "I wasn't upset. I was impressed," she testified, noting that her father allowed Greg to use his apartment to store stolen television sets.

Before long, Linda said, Scarpa not only gave her the details of his lesser crimes, he disclosed the murders as well, admitting that by 1962 he'd already committed "about twenty."[9] As a point of comparison, Sammy "the Bull" Gravano, John Gotti's underboss in the Gambino crime family, considered one of the most violent killers the Mafia ever produced, pled guilty in 1991 to a lifetime record of nineteen murders.[10] In 1962, with twenty hits under his belt, Greg Scarpa was only twelve years into a career that would last more than four decades.

Linda Diana Schiro Scarpa

By the late 1960s, Scarpa was still married to Connie Forrest, the mother of Gregory Jr. and three other children: Deborah, who was two years older than Junior; Bart; and Frankie, who was born in 1963.[11] Linda, whose maiden name was Diana, testified that she was still living with her father and wanted to have children by Scarpa Sr., so she married Charlie Schiro, who had no idea "Little Linda" (born in 1969) wasn't his own daughter. Linda gave birth to Joey, a second child by Greg, in 1972, the year before Senior formally separated from Connie and moved her to a farm in Lakewood, New Jersey.

Charlie Schiro raised Little Linda and Joey as his own, but after he learned the truth about Linda's relationship with Scarpa, he divorced her.[12] At that point she moved in with Scarpa at the house on Avenue J where Lin DeVecchio started meeting him several years later.

Then in 1979, after she and Scarpa were living together with their two kids, Linda spotted Mazza, who was then an eighteen-year-old delivery boy for Danza's market on Fifty-Fifth Street in Brooklyn. She was in her early thirties at the time.

In her interview with me, Linda insisted that she and Greg Sr. enjoyed "a beautiful sex life." But as she put it, "you know how sometimes you'll watch a movie and you'll see [somebody] who might turn you on? That's how it was with Larry. He was really so cute. He started delivering groceries to my house."

Before she and Mazza began their affair, however, Linda insists that she cleared it with Scarpa: "I just told [him] that there is this really nice delivery boy . . . and I would like to go to bed with [him]."

Incredibly, the volatile, highly territorial Scarpa, who had killed a man for insulting his son, gave her his blessing. "He said, 'Sweetheart, whatever makes you happy, that's what you do,'" she told me. "So we started and Greg knew."

And it wasn't just that Scarpa *knew*. According to Schiro, he was often at home when she and Mazza had sex. "Larry would come and we would make love and either Greg was in another room or he was down in the basement and that's how it went, but Larry didn't know that Greg was in the house. . . . In Larry's mind he was away."[13]

Mazza was also unaware, at the time, that Linda's common-law husband was a senior capo in the Colombo crime family.

In a detailed 2012 interview with Brad Hamilton for the *New York Post*, Mazza revealed the details of his first encounter with Schiro. One

day as he was dropping off groceries, Mazza said, Linda asked him, "Do you fool around?"[14] According to Mazza, he shot back, "Of course . . . what do you think, I'm *gay*?" She then reportedly invited him to stop by the house later. When he arrived, according to Hamilton, she was dressed in a sexy black jumpsuit. Schiro served him wine and M&M's. "The next thing you know we were on the couch getting hot and heavy," Mazza said.

Larry Mazza after he started working with Greg Scarpa Sr.

Mazza told Hamilton that at first he assumed Linda's husband was a "Jewish doctor." Then, one night when he came home, Mazza saw Scarpa get out of a brand-new black Cadillac. He was wearing sunglasses and a medallion and flashing an enormous pinky ring. "I knew something was a little off," Mazza said.[15]

Still, the affair escalated, with the buff eighteen-year-old meeting his Mafia Mrs. Robinson in cars and hotel rooms as well as the home on Avenue J. "We had the house four or five nights a week," he told Hamilton. When he found out he'd been carrying on an affair with the common-law wife of a Colombo capo, however, Mazza later testified that he decided to come clean. He asked for a sit-down with Scarpa, knowing full well that in the Mafia having sex with a made man's wife wasn't just "taboo," it was grounds for elimination.[16]

By that point, Scarpa had been treating him "like a son," so Larry figured he might have a chance to survive.[17] But his confession was accompanied by some bone-chilling tension after the meeting was set for Scarpa's office at the Wimpy Boys club—the same spot where Dominick Somma had been executed.

When Larry walked in, Scarpa was behind his desk. Mazza told Hamilton that there was a particular chair in that office where Greg would have people sit if they were going to get whacked. Another crew member would be hiding in a closet behind it, and if whoever Scarpa was questioning gave the wrong answer, the confederate would spring out and kill him.[18] As Scarpa nodded for Larry to sit in that chair, Mazza's heart was pounding. He could have been hit from behind, or Scarpa might have acted as he had with Big Donny and shot him dead on the spot. By then Larry knew that Greg had the temperament of a pit viper and he was murderously protective of his family.

The tension rose as the two men eyed each other. Mazza waited for the Killing Machine to pronounce his sentence upon him. But then, finally, Scarpa said, "As long as it stays between the three of us, it [can] continue."[19]

In his 2012 *Post* interview, Mazza speculated about why Scarpa had been so tolerant. While living with Linda, he realized that the Mafia killer was still carrying on a series of affairs, including his clandestine marriage to former beauty queen Lili Dajani.

"Maybe it was selfish," said Mazza. "[Greg] was seeing all these other girls and those . . . nights I would be with Linda."[20]

But it's clear that Greg Scarpa Sr. saw Mazza as more than a sexual stand-in. He developed a real affection for the younger man, and after that conversation at the club, Scarpa embraced the delivery boy as one of his own. In fact, Scarpa even got Mazza a job at Hewlett Supply, a legitimate fire-extinguisher company he reportedly controlled, and later he set up him up in a body and fender shop called Love Collision.[21]

"The Last Time I Saw Eli"

According to Mazza's sworn testimony in the DeVecchio trial, the owner of the small garage was a man named Eli Ackley. At one point, Scarpa loaned Mazza $10,000 to buy a 50 percent interest in the business. Before long, with vigorish, or interest, the debt had grown to $23,500, and Love Collision was losing money. Mazza knew nothing about repairing cars, and he testified that Ackley had a "cocaine problem," so Scarpa called Eli in for what Larry called a "riot," or reprimand. He used "hard words," Mazza testified, "because of the coke and destroying cars and ruining the business." When asked what happened to Ackley, Mazza replied: "That was the last time I saw Eli."

After the failure of Love Collision, Mazza says he tried other legitimate jobs. He got his insurance broker's license and enrolled in John Jay College. He even drove a school bus for a time. But pretty soon the lure of mob money became too tempting. He began as a courier running numbers; then, with Greg's backing, he started "putting money on the street," running his own loan-shark business. He also helped run a daily numbers racket. In return for dollar bets, the payoff could be $500. But Scarpa's illegal operation was in competition with the New York State Lottery, so Senior went to extremes to keep merchants from installing the state-operated machines. "One [business] got a truck driven through their storefront," Mazza told *Post* reporter Hamilton.[22]

Eventually, Mazza and an associate, Jimmy Del Masto, took over a sports-betting operation that serviced professional gamblers who risked five to ten thousand dollars a game. They became so successful, according to John Kroger, the former Eastern District prosecutor, that by the late 1980s they were "producing some fifty thousand dollars in weekly profit—two and a half million dollars a year."[23]

In any deal with the devil, though, there's a price to pay. And after Greg Scarpa started treating Larry like a second son, he also started schooling him in more violent crimes. "Little by little," Mazza testified, "I started getting involved in other things." Mazza started working with "Joe Brewster" DeDomenico in the bank burglary Bypass crew, which looted safe-deposit boxes.[24] Later he became a driver, taking Scarpa to various "scores."

In time he graduated to driving a "crash car"—a backup vehicle used to interdict the police during getaways. Finally, after a long period of what he called "grooming," Scarpa started sending him to murder scenes.

"He would ask me to [arrive] after [the killing] and check for witnesses and [the] police response," Mazza testified. "Ultimately I became a shooter." By the time the third Colombo war broke out in 1991, Larry Mazza, the middle-class son who had enrolled in college to make his father proud, became Greg Scarpa Sr.'s principal killing partner. "I was his right-hand man," Mazza said under oath. "I was very close to him." At that point in his testimony, the DA asked how many people Scarpa had confessed to killing. Mazza looked down sheepishly and said, "He told me he stopped counting at fifty."

The Costa Rican Job

According to Linda Schiro, sometime in the early 1980s, Scarpa went on another mission for the FBI. This time it took him out of the country, "down to Costa Rica to bring back Tony Peraino," she told me in an interview.[25] She made a similar statement under oath during the DeVecchio trial.[26]

Anthony "Big Tony" Peraino was a three-hundred-pound made member of the Colombo family who had struck it rich with his brother Joseph in 1972 after they invested $25,000 in the production of the legendary pornographic film *Deep Throat*.[27] By the mid-1970s, this extremely explicit film,

Anthony Peraino

which the Perainos distributed themselves, had grossed $25 million, allowing the brothers to build what a U.S. attorney general's report called "a vast financial empire, that included ownership of garment companies in New York and Miami, investment companies, a 65 foot yacht in the Bahamas, 'adults only' pornographic theaters in Los Angeles and record and music publishing companies on both coasts."[28]

"Big Tony" and Joseph were the sons of Giuseppe Peraino, a bootlegger and associate of Salvatore Maranzano. He was the godfather who made Joseph Valachi and Cargo Joe later served as his bodyguard.[29] Considered the first real "boss of bosses," Maranzano had fought for control of U.S. Mafia operations in the early 1930s.

His principal opponent back then was Joe "the Boss" Masseria, a boorish Sicilian immigrant who rose to power after the passage of the Eighteenth Amendment, which banned the sale of alcohol, in 1920. In what became a pattern for betrayal and assassination emulated in the 1950s by Carmine Persico and the Gallo brothers, Masseria was killed on April 15, 1931, at a Coney Island restaurant after being set up by one of his young lieutenants, Salvatore "Lucky" Luciano.

Maranzano, who had come from a strict Sicilian Mafia tradition, designed the rigid structure of the modern Cosa Nostra around the hierarchy of ancient Roman legions. But after promising Luciano equality, Maranzano reneged, just as Profaci later would with the Gallos, and ordered that Luciano be machine-gunned to death.[30]

But Luciano, the man many believe to be the first real criminal genius in the U.S. underworld,[31] got word of the plot and beat the boss at his own game, engineering Maranzano's assassination. In the elaborately planned hit the killers posed as IRS agents who had come to audit Maranzano's books at his lavish offices in the old New York Central Building atop Grand Central Terminal.* On September 10, 1931, with the help of his Jewish cohorts Meyer Lansky and Benjamin "Bugsy" Siegel, Luciano executed the bloody plot that left Maranzano dead from multiple knife and bullet wounds.

In the wake of the hit, Luciano divided the spoils and organized what emerged as New York's current Five Families, with Joseph Profaci as the boss who enjoyed the greatest longevity. The Peraino brothers, whose father had been murdered in 1930, eventually became made members of Profaci's borgata, and by the early 1970s, with the success of *Deep Throat*, Anthony Peraino, his brother "Joe the Whale," and Joe's sons Louis "Butchie" Peraino and Joseph Jr. were generating millions of dollars via their national network of adult theaters, peep shows, and bookstores—with a portion of the proceeds being "kicked up" to Carmine Persico.[32]

---

* Known today as the Helmsley Building.

MIPORN and the FBI

In 1975, the senior Peraino brothers were convicted of conspiracy to distribute *Deep Throat.* The following year, Big Tony was convicted of shipping video-tapes of the film across state lines. By 1977, the FBI commenced a sophisti-cated undercover operation dubbed MIPORN, in which two agents posing as sex-film producers and distributors set up a warehouse equipped with hidden mikes and cameras that recorded dozens of adult-film traffickers.[33]

With the Feds after him, and facing prison, Anthony jumped bail and disappeared for the next five years. Though many assumed he had gone on the lam to Italy, for at least part of the time he was hiding in Costa Rica.

By 1980, the porn industry had become a $4 billion annual enterprise and "a major income maker for La Cosa Nostra, after gambling and narcot-ics."[34] Soon the staggering profits from *Deep Throat* set off an independent turf war within the Colombo family.

Initially, the Perainos bought out the film's director, Gerard Damiano, for a mere $25,000 (the cost of production), depriving him of millions. In 1976, Robert J. DeSalvo, an ex-con who had acted as a front for Anthony and Joseph,[35] disappeared and was presumed murdered.[36] A year later,

The original movie poster

while their uncle Anthony was still at large, Joseph Peraino Sr.'s sons Louis and Joe Jr. were each sentenced to a year in prison and fined $10,000 at an obscenity trial in Memphis that focused on *Deep Throat.*[37]

With mounting pressure from the Reagan administration to bring Anthony to justice, the FBI once again sent Greg Scarpa on a secret mission. According to Linda Schiro, they furnished him with a fake passport and a phony Nevada driver's license.[38] He was then flown to Costa Rica, where he located Big Tony Peraino and rendered him back to the United States. Sentenced to ten months and fined $15,000, Peraino ultimately died of natural causes in 1996. His brother and nephew weren't so lucky.

Murder of a Former Nun

Ultimately *Deep Throat* would go on to gross an estimated $600 million.[39] The huge profits from the film, and the Peraino porn network it created, spawned another internecine war within the embattled Colombo family. Anthony claimed that not only had he been robbed by his brother, but by implication the family had been cheated as well, with insufficient profits finding their way up the food chain to Carmine Persico.

On January 4, 1982, a hit team, reportedly dispatched on Persico's orders, cornered Joe Peraino and his son Joe Jr. in the Gravesend section of Brooklyn. In a desperate effort to escape, the Perainos burst into a house at 431 Lake Street. At that moment, Louis Zuraw, an innocent accountant, was watching TV in the living room; his wife, Veronica, was folding laundry on the second floor. Suddenly, they heard what sounded like "fireworks" outside, and the front door flew open. The Perainos ran inside, followed by men firing shotguns. As they rushed up the stairs, stray pellets from one blast struck Veronica Zuraw in the head, killing her instantly. Joe Peraino Jr. was also killed in the attack; his father was hit but survived, paralyzed by his injuries.

The incident made headlines because Veronica had been a former nun for the Diocese of Brooklyn before leaving her order and marrying Louis. At the time of the shooting, a police officer told a reporter for the *New York Post*, "One minute he's watching TV and the next minute he gets up and his wife's head is blown off."[40] Given the mob connection, witnesses were reluctant to come forward, and the double murder soon became a cold case. Louis died four years later, never knowing the true reasons behind his wife's death.

The day after the shooting, Lin DeVecchio wrote the following 209 report, which was addressed to FBI Director William Webster:

ON JANUARY 5, 1982, SOURCE ADVISED THAT THE "HIT" ON JOSEPH PERAINO, JR., AND THE ATTEMPTED "HIT" ON PERAINO'S FATHER, JOSEPH PERAINO, SR., THE PREVIOUS EVENING IN BROOKLYN, WAS DONE BY MEMBERS OF ANDREW RUSSO'S CREW AND NOTED THAT CARMINE PERSICO AUTHORIZED THE CONTRACT ON THE PER-AINO'S [*sic*].

THE SOURCE PROVIDED FURTHER REASONS AS TO THE HIT OF THE TWO PERAINOS NOTING THAT THEY WERE DEALING IN NARCOT-ICS AS WELL AS PORNOGRAPHY AND ALSO NOTING THAT JOE PERAINO, JR., HAD FAILED TO CARRY OUT A "HIT" GIVEN TO HIM. . . . THE SOURCE ALSO ADVISED THAT [AMONG] THREE INDIVIDUALS . . . PRESENT AT THE SHOOTING OF THE PERAINO'S [*sic*] WAS ███████████ ANTHONY RUSSO, THE SON OF ANDREW RUSSO.[41]

We don't know how much Greg Scarpa told Lin DeVecchio about the incident. But given Linda Schiro's sworn account of Scarpa's involvement in Anthony Peraino's extradition from Costa Rica, the report appears to be vastly incomplete.

We've included the details of the violent attack on father and son in this section of the book because the 209 above offers a new insight into Lin DeVecchio's reporting on "34." Also, we now have additional evidence on the Peraino attack, related to federal prosecutors by a notorious capo who surfaced again as the third war unfolded a decade later. Those details also shed light on the quality of DeVecchio's reports on Scarpa Sr., which went to the FBI director.

Salvatore "Big Sal" Miciotta, a Colombo captain who would fight on the Orena side during the 1991–1993 war and eventually became a federal witness, later admitted to prosecutors that he was a member of the Peraino hit team on the night of the double murder. At the time of his debriefing, he reportedly named multiple accomplices in addition to the Russos, who were identified in Scarpa's report to DeVecchio. In a detailed *Village Voice* story on Miciotta's confession to the Feds, reporter William Bastone wrote that the participants in the murder plot also included Colombo stalwarts John Minerva, Vincent "Jimmy" Angelino, and Frank Sparaco.[42]

Bastone's story also cited an FBI memo on Miciotta's confession, which stated that "'Miciotta shot and killed Peraino Jr., who was standing to the right of his father, while Angelino shot and wounded Peraino Sr.'"

The report then noted, "'An innocent female bystander living in the house was also killed when she was hit with buckshot.'"

What the January 5, 1982, 209 Didn't Say

But DeVecchio's 209 report appeared remarkably incomplete in the context of these two questions: Was it possible that "34's" contacting agent would be ignorant of Scarpa's clandestine extradition trip to Costa Rica? Was it possible that Lin was unaware of the homicide of the former nun Veronica Zuraw, whose death had been widely publicized in the tabloids? A portion of that 209 is redacted, so we don't know for sure whether Scarpa named either Miciotta or Minerva. But that report to the FBI director seemed to omit as much information as it contained.

In addition, DeVecchio's later 209s and teletypes sometimes included false and misleading details—particularly at the height of the third Colombo war. That point was emphasized by Special Agent Chris Favo, DeVecchio's immediate subordinate in the C-10 squad. Testifying at a 1995 trial, Favo admitted that the agents in C-10 had been "duped" by Gregory Scarpa Sr.[43] As a result, the FBI officials reading DeVecchio's communiqués on "34" often got a distorted picture of what was actually going on inside the Colombo crime family.

For example, in the 209 on the Peraino hit, Scarpa attributed the attack to the allegation that they "were dealing in narcotics as well as pornography." But the family, under Joseph Colombo and Carmine Persico, had reaped millions from the distribution of *Deep Throat* alone, so the idea that they objected to smut defies belief. More important, as we'll see in a series of 209s from the early to mid-1980s, DeVecchio repeatedly included statements from Scarpa indicating that the sale of drugs was forbidden within the Colombo family, when in fact the early Mafia prohibition had been abandoned with the explosive use of heroin and cocaine and Scarpa himself made millions from their sale.

But an official at FBI Headquarters reading DeVecchio's reports on "34" would never have known that. While Lin continued to assert that Scarpa had "furnished no information known to be false," we can now state with certainty that many of the disclosures contained in DeVecchio's 209s on Scarpa were outright lies. Did DeVecchio know them to be false? We can't say for sure. Yet there isn't a word in the hundreds of pages of teletypes and 209s from 1980 to 1992 even *suggesting* that the Killing Machine was also a drug czar, even though Scarpa fingered other competing capos for selling dope. And as we're about to see, by the mid-1980s the Scarpa family was knee-deep in the cocaine trade.

Chapter 14

TWENTY GRAND
A WEEK

The following are excerpts from a series of FBI 209 memos filed by Supervisory Special Agent Lin DeVecchio on information passed to him about the Colombo crime family by Top Echelon Criminal Informant Gregory Scarpa Sr. between mid-July 1981 and July 1982. The memos reinforce "34's" continuing insistence that drug sales were forbidden not only by the Mafia Commission but by the Colombo family in particular.

> July 14th, source advised that Colombo capo JOHN "IRISH" MATERA was "hit" during the past week on authorization from . . . CARMINE PERSICO as a result of a private deal involving narcotics.[1]
>
> July 28th, source advised that COLLIF DI PIETRO was "hit" as a result of his narcotics activities, particularly handling large quantities of cocaine. . . . The bosses of the five New York LCN families have recently reiterated their opposition to family members handling narcotics.[2]
>
> Sept. 17th, source advised that Gambino capo JOHN GOTTI is currently in hiding as a result of his handling narcotics. Source noted that

a recent crackdown by the National Commission on LCN handling of narcotics resulted in the hits of numerous LCN members, and GOTTI apparently has word that his previous activities may result in his demise.[3]

January 21, 1982, source advised that the recent attempted hit of ██ ██████████ may well have been the result of ███████████ dealing in narcotics. The source noticed that it is quite possible that this work was done in part by Angelo Mazzola, who himself, was recently killed.[4]

March 29, 1982, source . . . advised that Colombo member ANTHONY AUGELLO . . . is heavily involved in a large scale heroin distribution operation.[5]

In these reports, Gregory Scarpa Sr. used his access to the FBI brass, through Lin DeVecchio, to paint a picture suggesting that drug dealing was still forbidden under the same Mafia rules he'd leaked to Hoover in 1962. But nothing could have been further from the truth. Not only were top bosses like Vito Genovese convicted of heroin trafficking as early as 1959, but from 1975 onward—five years before DeVecchio reopened Scarpa—Cosa Nostra was smuggling millions of dollars of China White heroin into the United States each year via the Mafia network known as the Pizza Connection, a $1.6 billion pipeline that wasn't shut down until 1984, two years after that 209 on Anthony Augello.[6]

All of this points to how, with the knowing or unknowing assistance of Lin DeVecchio, Scarpa was able to divert attention away from himself and incriminate mob leaders around him, just as he'd done in the early 1970s with Joseph Colombo and Joe Jr. As a result of Augello's activities, and whatever investigative help the Bureau may have received from Greg Scarpa Sr. pursuant to the Title III wiretap, Little Allie Boy Persico, the boss's son, was arrested on a heroin conspiracy charge. Although he was later acquitted,[7] the younger Persico's legal troubles had deadly consequences for Augello, who called his family from a pay phone to say good-bye and then shot himself.[8]

Bricks of Coke

But even as he fingered the competition, Greg Scarpa Sr. was raking in millions from his own narcotics activity. At the early-1990s trial of Colombo capo William "Wild Bill" Cutolo, Larry Mazza, Scarpa's trusted right arm, testified that Greg stored bricks of cocaine in a file cabinet leading to a basement apartment, right up until he was arrested in 1992.[9] Mazza went on to testify that Scarpa "encouraged his children to deal in narcotics" and even grew large quantities of marijuana at his New Jersey farm.[10]

According to Mazza, from the mid-1980s on, Greg Scarpa's sons, including Greg Jr., were "involved in the drug operation."[11] Mazza revealed more in his debriefings to FBI agents after he agreed to cooperate in 1994. He said that Scarpa had begun his drug-dealing activities by "taxing" existing dealers 25 percent of their take. It was Scarpa Sr.'s "belief," said Mazza, "that the streets belonged to the Colombo Family and the drug dealers would be required to pay." But then Senior "got greedy and decided that [his crew] should also be the source for the drugs."[12]

```
UNITED STATES DISTRICT COURT
EASTERN DISTRICT OF NEW YORK

- - - - - - - - - - - - - - - -X

UNITED STATES OF AMERICA

    - against -

GREGORY SCARPA, JR., et al.,

            Defendants.

- - - - - - - - - - - - - - - -X

EASTERN DISTRICT OF NEW YORK, SS:
```

The caption on the sealed affidavit in the 1987 DEA case against Greg Jr. and the Wimpy Boys crew.

Former Assistant U.S. Attorney John Kroger, who later prosecuted Greg Scarpa Jr. for drug dealing, writes in his memoir *Convictions* that this led to more murders. In 1985, after initially taxing a marijuana dealer named Peter Crupi, whose "drug spot" was Staten Island College, Greg Jr. reportedly decided on a "hostile takeover" and Crupi was gunned down on August 2, 1985.[13] Within weeks, according to Kroger, Scarpa's crew was servicing a thousand customers a night with profits of $20,000 a week—from dime-bag pot sales alone.[14] That represented an annual gross of $3,640,000. Eventually, writes Kroger, "charmed by the easy money, the crew diversified their product line, selling kilos of heroin and cocaine at wholesale prices to dealers all over the city."[15]

The final aspect of the takeover came with the murder of rival drug dealer Albert Nacha, twenty-two, whose body was found lying faceup in Clove Lakes Park on Staten Island on December 10.[16] Clutching a five-dollar bag of pot in his hand, Nacha had been shot three times in the head and once in the chest at close range.[17] According to Kroger, the message was clear: Scarpa's crew now ran the dope business in that part of Staten Island.

There wasn't a word in any of Lin DeVecchio's 209s or teletypes to the FBI during this period about the multimillion-dollar narcotics enterprise Greg Scarpa Sr. was running out of his Wimpy Boys social club headquarters.[18] But that lapse pales in the face of the evidence that later surfaced suggesting that DeVecchio himself leaked information to "34," warning him of an impending bust against Greg Jr. and his crew.

By the fall of 1987, agents from the Drug Enforcement Administration (DEA), which had been tracking Greg Jr.'s movements independently, had developed such a formidable case against him that the U.S. attorney for the Eastern District of New York prepared an indictment against Junior and crew members Billy Meli, Kevin Granato, Nicky DeCarlo, and Cosmo Catanzano. Carmine Sessa, the former consigliere of the Colombo family, later testified that he'd sold cocaine for Greg Sr. and that the elder Scarpa not only had prior knowledge of the coming arrests, but that he'd told Sessa ahead of time "who was getting arrested."[19]

According to Meli, Greg Jr. met him outside the Wimpy Boys club and said that his father "had a friend who was an FBI agent."[20] He then pulled out a handwritten list of names, Meli said, containing all of the Wimpy Boys crew members who were about to get busted. Greg Jr. then told Meli that his father had learned from this "agent" that the DEA expected Catanzano to cooperate.

Another member of Scarpa's crew, Mario Parlagreco, told the FBI in 1994 that there were actually two lists of names. "Approximately three and a half to four months before his arrest . . . Greg Scarpa Sr. warned him that the DEA was going to arrest Greg . . . Jr. and other members of [his] crew."[21] At the time of his initial contact with Senior, he said, Parlagreco's name was not on that list. But a month later, Greg Sr. showed him a *second* list containing his name and that of his brother. Greg Jr. later testified under oath that this second list had been furnished by Lin DeVecchio.[22]

Digging a Grave

After receiving instructions that "no one was allowed to go on the lam to escape arrest," Meli was then told that he should "be prepared to kill Catanzano" and that his body was to be buried "so it would not be found." Meli later told Special Agent Howard Leadbetter II, who debriefed him, that Greg Jr. confirmed that "the decision had been made to kill Catanzano" and that Meli should start looking for a place to bury him.

A few days later, Meli said, he and Kevin Granato found "an isolated spot off of Arthur Kill Road" and dug a grave. Mario Parlagreco also confessed to being in on the plot.[23] Before they could execute the contract, though, everyone on the list but Greg Jr. got arrested.[24] Tipped by his father's "FBI agent" source, said Meli, Junior then took off and became a fugitive.

Almost immediately, Assistant U.S. Attorney Valerie Caproni, who was supervising the prosecution of Junior's crew, reached out to the FBI for help in locating him. But she later complained that "neither the EDNY, DEA nor the NYPD received any positive information back from the NY FBI's Colombo LCN Squad regarding Scarpa's crew."[25]

Lin DeVecchio was just about to take over that squad, and already the DEA had developed compelling evidence that Greg Scarpa Sr. was in regular contact with the FBI's New York Office. According to Caproni, they'd set up a "pen register," which tracked calls from a phone in Senior's house to 26 Federal Plaza, where the Bureau's NYO was now located. She later told FBI agents that "it was her belief that Scarpa Sr. was an FBI informant" and that "the NY FBI was not cooperating with the EDNY in locating Scarpa Jr. in view of the confidential relationship [he] had with the FBI."[26]

Greg Scarpa Jr. was finally located after his fugitive status was publicized on the Fox television series *America's Most Wanted.* He'd been hiding out in Florida under the alias Salvatore Perri.[27] Larry Mazza later told federal agents that he visited Greg Jr. in Florida, but following the *Most Wanted* exposure, his father had Junior moved to New Jersey. After hiding out with his wife, Maria, who used the alias Tracy Hill, the younger Scarpa was spotted at a motel in Lakewood, New Jersey, near the senior Scarpa's horse farm. On August 29, 1988, Junior was arrested by DEA agents.[28]

After Greg Jr. was taken into custody, Assistant U.S. Attorney Caproni met with Lin DeVecchio. She questioned him about "a number of homicides she believed Scarpa's crew had committed."[29] But she insisted later that the information DeVecchio gave her was "of little prosecutive value."[30]

In a sworn statement in 1995 given to FBI agents from the Bureau's Office of Professional Responsibility (OPR), during what amounted to an internal affairs investigation of his relationship with Greg Scarpa Sr., DeVecchio stated the following:

"I emphatically denied then and today ever making any statement to Scarpa Sr. that I was aware that DEA was going to charge his son, or anybody else for drug violations."[31] In his recent book, when explaining why the FBI had been so slow to respond to Caproni's requests for help in apprehending Greg Jr., Lin writes:

> As it turned out, the DEA referral to open a fugitive case on Gregory Jr. had been made to headquarters in Washington, DC, but no referral had been passed on to our New York fugitive squad. It had fallen through the cracks of the FBI and the DEA.

Eventually, Greg Jr. was tried, convicted, and sentenced to twenty years in prison for racketeering and drug sales.[32] In a sworn affirmation in April 1995, Caproni stated that "there is some reason to believe that . . . in 1987, DeVecchio told Scarpa that the DEA planned to arrest Gregory Scarpa Jr. and his crew. This information was conveyed in advance of the arrests and led to Scarpa Jr. becoming a fugitive. Further, Scarpa [Sr.] correctly knew that . . . Cosmo Catanzano was a 'weak link,' who might cooperate . . . if arrested."[33]

In fact, were it not for the DEA's actions in arresting him, Catanzano may well have ended up in that grave by Arthur Kill Road.

Watching Surveillance Tapes

Without naming DeVecchio, Larry Mazza provided the Feds with further evidence that Greg Scarpa Sr. had been tipped to the DEA bust by a law enforcement source. He confessed that "sometime in 1987 . . . before the DEA arrests," he was at the home Greg Sr. shared with Linda Schiro and they were watching official surveillance videos taken outside the Wimpy Boys social club. Mazza told the Feds he was "surprised that Scarpa Sr. had these tapes and had no idea how he received them." But in a 2004 hearing Greg Jr. said under oath that his father "obtained [the video] from Agent DeVecchio."[34]

According to Mario Parlagreco: "Based on a discussion with his law enforcement 'guy,' [Greg Sr.] believed there was a bug in the club." After ordering Carmine Sessa to sweep the premises, a rectangular-shaped black bug was found. After that, Parlagreco said, "Scarpa Sr. asked everybody to come outside of Wimpy's and told them not to do business in Wimpy's because of the location of the bug."[35]

How did Scarpa become aware of the bugs? In his book *Convictions,* former federal prosecutor John Kroger names Lin DeVecchio as the source. Kroger writes that DeVecchio "told Senior [that] the Wimpy Boys had been bugged, foiling a New York State investigation in the process."[36]

"In all agent-informant relationships," Kroger writes, "the government is supposed to ensure that information flows in only one direction, from the informant to the 'controlling agent.' According to several witnesses from the Mafia and the FBI, DeVecchio ignored this basic rule. In the mid 1980's, according to these witnesses, he began to disclose confidential law enforcement information to Gregory Scarpa Sr."[37]

Kroger insists that "DeVecchio's motives, at least initially, were sound," noting that "in the 1980's Mafia informants were hard to come by, so having Senior on the payroll was a huge break." But he concludes that "over time . . . DeVecchio seems to have lost his moral bearings."[38]

In his own book, while steadfastly denying that he ever leaked any FBI intelligence to Scarpa, Lin DeVecchio nonetheless plays down the significance of the Scarpa drug operation, using commentary from retired SSA Chris Mattiace, who ran the Colombo Squad before him, to assess the significance of the DEA case.

The Dead-End Kids

"What were they involved in?" writes Mattiace, discussing the Wimpy Boys crew. "Shaking down kids who sold pot and coke to other kids! We had absolutely no interest in such a case. Greg Scarpa himself was not big enough for our interests at the time, much less his son and the Dead End Kids. . . . I didn't know that Scarpa was a source for anyone, much less Lin. Lin didn't get my Colombo squad until Gregory Jr. was already more than two months gone."[39]

But one FBI agent who worked under Mattiace had a different recollection when interviewed by agents during that OPR investigation into whether DeVecchio had crossed the line and leaked intel to Scarpa.

Special Agent Michael Tabman stated, "In . . . February of 1987, I was assigned to work for SSA Christopher Mattiace. . . . I was assigned to investigate the Scarpa crew." Later that year Tabman was present at a meeting at the DEA office in Manhattan when he learned that their investigation was nearing completion. According to Tabman, the "arrest of members of the Scarpa crew, including Gregory Scarpa Jr.[,] was imminent."[40]

Tabman went on to say that in "November or December of 1987 . . . the Mattiace squad was absorbed into SSA Lindley DeVecchio's squad." During this time, he recalled "having discussions with SSA DeVecchio regarding the Scarpa crew and the DEA case."[41] Tabman remembered DeVecchio "being very interested in this matter." So, despite Mattiace's comments in DeVecchio's book—that his squad had "absolutely no interest" in the investigation—Tabman's account suggests that DeVecchio was at least *aware* that Gregory Jr. was a DEA target. Further, Mattiace's admission that he knew about Scarpa's marijuana operation seems to contradict DeVecchio's sworn OPR statement. In that document, echoing the earlier 209s he sent to Washington, DeVecchio made this affirmative statement: "I had no idea that Scarpa Sr. or Scarpa Jr. were involved in drug distribution. It was my understanding the Colombo Family had a disdain for drugs."[42]

"In that single statement," says former FBI agent Dan Vogel, "Lin DeVecchio raises a serious question about his credibility. Given what's known about Scarpa's extensive drug operation, it defies belief that the supervisory special agent who was supposed to 'control' him didn't know he was committing these crimes—especially when you look at the statement of Chris Mattiace, who admitted knowing about the Staten Island College operation. How do you gross $70K a week under the watchful eye of your contacting agent and have him miss that?"[43]

As to Mattiace's characterization of the Staten Island drug operation as a kind of "Dead End Kids" enterprise, Tabman underscored the lethal nature of it in his OPR statement:

> We became involved in the investigation in a series of murders and we did a flow chart regarding the relationship of the decedents. These relationships all involved Gregory Scarpa Jr. It seemed as though each time we identified a potential subject in these cases that subject was found deceased after identification. I remember this occurring on approximately three occasions, one in particular involving a blond haired subject, who was found deceased the day after we determined his identity.[44]

Putting aside whether SSA Lin DeVecchio leaked any of that intelligence back to Greg Scarpa Sr., could DeVecchio, who had monthly and sometimes weekly meetings[45] with Scarpa, have been so clueless about the fact that his informant was running a multimillion-dollar marijuana, cocaine, and heroin operation? Was he really so naïve as to believe that the Colombos "had a disdain" for such a lucrative enterprise? The operation had begun with the murder of a pot dealer. It had grown into a $10,000-a-night enterprise that was considered such a public threat that Valerie Caproni expended significant resources to put Scarpa Jr. behind bars. Yet in his book Lin DeVecchio seems to downplay its importance, and none of his 209s to Washington ever hinted that Scarpa Sr. was linked to drug trafficking.

The Wimpy Boys

In the sworn statement he gave to agents during his OPR (internal affairs) investigation in 1995, DeVecchio confirmed that "Scarpa Sr., operated Wimpy Boys Club on 13th Avenue in Brooklyn, New York during the 1980s."[46] In his memoir, when he describes the first time he approached Scarpa outside his house on Avenue J in June 1980, DeVecchio writes, "I knew roughly what time he headed off to his Wimpy Boys Athletic Club, where he held court and conducted business."

In July 1986, the Brooklyn DA filed a thirty-page sworn affidavit seeking to extend wiretaps at the club. In the affidavit, Assistant DA Marlene

Scarpa outside the Wimpy Boys club, 1986 (FBI surveillance video)

Malamy cited pages of transcripts from previous bugged conversations involving Scarpa Sr., Larry Mazza, and other associates discussing drug dealing and loan sharking. Based on that surveillance, she wrote, "We are now in a position to state with certainty that SCARPA conducts his business on almost a daily basis from the above-captioned premises."[47]

On or about January 9, 1988, federal prosecutors in Brooklyn obtained copies of the Wimpy Boys eavesdropping tapes.[48] So that location was clearly known to DeVecchio and prosecutors in Kings County and the Eastern District as Scarpa's headquarters. But testifying under oath in 1998 at Greg Scarpa Jr.'s trial, under cross-examination by defense attorney Larry Silverman, Lin seemed to deny it.[49]

> **Silverman:** During the time period, sir, from 1980 to 1987, during that time period was the Wimpy Boys Club Mr. Scarpa's place of operation?
> **DeVecchio:** I have no idea.

In that trial—just as in the 1997 Vic Orena hearing, when he answered, "I don't recall," or words to that effect, more than fifty times—Lin DeVecchio was testifying pursuant to a grant of immunity.[50] As such, he could not be prosecuted for any admissions he might have made about his relationship with Greg Scarpa Sr. Whether that immunity extended to perjury is a question for legal scholars to ponder. But his contention that he had "no idea" whether his informant Scarpa was using the Wimpy Boys club as his "place of operation" seems clearly disingenuous, especially given the account in his 2011 book.

Mario from the Deli

There's another detail in DeVecchio's book that suggests he wasn't entirely forthcoming in the reports about "34" that he sent off to Washington. Mario Parlagreco was a key member of the Wimpy Boys crew who participated not just in multiple drug deals but in other crimes, such as the conspiracy to murder Cosmo Catanzano and bury his body. In his book, DeVecchio goes into detail about how Parlagreco happened to join the Thirteenth Avenue crew. As Lin tells it, Mario's father ran a deli with a "partner" whose son got released from jail. The son was then supposed to come to work at the deli:

> Only he thinks all he has to do all day is smoke pot, put his hand in the till for money, and let Mario take care of the business. Mario's father goes to his partner and says either you buy me out or I buy you out. The partner took over the deli then welshed on the $50,000 purchase price.[51]

In DeVecchio's version of events, Mario went to the Wimpy Boys club, and Greg Sr., acting as a kind of benevolent Don Corleone, "had a sit-down with Mario's father's partner and got all the money Mario's parents were entitled to." After that, DeVecchio writes, "Scarpa announced to . . . Mario that he's now with the crew."[52]

It's a great story that's true in part, but a couple of key elements are missing from both DeVecchio's book and any 209s he might have sent to Washington at the time.

First of all, the "partner" in the deli was none other than Joseph Peraino Sr., the porn king and *Deep Throat* producer whose brother Anthony had been rendered back to the United States from Costa Rica by Greg Sr. The "son" who smoked pot and stole was Joe Jr., who was killed in that attempted hit on his father that took the life of Veronica Zuraw, the former nun—an incident DeVecchio described only in part in his 209 report in 1982.[53]

According to an FBI 302 memorializing Mario Parlagreco's debriefing after he became a cooperating witness in 1994, the $50,000 represented the bond that Mario's father had put up to spring Joe Jr. from jail.[54] In that detailed eight-page 302, Parlagreco recounts how he "thought it was interesting [that] Scarpa Sr. continued to do business in the club involving the collection of shylock money and other criminal efforts" after he knew that bugs had been planted.

"Parlagreco stated that a lot of people thought it was strange that Scarpa Sr. . . . rarely, if ever, got arrested while others did. . . . A number of Parlagreco's associates surmised that Scarpa Sr. was cooperating with law enforcement, but nobody wanted to challenge him about it as he was a dangerous man."

The connection between Mario Parlagreco, his father, and the Perainos was significant. It was certainly the kind of interfamily intelligence that DeVecchio's FBI superiors in Washington would have wanted to know. So why didn't DeVecchio include it in his 209 on Joe Peraino Jr.'s shotgun murder in 1982? It's another example of how, when it came to the Colombo crime family, FBI officials got only part of the story.

As the head of two organized crime squads in the FBI's New York Office, Lin DeVecchio was in a position to document the full depth and breadth of Gregory Scarpa Sr.'s hugely lucrative and violent criminal activity. But he didn't. Instead, he was extremely protective of his source—so much so that, when another branch of the government threatened to put Scarpa away for years, Lin went out of his way to keep him on the street.

Chapter 15

ENTER THE
SECRET SERVICE

On the Ides of March 1985, not long before the DEA began its investigation of Greg Scarpa Sr.'s drug operation, which was grossing $70,000 a week, the FBI rewarded him with a $15,000 bonus.[1] In a teletype nearly two weeks earlier, the Bureau's New York Office justified the bonus to "34" because of what was described as the "vast quantities of singular information concerning the Colombo Family which has directly led to 17 affidavits in support of Title III intercepts and 50 re-authorizations of these intercepts."[2] Now even as he was continuing his loan-sharking, gambling, and drug operations, Scarpa was acting to eliminate his principal competition in the Colombo family—the boss Carmine Persico, who'd been arrested the previous October along with his underboss, three capos, and other family members in operations the Feds dubbed ECLIPSE STAR and STARQUEST.[3]

From the time he was opened in 1962, the FBI had paid Greg Scarpa a total of $96,475,[4] not counting the tens of thousands in reward "kickbacks" he'd earned via Tony Villano, and that March 2, 1985, teletype was filed in order to justify the latest bonus. In the five-page memo, the New York Office also credited Scarpa with assisting in the takedown of Genovese family boss "Fat Tony" Salerno.[5] The NYO reported that "the result" of Scarpa's intel was "the saving of countless thousands of man hours in investigative time," providing "a window into the inner workings of the most significant organized crime group in the country."[6]

The view through that "window," of course, was entirely from the perspective of a drug-dealing murderer who had everything to gain by removing his Colombo competitors—but neither DeVecchio nor the New York SAC who signed most of the airtels and 209s to DC ever mentioned that. Instead, that March 2 teletype closed with a reminder to the brass at Bureau Headquarters that "sources of this caliber are extremely rare in the FBI and serve as a tribute to the informant . . . program."[7]

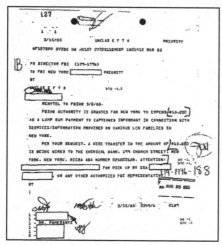

FBI teletype authorizing wire payment of $15,000 to Scarpa Sr., March 15, 1985

The 209 ended with a request that Scarpa's $15,000 bonus be sent by wire or separate check. It was a fee worth more than $32,000 in 2013 dollars.[8] On March 15, FBI Director William H. Webster himself authorized a wire transfer for the payment to be sent to Chemical Bank on Church Street in Lower Manhattan to be picked up by a supervisory special agent whose name was redacted from the memo.[9]

But using a habitual criminal like Greg Scarpa Sr. was a risky prospect, and less than eight months after the Director's endorsement of his work, another branch of the U.S. government sought to lock him up again.

The Bogus Plastic

On November 5, 1985, an undercover agent from the U.S. Secret Service met with Scarpa at the Wimpy Boys club and sold him three hundred blank credit cards—150 Visas and 150 MasterCards—for $9,000. The cards were complete with "holograms" and "mag stripes," and if embossed with fake names and numbers could have been used to gross Scarpa up to $1.5 million. His MO was to send members of his crew out to large box stores in New Jersey and have them max out the cards buying televisions, home appliances, and other expensive, resalable merchandise. It was an ingenious, 1980s kind of white-collar hijacking that produced the sort of exponential profits Scarpa Sr. loved. But after he counted out the cash to the undercover agent in the club, Greg was coaxed outside to pick up the phony "plastic."

Suddenly he was surrounded by uniformed agents, guns drawn.

Without putting up a fight, Scarpa was arrested by a backup team, taken into custody, booked, and printed.[10] After his release on a $300,000 bond, he admitted to Edward A. McDonald, the EDNY Strike Force attorney spearheading the case, that he was a confidential informant.[11] That triggered alarm bells between the FBI's NYO and Headquarters. On December 18, FBI Director Webster sent a teletype to New York acknowledging that FBI HQ had received Scarpa's fingerprints and issuing a series of pro forma questions as if Scarpa was a typical CI.

Among the boilerplate questions, which were non-gender-specific:

- Was the arrest related to his/her assignments as an FBI Informant?
- Has any attempt been made to intercede on behalf of the Informant?
- Do you anticipate making an effort to intercede for the source in the future?
- Furnish justification for continued use of Informant.[12]

The canned response almost suggested that Webster, who had approved a $15,000 bonus for Scarpa just months before, had never even heard of him. It was as though the Director had turned into *Casablanca*'s Inspector Renault, announcing that he was "shocked, shocked to find gambling going on here" before accepting his winnings.

The next memo to Washington, from the Colombo Squad, not only misstated the details of the Secret Service undercover operation as outlined by Assistant U.S. Attorney McDonald; it seemed almost to mock the senior Strike Force attorney.

Rather than confirming that Scarpa had counted out the $9,000 in "buy" money before his arrest, consummating the deal, the memo stated merely that "the Source agreed to look at samples on the day of the arrest."[13]

Then, in relating a conversation between McDonald and Scarpa at the office of the Secret Service after his arrest, the memo quoted McDonald as saying that "the FBI was known to have a love affair with their informants," emphasizing that "the Source would not get 'a pass in this case.'"

According to the memo, McDonald then offered to let Scarpa into "the Witness Security program in return for his cooperation and subsequent testimony [but] The Source refused this offer." The memo then asserted that "the NYO had several conversations with McDonald subsequent to the arrest" and that, after one meeting involving NYO agents, McDonald, Assistant U.S. Attorney Norman Bloch, and the Secret Service agents, "the EDNY dismissed the original complaint and made attempts" to hold off on an indictment.[14]

A Special Lawyer for Scarpa

After it was determined that "it was not safely possible to discuss Source's relationship with the FBI" with Scarpa's own lawyer at the time, Greg Sr. retained an attorney named William Kelleher. According to the memo, Kelleher advised that Scarpa should continue his relationship with the Bureau and that "further contact will assist the source against a possible indictment." The name of Scarpa's Bureau contact, an SSA, is redacted in the memo, but there's little doubt it was Lin DeVecchio.[15]

The memo goes on to predict that, "through efforts of the NYO with respect to organized crime investigations beneficial to the EDNY," Scarpa would be removed "from any further threat of prosecution."

The memo to the Director concludes with the announcement that "the NYO will continue to operate this source in the normal manner [and] that only SSA ████████████ and not Secret Service or the EDNY has approval from Source's counsel to contact the source." Adding an incentive for the

Eastern District to dismiss the case, the memo finishes with the promise that "the EDNY can be furnished with significant information from the Source to result in no further prosecutive action."

The next memo from the FBI director confirming Scarpa's continued status as a TE informant ends with an admonition that was almost comical given Greg's criminal history: "Source should be admonished," he warns, "not to get involved in any future unauthorized criminal activity."[16]

"We can only imagine the hysterical laughter from Scarpa Senior, if, in fact, Lin DeVecchio ever delivered that warning," says former Special Agent James Whalen, who worked in the NYO. "That's if [DeVecchio] could even do it with a straight face. At this point, given the lengths the Bureau had gone to in order keep him out of jail, Scarpa had to be thinking to himself that he could get away with murder."[17]

The lengths DeVecchio went to in defense of "34" in this case are worthy of note because he later testified under oath that he typically didn't go out of his way to shield informants from prosecution.[18] This is what the former SSA admitted to during his 1995 OPR investigation:

> Scarpa Sr. told me he had already advised [Assistant U.S. Attorney Edward] McDonald that he was cooperating with the FBI. I prepared a document which explained his contributions, obtained approval from FBIHQ to make the disclosure, and I consulted with Ed McDonald, the head of the Organized Crime Strike Force (OCSF), in Scarpa Sr.'s behalf.[19]

Lin also admitted that he made "an official contact with Judge I. Leo Glasser, who heard the USSS [Secret Service] credit card case against Scarpa Sr." DeVecchio went on to state that he "made that approach with AUSA Norman Bloch . . . and the contact was endorsed by the FBI."[20] Bloch, who was special counsel to the Strike Force at the time of Lin's intervention, later went into private practice with DeVecchio's longtime attorney Douglas Grover, who was also a former Eastern District prosecutor.[21]

But despite DeVecchio's intervention and Scarpa's TE status, Strike Force attorney Ed McDonald was not going to drop this case without a fight. He pressed the matter before a grand jury and a four-count indictment was returned. It included a count accusing Scarpa of possessing "more than 15 counterfeit access devices" with "intent to defraud"—devices that would have allowed him to activate the bogus cards.[22]

Agents Behind a Mirror

The conflict between the FBI's New York Office, in its effort to protect Greg Scarpa Sr., and the Brooklyn Strike Force, in its effort to prosecute him, soon grew so pointed that high-level Justice Department officials had to get involved. The Bureau fired first, in a memo that was not only critical of Ed McDonald but seemed to suggest it would be impossible to prosecute Scarpa without revealing his TE status.

The memo also implied that the Secret Service agents wanted to poach Greg Sr. as a source. The author was Steve Pomerantz, chief of the FBI's Investigative Support Section at the Bureau's Headquarters. The memorandum, dated April 22, 1986, was sent to Paul E. Coffey, the deputy chief of the Organized Crime and Racketeering Section of the Criminal Division at Justice.

> Mr. McDonald may have disclosed source's informant status to the USSS and may have attempted to utilize the FBI informant independent of FBI control and direction. Both the unauthorized disclosure of the informant's relationship with the FBI and the attempt to operate him . . . by the Eastern District Strike Force, if these events actually took place, are of concern to the FBI.[23]

"In other words, McDonald and company had better keep their hands off Scarpa," says former agent Dan Vogel. "This was Headquarters' way of making it clear that '34' wasn't going to be prosecuted without a fight."[24]

A week later Coffey fired back, noting that during McDonald's initial meeting with Scarpa, Greg boldly pointed to a two-way mirror in the room, asserting that Secret Service agents were no doubt monitoring the exchange, during which his TE informant status was revealed.[25] Coffey continued:

> At no time, to my knowledge, has the Brooklyn Strike Force used this prosecution as a vehicle to coerce the informant's cooperation with the

Secret Service. In fact, the Strike Force has consistently sought dialogue with Mr. Kelleher whereby the informant could be prosecuted without breaching his confidential relationship with the FBI.

"These two memos are indicative of the stakes that were involved here," says former agent Vogel. "The Strike Force and the Secret Service saw Scarpa Sr. as a Class A bad guy who needed to get put away, but New York and HQ were treating him like he was the Bureau's most important tool in the fight against the mob."

In the meantime, DeVecchio seemed to have Scarpa working overtime to furnish new incriminating evidence on other Mafiosi that might serve to reinforce his value to the Feds. In a six-page 209 on March 18, he cited eleven separate pieces of new intelligence "since [source's] arrest by [the] U.S. Secret Service on November 5th."[26] Most of it was directed at the Gambino and Bonanno families.

Apparently, Scarpa himself was confident that DeVecchio's intervention with Judge Glasser would pay off. In a sworn affidavit in 1998, Linda Schiro stated that "prior to his sentencing, DeVecchio told Senior that he would receive a sentence of probation from the judge."[27] Greg Scarpa Jr. also reiterated his father's confidence. At a January 2004 hearing, Junior testified under oath that his father had told him "he would just be getting probation" after pleading guilty to credit card fraud.[28] During his own trial in 1998, Junior testified that the deal was made by Lin DeVecchio, "because [Scarpa Sr.] was a Top Echelon informant."[29]

Judge I. Leo Glasser himself revealed that DeVecchio had intervened with him on Scarpa's behalf, and he noted that Greg Sr., who by then had been diagnosed with HIV, "did not have long to live."[30]

Whether it was because of DeVecchio's intervention or some other back-channel effort, on June 18, 1986, a deal was cut. On paper Scarpa was looking at seven and a half years in prison and a $250,000 fine,[31] but Judge Glasser allowed him to plead guilty to one count in the indictment. He was sentenced to five years' probation and a $10,000 fine—a virtual slap on the wrist.[32] If it was Lin DeVecchio who played the AIDS card with the judge, it worked. But rather than succumb in a matter of months, as Glasser expected, Greg Scarpa lived for another *eight* years.

Extortion and Credit Card Theft

Still, Ed McDonald, the tenacious Brooklyn Strike Force attorney, would not let the matter pass without comment. On July 22, 1986, in a scathing four-page letter to Judge Glasser, who approved the plea deal, McDonald chronicled Scarpa's stunning criminal history, from his first arrest for possession of a firearm in 1950 up through the latest credit card bust. As McDonald noted, "within the last two years, using the Wimpy Boys Social Club as his headquarters, Scarpa has supervised efforts by members of his crew to extort protection money from local merchants through the use of physical violence." Given Scarpa's criminal history, McDonald went on to recommend that he "be sentenced to a period of incarceration and a substantial fine," describing him as "one of the biggest distributors of counterfeit credit cards in the New York metropolitan area."

DeVecchio described the credit card case this way in his memoir:

> The only time [Scarpa] got any help from me was when he was arrested by the Secret Service for buying counterfeit credit cards from a wired cooperating witness. It was a sting. My lawyer Doug Grover's law partner Norman Block [sic]* was the federal prosecutor. . . . I got Scarpa's approval and my supervisor's approval to go to headquarters for permission to reveal his TE status to Block and for Block and me to go to Judge I. Leo Glasser and tell him privately in the judge's chambers. Which we did. They made the decision from there to give Scarpa probation.

Six years after he intervened on behalf of Scarpa in that credit card case, however, DeVecchio seemed to suggest something different when he was under oath. In the November 1992 murder trial of Carmine Sessa's brother Michael, DeVecchio testified for the government as an expert witness. Although he didn't mention Scarpa by name, DeVecchio gave an account that appears inconsistent with that passage from his book.

---

* Grover's partner's name is spelled Bloch; the error appears in *We're Going to Win This Thing.*

In the following excerpt from the trial transcript, he's being cross-examined by the defendant's attorney Gavin Scotti:

> **Scotti:** Does the Bureau reward these informants sometimes for the information they give?
> **DeVecchio:** It does, yes.
> **Scotti:** Do those rewards sometimes take the form of cash payments?
> **DeVecchio:** Yes it does.
> **Scotti:** Do those rewards sometimes take the form of helping informants out of jams, when, for example, an informant might get picked up by some other . . . law enforcement officer, brought in for questioning and the informant says, "Call up Agent DeVecchio. I work for him." Does the informant sometimes get a little help from the FBI, see if you can cut this fellow a break, he's a good informant for us?
> **DeVecchio:** No.
> **Scotti:** You never did that? . . . You've never told anybody, this is a very valuable informant for us, he is in the middle of a very intricate investigation, and it would really help us out an awful lot if you could see your way clear to cutting him loose or letting him back out on the street to help us?
> **DeVecchio:** I've not done that.
> **Scotti:** You've not done that?
> **DeVecchio:** That's correct.[33]

Nearly five years after that testimony, DeVecchio's comments came back to haunt him. At a hearing for Vic Orena, the former Colombo acting boss who was convicted of murder—based in part on evidence allegedly planted by Greg Scarpa—defense attorney Gerald Shargel referred to Lin's testimony in the Sessa case:

> **Shargel:** Do you remember November of 1992 . . . testifying in this courthouse . . . against Michael Sessa?
> **DeVecchio:** I may have testified. I made a lot of testimony.
> **Shargel:** Let me show you what I will have marked . . . as B for identification, transcript of November 2nd, 1992 and ask if that refreshes your recollection as to whether you testified there?
> **DeVecchio:** Yes.

Shargel: Do you remember on page 119 giving this answer:

QUESTION: You've never told anybody, this is a very
valuable informant for us, he is in the middle of a very intricate
investigation, and it would really help us out an awful lot if you
could see your way clear to cutting him loose or letting him back
out on the street to help us?
ANSWER: I've not done that.
QUESTION: You've not done that?
ANSWER: That's correct.

Do you remember giving those answers to those questions?
DeVecchio: Yes.
Shargel: Those were lies, weren't they Mr. DeVecchio?
DeVecchio: No, they were not.
Shargel: Wasn't it a fact that just two months before, you asked these prosecutors to cut Gregory Scarpa a break because of the information he had given you?
DeVecchio: I requested they consider that.
Shargel: Wait a minute. You requested they consider that?
DeVecchio: Let him out on bail. That's what I said.
Shargel: You've lied before to cover your own tracks, haven't you?
DeVecchio: I have not lied at all Mr. Shargel and I resent that. I have not lied.[34]

We'll leave it for the reader to decide what to make of Lin DeVecchio's testimony in those court proceedings. By the summer of 1986, however, one thing was clear: Thanks to his intervention, Greg Scarpa Sr. was "back on the street." And, despite the warning from FBI Headquarters that he was "not to get involved in any future unauthorized criminal activity,"[35] Scarpa continued to break the law in a ruthless ongoing enterprise that included numbers running, loan sharking, hijacking, extortion, and murder, while presiding over the multimillion-dollar narcotics operation that led to the arrest of his son's crew the following year.

With the dismissal of the credit card case, Scarpa had now beaten three separate indictments brought by federal prosecutors working with strike forces in Chicago, Newark, and Brooklyn. Despite his health problems, the Grim Reaper had every reason to feel untouchable.

It's fair to argue that with his criminal record, and absent the FBI's help in thwarting the Secret Service charges, Scarpa Sr. might have been sentenced to a full seven years. Given the virus in his system, that could have amounted to a death sentence.

If he'd been locked down in a federal prison, however, he would never have been able to instigate the third Colombo war—and twelve people killed between 1991 and 1993, not to mention two other probable war-related Scarpa hits, might still be alive.[36] That's not an unfair assumption, given the evidence we'll produce that Scarpa not only fomented the conflict but pulled the trigger himself, or ordered it pulled, in six of the homicides and a number of the other shootings.

Long before he fired the first shot in that war, however, Greg Scarpa committed murder again. And this time the victim was one of his most loyal and devoted crew members: Joseph DeDomenico, also known as Joe Brewster.

Chapter 16

DEATH OF A
SECOND SON

Joe DeDomenico went way back with Greg Scarpa Sr. In fact, when Linda Schiro first met Scarpa at the Flamingo Lounge in 1962, nineteen-year-old Joe was already close to Greg.[1] Carmine Sessa, Scarpa's wartime consigliere, was one of Joe's best friends. He later testified that they'd been doing scores together since they were in their early teens.[2] Along with brothers John and Joe Saponaro and Bobby "Zam" Zambardi, they were five kids from the mean streets of Brooklyn who started out stealing cars and hijacking trucks, then learned to rob banks and kill on the orders of their capo, Greg Scarpa Sr.

Sessa remembered that, as far back as the 1960s, when a witness "flipped" on a case involving stolen bonds, Scarpa and Joe Brewster "killed somebody" to make it go away.[3] (That was the rubout that may have taken the life of Jerry Ciprio.) In June 1974, DeDomenico was arrested with Scarpa in that sale of $4 million in counterfeit IBM stock certificates developed by the Newark Strike Force,[4] another case that was ultimately dismissed.[5] The Killing Machine so trusted Brewster that Joe was a witness to two separate homicides Scarpa was involved in within the first six months of his reopening by Lin DeVecchio in 1980: the precipitous murder of Dominick "Big

Donny" Somma at the Wimpy Boys club in August and the slaying of former abortion doctor Eli Shkolnik on December 3. Over the years, Scarpa became so friendly with DeDomenico that Greg was the best man at Joe's wedding and godfather to his son.[6]

One of DeDomenico's specialties was bank burglaries, and from the early 1970s forward he worked two separate Bypass crews: one for Scarpa and the other for Greg's lifelong "compare," Anthony "Gaspipe" Casso, who was then a capo in the Lucchese family. As we'll see, during Lin DeVecchio's murder trial, his lawyers suggested that it was DeDomenico's defection from Scarpa to another Bypass crew that led to his death. But the evidence uncovered in this investigation indicates that Scarpa Sr. not only worked with Casso, and shared in the profits from some of his scores, but "34" also used his FBI connections to provide Casso with intelligence. At the same time Joe Brewster DeDomenico swung back and forth between both crews.

In the 2008 book *Gaspipe: Confessions of a Mafia Boss,* by the late Philip Carlo, Casso identified Joe Brewster as one of his crew members at the time of a 1972 incident that Scarpa helped resolve. According to Casso, he was driving on the Belt Parkway in Brooklyn with his wife, Lillian, and his daughter Jolene when suddenly he was "surrounded by unmarked FBI vehicles . . . driven by stone-faced agents." After being summarily jerked from the car, he was cuffed and taken into custody. According to Casso, Joe Brewster and another member of his crew were arrested the same day.[7]

After putting up the bail money for Joe and getting back on the street himself, Casso reached out to Scarpa, whom Carlo described as "a fierce war captain in the Colombo crime family who was known by a select few to have good friends in law enforcement." Learning through his attorney that the Feds had a "snitch" named Bobby Dennish who was going to flip on his burglary crew, Casso reportedly met Scarpa Sr. at his own social club on Bath Avenue in Bensonhurst and asked for help finding Dennish.

Senior said he'd get back to him, writes Carlo, and when they met two days later at Mary's, a restaurant on Eighty-Sixth Street, Scarpa told Casso that, according to his FBI control agent (Anthony Villano at the time),[8] "Dennish was stashed in Topeka, Kansas." As Carlo tells it, Casso was able to get word to Dennish that if he "threw the case, did not ID him or the others in open court, he'd take care of him." And he did: The charges were dropped.

But like Scarpa, Casso wasn't the type to leave loose ends. A source with specific knowledge of the case told me that Dennish was later lured back to JFK airport with a free airline ticket, where he was picked up by none other than Joe Brewster and murdered.[9]

In *Gaspipe,* Carlo writes that over the years "Scarpa and Casso did more and more business together, hijacking valuable trucks and stealing all kinds of goods from Kennedy Airport."[10] Scarpa even reportedly offered to sponsor Casso in the Colombo family when "the books were opened," but Anthony "politely declined" and went on to become acting boss of the Luccheses. Casso himself later pled guilty to his role in fourteen murders and was implicated in another twenty-three.[11] In the Mafia pantheon of epic killers, that put Casso on the same level as Gambino consigliere Sammy "the Bull" Gravano, who pled to nineteen homicides.[12]

Still, Joe DeDomenico remained a strong mutual connection between the two ruthless mobsters. When I interviewed Casso, he told me that Scarpa used to give him "tips" on scores.

"Diamonds and jewelry, stuff like that," said Casso. "And I'd take Joe Brewster with me. He'd come work for me. And Brewster would go breaking in."[13] Casso further insisted that Scarpa trusted Brewster as much as he trusted his own son.

"Brewster was the guy who really knew everything," Casso told me. "Part of that was 'cause Junior was locked up for a lot of years, so the only two people who knew everything about Greg Senior were Joe Brewster and his girlfriend Linda." In fact, when Linda Schiro testified at the DeVecchio murder trial in 2007, she recalled that Scarpa "loved Joe Brewster like his own son."[14]

The Murder of Bucky

According to Carmine Sessa, the Colombos' wartime consigliere, Joe DeDomenico took part in four separate bank burglaries that Sessa was involved in from 1980 to 1984. The first was the Dime Savings Bank heist that led to Dominick Somma's death.[15] According to Sessa, it was DeDomenico's quick thinking during that aborted robbery that allowed the crew to escape.

The next burglary was a successful $1 million heist at a bank on Northern Boulevard in Queens, which yielded "gold bars, diamonds, jewelry and cash." Sessa's personal cut was $48,000 to $50,000.[16] He told the agents that the crew on that score included Brewster, Gus Farace (Scarpa Sr.'s nephew), and Bobby Zambardi, who used jackhammers to penetrate the vault. This time, the outside lookout working with Greg Jr. was Robert "Bucky" DiLeonardi, and just like "Big Donny" Somma, he ended up dead.

In fact, DiLeonardi's rubout was an eerie precursor to Brewster's eventual demise. According to what Sessa told the agents, Scarpa ordered DiLeonardi executed "because he had been overheard bragging about crimes in which he had participated," including "bank robberies."

The hit team dispatched by the Grim Reaper this time reportedly included Sessa, Greg Scarpa Jr., and two members of Senior's Wimpy Boys crew: Billy Meli and Kevin Granato.[17] The plan was for Bucky to drive Junior and Sessa to see somebody on Staten Island because Junior "had a problem to settle." Meli and Granato would follow in a separate car.

According to Sessa, on the day of the hit DiLeonardi picked him up with Junior in his own car and drove across the Verrazano Narrows Bridge from Brooklyn. When they reached Hylan Boulevard on Staten Island, they turned onto a side street near Russo's restaurant, where the younger Scarpa told Bucky to pull over. Suspecting nothing, DiLeonardi complied—at which point, according to Sessa, Greg Jr., who was sitting in the backseat, shot him "several times in the head, killing him." After the hit, Junior and Sessa reportedly left the vehicle and joined Meli and Granato in the getaway car. They then drove toward Junior's house on Holten Avenue and tossed the murder weapon into Wolfe's Pond.

In a strangely prophetic conversation, Sessa told his FBI debriefers that he discussed the murder later with Joe Brewster, who told him that "everybody has to follow orders or be killed themselves." At some point after that, Brewster himself started disobeying his capo, Greg Scarpa Sr., and once that happened—"son" or no son, best man or not—in Senior's ice-cold words, "he had to go."

DeDomenico's next bank job with the Scarpa crew was the successful robbery of a bank in Queens, with Zambardi, Granato, Sessa, and a fourth accomplice named Joseph Figueroa. By Sessa's account, Figueroa had also been in on the Dime Savings job.

This time the split was $15,000 to $20,000 per man, with the lion's share of the proceeds getting "kicked up" to Greg Sr. DeDomenico had a contact at ADT, the alarm company, and the crew learned how to bypass alarm systems so they could get into banks during off hours. The system had worked in two of the scores, failing only during the 1980 Dime job. In February 1984, when Greg Sr. decided to hit the same bank again, they used a police scanner to tip them off to any law enforcement presence.

According to Sessa, the crew this time consisted of DeDomenico, Greg Jr., Zambardi, Figueroa, and Anthony Frezza, who went on later that year to drive Mary Bari to her death, only to get whacked himself. The Bari murder was another homicide where Senior and Junior would trust both Carmine Sessa and Joe Brewster to keep quiet.

But on February 18, during their second burglary at the Dime, the police scanner went off and the crew fled. Joe Brewster, the seasoned thief, had his car parked behind the bank. He got away clean with Sessa and Bobby Zam. Out of loyalty to Figueroa, though, they doubled back to pick him up—only to get boxed in by NYPD patrol cars. Sessa, Zambardi, and Brewster were pulled from their vehicle, questioned, and arrested.

What Was Missing

In the four years since Lin DeVecchio had started sending 209s to Washington based on his debriefings of Greg Sr., there was very little in them about Scarpa's activities as a bank robber. So, again, the question is, what did DeVecchio know, and when did he know it?

The first 209 that even hinted at such activity—given Brewster's links to Scarpa—was in mid-December 1981. It recounted a meeting from the previous March:

ON MARCH 4TH, 1981 SOURCE ADVISED THAT JOE BREWSTER IS NOT CONNECTED WITH ▮▮▮▮▮ BUT NOTED THAT THE BURGLARY AT THE CHASE BANK ON THE WEEKEND OF JANUARY 17–19TH WAS DONE BY ▮▮▮▮▮ CREW. SOURCE ALSO ADVISED THAT ▮▮▮▮▮ ADT EMPLOYEE IN NASSAU COUNTY WHO HAS BEEN SUPPLYING ▮▮▮▮▮ WITH INFORMATION ON BANK ALARMS.[18]

Since most of the key information in that report was redacted, we don't know what crew Scarpa was referring to or who was getting the information from ADT. The next mention of a bypass robbery came two years later:

ON MARCH 5TH, 1983 SOURCE ADVISED THAT THE RECENT ROBBERY OF 900 POUNDS OF GOLD IN THE JEWELRY DISTRICT WAS HANDLED BY MEMBERS OF THE COLOMBO FAMILY, FRANK BEANSIE MILLER'S CREW. SOURCE SAID THE BURGLARS HAD TO HAVE INSIDE INFORMATION PARTICULARLY IN BYPASSING THE ALARM SYSTEM.[19]

Frank "Beansie" Miller, also known as "Frankie Beans," was another member of the Colombo family who divided his time, like Joe Brewster, between scores for Anthony Casso and Greg Scarpa. In fact, in Philip Carlo's book, Gaspipe went into detail about how his "B&E crew" would "meet at Frankie Beans's finished basement . . . in Bensonhurst where the eight-by-ten black-and-white [surveillance] photos they'd taken . . . were posted on a large blackboard" in preparation for each job. "The gang would actually buy the same alarm system as that in the bank," wrote Carlo, "so they could practice on the safe in preparation to dismantle the bank's alarm."[20]

Using crew members from the Colombo borgata, including Miller and DeDomenico, Gaspipe admitted to stealing "millions of dollars" in these heists. In a single robbery of a Chemical Bank on Canal Street in Manhattan, Carlo writes, Casso's Bypass crew "made $10 million."

"That's the kind of fortune Scarpa and Casso were making," says defense attorney Flora Edwards, "as they shared these crew members. The solving of bank robberies is at the core of the FBI's work. So where was the Bureau while all of this was going on, particularly when one of Casso's partners in crime was a Top Echelon informant?"[21]

Nearly a year went by before Lin DeVecchio made another report about a burglary in his Scarpa 209 memos. This time, after the arrest at the Dime Savings Bank, Scarpa was forced to admit that the botched score had taken place. But that 209, which other agents in the Bureau had access to, included two pieces of misleading information:

On 2/28/84 ▮▮▮▮▮▮▮▮ advised Supervisor R. Lindley DeVecchio that JOE BREWSTER, BOBBY ZAMBARDI, and CARMINE

SESSO [*sic*] are connected with GREG SCARPA but are not members of the Colombo Family. The source said the word on the street is to have no conversation concerning the attempted bank burglary inasmuch as the above individuals have been arrested. The source said that COLOMBO capo ANTHONY SCARPATI would had to have authorized a bank burglary, and SCARPA could not have made this decision on his own.[22]

First of all, the source of the report is clearly Scarpa, whose name is redacted. DeVecchio identifies the crew as being "connected" to Scarpa—perhaps as a way of diverting attention away from Greg Sr. as his CI. But the allegation in that 209 that no one was talking about the failed heist was disingenuous. Scarpa knew every detail, since his own crew had attempted the job. The most misleading aspect of that 209, however, involved the two suggestions in the last sentence: that Anthony "Scappi" Scarpati would have had to approve the robbery, and that Scarpa couldn't have acted on his own.

Denigrating "Scappi"

As noted earlier, despite the fact that Greg Scarpa Sr. is referred to repeatedly in the airtels from the early 1960s as a capo, caporegime, or captain, Lin DeVecchio insists in his book that Scarpa "would never agree to be a capo because it would draw too much attention to himself. He remained a soldier under capo Anthony . . . Scarpati."[23]

Scarpati was just four years older than Greg. At sixteen he'd been a member of the notorious South Brooklyn Boys gang, and one night in 1950, after a *West Side Story*–like rumble with a gang called the Tigers, he was charged with murder in the shooting of an eighteen-year-old. Also arrested in the incident was a young Carmine Persico.[24] Persico and Scarpati later joined the Profaci crime family.[25] Decades after that, Greg Scarpa Sr. used Scarpati to hide behind as his nominal captain, seeking to divert attention away from himself by posing as a lowly soldier who had to seek Scappi's permission for any significant crime. Within the family, however, Scarpa was known to routinely humiliate Scarpati in front of other members and associates.

Vic Orena Jr. and his brother John, the sons of the acting family boss who was Greg Scarpa's primary target during the third war in the early 1990s, told me in an interview that Scarpa often treated Scarpati brutally.

"Greg was supposed to answer to Scappi," said Vic Jr., "but Carmine Sessa [said] that Greg would abuse him."

"He would literally yell at him," said John Orena, "calling him a piece of shit to his face."[26]

Further, Scarpa's own reports to DeVecchio make clear that he had zero loyalty to Scarpati. In fact, in several 209s, Scarpa actually gave the FBI the information agents needed to set up wiretaps on his so-called capo. In November 1982, DeVecchio filed this memo to Washington based on what Scarpa had told him:

> SCAPPY CAN BE FOUND ON A DAILY BASIS AT THE NESTOR SOCIAL CLUB, FIFTH AVENUE AND PRESIDENT STREET, BROOKLYN, WHICH HE USES AS A LOCATION TO HANDLE HIS NUMBERS OPERATIONS, SPORTS BETTING OPERATION AND LOANSHARKING OPERATION. THE SOURCE ADVISED THAT . . . HE IS VERY CONSCIOUS OF SURVEILLANCE IN THAT AREA AND ALWAYS HAS LOOK-OUTS AT EITHER END OF THE BLOCK.[27]

Later, Scarpa went so far as to give DeVecchio the phone number to Scappi's social club, along with the location of a phone that might be tapped.

> THE SOURCE NOTED THAT ■■■■■■■ ARE CLOSE TO SCARPATTI, AND THAT ■■■■■■ HANDLES SOME OF SCARPATTI'S ACTION. THE SOURCE ALSO CONFIRMED THAT TELEPHONE NUMBER 638-4418 IS THE TELEPHONE USED AT THE NESTOR SOCIAL CLUB, ALTHOUGH IT IS LISTED TO AN UPSTAIRS APARTMENT.[28]

"If Scarpa Sr. had an ounce of respect for Scappi, or any loyalty to him, he would have never ratted him out like this," said Andrew Orena, the youngest son of the imprisoned boss, who has spent years working to prove his father's innocence in a murder he claims was set up by Scarpa.[29] We'll examine that issue more closely in Chapter 22.

In the meantime, the 209s on Scarpati and the bypass bank burglaries demonstrate that Scarpa's reports on the cases, which gave FBI officials an inside look at the Colombo crime family, were routinely being distorted by the Grim Reaper to serve his own interests, and his handler, Lin DeVecchio, was reporting those distortions directly to FBI officials in Washington.

An FBI chart from 1984, which DeVecchio published in his book under the title "Colombo Crime Family 1984," shows Scarpati as a capo. But it lists both Scarpas, Senior and Junior, as mere soldiers.[30]

And it wasn't just the DC brass who were getting a distorted picture. Other supervisors in New York were similarly deceived. In his memoir Lin DeVecchio quotes Chris Mattiace, the SSA who preceded him as head of the Colombo Squad in the NYO. In Mattiace's view, Greg Scarpa Sr. was merely a lowly soldier, unworthy of his attention.

"At that time [1987] we were only interested in capos and above," says Mattiace. "Our whole effort in every squad was focused on bringing down the hierarchy of each family. Here was a case with a single soldier [Scarpa] and a bunch of associates."[31]

With Scarpa Sr. as the principal source on his own activities, the FBI leadership was getting a twisted view of his actual position in the family. It's no surprise, then, that when the relationship between Senior and his trusted "son" Joe deteriorated to the point of Brewster's execution, Lin DeVecchio's report to Washington didn't even *hint* at Scarpa's role in the murder.

Getting Dressed Up to Die

The details of the final hours of Joe DeDomenico's life are quite similar in the accounts given by Lin DeVecchio in his book and the Brooklyn prosecutor who set out to convict Lin for complicity in the murder in 2007. Sometime on September 17, 1987, Joe Brewster was asked by Greg Scarpa Sr. to put on his best suit. He was going to be driven with Greg Jr. to a special event. Some hours later, Joe waited with Junior at a bar/restaurant to be picked up, and when a white Oldsmobile Cutlass arrived they got in. Unbeknownst to Joe, it was a stolen car, and earlier that day a gun had been hidden beneath its front floor mat. Greg Jr. was in the shotgun seat; Brewster sat behind him—never suspecting that he had only minutes to live.

At some point, after they pulled away, Junior reportedly retrieved the weapon, spun around, and shot DeDomenico at virtual point-blank range. In an instant, he had killed the man who stood as godfather to his own daughter—the trusted crew member who had been sponsored for membership in the family by his own father. Wiping away the brains and blood, Junior then reportedly turned to face the windshield as the Cutlass drove to Mario Parlagreco's garage. There it was wiped down of fingerprints and driven to Seventy-Second Street in Bensonhurst, where it was left with the motor running, Joe Brewster's corpse still slumped in the backseat.[32]

The Joe DeDomenico death car

In their respective accounts, DeVecchio and the Brooklyn DA seemed to agree on the motives for the slaying: Brewster's increased used of cocaine, his refusal to do a murder on Greg Sr.'s orders, his new-found interest in religion, and his refusal to cut Senior in on burglary scores he was reportedly doing on his own. As we'll see from the testimony of those close to DeDomenico, however, those problems had been festering for several years after his February 1984 arrest for the second Dime Savings Bank robbery attempt. The question is, what triggered his murder three years later? What caused Scarpa's actual son to kill his adopted "son," Joe?

In his book, DeVecchio hypothesizes that a leak through a Colombo family lawyer led to the brutal murder. But Linda Schiro, the one person Anthony Casso insisted that Scarpa trusted as much as DeDomenico, testified at DeVecchio's trial that it was Lin's confirmation of Scarpa's suspicions that sealed Brewster's fate.

The apparent conflict between Schiro's trial testimony and statements she'd made a decade earlier in a recorded interview led to the summary dismissal of the charges against DeVecchio. The 1997 interview tapes produced by reporter Tom Robbins suggested that Schiro had cleared DeVecchio in the DeDomenico homicide. But as we'll see in Chapter 42, a more careful comparison between what she said on the stand and what was recorded on those tapes now demonstrates that when it came to Brewster's homicide, Linda Schiro was consistent in both instances.

DeVecchio's Version of Events

In his book, Lin devotes three pages to the murder of Joe DeDomenico. He provides an italicized account of the death, with heretofore undisclosed details, in a style similar to his dramatized introduction on Mary Bari's death. In this account, Joe Saponaro, a Scarpa crew member, is driving the stolen Cutlass when it picks up Brewster and Junior.

According to DeVecchio, after the cleanup of the death car in Parlagreco's garage, a three-car convoy, including two separate "crash cars" driven by Billy Meli and Kevin Granato, accompanied Saponaro to Seventy-Second Street for the body disposal. After that, they all convened at Romano's restaurant—the same place where Scarpa had dinner after Mary Bari's murder.

But at that point, writes DeVecchio, "Joe Sap had left Kevin Granato's own personal car keys in the stolen Cutlass with the dead body in the back-seat," so "Billy Meli and another associate, Joe Savarese, ran out of Romano's and drove to the Cutlass. Luckily, Joe Brewster's body had not been spotted in the backseat."

Whatever the source of those details, it should be noted that DeVecchio's official report to the Bureau on DeDomenico's death was considerably shorter:

> ON SEPTEMBER 17TH, 1987, SOURCE ADVISED THAT JOE "BREWSTER" DE DOMENICO WAS HIT . . . DUE TO HIS ASSOCIATION AND NARCOTICS DEALINGS ▮▮▮▮▮▮▮▮. FURTHER, BREWSTER ALSO MADE A BURGLARY SCORE AND FAILED TO CUT IN HIS CAPO, AND THEN DENIED THAT HE HAD PARTICIPATED IN THE BURGLARY. THE SOURCE SAID THAT JUNIOR PERSICO ORDERED THE HIT AS A RESULT OF THE ABOVE.[33]

In his book, Lin claims that Greg Sr. had to clear the murder with Anthony Scarpati, who was then "in jail in the South." In fact, he writes that on two occasions Mario Parlagreco accompanied Greg Jr. to visit Scappi to get his blessing. He even alleges that, on the second visit, Scarpa Jr. "was given permission for the rubout by Junior Persico by way of Scappi." Larry Mazza later described Brewster's alleged religious conversion as a drift that rendered him "a step away from being a rat,"[34] and in his book DeVecchio supplies an appropriate quote from Scappi: "If he found God, it is time for him to join God."[35]

But would a murderous capo like Greg Scarpa have taken the time to get the Brewster hit cleared by another capo—especially one like Scappi, whom he reportedly treated like dirt? Would he have let Carmine Persico, the family boss, know just how far off the reservation his own trusted crew member Joe DeDomenico had gone? What did it say about Senior's ability to control his crew if the man he trusted to be godfather to his own grandchild had become such a liability?

As we've noted repeatedly, the airtels recording Scarpa's comments during the 1960s and '70s refer to the enmity and "bad blood" that existed between Scarpa and the Persico faction of the family. Why would Greg Sr. expose such a vulnerability to the Snake when he routinely whacked those around him who got out of line—like Dominick Somma and Bucky DiLeonardi—without Persico's say-so?

Furthermore, how credible was it that Carmine Persico, who controlled a family that grossed millions of dollars a year from drug dealing, would order the murder of a valuable earner like Brewster because he was selling narcotics?

"In order to continue to sell Scarpa Sr. as a truthful and stable CI, DeVecchio had to convince the Director and other FBI officials that Brewster's death was the result of his drug deals and that the murder was sanctioned at the highest level by the family boss," says Flora Edwards.[36] In his book, while denying that he had anything to do with Brewster's death, Lin seems to blame it on a leak in the EDNY that found its way to a lawyer for the Colombos.

> In my opinion, most of our leaks came from the Eastern District and I said that loudly and often over the years, and I was not the only agent to say so. There was something about Brooklyn that seemed to crave attention like a spoiled child.[37]

Chapter 17

THE CASE OF CASES

If the borough of Brooklyn was a "spoiled child," in Lin DeVecchio's words, it was also a Mafia killing ground. In 1987 alone there were ten separate gangland-style murders in Kings County, and at least two of them touched Greg Scarpa directly.

As the New Year commenced, "34" was also directly linked to a triumph for the Feds. On January 13, three of the five New York bosses were sentenced in the Mafia Commission case,[1] a prosecution that Rudolph Giuliani, the U.S. attorney for the Southern District, had predicted would "crush" Cosa Nostra.[2] Dubbed the "case of cases," the Commission trial, which had lasted three months in 1986, was based largely on wiretaps connecting the bosses and their underlings to murders and a bid-rigging scheme in the construction industry that netted $1.27 million for the mob.[3] Key to that aspect of the RICO "enterprise" was Colombo soldier Ralph "Ralphie" Scopo, president of the New York Concrete Workers District Council, who had demanded a kickback of 2 percent on every concrete bid under $2 million.

The business of the so-called concrete club was reportedly conducted by Scopo, Colombo underboss Gennaro "Jerry Lang" Langella, and capo Dominick "Donnie Shacks" Montemarano in the back of the Casa Storta restaurant in Bensonhurst. The Feds were able to eavesdrop on the club's secret conversations as a direct result of intel Scarpa leaked to DeVecchio, which paved the way for the government's Title III wiretap warrants.

After that, the Bureau's elite Special Operations Group (SOG) went into the restaurant and installed a bug in the ceiling above the table where Langella and Scopo conspired to rig the bids.[4] Scarpa also went so far as to supply the Feds with Langella's home address and phone number.[5]

Each of the three bosses convicted in the case, Anthony "Fat Tony"

Carmine Persico, Anthony Salerno, Anthony Corallo

Salerno of the Genoveses, Anthony "Tony Ducks" Corallo of the Luccheses, and Carmine Persico of the Colombos, got one-hundred-year sentences.* Persico, whom Scarpa was instrumental in "ratting out," actually represented himself pro se during the trial. Facing the jury during his opening argument, he shuffled his papers and exclaimed, "Please bear with me. I'm a little nervous." But his self-effacing strategy backfired,[6] and with the conviction of Persico; Langella, who got sixty-five years; and Scopo, who also pulled a hundred-year stretch, three key players in the Colombo hierarchy above Greg Scarpa were removed.

The conviction of these men, dubbed the Mafia's "Board of Directors," garnered page-one headlines and propelled Giuliani into the national spotlight. "Our approach is to wipe out the five families," said the tough-talking future mayor. *Time* magazine called the trial, which he personally prosecuted, "the most significant assault on the infrastructure of organized crime since the high command of the Chicago Mafia was swept away in 1943."[7]

At that point, Giuliani's 1976 decision to spare DeVecchio from indictment in the German Luger case must have seemed prescient. As a result of the bounty of intel reaped from his source, DeVecchio was appointed

---

* Two months earlier Persico was sentenced to an additional thirty-nine years in a separate prosecution.

supervising agent on the Commission case.[8] He was already running the Bonanno Squad, and in late 1987 he was rewarded with C-10, the Colombo Squad, which he took over from Chris Mattiace. In his book, Lin refers to this period, with its series of legal successes, as "our championship season."[9]

He then goes on to describe an FBI 209 he wrote, sourced by Greg Scarpa Sr., in which the Commission bosses reportedly discussed a plot to assassinate Giuliani, the mob-busting prosecutor who had saved him from the ATF's illegal gun sale charges.

> On September 17, 1987, source advised that recent information disclosed that approximately a year ago all five NY families discussed the idea of killing USA RUDY GIULIANI. JOHN GOTTI and CARMINE PERSICO were in favor of the hit. The bosses of the LUCCHESE, BONANNO, and GENOVESE Families rejected the idea, despite strong efforts to convince them otherwise by GOTTI and PERSICO.[10]

When that 209 was introduced by Lin's defense team during his murder trial in 2007, it created a small media storm. In a story headlined "Crime Bosses Considered Hit on Giuliani," *New York Times* reporter John Sullivan wrote that Giuliani "came within single vote of having a contract put on his head by the leaders of the five New York organized crime families."[11]

"That was one vote I guess I won," quipped Giuliani, who, by 2007, was considering a bid for the White House.[12] Suggesting that he took the threat in stride, Giuliani's campaign released a statement in which he said, "You get used to living with it. You say to yourself, 'It's worth doing what you are doing and it's always a remote possibility.'"[13]

The 209, penned by DeVecchio, was part of six hundred pages of memos documenting his contacts with Scarpa turned over at trial that day, October 24, 2007. But two days later, a story by *Times* reporter Michael Brick raised questions about the legitimacy of the threat. Under the headline "'80s Plot to Hit Giuliani? Mob Experts Doubt It," Brick quoted former Assistant U.S. Attorney Andrew McCarthy, the lead Southern District prosecutor on the 1995 "Day of Terror" case, as noting that "the Sicilian Mafia killed Italian judicial magistrates and police officers, [but] the American Mafia didn't do that. . . . In the United States, their general M.O. was that killing prosecutors and cops could do nothing but bring harm."[14]

Brick, who covered the DeVecchio trial, also quoted "Gang Land" columnist Jerry Capeci as disputing whether "John Gotti would have gone along with the proposal."[15] Was the plot real or a Scarpa fabrication? It's impossible to say for sure at this point. But the date that the alleged threat found its way into a DeVecchio 209 is curious. It was the same day Scarpa had his closest crew member, Joseph DeDomenico, killed.

"Was it meant to deflect attention away from the significance of Brewster's murder?" asks defense attorney Flora Edwards.[16] It's impossible to say, but it's worthy of mention that both reports—Brewster and Giuliani—supposedly came from Scarpa Sr. on the very same day.

The Death of Sal

Nine months earlier on January 14, 1987, one day after the sentencing of Carmine Persico, Gregory Scarpa's older brother Salvatore "Sal" Scarpa was gunned down. Sal was sitting in a social club at 1275 Seventy-Fourth Street in the Dyker Heights section of Brooklyn ten minutes before midnight when five armed gunmen came in for what seemed at first to be a robbery.[17]

After they forced the patrons to lie on the floor while they confiscated their money and jewelry, Sal Scarpa was shot once in the back of the head by one assailant, who was wearing a mask. The other four members of the crew were said to be African American, and before they fled the club one of them yelled out, "Howard Beach!"—a reference to an infamous racial attack just a month earlier, when three young black men were attacked in the largely Italian neighborhood in Queens after their car broke down. Wielding baseball bats and spewing racial epithets, a gang of white teens descended on the three young men, beating one of them severely, and another, twenty-four-year-old Michael Griffith, was killed after being hit by a car on the Belt Parkway while escaping from the attackers.[18] Charles Hynes, who went on to become the Brooklyn DA, was appointed a special prosecutor in the case,[19] in which twelve suspects were indicted.[20]

On the night of Sal Scarpa's murder, though, there was no compelling reason to believe that race was the prime motive. Neither, it seemed, was robbery. After Sal was shot at close range, his body was found with his watch, a gold pendant, and $313 in cash intact.

Salvatore and Gregory Sr. were the sons of first-generation immigrants from the village of Lorenzaga in the *comune* of Motta di Livenza near Venice. Greg was made in 1950 and Sal is believed to have preceded him into the Profaci family.

At the time of his death, Sal was free on bail awaiting trial for cocaine possession. It was just the latest in a series of charges dating back to the 1950s that rivaled those of his younger brother Greg. The newly released FBI files show that the two brothers were in on the December 1959 tractor trailer heist for which Greg was arrested.[21]

As noted earlier, Gregory quickly agreed to inform for the Bureau but severed his ties after agents pressed him on the whereabouts of Sal, who'd escaped.[22]

His loyalty didn't last long. By late November 1961, after he was reopened, Greg named Sal, along with Carmine Persico, Hugh "Apples" McIntosh, and Salvatore Albanese, as "criminal associates."[23] Beyond that, in the 1,153 pages of newly released airtels and 209s from Greg's file, there are very few references to Sal, who went on to became a capo in the family.

Sal Scarpa's name didn't surface in the press until twenty years later, when he was indicted with Charles LoCicero, son of the Sidge, in a quarter-million-dollar scam involving a fraudulent maintenance contract for the old Brooklyn Navy Yard. After the yard was closed by the Pentagon, the City of New York paid $24 million for the site in 1964 for use as an industrial park. But it proved slow to attract tenants and soon became a feeding trough for the Colombo crime family.[24] On February 10, 1981, LoCicero and Sal Scarpa were accused in a complex $250,000 bogus billing and kickback scheme uncovered by the city comptroller.[25] But two years after an audit found "widespread fraud and mismanagement" at the 265-acre park, no one had been brought to trial.[26]

Charles LoCicero, the uncle of Richard, who was brutally murdered in the Paine Webber securities theft case, was listed as "special projects and safety coordinator" for the park, while Sal was on the books as an "elevator contractor." The 1981 indictment named him in fourteen counts of alleged bribery, forgery, and grand larceny. He ended up pleading guilty to eleven counts in October 1983 after more than $500,000 in elevator-repair bills he'd submitted had been paid by the corporation running the park. It's unclear from the published record if Sal did any jail time or what fines he may have paid, but the comptroller's investigation revealed that he'd been doing business out of a five-by-eight-foot office in the rear of a Brooklyn espresso shop.[27]

A Case of Fratricide?

While Sal Scarpa's murder was never officially solved, Angela Clemente, the forensic investigator responsible for the release of the Scarpa FBI files,[28] believes she has identified the shooter, and she insists that Greg Scarpa Sr. himself was behind the rubout.[29] Clemente, who has worked for years to clear the names of several Colombo family members convicted after the 1991–1993 war, is one of the most knowledgeable researchers on the relationship between Lin DeVecchio and his Top Echelon informant.

In 2004, she unearthed dozens of FBI 302 memos documenting the undercover work of Greg Scarpa Jr. in an eleven-month FBI sting of al-Qaeda bomb maker Ramzi Yousef at the federal jail in Manhattan from March 1996 to February 1997.[30] That initiative is covered in detail in Chapter 38.

After DeVecchio's indictment on March 30, 2006, Clemente was cited by reporters for the *New York Post* and the *Daily News* for her contributions to the DA's investigation.[31] According to a *New York Times* piece on Clemente's 2008 lawsuit to force the release of the Scarpa files, "the Brooklyn district attorney's office . . . said her work on Mr. Scarpa was instrumental in helping the office file quadruple murder charges against Mr. Scarpa's former F.B.I. handler, Roy Lindley DeVecchio."[32] Clemente was also singled out for her "invaluable assistance" by Special District Attorney Leslie Crocker Snyder in her 2008 report, declining to indict Linda Schiro on perjury charges.[33]

In a report posted on her website in 2006, Clemente, whose principal source was retired NYPD detective Tommy Dades, identified Sal Scarpa's killer as one Philip "Philly Boy" Paradiso.[34] What makes that connection interesting is that Dades and Brooklyn Assistant DA Mike Vecchione, DeVecchio's prosecutor, had earlier linked Paradiso to Jimmy Hydell, one of the principal victims of Anthony "Gaspipe" Casso, Greg Scarpa Sr.'s longtime partner in crime.[35] As we've already established, Joe Brewster

DeDomenico worked for Casso and Scarpa in different permutations of their Bypass crews, and in this investigation we've found a number of links between Scarpa's homicides and the string of murders executed on Casso's orders in what became known as the Mafia Cops case.

Indeed, just weeks after Brewster was slain, the tenth victim in the series of mob-related hits in 1987 was John Otto Heidel, a convicted forger who, like DeDomenico, worked for both the Colombo and Lucchese families.[36] Heidel was shot eight times while changing a tire at Thirty-Fifth Street and Avenue U in Brooklyn at four fifteen on the afternoon of October 8.[37] After shooting Heidel in the chest, buttocks, and back, the killers fled in a light blue 1983 Oldsmobile. In Philip Carlo's *Gaspipe*, Casso identifies Heidel as a member of the same Bypass crew Brewster had worked for.[38]

Anthony "Gaspipe" Casso, 1989

During this three-week period in the fall of 1987 between the murders of Brewster and Heidel, we get the first real indication of the link between the DeVecchio-Scarpa scandal and the case involving retired NYPD detectives Louis Eppolito and Stephen Caracappa, known as the Mafia Cops.

The U.S. attorney for the EDNY alleged that Eppolito and Caracappa, convicted of receiving up to $375,000 in bribes from Anthony Casso, "directly participated in, or aided and abetted, eight murders, two attempted murders, one murder conspiracy, several instances of obstruction of justice, drug distribution and money laundering."[39]

In naming Philly Boy Paradiso as the shooter in the Sal Scarpa murder, Clemente claims that Greg Scarpa Sr. was behind his own brother's rubout, because at that point in January 1987 Sal "told someone that he thought Greg was an informant."[40]

Knowing how bloodthirsty Greg Scarpa was, I was skeptical when I first heard Clemente's theory, because Scarpa had always been murderously protective of his family. Indeed, he'd initially withdrawn from informing for the Bureau back in 1960 after they pressed him on his brother Sal's whereabouts. But relationships change over time, and the research I've now done has convinced me that Clemente's assessment is correct.

The first piece of new evidence came from an FBI 302 memo dated May 24, 1994, memorializing the debriefing of Joseph Ambrosino.

Known as "Joey Brains," Ambrosino had previously testified that he entered "the family" by first associating with Sal Scarpa. He began working for him in 1976 and did a variety of crimes including burglary and assault.[41] Later, he became a full-time member of Greg Scarpa's Wimpy Boys crew. But when he was interviewed by SSAs R. Patrick Welch and Robert J. O'Brien in 1994, Ambrosino told them that "Sal Scarpa and Scarpa Sr. had a love/hate relationship."[42]

Ambrosino said that Sal had initially defended his brother. During the 1970s, he reported, "there was a rumor on the street that Scarpa Sr. was an informant." When Ambrosino brought that up to Sal, the elder Scarpa admonished him, saying that "nobody could prove the rumor and that if you couldn't prove somebody was a 'rat' you shouldn't be making statements about the person you suspect."

As the years passed, however, and Greg Scarpa continued to dodge every federal charge he was indicted for, the rumors persisted. It was only logical to wonder whether he was getting some kind of inside help from the government—and it was common knowledge among wiseguys that no one got a pass on an indictment without some kind of reciprocation.

Anthony Casso, who committed a number of crimes with Greg Scarpa Sr., knew him well, so I reached out to him and asked whether he thought it was possible that Greg could have been involved in his brother's murder. Casso was quick to respond: "Greg was *totally* responsible for Sal's death," he wrote me. "Sal was telling people that Greg was an informant."[43] Casso was also emphatic about Scarpa's motive in the killing of his trusted soldier Joe DeDomenico. "Greg was afraid that Brewster would reveal him as an informant," Casso wrote.[44]

In a May 2012 interview with the *New York Post*, Scarpa's daughter Little Linda Schiro was quoted as telling a reporter that she believed "her father's murder victims included Scarpa's own brother Sal, her uncle."[45] So the evidence suggests that, within the space of nine months, Scarpa's fear of being exposed as an FBI "rat" drove him to kill not just his brother but the loyal crew member he'd treated like a second son.

First Sparks, Then the Bomb

In Cosa Nostra, as in any warlike society caught in a cycle of revenge, killing begets killing, which leads to more killing. To fully appreciate the trajectory of homicides that led to the murders for which the Mafia Cops were convicted, we need to revisit the assassination of Big Paul Castellano, the boss of the Gambino family.

The only reason Castellano didn't get the same hundred-year sentence as his peers in the Commission case was that he never made it to trial.[46] He was gunned down outside Sparks Steak House in Manhattan on December 16, 1985, in a bold move by capo John Gotti to take over as godfather.

As Gotti's soon-to-be underboss, Salvatore "Sammy the Bull" Gravano, later testified, the two of them watched behind the tinted windows of a Lincoln parked on the northwest corner of Third Avenue and Forty-Sixth Street in Manhattan as Castellano's black Lincoln pulled up in front of the restaurant, driven by his aide and bodyguard Thomas Bilotti. When they got out, four gunmen wearing "white trench coats and black Russian hats" came out of the shadows and started firing, leaving both men dead.[47] Each was shot six times in the head and torso.[48]

As Anthony Casso tells it, Gotti's audacious move had not been sanctioned by the Commission. Thus, "Gotti would have to pay and pay dearly," wrote his biographer Philip Carlo. "Castellano was not just a boss, he was the boss of bosses and he'd been shot down in the street like some errant punk."[49]

Within twenty-four hours of the murder, Greg Scarpa Sr. told his contacting agent Lin DeVecchio that "the hit on Paul Castellano, Gambino boss, and Thomas Bilotti was set up by John Gotti and Frank DeCicco."[50] As we'll see, DeCicco, another Gambino capo, would soon pay a heavy price for his association with Gotti.

After the double hit, Anthony Casso says he was summoned to a meeting on Staten Island at the home of Lucchese consigliere Christie "Tick"

Funari. There, he says, two members of the Commission, Lucchese chief Tony "Ducks" Corallo and Vincent "Chin" Gigante of the Genoveses, "placed a bull's eye on John Gotti's . . . head."

The contract was given initially to Genovese soldiers from New Jersey, but the man who would later be known as the "Teflon Don" proved hard to kill. Eventually, says Gaspipe, he got the job.[51]

Though the intended hit was later attributed to members of the hyper-violent Westies gang,[52] Gaspipe insists that the man he used for the would-be rubout was Herbert "Blue Eyes" Pate, an ex-cop who was an explosives expert.

On the afternoon of April 13, 1986, Pate drove to the Veterans and Friends Social Club in Dyker Heights, Brooklyn, where Gotti was supposed to be attending a meeting with DeCicco. Known as "Frankie Hearts," DeCicco had conspired with Gotti to lure Castellano to the steak house rubout and his future in the reconfigured borgata seemed bright.

But while the parties met inside the club, Pate attached a bomb to DeCicco's Buick Electra. Then, believing he'd seen Gotti get into the vehicle with Frankie after the meeting, he pushed a button on a detonator. A blast rocked the neighborhood. DeCicco was killed instantly, and the man Pate mistook for Gotti—Frank Bellino—was severely injured.[53]

As it turned out, Gotti never showed up for the meeting. Sammy Gravano, who rushed over to DeCicco after the bomb went off, gave this account: "When I heard the explosion, I didn't think of a car. It was so fucking powerful, it sounded like a whole building blew up. . . . I came out of

the club and Frankie's car is in fucking flames and there's Frankie Hearts with the blood shooting out of his feet."[54]

After that botched hit, Casso says, "John Gotti prepared for all out war."

Frank DeCicco's Buick after the bombing

Chapter 18

I SHOT HIM
A COUPLE OF TIMES

Now the bull's-eye was on Casso. Five months later, on September 14, 1986, a quiet Sunday afternoon, he was sitting in his tan Lincoln Town Car finishing an ice cream cone when he spotted a dark-windowed car pulling up beside him. Before he could reach for his gun, bullets and buckshot tore into him. By Philip Carlo's account, Casso "got low and rolled catlike to the passenger side," opening the door. Wounded, he then fled in a zigzag pattern as the shooters, Jimmy Hydell and Nicky Guido, kept firing.[1]

Hydell was a low-level Gambino associate. Sammy Gravano later told the Feds that he had been "conned into thinking that Gaspipe should be killed in retaliation for DeCicco's murder." The Gambino capo who sent Hydell after Casso was Michael "Mickey Boy" Paradiso, who happened to be the brother of Philly Boy Paradiso, the alleged shooter of Sal Scarpa— another example of the few degrees of separation between these Mafia murders.[2] In *Friends of the Family*, the book he later wrote with Brooklyn Assistant DA Michael Vecchione, Detective Tommy Dades says he first uncovered the links between Casso and the so-called Mafia Cops when he got to know Betty Hydell, Jimmy's mother.[3]

"Jimmy Hydell was a stone-cold killer," wrote Dades. "He even arranged the murder of his longtime girlfriend, an innocent young woman named Annette DiBiase. . . . A friend of his shot her in the head five times and buried her in the woods."[4]

Once he'd identified Hydell as one of his assailants, Anthony Casso took swift and brutal action.

In a 1998 prison interview, Casso told Ed Bradley on *60 Minutes* that he hired NYPD detectives Lou Eppolito and Stephen Caracappa to kidnap Hydell. "Louis and Steve . . . put him in the car. . . . The kid thought they were taking him to the station house. But they took him to a garage [where] they laid him on the floor. They tied his feet, his hands cuffed, put him in the trunk of the car. The police car comes in, the guy's kicking in the trunk. He's making noise. I took him to a place that I have pre-arranged. . . . Sat him down. I wanted to know why I was shot, and who else was involved." After that, Casso said, he shot Hydell.

"I didn't shoot him in the head. That was somebody's house. You make a mess. . . . No, I shot him a couple of times."

"What's a couple?" asked Bradley.

"More than a couple," Casso replied. "Maybe I shot him ten times, twelve times. . . . At that time, I gave Louis and Steve, I think, forty-five thousand dollars for delivering him to me."[5]

Eppolito and Caracappa were also accused of working for Casso in seven other homicides, including the murder of an innocent young man named Nicky Guido who happened to have the same name as the mob-connected would-be assassin who had fired at Casso with Hydell. During a police records search of suspects, Caracappa reportedly turned up the wrong Nicky Guido's address; Casso then dispatched three killers,[6] via his associate Burt Kaplan. They visited the house of the wrong Nicky, who lived on Court Street in Brooklyn, and shot him outside his home on Christmas morning 1986.[7]

Casso admitting to the Hydell murder to Ed Bradley

The Mafia Cops. Version 2.0

On March 9, 2005, in announcing the indictment of the heavyset Eppolito and the tall, gaunt Caracappa—dubbed "Fat and Skinny" by Casso[8]—Brooklyn District Attorney Charles Hynes called the case "one of the most shocking examples of criminal activity [he'd] ever witnessed."[9] On March 30, 2006, just over a year later, while announcing the four-count murder indictment against Lin DeVecchio, who was accused of leaking key FBI intel to Scarpa that led to four deaths, Hynes used an almost identical phrase, calling the DeVecchio case "the most stunning example of official corruption [he had] ever seen."[10]

But the two cases had remarkably different outcomes.

The Mafia Cops case had been developed for months by Dades, Vecchione, and Joseph Ponzi, head of the DA's Investigations Unit. But it was eventually removed by the Feds to the Eastern District, and it was in federal court that Eppolito and Caracappa were ultimately convicted on racketeering, extortion, and the murder counts.[11] They drew life sentences that were later upheld on appeal.[12] Homicide is a state crime, and Dades and Vecchione were bitter that the multiple-murder case had eluded them. They make it clear in their book that they believed the case was usurped by Mark Feldman, a senior assistant U.S. attorney in the Eastern District.

After claiming that Feldman promised to let him try the Hydell murder first, before the Feds prosecuted Eppolito and Caracappa, Vecchione writes that Feldman reneged. In fact, he calls the AUSA's behavior "such an act of cowardice and betrayal that I couldn't find the words to explain it."[13]

Because the case was moved to federal court, for reasons we'll discuss, Anthony Casso was denied a chance to take the stand against the cops. So the Feds used Burt Kaplan as their principal witness to prove the charges.

"At least at that point," says Andrew Orena, "Hynes's office still had the DeVecchio case. It was Vecchione's chance for payback for what happened with the Mafia Cops. But as we later found out, when Lin's case blew up, that wasn't to be."[14]

The common denominator between the two scandals was Anthony Casso, and based on what he told me during our interview on September 23, 2011, we can now rewrite part of the story surrounding "Fat and Skinny," described by Dades and Vecchione in their book as "the two worst men ever to wear the badge of the NYPD."[15]

According to the account by Dades and Vecchione, when Casso first sought the names of the men who'd tried to kill him, "Burt Kaplan . . . told him that he had cops inside the Sixty-third Precinct, where the assassination attempt had taken place. Kaplan eventually handed Casso a manila envelope containing all the crime scene photos and reports—and the names of the men who had tried to kill him: Jimmy Hydell . . . and Nicky Guido."[16]

Calling Kaplan a "Liar"

But when I spoke to Casso via phone from a Supermax prison, he insisted that he first got the identities of his would-be killers from another source: Greg Scarpa Sr.

Casso said, "When Kaplan got on the stand [at the Mafia Cops trial], he testified that he met me after I got shot in [19]86, two to three weeks later, by a park in Brooklyn, and he brought me the envelope from the two detectives with all the photographs of the people who shot me and all kinds of information. But that was a lie. A total lie. When I got shot, it was on a Sunday. Greg Scarpa reached out for me the next day, Monday, and I knew who shot me, I knew everybody who shot me, I knew everybody's name. Jimmy Hydell. It was given to me that Mickey Boy Paradiso was involved. There were four people involved in the actual shooting. One kid was a young kid. They used him to drive a backup car, so I didn't hunt the kid. I let him go."[17]

When I asked Casso who supplied Scarpa with that intelligence, he named Lin DeVecchio. "Did Scarpa tell you that Lin was the source of the information?" I asked.

"No, but Joe Brewster did," Casso said. "Joe Brewster was Scarpa's right-hand man. When Greg went to meet DeVecchio a lot of the time Joe Brewster was with him. One time I'm driving by the Veterans Hospital in Brooklyn and I saw Joe Brewster walking along outside the fence in the parking lot. I pulled my car over. I got out to talk to him, and on the other side there's the Fed. It was Greg Scarpa talking to DeVecchio. That's about the first time I even heard about DeVecchio—like, his name. Joe Brewster told me, 'Here, don't let Greg see us, he's in there talking to that guy.' I don't know if Brewster ever knew that Greg was an informant. I think he thought he was just getting information from Lin."

Casso later told me that after he was shot, it was Greg Scarpa Sr. and not Burt Kaplan who identified his shooters. "Greg brought me the information," he said, "and at that time I knew Greg was getting [it] from the FBI."

Casso insists that if the defense in the Mafia Cops case had called him to testify, he could have "proven Kaplan was lying about that part of the story." For reasons we'll discuss later, however, the ex-Lucchese boss was never asked to testify.

Casso also told me that he offered to testify for Michael Vecchione at Lin DeVecchio's trial in 2007. If that had happened, his presence on the stand would have represented a living, breathing witness to Greg Scarpa Sr.'s crimes—a Mafia boss who was ready to finger Lin for the leak that led to the death of Jimmy Hydell. However, the Brooklyn DA never called him, and the trial fell apart.

Still, Casso's new revelations underscore the significance of the string of murders in 1987 that began with the death of Sal Scarpa in January and ended with the October slaying of John Otto Heidel, another associate of Gaspipe's who worked in the same Bypass gang as Joe Brewster, killed just a few weeks before him.

The Real Grim Reaper

As a man who sent 666, the so-called Number of the Beast, to the pager of his consigliere each time he made a significant kill, Gregory Scarpa Sr. must have believed in the devil. But he also believed in God. In fact, he invoked the name of the deity multiple times in the late 1980s after it became clear that the HIV he'd contracted in 1986 had turned into full-blown AIDS.

At that point he was given only months to live,[18] but he stuck it out until the summer of 1994. By then he had lost more than a hundred pounds and degenerated to the point where he had the grayish pallor and sunken eye sockets of a death camp inmate.[19]

The full story of how the real Grim Reaper caught up with Greg Scarpa is a fascinating study of "34's" own tenacity and grit. He not only stayed alive for years after doctors had predicted his death, but as the virus weakened his body, he became the violent field general in the third Colombo war—roaming the Brooklyn streets, shooting victims, and taking human life at a rate that outpaced any of his previous murder sprees. At one point, Scarpa even broke house arrest and waged a running car-to-car gun battle—at a point when most AIDS patients would have been lying in a hospice.

Years before, in a deposition, Scarpa explained his longevity this way: "The sign of my birth is Taurus, which is a bull. Take it from there."[20] He described himself as rarely sick, but for him the beginning of the end came after he developed a stomach ulcer. He denied that it was linked to any tension or the anxiety that came from his life in the mob, and no doctor ever made a definitive diagnosis. But the ulcer was the apparent by-product of large quantities of aspirin Greg started taking after back surgery in the late 1970s.

"Depending on how I felt at the time, it would average out to . . . four to six aspirin a day,"[21] he told lawyers who questioned him after he filed a negligence action against Victory Memorial Hospital in Brooklyn. The lawsuit stemmed from his hospitalization in August 1986, during which he received AIDS-tainted blood from a transfusion.

In multiple depositions, Scarpa and Linda Schiro described the day when he developed internal bleeding, growing so weak that he almost passed out. Until then, they insisted, Scarpa was at the peak of health. "He was never sick, never colds, anything," Linda swore under oath during one deposition.[22]

In addition to their account of Greg's medical circumstances, those depositions also reveal how Scarpa, long a top captain in the Colombo family, presented himself to the outside world. In one session, he described his occupation as that of a self-employed "professional gambler."[23] At the point he was hospitalized for the ulcers, he said he made "approximately . . . $700 to $750 a week."[24] That was just months after Scarpa was indicted as one of the largest traffickers in counterfeit credit cards in New York—following that incident in which he paid an undercover agent $9,000 in cash.

On the public record, however, Scarpa was consistent. In 1984 and '85, he filed tax returns with the IRS listing his occupation as "gambling."

On the 1984 1040 he declared an income of $27,400 and a year later that number had grown to $36,200, which broke down to roughly $700 a week.[25] Scarpa told the lawyers representing the hospital that his last official job had been at the age of twenty-seven or twenty-eight, when he was "employed by the United Furniture Workers of America, Local 76."[26] That was a few years before he began working with Charlie "the Sidge" LoCicero, who, Scarpa later told the Feds, had burned down Florentine Furniture to destroy IRS records.[27]

Internal Bleeding

According to Linda Schiro, the first sign that Scarpa was in medical trouble came on a weekend in August 1986. Greg looked "pale and very weak," she said; his color had turned "gray," and his stools were black. That Monday she drove him to see his doctor, Emanual Schiowitz, who found blood in Scarpa's stool.

Schiowitz suggested that he be hospitalized. They chose Victory Memorial, said Linda, because Greg had had his back surgery there and because it was "right in the neighborhood."[28] After his admission to the hospital, Greg deteriorated rapidly, said Linda. He began feeling sick and dizzy. He was losing blood, and after several days the doctors told her that his condition was "life-threatening."[29]

By the following Saturday, Linda said, one of the doctors insisted that Scarpa "needed an operation or he would die. He would bleed to death."[30] The hospital called in Dr. Angelito Sebollena to perform "emergency" surgery to stop the internal bleeding. Linda insisted that "Greg didn't want the surgery," but in later depositions Scarpa admitted that he was passing out and semiconscious by then.

Linda said they got a second opinion from another doctor, who told her that "if he didn't have that operation, he would probably die."[31] But before the surgery, Scarpa underwent a series of transfusions using blood donated by family and friends, including several Mafia associates. As Greg later testified, they used the unscreened blood because Linda was told by nurses at Victory Memorial that "she would be putting [Greg] at risk by getting hospital blood."[32]

But after the surgery, which Scarpa claimed in his lawsuit was botched, Schiro said he developed a heavy fever and was "half dead."[33] At that point, she said, Scarpa passed out and she had to drag him to his bed. Soon "everybody was in a panic because there was blood coming out from his mouth, from his nose, from all over." According to Schiro, Sebollena said, "Don't worry. I have everything under control."[34] But Linda finally hired a private ambulance and rushed Senior to Mount Sinai Hospital in Manhattan, where he was stabilized.

The Fatal Transfusion

A few weeks after his release from Mount Sinai, Scarpa was recuperating when he said he got a phone call from Dr. Schiowitz. The call began, said Greg, "with the usual niceties . . . and then he says, 'I have some news to tell you, but you shouldn't get too upset about it.' So I said, 'What's that?' [And] he says, 'You contracted the HIV virus from some blood that you received. You shouldn't get over-anxious about it because it doesn't mean that you will get AIDS.' "[35]

Scarpa, whom Lin DeVecchio described as "fearless," nonetheless called that diagnosis "devastating."[36] He later told lawyers that in short order he was able to determine who the source of the tainted blood was: Paul Mele, a reputed mob associate who had donated blood prior to Greg's surgery. Mele, whom Scarpa had known since he was seventeen, was a weightlifter who was believed to have taken intravenous steroid injections. Shortly after Scarpa got the news from his doctor, Mele, only twenty-eight at the time, died of AIDS-related pneumonia.[37]

Initially, Scarpa said that his blood's T-cell count was normal, but by 1991 it had plummeted to almost zero; he had full-blown AIDS.[38] Typically, once the measure of T cells in the blood drops below two hundred, cellular immunity is lost.[39]

By August of that summer, Scarpa was taking the drug AZT and experiencing severe side effects. "Each morning I would find myself in a condition where I would be almost like to a point of passing out," he said during a second deposition. "I would become very dizzy. It was hard for me to just . . . stand."[40]

At that juncture, he said, his doctors switched him to Virex, an antiretroviral drug that had none of the same side effects. Later, when asked if he'd had any problems with pneumonia, the illness that killed Mele, Scarpa responded that he hadn't. Then he said, "Thank God." For a man who'd been so cold-blooded about taking human life, Gregory Scarpa was now on the receiving end.

"Anybody else would have been dead at that point," says his daughter Little Linda, who spoke to me after the DeVecchio trial. "But not my father. He had amazing, amazing strength in him." So much so that, as the 1980s wound down, he started preparing for what would become the most violent and bloody conflict ever for control of the Colombo crime family.

Before that happened, however, Scarpa had to endure another trauma: the massive manhunt for his nephew Costabile "Gus" Farace, a member of the Wimpy Boys crew who was eight months out of prison when he gunned down an undercover DEA agent.

Chapter 19

MURDER ON
THE OVERPASS

By every published account, DEA Special Agent Everett Hatcher died a hero.[1] The forty-six-year-old African American agent had been with the Drug Enforcement Administration for twelve years. He was a lieutenant colonel in the U.S. Army reserve, following a six-year tour in Germany as a deputy provost marshal.[2] After finishing his active duty, Hatcher returned to New York City to teach in the public school system. In 1974 he earned a master's in education from Boston College but was drawn back to law enforcement, working as an investigator for the Manhattan DA before signing on with the DEA.[3]

Hatcher had done hundreds of undercover narcotics buys over the years, tracking Pakistani heroin traffickers and infiltrating deadly drug operations in Harlem. He'd earned multiple Special Achievement Awards. He was a weapons expert and a firearms instructor. So if any veteran operative could have walked away from what, on the surface, appeared to be a routine "third pass" meeting with a lower-tier drug dealer, it was Everett Hatcher.

On the other hand, there are serious questions about Hatcher's murder on the night of February 28, 1989, that remain unanswered—at least on the public record. Hatch, as he was known, had been working out of the FBI's offices at 26 Federal Plaza on a joint Bureau-DEA investigation of fifty-eight-year-old Gerard "Gerry" Chilli, a capo in the Bonanno family who was believed to be moving large quantities of cocaine.

Gus Farace (pronounced "fa-RA-chee") was a Colombo family associate who'd met Chilli in the Arthur Kill Correctional Facility on Staten

Everett Hatcher, Gus Farace

Island while serving a seven-year stretch for the vicious murder of a young black teenager in 1979.[4] After he was paroled in June 1988, Farace started dealing again. He was then twenty-eight, six foot three and two hundred twenty pounds, with the bulk of a steroid-using bodybuilder. In the Chilli operation, Hatcher was posing as a drug-buying, gun-selling ex-army colonel who'd gone rogue. The goal was to induce Farace into making a sale so that the Feds could flip him into informing on Chilli, who was reportedly running a cocaine-distribution ring that stretched from Florida to Staten Island.[5]

According to the memoir of Robert M. Stutman, the DEA's former chief in New York City, Hatcher first met with Farace on February 8, 1989. Two days later he bought just over an eighth of an ounce of coke from him to establish his bona fides as a criminal. The third meeting was intended to set the hook in Farace. Hatcher had reportedly suggested he'd be buying "weight" from him at the kilo level.[6]

But there were warning signs. As Stutman tells it in his book, written with veteran ABC News producer Richard Esposito, Hatcher was unhappy working at the FBI's NYO. He reportedly clashed openly with Dan Miller, his FBI supervisor, who complained to him about the time it was taking to set up Farace, and the cost: $2,500 in buy money.[7] Further, according to Stutman, there was a possibility that Hatcher's cover had been blown.

The introduction to Hatcher, whom Gus called "the Colonel," had been made for him while Farace was still an inmate at Arthur Kill. That meeting had reportedly been brokered by one William "Rebel" Liberty. But according to Stutman, another mob associate of Gus's had called and left a message with Farace's wife that the Colonel was "bad"—meaning he was either "a government informant or a federal agent." That information would take on deadly significance as the operation unfolded.

Later, Farace's cousin Dominick confessed that Gus had told him, "If the Colonel is bad, I'll do what I gotta do. Nobody is putting me back in fucking jail." It's doubtful that Hatcher would have gone through with the meeting if he'd known he'd been made as a possible informant, and it's clear that he had no knowledge of Farace's racially motivated manslaughter conviction. Retired DEA Special Agent Mike Levine, who spoke to Hatcher just hours before the killing, told me that "Everett was completely unaware that Farace had done time for the murder of another black man. If he'd known that, he would have been on hyper-alert."[8]

"A Flurry of Mistakes"

On the night of the meeting, which Farace set with Hatcher for nine P.M., Gus came armed with a stainless steel, snub-nosed Ruger Security Six .357 Magnum. In order to maintain his cover, Hatcher locked his machine gun, badge, and DEA credentials in the trunk of the Buick Regal he was driving and stashed his Glock in the glove compartment. Farace had selected a deserted overpass above Staten Island's Route 440 on Bloomingdale Road, an area that gave the three DEA backup units no chance for line-of-sight surveillance.[9] Hatcher's only protection was a T-4 voice transmitter, which had failed during an earlier meeting with Farace.

After the backup team took up positions near the overpass, the first unit, which included FBI supervisor Miller and DEA supervisor Claudia Pietras, reportedly saw the tan-colored van Farace was driving as it approached the meeting point. But they soon lost sight of the van as it pulled up behind Hatcher's Buick. Meanwhile, DEA agents Larry Hornstein and Wade Baldwin, a twenty-two-year-old rookie, waited nearby in a Mercury Cougar. A fifth agent, Tom King, was also nearby. But none of them had "eyes on" the rendezvous point. All they could make out on the faulty T-4 were parts of a conversation suggesting that the two vehicles were moving to another location, which sounded like "a diner or a restaurant." The team caught sight of the van as Hatcher followed but reportedly lost it at an intersection.

As Stutman tells it, "What had begun as a routine meeting between Hatcher and a drug dealer had now collapsed amid a flurry of mistakes. . . . The backup team was out of position, the equipment had failed and the undercover agent had moved when he was expected to stay in one place. It didn't help that the meeting had been held against a backdrop of friction between Hatcher and the FBI Supervisor on the case."[10]

An hour later, when the two units finally doubled back to the overpass, they found Hatcher sitting in his car at the original location. The Buick was in drive, but the agent's left foot was pressed against the brake. He'd been shot dead with four heavy-caliber rounds from Farace's .357 Magnum. One had struck him in the eye, another in the left ear.

Within days, a five-hundred-man task force was set up to find Farace, including four hundred agents from the DEA's New York Office and another hundred FBI agents from 26 Federal Plaza. They fanned out in a manhunt that spread across fifteen states and extended to the Cayman Islands. Hatcher was the first DEA agent killed in New York since 1972, but in the previous six months since the drug war had escalated, three other agents had been wounded.

The brutal murder of the gentle, bearlike Hatcher was the last straw.

The Feds launched an immediate crackdown on organized crime, with raids on social clubs and bookie joints that yielded two dozen arrests. President George H. W. Bush even made a special trip to New York to console Hatcher's widow, and Stutman purportedly visited the home of John Gotti in a failed attempt to enlist his help in the manhunt.[11]

It took another nine and a half months to catch Farace, but the "justice" that was done had little to do with anyone in official law enforcement. In fact, Farace was gunned down Mafia style. Although Stutman's book links Gerry Chilli to the death, the evidence uncovered in this investigation suggests that one prime suspect should have been Greg Scarpa Sr.

One of the "Bad Boys"

To appreciate just how close Gus Farace was to Scarpa, you have to consider the family ties that bound them. Gus was the nephew of Connie Forrest, Scarpa's first and only legal wife. She lived on a horse farm near Lakewood, New Jersey, where two of her sons by Greg trained as sulky drivers.[12] That farm was one of the places the joint DEA-FBI task force searched for Farace, but unbeknownst to them, he'd been hidden by Gerry Chilli's daughter Babe Scarpa, the widow of Alfred Scarpa, another relative on Greg's side who'd been gunned down a year earlier.[13]

The other co-conspirator in Hatcher's murder, present in the van on the night of the shooting, was Gus's cousin Dominick, the son of Frank Farace. Even though he was on Connie's side of the family, Frank was so close to Gregory and his son that he was living with them at 1064 Fifty-Eighth Street in Brooklyn in October 1969 when the three of them got arrested in the J&B whiskey hijacking.[14] Interestingly, when he testified about that bust during his second racketeering trial in 1998, Greg Scarpa Jr. mentioned most of those seized during the $70,000 theft, but left his uncle Frank out of it.[15] Junior was then facing his second set of federal charges in a decade, and his cousin Gus, the mad-dog killer of a hero drug agent, wasn't a family member he wanted to claim.

Still, Farace's ties to the Scarpas, father and son, were very close.

By 1979, Gus had become a regular member of the Wimpy Boys Bypass crew. Carmine Sessa included him as one of the burglars in the break-in of the Dime Savings Bank that resulted in the sudden rubout of Big Donny Somma.[16] But Gus had even closer ties to the Wimpy Boys crew. His cousin was Mark Granato, the brother of Kevin, who was indicted in the DEA bust with Greg Jr. in 1987. Kevin was one of the Wimpy Boys crew members who had dug the grave for Cosmo Catanzano.

Billy Meli, another member of the crew, later told FBI agents that, after his release from prison in 1981, he was introduced to Greg Scarpa Jr. by Kevin Granato and Gus Farace, who "used to hang out at a bar called On the Rocks" that Scarpa and his son owned on Staten Island.[17]

Two years before that, on October 8, 1979, Gus Farace, Mark Granato, and two other young Italian bullies who called themselves the "Bad Boys" had participated in a notorious gay-bashing rampage. They kidnapped two black teenagers at a club in Greenwich Village, then drove the terrified teens, ages sixteen and seventeen, to Wolfe's Pond Park on Staten Island, where they spent hours beating them. After reportedly forcing one of the boys to perform oral sex on one of the gang members, Farace clubbed him with a piece of driftwood, then shot him to death. The second victim jumped into the pond and escaped. Based on his testimony, Farace was later convicted of manslaughter and sentenced to seven to twenty-one years.[18] He'd been paroled for just over eight months when he fired the fatal shots into Hatcher.

In two expansive articles on Everett Hatcher's murder written for *New York* magazine, journalist Eric Pooley offered extraordinary details on the manhunt for Farace. Gus hid out in various safe houses on Staten Island; in Brewster, New York; and finally in an apartment on Manhattan's Upper East Side. While on the lam, he got money and resources from relatives and friends via a secret system of "mail" drops. Pooley and Stutman each describe the DEA's efforts to turn Chilli against Gus, but it's also clear that Farace had been abandoned by his uncle Greg Scarpa Sr. almost from the moment he fired on Hatcher.

"Like a Jungle Out There"

On March 4, just days after the shooting, Scarpa did something almost unheard of for a mob capo: He granted an interview to the New York *Daily News* in which he denounced his fugitive nephew. After first being outed as Farace's uncle by the *Daily News*'s David J. Krajicek,[19] Scarpa spoke to the crime reporter by phone. He told Krajicek that his family was no longer close to Farace. They hadn't even attended his recent wedding or his father's funeral. Calling Gus "a nothing; a nobody," Scarpa made it clear that, in killing a federal agent, Farace had crossed the line.[20]

"I feel that this type of thing shouldn't be," he said, likely worried that his own son, recently sentenced in the 1987 DEA case, might be punished further by being sent to a federal prison far from New York.[21]

"They could put him in Alaska, for Christ's sake," Scarpa told Krajicek, who gives an account of the unprecedented interview in his 2012 book, *Gotti and Me: A Crime Reporter's Close Encounters with the New York Mafia.*[22]

During their brief talk, Scarpa, one of the most bloodthirsty criminals in Cosa Nostra history, came off sounding like a dyed-in-the-wool Republican: "Once you start killing law enforcement people, it'll be like a jungle out there," he told Krajicek. "These people [like Hatcher] are there to keep law and order. Once you take law and order away, we become uncivilized people, behaving like animals. We need law and order, bottom line." Scarpa summarily disowned Farace in the interview. "My son wants nothing to do with him," he said. "You put the two of them in a room together, only one's going to walk out."[23]

Within days of Hatcher's murder, Gus Farace was added to the Bureau's Ten Most Wanted List. And yet, despite the fact that one hundred agents in the NYO were tracking Farace and their number one TE informant had publicly condemned him, the two references to the Hatcher killing in Lin DeVecchio's 209s during this period were cryptic and heavily redacted.

Last Name Unknown

The first reference came in a 209 dated March 13, 1989, almost two weeks after the bloody shooting. We're reproducing the relevant section of DeVecchio's report in the figures here and on the next page to illustrate that the FBI redacted virtually every key name in the document released, making it difficult, if not impossible, for any outside investigator to determine whether Scarpa admitted any of his *own* direct connections to Farace during his debriefings.

The designation "LNU" stands for "Last Name Unknown." The next page of that 209 underscores just how close Scarpa was to Farace at the

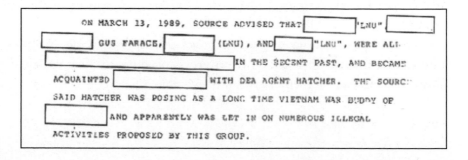

ON MARCH 13, 1989, SOURCE ADVISED THAT ☐ "LNU" ☐ ☐ GUS FARACE, ☐ (LNU), AND ☐ "LNU", WERE ALL ☐ IN THE RECENT PAST, AND BECAME ACQUAINTED ☐ WITH DEA AGENT HATCHER. THE SOURCE SAID HATCHER WAS POSING AS A LONG TIME VIETNAM WAR BUDDY OF ☐ AND APPARENTLY WAS LET IN ON NUMEROUS ILLEGAL ACTIVITIES PROPOSED BY THIS GROUP.

THE SOURCE SAID THAT HATCHER AND FARACE WORKED OUT A DEAL
INVOLVING NARCOTICS, AND AT SOME LATER TIME BECAME SUSPICIOUS
THAT HATCHER WAS IN FACT AN INFORMANT. THE SOURCE SAID THE GROUP
█████████████████████████ AND ASSUMED THAT
HATCHER HAD BEEN KNOWINGLY INTRODUCED TO THE GROUP FOR THE
PURPOSE OF EXPOSING THEIR ACTIVITIES. THE SOURCE SAID HATCHER
WAS KILLED AS A RESULT OF THIS BELIEF THAT HE HAD SET UP FARACE,
AND WAS GOING TO EXPOSE HIS ASSOCIATES.
THE SOURCE SAID THERE WERE AT LEAST TWO OTHER INDIVIDUALS
WITH FARACE WHEN HE SHOT HATCHER.

time, because when the memo was written, Greg had already learned that
Farace suspected Hatcher of being a snitch. That was a detail he could have
learned only from Farace himself, his cousin Dominick, or someone very
close to them.[24]

In his book, however, DEA chief Stutman downplays the full significance of the Scarpa-Farace connection. He writes that Gus was tied to a
"loosely linked network of young thugs who called themselves the Wimpy
Boys," apparently not realizing that the network was tightly controlled by
Scarpa Sr.[25]

Their drug "business was a shambles," he writes, "and most of the ring's
members were in prison."[26] But he somehow doesn't mention the fact that
the actual ringleader (Senior) was not only free but prospering, having
beaten the Secret Service credit card case with the help of Lin DeVecchio.

Stutman does note that "for two days after the murder [government]
raiders interrogated every Wimpy Boy connected with Farace." But was
Scarpa interviewed by any agent besides DeVecchio? We don't know.
Stutman also writes that "all telephones connected to Farace's associates
were placed under electronic surveillance." But he never tells us whether
anybody at 26 Federal Plaza actually traced *Scarpa's* calls, even though the
killer regularly phoned the FBI's NYO via what was known as the "Hello"
line located in the C-10 squad on the twenty-second floor.[27] That was the
Colombo family squad then run by Lin DeVecchio.

Chapter 20

A CONNECTION
BY BLOOD

In examining who was actually behind the rubout of Gus Farace, former New York DEA chief Robert Stutman does not name Greg Scarpa Sr. as a suspect and seriously underestimates his capabilities. Dismissing the Scarpas as a threat, he writes, "The father was ailing, his power almost gone; his son's influence limited by a jail cell."[1] Considering that within two years Senior would be the principal antagonist in the third war for control of the Colombo family, wiping out as many as six rivals himself, the idea that his power had diminished, as Stutman suggests, seems naïve.

Since he had no idea that Greg Sr. was an informant for the FBI, Stutman fails to appreciate the help "34" might have been in locating Gus. Instead he insists that the break in the case came from Gerry Chilli. "We . . . returned to pressuring a small network of people very close to Gerry Chilli," Stutman writes. " 'We want Gus,' we told them."[2] Stutman then claims that one of the Chilli associates who buckled under DEA pressure was Frank Farace, Dominick's father. But the former DEA chief seems unaware of the fact that Frank was so close to the Scarpas that he'd actually lived in their house and he'd been arrested with Senior and Junior in the J&B hijacking.[3] David Krajicek had already revealed that link in his *Daily News* piece.[4]

Still, Stutman insists that Chilli was the precipitating force in Gus Farace's demise, writing that "Frank Farace reached out for Gus's mailman Louis Tuzzio," who "caved in and decided to deliver Farace to the mob."[5]

But the Colombo associate who ferried Gus to Tuzzio was none other than Joseph Scalfani, a childhood friend of Farace's who ran the Narrows Bar & Grill on Staten Island. On the night of November 18, 1989, Gus, now with a heavy beard, was holed up in his Upper East Side safe house watching *The Godfather* on video when Tuzzio, twenty-five, called him to a meeting at his mother's house on Eighteenth Avenue and Eighty-First Street in Brooklyn.[6]

Scalfani picked him up, and as they arrived at the house in Bensonhurst, a light blue van rolled up next to them. Not even suspecting he was being set up, Gus rolled down the window. Suddenly a hail of gunfire erupted, striking Farace multiple times. Scalfani was also hit, but he slid out the passenger door and escaped. A total of sixteen rounds from .380 and nine-millimeter pistols were fired. The ox-like Farace, who was struck in the face, neck, abdomen, buttocks, and pelvis, took eleven rounds and died on the way to the hospital.

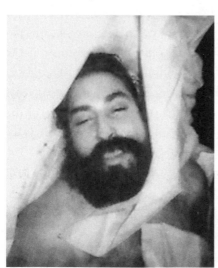

Farace after the hit

In January 1990, Tuzzio was shot to death. Seven years later, two men described by prosecutors as associates of the Lucchese family pled guilty to Farace's murder. The Feds claimed that at the time of the killing they were working on the orders of Anthony Spero, then a boss in Gerry Chilli's Bonanno family.[7] In 2001, Spero was convicted in Tuzzio's death.[8]

In his book, Stutman celebrates the Mafia "justice" that was done in this case. "Federal agents are not supposed to applaud mob executions," he writes, "but I was glad he was dead. He didn't deserve a trial."[9] Many law enforcers might have agreed with him, but despite the links to the Bonanno family in Farace's rubout, Stutman, the highest-ranking DEA official in New York at the time, ignores the possibility that the puppet master Greg Scarpa Sr. may have been involved.

The Grim Reaper's MO

Not only had Scarpa, a close relative of Farace's and his boss in the Wimpy Boys crew, taken the unprecedented step of denouncing him publicly, but his son Greg Jr., whom Senior had killed for in the past, was in jeopardy in the prison system as long as Farace remained at large. Shooting from a van was a technique Scarpa used repeatedly during the 1991–1993 war. And there was an even closer link to Greg Sr. that Stutman seemed to miss: In the transcripts of his lawsuit against Victory Hospital, Scarpa had testified that the man who ended up chauffeuring Gus to his death had been one of the few associates he'd trusted to donate blood during his 1986 transfusion: Joseph Scalfani.[10]

Scalfani survived the shooting and went on to become an associate of the Gambino family. He ended up carrying on the Wimpy Boys tradition by allegedly running a major marijuana and cocaine distribution ring out of Staten Island. As recently as August 11, 2011, Scalfani was arrested by DEA agents.[11]

As to Scarpa's links to Gus Farace's murder, it should be noted that Frank Farace demonstrated much more loyalty to Greg Sr. than he showed to Bonanno capo Gerry Chilli. Not only was Frank proposed for membership in the Colombos in June 1991, but during the war he became an active soldier in the Persico faction, run by Scarpa Sr.[12]

With respect to Anthony Spero's involvement in Farace's murder, that doesn't rule out Scarpa as a co-conspirator. During Lin DeVecchio's trial, Carmine Sessa, the former consigliere of the family, admitted that he'd used his contacts in a photo-processing store to provide Spero with surveillance photos the Brooklyn DA's office was getting developed.[13]

In that instance, the contact was Joey Ambrosino, another member of Scarpa's Wimpy Boys crew.[14] So, just as with Anthony Casso and the Lucchese family, Greg Sr. was willing to facilitate interfamily business when it suited his interests.

In my communiqués with Casso, he told me that after Hatcher's mur-

der "Greg told Farace to go into hiding."[15] And there was one other factor
that might have motivated the Grim Reaper to take a direct role in Farace's
death. According to what Carmine Sessa told FBI agents after he became
a cooperating witness, Gus Farace was an eyewitness to Scarpa's murder of
Dominick Somma in August 1980—the first murder we know of that was
committed by "34" after he was reopened by Lin DeVecchio. What would
have happened if Gus had been taken alive by DEA agents and flipped?
Would he have given up his uncle Greg to save himself?

I asked Little Linda Schiro if she thought her father had played a role
in Farace's killing. She said it was a distinct possibility. "I wouldn't put it
past my father," she said, "particularly considering how close Gus was to the
Granato brothers and how that murder [of DEA agent Hatcher] could have
really hurt Junior in jail."[16]

And what did Greg Sr. himself have to say on the matter? When David
Krajicek asked him whether he'd ordered the hit on his nephew, the reporter
recalled, "He was quiet for a moment before finally saying, 'Next question.'"[17]

Why Didn't "34" Do More?

Lin DeVecchio referred to the Hatcher murder in only one other 209. That
report, again heavily redacted, was dated January 30, 1990, ten weeks after
Farace's death:

> ON JANUARY 30, 1990 SOURCE ADVISED THAT ▮▮▮▮▮▮▮ HAS RECENTLY
> BEEN TALKING ABOUT THE "HIT" ON GUS FARACE, AND SAID THAT
> THE OPERATION WAS SET UP BY LOUIS TUZZIO AT THE REQUEST OF
> ▮▮▮▮▮▮. THE SOURCE SAID THAT ▮▮▮▮▮▮ WAS SUPPOSED TO
> BE ONE OF THE SHOOTERS AND WAS AWARE OF THE IMPENDING HIT
> ON FARACE BUT HAD NO IDEA THAT HE WAS TO BE INCLUDED. AS A
> RESULT OF ▮▮▮▮▮▮ BEING SHOT, AND THE FACT THAT ▮▮▮▮▮▮
> IS A GAMBINO MEMBER, JOHN GOTTI ORDERED THE KILLING OF LOUIS
> TUZZIO.[18]

Unless his was one of the redacted names, Scarpa's account left out any connection between himself and his nephew. But in a line sure to excite the FBI

brass, which was obsessed with "getting" John Gotti, the 209 blames the Tuzzio murder on the Gambino boss.

Despite the anemic file on "34's" discussion of the Hatcher homicide, Lin went out of his way at the end of that 209 to note that his source had "provided extremely singular information on the murder of federal fugitive Gus Farace."

The question is whether DeVecchio sought to press Scarpa for help in the manhunt for Farace, and if he did, whether Scarpa reciprocated. Why had it taken nine and a half months for Mafia killers to catch up with Gus, who was so close to his uncle Greg that Scarpa knew Farace had suspected Hatcher of being an informant? We don't know whether the DEA was privy to any of those 209s—or, if they were, whether the memos were similarly redacted.

"The only possible justification for allowing a killer like Scarpa to stay on the loose," says retired DEA Special Agent Mike Levine, "is for the help he might offer in a case like this. If Scarpa had done anything affirmative to help the FBI find Farace you can bet it would have been in those memos to the Bureau in DC. Instead, all we get are a few lines on one of the most violent murders of a DEA agent in recent New York memory."[19]

The Murderous 1980s

Whether or not Greg Scarpa Sr. played a role directly or indirectly in the murder of his nephew Gus, the record of homicides associated with "34" in the first ten years he was "controlled" by Supervisory Special Agent Lin DeVecchio is startling. The following chart lists seventeen murders directly attributed to Gregory Scarpa Sr. from June 1980, when he was reopened, to the end of 1989:

Dominick Somma	August 1980
Eli Shkolnik	December 1980
Robert "Bucky" DiLeonardi	July 1981
Alfred Longobardi, limo driver	July 1982

Sal Cardaci	January 1983
Jose Guzman, limo driver	1983
Loan shark "victim" killed at Occasions	Date unknown
Albie Variale	July 1983
Mary Bari	September 1984
Peter Crupi	August 1985
Anthony Frezza	October 1985
Albert Nacha	December 1985
Michael Yodice and Jose Lopez	December 1986
Ray Shapiro	Date unknown
Sal Scarpa	January 1987
Joe DeDomenico	September 1987

With the exception of Sal Scarpa, whose murder by his brother was confirmed by Anthony Casso and Little Linda Schiro, I've been able to document every one of these homicides independently via trial transcripts, FBI 302s, or other official sources—except for Variale, Yodice, Lopez, and Shapiro, who were named as Scarpa murder victims by Judge Pierre Leval of the Second Circuit in the appeal of Greg Jr.'s 1989 DEA conviction.[20] Of those seventeen homicides, however, the only ones mentioned in Lin DeVecchio's 209 reports to Washington were Dominick Somma, Joseph DeDomenico, and Peter Crupi.

As noted earlier, neither the Somma nor the Brewster reports implicated Scarpa. The most glaring omission, of course, was any report marking the homicide of Sal Scarpa, whose murder was covered by the *New York Times* in two separate stories. The first story appeared two days after his death on January 14, 1987.[21] The second came on October 10, when the elder Scarpa's hit was cited in an article on the ten mob-related rubouts in Brooklyn that year.[22]

The headline of the second piece was "Puzzle of Gangland-Style Killings Eludes Brooklyn Police," and it could hardly have been missed by special agents in the FBI's New York Office who worked organized crime. Lin DeVecchio, who was already running the Bonanno Squad and about to take over the Colombo Squad, surely saw it. Greg Scarpa Sr. was arguably the most important TE informant in the NYO.

How was it, then, that in DeVecchio's 209s to Washington, which reported dozens of other details from Scarpa on the Colombo family, the murder of his own brother wasn't mentioned? If it was, it wasn't included in the 1,153 pages of newly released files on DeVecchio's notorious informant. Even if Lin was ignorant of the fact that his star informant had committed the murder, how could such a high-profile rubout relating to another Colombo capo seemingly go unnoticed?

The next omission in DeVecchio's 209s arguably rises to the level of a distortion. It involves the murder of Staten Island drug dealer Peter Crupi, who was shot on August 2, 1985, as part of the takeover by the Scarpas of his distribution network on Staten Island. The rubout of Crupi, along with Albert Nacha, was cited by the EDNY U.S. attorney in the 1987 DEA case against Greg Jr. and his crew. It was that pending indictment that turned Junior into a fugitive. Yet the first reference to Crupi in one of DeVecchio's 209s didn't come until February 22, 1989, more than three and a half years later. In a six-page teletype to the FBI director, sent in March 1989, reporting on his debriefings of Greg Scarpa Sr. ("Source"), DeVecchio writes:

> ON FEBRUARY 22ND, 1989 SOURCE ADVISED THAT PETER CRUPI, A SMALL TIME MARIJUANA DEALER WAS KILLED BY A RIVAL DRUG DEALER JIMMY DUNNE IN A RIPOFF OF $25,000.00 BUY MONEY. THE SOURCE SAID DUNNE WAS KILLED IN TURN, BUT NOT BY ANY MEMBERS OF THE COLOMBO FAMILY. THE SOURCE SAID THE HIT ON DUNNE WAS PROBABLY HANDLED BY THE BRENNAN CREW, WHO AT ONE TIME HANDLED ALL THE MARIJUANA DISTRIBUTION IN THE BENSONHURST AREA OF BROOKLYN.[23]

Consider this report of a Scarpa Sr. debriefing by Lin DeVecchio against what we now know to be the truth. First, the date suggests that it was fresh intelligence, not information on a murder from 1985. Second, it ignores the alleged involvement of Greg Scarpa Jr. in the homicide. Third, the representation of Crupi, who ran a network grossing $10,000 a night, as a "small time" dealer is another distortion.

Should Lin DeVecchio have known about all of that? He was well aware of the DEA charges facing Greg Scarpa Jr. and his crew. In fact, he was later accused of leaking them to Greg Sr. Further, a November 1987 *New York Times* story on the crew's arrest listed the murders of Crupi and Nacha among the racketeering "acts" Junior was being charged with.[24] So it was clearly public knowledge. How could Greg Sr.'s principal FBI contacting agent—a supervisor then running two organized crime squads—allow FBI officials to think that Peter Crupi's rubout had taken place so recently and was unrelated to the activities of their star informant?

Could it be that Lin DeVecchio was sanitizing his 209s on "34" to shield his source? If so, that would constitute a serious violation of the Attorney General's Guidelines and could have amounted to obstruction of justice.[25]

As to the sixteen other murders during the 1980s committed by Scarpa himself or by others at his direct order, is it possible that DeVecchio was unaware of Scarpa's connection to *any* of them? In his own book, DeVecchio concedes that he knew about Scarpa's role in the murder of the limo driver who attacked Little Linda Schiro.[26] Could he have been clueless about "34's" roles in the other fifteen?

But if he *was* aware, that information never found its way into DeVecchio's 209s. Was he actively hiding Scarpa's involvement in those murders? Or did Lin DeVecchio have another motive in turning a blind eye to Scarpa's death toll?

As the years passed, homicide was the Grim Reaper's best cover. It insulated him from suspicion within his own family that he might be an FBI "rat." Testifying at DeVecchio's trial in 2007, consigliere Carmine Sessa actually gave the Bureau more credit than it deserved. The fact that Greg did "so much work," he said—meaning so many hits—caused other members to question whether he "could . . . be cooperating."[27] The hardened wiseguys in Greg's circle couldn't believe that the FBI would tolerate that kind of murderous behavior in a confidential informant.

Now, as 1989 came to a close, Greg Scarpa might have been dying of AIDS, but he wasn't showing any signs of slowing down. In fact, as the other members of the Colombo crime family were about to find out, the Killing Machine was just gearing up for his final onslaught.

PART III

Chapter 21

RUMBLINGS OF WAR

By 1991, Gregory Scarpa Sr. had earned a new nickname. Though he'd been given only months to live back in 1986,[1] he'd survived another five years and was strong enough to become the battle commander in the third war for control of the Colombo crime family. So his mob associates, who had long known Scarpa as "the Mad Hatter" and "Hannibal Lecter," now began referring to him as "General Schwarzkopf," after the relentless U.S. Army general who had led the coalition forces in Operation Desert Storm.[2]

Despite the ravages of HIV, with his T-cell count continuing to plummet, Scarpa was later described by a federal judge as "a prolific killer" who was "perhaps the most violent combatant in the war."[3] Multiple defense attorneys would later contend that Scarpa was "aided and abetted" in his "criminal pursuits" by Lin DeVecchio.[4] A series of federal appeals courts disagreed with that conclusion. But, after considering the research uncovered in this investigation, we'll let the reader decide to what degree, if any, DeVecchio was culpable.

In a 1992 indictment, federal prosecutors effectively blamed acting boss Vic Orena Sr. (a.k.a. "Little Vic") for the "violent internal war in the Colombo family." Arguing that "various members and associates" of the family "had become increasingly disenchanted" with Orena, the Feds alleged that he had been "retaining too great a share of money generated by" the borgata's "illegal activities" and was bent on becoming "the official boss," a position held by the imprisoned Carmine Persico.[5]

Virtually every media account of the war accepted this premise,[6] which was reported by veteran Mafia columnist Jerry Capeci just months before the violence broke out openly in the fall of 1991. In a piece entitled "Colombos Set to Play Family Feud," Capeci wrote, "Sources say the feud stems from Persico's desire to turn the crime family over to his son Alphonse, a reputed capo not scheduled to be released from federal prison until July 1993, and Orena's desire to keep it for himself."[7]

As the OPR internal affairs investigation later revealed, one of Capeci's alleged "sources" at the time was Lin DeVecchio.[8]

But the true origin of the third Colombo war can be traced back to the power vacuum created by Greg Scarpa's leaks of Colombo intelligence to the Bureau. That gave the Feds the probable cause they needed in the mid-1980s for the wiretaps that fueled the Mafia Commission case. After Carmine Persico was sentenced to 139 years in prison, an opening was created at the top of the family, which Scarpa brilliantly exploited. As we'll see, while Persico and his son repeatedly trusted Vic Orena with the stewardship of the family in their absence, Scarpa made a series of moves in the background that put pressure on Orena and his most loyal captains. Those actions also sparked jealousy among Persico loyalists. The end result was that Scarpa's machinations, aided by inside intelligence from the FBI, created a false schism in the Colombos that pitted the twenty-five to thirty Persico soldiers and capos against the seventy-odd members who saw Little Vic as the lawful godfather pro tem.

In fact, new evidence uncovered in this investigation suggests that Scarpa first used Carmine Sessa as a mole to get close to Orena, then manipulated Sessa into making an attempt on Orena's life, which was botched.

But Scarpa, the master strategist, had a backup plan. If Orena couldn't be removed by force, he would be framed. Compelling new evidence demonstrates that "34," the FBI's Top Echelon informant in the Colombo family, conspired to commit a murder that implicated Vic Orena Sr. in a crime he didn't commit. It was the grisly rubout of Colombo gambler, loan shark, and restaurateur Tommy Ocera.

Taking Out Little Vic

At the height of the war, after several failed attempts on his life, Orena was convicted of Ocera's murder. He was sentenced to concurrent life terms in prison and fined more than $2,250,000.[9] But the evidence we've developed shows multiple links to Scarpa Sr. in Ocera's rubout. Not only was there proof that Scarpa stalked him, but Greg Jr. himself has confirmed that his father had guns planted at a safe house where Orena was hiding during the war—evidence seized by the FBI that led to Orena's guilty verdict and life sentences.[10] Thus, in the end, "34," the Machiavellian plotter, succeeded in getting the Feds to do in court what he couldn't accomplish in the street through Sessa: namely, taking Little Vic out of play.

Although Orena appealed the verdict and sought a new trial multiple times, he was repeatedly turned down by Judge Jack B. Weinstein, the former chief judge of the Eastern District, who also rejected multiple arguments by defense lawyers who effectively blamed the war on a conspiracy between Greg Scarpa Sr. and his FBI handler Lin DeVecchio. In a 101-page decision rejecting Orena's first petition in 1997, Weinstein described the evidence against Orena at trial as "overwhelming."[11]

Then, after new evidence surfaced revealing DeVecchio's questionable relationship with Scarpa, Orena petitioned again for a new trial. But Judge Weinstein rejected that motion as well.[12] Vic Orena's indictment was one of the first of seventy-five brought by the Feds in connection with the third Colombo war,[13] and in a related case in 2001 Weinstein made it clear that pursuing the Scarpa-DeVecchio scandal further might cause those other prosecutions to "unravel."[14]

Today, at the age of seventy-eight, Orena is serving his life sentence at the U.S. penitentiary in Terre Haute, Indiana. At this point, with his appeals exhausted, he has little hope of seeing the light of day outside prison. But while he may be guilty of other, lesser Mafia crimes, a compelling case can be made for his innocence in the Ocera murder—particularly in light of what we now know about Greg Scarpa's leading role in propagating the war.

One of the Jolly Boys

In order to examine fairly whether Vic Orena was framed for the Ocera killing, it is helpful to measure his style of management in the Mafia against that of Greg Scarpa. "Vic was essentially a nonviolent racketeer who was an incredible earner," says one lawyer who represented him.[15] Short and stocky, with piercing green eyes, Orena made millions at the height of his career as an acting boss through loan sharking, labor racketeering, and a scheme to siphon profits from gasoline taxes. But he refused to deal in narcotics, and before the war was sparked—by a threat to *him*—he never even carried a gun. Orena was a brilliant businessman who reliably kicked his profits up to Persico, which is why the Snake trusted him to be acting boss. But he was a serious impediment to Greg Scarpa, who sought to dominate the family, and new evidence demonstrates that Scarpa Sr. conspired to take him down.[16]

I did an extensive series of interviews with three of Orena's five sons: Andrew, a film producer who was never involved in the mob, and his older brothers, John (known as "Johnny Boy") and Vic Jr., both of whom were made members of the Colombo family. By 2007, when we first talked, the latter two had each been paroled after serving prison sentences.

Often referred to as "Vic Jr.," Victor, the son, was christened Victor Michael Orena. (His father was Victor John.) The younger Vic had been a Colombo captain. As we'll see, both he and John were initially acquitted by a jury in 1995 after evidence of the Scarpa-DeVecchio relationship surfaced.[17] It proved to be a stunning rebuke for the Feds and an embarrassment that threatened all of the Colombo war cases.[18] But the brothers were later convicted of other mob-related crimes. The three older sons and their younger brothers, Peter and Paulie (also "civilians"), have worked for years to establish their father's innocence in the Ocera murder and secure his release.

Born Vittorio Orena on August 4, 1934, the elder Orena earned the nickname Little Vic after anglicizing his name to Victor.[19] When he was five years old his father died, and according to Andrew, it affected him deeply:

"My grandfather was dying of tuberculosis," he told me, "and my father was at his bedside. When my grandfather got thirsty he would ask him for water and my father would run and get it. One day when he was close to the end, my grandfather said, 'Vito, *acqua* . . .' And when my father came back, *his* father said, 'I'm not gonna need it. I just saw the Lady in White,' meaning the Virgin Mary. So when he died, my father took it as a sign that God was not really there for him. After that, without a strong male figure to guide him, he took another path in life."

Vic's antipathy toward the church only increased, Andrew said, after he was sent to Lincoln Hall, a reform school that the *New York Times* referred to as "a Roman Catholic home for maladjusted boys."[20]

By the time he became a teenager, Vic was running with the Jolly Boys, described by Vic Jr. as "a classic 1950s gang of Italian and Irish kids" who rumbled with other gangs. "It was all leather jackets and zip guns," he said. "They did a series of petty crimes. But it was around this time that my father experienced a real humiliation from the cops."

"He was always a snappy dresser," Andrew said, picking up the story. "He loved clothes and prided himself in his appearance. He had a great head of hair, which he combed in a pompadour like they did back then. But one day my father took a pinch for some minor offense and the police said, 'Come here, you little Guinea bastard.'"

"They took him into the precinct and shaved off all his hair," said Vic Jr.

After that, said Andrew, Little Vic got a box of cherry bombs and exploded them in front of the police station. "And that only got him in more trouble."

Unlike other street gang veterans like Carmine Persico and Anthony Scarpati, who joined the Colombo family with lengthy police records, Orena's rap sheet was relatively clean. According to longtime *New York Times* reporter Selwyn Raab, Orena had "minor busts for gambling and one for perjury, without prison time." The longest he served was a four-month stretch in a Long Island jail for loan sharking.[21] Even Lin DeVecchio described Orena in his memoirs as "a successful loan shark, bookmaker, construction mogul and waste-hauling tycoon," but "not a volatile hair trigger like some."[22]

Vic Orena, 1980s

Little Vic soon became known for his business acumen. By 1987, an FBI 209 from Lin

DeVecchio noted that "Vic Orena is heavily involved in the gas tax scam operation on Long Island."[23] Initially developed by Russian gangsters, who controlled hundreds of gas stations in the New York area, the scheme resulted in the theft of up to thirty cents a gallon siphoned off by the Colombos, who had muscled in on the Russians' action. Astonishingly, the IRS estimated that up to $1 billion a year in federal tax revenue was being lost, with 10 percent of that—or $100 million a year—going to the mob.[24]

In 1986, Michael Franzese, the Colombo capo who first tapped into the scam after being asked to collect a $70,000 debt, was listed as number eighteen on *Fortune* magazine's list of the "fifty most wealthy and powerful mob bosses."[25] And while Vic Orena Sr. wasn't quite in that league, he was still raking in millions a year for the borgata.

Old-School and Anti-Drugs

As one indication of Vic Orena's earning power, Kenneth Geller, a Long Island accountant who confessed to his role in a murder conspiracy[26] and falsifying up to three thousand tax returns,[27] once borrowed $1 million from the Orenas. Geller used the money, in turn, to make loans at usurious rates in an effort to feed his gambling habit. At one point, he admitted that he was paying the Orenas $12,200 a week in vigorish, or interest, on those loans.[28] But Geller wasn't making the payments under the threat of physical harm, like Scarpa's clients. Even though the government portrayed him as a "victim,"[29] in more than one hundred undercover recordings Geller made for the FBI of his dealings with John Orena, not a single one showed any evidence that he was being leaned on or physically pressured to pay the vig.[30]

Further, in none of those tapes or the dozens of other hours of surreptitious recordings entered as evidence by the Feds at Vic Sr.'s 1992 trial was there a hint that Orena or his sons sold narcotics.

"He was making this kind of money without having to resort to drug dealing," Andrew told me. "When it came to dope, my father was totally against it. He not only refused to sell it, but he wouldn't tolerate anybody dealing it in the family."[31]

Even Joseph "Joey Brains" Ambrosino, one of the government's main witnesses against Vic Sr. in the Ocera trial, described a meeting at a restaurant in March 1991 attended by Robert "Bobby Zam" Zambardi, a longtime member of Scarpa's Wimpy Boys crew, and his stepson "Jerry Boy" Chiari,[32] whom he was proposing for induction into the family. According to Ambrosino, Orena told Chiari that "if he behaves himself and . . . gets out of the drug business, that he [Orena] would make sure he got 'straightened out,'" i.e., "made."[33]

To underscore his father's antipathy to drug dealing, John Orena told me a story about a phone call he got one night from his father in 1990.

Vic Sr. wanted John to drive him to a prison to pick up an old friend who had just been paroled after serving eighteen years for armed robbery. "This guy had nobody else to pick him up," said John, "so he called my father. We drive to the prison and the guy gets in the car. Right away he says to my father, 'Vic, if you don't mind, I gotta ask your advice. I just got out of jail. I'm broke, I have two kids to support, and I got a chance to make some money.' And my father knows where the guy's goin' with this. He says, '*That* business?' Meaning drugs. And the guy says, 'Yeah.' My father shakes his head and says, 'Listen, you have a son?' The guy says, 'Yeah.' My father asks, 'How old?' The guy says, 'Twenty-one, twenty-two.' And my father looks him straight in the eye and says, 'Then why don't you go home and kill him?' And the guy can't believe it. He looks at my father and says, 'Vic, what're you *talkin'* about? Why would I—' And my father cuts him off. He says, 'You might as well do it. Shoot him. 'Cause if you're sellin' dope, you'll be killin' somebody *else's* son.'"

"That's how dead against it he was," said Vic Jr.

"He looked at it with that old-school mentality," said Andrew. "It was antifamily. It tore people apart. You remember that scene in *The Godfather* where Don Barzini wants to sell it to the blacks and another boss calls them 'animals'? Well, my father didn't see it like that. He grew up with black kids. He lived with Jewish people. He was one of the most tolerant men I ever met, and he just drew the line when it came to drugs."

"It was a matter of principle," said Vic Jr. "But my father was also a practical man and he knew that drugs would be the end of this thing they had." According to Vic's three older sons, whom I interviewed, it was their father's intolerance for drug dealing that ultimately put him on a collision course with Gregory Scarpa.

From Soldier to Boss

In order to understand fully the role that Greg Scarpa Sr. played in instigating and waging the third war, it's necessary to go back and examine the path taken by Vic Orena Sr. in the Colombo family, where he'd been a trusted and favored surrogate of the Persicos until the conflict broke out. It's also important to consider that until the violence erupted in 1991, Greg Sr. had worked for years to undermine Carmine Persico's position in the family. The newly released files document how Senior—who claimed to be fighting for the "Persico faction"—routinely informed on the Snake.

As far back as August 1967, Scarpa told his FBI handlers that Persico was "operating a large numbers operation in Brooklyn."[34] In 1970 Anthony Villano, Senior's third contacting agent, noted that "there has always been 'bad blood' between [SCARPA] and PERSICO."[35]

During the second war with the Gallos, Scarpa not only suggested that Persico may have had a role in the attack on Joseph Colombo,[36] but he pointedly blamed Persico for the rubout of Crazy Joe Gallo in 1972.[37] And ultimately it was "34" who provided the lion's share of probable cause that resulted in Persico's century-long sentence in the Commission case.[38] A 209 sent to FBI Headquarters in Washington after Scarpa's death in 1994 even reported that Greg Sr. "hated the Persicos."[39]

"Does that sound like the kind of loyalty that would have inspired Greg Scarpa to kill for Carmine Persico?" asks Vic Orena's former attorney Flora Edwards. "Of course not."[40]

On the other hand, the 209s demonstrate how Vic Orena was given more and more responsibility by "Junior" Persico shortly after the boss drew back-to-back sentences of thirty-nine years in November 1986[41] and one hundred years in January 1987.[42] After the first sentence, a three-man ruling "committee" was set up by Persico to run the family's day-to-day operations. The troika consisted of Vincent "Jimmy" Angelino, Joseph "Joe T" Tomasello, and Benedetto "Benny" Aloi, who later became consigliere.[43]

At that point, Orena, who joined the borgata in 1980,[44] had been a trusted soldier in the crew run by Carmine Persico's son Little Allie Boy. But when both Periscos went off to the U.S. penitentiary in Marion, Illinois, Orena was elevated to acting capo of that crew.[45]

Carmine had originally intended to appoint his brother Alphonse as the family boss in his absence. "Big Allie," as he was known, was the boyfriend of Mary Bari, and it was the alleged fear that she would disclose his location that had led to her death. As noted, though, Alphonse Persico skipped out on a loan-sharking charge in 1980, forfeiting a $250,000 bond,[46] only to be captured and sentenced to twenty-five years in December 1987.[47]

And so, with Big Allie unavailable to run the family, Little Allie Boy not due for release until 1993, and "Jimmy" Angelino also facing jail, in the summer of 1987 Carmine Persico reconfigured the ruling "committee" to include Aloi, Joseph "Jo Jo" Russo, and Vic Orena.[48]

Sometime that fall, Vic Jr. was also inducted into the family.[49]

By April 8, 1988, as a result of Vic Sr.'s continuing loyalty and earning power, Persico finally decided to elevate him to "acting boss," scrapping the three-man control structure.[50] At that point, Benny Aloi was appointed underboss and Angelino, still free at that time, was made consigliere. But Persico, the imprisoned family boss, so trusted Orena that he invested him with a crucial power: Without seeking permission from the Snake, Orena could induct new soldiers to grow the family's ranks.[51]

"I can't emphasize enough how significant Carmine's trust was in my father," said Andrew Orena.[52] "A boss doesn't hand the keys to the family to a nonrelative unless he knows for sure that he won't betray him."

In his epic study of the Mafia, *Five Families*, Selwyn Raab offered some insight into why that happened for Vic Sr. "Orena was well regarded among the Colombo cognoscenti for his business acumen," he wrote. "A mobster with decades of unfailing service to the Persico wing of the family, Orena skillfully handled major loan-sharking and labor rackets, principally on Long Island."[53]

But the rap by the Feds would soon be that Vic's ambition got the best of him. The government's position, and the theory argued by federal prosecutors in all the Colombo war cases, was that Vic Sr. ignited the third war in a move to become the official head of the borgata. Lin DeVecchio expressed that position best in his book:

As obsessed as Junior was at installing his heir apparent as Boss, Orena became equally obsessed with making his acting Boss job permanent.[54]

But the very FBI 209s that Lin DeVecchio wrote documenting the war from Scarpa's perspective also reveal "34's" behind-the-scenes moves to destabilize the family and dominate the Colombos. Nearly three decades earlier, one of the first airtels to J. Edgar Hoover detailing Scarpa's role as a Top Echelon informant had predicted that a bid by Greg's padrone Charles LoCicero to take over the borgata "would place this source [Scarpa] . . . at the top operational level" of the Colombos. By 1989, using Carmine Sessa as his surrogate, Scarpa launched a plan to put himself in that position. It started, the evidence shows, with the brutal murder and burial of Tommy Ocera.

Chapter 22

DEATH BY WIRE

In the fall of 1989, Tommy Ocera was one made member of the Colombo crime family who seemed to have it *made.*[1] He was part owner of the Manor, a successful restaurant and catering hall in the upscale suburb of Merrick, Long Island.[2] He earned income from a refuse-carting business[3] and owned a part interest in a gasoline supply company.[4] He had a successful loan-sharking "book"[5] and he ran two gambling clubs.[6] A former prizefighter, Ocera was having an affair with Diane Montesano, an attractive retired flight attendant for TWA who was now manager of his restaurant.[7]

But five weeks later, after a tiny slip-up in which his loan-shark records were seized by law enforcers, Ocera disappeared. According to the Feds he was suspected of skimming from the Colombo family and brutally slain. Two years later, his body was discovered, strangled with a wire and stabbed in the neck. His remains had been shoved into a car trunk before being dumped in a shallow grave.

It was Vic Orena's conviction for Ocera's murder that put him away for life. But new evidence developed in this investigation raises a question: Was Tommy just another casualty of the dangerous wiseguy life, or was he a pawn in Greg Scarpa's larger strategic plot to dominate the family? Whatever the answer, one thing is clear: The story behind Ocera's rubout played out like a graphic episode of *The Sopranos.*

The Five-Martini Lunch

The Manor restaurant opened for business on Columbus Day 1988. Tommy Ocera was the only one of the three partners who'd run a restaurant before, but over the next eleven years more than thirty-six thousand customers enjoyed the Manor's Italian cuisine.[8] Every Monday night, according to Diane Montesano, whose husband, Anthony, was a co-owner, Tommy's "friends" would come by. Among the most prominent were Vic Orena and his sons, who often took one of the two large tables in the back. Later in December, when Carmine Sessa's brother Michael got made, his induction ceremony took place at the Manor. Among the other associates who swore a blood oath to the borgata that night was Vincent "Schwartzie" Cascio, who frequently drove for Little Vic.[9]

Ocera often divided his time between the restaurant and his Long Island gambling clubs, located on Merrick Road and Post Avenue. They featured card games and Joker Poker machines. Tommy also had loan-shark money "on the street," and he regularly got envelopes from a man who was in the carting business, which at that time was dominated by the Lucchese and Genovese families.[10] Then, in early October 1989, something happened that marked the beginning of the end for Tommy Ocera.

On October 5, investigators for the Suffolk County Police served a search warrant on the Manor. Raiding Ocera's office, they confiscated a series of business records, including a "Week-at-a-Glance" appointment book that was sitting in the open on Tommy's desk. Diane Montesano, who'd left her husband five months earlier, was at the restaurant at the time of the raid. By now she was romantically involved with Ocera.

Four days later, Ocera drove Montesano to the police department in an effort to get the records back. Detectives returned a desk calendar marked with upcoming catering events and a business checkbook, but Tommy was shocked to learn that they'd decided to hold on to the small appointment book. In it, according to the Feds, along with the names and phone numbers of vendors who supplied the restaurant, was a series of Ocera's hand-written notes detailing various shylock loans.

After leaving the detectives, Ocera was so worried about those records that he went to a restaurant with Montesano and tossed down five martinis in rapid succession. Since he was too drunk to drive, she drove him back to her place to let him sleep it off. As she later testified under oath, Montesano then went back to work.

Later that night Vic Jr. and John Orena visited the restaurant. They asked to speak to Tommy, so Montesano took them to see him, driving to her house with the two brothers following in their own car. At that point, Montesano sensed no hint of any threat to Ocera. She later testified that Vic Sr. always behaved like "an absolute gentleman" when he came to the restaurant,[11] and she had no reason to suspect that his sons would act otherwise. She let Vic Jr. and John into her house, where Tommy was sobering up, then drove back to the Manor and closed up for the night.

Things stayed quiet for the next two weeks and no evidence was ever presented by the government that Tommy felt threatened at that point. Then, on the night of October 22, Diane Montesano and Ocera were leaving the club around one thirty A.M. after closing for the night. Diane was carrying the cash receipts from the restaurant, which she was taking home to deposit the next day, so Ocera walked her to her car.[12]

As they approached their vehicles, Montesano noticed two cars across the street parked in the lot of the nearby Long Island Rail Road station. "I knew there were no trains coming in or leaving at this time," she later testified.

Tommy got in his car and pulled out of the restaurant lot first, but Diane was concerned that there might be a break-in at the restaurant. So rather than following Ocera, she boldly drove across to where the two cars were parked. As she approached them, she noticed that each car had dark tinted windows. The headlights were off but the engines were running. One of the cars had a broken taillight, she testified, and she could just make out "two figures" in each vehicle. She was "concerned," she said, "because [she] carried all the monies from the restaurant."

Now, having lost sight of Ocera's car, Montesano headed home. Since "there was not a direct route to [her] house,"[13] she followed a series of side streets that "curved and turned"—until suddenly she came upon a Cadillac in front of her with New Jersey plates. Later, Montesano would recall that it was one of the two cars from the railroad station. Apparently the driver knew the way to her house, and as he drove past a streetlight, Diane could just make out his face. She later picked his picture out of a series of FBI surveillance photographs of Colombo family members.

It was Gregory Scarpa Sr.

Driving at Her Head-On

The Caddy turned off on a side street, she said, but when she got home a few minutes later she noticed the other car from the LIRR station parked "directly in front" of her house. Afraid that she might get cornered in her driveway, Montesano drove past it, when suddenly, "a car came towards [her] with its lights off," then "put on [its] bright headlights."

The streets were wet and covered with leaves. As the vehicle came at her head-on, Diane was forced to swerve up onto the sidewalk.

"I almost lost control of my car," she testified. But somehow she managed to drive past the car, roaring up the street and quickly turning. Then suddenly, she found herself once again confronting the Cadillac. "The car that I had been following with the New Jersey plates . . . had turned in the opposite direction and was now in front of me," she said.

Somehow, Montesano was able to get past it. Then, about two minutes later, she encountered Tommy Ocera, who was now approaching her house in his vehicle. Ocera quickly parked and got into her car. She told him what had happened and switched off her headlights. For the next few minutes, she said, they drove quietly through the back streets of her neighborhood trying to assess the situation.[14]

At that point Ocera suggested that they drive to Brooklyn, but when they approached the entrance to the Southern State Parkway, they were surprised to see that one of the cars from the LIRR station—the one with the broken taillight—was half a block in front of them.

Tommy quickly told her to keep going and they found the next parkway entrance. Montesano testified that they drove for a few miles, then pulled off the Southern State and went to an all-night diner. From there, she said, Ocera called his daughter Tracey, who lived with him. He told her to "lock the doors and stay in the bedroom" until he arrived. After that, Diane and Tommy drove back to the Manor to make sure there hadn't been a break-in.

They then returned to Diane's place so Ocera could pick up his car. It was now about four thirty A.M.

Montesano approached her front door warily and unlocked it. There was no sign of any forced entry as Tommy accompanied her inside. He stayed for a while and Montesano gave him a shotgun that her husband had kept for home protection. As he drove home, Montesano later testified, Tommy stayed on his car phone and talked to her all the way. When he got inside his house and saw that his daughter was safe, he called Diane. "Everything was fine," he told her.

According to Montesano, they both worked the next night. Vic Orena Sr. came in with a small party, including his driver Schwartzie Cascio. At one point, the incident from the night before came up. Vic seemed to laugh it off. He joked with Montesano that she was "a very good driver" and maybe he could hire her to replace Schwartzie.[15] In her testimony at Vic Sr.'s trial, she expressed no sense of any threat from the acting boss, who she insisted had treated her cordially.[16] Nor did she indicate that Tommy Ocera was concerned about retaliation from Orena or his sons. But after that night, at what she described as Ocera's "request," she and Tommy started parking their cars away from each other in the restaurant lot.

A few weeks later, on the night of November 12, Montesano and Ocera went to a small club near the restaurant after work to hear the piano player from the Manor, who was performing a solo engagement. Ocera seemed to be in a good mood, she said. He bought a round of drinks for the pianist and the people sitting at the bar. Later he accompanied Diane back to her place and stayed for a few hours before leaving.

It was the last time she saw him alive.

The Feds' Account of Ocera's Hit

On April Fools' Day 1992, at the height of the third Colombo war, Vic Orena Sr. was arrested for Tommy Ocera's murder. He was seized in the basement of the house of his girlfriend, Gina Reale, the daughter of a Gambino family associate.[17] Orena's sons Andrew and John were with him at the time.

There were four shotguns in the house, which they contend were for protection. By that point Greg Scarpa had already murdered one member of their faction, and six weeks later he'd rub out a second. At the time of the arrest, based on the word of James Fox, then the assistant director in charge of the FBI's New York Office, the *New York Times* reported that "two assault rifles" were seized at this house, but that was untrue.

The Feds later claimed to have found "a small arsenal" at the safe house,[18] but the only other weapons discovered were six handguns and two magazines curiously found in a plastic garbage bag under an open deck behind the house.[19] A single latent fingerprint was lifted from the bag, but it failed to match any of the "various subjects of the investigation," including Orena.

Later, when Vic's lawyers requested the bag for analysis, it had gone missing.[20] Gregory Scarpa Jr. would later testify that the guns were planted by his younger brother Joey under the direction of his father, Greg Sr.[21] At the time of the arrest, the yard around the house was open, with no fence preventing access to the deck.[22] Yet, in attacking the defense's planted-gun theory, prosecutors at Orena's trial showed the jury pictures of the backyard *after* it had been fenced in.[23]

Also seized at the house were a number of cell phones, bulletproof vests, and Cole reverse phone number directories, which the Feds argued Vic Sr. and his sons were using to hunt their rivals on the Persico side of the family. But as we'll see, despite some retaliatory attacks, the Orena faction largely spent the war playing defense, while Scarpa, in his General Schwarzkopf mode, amped up the death toll.

When it came to the Ocera murder, the U.S. attorney for the Eastern District provided no direct evidence linking Vic Orena to the crime. The best the prosecutors could offer was a case built entirely on circumstantial evidence and hearsay.

Freelance Undertaker and Killer

According to the Feds, one of the lead killers in the Ocera murder was Giachino "Jack" Leale, a florist and undertaker.[24] But the U.S. attorney was forced to tell the story of Ocera's brutal rubout through the testimony of Michael Maffatore and Harry Bonfiglio, two low-level Colombo henchmen, whose description of the killing came via second- and thirdhand hearsay information. Facing life sentences, both men had cut deals with the

Feds, and they made far-from-reliable witnesses. Maffatore, an eleventh-grade dropout, was a self-described dealer and user of angel dust (PCP) who admitted that the drug often made him "see things that [weren't] really there."[25] Meanwhile, the sixty-two-year-old Bonfiglio confessed that he'd experienced "memory loss" after a stroke.[26]

Throughout the trial, Orena's aggressive attorney Gus Newman repeatedly objected to the pair's hearsay testimony, but Judge Weinstein overruled most of his objections under an exception to the Rule Against Hearsay for co-conspirators. Newman argued that these lower-tier Colombo associates could hardly be considered *co-conspirators* of Vic Orena—particularly once the war had started and they were on the other side. But Weinstein rejected that argument, finding that "the ongoing Colombo conspiracy was continuing and that these conversations were in aid and during the continuance of the conspiracy."[27]

Such rulings from Weinstein helped prosecutors Andrew Weissmann, George Stamboulidis, and John Gleeson to convict Orena for the Ocera homicide based in part on their witnesses' hearsay accounts.

Maffatore, who admitted committing arson and robbery, had also dealt cocaine and pot and did time for smuggling three hundred pounds of marijuana into New York.[28] As recently as January 1991, he'd been jailed after back-to-back coke sales to undercover cops and was facing life in prison as a "persistent felon." On the stand, Maffatore admitted that in the fall of 1989 he was on a work release program for a previous offense and was supposed to be working at a pizzeria by day, but in fact he was driving for Leale, the mortician-florist, whom he'd met on July 4.

Leale, who was reportedly a made guy,[29] lacked the funds to own his own funeral home, so he did freelance wakes for various underworld associates.[30] Maffatore had been introduced to Leale by Jack's brother-in-law Harry Bonfiglio, a ninth-grade dropout who'd formerly driven brewery trucks. Maffatore lived near Bonfiglio in Middle Village, Queens. While Bonfiglio admitted he'd never met Tommy Ocera, Maffatore said he'd met him twice after driving Leale to meetings at the Manor in October 1989.

Maffatore also ran into Ocera a third time, he said, when he visited one of Tommy's gambling clubs. At that point, he claimed that he'd also met Pasquale "Patty" Amato, an associate of Vic Orena Sr.'s who was purportedly Leale's capo.

Central to the testimony of both Maffatore and Bonfiglio was a trip they claimed to have taken with Leale sometime in November 1989, after Leale was allegedly contacted by Little Vic.

Each of them testified that they'd driven with Leale to a "social club" run by Orena in Cedarhurst, Long Island.[31] After Leale left the car, which Maffatore was driving, the pair claimed that he met with Vic Sr. for a "walk-and-talk" lasting about fifteen minutes.

Maffatore said that when the acting boss and the soldier reportedly returned to the car, he heard nothing of the conversation.[32] But Bonfiglio, who was sitting just behind him in the backseat, insisted that he somehow overheard Vic say, "I want this thing taken care of."[33] In Maffatore's version of events, Leale got in the car and waited five minutes before telling them that he'd received "a contract" to kill Tommy Ocera. As Bonfiglio told it, Leale disclosed the alleged contract as soon as he entered the vehicle.

The jury was left to decide how plausible it was that a Mafia boss would order a low-level soldier to undertake a hit—not to mention allowing two even lower-level crew members to overhear him. But Maffatore went further, claiming that after the Orena meeting he drove Leale to Ocera's gambling club on Merrick Road, where he met "Big Patty" Amato. At that point, Maffatore said he overheard Amato telling Leale that "they didn't want [Ocera's] body found."[34] Bonfiglio was also supposedly present, but he claimed he was "in the kitchen" and wasn't privy to that exchange.

Nevertheless, Maffatore testified that on the night of November 13, 1989, he got a call from Leale instructing him and Bonfiglio to meet Leale the next day at his house and bring their own cars. Maffatore drove a Ford LTD and Bonfiglio a four-door Dodge Aspen. The next morning, after they arrived at Leale's place, Leale reportedly told Bonfiglio to leave the Aspen. He'd meet them later at a diner.

According to Maffatore, "Jackie [Leale] showed up about 10:30 A.M. with Tommy['s body] in the trunk of the car."[35] He then purportedly instructed the two of them to drive the car back to their neighborhood in Queens and wait for his call. Maffatore said that he balked because his trunk was ajar, but Leale insisted.

Later, Bonfiglio testified, he drove all the way back to Middle Village along the Southern State Parkway on Long Island with a part of the body bag containing Ocera's remains "exposed."

Chapter 23

BRAINS, BUTCHER, AND BULL

According to Maffatore's testimony, the car sat outside Bonfiglio's house on a public street in Queens for more than ten hours. Later, when Harry's wife asked to use it, he refused to let her and told her it was "because there [was] a body in the trunk."

At that point she "ran in the house" screaming.[1]

Later that night, after buying picks and shovels, the two men reportedly drove with Harry's son and his friend George to Forest Park in Queens. There they dug a hole, but Maffatore said that as they carried Ocera's remains, they dropped them and the body bag went "down the hill." They finally buried the corpse in a shallow grave and went back to Bonfiglio's house, only to discover that they'd forgotten the pick they'd used to dig the grave. So rather than leave one of the burial tools at the site, Maffatore said, he went back to retrieve it. According to Bonfiglio, two days later Leale was given both of Ocera's gambling clubs as a reward for his participation in the hit.[2]

Neither of these two witnesses for the Feds was a party to Ocera's murder. The only thing they could testify to with any certainty was the burial of the body. Nonetheless, the jury was permitted to listen as Bonfiglio claimed that Leale and Amato met Ocera at Amato's house and "Patty put him down" while "Jack whacked him"—purely hearsay, since Bonfiglio was not there at the time.[3] Similarly, Maffatore admitted that all the information he had about Vic Orena had come indirectly from Jack Leale.

But Leale, who would have been a better witness, never took the stand. And for good reason: Jack the undertaker had himself been murdered on or about November 4, 1991, in what turned out to be the first homicide of the third Colombo war.

At that time, Lin DeVecchio filed the following 209 based on what he'd heard about the killing from Greg Scarpa:

> The recent hit on JACK LEALE was done by the ORENA faction of the COLOMBO Family, although the PERSICO side was as anxious to have LEALE "hit." The source said LEALE made the fatal mistake of relying on too many non-made individuals to dispose of TOMMY OCERA's body, which was subsequently found by the FBI. The source said LEALE was obviously set up by someone he trusted.[4]

In his book, *We're Going to Win This Thing,* DeVecchio quotes from that 209—but tellingly leaves out the last line about Jack's being "set up." That might be because the likely candidate for the person "he trusted" was DeVecchio's own informant, Greg Scarpa. As demonstrated in the numerous 209s that DeVecchio filed throughout the war, either Scarpa misled his control agent about murders he was committing himself, or DeVecchio knew about his informant's activities and filed incomplete reports about them to his superiors. In either scenario—whether Lin acted with intent or negligence—it's clear that Greg Scarpa was controlling the flow of intelligence and spinning it his way.

With Leale dead, the Feds had to rely on Maffatore to speak for him, but the former PCP dealer's testimony alone would have been insufficient to convict Orena without corroboration. So the FBI induced him to wear a wire on Bonfiglio, who was arrested and indicted as a co-conspirator. Though at first Harry was unwilling to cooperate, once he was tried and convicted in January 1992 Bonfiglio finally agreed to flip. Significantly, Maffatore admitted under cross-examination that while Bonfiglio mentioned Patty Amato and Jackie Leale many times in surreptitious recordings, he never mentioned Vic Orena.[5]

At one point in the tapes, Bonfiglio joked to Maffatore that if he'd been caught with the body in his trunk, "[a] hundred fuckin' years I would have got. They would have melted the key."[6] While both witnesses were facing life sentences before their testimony against Orena, each admitted that, based on the deals they'd cut with the Feds, they could end up with "zero" jail time.

Another witness who testified, "Joey Brains" Ambrosino, added different details about the murder, but they were thirdhand. Ambrosino claimed that Carmine Sessa had told him that the murder in Patty Amato's house involved Leale; Thomas Petrizzo, a Colombo captain loyal to Vic Sr.; and Frank "Chickie" Leto. Since Sessa wasn't present at the murder either, Ambrosino was two steps removed from the rubout. But that didn't stop him from adding at least one new detail: that Ocera had been stabbed "in the neck."[7]

In return for his testimony, the thirty-five-year-old Ambrosino, who was facing twenty years, admitted that he could get no jail time at all— despite his confessed participation in the murder of Anthony "Bird" Collucio, a member of Michael Sessa's crew.[8] Then, in the absence of any physical evidence tying Vic Orena to the execution or disposal of Tommy Ocera, the Feds sought to bolster the case with the testimony of two high-level Mafia turncoats: Sammy "the Bull" Gravano, the former underboss of the Gambino family who became famous as the principal witness against John Gotti Sr., and Alphonse "Little Al" D'Arco, the former acting boss of the Luccheses.

The Star Witnesses

At the opening of Orena's trial, the Feds actually attributed three separate motives to him for the slaying. At first they said that Ocera was skimming profits from a carting company, but they were never able to link Orena to that enterprise. Next they claimed that Orena was concerned that, having lost the loan-sharking records, Ocera might be convinced to flip in return for immunity from the crimes they recorded.

But the fact that Orena and his sons had visited the Manor after the DA seized the records undercut that theory. "They wouldn't have shown

themselves anywhere near Ocera if he'd been targeted for a hit," says Flora
Edwards, Orena's former attorney. "It also defies belief that Vic Jr. and John
would have asked Diane Montesano to take them to see Tommy if they had
even *contemplated* eliminating him, since she would have been a witness."[9]

Indeed, in the separate trial of Pasquale Amato, Diane Montesano
testified that she never heard him threaten Ocera "in any way." She said
she never heard Tommy complain about Amato, and though she admitted
that they were "business friends," she insisted that neither owed the other
any money—thus undermining the government's loan-shark theory.[10] But
the motive to which the Feds devoted the most time at Orena's trial was
the allegation that the Ocera rubout had been executed as a favor to John
Gotti Sr.

The Gambino boss was allegedly "ripping mad" that Ocera had killed
Greg Reiter, the brother of Michael Reiter, who worked in Tommy's two
gambling clubs. The Reiter brothers' father, Mark, was a Gambino member
who was then serving a life sentence. According to the Feds, Gotti was concerned that Ocera's alleged murder of Greg Reiter might cause the imprisoned father to cooperate with prosecutors. So they argued that Gotti leaned
on Vic Orena to take care of the problem.

Salvatore Gravano, Al D'Arco

In order to sell that theory,
the Feds trotted out Gravano,
whose testimony against his former friend and boss had finally
resulted in the conviction of the
"Teflon Don" after three previous
attempts had failed.[11] The "second seat" prosecutor in Gotti's
1992 trial[12] was John Gleeson,
who was one of the three assistant U.S. attorneys prosecuting
Vic Orena seven months later.
Now, taking the stand against
Orena, Gravano claimed that Little Vic had actually visited Gotti at his
Ravenite Social Club on Mulberry Street in Little Italy on the night of
January 10, 1990. Alleging that Gotti "seemed agitated" before the meeting, Gravano insisted that Orena spoke to the Gambino boss privately, and

that after he left Gotti appeared calmer.[13] According to Gravano, Gotti Sr. later told him that "they whacked that Tommy Ocera."

Similarly, Al D'Arco claimed that at a December 1989 dinner for Lucchese and Colombo family leaders Orena had bragged to him that he'd had Ocera "whacked" as a favor to Gotti because Ocera had killed Reiter. Again, both of these claims represented little more than hearsay by the witnesses. And there was significant evidence to contradict the Reiter motive in the Ocera slaying.

Killed by the Butcher

In his compelling biography *The Butcher: Anatomy of a Mafia Psychopath*, the late organized crime author Philip Carlo directly attributes Greg Reiter's murder to vicious Bonanno capo Tommy "Karate" Pitera.[14] In June 1992, Pitera was convicted on eighteen of nineteen homicide counts he'd been charged with. But he was never indicted for Reiter's murder, because the body was never found and the only witness to the murder, Michael Harrigan, had been killed.[15]

Still, Carlo's account leaves little doubt that Pitera killed Reiter with a shotgun blast to the head. He then buried his body in a remote wildlife sanctuary in Nassau County, Long Island. Carlo writes that Mark Reiter, mistakenly convinced that his son had been killed by another drug-dealing mob associate named Billy Bright, actually paid $5,000 to a member of the Aryan Brotherhood, who allegedly stabbed Bright to death at the U.S. penitentiary in Atlanta.[16]

In fact, after Orena and Amato were found guilty for Ocera's murder, Gravano testified in the prosecution of Bright's alleged killer, Jack Stancell.[17] In doing so, Sammy the Bull effectively *recanted* the testimony he'd given in Vic Orena's trial, in favor of the Feds' new theory that Mark Reiter had hired Stancell to kill Bright. At that point in 1996, four years after Orena's conviction, Gravano actually testified that the Ocera homicide was not connected to Greg Reiter's disappearance—completely undermining one of the government's principal theories for Orena's motive in the Ocera murder: that he'd done it as a favor to John Gotti.

"Tommy Ocera had nothing to do with Greg Reiter's murder," Andrew

Orena told me. "And as to their story that my father visited Gotti at the Ravenite, all they could produce was three seconds of video which they claimed showed him leaving the club on January tenth. They had multiple bugs inside the club recording conversations that night but didn't get a word of my father. Nor did that video show Sammy Gravano entering or leaving the club on that date. My father's conviction for Tommy's murder was an absolute frame, and in addition to Gravano, the Feds shamelessly used Al D'Arco, who would have said anything to keep his plea deal and escape prison."[18]

D'Arco, who was at the same level in the Mafia hierarchy as Vic Orena, had testified in a dozen Mafia trials. He was rewarded by the Justice Department with a one-day jail sentence.[19] Meanwhile, as noted, after admitting to nineteen homicides, Gravano served only five years.[20] But Sammy the Bull, whose testimony led to thirty convictions and the imprisonment of twenty-three mob leaders and their associates,[21] was later exposed as a drug-dealing liar.

The *New York Times* described Gravano as "the most devastating witness ever used against the mob,"[22] but he'd signed a plea deal with the Feds that was predicated on his sworn insistence that he'd never sold narcotics, and he testified to that multiple times under oath. There was also compelling evidence that Gravano had committed many more than the nineteen hits he admitted to—as many as forty-four, according to former Lucchese boss Anthony Casso, who told FBI agents after his defection that he'd sold drugs to Gravano for years. But then, after cutting a plea deal in which Casso agreed to testify against other mob associates, the Feds suddenly reneged on it. In *Gaspipe,* Philip Carlo wrote about Casso's prospective testimony:

> All the attorneys at the Justice Department knew that if Casso was put on the stand in a court of law and told about how he dealt drugs with Gravano, told that there were more murders than the nineteen Gravano had admitted to . . . this would immediately create fertile ground for all the defense attorneys representing the people Gravano put away to file appeals creating a nightmare for the Justice Department and an embarrassment of monumental proportions.[23]

In interviews and correspondence with me for this book, Casso insisted that "Gravano lied with impunity on the stand when it came to his murders and drug dealing." He claimed that Sammy the Bull once offered to sell him $160,000 worth of China White heroin.[24] And years after his sworn testimony, following his release from prison, Gravano acted in a way that corroborated Casso's allegations. In February 2000, Gravano was arrested in Phoenix with his wife, son, and daughter for running a ring that sold up to twenty-five thousand tablets of the illegal drug ecstasy each week.[25] Convicted in 2002, Gravano is now serving a nineteen-year sentence at ADX Florence, the same Supermax prison where Casso was initially housed.

But Gravano isn't the only star federal witness who Casso claims was a fabricator. "Al D'Arco had become known as a chronic liar," Carlo quotes Casso as saying in his book. D'Arco had testified against Genovese boss Vincent "Chin" Gigante, but Casso insisted that Little Al had "never been to any meetings at which the Chin was present."[26]

In his correspondence with me, Casso wrote that "D'Arco had decided to become an informant in 1990, but knowing well that the Lucchese family had a mole in both the Brooklyn and New York Offices of the FBI, D'Arco had taken precautionary measures by turning himself in to Federal agents in the Bureau's New Rochelle Office."[27] Further, at Orena's trial D'Arco also gave the impression that he'd never been a serious drug dealer. But new evidence surfaced later that he was heavily involved in the sale of narcotics dating back to 1989.[28]

Scarpa's Backup Plan

Given the absence of any direct evidence linking Vic Orena to the crime—and given the suspect nature of the testimony against him by Maffatore, Bonfiglio, Gravano, and D'Arco—the question is, who was behind the death and burial of Tommy Ocera?

In his summation at Orena's trial, Assistant U.S. Attorney John Gleeson actually identified Greg Scarpa as "probably" one of those who had followed Ocera and Montesano.[29] He also suggested that someone "tried to get Greg Scarpa to kill [Ocera] . . . but it failed."[30] In the Colombo war that followed, Scarpa proved to be the absolute enemy of Vic Orena, so he would never have done Orena's bidding or executed a murder contract at Orena's behest.

But if Scarpa killed Ocera, what was his motive? Why did he want him dead? The answer came from his son Greg Jr. in a sworn affidavit on July 30, 2002.

> In the late 1980's my father visited me in Lewisburg [federal prison] and told me that DeVecchio told him that Tommy Ocera was spreading rumors that my father was an informant and that Ocera himself may be a "rat." My father never received any order from Victor Orena to kill Tommy Ocera. The story that Ocera was killed on Orena's instruction was invented after-the-fact by my father and DeVecchio to frame Orena when the Colombo Family war began.[31]

Greg Jr. made a similar statement during live testimony at a hearing for Vic Orena in 2004. Testifying from the Supermax prison via a live video feed, Junior was asked if he knew how Tommy Ocera had died. "My father killed him," he said.

Scarpa from FBI surveillance video

Repeating what he'd written in his affidavit, the younger Scarpa explained that his father had received the information about Ocera's being an informant from "his friend 'D,'" a code name for DeVecchio. At that point, Greg Jr. testified, "he had to do what he had to do with this guy." When asked what that meant, he replied, "[It] means he had to kill him, otherwise his [Greg Sr.'s] life would be lost."[32]

If Greg Scarpa Jr. is to be believed, his father cleverly used the Ocera rubout to kill two birds with one stone. He eliminated a potential "rat" who might have exposed his own informant status, and he implicated the acting boss of the family, who was his principal obstacle to a family takeover. And, according to Greg Jr., he did all this with the help of his FBI contacting agent. In that same sworn affidavit, Junior wrote:

> DeVecchio provided my father with the addresses of the men who were loyal to Orena. As a result of the attacks [during the war], Victor Orena

went into hiding. DeVecchio and my father had a plan to plant guns at the house where Orena was staying to ensure Orena's arrest and conviction. Orena's arrest was supposed to be a "trophy" for DeVecchio. My father told me that he and DeVecchio rode in one car and my half-brother Joey drove another car, which carried the guns in the trunk. They parked some distance from the house and my father and DeVecchio watched while Joey planted the guns under the deck.[33]

Greg Jr. testified to those same details at the 2004 hearing before Judge Jack B. Weinstein. But eight days after Junior's video testimony, Weinstein found him to be "not credible."[34] The judge, who had presided over Orena's trial in 1992, had also refused to grant Vic a new hearing the first time Orena brought up the alleged corruption between Greg Scarpa Sr. and DeVecchio.[35] Back in 1997, in rejecting Orena's petition for a new trial, Judge Weinstein cited his reasoning in that 101-page decision:

> Orena and Amato contend that it was not they—the convicted criminals—but ex-F.B.I. Special Agent R. Lindley DeVecchio who conspired with one of the defendants' associates—the murderer Gregory Scarpa—to cause the killing of their partner, the loan shark, Thomas Ocera, and to instigate an internecine mafia war. The evidence to prove this bizarre, but not entirely implausible, contention, defendants argue, should have been supplied to defense counsel so that they could rely on the jurors' rationality or befuddlement (they claim either provides a justifiable basis for reasonable doubt) to achieve a verdict of not guilty, or at least disagreement sufficient for a mistrial. . . . Scarpa has died in prison and can provide no help on the facts. DeVecchio, having been allowed to resign from the F.B.I. . . . was granted immunity, all documents relevant to his background were revealed, and he was subjected to fierce examination by defense counsel. Despite the seamy aspects of law enforcement revealed by the record, . . . defendants' factual assumptions and legal theories are unpersuasive.

But at the time of Orena's 1992 trial, *none* of the evidence of Scarpa's informant status, or DeVecchio's alleged role in leaking intel to him, was known to the defense. Thus, not all documents "relevant to [DeVecchio's] background" were revealed. Nor did Orena's lawyer get a chance to subject Scarpa's control agent to the kind of "fierce examination" he might have, since DeVecchio merely testified to the structure of the Mafia and the course of the third war.

Even after the shocking evidence of Lin's questionable relationship with "34" was revealed in the 1994 OPR investigation, Judge Weinstein was not persuaded. A decade later, in 2004, he concluded:

> Orena and Amato now present further "evidence" in a renewal of their attack on their convictions. . . . The only relevant support for their contentions of any significance are the alleged confessions of Scarpa to his son, Gregory Scarpa, Jr., a convicted murderer and a made member of a mafia family, that it was the father and DeVecchio, not defendants, who killed a fellow gang member and organized the mob war.[36]

Earlier, during Orena's trial, Judge Weinstein had allowed the admission of second- and thirdhand hearsay from low-level Colombo associates Maffatore and Bonfiglio to convict the acting boss. Each witness had a massive motive to lie for the Feds, since they would each receive drastically reduced sentences in exchange for their testimony. On the other hand, Greg Scarpa Jr., the son of Orena's principal enemy, had no reason to distort the truth and no real hope of reduced jail time. At that 2004 hearing he testified to specific details his father had told him about his plan to frame Orena for the Ocera hit.

If any Mafiosi ever fit the definition of "co-conspirators," Greg Scarpa Sr. and his son would arguably qualify—thus allowing admission of Junior's testimony under the exception to the Rule Against Hearsay. But now, seeming to contradict his earlier logic, Judge Weinstein found Greg Jr.'s testimony not credible because he'd learned the details secondhand from his father:

> The only substantial information Scarpa, Jr. had was furnished to him orally by his parent. The son, if he is credited at all, was told by his sire what DeVecchio was doing for the mob and what the elder Scarpa was doing for DeVecchio. The son observed nothing that took on significance without the father's extra-judicial statements. Since both Scarpas were sentenced to federal prison, where the father died, and the son is serving an almost endless sentence, they had good reason to want to further dam-

age the reputation of the F.B.I. and to help their erstwhile friends, and sometimes adversaries, Amato and Orena.[37]

What's astonishing about that last statement is Judge Weinstein's description of Vic Orena as Scarpa's "erstwhile friend." At no point during Orena's trial before him, nor in any evidence furnished by the Feds on appeal, was there ever a *hint* that Scarpa had been anything but Vic Orena's mortal enemy.

As we'll see in the chapters ahead, Scarpa Sr. conspired against Orena with all the guile that Shakespeare's Iago showed in plotting to destroy Othello. But Jack B. Weinstein, one of the most brilliant legal minds in the federal judiciary, was unwilling to follow the path of his EDNY colleague Judge Charles Sifton, who granted new trials in 1997 for Colombo underboss Joseph Russo, his brother Anthony, and crew member Joseph Monteleone after similar evidence of the allegedly corrupt Scarpa-DeVecchio relationship came to light.[38]

Weinstein saw the interaction between DeVecchio and Scarpa differently and in 2001, as noted, he declared, "There's a time to end all of these cases."

In effect he was saying enough was enough—that further probing into the alleged "unholy alliance" between "34" and Mr. Organized Crime could cause other Colombo war-related cases to "unravel."[39]

"The evidence that DeVecchio was providing illegal information to Scarpa was absolutely overwhelming," says Flora Edwards. "But so was the perception in the New York judiciary that you do not go easy on the mob."[40]

Defense attorney Alan Futerfas, who mounted Vic Orena's initial appeal, agreed. "There was a belief in this city for years," he says, "that the Mafia controlled construction, the fish industry and the waste industry. People like Rudy Giuliani made their careers by breaking that perceived control. Now, the Colombos constituted a large series of prosecutions. And no matter what we presented in the way of government misconduct—obstruction of justice and withholding of evidence—the appellate courts were not going to let these men out of jail."[41]

In his singular drive to dominate the Colombo family, the ingenious Greg Scarpa Sr. had constructed two scenarios to eliminate Vic Orena. Plan A was to remove him by force. Barring that, however, the grisly murder and burial of Tommy Ocera would provide the Feds with another way to remove him for good.

Now, having laid the groundwork for plan B with Ocera's rubout, the Killing Machine put plan A in motion. The surrogate he would use to pull the trigger was his longtime Wimpy Boys crew member Carmine Sessa, who by 1991 had worked his way into Orena's good graces. Orena had come to trust Sessa so much, in fact, that he'd made him consigliere of the family. But in the treacherous ways of the Mafia, the "kiss of death" was usually delivered by a friend—and as the summer approached the unsuspecting Orena had no idea that Sessa was putting together a crew to gun him down.

Chapter 24

COUP D'ÉTAT

Since the seventh century B.C., in ancient Athens, criminal law has recognized two principal definitions of homicide: murder, which involves the intent to kill, and manslaughter. The distinction, which was literally carved into stone in the fifth century A.D., concerns degrees of culpability.[1] Just how responsible one human being is for causing the death of another is measured by what the law calls "mens rea," which literally translates as "guilty mind."[2] While the prosecution of murder is typically a state responsibility, federal law defines it as "the unlawful killing of a human being with malice aforethought."[3] The essential element of the crime is *intent,* and the New York Penal Code is typical of other state statutes. Since "murder in the first" is usually reserved for the killing of a police officer, a person is guilty of "murder in the second degree" when "with intent to cause the death of another person, he causes the death."[4]

Manslaughter, on the other hand, is measured by degrees of criminal negligence. Typically, voluntary manslaughter involves a crime caused by a person who could reasonably foresee the consequences of his actions and was thus "reckless" in not acting to stop it. As the fulcrum of culpability for murder moves between intent and omission, the most important factor in determining guilt is whether the accused could have or should have *predicted* the consequences of his actions.

An individual with a high blood alcohol level who gets into a car and causes an accident resulting in death is more culpable on the sliding manslaughter scale than an individual who simply drove sober but nonetheless killed another person.[5] In New York a driver will be charged with vehicular manslaughter in the first degree when he drives with a BAC of .18 or above, which is more than twice the legal limit of .08.[6]

But whether one acts with intent or negligence, those two legal definitions of murder have something in common: One person acts and another person ends up dead. When it came to Gregory Scarpa Sr., few made members of the underworld acted with such intentional disregard for human life. The question is, was Lin DeVecchio, his contacting agent, guilty in any way for failing to stop him?

In 2006, when the Brooklyn district attorney indicted DeVecchio, he was charged with four counts of second-degree murder under section 125.5 (1) of the New York Penal Code. The DA alleged that "in concert with other persons, namely Gregory Scarpa Sr. . . . [he] did solicit, request command, importune and intentionally aid in the deaths" of Mary Bari, Joseph "Joe Brewster" DeDomenico, and two others we'll examine in the pages ahead.[7]

When that case was dismissed on November 1, 2007, under the constitutional prohibition against double jeopardy, DeVecchio was forever free from prosecution for those "intentional" crimes.

But in light of the evidence uncovered in this investigation it's now fair to ask whether, in his twelve-year interaction with Scarpa, during which the Killing Machine was responsible for more than twenty-five homicides,[8] Lin DeVecchio was *criminally negligent*. Even if he didn't act with *intent* in those murders, judged against the standards for manslaughter, the question can be stated as follows: By allowing Greg Scarpa to stay on the street after he had passed DeVecchio information about his rivals, should Lin DeVecchio have *foreseen* that Scarpa might cause the death of those victims? That question takes on new relevance in light of Lin's admission in his book that "In my heart, as Scarpa's handler, of course I knew he was doing hits."[9]

In the simplest street terms, did DeVecchio allow "34," his coveted Top Echelon source, to get away with murder?

In order to answer that question we need to review the dozens of teletypes and 209 reports that DeVecchio sent to FBI officials memorializing Scarpa's debriefings and measure them against the now-established facts of what actually happened in the months leading up to the third Colombo war, which began in June 1991.

Two Knights and a Pawn

To appreciate how Greg Scarpa Sr. instigated that conflict, consider how he first conspired against two of the family's most powerful captains. By 1990, with Vic Orena well established as Carmine Persico's designee for acting boss, Scarpa had two immediate rivals: William Cutolo and Nicholas Grancio.[10]

Cutolo ran an enormous loan-sharking operation, with more than $2 million on the street.[11] A former Teamster official, he had been accused of labor racketeering with links to District Council 37, New York City's largest municipal union.[12] Known as "Billy Fingers," Cutolo often wore western boots and sometimes even a cowboy hat, earning him a second nickname: "Wild Bill."

Across Brooklyn, "Nicky Black" Grancio was a gregarious capo who presided like a benevolent don over his neighborhood near Avenue U and McDonald Avenue in Brooklyn. "He was one of those bigger-than-life guys who would take an entire pizza, fold it over like a slice, and eat it," said Vic Orena Jr. of bald-headed Nicky, who was fiercely loyal to his father.[13] Both men—Cutolo and Grancio—would eventually be murdered. But at first Scarpa set out to give Lin DeVecchio enough dirt on Cutolo to get him removed by the Feds. The pawn in this game was Carmine Sessa, who, with Scarpa Sr. as the chess master, moved from made guy to consigliere in just over three years.

Few gangsters in the annals of organized crime enjoyed the rise through the ranks experienced by five-foot-four Carmine Sessa. Even Lin DeVecchio, in his book, describes Sessa's trajectory as "meteoric."[14] Although DeVecchio mistakenly writes that Sessa was "straightened out" in 1988,[15] his own 209 to Washington dated March 13, 1987, reports that Carmine (whose name was misspelled "Sesso") was made on that date, along with Robert "Bobby Zam" Zambardi.[16] Both Sessa and Zambardi had participated in the bru-

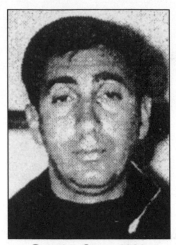

Carmine Sessa, 1980s

tal slaying of Mary Bari at Carmine's club Occasions,[17] the site of Scarpa's previous rubout involving a loan-shark victim.[18]

At Lin DeVecchio's 2007 murder trial, Sessa confessed to his role in thirteen homicides over the years,[19] ultimately pleading guilty to four: Bari; Anthony Bolino, whom he claimed he killed as "a favor" to Anthony Casso;[20] Jimmy Angelino, the family consigliere—a hit we'll detail shortly; and Anthony "Bird" Collucio, a shylock who was a member of Michael Sessa's crew.[21] That was the murder in which "Joey Brains" Ambrosino also admitted his involvement.[22]

Carmine initially fingered his brother in that hit,[23] and since his conviction in 1992, Michael has been serving life for the murder, which he insists he didn't do. But it's fair to say that after years of doing hits and burglaries in the Wimpy Boys crew, once he was sponsored for membership by Greg Scarpa, Carmine's movement up the Colombo ladder was unprecedented.

After getting his button in March 1987, Sessa was designated a captain just seventeen months later, in August 1988. He took over the crew formerly headed by Carmine Persico's own brother Teddy.[24] Less than a year after that, in May 1990, Sessa was anointed consigliere—the number three position in a family of 130 members.[25]

"Nobody moves that fast through the organization without some kind of outside help," said Vic Orena Jr.[26] "Carmine had always been what we called one of 'the disciples of Scarpa.' He was Greg's boy. Always a spear carrier. Never a leader. And now, suddenly there is the perception that he is some kind of ninety weight in the family.[27] But what was really going on was that Scarpa was in the background pulling the strings and he put Carmine on the white horse to make it look like he was leading the charge."

Thirteen months after being designated the family's "counselor," Sessa took part in the plot to murder Vic Orena, the botched hit that touched off the new Colombo war.[28]

Long before that, however, Sessa got so close to the Orenas that he was considered a member of their family with a small "f."

"He was always hanging out with us," said Andrew. "He'd visit me in the Pontiac dealership I had in Cedarhurst [Long Island]. My father had a fifty-foot yacht and everybody would joke that Carmine used it more than we did." Indeed, Lin DeVecchio filed a 209 dated June 13, 1989, fourteen months after Vic Orena was elevated to acting boss, noting that:

> CARMINE SESSA RECENTLY SOLD HIS HOUSE IN BROOKLYN AND MOVED TO LONG ISLAND TO BE CLOSER TO VIC ORENA. SOURCE SAID SESSA AND ORENA HAVE BEEN VERY CLOSE AND SESSA IS BECOMING A MAJOR POWER IN THE COLOMBO FAMILY DUE TO ORENA'S POSITION.[29]

When Sessa first got made in March 1987, under the sponsorship of Greg Scarpa, he went into Vic Orena's crew.[30] At one point, Sessa appeared to be so supportive of Orena that he tried to go into the produce business with him, but the idea was reportedly rejected by Jimmy Angelina, who was consigliere at the time.

The question is, in the lead-up to the war, when Sessa not only conspired to kill Orena but became one of his chief adversaries and eventually took over as acting boss, was he being manipulated by Greg Scarpa?

The evidence we've uncovered suggests that he was.

For one thing, absent a push from Scarpa, Sessa had every reason to be supportive of Little Vic Orena. Orena had been incredibly generous to Carmine. Not only did Vic preside over Sessa's rapid promotion from soldier to capo, but he made him consigliere. Orena even loaned Sessa $130,000 to start his own loan-shark book, independent of Greg Scarpa, after Carmine became more fearful of Scarpa following the death of his close friend Joe Brewster. Sessa later testified at DeVecchio's trial that he "wanted to distance" himself from Scarpa.[31]

So Orena gave him the money to pay back Scarpa, who was charging him "two points" of vig. In fact, Little Vic was so generous to Sessa that he charged him only half a point on the first hundred thousand, and one point on the thirty thousand balance.[32] As such, Sessa was actually able to make money on the transaction and retire his debt to Scarpa. The diminutive Sessa often made his payments to Orena near Stella's Restaurant on Long Island, a location that would take on historic significance as the war began.

But whatever affection and loyalty Carmine Sessa might have had for Vic Orena Sr., it was far outweighed by his fear of the Grim Reaper.

"Sessa had killed multiple people on Greg's orders," says Orena's former attorney Flora Edwards, "so Greg had that hold over him. And, given his status as an FBI informant, [Scarpa] could have dropped a dime on Carmine anytime."[33]

The Body in the Candy Store

At one point in the late 1980s, it became clear to Sessa that one hit in particular made him vulnerable since Greg Sr. literally knew where the body was buried. It was the murder of Sal "the Hammerhead" Cardaci, which Scarpa had ordered in January 1983.[34] Fearful that Cardaci was going to "rat" on crew member Billy Meli, Scarpa had lured him to Mike's Candy, a store Senior owned down the street from his social club. Sessa then shot him with a .357 Magnum and buried his body in the basement using quicklime.

During a debriefing in 1994, Sessa told FBI agents that sometime after Vic Orena took over as acting boss, Anthony Casso informed him that "Gregory Scarpa Sr. was a snitch."[35]

At that point Sessa trusted Orena enough to pass the news on to him, so Orena advised that he move Cardaci's body. Sessa then undertook what amounted to a black-bag job, secretly entering the candy store with Bobby Zam and others, who helped him dig up the remains. But there was a hitch.

As they were moving the deteriorated corpse out to a car, Joey Scarpa, Greg's youngest son, happened by. He didn't see the body and said nothing, but later his father grilled Zambardi about what they were doing in the store.

Zam feigned ignorance and Sessa did the same when Scarpa asked him on two other occasions if he'd dug up the body. Terrified of Greg, with whom he'd killed two people in his own club Occasions, Sessa just clammed up.[36] "But there's no doubt that Scarpa held the knowledge of Cardaci's murder over Sessa like a guillotine," said Andrew Orena, "and he could drop it at any time. I know that Carmine cared for my father, but when it came to his own survival he was going to follow Scarpa, and when Greg snapped his fingers, Carmine jumped."[37]

Targeting Wild Bill

While Scarpa was encouraging Carmine Sessa to betray Vic Orena behind the scenes, he was openly critical of one of Vic's most trusted captains, William Cutolo. It was purportedly a crew sent by Wild Bill that fired the

Wild Bill Cutolo

first shots at Scarpa during the war, but in the years leading up to that November 1991 incident, "34" gave the Feds the kind of inside intelligence they needed to indict and convict Cutolo if he couldn't be brought down by force.

In much the same way he had been undermining Carmine Persico with his Bureau handlers since the early 1960s, Scarpa started providing DeVecchio with significant intelligence on Cutolo in 1989, after Wild Bill became Orena's underboss. The following excerpts from teletypes and 209s DeVecchio sent to Washington demonstrate how Greg not only helped the government track Cutolo's rise in the family but also gave the FBI enough details to obtain wiretaps on the flamboyant capo, who was one of Scarpa's two chief rivals.

ON AUGUST 1, 1989 SOURCE ADVISED THAT BILLY CUTOLO CONTINUES TO USE SECRETS [LOUNGE] 62-01 11TH AVENUE BROOKLYN, NEW YORK TO MEET WITH HIS CREW AND DISCUSS ILLEGAL ACTIVITIES TO INCLUDE LOANSHARKING LABOR RACKETEERING AND EXTORTION.[38]

ON NOVEMBER 16TH, 1989 SOURCE ADVISED THAT WILLIAM CUTOLO . . . HAS GAINED CONSIDERABLE POWER AND INFLUENCE IN THE FAMILY IN A SHORT PERIOD OF TIME, IN PART DUE TO HIS INFLUENCE IN UNION ACTIVITIES AND HIS SKILL AS A MONEY MAKER FOR THE FAMILY.[39]

ON DECEMBER 25TH, 1989 SOURCE ADVISED THAT WILLIAM CUTOLO FINANCES SHYLOCK LOANS THROUGH SEVERAL LOANSHARKS WHO MEET HIM AT SECRETS LOUNGE. . . . SOURCE ADVISED THAT THOSE VICTIMS WHO DO NOT MAKE THEIR PAYMENTS ARE THREATENED OR PHYSICALLY BEATEN. SOURCE HAS OVERHEARD CUTOLO DISCUSSING LOANSHARKING MATTERS ON HIS MOBILE PHONE.[40]

Keep in mind that Greg Scarpa, DeVecchio's principal source, was engaging in the same kind of violent extortion of loan-shark victims even as he was ratting on Cutolo for doing the same. As far back as 1986, a wiretap in the Wimpy Boys club picked up Scarpa saying, "If I don't have my money by Thursday, I'll put him right in the fucking hospital. . . . I wanna break his mother's face and break his fuckin' legs and arms."[41]

"When it came to collecting on the vig," said John Orena, "the only difference between Greg and Billy was that Scarpa was the FBI's inside man."[42] And there's little doubt that just as Scarpa badmouthed Cutolo to the Feds, he was also spreading poisonous rumors about him throughout the family. It was the same approach he'd used years earlier to denigrate Charlie "the Sidge" LoCicero. And by 1990, Scarpa's efforts to undermine Cutolo were starting to pay off:

JUNE 12TH, 1990 [SOURCE] ADVISED BILLY CUTOLO HAD BEEN KNOCKED DOWN FROM THE UNDER BOSS POSITION. . . . SOURCE SAID [CARMINE] PERSICO FEARS OTHER MEMBERS INCLUDING CUTOLO OF GAINING TOO MUCH INFLUENCE IN THE FAMILY AND SHUTTING HIM [PERSICO] OUT IN TIME.[43]

By July 23, Scarpa had furnished the Feds with enough probable cause to renew Title III wiretaps on Cutolo. And by September, Cutolo was forced to withdraw from Teamsters Local 861—based on an affidavit supplied by Lin DeVecchio.[44]

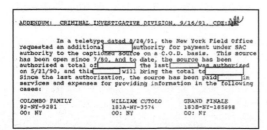

The Feds seemed so determined to target Cutolo that Scarpa received a payment in September 1991 for three separate "cases," or operations, for which he was supplying intel. One op was broadly named

"Colombo Family," one focused exclusively on Cutolo, and one bore the curious name "Grand Finale."[45]

"That was an interesting designation," says Flora Edwards, "because the principal theory of defense lawyers after the war was that it had been instigated to install Scarpa as boss, and in the eyes of the Feds that could have represented a final curtain on the Colombos, because they would have had a TECI with a seat on the Commission."

After Wild Bill Cutolo's diminishment in the family, the next immediate threat to Scarpa was the acting boss himself, Vic Orena. "It's important to understand the difference in the culture of the family back then," said Andrew Orena. "My father is out on Long Island. He's a nonviolent moneymaker who is vehemently anti-drugs, and Scarpa has been making a fortune selling dope since the mid-1980s, when his crew was sent away. Cutolo was one of my father's strongest capos, along with Nicky Black [Grancio]. Eventually Greg knows that my father is going to have a problem with the violent way he does business, so he starts making moves, using Carmine Sessa to eliminate my dad."[46]

Polling the Captains

Perhaps not wanting to admit that he was Scarpa's pawn in the violent battle about to ensue, Sessa gave a different account of this story—claiming that his change of heart regarding Vic Orena began in 1988, when he was asked to kill consigliere Jimmy Angelina. Testifying at Lin DeVecchio's trial, Sessa insisted that Vic Orena had asked Angelina to "poll the captains" in the family to see if they still supported Carmine Persico as boss.[47]

Sessa then claimed that after Angelina took the poll, forces loyal to Orena, including underboss Benny Aloi and Bill Cutolo, asked him to murder Angelina. "Benny Aloi asked me how would [I] feel if Jim Angelina wasn't around anymore," Sessa testified.[48] Claiming that he voiced no opinion either way, Sessa then confessed that, after one failed attempt, he eventually shot Angelina in the stairwell of a building with Cutolo nearby. After that Vic Orena promoted Sessa to fill Angelina's shoes as consigliere. Later Sessa claimed that when Orena came to him in 1991 and asked him to poll the captains *again,* he began to worry. "I didn't want the same thing to happen to me that happened to Jimmy," he said.[49] That was the Feds' theory for why Carmine Sessa turned on Vic Orena and started the Colombo war.

But one of the recently released FBI 209s suggests otherwise. In a teletype dated November 29, 1988, DeVecchio says:

> Source advised that JIMMY ANGELLINO [*sic*] was recently "hit" on orders from JUNIOR PERSICO.[50]

In other words, Angelina's murder wasn't Vic Orena's idea. It was sanctioned by the boss himself: Carmine Persico. In that 209, DeVecchio also reported that "Vic Orena and Benny Aloi were fully aware of the hit."[51] But awareness is a far cry from instigation, and it would have been an act of war in itself if Vic Orena, the acting boss, had unilaterally taken out Carmine Persico's consigliere without his permission. "The idea that Carmine Sessa suddenly did a hundred-and-eighty-degree turn on Vic Sr. because he was worried about polling the captains doesn't wash," argues Flora Edwards. "When Vic asked Sessa to do what Angelina had done, he was simply seeking a vote of confidence from his captains. In no way was he suspicious of Sessa at that point."

In fact, Sessa later admitted that Orena had suggested he include Teddy Persico in that poll. "If Vic was conspiring to take over the family," says Edwards, "the last man he'd tell Sessa to brief would be Junior's own brother. But he wasn't. That 'polling' excuse was what Scarpa Sr. came up with to justify Carmine's move on Vic."[52]

Later the Feds went along, spinning the "polling" story into a purported coup d'état attempt by Orena to bring down Carmine Persico as boss. One of the 302s describing a Sessa debriefing in 1993 says:

> SESSA polled Colombo LCN Family Captain THEODORE PERSICO, who was upset that ORENA advocated that CARMINE PERSICO should be removed but told SESSA to continue polling the captains as ORENA had requested. THEORDORE PERSICO resolved to contact his brother, CARMINE PERSICO, and advise him of ORENA'S intentions.[53]

This second polling of the captains took place on June 14, 1991, at the wedding of Vic Sr.'s son Peter, a civilian—hardly the place one would expect the acting boss to put a plot in motion to take over the family. As recently as

June 5, Orena had approved Carmine's brother Michael as an acting capo.[54] So there was no indication at that point that Vic Sr. thought of Carmine Sessa as anything but loyal.[55]

"At that wedding we noticed that Carmine wasn't himself," said Andrew Orena. "But we certainly didn't think things had reached the point of [his] betraying my father." In fact, another Sessa 302 notes that "a day or two after Peter Orena's wedding Sessa met Orena and Orena Jr. and [Vic Sr.] concluded the meeting by attempting to persuade Sessa that everything would work out and that Sessa had nothing to fear."[56]

"But Carmine Sessa was always paranoid," says Vic Orena Jr. "Who wouldn't be, after spending years in Scarpa's crew, when you didn't know when you walked into Wimpy Boys whether Greg would pull a gun and shoot you dead?"

Joey Ambrosino, a member of that crew, testified that Sessa was so cautious that he used hand gestures to communicate, using a V to represent Vic Orena and three fingers to represent Cutolo, who was missing a finger.[57]

So despite the assurances from Vic Sr., Carmine Sessa came to believe that there was a plot against him. That "plot" was suggested to him, according to Ambrosino, by "another captain."

Supposedly, Sessa was going to be invited to an induction ceremony on Friday night, June 21, during which two new members would be "made." But on the way to that ceremony "he and Richard Fusco [another capo] would be killed."[58] As Andrew Orena asks today: "Who was this capo who put the bug in his ear? There's little doubt in my mind that it was Scarpa, feeding on Carmine's paranoia, convincing him that getting a vote of confidence from the captains for my father meant a death sentence for him. It was ridiculous."

According to one of his FBI debriefings, on or about June 18, 1991, three days before the induction ceremony, Sessa went to Romano's restaurant in Brooklyn to meet with Cutolo and Grancio, two of Vic Orena's most loyal captains. During the meeting, Sessa said that acting underboss Joe Scopo had announced that Vincent "Chickie" DeMartino and James "Jimmy O'Toole" Spitaleri would be inducted that Friday, and that Scopo would arrange to have Carmine brought to the ceremony.[59] "Of course he was invited," said John Orena. "Carmine was consigliere and it was natural for him to attend. But the paranoid wheels greased by Scarpa started turning in his head. He left that meeting at Romano's deciding that he was going to be whacked."

And so, acting either on his own or at Scarpa's behest, Sessa decided to make a "preemptive strike." On June 20, 1991, the night before the induction ceremony was scheduled to take place, he drove to Cedarhurst, Long Island, with one of his fellow Scarpa crew members, Bobby Zambardi. Along with another capo, John Pate, they headed toward Stella's Restaurant, which Vic Orena frequented. The plan was to follow him when he left, link with another car full of shooters, and "take him out." As Sessa later explained at Lin DeVecchio's trial, "I felt at that induction ceremony they were going to kill me. So we decided to kill Vic Orena first."[60]

Chapter 25

PEARL HARBOR

Carmine Sessa's coup d'état attempt involved two hit teams. In a plot that seemed derived from the final scene in *The Godfather,* Sessa planned to decapitate the family leadership, killing not just Vic Orena but underboss Joe Scopo in simultaneous hits that would take place miles apart. If successful, those parallel strikes would have left Sessa—the family's number three official—as the effective street boss of the Colombos, or at least the figurehead if Greg Scarpa was pulling the strings. As we detail the plans for this two-pronged attack, keep in mind that Sessa—who was not known for strategic thinking—purportedly put the complex operation together in less than forty-eight hours after deciding on June 18, with little basis in fact, that he would have to kill or be killed.

"Joey Brains" Ambrosino, another Wimpy Boys crew member and Scarpa surrogate, said that at around noon on Thursday, June 20, he got beeped by Carmine's brother Michael, who told him to come to his house. The Sessa brothers were waiting there, along with Colombo associate Lefty Sangiorgio. Ambrosino said that Carmine told him he "needed some help"—that he had to "murder some people that night."[1]

The plan was for them to meet capo John Pate and some of his crew members at seven P.M. and split into teams. Carmine Sessa, Pate, and Zambardi would make up the surveillance detail. Once they located Orena, they would contact an armed "backup team"[2] consisting of Michael Sessa, Sangiorgio, and members of Pate's crew. This second team would then go into action and "do the work."

Meanwhile, a third team of shooters would target Scopo, who frequented Turquoise, a Brooklyn club, on Thursday nights.[3] "Our plan was to kill Joey Scopo when he left Turquoise and at the same time, Carmine, Bob, and Johnny Pate and their crews were going to murder Vic Orena," Ambrosino testified.[4]

As a federal prosecutor later noted, however, "the plan was a complete disaster. It didn't come off."[5] After driving around for more than five hours searching in vain for Orena,[6] Sessa's recon team was stopped at a traffic light in Floral Park, Long Island, when Vic Orena happened to pull up next to them in his Mercedes.[7] He'd left Stella's Restaurant and was on his way home to nearby Cedarhurst, alone and unarmed. Sessa, Pate, and Zambardi were all wearing baseball caps to obscure their identities. But when they looked over and saw the acting boss in the lane next to them, they quickly peeled off to the left as the light changed, and Orena sped forward.[8]

According to Vic Jr., his father normally drove a Lincoln but that night he was in a Benz that had recently been driven up from Florida. "When he saw these guys, who were all Scarpa minions," said Vic Jr., "he knew at that moment they were up to no good."[9]

"We were hoping that he didn't identify us," the hapless Sessa later testified. "But it appeared that he did."[10]

Within minutes, Orena had made it safely home. "As soon as my father got on the phone, he called me because his first fear was that I was gone," said Vic Jr. "That they'd hit me and John. So he said, 'Check with your brother. I'm gonna meet you at the house.'"

At that same moment, in Brooklyn, Ambrosino waited at a diner with Michael Sessa and three other crew members, including Frank Farace, Greg Scarpa's "cousin" by marriage and the uncle of the murderous Gus Farace. Hank Smurra, who worked at Turquoise, arrived to inform them that Scopo hadn't shown up at the club that night.

"So me and Michael drove to [Scopo's] home," said Ambrosino. "His car was in the driveway." Realizing that they'd lost the opportunity to kill the underboss, they beeped Carmine Sessa, who told them how "Vic Orena had got home early, and they got spotted."

Back on Long Island, Vic Sr. assessed the situation with his two sons. "Once we knew his house was safe," said John, "my father sent everybody else in the family out to Montauk because this was an act of war. From that moment on, nothing for us was ever the same."[11]

"Sessa, Zambardi, and Ambrosino were all Scarpa's [crew]," added Vic Jr. "There is no way Carmine would have made a hit attempt like this without clearing it with somebody more powerful in the family. We know he didn't ask Junior Persico, so he was following orders from somebody else. He'd been Greg's boy since he first joined the Wimpys crew in the early 1980s. Greg had sponsored him for membership in the family. Now we realize that we're dealing with the Grim Reaper. He wants my father dead. He wants Joe Scopo gone. And we never saw it coming."

"Believe me," said Andrew, "if my dad had suspected for a second that there was a problem, or if he'd actually planned to take out Carmine at that induction ceremony, do you think he'd be driving home alone? Unarmed? No way. For us this was Pearl Harbor."

To the Mattresses in Jersey

After the aborted hit attempt, Carmine Sessa and the various crews took off for New Jersey and went into hiding. They stayed first at a Holiday Inn, where they were joined by Teddy Persico; then they moved to a nearby Hilton, trying to assess the fallout.[12] An FBI 302 memorializing a Sessa debriefing detailed what happened next:

> SESSA, PATE, and ZAMBARDI all realized there was no explanation for their presence near ORENA's house, and they were all in serious trouble.[13]

But rather than demanding retribution or escalating the conflict, Vic Orena sought to *defuse* it by appealing to the Commission, which was created, in part, to resolve such internecine disputes. "Right away my father wanted the other families to intervene," said Vic Jr. A meeting was held at a Manhattan hotel, attended by representatives of the Genovese, Lucchese, and Gambino families. (At that time, the Bonanno family had been ostracized by the

Commission.) According to an FBI 302 on one of Sessa's debriefings, Little Al D'Arco represented the Luccheses and John Gotti Jr. was among three capos from the Gambinos.[14]

Vic Orena met with the Commission representatives first and Carmine Sessa followed him. Given Sessa's unsanctioned unilateral infraction, when it came time for him to face the impromptu tribunal, he agreed that he would step down as consigliere if asked. After a number of Colombo captains were interviewed, it became clear at that point that the family had now broken into two factions, so the Commission ordered a truce prohibiting any killing. As Sessa later admitted to FBI agents, "all the families would attack anyone who broke the truce."[15]

At Orena's trial, Assistant U.S. Attorney Andrew Weissmann insisted that Vic was now the aggressor. "Vic Orena was very quick to run to the other families and to tell them that there was this plot to kill him," he said. "He wanted to get their support so that he could be declared the official boss. He also wanted their permission to kill the members of the Colombo Family who had aligned themselves with Junior Persico."[16]

But the Orena sons insist that just the opposite was happening. "We went into a totally defensive position," said Vic Jr. "I didn't even know how to handle a gun. I literally had to buy a gun book and read it, to learn how to fire a shotgun. We didn't carry handguns because the FBI and NYPD were arresting people who were packing, so we just did our best to protect our homes and our families. In no way did my father authorize anything aggressive. There's no way we were going to break the peace."[17]

"Meanwhile, throughout that summer," said John, "guys were reaching out to us from the other side and we'd meet and they were telling us, 'We don't want a war.' We were hopin' that, whatever happened, the FBI would step in to stop any violence before it started."[18]

In fact, a month after the attempt on his life, Vic Sr. attended a wake with sixty to seventy members of the family, at which he urged those bent on violence "to come in."[19] The meeting took place in a side room at a funeral home during the wake of "Joe Sap" Saponaro, whose brother John had died of natural causes the previous March.[20] Scarpa Sr. himself actually attended that wake, and Orena, the trusting acting boss, never catching on that Greg was the agent provocateur behind the war, interpreted his presence as a positive sign.

But as "Joey Brains" Ambrosino later testified, Scarpa was "just being a spy for the Persicos" and "made believe that he was aligned with" the Orenas.

Keep in mind that Scarpa, the chess master, wasn't just the principal *instigator* in the war, he was also the principal *interpreter* of events for the FBI. As such he was able to get his contacting agent Lin DeVecchio to spin the "intelligence" from his self-serving point of view. On August 13, DeVecchio sent the following 209 to Washington, painting Vic Orena as the aggressor, bent on assuming "full control" of the family, and quoting his "source," Scarpa, as stating that "the logical move" for the Persico side would be "to take out VIC ORENA."

ON AUGUST 13, 1991, SOURCE ADVISED THAT "LITTLE VIC" ORENA IS TRYING TO ASSUME FULL CONTROL OF THE COLOMBO LCN FAMILY BY HAVING CARMINE PERSICO RELIEVED OF HIS POSITION AS BOSS. THIS HAS CAUSED A MAJOR DIVISION WITHIN THE FAMILY. . . .

THE SOURCE SAID CARMINE SESSA HAS ALSO BEEN REPLACED BY VINNIE ALOI AS ACTING CONSIGLIERE, AND JOEY SCOPO IS ACTING UNDERBOSS. THE SOURCE NOTED HOWEVER THAT ACCORDING TO LCN TRADITION, THERE ARE ONLY THREE WAYS TO CHANGE A FAM-ILY BOSS: 1) BY DEATH (PERSICO IS IN PRISON); 2) BY THE BOSS VOLUN-TARILY STEPPING DOWN (NOT LIKELY IN PERSICO'S CASE); AND BY A VOTE OF THE COMMISSION TO RELIEVE THE BOSS.

THE SOURCE SAID VIC ORENA IS EXPECTING THE OTHER FAMI-LIES TO BACK HIM, HOWEVER, THE OTHER FAMILY BOSSES ARE NOT GOING TO DEPOSE A JAILED BOSS SINCE ALL THE FAMILY BOSSES ARE CURRENTLY IN JAIL, PLUS CARMINE PERSICO HAS ALREADY PUT OUT THE ORDER TO HAVE VIC ORENA HIT. THE SOURCE SAID THE LOGICAL MOVE WOULD BE TO TAKE OUT VIC ORENA AND BENNY AND VINNIE ALOI, AND LEAVE THE POSITION OF BOSS OPEN UNTIL "LITTLE ALLEY" [*sic*] PERSICO IS RELEASED FROM PRISON.

THE SOURCE SAID THE FOLLOWING ARE SIDING WITH ORENA:

JOEY SCOPO
NICKY GRANCIO
TOMMY PETRIZZO
PATTY AMATO
VINNIE ALOI
BILLY CUTOLO
CHARLEY PANARELLA[21]

Vic Orena's two strongest allies in that group were Nicky Black Grancio and William Cutolo. At that point, several months after Sessa's botched hit attempt, having been unable to give the FBI enough intelligence to indict Cutolo, the Orena brothers contend that Scarpa conspired to eliminate "Billy Fingers" by force.

The Move on Wild Bill

Larry Mazza, who was Greg Scarpa's principal killing partner, later testified that Scarpa had outfitted a special station wagon with hidden compartments for a rifle and other guns. Senior also used a van. At some point in the early fall, he started trolling the streets of Brooklyn looking for targets.[22]

According to Mazza, Scarpa had two informants inside Cutolo's crew: Joseph "Joe Legs" Legrano and Robert D'Onofrio. Mazza testified that they "would call" Scarpa "from time to time telling the things that were talked about in Billy's club."[23]

"Billy lived near Greg," said Vic Jr., "and on the road one day he sees Scarpa layin' down in a car with a gun. So he bolts from the spot. He isn't armed at the time. But the car goes after him. There's a chase through the streets of Brooklyn, but Billy gets away."

"A few days later," said John, "this kid who drives Billy around is walkin' down the street and Scarpa, who is in a vehicle, sees him. The kid is on foot. He doesn't have anything on him. No protection and he's not a tough guy. But Greg chases him with the car for three blocks. The kid is scared to death. Finally he runs up on somebody's stoop and starts poundin' on the door, and the car pulls away. They tried another two or three times to make a move on this kid. So now Billy is thinkin' to himself that if he doesn't stop Scarpa, Scarpa's gonna stop him."[24]

In the spring of 2011, while promoting his book, Lin DeVecchio recited the conventional wisdom that it was the "Orena faction" that "fomented the war."[25] He told a radio talk show host, "The war actually started with [an] attempt to kill Scarpa, because he was a feared member of the Persico faction and the Orena faction really wanted him out of the way. So on November eighteenth they tried to kill him as he was leaving his house."

William Cutolo is credited by the Feds with engineering that "attack" on November 18, and as we'll see, serious questions have been raised about its very legitimacy. But before we get there, it's important to examine the various 209 reports that Lin DeVecchio filed in the weeks leading up to that incident.

On October 9, quoting Scarpa as his source, DeVecchio sent a memo to his FBI superiors that clearly painted Vic Orena Sr. as the principal antagonist in the Colombo family conflict. But in fact the evidence suggests that Orena was going out of his way to stop the conflict short of violence. On October 6, Orena actually went to Teddy Persico's house to discuss resolving the split, accompanied by his sons Victor and John, underboss Benny Aloi, and three other capos, including Nicky Grancio. For Orena to visit Persico's turf on a peace mission was a clear gesture of conciliation.[26]

At that time, Orena claimed up to one hundred made members of the family versus twenty-five to thirty who were supporting Persico.[27] He was in such a strong position that he should have been able to resolve the conflict without bloodshed. A war would threaten the earning power of every associate, soldier, and captain. "Blood was bad for business," said Andrew Orena, "and most of the people in the family knew what a good businessman my father had been. So why risk all that?"[28]

But Lin DeVecchio, passing on Scarpa's intel, described the meeting this way:

> The source said Teddy PERSICO opened the meeting by asking Benny ALOI if those members backing VIC ORENA recognized CARMINE PERSICO as the COLOMBO Boss. ALOI said PERSICO was regarded as a Boss, but VIC ORENA speaks for the COLOMBO Family. At that point Teddy PERSICO said that CARMINE PERSICO was the official boss, and not ORENA, and demanded all the money that the PERSICO's [sic] should have gotten over the past several years that had gone to ORENA.[29]

According to DeVecchio's 209, "The ORENA faction said that they were there to resolve any differences and that a meeting should take place." But the memo went on to describe the inflexible stance taken by the "PERSICO faction."

TEDDY PERSICO said that until that side recognized CARMINE PERSICO as the official boss, and ORENA would no longer be the acting boss, there would be no further discussions.[30]

Again, this was Scarpa Sr.'s take on the conflict. The FBI was getting most of its intelligence on the war from its principal antagonist, who by now was an expert at playing his Bureau handlers. So now, ever the tactician, "34" added a new element to the equation: John Gotti.

Since 1987, "getting Gotti" had been the "top investigative priority" of the FBI's New York Office,[31] and dozens of Scarpa's debriefing reports contained dirt on the Gambino boss. Now, on October 9, 1991, a second 209 filed by Lin raised an ominous new prospect: that Vic Orena was really just a Gotti pawn. As noted, the Feds would advance that premise during Vic Sr.'s 1992 trial, arguing that one of the principal motives for the Tommy Ocera hit was Orena's desire to appease Gotti—a theory that was later entirely discredited.

But now, in the fall of 1991, sourcing Scarpa, DeVecchio filed a report with Washington suggesting that the "Dapper Don" was taking sides in the Colombo war.

> On October 9, 1991, ████████ advised SSA R. LINDLEY DE VEC-
> CHIO that JOHN GOTTI has circulated a list of approximately twenty-
> five (25) COLOMBO members loyal to CARMINE PERSICO, and
> advised all GAMBINO members to have no contact in business or oth-
> erwise with these individuals. The source said as a result of this list all
> COLOMBO members so mentioned who have illegal activities together
> with GAMBINO members, are now keeping the proceeds of these busi-
> nesses, and not sharing them in their respective counterparts.[32]

On November 4 DeVecchio went further, suggesting (per Scarpa) that Gotti was actually using Orena in a plot to take over the entire Colombo family— a goal that defies belief, given the long-established five-family structure of the Mafia Commission.

> On November 4, 1991 ████████ advised SSA R. LINDLEY DE VEC-
> CHIO that . . . GAMBINO Boss JOHN GOTTI has been manipulating

ORENA for a long time and is anxious to have this dispute resolved in ORENA's favor so he can assume control of the COLOMBO Family's activities.[33]

But that 209 is even more telling for another reason: In it, "34" names *himself* as a possible Orena target and states that William Cutolo would be a "likely victim" from the Orena faction:

> The source noted that JOEY SCOPO and possibly BILLY CUTOLO would be likely victims on the ORENA side, and that CARMINE SESSA and GREG SCARPA, SR. would be the ORENA's side pick to be hit.

After threatening Cutolo for many weeks, Scarpa seemed to be setting the stage now for the "attack" outside his house on November 18 that DeVecchio later claimed had "fomented" the war. But Scarpa made another allegation in that November 4 report, suggesting that the Cutolo attack wasn't the first violent outbreak in the conflict. According to Scarpa, the initial bloodshed came two weeks earlier with the murder of Giachino "Jack" Leale, one of the killers of Tommy Ocera. In that same 209, Scarpa blames Vic Orena for Leale's rubout:

> On November 4th, 1991 SOURCE advised that the recent hit on JACK LEALE was done by the Orena Faction of the COLOMBO family. . . . The SOURCE said LEALE was obviously set up by somebody he trusted.[34]

The question is whether that somebody was Scarpa himself. The evidence we've uncovered suggests that Scarpa not only "stalked" Ocera but participated in the murder and later sought to frame Vic Orena for it. If Leale was a conspirator to Scarpa's garroting of Ocera, then Scarpa would have had a strong motive to want him dead—and killing him in the fall of 1991, during a Commission-ordered truce, would have made it look like the Orenas had broken the peace.

"There is no way that my father would have sanctioned the killing of Jack Leale," said Andrew Orena. "There was too much to lose. Contrary to what Scarpa was telling Lin, my father had the backing of the Commission and he was desperately trying to broker a resolution before shots were fired. The last thing he would do was get anywhere near a hit like that."[35]

Shootout on Eighty-Second Street

On the morning of November 18, 1991, Little Linda Schiro, Greg Scarpa's daughter by his common-law wife, Linda, was getting her infant son Freddy dressed to go out shopping. Her father reportedly had three crew members with him as he left the house: Joseph "Joe Fish" Marra, Carmine Sessa's brother Larry, and Dean Capiri. The Lincoln they were driving was parked behind Big Linda's Mercedes.[36]

According to the testimony Big Linda gave at Lin DeVecchio's trial in 2007, Greg Sr. helped his daughter take his grandson out and put him into a baby seat. He then took off with his crew in the Lincoln. Just then, as Little Linda was about to pull into the street behind them, she said she saw a van come out of nowhere, "speeding up the block."

"I cut the van off," she told a television interviewer in 2011.[37] "My father's car gets to the stop sign and I'm behind his car and this van is behind me. I leaned down to get the portable radio and I heard popping sounds, and as I looked up I saw a whole bunch of guys dressed in black from head to toe. Black hoods, black ski masks, shooting up my father's car." The Lincoln was stopped at the corner of Eighty-Second Street because it had been cut off by a panel truck.[38]

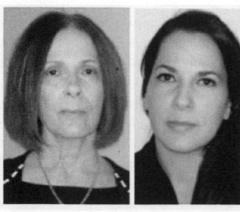

Big Linda and Little Linda Schiro, 2007

"It was like something out of a Mafia movie," said Schiro. "I got in the way between the van and my father's car because if I wasn't there, nobody in that car would have had a shot [at survival]."

Moments later, Little Linda grabbed her son and ran back into the house. When Big Linda opened the door, she said her daughter was screaming, "Mommy, I think they killed Daddy." But Scarpa and the three crew members had been able to drive around the panel truck and escape.[39] About ten minutes later, Little Linda said her father came back. "We both looked at each other," she said. Then he told her, "Every single person involved [in this] is going to pay."

A team of FBI agents quickly arrived on the scene. In short order, they determined that the panel truck had been rented in Queens. Based on a description of the van that came from Scarpa loyalists, they identified two of Cutolo's crew members, Vincent "Chickie" DeMartino and Frank Ianacci, who were seen earlier that day getting into a similar van. They'd left their car at a social club at Seventy-Seventh Street and Thirteenth Avenue, five blocks away, and were later reportedly spotted returning to it after the hit attempt.

All that information was contained in a 1992 FBI 302 describing the debriefing of Carmine Sessa. Curiously, Sessa told Agents Jeffrey Tomlinson and Howard Leadbetter II that later on the day of the ambush, Scarpa had told him that it was DeMartino and Ianacci who had attacked him—which was suspicious, since the assailants' faces had been covered.

Special Agent Chris Favo, DeVecchio's immediate subordinate in the C-10 (Colombo) squad, later told OPR investigators that he was the source of the panel truck rental details and that he'd given that information to DeVecchio.[40]

Larry Mazza, who would soon embark on a killing spree with Scarpa, later told agents that Senior found out where the panel truck had been rented from "his law enforcement guy." In his debriefing, Mazza suggested that this source had been "the Girlfriend"—a code name that multiple witnesses have said Scarpa used for Lin.[41]

Then, the day after the incident, Lin DeVecchio sent this 209 to Washington using Scarpa Sr. as his source. In it, "34" cites himself as the target of the attack.

An attempt to "hit" GREG SCARPA was made on November 18th, 1991 by members of the ORENA faction of the COLOMBO Family. SOURCE said there were several shooters and SCARPA's daughter was almost shot in the attempt. The SOURCE did not know which crew attempted the "hit" but noted that this would start the shooting war between the two factions.[42]

There it was: the official announcement, from the very source who had engineered Carmine Sessa's first attempt to kill Vic Orena, that the attack on Eighty-Second Street would now trigger "the shooting war." Since the other families seemed unwilling to challenge Vic Orena, Scarpa was now using the attempted hit as a justification to retaliate—and he would do it with a vengeance. As his daughter later put it, "After that incident, that was the end of anything normal in our family. Once those people did that in front of us, he became an absolute irate maniac."[43]

The Killing Machine was about to go into overdrive.

Chapter 26

GO OUT AND KILL SOMEBODY

The next move by the Persico faction was another attempt to kill Vic Orena. On or about November 23, five days after the shootout in front of Scarpa's house, Wimpy Boys member "Joey Brains" Ambrosino was with Michael Sessa on Staten Island. According to Joey, Michael's brother Carmine called and told them that Vic Orena had been spotted with Joe Scopo and Orena capo Thomas Petrizzo on the street in front of a funeral parlor at 101st Avenue in Ozone Park, Queens.

Quickly moving into action on Carmine's orders, Ambrosino beeped John Pate, Bobby Zambardi, and Bobby Zam's stepson "Jerry Boy" Chiari, the kid Vic Orena had promised to induct into the family if he stopped selling drugs. Now, Chiari was being summoned to kill him. As Ambrosino later testified, the second crew was instructed to bring "all the equipment" and link with Carmine, Michael, and Brains at a Rockaway Parkway diner. The "equipment" consisted of "machine guns, handguns [and] bulletproof vests."[1]

But after beeping Zambardi up to eight times with no response, Ambrosino said, Pate's crew didn't arrive at the diner until after five P.M.

When Carmine Sessa pulled up to meet them, he announced that Orena, Scopo, and Petrizzo were gone. At that point, according to Ambrosino, Carmine yelled at his brother for assembling the murder squad too late.[2] The next day, when word of the second murder plot against Orena filtered back to his faction, some of Cutolo's crew reportedly took action. The victim was Hank Smurra, the same capo who had initially targeted Joe Scopo at Turquoise. Carmine Sessa later related the events leading up to his death to FBI agents.

According to Sessa, after two failed moves on Orena, he was "concerned about Persico loyalists becoming targets."[3] With their faction outnumbered three to one, it was time to find new places to hide. So he instructed Smurra to drive to Staten Island and look for safe houses.[4] Sessa later told the agents that Smurra said he'd be accompanied by a man named "Leo" (last name unknown), whom Carmine didn't know. Sessa said he was "cautious." But Smurra insisted he'd be "okay . . . with Leo."

Later that day, when Smurra returned to Brooklyn, he was shot to death. His body was found in his car in the Sheepshead Bay area.[5] Masked gunmen had approached the vehicle and pumped three shots into his head while he was still behind the wheel.[6] Sessa later told Bureau agents that he'd heard secondhand from Michael "Black Mike" Calla that the shooters included "Chickie" DeMartino, one of Cutolo's crew members who had allegedly made the move on Greg Scarpa outside his house.[7] Ambrosino also testified later that Calla had identified DeMartino as Smurra's killer.[8]

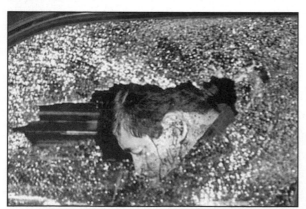

Hank Smurra after being shot to death as he sat in his car

The day after Smurra's murder, Lin DeVecchio filed a 209 in which "34" warned that "the PERSICO faction will doubtless retaliate soon." Scarpa added that "ski masks are being worn since neither side is sure of the ultimate settlement of this dispute and the actual shooters don't want to be identified for fear of future reprisals."[9]

In this case, Scarpa's prediction of a retaliation was dead-on. Hank Smurra's death represented the second murder in the third Colombo war, following the hit on Jack Leale, who was killed on November 4. Whether or not Scarpa was responsible for that hit, the FBI's star informant was now about to take control of the war away from his surrogate Carmine Sessa, who had blown two attempts on Vic Orena.

During Lin's 2007 murder trial, Sessa admitted that he had "learned the ways of the Mafia through Mr. Scarpa [his] sponsor."[10] But apparently he hadn't learned enough. Scarpa's next move was an elaborate plot that would leave nothing to chance. He wasn't simply going to wait around for a target of opportunity, as Sessa had done with Vic Orena. This time, the Mad Hatter would drive the action.

The Impossible Mission

On November 28, Thanksgiving morning, ten days after the purported attempt on his life by Cutolo's shooters, Greg Scarpa was at a safe house on Staten Island.[11] He stood watching as the members of his crew disguised themselves as Hasidic Jews, dressing all in black with full beards, frock coats, and the round fur *shtreimel* hats Hasidim wear over their long curling sideburns, known as *payot*. Scarpa had gotten word from his two spies in Billy Cutolo's camp[12] that later that morning Cutolo would be celebrating the holiday at the home of his girlfriend's grandmother in a Hasidic neighborhood of Brooklyn.[13] So, in a plot right out of Scarpa's favorite television series, *Mission: Impossible*,[14] his costumed crew would be walking near the house with TEC-9s and other weapons hidden in their coats. When Cutolo emerged from his car to enter the holiday dinner, he would be assassinated.

Ambrosino later testified that the Hasidic costumes were picked up by Anthony "the Arab" Sayegh, a member of their crew.[15] They were reportedly kept at the home of Larry Fiorenza's girlfriend. On the morning of the plot, as the members of the hit team suited up, Ambrosino testified that he got a call from Fiorenza, who told him to "go buy the *New York Post*."

That very morning, the *Post* had run a story by reporter Murray Weiss alleging that Scarpa had been a government informant. So the plot was canceled.[16]

The stories within the family about Scarpa's being a government snitch dated back to the 1960s, and they continued to dog Greg Sr. as he operated with virtual impunity, avoiding federal charge after federal charge.

"This is a guy who seemed to walk between the raindrops," said one lawyer who represented Scarpa but asked not to be identified.[17] Anthony Casso told me that Scarpa's motive for killing both his own brother Sal and Joe Brewster DeDomenico, whom he thought of as a son, was that he suspected them of spreading rumors that he was a government informant. Now this latest *Post* story was threatening to derail Scarpa's plan to eliminate Vic Orena.

Carmine Sessa later testified that he was worried the allegations in the *Post* story might be true, and he had good reason to feel that way. After he became a cooperating witness in 1993, Sessa told FBI agents of the many indications he'd had over the years that Scarpa had an official source who protected him.

As early as the 1980s, Sessa said, Greg Jr. told him that his father "had someone in law enforcement providing him with information."[18] Not only did Sessa confirm how Scarpa had received the list of Wimpy Boys crew members about to be arrested by the DEA in 1987,[19] but a year later, after he and Joe Brewster and Bobby Zam were busted for a bank robbery, he told agents that "Scarpa Sr. had some influence to keep his crew on the street," and that he had "an angel looking after him."[20] Sessa also said he was "amaze[d]" that Scarpa didn't "hesitate" to discuss criminal activities inside the Wimpy Boys club, even though he'd warned Sessa that it had been bugged.

"That made Sessa suspicious about Scarpa Sr.'s relationship with law enforcement," the agents wrote in their 302.[21]

But now, on Thanksgiving Day 1991, as the crew suited up to take out Cutolo, Sessa had to placate the other family members who were worried that if Greg Sr. was a snitch, they might be in jeopardy. So he sought out "Joe T" Tomesello, the capo who had been appointed part of a three-man ruling panel by Junior Persico back in 1986. Tomesello, a family elder, had a solution. "To settle everybody's mind," he suggested, Sessa should tell

Scarpa to "go out and kill somebody on the Orena faction . . . to prove himself."[22] As Sessa later testified during Lin DeVecchio's trial, the sense among the family members was that the FBI would *never* allow a confidential informant to commit murder. So to deflect the criticism and prove that he wasn't "a rat," Scarpa should "go out and do a piece of work."[23]

Now that he had to prove to the Persico loyalists that he wasn't an informant, Scarpa was even more motivated, so he went off on a rampage, trolling the streets of Brooklyn with Larry Mazza and Jimmy Del Masto in his tricked-out murder wagon and killing or wounding one person per week between early December 1991 and January 1992. "Here we have a paid government informant," says Flora Edwards, "who is acting more like a secret government *agent* and to protect his cover he feels compelled to kill. From this point on, the blood he spilled is now on the hands of the FBI as well."[24]

Taking Out Tommy Scars

Scarpa's next victim turned out to be an aging gangster who was in the wrong place at the wrong time. On December 3, 1991, at 9:38 A.M., Greg was cruising past the Mother Cabrini social club at 2284 McDonald Avenue in the Gravesend section of Brooklyn,[25] when he thought he spotted Nicky Grancio, one of the Orena capos he saw as a threat.

As it happened, the man Scarpa saw was thirty-eight-year-old Joey Tolino, Grancio's nephew, who resembled his uncle. Tolino was standing talking to Gaetano "Tommy Scars" Amato, a seventy-eight-year-old member of the Genovese family. From his passing van, driven by Jimmy Del Masto, Scarpa gave Mazza the word to fire, and a volley of bullets hit Tolino and Amato, killing the old Genovese soldier where he stood and wounding Tolino in the foot.[26]

It was the fourth war-related shooting in two weeks. On November 28, Carmine's brother Larry Sessa, who had been with Scarpa during the alleged hit outside his house, was chased by a group of gunmen while he walked down Eighty-Sixth Street. As they closed in on him, a car driven by Ron Calder, another Persico loyalist, pulled up and Larry jumped in. Speeding off, Calder was shot in the shoulder and hand, then lost control of the car, running into four innocent pedestrians on the sidewalk, who were also injured.[27]

Now, on the morning of Amato's slaying, law enforcement sources were quoted in the *New York Post* as predicting an extended conflict.

"The whole family is in turmoil," one source said. "This is not going to end easily."[28]

The very next day, another aging wiseguy, seventy-nine-year-old Rosario "Black Sam" Nastasi, a longtime Colombo bookmaker, was shot around one A.M. while playing cards at the Belvedere Social Athletic Association at 985 Sixty-Third Street in Bensonhurst.[29] His girlfriend, forty-seven-year-old Kay Duggan, was wounded in the attack. She was later treated for a superficial chest wound at Maimonides Medical Center and released. With two bystanders now caught in the crossfire, this open mob war on the streets of Brooklyn was starting to produce unmistakable collateral damage.

In a 209 filed the day of the Nastasi hit, Lin DeVecchio blamed the "turmoil" entirely on the Orena faction—with no mention of the drive-by shooting of Amato, which had been reported in the *Post,* or the role his source, Scarpa Sr., had played in it.

> On December 5th, 1991, ▮▮▮▮▮▮▮▮ advised that . . . the current turmoil within the COLOMBO Family is caused by ORENA wanting to be the official Boss and to that end has approximately five Capos backing him. As a result of this internal conflict, two COLOMBO members aligned with PERSICO, HANK SMURRA, and ROSARIO NASTASI, were recently killed. Further, an attempt to kill GREGORY SCARPA Sr., a COLOMBO member loyal to PERSICO, was made without success, and all of the hits and attempts were authorized by VIC ORENA.[30]

The day after Nastasi's murder, Scarpa struck again. This time, he fired a rifle from his van at Vincent Fusaro, the thirty-year-old night manager of the Venus Diner in Bay Ridge, Brooklyn, who was a member of Cutolo's crew. According to Larry Mazza's testimony at Teddy Persico's subsequent trial, Mazza was coming back from a numbers pickup with Scarpa and Jimmy Del Masto when they spotted Fusaro stringing Christmas lights with his wife outside his house in the Bath Beach section of Brooklyn. It was 3:35 on a Friday afternoon.[31] Mazza described what happened next:

Greg had a rifle on him. Most of us had pistols, and he told us to stop, he was going to shoot him, but Jimmy [Del Masto] kept going, certainly not prepared for that. And Greg told us to go around the block. And he told [us] to cover our license plate. [We] had tape in the car [to] cover the plate. We went around the block, but we never stopped to put the tape on. Everybody was jittery. As we pulled up, Greg opened the window and fired three shots . . . hit Fusaro and killed him.[32]

"It was a hell of a shot," Mazza later said in a 2012 *New York Post* interview. "Guy went down like a sack of potatoes." But as a measure of Senior's

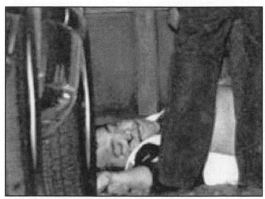

Vincent Fusaro after being shot by Greg Scarpa Sr.

thoroughness and brutality, Mazza said that he "shot him two more times— once in the neck and once in the body."[33] Scarpa later admitted that he used an M1 carbine in the attack.[34] Fusaro, who had no criminal record, was hit in the head and died instantly.[35] His terrified neighbors wouldn't talk to the police.

"In this neighborhood, mum's the word," said one man, who refused to give his name to a reporter. According to the *New York Times,* both Police Commissioner Lee P. Brown and Brooklyn DA Charles Hynes would not yet characterize the violence, which had already claimed three lives, as part of a "mob war."[36]

That same *Times* piece, quoting "the authorities," reported that "Mr. Orena has decided to take the family over for himself, an action that has divided the Colombo organization and brought other families into the action."

At that point, other than the mistaken murder of Genovese member Amato, there wasn't a shred of evidence that any of the "other families" had gotten involved in the violence. But the *Times,* like the two New York tabloids, was getting much of its law enforcement information from the Bureau—and the FBI was getting its *mis*information from Greg Scarpa. So the false story that Vic Orena was principally responsible for the burgeoning war continued to dominate the coverage.

The Black Sheep

On December 17, the *Times* ran a story on a move by DA Hynes to subpoena twenty-eight Colombo members to a grand jury. Quoting one mob lawyer, who called it a "publicity stunt," reporter Robert D. McFadden cited "law enforcement officials" as attributing the violent incidents to the "power struggle between Carmine Persico . . . the imprisoned boss and Mr. Orena." Citing "the authorities" as his source, McFadden reported that Orena had "refused orders, among other things to share profits and relinquish control of the family to Mr. Persico's son Alphonse."[37]

A week earlier, Selwyn Raab had reported a similar allegation in a *Times* story under the headline "Even to the 5 Families, the Fighting Colombos Have Been Black Sheep."[38] Calling the recent shootings "the worst outbreak of Mafia violence in three decades," Raab revisited the two previous Profaci-Colombo conflicts, noting that "even within the violent councils of America's Mafia, authorities say the Colombo crime family has long been feared as an erratic, troublesome gang." He then reported the theory, spun by Scarpa and communicated to FBI brass by DeVecchio, that the latest conflict "stemmed from Mr. Orena's refusal to share illicit profits with Mr. Persico's allies."[39]

But what Raab could not have known at that point was that, of the Five Families, the Colombo borgata was the only one with an inside FBI agent provocateur. A violent killer who used his special position with the Feds to destabilize the family from within.

During Lin's 2007 murder trial, Mark Bederow, one of his lawyers, described Greg Scarpa as "treacherous," "deceitful," and "a master liar."[40] Until the disclosure of the 1,153 pages of heretofore secret files on "34," detailed here for the first time, no one in the outside media—including veteran organized crime reporters like Selwyn Raab—had any real sense of the depth of Scarpa's treachery when it came to selling out his Mafia brothers.

"This refusal-to-share-the-profits story was pure Scarpa," said Andrew Orena. "It was a fabrication enhanced by the Feds. Naturally, when the family split apart after the attack on my father, the funds that might have gone to Junior Persico were put on hold, but not *before* that. This was another one of the stories planted by Greg and put out by the Feds that the media picked up on."

Andrew said emphatically, "When my father asked Carmine Sessa to poll the captains in the spring, he included *Teddy Persico*. If he was trying to cheat Junior or stage a kind of power grab, he never would have done that."[41]

As to who was really behind this new war, Greg Scarpa Sr. would eventually plead guilty to the murders of Fusaro and two others during the conflict.[42] Larry Mazza would confirm Scarpa's participation in the murder of Tommy Scars. And we'll examine probative evidence that Scarpa was directly linked to two more homicides—making him responsible for one-third to one-half of the first twelve murders in the conflict. But at this point nobody in the media, and few inside the Bureau, understood the dominant role he was playing as the field general responsible for much of the violence.

The Bagel Shop Killing

Two days after Fusaro's murder, the civilian toll in the escalating war grew again. On the morning of December 8, James Malpeso, the twenty-one-year-old son of Colombo soldier Louis "Bobo" Malpeso, was shot.[43] After he was dropped off at Coney Island Hospital with a gunshot wound to the chest, forces loyal to his father struck back almost immediately and with tragic consequences.[44] Anthony Libertore and his son Christopher, who reportedly served as the elder Malpeso's bodyguards, entered the Wanna Bagel Shop at 8905 Third Avenue in Brooklyn, which was reportedly owned by two members of the Persico faction: Anthony Ferrara and Frank Guerra.[45]

Mistakenly thinking one of the owners was behind the counter, the father-son hit team opened fire, killing eighteen-year-old Matteo Speranza, a worker in the shop who had absolutely nothing to do with organized crime.[46] Speranza, the innocent son of an Italian immigrant, was the fourth person killed in six days.

The Libertores later became government witnesses, testifying at a federal trial against Malpeso, who was convicted of loan sharking and stock manipulation after the jury deadlocked on the murder charges. In a heartfelt outburst during the trial, after Chris Libertore admitted shooting Matteo twice in the face and four times more to make sure he was dead, Umberto Speranza, the dead teenager's father, jumped up sobbing and yelled, "You bastard, you killed my son!"[47]

In 1931 Edward Doherty wrote a now-famous piece for *Liberty* magazine chastising Americans who idolized gangsters like Al Capone. Doherty noted how Americans seemed to justify their murders with the phrase, "they only kill each other."[48] But in the first days of December 1991, while the shooting of Gaetano Amato, a made guy, and the girlfriend of "Black Sam" Nastasi, might have been written off because of their association with the Mafia, the slaying of young Matteo Speranza was proof positive that the violence unleashed by Greg Scarpa Sr. had now touched the public in a bloody and brutal way

Until now, Lin DeVecchio had been able to appease FBI officials in Washington with "34's" self-serving spin on the war. But the murder of Matteo Speranza seemed to alter the level of scrutiny. This time, when he visited Scarpa at his home on Eighty-Second Street, DeVecchio took along two special agents from the C-10 Colombo Squad, Raymond Andjich and Jeffrey Tomlinson, who accompanied him there two more times.

In his memoirs, Lin explains these exceptions to his one-on-one protocol with Senior this way: "To make it look like an official FBI visit in case anyone saw me go into his house, I took along an FNG, a follower of Favo, a partner of Favo, and, like Favo, a man without a knack, Ray Andjich."[49] In the FBI's New York Office, "FNG" was an informal term used to describe less experienced agents. It stood for "Fucking New Guy."

The subtitle of DeVecchio's book, *We're Going to Win This Thing,* is *The Shocking Frame-up of a Mafia Crime Buster,* and Lin makes it clear in that memoir that he considers Special Agent Chris Favo, his immediate subordinate in the C-10 squad, one of those who set him up.[50] In January 1994, Special Agents Favo, Andjich, Jeffrey Tomlinson, and Howard Leadbetter would come forward with suspicions that DeVecchio had passed intelligence to Scarpa. Their allegations would lead to the opening of the OPR internal affairs investigation of their boss, which lasted thirty-one months.

In his book, DeVecchio describes his treatment of Andjich at Scarpa's house as if he were dealing with a child: "I parked Ray Andjich in the living room in front of the TV and sat down in the kitchen with Scarpa."[51] The 302 report memorializing that meeting, which DeVecchio, Andjich, and Tomlinson filed jointly, would later become known infamously as "the Kitchen 302," because DeVecchio later insisted that the TV in the living room made it impossible for Andjich (and by implication Tomlinson) to overhear what he was discussing with his informant.

According to that 302, Scarpa denied any knowledge of the "internal war" within the family and claimed Cutolo's crew must have been "mistaken" in its attack on him:

> On December 10, 1991, Supervisory Special Agent R. LINDLEY DEVECCHIO, Special Agent (SA) RAYMOND ANDJICH, and SA JEFFREY W. TOMLINSON contacted GREGORY SCARPA, SR. at his residence, 1243 82nd St., Brooklyn, NY where they identified themselves as FBI agents. . . .
>
> SCARPA was provided with details of the Witness Protection Program in view of the recent attempt on his life, but declined any help from the government and stated that any past incident involving a shooting was a case of mistaken identity and he believed himself to be in no danger. . . .
>
> SCARPA denied any knowledge of a COLOMBO Family internal war and said if he ever felt he needed help from the federal government, he would not hesitate to contact one of the above agents.[52]

DeVecchio may have brought along other agents to the meeting, but the fact that he "parked" them where they couldn't overhear his debriefing was telling. As noted, Department of Justice guidelines mandate that at the first sign that a confidential informant has committed an act of criminal violence or is suspected of planning to commit one, the U.S. attorney must be brought into the loop. If Andjich and Tomlinson had become aware that Scarpa was linked to the new round of violence, they would have been required to alert the EDNY.

In 1995, during Lin DeVecchio's OPR investigation, Chris Favo claimed that his boss's December 10 report was "fictitious," created to "protect" Scarpa from being readily identified as a source.[53] This allowed the Feds to argue, later, that Scarpa's characterization of the Eighty-Second Street shootout as a "case of mistaken identity" was untrue. Still, on the day after that 302 was filed, DeVecchio filed a much more detailed 209 in which he described what he had learned from Scarpa in that kitchen. It was a report full of half-truths and misinformation that utterly obscured Scarpa's culpability in the war.

On December 11, 1991, SCARPA SR advised SSA R. LINDLEY DE VECCHIO that the main shooters from Billy CUTOLO's crew, who were responsible for the hits on HENRY SMURRA, and ROSARIO NASTASI, and the attempts on GREG SCARPA and LARRY SESSA were VINCENT "Chickie" DIMARTINO [*sic*], FRANK IANNACI, and "Nigger Dom." The source noted that in several instances, particularly with the attempt on LARRY SESSA, numerous other individuals were involved from CUTOLO's crew.

The source said the hit on GAETANO AMATO was an accidental shooting by the PERSICO faction when attempting to hit JOSEPH TOLINO. The PERSICO faction contacted the GENOVESE Family and expressed their apologies for the shooting, and were told by officials of the GENOVESE Family that it was regrettable about AMATO, but he should have known better than to be in a COLOMBO location and there would be no retaliation. The source said the PERSICO side believed them to be members close to NICHOLAS GRANCIO at that location prior to the shooting.

The source said an attempt was made to hit JOEL "Joe Waverly" CACACE on December 4 or 5, 1991 by the PERSICO faction, several shots were fired by the PERSICOs and CACACE, but no one was injured.

The source said the hit on VINCENT FUSARO was done by the PERSICO faction, and noted that FUSARO, although not a button, was one of BILLY CUTOLO's main shylocks, and was very close to CUTOLO.

Concerning the shooting of JAMES MALPESO. . . . Source said this shooting appears to be a separate incident related to a bar fight, although COLOMBO member LOUIS MALPESO, SR. is on the ORENA Side.

The source said that the Killing of SPERANZA, who worked at the bagel shop on Third Ave. was not done by the PERSICO faction. The source said that there are indications that TEDDY PERSICO had some connection with this bagel shop, and that the ORENA faction shooters apparently mistook the kid to be related to the owner or in some way connected to the PERSICOs.

The source said CARMINE SESSA, JOE TOMASELLO, and JO JO RUSSO are currently speaking for the PERSICO faction. Source advised that there is to be a sit-down next week between the two factions in an attempt to resolve the dispute, however, if it can't be settled amicably, there would be more hits. The source said that law enforcement pressure may slow down the active shooting but it would resume in short order unless some of the players are killed or indicted as a result of current federal investigations.[54]

Missing from the report was any word of Scarpa's direct role in the murders of Amato and Fusaro and his role in the shooting of Joe "Waverly" Cacace, which was later confirmed.[55] But the most telling aspect of that 209 was in the very last sentence: Scarpa Sr. was predicting that, unless various "players" were killed or indicted, the violence would go on—and he certainly wasn't talking about himself as a victim or arrestee.

With that 209, Scarpa, and by implication his handler DeVecchio, was signaling to FBI officials that it was the "Orena faction" that had to be stopped, otherwise the bloodshed would continue. There was never even a suggestion that "34" himself had instigated the conflict, or that he had personally escalated it to the point where innocent people were dying.

As far as Washington knew from those 209s, Vic Orena was the aggressor—and federal prosecutors in Brooklyn soon bought into that story.

The 209 ended by noting the existence of "current federal investigations," but until the outbreak of shooting after Carmine Sessa's initial attempt on Orena, there *hadn't* been any investigations of significance.

How do we know that? Because a senior federal prosecutor in the EDNY has admitted to it. In his epic Mafia history, *Five Families,* Selwyn Raab quotes EDNY Assistant U.S. Attorney John Gleeson (now a federal judge) as saying, "We had very little on the Colombo family [prior to the start of the war]. We were struggling along, there was nothing big in the works."[56]

But soon, as a result of the violence Scarpa engineered, the Eastern District would issue up to seventy-five indictments. With the death toll mounting, Gleeson and fellow AUSAs George Stamboulidis and Andrew Weissmann started working overtime to make cases—and the most significant early indictments were directed at the Orena faction.

On December 19, 1991, as Greg Scarpa Sr. fed Lin DeVecchio more "intelligence" that diverted the focus away from himself, he hammered away at Wild Bill Cutolo, the capo he'd first sought to get indicted:

On December 19, 1991 ████████ advised SSA R. LINDLEY DE VEC-
CHIO that the PERSICO faction is only looking to hit ORENA faction officials, and members connected to Billy CUTOLO. Source said
CUTOLO's crew is not highly regarded as a result of the hits on Black
Sam NASTASI, and on the kid who worked in the bagel store. The source
said numerous members have questioned CUTOLO's methods, noting
that killing "civilians" has brought a lot of law enforcement pressure to
the day to day criminal activities.[57]

There was no mention of Gaetano Amato's murder by Scarpa or how close
Vincent Fusaro's wife might have come to the bullets from "34." Cutolo,
who had allegedly made the move on Scarpa outside his house, was now
being blamed for the murder of Matteo Speranza—despite the assertion in
DeVecchio's last 209 that the shooting of James Malpeso, which supposedly
triggered the bagel shop killing, appeared to be "a separate incident related
to a bar fight."

At this point, the FBI and the federal prosecutors they serviced were
bent on removing Vic Orena and his captains, convinced by Scarpa that
they were the aggressors in the war. The spin against Orena was so pronounced that in DeVecchio's final 209 of the year, he told his FBI bosses
that there was one sure way to end the conflict:

> The source said the current dispute is unacceptable to all in the PERSICO
> faction, and they want to resolve it as soon as possible. The source said
> that unless ORENA accepts the proposals, after review by Junior PER-
> SICO, the shooting war will continue until one or more of the principals
> on either side is killed. The source noted that an arrest of VIC ORENA
> would temporarily halt the shooting war.[58]

It would be another four months before the Feds made good on that final
suggestion by Greg Scarpa. Having twice failed to execute his plan A and
have his rival Vic Orena killed, Scarpa now initiated plan B: Orena would
soon be arrested for murder, and as we'll see, the evidence uncovered in this
investigation suggests that he was framed.

Chapter 27

THE HIT
ON NICKY BLACK

With the coming of the New Year, and no end to the war in sight, the principal campaign to stem the violence was waged by the Organized Crime Investigation Division (OCID) Task Force. A group of elite detectives from the NYPD's Organized Crime Control Bureau (OCCB) were assigned to work out of the FBI's New York Office at 26 Federal Plaza. Their immediate goal was to arrest as many members of the Colombo family as possible and get them off the streets. Two weeks earlier, Kings County DA Charles Hynes had vowed, "We're not going to allow this county to become a shooting gallery where innocent people are being gunned down."[1] But Hynes's effort to haul dozens of Colombo wiseguys before a grand jury had little effect.[2]

The arrest strategy, by contrast, soon began to pay off. Since being a member of the Mafia wasn't a state crime, the OCID's main tactic was to lock up the made men and associates for "carrying"—that is, for illegal possession of handguns.

In the course of the war, 123 such gun arrests were made.[3] Nearly a third of them were the work of Detectives Joe Simone and Pat Maggiore, a pair of street-smart Italian American cops who had spent years working undercover narcotics and other NYPD specialty units.[4]

On December 16, Simone and Maggiore arrested "Chickie" DeMartino and two other Colombo associates for carrying nine-millimeter semiautomatics. They'd spotted DeMartino and followed him to Avenue U and East Fourth Street in the Gravesend section of Brooklyn. There they watched as DeMartino linked with twenty-four-year-old Michael Spataro of Staten Island and thirty-four-year-old Gabriel Scianna of Brooklyn, who were reportedly trying to break into a Cadillac using a wire hanger.[5]

All three arrestees were named in a routine police blotter story in the *Staten Island Advance.* But the full significance of that NYPD pinch didn't become clear until Greg Scarpa weighed in. In a 209 dated January 7, 1992, sourcing Scarpa (though his name was redacted in the released version), Lin DeVecchio wrote that all three of the suspects collared by Simone and Maggiore were part of the same Cutolo hit team that allegedly sought to kill "34" and later succeeded in killing Hank Smurra and "Black Sam" Nastasi.

> On January 7, 1992, ▮▮▮▮▮▮▮ advised SSA R. LINDLEY DE VEC-CHIO that GABE SCIANNA . . . is an associate of BILLY CUTOLO, and was a member of the "hit team" composed of VINCENT DEMAR-TINO, MICHAEL SPATARO, FRANKIE IANNACCI, "NIGGER DOM," and SCIANNA. The source said they were responsible for the hits on HENRY SMURRA and BLACK SAM NASTASI.[6]

The fact that these arrests were made by this particular team of detectives is hugely significant in the overall story of the Scarpa-DeVecchio scandal, because, as we'll see, the Feds later falsely accused Joe Simone of leaking key intelligence to the mob—a ploy some defense attorneys believed was designed to take the heat off Lin DeVecchio. But more immediately, Simone and Maggiore would play major roles in the next significant incident in the war—Greg Scarpa's murder of Nicholas Grancio. It took place on January 7, the same day SSA DeVecchio filed that 209 on the DeMartino arrest.

The Cop from Gravesend

Joe Simone was born in the Italian neighborhood near West Sixth Street and Stillwell Avenue in Brooklyn known as Gravesend—a name that seemed fitting when it became the site of many of the homicides during the third Colombo war. After spending the first part of his childhood there, Simone's parents moved him to Flatbush at the age of six—another Brooklyn neighborhood where the Mafia was well entrenched.

"We lived on a block where you were either a cop or a fireman or you got made," he told me in the first of a series of interviews.[7] And it was during his teenage years that Joe was first approached to make that third choice. It came at a time when his family was in dire financial straits. His father had just died, and Joe's mother was about to lose their house. "There was a guy name Louie who lived across the street," he remembered. "He says, 'All you have to do for me is drive and you can make seventeen thousand dollars a year.' That was real money back then. But when I told my mother, she gave me a crack across the face and said, 'Don't get involved with those people.'"

Joe's uncle was a first-grade detective with the NYPD. So after passing the entrance exam, Simone became a uniformed patrolman, beginning his career as a beat cop in the Seventieth Precinct. He later distinguished himself in the Seven-O's Anti-Crime Unit, collaring arsonists, rapists, and murderers.[8] After years in Manhattan South Narcotics he finally earned his gold detective's shield,[9] eventually joining the elite OCID unit—an NYPD-FBI task force designed to partner street-hardened cops like Simone and Maggiore with inexperienced FBI agents from around the country.

Simone's immediate boss was Chris Favo, DeVecchio's number two. An Italian American Notre Dame graduate with a law degree, Favo came to New York, according to Simone, with little or no sense of the street.

"I helped to educate him," he said. "Chris knew that I knew a lot of wiseguys. One time he came up to me and he had a picture. He says, 'Do you know this guy?' And I say, 'Yeah, that's Bobby Attanasio.' He asks me, 'How do you know him?' And I say, 'His kid and mine played touch football together.' At the time, [Attanasio] was a soldier in the Bonanno family. His brother was a capo. Another time, Favo shows me a picture—'Who's this guy?' I say, 'Joey Ida. He lives about eight blocks away from me. He's Jimmy's brother.' Then Favo asks me, 'Is he a made guy?' I say, 'Yeah. His brother's a [Genovese] capo and he ended up being a street boss.' Now he's doing three life sentences. I knew these guys and they knew me," Simone recalled. "They knew what side of the street I walked on. There was an association, but I never crossed the line."

Once, when his mother was in the hospital, one of Bill Cutolo's associates asked if there was anything his captain could do. "I said, 'Thanks. No. Just prayers,'" said Simone. "The next day this kid from a florist came with a basket maybe four feet wide and three feet high with a card, 'Best wishes to your mom,' signed 'Billy Cutolo and friends.' And my mother, who was as honest as the Virgin Mary, said, kidding, 'I hope I don't find a horse's head under my bed.'

"The Colombo people knew I was a cop, but they just felt more comfortable telling me things because I was a neighborhood guy and knew how they operated. There's no way they would have trusted some agent from the Midwest just 'cause he was Italian."

And it wasn't simply a matter of trust. Simone and Maggiore had extraordinary operational skills. Once, during a tour of Bensonhurst and Gravesend, Simone showed me the exact spot where he and his partner had followed Vincent DeMartino.

"Chickie gets out of his car and he walks over to these two guys jimmying the Caddy," Simone recalled. "So Pat and I jump out, flip out our shields, and say, 'Stop! Police.' We order them to bend over, hands on the car. One guy's kissing the trunk. The other two have their hands on the hood. We catch them in the act, so we search them and right off we find the guns. If it had been the Bureau they wouldn't even have *approached* them without a half dozen guys with machine guns and vests."

So at the height of the war, as the violence increased, the FBI used OCID detectives like Simone and Maggiore to follow Colombo members with two goals in mind: arrest anybody who was "strapped," and protect those who weren't from gunfire. One of the Orena captains they were assigned to follow was Nicky Grancio. Next to Wild Bill Cutolo, Nicky Black, named for the dark circles under his eyes, was the capo who posed the biggest threat to Greg Scarpa.

On the afternoon of Tuesday, January 7, the two detectives were in a white FBI-issued Nissan Maxima, tailing Grancio, who was behind the wheel of a new Toyota Land Cruiser. Sitting next to Grancio was his nephew Joey Tolino, whom Scarpa had wounded a month earlier in the shootout that killed Tommy Scars Amato. At twelve forty-five P.M., Grancio and Tolino rolled up to a social club run by Alphonse "Funzi" D'Ambrosio, another capo loyal to Vic Orena. The location was near the intersection of McDonald Avenue and Avenue U in Joe's old neighborhood of Gravesend.[10]

"We had him under observation from two angles," Simone told me. "Pat and I were watching him from our car and up above in an apartment overlooking the club the Bureau had what we called a 'perch' known as Plant 26. There was a camera and recording equipment up there manned by a couple of agents. We knew the heat was on Nicky, so we were keeping him under virtual round-the-clock surveillance."

Simone's Daily Activity Report (DAR) from that date confirms that he and Maggiore sat on Grancio until 13:30, or 1:30 P.M. At that point the two detectives got what Simone later described as a "strange call."[11]

Daily Activity Report, Det. Joe Simone, Tuesday, January 7, 1992

"Out of the clear blue," said Joe, "Favo calls and tells us all to come back to Federal Plaza for a team meeting. Now, this is unusual, since it's two in the afternoon and we normally meet at the end of the day."[12] As outlined in Simone's DAR, reproduced here, he and Maggiore and the FBI surveillance team withdrew and headed back to 26 Federal Plaza for the meeting with Favo, which lasted from 14:00 to 16:00 (2:00 to 4:00 P.M.).

What happened next would be widely disputed over time. What is certain is that, sometime after the FBI agents and the two detectives had withdrawn, Greg Scarpa Sr., who had been trolling the streets of Brooklyn, passed by in a rented mid-size blue sedan driven by Jimmy Del Masto.[13] Scarpa was in the shotgun seat with the M1 carbine he'd used to kill Fusaro. Larry Mazza was in the back with a twelve-gauge double-barrel riot-control shotgun. According to details Mazza gave reporter Brad Hamilton for a *New York Post* story, the sedan was tricked out like a police surveillance vehicle.

"We had a big walkie-talkie and coffee cups in the window and a blue police siren," Mazza recalled.[14]

Mazza, who is now fifty-two, later testified that they had been "driving around different areas where we thought we can find some . . . Orena faction people."[15] Driving past the club, they spotted a car belonging to Funzi D'Ambrosio, another Orena capo and thus a potential target. "So we went around the block," said Mazza, and "parked in a position where we can watch the club [and] see when he would come out."[16]

At some point, Mazza said, he "spotted Nicky Black's truck." When he pointed it out, Scarpa said, "Let's get him." At that point, said Mazza, "Jimmy started driving. As we got toward the corner, Grancio pulled away." He made a left on Avenue U, so they followed the Land Cruiser as Grancio drove around a small triangle of land known in the neighborhood as Billy Grove Square. Just then, Grancio pulled over and Anthony Bianco, a twenty-six-year-old Colombo associate, came out of the club. Bianco walked toward the Toyota, said Mazza, and leaned on the driver's side to talk with Grancio and Tolino.

In an interview with me, Mazza said that Scarpa "got one shot off and then the clip fell out [of the M1]."[17] So Mazza rolled down the window and brandished the riot gun, which they'd stolen from a police car in Lakewood, New Jersey, near Scarpa's farm.

"I was close enough I could have smacked him," he said. "I aimed right behind his ear." Mazza says the blast caused Grancio's nose to hit the windshield.[18] Nicky Black was killed instantly. Bianco was wounded and rushed to Coney Island Hospital. Tolino later told Simone that "he ended up with brain matter all over him." "We even recovered one of Nicky's teeth from the wall of a house fifteen feet away," Simone told me. "It was gruesome."

Simone and Maggiore were still in their meeting at 26 Federal Plaza when they got word that the man they'd been trying to protect earlier was now dead. They rushed back to the scene and caught up with Tolino at a nearby precinct, where he admonished them for pulling back the surveillance.

"He said to me, 'Man, you guys were fol-

Nicholas Grancio after the murder

lowing us all this time and all of a sudden you disappear and they whack Nicky,'" said Simone. "I didn't have the heart to tell him at the time that we got pulled back for a team meeting in the Ivory Tower at 26 Federal."

Simone insists that it was "highly unusual to have a meeting like that at midday on a Tuesday. Usually we had them on Fridays," he said. So why was surveillance withdrawn from Grancio at that particular time? Could the withdrawal have had anything to do with Greg Scarpa's "law enforcement source"?

Mazza ended up pleading guilty to the Grancio murder and two other war-related homicides committed with Scarpa. He was sentenced to ten years in prison. In 2002, after getting paroled, Mazza met defense attorney Flora Edwards at a Hilton hotel in Orlando, Florida, near where he was living. According to Edwards, Mazza told her that after Scarpa first spotted Grancio outside the club that day, he became concerned about the police surveillance.

"They wanted to kill Grancio," she said, "but they couldn't get a clear shot at him because the cops were all over him." Then, said Edwards, "Scarpa Sr. borrowed Mazza's cell phone and called somebody named 'Del.' He said, 'What the fuck is going on here? The whole world's here. Do something.'"[19]

Mazza's Conflicting Accounts

In May 2003, Mazza was interviewed by the late Dr. Stephen Dresch, a Michigan-based PhD who was working at the time with forensic investigator Angela Clemente. The two of them were probing the Scarpa-DeVecchio relationship with the hope of presenting their findings to a congressional committee. In 2004, on the twelfth anniversary of Grancio's death, Dresch appeared at a hearing for Vic Orena. On the stand under oath, Dresch said that when he met with Mazza in Plantation, Florida, in 2003, Mazza told him that on January 7, 1992, after locating Grancio, whom he and Scarpa intended to "eliminate," they "observed that he was under surveillance."

According to Dresch, Mazza went on to say that "Mr. Scarpa became upset and immediately called . . . his law enforcement source [and] essentially . . . demanded the surveillance team be withdrawn from the location."[20] Mazza and Scarpa then "returned to the scene, discovered that the surveillance had been terminated and they proceeded to terminate Mr. Grancio." In other words, according to Dresch, Mazza told him that the van made *two* passes at the Land Cruiser that day: one before the law enforcement surveillance was removed and one after, when the fatal shot was fired.

But Mazza himself also testified at that same hearing, before Judge Jack B. Weinstein, and his account of the murder conflicted with what Dresch said he'd told him. First, Mazza stated that he "didn't notice any surveillance on Nicky Grancio that day."[21] Second, while he admitted that Scarpa had made "phone calls," he agreed with a federal prosecutor that "from the moment [he] first saw Mr. Grancio 'til the moment he was killed, there was no time to make any phone calls."[22]

In 2008, after Nicky Black Grancio's widow, Maria, filed a wrongful death suit against Lin DeVecchio and Chris Favo, a federal judge dismissed it, largely because of Mazza's testimony at that 2004 hearing.[23] "Mrs. Grancio's claims hinge on Mazza," Judge Frederic Block wrote.[24] In granting the government's motion for summary judgment, Block noted that both DeVecchio and Favo "concede that Simone and Maggiore left their post at Favo's request. They deny however that the request was part of a murder conspiracy with Scarpa."

In a sworn affidavit submitted in conjunction with the lawsuit, DeVecchio insisted that he never "receive[d] a telephone call, or any other form of communication from Gregory Scarpa Sr. in which [he was asked] to remove or terminate any surveillance of Nicholas Grancio."[25] Favo submitted a similar affidavit in which he stated that "DeVecchio did not ask [him] at any time to undertake any effort to terminate any surveillance on January 7, 1992."[26]

Interestingly, however, Favo insisted that neither Simone nor Maggiore had told him "that it was important to maintain surveillance on Grancio . . . or that they had Grancio under surveillance to protect him or to prevent his murder."[27]

"If nothing else, that last point suggests gross incompetence," says Flora Edwards, whose motion seeking a new trial for Vic Orena had prompted that 2004 hearing. "By January 7, 1992, there were five previous homicides and a half dozen casualties in the war," she said in an interview. "Joey Tolino himself told Detective Simone how he'd expected the Feds to protect him. So it strains belief for Favo to suggest that he didn't think Nicky was in danger."[28]

Further, in his order dismissing the Grancio case, Judge Block cited a *Daily News* article by Greg B. Smith and Jerry Capeci from October 30, 1994. Under the headline "Mob, Mole & Murder," the piece reported:

> On January 7, 1992, Scarpa met again with DeVecchio. Later that day, he [Scarpa] executed Nicholas (Nicky Black) Grancio in Gravesend. "This one's for Carmine!" Scarpa shouted as he shot off his rival's face.

DeVecchio's 209 of January 7, on the killing of Hank Smurra and Sam Nastasi, proves that DeVecchio met Scarpa that day,[29] and the account by Smith and Capeci appears to be credible. How would they know of Lin's meeting with "34" on that date? Because, according to the account of Chris Favo during DeVecchio's OPR, Lin regularly discussed Colombo Squad details with Jerry Capeci.[30]

"Greg Smith interviewed me in 2003," said Andrew Orena, "and he told me that during the war Lin spoke to Capeci almost every day. So if Capeci was reporting that Lin DeVecchio had met Scarpa *prior* to the Grancio hit, how is it possible that Lin, Favo's supervisor, and Favo himself didn't sense that Grancio might be in danger?"[31]

But the most authoritative evidence that the Feds were fully aware of the danger to Nicky Black surfaced at the trial of William Cutolo in October 1994. During those proceedings, the government actually admitted that, on the day before Grancio was shot, a New York State detective named Matthew Higgins, who was assigned to the joint OCID, "tried to warn . . . Mr. Grancio . . . about information that [he] might be the target of a murder conspiracy."[32]

And that raises the question of why Lin DeVecchio and the agents under him didn't monitor Greg Scarpa's movements more closely. In that December 1991 "Kitchen 302," DeVecchio had recounted the following warning:

> Despite his position, SCARPA was advised that his actions would be closely monitored by law enforcement, and was warned about his potential liability of being on federal probation.

Since he was still on probation for the 1986 credit card case, the Feds had a lot of leverage with Scarpa—or they should have. Even if they perceived that Grancio, one of his chief rivals, wasn't in jeopardy, why not keep the Grim Reaper on a shorter leash?

And there are other questions: Why, in his 2004 hearing, did Larry Mazza seem to dial back on what he reportedly told Flora Edwards and Dr. Stephen Dresch in May 2003? Edwards insists Mazza was telling the truth the first time, but that he later got worried about the consequences. "I'm afraid of the FBI," she says he told her later. "They're gonna trump something up. I'm gonna end up back in jail if I'm lucky, and if I'm not lucky, they'll kill me."[33] And, in a sworn affidavit submitted for the Grancio lawsuit, Mazza *did* claim that on the day of Grancio's murder Scarpa "made multiple calls to a person whom he addressed as Lin."[34]

After initially assuming that "Lin" referred to Linda Schiro, Mazza went on to state that he "now believe[d] that 'Lin' could have been Lindley DeVecchio."[35] In petitioning Judge Block not to dismiss the case before he could undertake discovery, Mrs. Grancio's lawyer, David Schoen, argued that they could get to the truth of what happened by obtaining "all phone records related to Scarpa's calls to DeVecchio." Flora Edwards insists, "If we could have gotten a look at the cell records of Larry Mazza's sister, whose phone Scarpa used to call this person 'Lin,' we'd know for sure if the Feds had acted to withdraw that surveillance."

But citing that phone record request, among others, Judge Block concluded that "Mrs. Grancio's counsel has failed to articulate how the discovery sought could be expected to create a genuine issue of material fact, other than a conclusory assertion . . . support[ing] an inference that DeVecchio and Favo acted improperly."[36] He also declared that Dresch's testimony at the 2004 hearing and a subsequent declaration by Flora Edwards were "inadmissible hearsay."[37]

What Did Lin Know?

And when did he know it? Those Watergate questions take us back to the issue of foreseeability. By January 7, 1992, given the amount of violence directed at both sides in the war, should DeVecchio's deputy Chris Favo have pulled the plug on *all* surveillance covering Nicky Black? Keep in mind that, in addition to Simone and Maggiore, several FBI agents watching from Plant 26 overlooking D'Ambrosio's social club were also called back to headquarters. Was it really necessary to bring them *all* back for a team meeting? That one act by Favo had the undeniable consequence of leaving Nicky Black fully exposed. Shouldn't Favo and his boss, DeVecchio, have foreseen the danger Grancio would face if his entire surveillance detail was removed?

Even if DeVecchio never got a call from Scarpa, as he insists, and Favo didn't pull the surveillance teams away in response, Lin had to know that Grancio was a prime target for the Grim Reaper.

How can we say that for sure? Because we now have the 209 that Lin wrote on January 8, 1992, the day *after* the murder. It's clear from this memo that DeVecchio understood the importance of "Nicky Black" to Vic Orena:

> On January 8, 199[2] ▮▮▮▮▮▮▮▮ advised SSA R. LINDLEY DE VEC-
> CHIO that the "hit" on NICKY GRANCIO was done by the PERSICO
> faction of the COLOMBO Family. The source said GRANCIO was the
> main go-between for VIC ORENA and was a very influential ally of
> ORENA's.[38]

Once again, quoting Scarpa, DeVecchio writes that the homicide was done by the "PERSICO faction," without naming his own informant. But even if we ignore that lapse, or write it off as negligence on Lin's part, we're confronted with that line in the Greg Smith–Jerry Capeci piece, "This one's for Carmine!" The line referred to Carmine "the Snake" Persico, in whose name Scarpa was supposedly waging the war. We know from testimony in the William Cutolo trial that right after he shot Grancio, Scarpa paged the other Carmine—Sessa—and punched in the digits 6-6-6 to let him know that "the work" had been done.[39] We know that Capeci spoke to DeVecchio regularly. Could he have learned about Scarpa's alleged cry of revenge *without* talking to Lin?

In my interview with Larry Mazza in January 2013 he shed new light on that issue, insisting that at the time he fired the shotgun blast that killed Grancio, Scarpa Sr. said nothing.

"This is what happened," said Mazza. "And it's the truth. He [Scarpa] never said a word. But after [the shooting] he told Carmine Sessa that he'd said that. 'This one's for Carmine . . .' OK? It was like he had to embellish it. But he never said it at the time."[40]

Clearly that embellishment by "34" was communicated to Lin DeVecchio, who cites the "Carmine" line in his book.[41] In any case, following the Grancio rubout, with details only the killer could have known (or made up), Lin had an apparent confirmation that "34" had participated in the grisly homicide. The question is, why didn't the FBI shut down Scarpa then and there and come clean to EDNY prosecutors, pursuant to DOJ guidelines? Despite mounting evidence that Scarpa had murdered one of Vic Orena's top captains, they did nothing to rein him in.[42]

After the hit on Grancio, Greg Scarpa Sr. went on to commit at least one more murder that he later admitted to, and he has been linked to two others. But it would take months before he was closed as a source—and even after that, Lin DeVecchio would lobby Washington successfully to reopen him. But DeVecchio's apparent lack of candor in that January 8 memo is the least of the unanswered questions connected to the death of Nicky Black. As we'll see, in the months ahead, as the FBI desperately sought to explain how so much intelligence was leaking out of 26 Federal Plaza and finding its way to the mob, they acted affirmatively to set up one of their own.

The Arrest of Detective Simone

On the morning of his retirement, following a stellar law enforcement career, federal agents appeared at Joe Simone's door and accused him of being a Colombo mole.

Not only were the charges patently false, as a federal jury later determined, but in an effort to convict him, FBI agents put Simone himself under the kind of surveillance that would have saved Nicky Grancio's life. On one occasion, eight separate FBI agents followed him to try to prove that he was secretly talking to wiseguys.[43]

One of the best law enforcement officers the Feds had against the Colombo crime family, Detective Joe Simone, was falsely branded a rogue cop. And, though he's been cleared of criminal wrongdoing, Simone has been fighting ever since to reclaim his NYPD pension and his good name.

We'll get to the details of that shocking story after we assess the continuing violence from the third war for control of the Colombo family.

Meanwhile, despite Greg Scarpa's prediction to Lin DeVecchio that Vic Orena's arrest would "temporarily halt the shooting," it went on long after Orena was locked up—proving that Orena wasn't the real problem. The third war for control of the Colombo crime family wouldn't come to an end until the Hannibal Lecter of Brooklyn was finally behind bars.

Chapter 28

CLOSING AND REOPENING "34"

Four days after the shotgun blast from Scarpa Sr.'s death car hit Nicky Grancio's head, Special Agent Chris Favo learned that "34" was responsible. We know that because of the sworn testimony of Detective Pat Maggiore in the 1994 trial of Bill Cutolo.[1] Favo himself testified at the same trial that his report to Maggiore on Scarpa's involvement came on January 11, 1992.[2] But despite the mounting evidence of Greg's direct involvement in the war violence, no search warrants were executed for his home or vehicles. He was never brought in for questioning or made to stand in a lineup. Other than Scarpa's debriefings like the one memorialized in the "Kitchen 302" and the 209s in which he gave misleading information, there was zero effort by the Bureau to interdict his murder spree. In fact, the FBI actually rewarded him.

On January 24, almost two weeks after Favo fingered Scarpa as Grancio's killer, Lin DeVecchio sent a detailed 209 to Washington. After falsely naming "Richie Fusco's crew" as responsible for the Grancio murder, he noted that, on December 5, "Bureau authority was granted for an additional $5,000 under SAC authority" to be paid to Scarpa. That payment was approved the very day before Scarpa gunned down Vincent Fusaro in front of his wife while he was putting up Christmas lights.[3]

But a week later, perhaps sensing that Scarpa's spiraling violence would eventually result in additional deaths, DeVecchio sent what retired FBI agent Dan Vogel described as a "cover your butt" memo to the New York SAC. It was framed as an eleven-point advisory to Scarpa, whose name was redacted.

Memorandum

To: SAC ████████████

Date: 2/3/92

From: SSA R. LINDLEY DEVECCHIO, C-10

Subject: ████████████

On 1/30/92, ████████████████ was again advised of the following:

(A) Assistance voluntary—informant's assistance is strictly voluntary and will not exempt him/her from arrest or prosecution of any violation of law except where such violations were approved pursuant to Attorney General Guidelines.

(B) Informant is not an employee or undercover Agent of the FBI.

(C) Informant's relationship must be maintained in the strictest confidence and the relationship is not to be divulged to anyone. The FBI will take all possible steps to maintain the full confidentiality of the informant's relationship with the FBI.

(D) Informant is to report positive information as promptly as possible.

(E) The informant was advised of pertinent FBI jurisdiction.

(F) The informant shall not participate in acts of violence.

(G) The informant shall not use unlawful techniques to obtain information for the FBI.

(H) Informant shall not initiate a plan to commit a criminal act.

(I) Informant shall not participate in criminal activities of persons under investigation except insofar as the FBI determines that such participation is necessary to obtain the information needed for purposes of Federal prosecution.

(J) All informant payments are income and taxable for Federal income tax purpose.

(K) Informant's relationship with the FBI will not protect him/her from arrest or local prosecution for any violation of Federal, state, or local law, except insofar as determined pursuant to Attorney General Guidelines.

"There's little doubt," says Vogel, "that at this point Scarpa had gone way past being an asset and had become a serious and dangerous liability. But apparently the supervisors above DeVecchio were still unwilling to pull the plug on him—so this memo, in which Scarpa was warned not to commit violent crimes, was a way for the brass to insulate themselves later on if the you-know-what hit the fan."[4]

Also at that point, DeVecchio decided to spread the risk. For the first time since 1980, he made an exception to his one-on-one relationship with Scarpa. Chris Favo, who first learned of "34's" identity in June 1991,[5] would now serve as Greg's backup contacting agent "in an emergency."[6] The admonitions in that February 3 memorandum were clear. Scarpa was forbidden from committing any acts of violence. But if, in fact, DeVecchio actually had the temerity to pass on those warnings to his charge, they had little effect. Scarpa was already planning his next hit.

On the day before he met with DeVecchio to receive that "advisory," Scarpa reported on Joel "Joe Waverly" Cacace, a Colombo capo with whom Greg had been feuding for five years, after Waverly began spreading rumors that Scarpa was an informant.[7] Now, in his self-serving debriefing with DeVecchio, Scarpa passed on the provocative intelligence that Cacace had "a club on East 14th Street and Avenue U," where he kept "an apartment upstairs which may now be used as a location for one of the 'hit' teams."[8]

Earlier, Scarpa had reported to DeVecchio that "an attempt was made to hit . . . CACACE on December 4th or 5th by The Persico Faction." But the 209 on that debriefing did not name Scarpa as the one who pulled the trigger.[9]

A few days after New Year's, the killing trio of Scarpa, Mazza, and Del Masto had spotted Waverly in his car on East Third Street and Avenue U in Gravesend and pulled alongside him. Scarpa attempted to fire a TEC-9 auto pistol but it jammed, at which point Cacace fired back from two feet away, shattering the window of their van. Scarpa literally had glass in his hair as the van sped away.[10] By late February, he was grinding his teeth for a chance to finish off Cacace.

Now on February 26, a little over three weeks after that memo reminding Scarpa that he was forbidden from participating in "acts of violence," he fired fourteen shots with a rifle as Cacace left his dry cleaner near the Party Room Social Club in Sheepshead Bay.[11] Although Cacace returned fire with a handgun, he was no match for Scarpa, who was an expert marksman. Cacace fell to the ground seriously wounded in the stomach and groin.[12]

Mazza, who had been listening to a police scanner, heard a report that a man had been shot and ambulances were on the way, so Scarpa's murder wagon sped off. Mazza later testified that they switched vehicles and returned to Scarpa's house.[13] Greg then reported the shooting to Carmine Sessa, noting that he'd hit Cacace a few times in the stomach.[14]

DeVecchio Warns "34" of an Arrest

The next day, Carmine Imbriale, a member of Carmine Sessa's crew, was arrested on a drug charge by veteran detective George Terra of the Brooklyn DA's office. Imbriale soon agreed to flip, not only to become a cooperating witness (CW) but also to strap on a wire and bravely go back into the street to try to incriminate other members.

In a phone conversation after the arrest, Terra told Chris Favo that Imbriale had attended a dinner the night before at a Red Lobster restaurant where Scarpa had bragged about wounding Cacace that morning.[15]

Then, after hanging up with Terra, Favo briefed his boss, Lin DeVecchio, on Imbriale's admissions. In an FBI 302 written during Lin's OPR, Favo made a stunning allegation about a phone call DeVecchio then received from Scarpa on C-10's "Hello" phone:

> During the briefing, DeVecchio received a telephone call. DeVecchio listened to the caller and then said, "I don't know what he's saying about you. We haven't even talked to him yet. The Brooklyn DA has him." From the context of the conversation I suspected he was talking to Scarpa. When DeVecchio hung up the phone I asked him who he spoke to and he stated it was "34" . . . a name which DeVecchio used when referring to Scarpa.[16]

Favo later testified that he was alarmed at this disclosure because it put Imbriale at great risk of being killed by Scarpa.[17] In fact, Favo was so concerned about the jeopardy that Imbriale was now in, thanks to Lin's "Hello" phone leak, that he suggested to DeVecchio that he should tell Scarpa he'd been overheard on a wiretap threatening the new snitch, and that "if anything happened to Imbriale, Scarpa would immediately be arrested."

Favo testified that at first he thought that DeVecchio had been merely "careless" in disclosing Imbriale's arrest to Scarpa, but over time he came to conclude that what DeVecchio had done, in potentially threatening Imbriale's safety, was "criminal."[18] In his memoir, DeVecchio writes that after that phone call Favo started "withholding significant information from [DeVecchio], his supervisor."[19]

Later, when he interviewed Imbriale himself, Favo learned that at that Red Lobster dinner Scarpa had literally "toasted" his shooting of Cacace, exclaiming, "This is one for the good guys."[20] That story only confirmed what Favo already knew in relation to the Grancio murder: that Scarpa was committing new acts of violence during the war, in violation of the February 3 memorandum.

On February 25, DeVecchio filed a 209 in which he quoted Scarpa as disclosing that "a contract to hit Frankie the Bug SCIORTINO had been put out from CARMINE PERSICO to his brother Teddy PERSICO, who, in turn, got word to Joe 'Fish' MARRA." Marra was a member of Scarpa's crew and was so close to Greg Scarpa that he'd been with him during the alleged shootout outside his house on Eighty-Second Street in November. According to that 209, Marra was told to "reach out" to a pair of Colombo associates to kill Sciortino, who was then serving time in a federal prison.[21]

That report became hugely significant because the contract passed to Joe Fish had to have come from Scarpa, his immediate supervisor in the family. To make matters worse, another Top Echelon informant had independently confirmed that Scarpa himself was involved in the murder plot.[22] That constituted another direct violation of one of the warnings in that February 3 memo—that Scarpa couldn't "initiate a plan to commit a criminal act."

So on February 27, the day after Scarpa "gut-shot" Cacace, DeVecchio's supervisor, Donald North, issued a directive for him to close Scarpa "immediately."[23] According to that closing memo, DeVecchio was instructed not to "initiate any contact with the source . . . and that [Scarpa] should remove himself from any involvement in the factional war."[24]

Naturally, the Mad Hatter ignored the warning.

The Pastry Shop Murders

On the night of March 25, John Minerva, a Colombo captain, was closing up the pastry shop he owned on North Broadway in Massapequa, Long Island.[25] He walked to his car, which was being driven by an associate named Michael Imbergamo. Shortly after Minerva got in, shots rang out and the two men were murdered.

Five days later, despite his inactive status, Scarpa contacted DeVecchio and blamed the killings on forces loyal to "Jo Jo" and Chuckie Russo, members of the Persico faction.

> March 31, 1992: The source said that the hit on JOHN MINERVA was handled by Jo Jo and Chuckie RUSSO's people. The source said MICHAEL IMBERGAMO who was shot with MINERVA was a COLOMBO associate and was purposely taken out along with MINERVA.[26]

As far back as January 1982, Scarpa had implicated the Russos in the attack on Colombo family pornographer Joseph Peraino Sr. and his son, who were on the receiving end of gunfire from a crew that included Minerva. It was that home-invasion shotgun murder that also led to the tragic death of the former nun Veronica Zuraw.[27] Now, in what became known as "the pastry shop murders," the supposed motive for the double slaying was that Minerva, a longtime Persico loyalist, had changed sides during the war.

But after Carmine Sessa began talking to the Feds new evidence surfaced suggesting the Russos weren't involved. Once he became a cooperating witness in 1993, Sessa reported that Minerva owed the Russos some $90,000 in a loan-sharking debt. That made him a highly unlikely target if they ever wished to collect.[28] In the Colombo family, where soldiers often changed loyalties to capos, a money debt routinely trumped a violation of allegiance as a factor in who lived or died.

Following their convictions, the Russos and a codefendant, Joseph Monteleone, argued that it was Greg Scarpa Sr. who was responsible for the Minerva-Imbergamo hit—and, in testimony at a later hearing, Greg Jr. agreed.[29]

The younger Scarpa testified under oath that the hit had been carried out by his father and "a kid" named Eric Curcio. Senior reportedly told his son that Curcio "took a shot" at Imbergamo and missed, so Junior's "father and this Curcio located him and took him out. The fellow in the car with him was also taken out," Junior said.[30]

The Russos and Monteleone argued on appeal that the Feds had withheld key exculpatory evidence in the form of DeVecchio's 209s, which would have proven to a jury that Scarpa had repeatedly lied to DeVecchio about other war murders he'd committed. So they were granted a new trial.[31] But the Second Circuit reaffirmed the guilty verdicts, concluding that the evidence of Scarpa's involvement in other murders was insufficient to clear the Russos for the Minerva and Imbergamo slayings.[32]

Years later, in 2011, new evidence surfaced calling their conviction into question. Frank "Frankie Blue Eyes" Sparaco, whom Colombo capo Sal Miciotta had fingered as one of the members of the 1982 Peraino hit team, admitted that he'd previously lied to the Feds about his role in the Minerva-Imbergamo killings. His admission caused headlines because of the revelation that at the time of the pastry shop murders, *Sparaco was also acting as an FBI informant*.[33] It was an extraordinary revelation. It meant that besides Greg Scarpa, the Bureau had a second CI during the Colombo war who was committing murders while passing information to Bureau agents.

The Russos' culpability was further called into question following a June 4, 2008, indictment by the U.S. attorney in Brooklyn, charging Thomas Gioeli, the acting Colombo boss, with the Minerva and Imbergamo hit.[34] On May 9, 2012, while convicted on racketeering and conspiracy charges, Gioeli was cleared of direct involvement in the pastry shop murders. The jury didn't believe that he'd pulled the trigger himself.[35]

If, in fact, Greg Scarpa was also the trigger man in the Massapequa double slaying, that would bring to six the number of homicides he was personally responsible for during the war—that is, half the body count during the initial phase of the conflict. But while he was still officially closed as a confidential informant, Scarpa's most notorious rubout in the war was yet to come.

Taking Orena off the Street

As far back as December 30, 1991, before the murders of Nicky Grancio and Minerva and Imbergamo, and before his attack on Joel Cacace, Greg Scarpa Sr. had told Lin DeVecchio that "an arrest of Vic Orena would temporarily halt the shooting war."[36] Yet the war continued long after the FBI stormed the home of Gina Reale, Vic Orena's "gumar," or mistress, on April 1 and put the cuffs on the acting boss. That dramatic April Fools' Day search and seizure was the incident that produced the black plastic garbage bag containing six handguns from under Reale's outdoor deck—guns Greg Jr. later insisted were planted by his father and brother Joey.[37] In fact, the younger Scarpa said that as Joey entered the yard to hide the guns, Lin DeVecchio watched him from a car with Scarpa Sr. "to make sure [Scarpa Jr.'s] brother would be O.K." In his book, DeVecchio calls those allegations part of a Mafia plot to "frame" him.[38] But there wasn't a single fingerprint on the guns discovered outside the house that linked them to the Orenas.

Lin DeVecchio (*far right*) as Vic Orena is "perp walked" post arrest

The Feds offered no explanation for why anyone would leave a bag of weapons in virtual plain sight outside in the elements at the end of winter, or why potentially incriminating firearms would be kept at all. As noted, the bag, which might have contained exculpatory prints, later disappeared.[39] Still, federal prosecutors, who described those guns as part of Orena's "small arsenal," laid them out on a table at the end of Vic's trial so that the jury members could see the kind of firepower brought to bear in the war ostensibly waged by "the Orena faction."

"Even though all my father had at that safe house were shotguns for defense," said Orena's son Andrew, "the sight of those weapons shocked the jury. They were a significant factor in the guilty verdict, which not only convicted my father for Tommy Ocera's murder but for waging the war that we now know was conducted largely by Scarpa Sr."[40]

In a *New York Times* story reporting Orena's arrest on April 2, Andrew J. Maloney, the U.S. attorney in Brooklyn, was quoted as describing Vic Orena as "a central figure in an internecine power struggle that has crippled the Colombo family." After quoting James Fox, the assistant director in charge (ADIC) of the FBI's New York Office, on the time and location of the arrest, the *Times* piece noted that "twelve firearms, including four loaded shotguns and two assault rifles, were seized at the site."[41] In point of fact, Special Agent Joseph Fanning, who testified for the government at Orena's trial, admitted that all four of the shotguns seized were found stored in closets at the time the FBI raided the house. All of them, he acknowledged, could have been purchased over the counter at sporting goods stores. Two of the shotguns had been bought respectively by Vic Orena and his son Andrew, and both men had filled out the requisite paperwork. A third shotgun—a twelve-gauge Remington—was more than twenty-five years old. These were hardly the type of weapons one would expect to find in the "arsenal" of a mob boss bent on waging a violent and aggressive war.[42]

The six handguns found outside, which included four semiautomatics and two revolvers, were dusted for prints; none matched the Orenas. As noted, the allegation by ADIC Fox that two "assault rifles" had been seized was entirely untrue.

Pushing to Reopen "34"

On the day after Orena's arrest, Lin DeVecchio started pressing hard for permission to reopen Scarpa. To make that happen, evidence now suggests that he misrepresented the facts behind Scarpa's participation in the "Frankie the Bug" murder plot. This is the background:

On March 3, the following teletype (or RETEL) went to FBI Director William Sessions, citing that other TE source's allegation that Scarpa was "involved" in the murder conspiracy.[43]

Although the copy we obtained was heavily redacted, a subsequent tele-

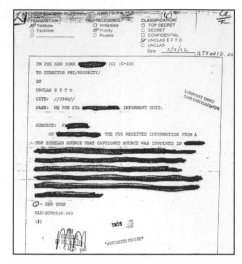

type proves conclusively that this was the alleged "contract" plot to kill "Frankie the Bug" Sciortino that DeVecchio reported in that 209 dated February 25.[44] But the day after Orena's arrest on April 2, in a memo to Sessions, DeVecchio represented that the information linking Scarpa to the Sciortino plot could not be verified. He then stated that "34" was being reopened.

> In view of the inability to verify the original information with respect to captioned source's involvement, coupled with the fact that all current sources are potentially in the same position as a result of constant shootings and attendant paranoia, NY is reopening this source.[45]

On April 7, relying on DeVecchio's claim, Sessions sent this teletype to New York:

> Authority for New York to initiate a suitability inquiry regarding the captioned individual [SCARPA] is hereby granted. FBI HQ is granting this authority with the understanding that the Allegations set forth in retel dated March 3rd, 1992 regarding the CI's possible involvement in a contract murder were unsubstantiated.[46]

"If Scarpa had been involved in that plot to kill Sciortino, in violation of that memo from February 3, the Feds never could have reopened him as a source," says defense lawyer Flora Edwards.[47] But the February 27 memo ordering Scarpa closed had left that door open, stating, "If at a future time the NYO can show that the information is unreliable or inconclusive with respect to captioned source's involvement in the conspiracy, this source will be reopened."

So the question is, was DeVecchio truthful with his superiors in New York and Washington with respect to Scarpa's involvement in the plot to hit Sciortino? In short, did he lie in order to get "34" reopened? The answer came during Lin's OPR in 1995, and the source was his number two in Squad C-10: Special Agent Chris Favo.

DeVecchio's Account Called False

On May 20 and 21, 1996, Vic Orena and Patty Amato sought to vacate their sentences at what is known as a 2255 hearing. During the proceedings, Judge Jack B. Weinstein, who had presided over Orena's trial, listened to testimony from a number of witnesses, including DeVecchio, Favo, Special Agents Tomlinson and Leadbetter, and Donald North, DeVecchio's supervisor in New York. Before closing Scarpa, North testified, he'd done some "cursory checks" and had been advised by another agent that Scarpa was "engaged in planning criminal activity." But when he spoke with DeVecchio, said North, the SSA was "adamant" that Scarpa "was not engaged in any violent activity."[48]

North reiterated that if he had been presented with evidence that "34" was engaged in violence, Scarpa would have been prosecuted "without question." Asked whether *any* circumstances during "a war or conflict or shootings" would "justify having a confidential informant go out and commit the crime of murder and get a pass," North insisted that "nothing" could "justify it."[49]

Despite DeVecchio's "adamant" assertions that his coveted source was not participating in the war violence, North testified that he'd ordered DeVecchio to submit that "closing teletype" on February 27. Then, in reliance on Lin's assurance that Scarpa was not involved in the "Frankie the Bug" murder plot, FBI Director Sessions acquiesced to "34's" reopening.[50]

But in a sworn statement filed in 1995 during DeVecchio's OPR investigation, Chris Favo, DeVecchio's immediate subordinate, effectively called him a liar. Even though the statement, which became part of the OPR file, has been redacted, it's clear what Favo was charging:

> I read SSA DeVecchio's teletype reopening Scarpa after he had been closed by ███████. This teletype indicated there was no merit to the information that Scarpa had participated in a conspiracy ███████. This teletype is false. SSA DeVecchio told me that Scarpa confirmed this information

██████████. It was shortly after Scarpa told DeVecchio this information that I heard DeVecchio on the "Hello" phone telling Scarpa to stay away from ██████████. DeVecchio later told me it was all he could do to keep Scarpa away from this source.[51]

The "source" was presumably that other Top Echelon informant who had implicated Scarpa in the Sciortino murder plot. Now, on April 22, despite Chris Favo's insistence that DeVecchio's exoneration of Scarpa in the Sciortino conspiracy had been "false," DeVecchio sent Sessions a teletype announcing "34's" reopening:

> A SUITABILITY AND PERTINENCE INQUIRY HAS BEEN CONDUCTED . . . AND CAPTIONED SOURCE IS CONSIDERED SUITABLE IN VIEW OF THE LONG-STANDING RELATIONSHIP WITH THE NYO AS A TOP ECHELON SOURCE.[52]

In that same teletype, DeVecchio wrote:

> ON APRIL 16TH, 1992 ASAC DONALD V. NORTH REVIEWED CAPTIONED SOURCE'S FILE, AND ON THE BASIS OF INFORMATION FURNISHED, DEEMED CAPTIONED SOURCE TO BE SUITABLE AND INFORMATION PERTINENT TO FBI JURISDICTION.

But in his sworn testimony at the 2255 hearing in 1996, ASAC North stated that he couldn't *recall* authorizing Scarpa's reopening. During direct examination by Orena's attorney Gerald Shargel, North went even further, admitting that he was "somewhat surprised when the prosecutors asked [him] if [he] authorized" Scarpa's reactivation and had "no recollection of [his] being reopened."[53] However, in his April 22 teletype to Sessions, DeVecchio implied that North had signed off on "34's" reinstatement. So the conflict between their accounts raises one of two prospects: Either North was being disingenuous or DeVecchio was.

Donald North died of a heart attack in 2005,[54] so I never got a chance to press him on whether he'd approved Scarpa's reopening, as DeVecchio suggested. In his book DeVecchio proudly writes, "On April 22, 1992, I won the right to reopen Scarpa."[55] What he doesn't mention at that point is that the Grim Reaper waited only a month before adding another corpse to his string of homicides.

Chapter 29

WHO'S GOING TO WIN THIS THING?

O n May 22, 1992, precisely thirty days after he'd been returned to active status as a Top Echelon FBI informant, Greg Scarpa Sr. executed a Colombo family member in a hit that not only inspired the title to Lin DeVecchio's book but created a Mafia tagline that would become so famous it ended up in the finale of *The Sopranos*.[1] This time Scarpa's target was a sixty-six-year-old wiseguy named Lorenzo Lampasi, a.k.a. "Larry Lamps."

By the late 1970s, Lampasi, who had an arrest record for loan sharking, gambling, and drunk driving, had become an owner of Abco Bus Company, which contracted with the New York City Board of Education to run a fleet of school buses. In a riveting investigative piece for *New York* magazine, Nicholas Pileggi traced Lampasi's mob pedigree back to 1963, when he was wanted for questioning in the garroting of Larry Gallo at the Sahara Lounge.[2] Since that was the intended hit in which Carmine Persico betrayed the Gallo brothers and cemented his position in the Profaci-Colombo family, Lampasi's participation in that plot should have earned him a solid place within the Persico faction during the war.

But Carmine Sessa would later tell FBI agents that one of the reasons for Lampasi's rubout was "his loyalty to [the] Colombo LCN Family acting boss, VICTOR J. ORENA."[3] As we'll see, there was little evidence that Lampasi had anything to do with Orena, so that motive doesn't ring true. The more likely reason that Larry Lamps was marked for death was that, like Sal Scarpa, Joe Brewster DeDomenico, and Joe Waverly Cacace before him, Lampasi had made the mistake of airing his suspicions that Scarpa was a government informant.

Indeed, during William Cutolo's trial in 1994, Sessa testified that Lampasi had told others that Scarpa had been cooperating with law enforcement.[4] At Vic Orena Jr.'s trial six months later, Sessa went even further, swearing under oath that Greg Sr. had been "furious" after Lampasi wrote to him and audaciously cited "34's" status as a CI.[5]

Earlier, Sessa had told FBI agents that an associate of Lampasi's named "Tony" owed Scarpa money, and that along with his repayment Lamps had sent Greg a letter threatening that if the money didn't erase Tony's problem, then he and Scarpa would have to "settle this in another manner." Then, according to Sessa, Lampasi wrote that he refused to speak to Senior in person because "there's bad rumors about [him] on the street."

At that point, according to Sessa, Scarpa went to "Joe T" Tomasello, a senior capo in the family, complaining that Lampasi had called him a "rat."[6] In Sessa's account, Scarpa asked Joe T for permission to kill Lampasi—but that doesn't sync with the unilateral way Scarpa did business. "He hadn't sought permission for a host of other murders, from Mary Bari to Joe DeDomenico," says Flora Edwards. "He wasn't about to start at that point." In any case, the Killing Machine started plotting Lampasi's death.

According to Sessa, Scarpa got Lampasi's home address from Tomasello, who was a partner with him in another bus company. Sessa said that because Joe T had a relative who worked there, Tomasello asked that the hit go down elsewhere.[7] The source of the address became a major issue during Lin DeVecchio's trial, when the Brooklyn DA alleged, via Linda Schiro, that Scarpa had obtained the location of Lampasi's house from his FBI handler.

But later, in the tapes produced by Tom Robbins, the most convincing exculpatory statement Schiro made came in relation to Lampasi: "When Lin is right, I give him right," she said. "He didn't tell Greg about Larry Lampasi."[8] However, even if we accept that DeVecchio had no *intentional* role in Lampasi's murder, the homicide took place just a month after he'd lobbied Washington to bring Scarpa back to full Top Echelon status.

Thus, DeVecchio's actions before and after the murder raise the question of whether he was criminally negligent—whether he should have had the foresight to know that, if left on the street, Scarpa would kill and kill again.

At this point in the war, DeVecchio knew of the aggressive and murderous role "34" was playing in the violence. The February 3 memo had represented a warning to Scarpa that he could no longer plan any criminal acts. Chris Favo, DeVecchio's number two, had become aware of Scarpa's role in the Grancio hit four months earlier. Lin was aware of Scarpa's involvement in the prospective "Frankie the Bug" hit. So why didn't DeVecchio, the supervisor of the Colombo Squad, move to shut down his source and arrest him? As noted, I made multiple attempts to interview DeVecchio for this book, but he never responded to my queries.

The Death of Larry Lamps

By May 1992, even the other two members of Scarpa's hit crew were growing weary of the bloodshed. Larry Mazza later testified:

> Jimmy [Del Masto] and I were staying at my parents' house in New Jersey. Greg had told us we had done enough and we were going to be able to stay in the background. We were getting fed up. We felt like we were being used and we went—way further than we ever wanted or expected to go. And he told us he would use Carmine's people when they went on their next attempt.[9]

At that point, according to Mazza, Scarpa contacted Carmine Sessa and asked him to assign Larry Fiorenza to the Lampasi murder squad. Fiorenza had reportedly been part of the crew in the aborted "Hasidic" plot to kill Bill Cutolo. But after Mazza and Del Masto had finished the surveillance on Lampasi's home and business, Fiorenza never showed.[10]

By the third week in May, Mazza and Del Masto had staked out Lampasi's bus company and his home. They had learned that he left for work each morning around three thirty A.M. They had also observed a gate outside his house that he had to manually open and close and went so far as to plan their escape route back to Scarpa's house once the murder had taken place.

Now, in the early-morning hours of May 22, with Fiorenza AWOL, Scarpa picked up Mazza and Del Masto, who had been with him during the murders of Amato, Fusaro, and Grancio. They drove to Lampasi's address and waited until four A.M., when he emerged from his house. He opened the gate, got in his car, and backed out. Mazza later gave this account of what happened when Lampasi went back to close the gate:

> Greg put the rifle out the window. He shot him. [Lampasi] went down. Jimmy started to drive away. Greg told him to stop. He wasn't sure if he was dead. He got out of the car. We both followed, and the three of us fired again.[11]

As Lampasi lay dying, he looked up at Scarpa standing over him. The tough old wiseguy, who had survived a 1973 shooting during the second Colombo war,[12] demanded to know why'd he been hit.

According to Carmine Sessa, who wasn't there at the time of the hit, Scarpa told Lampasi that "he'd picked the wrong side" in the war.[13] But in my interview with Larry Mazza he said that just like the "This one's for Carmine!" line, that was a fabrication.

"He never said that," said Mazza.[14] "Lampasi, who was being shot, said 'Why are you doing this?' But that statement from Sessa and the 'Carmine' line, which seemed to prove for the Feds that there were two factions in the war, made it into the record at the [war] trials. I couldn't believe it because neither of those lines ever happened at the time."

As to Carmine Sessa's assertion, it was in his best interest to tell the Feds what they *wanted* to hear: namely, that Lampasi had died because of his loyalty to Vic Orena. "The problem with that story," said Andrew Orena, "is that it doesn't hold up. Larry Lamps barely knew my father and he certainly wasn't loyal to him. He got hit because he was another loose end that Greg had to tie off—another family member who had the guts to say what many guys were starting to suspect: that Greg had stayed out of jail all those years because he was informing for the Feds."[15]

"He Had Lost Track of Who He Was"

Five hours after Larry Lampasi's murder, Chris Favo, who learned about it along with another war shooting that morning, briefed Lin DeVecchio in the C-10 squad at the FBI's NYO. Favo later described the conversation during the trial of John and Vic Orena Jr. Under cross-examination by attorney James LaRossa, Favo said that after hearing the news of Lampasi's rubout, DeVecchio "slapped his desk."[16]

> **LaRossa:** And you wrote down that he got excited about it. Didn't he?
> **Favo:** Yes.
> **LaRossa:** You said that he said to you, "We're going to win this thing," right? Meaning the war, right?
> **Favo:** Yes.
> **LaRossa:** Meaning the Persico side, right?
> **Favo:** Yes.

In a 302 dated February 6, 1994, Favo went further: "I told DeVecchio that as law enforcement we did not support either side in the war. DeVecchio then stated that was what he meant."[17] But during that trial of the Orena sons, Favo offered more details about his own thoughts on the significance of DeVecchio's comment:

> I had gotten the information about the two shootings in the morning. They both occurred before 9:00. It was approximately 9:00 when I went in to see Mr. DeVecchio. I walked in, I said my usual briefing, two shootings occurred, two Orena side people were shot, they're not really sure who did it and so forth. . . .
>
> As I started into that, he slapped his hand on the desk and he said, "We're going to win this thing," and he seemed excited about it. He seemed like he didn't know . . . we were the FBI. . . . It was like a line had been blurred . . . over who we were and what this was. . . . I just thought he was not—I thought there was something wrong. He was compromised. He had lost track of who he was.[18]

In his memoir, Lin acknowledged the exchange, adding that Favo had told him, "We're the FBI. We're not on either side," to which he agreed, writing it off as a harmless comment until it came back to haunt him years later, during his OPR investigation.

Apart from the propriety of a federal agent slapping his desk on news of a murder—be it a mob hit or not—what about that conversation? Was DeVecchio really rooting for the Feds, as he insists, or had he allowed his loyalty to Greg Scarpa to push him across a line?

There's no doubt that since 1980, Lin DeVecchio had gone to extraordinary lengths to keep Scarpa free. Later, federal prosecutors were forced to admit that DeVecchio may have passed crucial intelligence to "34," including the locations of potential war targets. But did he share his source's sentiments about which side should "win" the war?

We can get another insight into that question from an account given by Wimpy Boys crew member Joseph Ambrosino. Testifying at Teddy Persico's trial after the war, Ambrosino described a Scarpa speech that was eerily similar to Lin's "We're going to win" exclamation. According to Joey Brains, in January 1992, right after the Grancio murder, Scarpa convened a meeting of his crew at a Steak and Ale restaurant. This is the FBI account:

> Carmine Sessa was arguing with Bobby Zambardi, telling him that he had to pick up his efforts; that he had to get out of the house; that he had to participate. . . . Greg Scarpa was doing a lot of talking. He was saying . . . the only way we're going to win this war [is] if we stick together; that he's been in other wars before and we have to stick together, all of us have to work together, we can't not work with each other, else we're not going to get nowhere.[19]

So what was the "thing" Lin DeVecchio hoped "they" would win: the Feds' war against the mob, or Greg Scarpa's war against Vic Orena? As noted, defense attorneys theorized for years that Scarpa had fomented the war with DeVecchio's advice and consent. The purported goal was for Scarpa to eliminate the competition in the family so that he could rise to the rank of "boss," thus ensuring that the FBI had a confidential informant on the Mafia Commission. There's little doubt that, despite his failing health, no single member of the Colombo family had done more to further the war violence than their own Top Echelon Criminal Informant "34."

The very day after the Lampasi rubout, Vincent Giangiobbe, an associate of the Bonanno family, was shot to death. But months later, testifying at the trial of Vic Orena, Lin DeVecchio would include Giangiobbe's homicide in the total count of Colombo war dead.[20] Now, in June 1992, as the violence continued, the most revealing admission about Greg Scarpa's long-term goal came from Joseph Ambrosino himself.

"With Greg on Top . . ."

On June 4, the Feds installed a bug in Ambrosino's car. Over the next six days conversations were recorded documenting how "the Scarpa faction" continued to escalate the war. According to what can be heard on those tapes, less than two weeks after killing Lampasi, Greg Scarpa had put together an elaborate plan to kill William Cutolo in a bloody machine-gun rubout at a Staten Island intersection in broad daylight.

As Joey Brains later testified at the trial of Vic Orena, the plan was to manipulate a traffic light near Cutolo's girlfriend's house. Then, when "Wild Bill" was stopped at the intersection, the crew—consisting of Scarpa, Mazza, Del Masto, and Sessa—would flank his car. Using a stolen Audi on one side and a van on the other, they would pull out a machine gun and fire.[21] The hit was supposed to take place on Saturday, June 13. But once the FBI got word of the plot, via the wire, Ambrosino was taken into custody.

However, before his arrest, while he was driving around clueless about the FBI recording device in his car, Ambrosino had a conversation with a Colombo associate named Michael DeMatteo. The two of them discussed just how much money could be made once the war was over.

"With Greg on top, we'll see what we get," Ambrosino said, suggesting that after the conflict, which Scarpa had fomented, Greg would take over the family.[22]

At the time he decided to cooperate, Ambrosino had no idea how dangerous that decision was for him—particularly since he didn't know that Scarpa might have access to FBI intelligence and word of his defection might get back to "34."

In fact, within days of Ambrosino's decision to flip, Scarpa actually discussed a plan to kill Joey's mother and leave a note signaling that "this is what happens to 'rats.'"

Larry Mazza testified to that plan during Teddy Persico's trial.[23] But as reflected in a 209 filed by Lin DeVecchio in the fall of 1992, the ever-deceitful Scarpa tried to blame that plot on "Frankie Blue Eyes" Sparaco:

> There was serious discussion concerning some members of the PERSICO faction to kill Joey AMBROSINO's mother in retaliation for his coopera-tion with the government. The source Greg SCARPA put a stop to the plan and has advised the PERSICO faction that he has to be consulted before any further actions are taken in the war between the two factions. The source said Frank SPARACO was a major push behind the plan to kill AMBROSINO's mother.[24]

Even if Scarpa's account had been true, it would have represented another low for the FBI, because we've since learned that Sparaco too was a con-fidential FBI informant at the time of the war. But Mazza was closer to Scarpa at that time than any living person other than Linda Schiro, and he swore that the plan to kill Joey's mother had come from Greg himself.

The question is: How did Scarpa find out that Ambrosino had decided to play for Team Fed? The fact that he was arrested didn't necessarily mean he'd cooperate. The knowledge that Joey Brains had decided to flip was inside intel known only to the FBI agents and EDNY prosecutors who had turned him. How would Scarpa have known that Joey would become a CW to the point of ordering his mother killed in retaliation, unless someone on the inside had tipped him?

Further, this 209 represents the clearest example to date of Lin DeVecchio sending "intelligence" to Washington from his Top Echelon informant that was patently false—particularly the assertion that "Greg SCARPA," who actually *hatched* the plot to kill Ambrosino's mother, had "put a stop" to it.

Warning Mazza and Del Masto

As soon as Ambrosino started talking, he confirmed that Scarpa had mur-dered Amato, Fusaro, and Nicky Black. In fact, he told Favo that Greg "had been at all the meetings; he had been as active in the war as anybody."[25]

Four days after Ambrosino's arrest on June 10,[26] and based on the information he supplied, Larry Mazza and Jimmy Del Masto were indicted.[27] Yet Scarpa, the FBI's star informant, who had directed this killing pair, remained indictment-free. The question is, why?

At the time of Carmine Imbriale's arrest back in February, Chris Favo had insisted that he didn't have probable cause to lock up Scarpa.[28] But by June, with Ambrosino's disclosures and the recordings from his car, Favo had what he needed to get Senior off the street. In fact, he later admitted as much at the trial of Vic Jr. and John Orena,[29] testifying that Ambrosino's debriefings had convinced him that Gregory Scarpa Sr. was "the most violent and active in a group of many violent and active people."[30] Still, Favo acknowledged, the Feds decided not to indict Scarpa at that time.[31]

In June, once the charges against them had leaked out, Mazza and Del Masto went on the lam. In fact, Mazza, Scarpa's principal backup trigger man, wasn't arrested until February 9, 1993. In a letter to defense attorneys presented during the trial of the Orena sons, the Feds gave a hint as to why the two co-conspirators had known enough to take off. Prosecutors admitted that one of the disclosures DeVecchio "may" have made to Scarpa was that "there were arrest warrants outstanding for Mazza and Del Masto" and "that if they stayed away from their normal 'hangouts' they could avoid being arrested."[32]

As noted, following his arrest Mazza told FBI agents that Scarpa had a law enforcement source he referred to by a code name: "the Girlfriend." In fact, Mazza disclosed that this source regularly called Greg via a phone in the basement of the house on Eighty-Second Street that was registered to Linda Schiro's sister, and that the Girlfriend had leaked key information to Scarpa during the war. That intelligence included the addresses of "Big Sal" Miciotta and Joe Scopo, both Orena loyalists. Mazza also identified the Girlfriend as the source who had warned Senior about his 1986 credit card bust and the impending DEA arrests of Greg Jr. and crew in 1987. Further, Mazza told Favo and Special Agent Maryann Walker-Goldman, who debriefed him, that Scarpa had learned the address where the panel truck had been rented in the alleged shootout outside his house on November 18, 1991.

That was information that Chris Favo himself had developed after the ski-mask attack. With that revelation by Mazza, Favo knew for sure that intelligence gathered during the war by him and the other agents in Squad C-10 had found its way back to the Killing Machine. Now, regarding Scarpa's warning that Mazza and Del Masto were going to be indicted, Larry admitted this to agents Favo and Walker:

> THE GIRLFRIEND told SCARPA SR. that if there were no more shootings, MAZZA and DELMASTO might not be in too much trouble with the law.[33]

**DeVecchio at
26 Federal Plaza**

Defense attorneys later alleged that this proved DeVecchio knew, through Scarpa, that Mazza and Del Masto were responsible (with him) for many of the war shootings—otherwise why would Lin suggest to Greg that they would be safe if they laid low?

DeVecchio Erupts

By the end of June 1992, tensions were starting to mount inside Squad C-10 as Favo and fellow agents Howard Leadbetter, Jeffrey Tomlinson, and Ray Andjich gathered more and more evidence from cooperating witnesses that Greg Scarpa was getting special treatment from a law enforcement source. Andjich, whom DeVecchio had "parked" in front of the TV on several of his visits to Scarpa's house while DeVecchio conferred with "34" in the kitchen, later expressed his chagrin at this treatment:

> I could hear discussions between SSA DeVecchio and Scarpa Sr. but I could not hear all of the words. On one of the occasions I do recall Scarpa saying something about a murder or "hit" but I do not recall a specific comment. I found this to be an awkward situation and didn't understand why Scarpa Sr. could be saying something that I shouldn't be hearing since I'm involved in investigations as well.[34]

Andjich also complained about how limited one of DeVecchio's 209s was, recounting a debriefing of Scarpa for which he was present at the Eighty-Second Street house:

> On one of these occasions, SSA DeVecchio did prepare an FD-209 and presented it to me for review. As I recall there were only a few sentences on the FD-209. This meeting took approximately 30–45 minutes and less than half a page of content chronicled the contact.[35]

Emotions in the squad came to a head on June 25, 1992, when the Manhattan DA's office executed an arrest warrant for Scarpa loyalist John Pate in Point Pleasant, New Jersey. To ensure that members of Pate's crew were also held, the FBI arrested them on a federal warrant.[36] It was a bust that Favo had deliberately chosen to keep from his boss Lin DeVecchio until after it had gone down.

The next day when Lin learned of the arrest he erupted with anger. According to Special Agent Leadbetter, who was present in the squad, Lin yelled at Favo, "I've had it! You will not arrest another single individual without my specific approval!"[37] When the incredulous Favo asked Lin what he should do when they had to make arrests, DeVecchio told him, "Just do the paperwork." Favo later testified that he thought that comment by his boss was "ludicrous."[38]

Testifying at the same trial, Leadbetter acknowledged that he was struck by how "distressed" DeVecchio had been, but he didn't understand why until the later trial of Alphonse Persico. At that point he found out that just before Pate's arrest in New Jersey, Scarpa *himself* had been present with the crew and had narrowly escaped getting busted.[39] The implication was that DeVecchio was upset over the possibility that his star informant might have gotten pinched before he could have warned him to stay away from the site.

"The Guy—He Duped Us"

As he got more and more information from cooperating witnesses like Joseph Ambrosino, Chris Favo, whom Lin DeVecchio had appointed "case agent" for the war, began to realize just how worthless "34" had been in providing the FBI with useful intelligence. Not only had he failed to give them actionable intelligence, he had downright deceived them. This was Favo's testimony at the trial of Vic Orena Jr.:

> When Ambrosino came in and told us everything that Gregory Scarpa had been involved in and that we didn't know about . . . I mean—there were meetings that occurred that if [Scarpa] had told us about we could have had surveillance there, we could have gotten photographs, we could have planted bugs, we could have done a lot of things. The guy—he duped us. At that point, I wanted to arrest him, but we just—I didn't have the opportunity to. By that time I got the order [forbidding more arrests] I just can't go out and arrest him without telling Lin DeVecchio.[40]

By August, after Ambrosino came in, Favo could no longer, in good conscience, delude himself into thinking that Greg Scarpa had any intelligence value that outweighed his threat to public safety. But even then, Favo was concerned that if he moved on Scarpa he'd be accused of "insubordination." So he came up with another tactic. When he found out that the NYPD's OCID Task Force was going to arrest Greg Sr., he actually went to Lieutenant William J. Shannon,[41] the supervisor, and told him to *keep the time and date of the bust a secret* until just before it was to take place. Why? Because Favo didn't want to have the responsibility of informing Lin. Such was the junior special agent's sense, at that point, that his own boss couldn't be trusted with the information.[42]

As it turned out, Favo's fears weren't entirely unfounded. On August 30, when Shannon told him that Scarpa would be arrested the next day, Favo waited until the morning of the arrest to inform DeVecchio. At the same time, Favo had secretly arranged for "34" to be arrested on federal charges. During DeVecchio's OPR, Assistant U.S. Attorney George Stamboulidis, who helped prepare the indictment, told senior FBI agents that "he did not trust DeVecchio not to tell Scarpa; and therefore, DeVecchio was not advised of the arrest."[43]

Favo later testified that when he finally told DeVecchio about the arrest, DeVecchio was visibly upset. DeVecchio called Scarpa right away to warn him, Favo recalled, but he'd already left where he was.[44]

"When you think back on this, it's astounding," says Flora Edwards.

"Here is Chris Favo, the agent Lin had given top ratings to, whom he'd trusted as his number two in the squad—and he's literally having to go behind DeVecchio's back to keep him from warning this mad-dog killer. The only thing harder to believe than all of this is that it took Favo, Tomlinson, [and] Leadbetter another sixteen months before they finally went to their boss, Don North, to tell him the depth to which their own supervisor had been protecting the principal trigger in the war."[45]

In his later testimony, Favo stated that he wasn't more forthcoming about DeVecchio sooner because he didn't think anyone in the FBI would believe him:

> Deep in my heart, I believed that if I went to anyone and told them that there was a problem with Lin DeVecchio . . . they would regard this— Lin DeVecchio had been an agent for thirty years. He had been a supervisor for ten years. He was well known and was well respected. If I said this to somebody, they would take it about as well as I would take it if somebody came up to me and said my wife was unfaithful. They would not believe it. They would never believe it.[46]

Chapter 30

SCARPA'S WAR

Using Little Linda Schiro's metaphor from the Eighty-Second Street shootout that started the war violence, the arrest of her father on August 31, 1992, "was like something out of a Mafia movie." Even though he'd been reopened as an FBI source in late April, Scarpa had been lying low for months. Clearly aware of Ambrosino's defection and the indictments of Mazza and Del Masto in June, and with NYPD-OCID detectives camped outside his house with a warrant, Scarpa didn't show his face in public.

But that didn't stop DeVecchio from communicating with him. On July 9, several weeks before the bust of John Pate's crew, Scarpa told Lin that Carmine Sessa "had decided to remain in hiding."[1] Curiously, Scarpa's surrogate in the war had disappeared not long after word had gotten back to Greg about the Ambrosino wiretap. Four days later, on July 13, with DeVecchio's FBI agents prepping for the arrest of other "Persico faction" members, Scarpa told Lin that "a truce was called between the ORENA and PERSICO factions in view of the ongoing problems associated with a shooting war and the pressure being applied by law enforcement."[2]

Favo later testified that he asked DeVecchio at the time to pressure Scarpa to give up Mazza and Del Masto. According to Favo, Lin told him that he'd asked "34" to do that, but he'd refused to reveal their locations. The reason, Favo told a defense lawyer, was that Larry and Jimmy were "collecting loan shark payments for Scarpa."[3] The implication was that their arrests would interrupt the flow of vig back to Greg, so he needed them on the street.

Astonishingly, one of the disclosures that federal prosecutors made in 1995 was that DeVecchio may have assisted Scarpa in locating his loan-shark victims by providing him with their addresses.[4]

In his book, DeVecchio acknowledges that Favo did ask him to lean on Scarpa to turn over Mazza and Del Masto, but he cynically mocks Favo's requests. Referencing SSA Chris Mattiace, who ran the C-10 squad before him, Lin writes, "Maybe Chris Mattiace and I should have escorted Scarpa into the men's room for a little head-in-the-toilet-bowl persuasion."[5] "To me," said Andrew Orena, "that line in Lin's book raised the question we've always been asking: Who was 'running' who? Was DeVecchio and the FBI in charge of Scarpa Sr. or was it the other way around?"[6]

Demanding Payment in Cash

While Scarpa had been in virtual hiding since March, his lawsuit against Victory Memorial Hospital was coming to a head. On July 30, his AIDS-tainted-blood case alleging negligence by Dr. Angelito Sebollena had advanced in his favor. As it turned out, the Philippines-born doctor and his secretary were arraigned on charges of conspiring to have two male patients *killed* with injections of cocaine.[7] In a plot that seemed even more bizarre than the story of how Greg Scarpa had received the infected blood in the first place, Sebollena, forty-seven, had previously been charged with four counts of sodomy and six counts of sex abuse for allegedly attacking two male patients, ages twenty-four and twenty-five.

According to the criminal charges, Dr. Sebollena had fondled and sodomized the young men after sedating them during office visits. The July 30 complaint alleged that, after his release on bail in May, Sebollena conspired with his secretary to murder his two accusers by shooting them up with cocaine.

While Scarpa was off the grid, on August 17, the New York *Daily News* ran a piece reporting that he was due to testify against Sebollena in Brooklyn Supreme Court in pursuit of his $1.5 million claim against the hospital.[8] Two days later Scarpa took the witness stand in open court—and gave such riveting testimony that he caused one female juror to weep.[9] Now sixty-four, the Mafia capo, once a strapping 220 pounds, was reduced to 150. His eye sockets and cheeks were hollowed out and he had to stop continuously to catch his breath. Speaking quietly and directly to the jury, he compared himself to a man on death row:

> We all know that our Creator is somehow, someday going to uncreate us. . . . The best example I can give to what this is like is that I now know the feeling of a person that's condemned to death, and each time he walks the corridor to the execution, he gets a reprieve. But I do know each time that I walk down that corridor, I might not be coming back. . . . To have something like this is pretty devastating.

Scarpa emaciated by HIV at the time of his trial

At that point, according to *Newsday* reporter Patricia Hurtado, who covered the hearing, one of the six members of the civil jury began to cry and Linda Schiro ran from the courtroom in tears. Scarpa's testimony lasted more than four hours and he nearly broke down himself several times. Later, his personal physician testified that he had between two and six months to live.[10]

But a week later, Scarpa bounced back with the ferocity of a loan shark after Dr. Sebollena and the hospital agreed to settle his case for $300,000. Demanding the entire payment immediately, Scarpa literally insisted that the full settlement be delivered to him forthwith and in *cash*.

With respect to the fatal transfusion, Scarpa was quoted in the *New York Times* as saying, "I wasn't given ample warning. It was never something that should have been left to the prerogative of the patient."[11] After the verdict, Scarpa and Linda were surrounded by jury members. Several of them told reporters that if he hadn't cut the deal, they would have been inclined to give Greg Sr. a judgment "in the millions."[12]

Scarpa was jubilant after the victory, telling reporter Hurtado, "I'm going to line up all my kids around me and I'm going to play Santa in August and hand this stuff out," adding that he didn't know if he would "be around to play Santa in December." Hugging Linda, he also announced that he was "looking forward to a vacation in Florida and relaxing for the rest of my life."

But that wasn't to be. Scarpa's high-profile appearance in the Brooklyn courtroom had alerted state and federal prosecutors to his presence. Two days after the verdict, he was arrested on New York gun charges and federal racketeering and murder counts.[13]

According to Fred Dannen, who interviewed DeVecchio for his seminal 1996 *New Yorker* piece, "even after Scarpa's arrest, DeVecchio did not abandon his top-echelon source. He got in touch with prosecutors at the Brooklyn United States Attorney's Office to ask them to request bail for Scarpa."[14]

Assistant U.S. Attorney Andrew Weissmann, who would go on to prosecute Vic Orena Sr., told FBI agents in the course of DeVecchio's OPR that he was "incredulous" that anyone would want Scarpa out of jail. He said he believed that the court "should be told that Scarpa Sr. was a criminal while he was a confidential source."[15] Weissmann then said, "The U.S. Attorney's Office decided to bring the matter to the attention of Judge [I. Leo] Glasser who knew of Scarpa Sr.'s status as a confidential source from a previous case." That was the 1986 Secret Service credit card case, which resulted in a $10,000 fine and probation for Scarpa, rather than the $250,000 fine and the seven-year prison term for which he was eligible. That deal had been cut after Lin DeVecchio intervened with Glasser, who was told—even back then—that Scarpa had only a short time to live.

But Judge Glasser never got the case. Instead, after a bail hearing before Judge John L. Caden, it was assigned to Jack B. Weinstein, the same judge who would soon preside at the trial of Vic Orena Sr.

AUSA George Stamboulidis later told FBI agents that he had gotten calls from DeVecchio "attempting to let Scarpa out." He said that DeVecchio had told him that if the U.S. attorney's office would agree to release Greg on bail, that he "could be trusted and that he was not going anywhere since Scarpa had given DeVecchio his word."[16]

As Dannen recounted, at the bail hearing after Scarpa's arrest, Judge Caden was unaware of Greg's Top Echelon informant status. More surprisingly, so was Scarpa's lawyer at the time, Joseph Benfante, who expressed shock after learning that for years his client had been a secret FBI mole.

"That would be tantamount to me thinking that Mother Teresa is assisting Saddam Hussein," Benfante said, "because no F.B.I. informant goes out and engages in a Colombo war—it's insanity."[17]

At the initial bail hearing, Benfante argued to Caden that Greg's T-cell count had now reached zero—down from two thousand. He reiterated the prediction of Scarpa's doctor from the August trial that he had just months to live.

In a 302 recording his debriefing during DeVecchio's OPR, Judge Caden insisted that "no one from the government ever suggested that Scarpa was anything other than a crime boss who was a risk of flight." But he did admit that an official from the Metropolitan Correctional Center—the federal jail in lower Manhattan—had testified that "temperatures in the prison" might impact "Scarpa's problems with AIDS." So Scarpa was allowed to go home to Eighty-Second Street on house arrest wearing an ankle bracelet.[18]

If anyone in the FBI or EDNY was naïve enough to think that Scarpa's incarceration at home would stop the violence, however, they were mistaken. On October 7, Colombo associate Steven Mancusi was gunned down in a hit attributed to the war.[19] And before the year was out, "34" himself would go on another violent shooting rampage through the Brooklyn streets.

DeVecchio Threatens Favo

During the early fall of 1992, EDNY prosecutors held several meetings regarding Scarpa's status. Attending the meetings were AUSAs Weissmann and Stamboulidis, along with Scarpa, DeVecchio, and Special Agent Chris Favo. In the course of Lin's OPR, both Weissmann and Stamboulidis recounted their memories of those meetings for FBI agents. At the first meeting, attended by Assistant U.S. Attorney John Gleeson, Stamboulidis recalled, "DeVecchio did not want Scarpa indicted," but he was overruled.

At a second meeting, on September 27, Scarpa's Top Echelon informant status was revealed to Stamboulidis, who remembered how, at that point, Scarpa agreed to cooperate. But apparently SSA DeVecchio was not happy. Later at the same meeting, Stamboulidis remembered, DeVecchio "looked at Favo" and said, "If this ends up in an OPR, I'll have your ass."[20]

When it comes to the dozens of murders Scarpa committed on DeVecchio's watch, and the question of what DeVecchio knew and when he knew it, George Stamboulidis's memory is important. The first prosecution in this third Colombo war would be the trial of Michael Sessa in late October, and Lin DeVecchio would testify for the government as an expert witness, as he would in Vic Orena's trial in December. At each trial, the judge presiding would be Jack B. Weinstein. And the Feds would stick to their argument that the war was propagated by Orena, who was bent on taking over the family. But in neither prosecution would the jury know about DeVecchio's controversial relationship with the cold-blooded killer or get a hint of the compelling evidence the FBI and prosecutors now had that Scarpa was principally responsible for the war violence.

Naturally, in prepping him for trial, one of the questions prosecutors like Stamboulidis would want to ask DeVecchio was how much he knew about his source's role in the killings. If DeVecchio had known that "34" was whacking victims and yet allowed him to remain free—in defiance of the Attorney General's Guidelines—that information could have been very damaging to the government.

In his OPR debriefing, however, Stamboulidis told SSAs Kevin P. Donovan and Robert J. O'Brien that "at the time of his preparation of DeVecchio for his cross examination, he was told by DeVecchio that DeVecchio had never asked Scarpa if he was involved in any of the Colombo war killings."[21]

How truthful was that answer?

As we'll see, in at least two instances over the years when he was under oath, DeVecchio flip-flopped on the question of how aware he was of his source's murderous activities. Further, his immediate subordinate clearly knew. Chris Favo knew of Scarpa's involvement in the murder of Nicky Grancio four days after it happened. Favo even testified under oath in Vic Orena's 2255 hearing in 1996 that he'd told DeVecchio that "Scarpa, the confidential informant, had murdered Nicky Grancio."[22] But even if Favo hadn't told him, once he'd debriefed "34" immediately after the Grancio rubout, an experienced SSA like DeVecchio should have known that Scarpa had supervised the drive-by hit.

The AG's Guidelines mandated that when special agents became aware that their CIs were involved in violent activity—particularly crimes as egregious as murder—they were *bound* to inform their superiors and consult federal prosecutors right away.

Favo testified at that 1996 hearing that he couldn't remember if EDNY prosecutors had been brought into the loop following Grancio's hit, but that he certainly told his supervisor about Scarpa's role. His supervisor at the time was Lin DeVecchio.[23] The question is, what did Lin do with the information?

In 1995 and 1997, under penalty of perjury, DeVecchio gave conflicting accounts of what he knew about "34's" involvement in the Colombo war homicides.

At a hearing before Judge Weinstein in February 1997, under direct examination by defense attorney Gerry Shargel, DeVecchio discussed the Scarpa debriefing that gave rise to the 209 of December 11, 1991, blaming "the Persico faction" for "34's" murder of "Tommy Scars" Amato:

Shargel: Did he tell you who in the Persico faction had shot and killed Gaetano Amato?
DeVecchio: No. In this particular 209 he did not. Just said it was done by the Persico faction . . .
Shargel: Did you ask him whether it was Scarpa himself?
DeVecchio: No. I did not. . . .
Shargel: Never asked him that?
DeVecchio: That's correct. Never asked him that.
Shargel: Did you ever say to him you are my TE. You are my Top Echelon source. I'm paying you thousands of dollars. Can you go out and find out who did that?
DeVecchio: Yes. Sure. Absolutely I would say that to him. . . .
Shargel: Did he ever come back and tell you who did it?
DeVecchio: On some occasions . . .
Shargel: He came to you . . . Gregory Scarpa came to you and said . . . that the hit on Vincent Fusaro was done by the Persico faction? Did you ask him that day . . . who was it?

DeVecchio: Had he told me I would have recorded it.

Shargel: There is no record of it there [in the 209s].

DeVecchio: Obviously he didn't tell me. . . .

Shargel: You wouldn't do anything as absurd as lie, right? . . .

DeVecchio: Certainly not . . .

Shargel: So when Gregory Scarpa says to you that it was the Persico faction that did it, we are not talking about some large population right?

DeVecchio: Yes.

Shargel: At no time, according to your document there . . . on December 11th do you say to him "I'm not satisfied with 'the Persico faction,' I want to know who exactly did it so I can safeguard the streets of New York? . . ."

DeVecchio: I didn't ask him directly if he killed somebody, knowing he would not tell me that.

Shargel: He wouldn't tell you?

DeVecchio: Absolutely not. He wouldn't tell it to me. No informant will tell you.

Shargel: Did you ever ask him?

DeVecchio: No.

Shargel: So at no time, right up until the day he died in June of 1994, at no time did you ask Gregory Scarpa if he, in fact, committed murders?

DeVecchio: I don't recall talking to him about that up until that time. We may have had discussions but I don't recall it.[24]

Moments later, Shargel reminded DeVecchio of a sworn statement that he'd given twenty-one months earlier, in May 1995, during the OPR investigation.

> **Shargel:** On page 20 of the affidavit that you swore to you said, "I do recall asking Scarpa Sr., prior to his incarceration, who did the work, meaning who killed the four victims and wounded Waverly. He said he believed the violence took place as a result of spontaneity and not a plan, and he denied involvement in these killings." Do you remember saying that under oath?
>
> **DeVecchio:** If you have it printed, I have said it under oath obviously.

So did Lin DeVecchio ask Greg Scarpa about the murders or didn't he? In both instances, each time under oath, DeVecchio gave two different answers to that question: He didn't and he did. A few minutes later during that 1997 hearing, after discussing the FBI's practice of submitting its agents to polygraph tests, Shargel got DeVecchio to admit that the OPR investigators had asked him to take one.

Six months before that hearing, the Justice Department had concluded that DeVecchio's prosecution was "unwarranted." But that was only after he'd been given a grant of immunity that would have made it virtually impossible for him to be convicted for the underlying allegations in the OPR.

Before agreeing to testify at this subsequent 1997 hearing, DeVecchio had insisted again on a *separate* grant of immunity and Judge Weinstein had agreed to it. Now, as the hearing wound down, Shargel brought up the issue of the polygraph again:

> **Shargel:** There is no more prosecution. They are not going to prosecute you, right? Right?
>
> **DeVecchio:** Prosecute me for what?
>
> **Shargel:** For any of the crimes that they were investigating. You are not going to be prosecuted. You got a letter from the Justice Department.
>
> **DeVecchio:** They found out I committed no crimes to be prosecuted for.
>
> **Shargel:** You got immunity here today, right?
>
> **DeVecchio:** Yes.
>
> **Shargel:** My question to you now is, would you take an FBI polygraph test to determine whether or not you are telling the truth? Would you agree right now on the witness stand to take a lie detector test administered by the FBI or any expert on polygraph?
>
> **DeVecchio:** Why would I?

"Think about that response," says Shargel. "How could a supervisory agent with Lin DeVecchio's experience—a man who had taught informant development at Quantico—*not* have been aware at the height of the war that his principal TE informant was killing people on the streets of Brooklyn and not intervene to stop him? Whether or not Justice could have prosecuted him in the face of that immunity, or whether or not he would stand for a polygraph, how is it conceivable that he didn't know those murders were happening and not take immediate action to stop them?"[25]

Fredric Dannen, the author of that groundbreaking 1996 *New Yorker* piece on Scarpa and DeVecchio, read Lin's book and sent me this comment:

On page 166 of *We're Going to Win This Thing,* DeVecchio says it was his "sworn duty to prevent violence and stop the war if I could, and I took that duty very seriously." But starting on page 172, DeVecchio begins digging his own grave on this very point. He admits that Scarpa's team killed Nicky Grancio on January 7, 1992, and that Scarpa pinned the murder on Richie Fusco's hit squad. DeVecchio believed this misinformation—or willed himself into believing it—and he still manages to complain that "I got accused of being 'duped' by Scarpa over this one." What else do you call it? Later on the page [DeVecchio writes,] "In my heart, as Scarpa's handler, of course I knew he was doing hits." This is an extraordinary admission. DeVecchio told me in one of our 1996 interviews that he did *not* know Scarpa was a multiple murderer until after the Colombo War had ended.

The evidence presented thus far in this book demonstrates that Lin DeVecchio went to extraordinary lengths to keep the Killing Machine out of jail. Now, as 1992 came to a close, even while locked down on house arrest, "34" continued his shooting rampage.

The Shootout in Bay Ridge

Despite his prediction in August that he'd be dead by Christmas, by December Greg Scarpa was very much alive. But he was feeling the tension of wearing that ankle bracelet. Until his arrest, Scarpa had roamed the streets of Brooklyn as though he had a license to kill. Every time his family had been threatened—from Donny Somma's criticism of Greg Jr. during the 1980 bank robbery to the shots fired outside his house that purportedly threatened his daughter and grandson in 1991—Scarpa had reacted violently.

Now his cloak of invincibility was deteriorating. Even the Feds who'd protected him were now conspiring behind his back—or at least that's what he came to believe, as AIDS-related dementia began to affect him. His daughter Little Linda later confessed to an interviewer that the prospect of her father's vulnerability terrified her.

"Now I know that my father is not invincible and neither are we. We're open game in that life. Nobody is protected. Even though they're in the same Family they don't care. They kill each other."[26]

Four nights after Christmas, her brother Joey came home with a friend, twenty-one-year-old Joseph Randazzo, and told his father that he'd been insulted by a group of local drug dealers. One of them was an alleged crack seller named Ronald "Messy Marvin" Moran.[27]

Suddenly, the Grim Reaper erupted. "He was yelling and screaming," Linda remembered. "'These people think I'm sleeping?'" she recalled him saying. "'They think they can pull a gun on *my* son?' My father went wild."

At that point, despite his ankle bracelet, Scarpa grabbed a gun, bolted from the house, and ordered Joey and Randazzo to get in his car. He drove around the block until his son spotted Moran, and then Scarpa started shooting, chasing them with the car as Moran and another dealer returned shots. It was another open gun battle on the streets of Brooklyn. A total of sixteen rounds were fired by both sides.[28] Lin DeVecchio later claimed that Scarpa killed Moran's partner.

Messy Marvin later testified that he "had no bullets left in the gun. I was trying to . . . run in the house and he [Scarpa] was waving his gun

around, shooting it." But one of Moran's shots had struck Randazzo, who was in Scarpa's backseat. Another shot had struck Scarpa in the face, taking out his left eye. As he pulled the car to the curb, Joey bolted in a panic and took off. Remarkably, Scarpa got out, bleeding, and staggered home.

"I looked at him and I went 'Oh my God,'" Little Linda said. "I thought I was going to faint. . . . My father had AIDS and he didn't want me to touch him. . . . So now I'm saying to myself, 'Oh my God where's my brother?' So I ran out to the car and my brother's not there. But his friend's in the back, covered in blood. I was talking to him the whole time, trying to tell him help is on the way. I was in shock."

An ambulance was soon called. But before it arrived, Scarpa sat down in the house and patted

Joey Scarpa

his eye socket with a towel. He then downed a Scotch and was driven to the hospital by Larry Mazza.[29] Randazzo, who was taken in the ambulance, died two days later. Moran pled guilty to the murder in 1997.

As a measure of his devotion to Scarpa, Lin DeVecchio describes that incident with admiration in his book, claiming that during the gun battle Scarpa had evened the score:

> On December 29, 1992 . . . Scarpa's son Joey Schiro came home complaining about two rival drug dealers in the neighborhood who were encroaching and showing no respect for the Scarpa name. Greg Scarpa grabbed his gun and found the two dealers. A gun battle ensued. Scarpa killed one of them, but had his own eye shot out. Before he went to the hospital, he returned home and had a glass of Scotch. Come on, loosen up, you've got to admire the man.

That last line speaks volumes about how Lin DeVecchio seemed to regard Scarpa's death toll. Just a week earlier, in part because of DeVecchio's expert witness testimony, Vic Orena had been convicted not just of the Tommy Ocera murder but of racketeering and propagating the Colombo war—a conflict that Greg Scarpa, not Orena, fomented and waged. By the time that trial took place, agents like Chris Favo could no longer ignore the role the Bureau's star informant had played in the violence. Scarpa would soon plead guilty to three of the murders—Fusaro, Grancio, and Lampasi—and Mazza would plead to a fourth (Amato).

But it would be another year before Favo, Tomlinson, and Leadbetter could muster the courage to blow the whistle on their boss. The central question the OPR investigators would explore was whether Lin DeVecchio had intentionally aided and abetted Scarpa's rampage. The head of the FBI's New York Office would exert intense pressure to speed up the investigation, because of the ongoing embarrassment it brought to the office and the threat it posed to the Feds' many ongoing war cases.[30]

But based on the evidence uncovered in this investigation, one thing is clear: Whether or not it was the result of negligence on Lin's part, from 1980 to 1992 twenty-six people were killed directly by Scarpa, or by members of his crew at Scarpa's direction. More than half of the homicides Greg admitted to, before telling Larry Mazza he'd "stopped counting," occurred on the watch of SSA Roy Lindley DeVecchio, the man known in the media as "Mr. Organized Crime."[31]

Eventually, with his own agents coming forward to blow the whistle, the harsh light of scrutiny would be shed on Lin DeVecchio himself. But before that happened, a series of FBI agents and supervisors, working in conjunction with federal prosecutors, would go to extreme lengths to contain the potential damage.

PART IV

Chapter 31

A GRAIN OF SAND
ON JONES BEACH

By March 1997, nearly six years after Carmine Sessa's murder crew rolled up on Vic Orena—whose ambition, the Feds insisted, had triggered the war—seventy-five members of the Colombo family had been prosecuted.[1] As a measure of culpability in the conflict, forty of them were members of the so-called Persico faction. Literally the entire anti-Orena faction, from Greg Scarpa Sr. on down, was indicted, versus about thirty-five from Vic Orena's side, which had triple the number of members and associates at the time of the hostilities.[2] As noted, as late as 2001, Judge Jack B. Weinstein, who presided over many of the top cases, acknowledged that if the Scarpa-DeVecchio scandal continued to fester, many of those "war" prosecutions would "unravel."[3]

In the early fall of 1992, as the Feds were prepping the first Colombo war prosecution—the murder and racke-

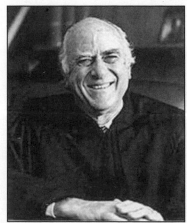

Judge Jack B. Weinstein

teering trial of Carmine Sessa's younger brother Michael—a number of FBI agents in the New York Office knew that Greg Scarpa had played a significant role in the violence. At the same time, federal prosecutors in Brooklyn knew that evidence had surfaced as far back as 1987 that "34" had a law enforcement source. By late February 1992, Special Agent Chris Favo suspected that Scarpa was getting intelligence from Favo's own boss, Lin DeVecchio.[4] Later, Favo's colleague Special Agent Howard Leadbetter II said he "began to believe that it was possible that SSA DeVecchio was attempting to interfere with or otherwise stall the development of the [Scarpa] investigation."[5]

But that fall, as EDNY prosecutors geared up to try the younger Sessa and Vic Orena, no one outside the Justice Department had any inkling of that—particularly the defense lawyers.

Under the doctrine expressed in the landmark 1963 Supreme Court decision *Brady v. Maryland*,[6] each of the accused had a constitutional right to receive any "material" exculpatory evidence that could help their defense.[7] Chief among that evidence would be proof that would allow the defense to impeach the credibility of a prosecution witness, and since Lin DeVecchio would testify for the government in both the Sessa and Orena trials, word of his alleged "unholy alliance" with Scarpa was arguably "material."

But when it came to the metastasizing Scarpa-DeVecchio scandal, none of that "Brady evidence" was forthcoming from the Feds.

"The idea that DeVecchio, a senior supervisory special agent in the New York Office who was running two squads, had been feeding intelligence to this killer who had then acted upon it would have been *hugely* exculpatory," argues Ellen Resnick, who later defended Vic Orena Jr. and represented his father on appeal. "But at that time, throughout the fall of 1992 and well into 1993, we didn't even get a whiff of that from the government."[8] Moreover, as Flora Edwards, who represented Vic Orena, insists, "the Feds didn't just *withhold* that information. Lin DeVecchio actually got on the stand in the Michael Sessa trial and misrepresented what he had done to protect Scarpa Sr."[9]

On November 2, 1992, DeVecchio testified as an expert witness for the government in *United States v. Michael Sessa,* the first Colombo war prosecution. Charged with racketeering and the murder of Anthony "Bird" Collucio, a loan shark and member of his crew, the younger Sessa was convicted largely on the testimony of Joseph Ambrosino, who had eagerly become a government witness after flipping in June.[10]

As previously noted, during Sessa's trial, Lin DeVecchio was cross-examined by defense attorney Gavin Scotti, and he pointedly denied having helped a confidential informant like Scarpa.* But five years later, Gerry Shargel got DeVecchio to admit under oath that, in fact, he *had* intervened so that "34" could be released on bail. When Shargel suggested that DeVecchio had lied during his Sessa testimony, the former SSA shot back that he "resent[ed]" the accusation.[11]

Why is the issue of DeVecchio's veracity so important at this juncture? Because if the jury had concluded that he'd lied, that might have made the difference between a verdict of guilt and one of innocence for Michael Sessa. During his summation, Assistant U.S. Attorney George Stamboulidis told the jurors *emphatically:* "If you believe any agent testifying lied for a second, if you even *entertain* that thought, come right back, let [Sessa] go."[12] Since Sessa was convicted and sentenced to life—with his jury clueless about the Scarpa-DeVecchio relationship—it's relevant to ask whether George Stamboulidis should have known that DeVecchio wasn't telling the truth when he denied intervening to help a confidential informant like Scarpa.

Consider the evidence uncovered in this investigation:

On March 31, 1992, several days before ASAC North ordered Scarpa closed, NYPD detectives Brogan and Willoughly, from the OCID Task Force, spotted Scarpa tossing a loaded handgun out of a moving vehicle. Since "34" was on parole in the credit card case, this was a violation that could have resulted in his immediate arrest. But Chris Favo later admitted under oath that "out of concern that the NYPD would force the FBI to arrest Scarpa for the gun," he called Stamboulidis at that time "and informed him that Scarpa was a source."[13]

Now, with respect to Stamboulidis's level of awareness at the time of the Sessa trial, consider this verbatim account of what he later told investigators during DeVecchio's OPR inquiry. It was written in the third person by FBI investigators:

---

* See Chapter 15.

STAMBOULIDES [*sic*] stated that he was told that the police were going to arrest SCARPA on a gun charge. STAMBOULIDIS stated that he told DEVECCHIO to let SCARPA get arrested and that based on the way DEVECCHIO described the situation and the possibility of revealing the identity of SCARPA as a source, that the state had a weak case. . . . STAMBOULIDES [*sic*] stated that he felt that SCARPA had called in a panic concerning the gun case. . . .[14] STAMBOULI DES [*sic*] stated that he did not trust DEVECCHIO not to tell SCARPA. . . . STAMBOU-LIDES [*sic*] stated that he subsequently had contact with DEVECCHIO regarding the indictment of SCARPA, and *he was advised by DEVEC-CHIO that SCARPA was more valuable on the street than in jail and that he had gotten calls from DEVECCHIO attempting to let SCARPA out on bail.*[15]*

That 302 documenting what Stamboulidis told FBI agents probing DeVecchio during the OPR in September 1994 is prima facie evidence that, *before* Stamboulidis's summation to the jury in the 1992 Michael Sessa case, he *knew* that Lin DeVecchio had misrepresented to attorney Scotti at that trial that he had never intervened to keep a confidential informant on the street. In fact, Stamboulidis knew that DeVecchio had intervened directly—and had even gone so far as to seek *the attorney's* advice on how to free Scarpa following his indictment on the NYPD's gun charge.

But later, at trial, Stamboulidis told the jury with a straight face that if they believed that any of the agents testifying had "lied for a second," they should acquit Michael Sessa.

When the jury came back, not only did they convict Sessa, but Judge Weinstein threw the book at him, sentencing him to two life terms plus an additional sixty years and fining him $2 million.[16] Although this was a murder conviction, it was in strong contrast to the wrist-slap Scarpa got in his 1987 credit card case: probation and a $10,000 fine, instead of the maximum seven-year prison term and $250,000 fine provided by law.[17]

"By the fall of 1992, the Feds faced a serious dilemma," says Flora Edwards, echoing an argument she later made before Judge Weinstein.

---

* Emphasis added.

"They had all these war cases to prosecute, and they knew, or had reason to know, that the principal instigator of the violence was their own informant. But they routinely misrepresented the full truth to juries. As a direct result, defendants like Michael Sessa and Vic Orena Sr. were convicted. You have to ask, where was Chris Favo and his band of agents back then? They were so concerned about the leaks in January 1994 that they blew the whistle on Lin, but beginning with the war trials in 1993, despite their misgivings about their boss DeVecchio dating back a year, these same agents began testifying for the government and they never even *hinted* at the alleged corrupt relationship between Scarpa Sr. and his contacting agent DeVecchio."[18]

"The record before the Court reveals a systematic government effort to bury every detail about Scarpa's informant status and his corrupt relationship with a supervisory special agent of the FBI."[19] That was the argument made by defense lawyer Gus Newman, in his 1996 motion asking for a new trial for Vic Orena.

But three years earlier, when he represented Vic Orena at trial, Newman had no idea about that alleged corruption when he cross-examined Lin DeVecchio, even though the Feds were obligated to disclose it under Brady rules. In his appeal brief, filed on January 16, 1996, Newman pointed out that

> DeVecchio well knew prior to the instant [Orena] prosecution all that Scarpa, [Carmine] Sessa and Mazza had done to incite and perpetuate the so-called war and all that he had done, for the previous ten years, to protect, assist and encourage Scarpa in his criminal activities. As the Supervisor for C-10, with the authority (which he exercised) to steer the investigation away from Scarpa, he personally influenced the direction of the investigation and the course of events which were ascribed to the "Colombo War."[20]

Newman also emphasized how much Chris Favo knew about Scarpa's violence by the start of Vic Orena's trial:

> He knew that Scarpa was an informant for the FBI whose handler was DeVecchio. He knew from Imbriale and Ambrosino that Scarpa had

committed more violence than any other individual associated with the so-called "war." He knew the content of the 209 reports in Scarpa's file and had already concluded that the FBI was "duped" by Scarpa's purported assistance. Finally, he knew by this time that his supervisor, Lindley DeVecchio, had been compromised—so compromised, in fact, that Favo withheld all information about Scarpa from him after May 1992.

By his own admission, the pieces had fallen together for Favo long before Mr. Orena's trial. Favo had witnessed: the disclosure to Scarpa of Imbriale's cooperation; DeVecchio's assistance to Scarpa in finding his loan shark victims and in protecting Mazza and Del Masto while fugitives during the war; DeVecchio's glee at learning that Lampasi was killed and his statement that he and Scarpa were "winning"; DeVecchio's order halting any further arrests after the Point Pleasant (NJ) incident for fear that Scarpa might be apprehended; and his opposition to the federal complaint and arrest of Scarpa on August 31, 1992.

And Favo admitted that his failure to report DeVecchio was not due to his uncertainty about DeVecchio's mishandling of Scarpa but, rather, his fear that DeVecchio's stature within the FBI meant that Favo would not be believed. Yet, Favo was so certain of DeVecchio's corrupt relationship with Scarpa that he could not report him for fear that Scarpa would be told and would flee. Favo continued to withhold information about what he knew for more than a year after Mr. Orena's trial had concluded.[21]

In his summation at Vic Orena's trial, Newman had argued to the jury that "there's no credible, direct evidence of Mr. Orena conspiring with anyone to kill [Tommy] Ocera . . . from any credible, believable source. There's no direct proof from a credible, believable source that Mr. Orena conspired with anybody to do anything to anybody from this so-called Persico faction."[22]

But the jurors who eyed the table full of guns—most of which came from the missing plastic bag found under the porch—were never told of Greg Scarpa Jr.'s sworn allegation that the six handguns were planted by his brother under the watchful eye of his father and Lin DeVecchio.[23] "They weren't told," says Newman, "because we didn't know those facts at the time of trial."[24]

Lin DeVecchio was the lead-off witness at that trial. He drew on his twenty-five years of FBI expertise to detail the war violence for the jury.[25] But the jurors had no inkling that Greg Scarpa Sr. had stayed out of jail for years and was literally free to instigate and wage the war from 1991 to 1992 because DeVecchio had gone to bat for him in the 1986 credit card case.[26] They had no clue that the address of Orena's girlfriend's Queens apartment, which was passed to Scarpa in January 1992, may have come from DeVecchio.[27]

For the jury's edification, the government prepared a huge chart tracking the war violence. Across the bottom of the chart was a series of red boxes, each one marking one of the war deaths. Assistant U.S. Attorney John Gleeson later admitted that Scarpa, "an accomplished killer," was "responsible for half of the red boxes on the bottom of the war chart."[28]

But the jury was never informed that during that streak of bloodshed, Scarpa was on the FBI's payroll and had even received cash bonuses for the "intelligence" he provided. In short, the FBI had in its employ the principal perpetrator of the violent crimes now being prosecuted in federal court.

As noted, Gleeson admitted to the jury in his rebuttal that on October 27, 1989, when Tommy Ocera and Diane Montesano were followed, "it probably" was "Greg Scarpa"[29] who was stalking them in the Cadillac. Gleeson went on to say that Vic Orena "tried to get Greg Scarpa to kill [Ocera] . . . assuming it was Greg Scarpa, maybe it was someone else, but it failed."[30]

"So here we have one of the senior EDNY prosecutors admitting that Scarpa Sr. was likely involved in the murder plot," said Vic Orena's son Andrew. "What an amazing admission by the Feds." What Gleeson never explained to the jury was why Vic Orena—Scarpa's mortal enemy during the war—would ever contract with him to kill Ocera. Why would Little Vic ask Scarpa to stalk Ocera and Montesano the night they left the restaurant? Why would he put himself in the debt of Scarpa, a drug-dealing killer he'd had little to do with before 1989?

Yet in Gleeson's rebuttal the government was admitting that it was "probably" Scarpa who took the first pass on Tommy Ocera. And if he tried to kill him once, it's fair to argue that he would have finished the job—providing the FBI with a perfect excuse for getting Vic Orena off the streets.

The Isolated Jury

Given the Feds' willingness to link Greg Scarpa Sr. to the stalking of Tommy Ocera, one of the most compelling revelations from the Vic Orena trial is how they isolated the jury from any suggestion that the Killing Machine was a Top Echelon source.

In recounting the war violence, AUSA George Stamboulidis told the jury, "On January seventh of 1992 . . . the Persicos kill Nicky Black."[31] Minutes later, he reiterated, after earlier testimony, that on "February twenty-sixth, Joe Waverly—Joel Cacace—was . . . shot and wounded." To remind the jury that it was Vic Orena who was on trial, he added that Cacace "was an Orena faction member."[32] But Stamboulidis never let on what he should have known at the time: that both acts of violence were committed by Gregory Scarpa Sr., the man who effectively *was* the "Persico faction."

Judge Jack B. Weinstein, who was on the bench for both the Sessa and Orena trials, issued a number of rulings during Orena's prosecution and motions for a new trial that seemed to favor the prosecution.[33]

In the absence of any physical evidence linking him to Ocera's murder, Vic Orena was convicted and sentenced to multiple life terms by Judge Weinstein—largely on the weight of hearsay evidence, which also sought to cast Orena as the lead protagonist in the war. The government's star witnesses, Little Al D'Arco and Sammy the Bull Gravano, also testified about Orena's alleged admissions regarding Ocera's death, which were entirely hearsay—and each of them was later proven to be to be a liar. Further, the government's theory that Orena killed Ocera as a favor to John Gotti was entirely discredited.[34]

In 1997, lawyers for Vic Orena and Patty Amato petitioned for new trials in light of these revelations and the evidence that had surfaced since their convictions establishing Greg Scarpa Sr. as the primary instigator of the war. Judge Weinstein issued a 101-page decision rejecting those motions.

Calling Orena and Amato "murderous criminals" who'd been convicted on "strong evidence," he wrote:

> Attempting to transform a troubling cloud of questionable ethics and judgment enveloping an F.B.I. Special Agent into a raging storm of reasonable doubt, petitioner-defendants move for dismissal of their indictments or for new trials. . . . The claim is that the government violated its disclosure obligations under *Brady v. Maryland,* after engaging in and covering up outrageous government misconduct.[35]

In that decision, Judge Weinstein acknowledged Orena's claim that "Gravano's testimony in another case, *United States v. Stancell,* 95 CR 503 (N.D.Ga.1996), constitutes newly discovered evidence that contradicts his and D'Arco's testimony, as well as the government's argument, at the Orena trial, that Orena's primary motive to kill Ocera was to please Gotti by retaliating for Ocera's murder of Greg Reiter."

Then he went further:

> During the *Stancell* proceedings and outside of the jury's presence, Gravano testified that the Ocera homicide had no connection to Greg Reiter's disappearance and murder. . . . Orena then points to another case, *United States v. Brennan,* 95 CR 941[,] . . . in which the government charged that defendant Robert Scott Brennan murdered Dennis Harrigan in retaliation for Harrigan's murder of Greg Reiter. Harrigan was murdered on October 1, 1991. . . . Thus, Orena now argues that the facts of *Brennan* and Gravano's *Stancell* testimony contradict the government's theory of motive for the Ocera murder case against Orena. If the elder Reiter believed, so the argument goes, that Harrigan and Bright were responsible for Greg's murder, then it makes no sense at all that Gotti believed that Ocera was responsible and communicated that to Orena. Further, Gravano's testimony in *Stancell* indicates that a different motive existed.

But having acknowledged all that, Judge Weinstein nevertheless concluded that "this argument misses the mark . . . the primary motive for the Ocera murder the government advanced at trial was Orena's concern that Ocera allow his loan shark records to fall into the possession of law enforcement."

Weinstein then concluded that "Orena's desire to ingratiate himself with Gotti was a subsidiary motive, not the principal one, as Orena now argues."[36]

The Prosecutor's Emphasis on the Gotti Theory

However, in that decision, Judge Weinstein, one of the smartest judges in the federal judiciary, seemed to overlook the emphasis that Assistant U.S. Attorneys Stamboulidis and Gleeson had placed on the testimony of D'Arco and Gravano in their closing arguments to the Orena jury. In his summation, which filled 150 pages of transcript, Stamboulidis cited D'Arco and Gravano or the Greg Reiter–Gotti theory on forty-four of those pages (nearly one out of every three), saying emphatically at one point, "Tommy Ocera had been murdered. The contract was fulfilled. Gotti got his favor."[37]

Further, in his rebuttal, AUSA Gleeson cited Gravano, D'Arco, or the Reiter murder motive in eleven out of forty-one pages (one in four)— reminding the jury of the pedigree of the government's witnesses: "You heard the big shots from the other families, Al D'Arco, Sammy Gravano," he said. "There are a lot of documents, a lot of physical evidence. I'm not going to go over all of them."[38]

So, while the Gotti "favor" theory may have represented a *secondary* motive, in Judge Weinstein's view, it was certainly front and center in the hours before the jury got the case.

Weinstein also rejected Orena's argument that "since the completion of the trials, new evidence has emerged that bears upon the credibility of both Gravano and D'Arco." He acknowledged Orena's contention that "Gravano lied about the full extent of his prior criminal conduct," including drug dealing and evidence in published reports that Sammy "the Bull" had engaged in two additional murders. Yet he dismissed this new information as "the evidentiary equivalent of a grain of sand on Jones Beach."

And when it came to the real "elephant in the room"—the fact that Lin DeVecchio had testified in detail about the war murders without informing the judge or jury that Greg Scarpa, the lead antagonist, was his asset— Weinstein minimized it, concluding, "On cross-examination, defense counsel offered no impeachment of DeVecchio regarding his truthfulness, bias or motive to obtain a conviction against Orena."[39]

But "how in God's name," asks Flora Edwards, "was Gus Newman supposed to attack Lin's credibility when *nobody* outside of the Justice Department had a clue at the time of that trial that Lin was conspiring with his own CI?"[40]

Now, as 1993 unfolded and more members of the Persico faction were arrested and agreed to cooperate, the details of Greg Scarpa's extraordinary get-out-of-jail-free card with the Feds became increasingly apparent. It would prove to be a year of conflict between the FBI agents at 26 Federal Plaza, who were making the war arrests, and the prosecutors of the Eastern District in Brooklyn, who had to bring them to trial. Chris Favo, a Jesuit-trained Roman Catholic, was perhaps the most conflicted of all. The problem the Feds now faced was how to explain the hemorrhaging leaks that had occurred for years.

Chapter 32

EXPECTING TO
GO HOME

On January 19, 1993, after thirty-two months as a fugitive, Anthony "Gaspipe" Casso, the acting underboss of the Lucchese family, was arrested in Mount Olive, New Jersey.[1] James Fox, the FBI's assistant director in charge in New York, called Casso "a psychopath whose name should be Mad Dog." Federal prosecutor Greg O'Connell called him "the most dangerous, cunning, ruthless Mafia leader left on the streets," and with Greg Scarpa Sr. finally behind bars, that may have been a fair assessment.[2] Casso and Scarpa had worked together on countless scores over the years, and Gaspipe himself told me that he used intelligence provided by Greg to hunt down the shooters who had attacked him in 1986.[3] Scarpa, he said, had actually handed him a file containing the names of the shooters—a file that he maintained came from Lin DeVecchio.

On the day of his arrest, by Casso's own account, he was taking a shower in his New Jersey hideaway when the Feds, clad in flak jackets and carrying machine guns, surrounded the house. They reportedly banged on the front door and shouted, "FBI! Come out with your hands up!"[4] In Phil Carlo's *Gaspipe,* Casso said that after the Feds kicked in the front door and stormed inside, he nonchalantly proceeded to get dressed in an upstairs bedroom while they shouted, "Anthony, give it up."

"I ain't coming down until I'm dressed," the hardened mob boss yelled back. So the fugitive arrest team rushed upstairs and cuffed him.

As a measure of the kind of wealth Casso had amassed over the years, the FBI found $375,000 in that safe house, another $200,000 in a safe-deposit box that Anthony had hidden away to pay for his daughter Jolene's wedding, and a third safe-deposit box containing half a million dollars in jewelry he'd bought for his wife, Lillian. When she heard that the house he'd been hiding in was owned by Rosemarie Billotti, a childhood girlfriend of Anthony's, Lillian reportedly wouldn't talk to him for months.[5]

Casso himself was just as stone-faced with the Feds after they locked him up. Initially he refused to cooperate until they offered him the kind of deal he knew they'd given Sammy Gravano—five years for nineteen murders. Gaspipe was also well aware of the decades-long leniency the Justice Department had shown toward his good friend Greg Scarpa, and he expected no less if he was going to betray Cosa Nostra.

Casso later concluded that it was his honesty about the extent of Gravano's drug dealing that ultimately caused the Feds to renege on the plea bargain agreement they offered him. But in the hours following his arrest, as he was transported to the Metropolitan Correctional Center (MCC), Gaspipe was confident.

The first cell they put him in was on Eleven North, the same tier where Scarpa was being held. At that point, Casso had every reason to expect that if he cooperated, the Feds would reciprocate. After all, Scarpa was dying, and his usefulness to the government was diminishing. In fact, he could even become a liability with the Colombo war trials ahead if his special relationship with Lin DeVecchio was exposed. On the other hand, Casso was in bulldoglike health. He had a photographic memory. And the hard drive in his head held a treasure trove of Mafia secrets.

Hospital Bed vs. Jail Cell

On February 4, 1993, Greg Scarpa Sr. was indicted for the murders of Fusaro, Grancio, and Lampasi. He was also charged with murder conspiracy stemming from the war and with a probation violation for the tossed gun.[6] Two weeks later, after being locked up as a result of his Bay Ridge shooting rampage, sixty-four-year-old Scarpa came before Judge Weinstein. Despite having broken house arrest, killing one person and causing the death of his son's friend, he audaciously reapplied for bail. At the hearing, Weinstein noted that since returning to the MCC Scarpa had offered credible medical evidence that his condition had "seriously deteriorated." Thus, despite his "proven dangerous propensities," Weinstein ruled that Scarpa could spend the rest of his days incarcerated in a hospital bed within a medical ward as opposed to a jail cell.[7]

Meanwhile, with its field general out of commission, the FBI started rolling up his various lieutenants. Larry Mazza had gone on the lam in June after Scarpa tipped off him and Jimmy Del Masto to their indictments, but on February 9 he was arrested in Florida. He soon agreed to cooperate with the Feds and convinced Del Masto to surrender.[8]

On April 4, Palm Sunday, Carmine Sessa, who'd been at large since July, was arrested while attending a secret meeting outside St. Patrick's Cathedral on Fifth Avenue in Manhattan. Chris Favo later told the OPR agents that as soon as the cuffs were placed on Sessa, Lin DeVecchio, who was present for the bust, "stated that he had to give Jerry Capeci a call so he could send a photographer over."[9] Once the arrestees were taken away, Favo was so concerned about DeVecchio's comment that he called Joe Valiquette, who was then the Bureau's public information officer in New York.

Reached at home, according to Favo's OPR 302, "Valiquette stated that Capeci would be out of town that week and was unlikely to contact him about the arrest."[10] Still, the incident pointed out Lin's apparent devotion to Capeci, whose weekly "Gang Land" column in the *Daily News,* according to Favo, benefited from DeVecchio's leaks.[11]

In that same 302, Favo told the investigating agents, "Throughout the course of the war, important investigative information was disclosed in Jerry Capeci's weekly column. . . . On several occasions SSA DeVecchio approached me or another agent with a specific question about the investigation of the war or the Colombo family and our answer to the question appeared in Capeci's column the following day with an attribution to a law enforcement source or federal law enforcement source."[12]

During the first three days after his Palm Sunday arrest, as Carmine

Sessa was being debriefed by Special Agent Jeffrey Tomlinson, Lin DeVecchio repeatedly came in to speak with the consigliere of the Persico faction. In his sworn statement to OPR investigators, Tomlinson later stated that he found this "rather unusual," since *he* was in charge of the debriefings. "Up to that point," he confessed, "SSA DeVecchio had been somewhat removed from the investigations and did not generally take such a high profile."[13]

Tomlinson stated that Sessa told him "he thought it was unusual that SSA DeVecchio spent so much time in the first three days after he was arrested, talking to him, and that Sessa got suspicious that SSA DeVecchio might be Scarpa Sr.'s law enforcement source."[14]

But in light of what we've uncovered in this investigation, DeVecchio's renewed attention to the war probe makes sense. After all, Carmine Sessa had been Greg Scarpa's surrogate in the conflict. He was now confessing to Tomlinson that he committed thirteen murders and that "Scarpa Sr. was involved in seven or eight of those homicides."[15] More important, as Tomlinson related in his sworn OPR affidavit, "at least two or three of the killings were done because Scarpa Sr. had told Sessa that the victim was going to cooperate or was cooperating with law enforcement authorities."[16]

Among Sessa's extraordinary revelations was the story of how, back in the 1980s, he had found what appeared to be a bug in a pay phone inside the Wimpy Boys club, and Scarpa had dismissed the news, telling Sessa, "It was not a bug and don't worry about it."* Later, when a private investigator confirmed that it was in fact a listening device, Sessa was "confused" as to why Greg didn't want to pursue the issue. This, said Carmine, made him "suspicious that Scarpa [might] be cooperating with law enforcement."[17]

Sessa also reported that his wife had picked up phone calls at Scarpa's house while he was hospitalized, and that the caller had identified himself as "Mr. Dello."† That caused Sessa to conclude that DeVecchio was Greg's law enforcement source.[18] Another revelation from Sessa during his debriefings was that "Scarpa Sr. had access to telephone numbers, subscriber informa-

---

* Earlier, Scarpa had expressed concern about bugs planted by the Brooklyn DA at the Wimpy Boys club, but he didn't seem worried about listening devices installed by the Feds.

† Another code name was "Del." Gregory Jr. said that his father sometimes referred to DeVecchio simply as "D."

tion and license plate registrations which he got from his law enforcement source."

Later in that same sworn statement, Special Agent Tomlinson admitted that, after Ambrosino's June 1992 arrest, when the FBI confirmed Scarpa's role in the murder of Nicholas Grancio, with corroboration from Carmine Imbriale, "he couldn't understand why . . . the source [Scarpa Sr.] would continue to be operated."[19]

On April 23, 1993, Greg Scarpa Sr. pled guilty to the weapons charge in Brooklyn Supreme Court. As part of a deal with the DA, in which he agreed to accept a guilty plea to federal racketeering charges, the tossed-gun charge—a felony—was reduced to a misdemeanor, and Scarpa was sentenced to a year in a Rikers Island hospital bed.[20]

In an apparent bid to counter critics who might complain about leniency for the killer, a DA's spokesperson said that Scarpa was "not expected to survive the year."

By 1993 Scarpa was down from 220 pounds to 160

On May 6, Scarpa came before Judge Weinstein, who was on the bench during the Vic Orena trial six months earlier when federal prosecutor John Gleeson admitted that Greg had "probably" been the one stalking Tommy Ocera and Diane Montesano.

At this point Weinstein had no idea of the depth of Scarpa's involvement in the war—but he listened as the FBI's star informant admitted to the murders of Fusaro, Grancio, and Lampasi. AUSA George Stamboulidis, who was present, had a much fuller picture of Scarpa's role in the war violence, but since homicide was a state crime, "34" was allowed to plead guilty to racketeering charges.

For Scarpa, the Killing Machine—who'd told Larry Mazza he'd stopped counting after fifty hits, *half* of which had occurred on Lin DeVecchio's watch—this plea was certainly a bargain. But although his HIV infection had turned into full-blown AIDS, Scarpa's expression of remorse at the hearing was limited.

Of all his horrific crimes, including the brutal slaying of Mary Bari, the spur-of-the-moment rubout of Donnie Somma, and the murders of his brother Sal and Joe DeDomenico, which he'd contracted to others, the only homicide Greg Sr. wanted to talk about was the killing of twenty-one-year-old Joseph Randazzo, Joey's friend who died after Scarpa's shootout on December 29. Although he may have been criminally negligent in that killing, it was one homicide that "34" didn't commit.

> **Scarpa:** I want to thank Your Honor, Mr. Stamboulidis, for the consideration and compassion that has been shown to me from the time of my original arrest. If the good Lord had given me the opportunity to change that particular night where this young boy died who hadn't even seen the dawn of life, I would certainly look to do it.

At that point, the judge noted that the parties had agreed to postpone the sentencing. There was a brief discussion of the defense's expectation that Scarpa would do his time at Rikers Island, the city's principal jail. Greg's lawyer, Stephen Kartagener, pointed out that Rikers had "one of the leading AIDS hospitals in the criminal justice system." He then asked that Scarpa be allowed "a very, very brief courtroom visit [with] his two-year-old grandson." Without objection from Stamboulidis, Weinstein granted that request and the hearing ended with the judge wishing the emaciated killer "good luck."

Physicians had repeatedly insisted that Greg Scarpa Sr. should have been dead years ago, but before the year was out he was back in front of Judge Weinstein asking that he be allowed to die at home. The Mad Hatter was hanging on with a tenacity that the Mad Monk, Rasputin, himself might have envied.

Before Scarpa's final sentence was pronounced, however, his status as a TE informant would be the subject of multiple meetings with the Eastern District Feds. His own fate was close to being decided, but his decades-long relationship with the Bureau was in danger of impacting the fate of multiple Colombo war prosecutions.

Scarpa "Had Nothing Left"

During the May 6 hearing before Judge Weinstein, Scarpa had presented himself as being at death's door. On August 27, though, he was healthy enough to call Lin DeVecchio from his Rikers Island AIDS ward and pass on a new series of allegations regarding his old nemesis Wild Bill Cutolo.

> On August 27, 1993, Former ████████ telephonically contacted SSA R. LINDLEY DE VECCHIO and provided the following information: Source said WILLIAM CUTOLO is a Capo in the COLOMBO LCN Family who was a strong supporter of VIC ORENA, and continues to be the main force in the ORENA faction. CUTOLO continues to meet at a club on 63rd street and 11th Ave. Brooklyn, New York where he discusses his illegal activities. . . . The source identified the following as being in CUTOLO's crew:
>
> FRANK IANNACI . . .
> JOSEPH "Jo Jo" RUSSO
> VINCENT DIMARTINO
> GABE SCIANNA . . .
> VINCENT FUSARO—Deceased
>
> The source said the above individuals have conducted loansharking activities for CUTOLO, and were sent out as "hit teams" during the height of the COLOMBO War.[21]

In his book Lin appears to disparage that report, describing it as "a lot of stale information." He then denigrates his heretofore trusted source by writing that "Greg Scarpa was well out of the loop at this point." As if to comment on Senior's deterioration from AIDS, Lin writes that Greg "had nothing left."

Then Lin writes that on September 29, he was "summoned to a meeting at Valerie Caproni's office." Caproni was the former AUSA who had supervised Greg Jr.'s 1987 DEA prosecution. Back then, she had crossed swords with the Bureau by dispatching U.S. Marshals to find Junior after he'd become a fugitive. In those days there was no love lost between DeVecchio and Caproni, and later, during Lin's OPR, she told investigators that she

Valerie Caproni

was "displeased with the FBI's efforts to locate Scarpa Jr."[22]

Caproni, a tough-talking Southerner with a masculine demeanor, had left the EDNY in 1989, but she returned to Brooklyn in 1992 and was put in charge of the Colombo family war prosecutions. She was later appointed chief of the EDNY's Criminal Division.[23] Now the relationship between DeVecchio and his source threatened to derail the war cases if the full truth of their association came out.

By the early fall, despite Lin's suggestion in his book that Scarpa Sr. had pretty much shot his load as a source, Greg Sr.'s attorney Stephen Kartagener made an audacious offer. He actually approached the EDNY and "proffered his client's cooperation in return for being released from prison."[24]

The September 29 meeting in Caproni's office was attended by Kartagener, Scarpa, DeVecchio, Chris Favo, and George Stamboulidis. Curiously, also in attendance was Special Agent James Brennan from the Lucchese Squad.

Calling "Gaspipe" the Source

At first glance, the attendance of an agent whose work didn't involve Colombo issues seemed unusual, since Greg Sr.'s secret status as a Top Echelon source was to be the principal topic of conversation. But as the meeting progressed, the reason for Brennan's presence became clear.

Lin later wrote that at the meeting, Scarpa Sr. appeared "emaciated. His skin was gray and he wore an eye patch."[25] After Greg made what DeVecchio called a "pitch" to cooperate, Lin reportedly left the meeting while Scarpa, his lawyer, and Brennan stayed behind.[26] As Caproni later told FBI investigators during DeVecchio's OPR investigation, she then asked Scarpa if he had a law enforcement source. But Greg reportedly denied it, insisting that "he received his law enforcement information from . . . 'Gaspipe' Casso," the Lucchese underboss, who'd been captured in January.[27]

That revelation seemed to clear DeVecchio as the source of the leaks.

In his book, Lin treats this Casso disclosure as his ultimate vindication. He writes that he never knew what happened in that meeting after he left until years later, when he was defending his reputation during the OPR. After reading Caproni's account, DeVecchio writes, "I did some long slow breathing to calm down. Then I put Caproni's OPR interview down, went to my garage, got out my motorcycle, and went for a long hard ride."[28] He goes on to contend that, since Casso had later confessed to FBI agents Rudolph and Brennan that he'd received intelligence over the years from disgraced detectives Lou Eppolito and Stephen Caracappa, and since Casso and Scarpa had shared members of each other's Bypass crews, it only made sense that intel from the Mafia Cops had found its way to "34" through Gaspipe.[29]

But in a subsequent 302, Caproni admitted that after Casso began cooperating he "told the interviewing FBI agents that he never provided any information to Scarpa Sr."[30] And, as we'll soon see, in the FBI's interviews with Gaspipe at La Tuna federal prison in the spring of 1994, Casso not only denied leaking intel to Scarpa, he actually accused *DeVecchio* of being one of the two "crooked agents" he'd received intelligence from over the years.[31]

It's worth noting that the idea of Casso as Scarpa's source could not have come as a surprise to the Feds. It's only logical that one of the participants at that meeting in Caproni's office must have had some advance warning that Gaspipe's name would come up; otherwise, why, out of the hundreds of agents in the FBI's NYO, would Jim Brennan—a Lucchese Squad agent, who later went on to debrief Casso at La Tuna—be asked to attend? And there's another question: Why would Scarpa, who'd been supplying the FBI with detailed information—truthful or not—off and on for thirty-two years, suddenly expect to get out of jail in return for "cooperating"?

In an e-mail exchange with me, Brennan, who retired from the FBI, said, "Caproni invited me to the 9/29/93 meeting because I was involved in the ongoing investigation of law enforcement leaks. In that meeting, Scarpa said he never received information from DeVecchio or any other FBI agent. Scarpa added that he did not know the identity of anyone in law enforcement allegedly providing information to Casso."[32]

Given all that the Feds had to lose from any further connection to Scarpa, Valerie Caproni passed on his offer to cooperate. But it's crucial to note that by now, as she supervised the seventy-five war prosecutions, Caproni's attitude toward Lin DeVecchio shifted from her critical stance back in 1987.

At this point, in 1993, the Scarpa-DeVecchio scandal was threatening to undermine many of her war cases. So keeping Lin in the fold was an important strategic move for Caproni. That may explain why, in a second major debriefing by OPR investigators in September 1994, Caproni seemed to go out of her way to note that "SSA DeVecchio did not try to apply any pressure to convince her or her assistants to enter into an agreement with Scarpa Sr. for his cooperation."[33]

The War Continues

Meanwhile, if anyone in the FBI's New York Office thought locking Greg Scarpa away in a prison ward on Rikers Island would end the Colombo war, they were mistaken. On the night of October 20, 1993, three weeks after Scarpa's offer of cooperation, Joe Scopo, the former Orena underboss who himself had been targeted with Vic back in June 1991, was shot to death by a team of hooded gunmen as he left his house in Queens.

Scopo was the son of Ralph Scopo Sr., the former head of the so-called concrete club who had been convicted in the Mafia Commission case as a result of Title III wiretaps for which "34" supplied the probable cause. The elder Scopo had died in prison the previous March; now the Persico faction added another name to the list of war deaths.[34]

Joe Scopo had been returning home with his nephew and future son-in-law when the masked assassins fired with a MAC-10 and a .380 semiautomatic pistol. Still in his car when they started shooting, Scopo bolted and ran, but he was hit twice in the abdomen and chest. His nephew was struck in the arm. A total of twenty-three shell casings were recovered following the fusillade. With Scopo's death, the war officially came to an end.

In varying media accounts, the number of deaths attributed to this third conflict in the Colombo family ranged from ten[35] to fifteen.[36] By November 1992, testifying as an expert witness at Vic Orena Sr.'s trial, Lin DeVecchio put the number of war deaths at ten, including Hank Smurra, Gaetano Amato, Sam Nastasi, Vincent Fusaro, Matteo Speranza, Nicholas

Grancio, John Minerva, Michael Imbergamo, Larry Lampasi, and Vincent Giangiobbe.

At that time, DeVecchio also testified that another "fourteen individuals had been shot," including the wounding of Colombo associate Steven Mancusi on February 7, 1992.[37] But on October 7 a second attempt was made on Mancusi, just as with "Joe Waverly" Cacace—and unlike Waverly, who survived Scarpa's second fusillade, Mancusi was murdered by unknown assailants, making him the eleventh victim in the war.[38] Joe Scopo's rubout in 1993 rounded out the official toll to a dozen murders—in half of which, as we've demonstrated, Greg Scarpa Sr. played a part.

Moreover, if one accepts the premise that "34" not only engineered the final Colombo conflict but preceded it with his "plan B" attempt to frame Vic Orena for the Tommy Ocera murder, then it's fair to include Ocera's homicide in November 1989[39] and Jack Leale's killing in November 1991,[40] bringing the death toll to fourteen.

Slipping in and out of Reality

On December 15, 1993, Greg Scarpa made one final pitch for a deal. Once again he was the Machiavellian strategist, hoping to parlay his medical condition into another excuse for avoiding jail time. Now, just months after he'd tried to trade his release for "cooperation," with his lawyer arguing that he still had valuable intel to offer the Feds, Scarpa sent Kartagener to insist that his client was suffering from "AIDS related dementia." As Scarpa stood beside him before Judge Weinstein's bench, Kartagener argued that Greg "was . . . slipping in and out of reality."[41]

Alleging that Scarpa was "getting into delusional states" as a result of "the drug therapy that he was undergoing," the attorney asked Weinstein to consider keeping Scarpa "in a medical environment until he may become ready for sentencing, which may never occur."[42]

But the judge responded, "Mr. Scarpa appears to me to be understanding exactly what I'm saying," and Scarpa quickly agreed, saying, "Yes, your honor."[43]

"Any prison sentence that's imposed here in this case, I submit is, of course, the equivalent of a death sentence," said Kartagener, "even if it's a year long." He went on to argue that a presentence report had indicated that Scarpa's "diseased body" would "warrant downward departure," or a shorter sentence. "That might sound ironic, when I make an argument like that on behalf of Greg Scarpa," the lawyer continued. "Mr. Scarpa's reputation precedes him into this courtroom."[44]

At that point, perhaps Kartagener should have stopped talking. But he went on to remind Weinstein that an EDNY judge had "showed . . . great humanity [and] allowed [Scarpa] to go home with an ankle bracelet once, and then he walked out the door and got shot in the eye."[45]

Renouncing the Mafia

Then, in a display of audacity befitting the legal representative of the most audacious mobster alive, Kartagener proceeded to ask Weinstein "to consider the possibility of allowing this defendant to go home with whatever security devices might be appropriate, to die at home."

"That's impossible," Weinstein shot back.

He then asked Scarpa if he wanted to add anything.

As if he hadn't been listening, Scarpa responded, "I expect to go home."[46]

"You're not going home. You're going to prison," the judge said. "You understand that?"

"Yes, your honor."

"If you want to say anything in amelioration of your crimes—"

"No, your honor. There's nothing more for me to say." And then, alluding to his years as a TE informant, Scarpa added, "I tried to help, your honor. I'm sure you're aware of that."

"Yes," replied Weinstein.

"But it just didn't work out."

"I understand that, but I want a statement from you on the record, that as far as you're concerned, you've cut off all ties to organized crime, and that you will do nothing in prison, or if you should leave prison, in connection with organized crime or any other criminal conspiracy. Is that clear?"[47]

It was like asking Hannibal Lecter to promise he'd never kill again. But Scarpa responded, "Yes, your honor . . . I thought there was a possibility of me going home."

"No. It's not possible," said the judge. "But I want you to renounce and abjure any connection you may have had with organized crime."

"I do renounce it, your honor."

The transcript doesn't record the expressions on the faces of the parties present, but one can only imagine them trading looks of bewilderment. Asking Gregory Scarpa to renounce his ties to the Mafia was like asking a great white shark to stop eating. But that's what happened.

Moments later, Valerie Caproni rightfully said, "I think Mr. Scarpa will say to you at this point whatever he thinks you want to hear, if he thinks it will get him out of jail. He desperately wants to go home."[48]

"I don't agree with that," Weinstein replied. He turned to face Scarpa. "Are you misleading me?"

"No, your honor," said Scarpa.

"I don't have that impression," replied the judge.

Gregory Scarpa was a sociopathic killer. Perhaps a psychopath. His protégé Larry Mazza later described him as "unscrupulous and treacherous."[49] Lin DeVecchio's own lawyer called him "deceitful," "a master liar."[50] Now, here was Jack B. Weinstein, the former chief judge of the Eastern District, a tough-talking New Yorker who had presided over dozens of organized crime trials—and he appeared to be buying Scarpa's story of newfound redemption.

At that stage in the hearing, Valerie Caproni called for an off-the-record discussion in the judge's chambers. When the parties emerged, Caproni hinted at what had been discussed: not just Scarpa's years as an informant but his deception.

"It was the abuse of trust of the Federal Bureau of Investigation that I thought should be called to your honor's attention," she said.

But then, mindful of Lin DeVecchio's role in the still-pending war prosecutions, she seemed to contradict herself.

"In all fairness to Mr. Scarpa, he has been quite an asset to the Federal Bureau of Investigation over the years."

Then, in another flip backward, she added, "It doesn't mitigate the fact that he was a killer during the war."[51]

Finally, after all of this, Weinstein was ready to pronounce sentence.

Noting Scarpa's role in the murders of Fusaro, Grancio, and Lampasi, he stated that the sentencing guidelines "call[ed] for a prison term of life."[52]

Then he added, "This defendant has terminal AIDS because of a blood transfusion and has had one eye shot out. He suffers punishment far beyond what this court can mete out. Despite the defendant's dreadful murderous conduct, and that of his gang, he is a person, a human being. While he has done acts worse than those of a wild animal we would forfeit part of our God-given humanity were we to ignore his status as a fellow human being. If he were sentenced to life he would have to go to a maximum security institution where he probably would have been denied what would be essential to his medical and other treatment during this terminal period. Ten years rather than life will permit a sentence with a more comfortable prison. The Court will recommend the defendant be imprisoned near the Metropolitan New York area so he can be visited by his family." The final sentence: "Ten years in prison. Five years of supervised release. A fine of $250,000, payable as Probation directs, and a special assessment of $100. Good luck."[53]

It was an act of mercy by a sitting federal judge for a Mafia killer who had been merciless over the years with dozens of his own victims. Scarpa then thanked Weinstein and Kartagener praised the judge for his "great humanity."

"I did what any other judge would do, I am sure," Weinstein added as Caproni moved to dismiss any other government counts.

In the end, having failed with his "AIDS dementia" argument, hoping to put off sentencing via an extended psychiatric evaluation, Scarpa, the master strategist, played the "death card" and won. Although Greg himself was facing his own "life sentence," there was an enormous disparity between his relatively light punishment and the multiple life terms, plus sixty years, plus the $2 million fine, that Weinstein had imposed on Carmine Sessa's brother Michael. All of that underscored the special treatment "34" continued to get from the Feds. The younger Sessa was a junior capo convicted of a single homicide. Scarpa had spent more than four decades in a career of murder, mayhem, and racketeering and left enough bodies in his wake to put him in the ranks of the world's top serial killers.

"It's beyond belief," says defense attorney Flora Edwards. "AIDS virus or not, Scarpa was given the federal equivalent of a love tap at this late stage, and by the same judge who showed absolutely no mercy to Vic Orena Sr."[54]

As for Scarpa's imminent death, he would continue to defy all the medical predictions.

Chapter 33

THE OPR

If any of the special agents who worked under Lin DeVecchio doubted whether he'd passed FBI intel to "34," those reservations must have ended in early January 1994, when Larry Mazza finally flipped and Chris Favo started debriefing him. The FBI 302 memorializing that interrogation, which began on January 7, later became known as the "Girlfriend 302," after the name Mazza said that Scarpa used to refer to his source. Most of the alleged leaks Mazza described were later disclosed by the Feds, and Lin DeVecchio was suspected of being that source.[1] The potential security breaches were so serious that, coupled with the allegations of Favo and fellow agents Tomlinson and Leadbetter, they prompted DeVecchio's internal affairs investigation by the FBI's Office of Professional Responsibility (OPR). The entire "Girlfriend 302" is reproduced in Appendix E, but some of its key revelations are below:

> One of the sources that supplied information on a regular basis was referred to as "THE GIRLFRIEND." The source would call him at home, as well as beep him. . . . SCARPA SR.'s wife, LINDA . . . referred to the source as "THE GIRLFRIEND" when giving messages to SCARPA SR. regarding phone calls. On occasions when the source beeped SCARPA SR., he would stop whatever he was doing in order to return the call.

When in his own home, SCARPA SR. always returned the calls to the "GIRLFRIEND" using the telephone in the basement. . . .

The information that SCARPA SR. received through his source(s) included, but was not limited to, the address of VICTOR ORENA's girlfriend's home in Queens, New York, including descriptive information that it was a white, two family home with aluminum siding. Shortly after SCARPA SR. is shot at, he learns that the panel truck used in the murder attempt was rented from Queens, New York . . . as well as SALVATORE MICIOTTA and JOSEPH SCOPO's addresses. He also received information regarding the scheduled drug arrest of GREGORY SCARPA JR. and his crew, and the scheduled Credit Card arrest of SCARPA SR. He received a copy of the Complaint issued against himself, and was told that his problems with the Law might disappear if he stayed out of trouble.

On one occasion, MAZZA was in SCARPA SR.'s house when he received a telephone call from "THE GIRLFRIEND" on the basement telephone. After the call, he told MAZZA that the "GIRLFRIEND" said that the members of the ORENA faction were very close to killing him.[2]

In another debriefing, Mazza told Favo and his colleague Special Agent Maryann Walker-Goldman:

One or two days after the arrest of CARMINE IMBRIALE . . . GREG SCARPA SR. told MAZZA that IMBRIALE . . . was cooperating. . . . SCARPA SR. also talked about killing IMBRIALE some time in the future.[3]

Mazza's revelations only corroborated what Favo and the other agents already knew. But they were potentially very damaging—particularly the intel on Joe Scopo. The fact that Scopo had been killed outside his home three and a half months earlier raised the prospect that Scarpa had learned of Scopo's address from his source in law enforcement. If that source was Lin DeVecchio—if he was the "Girlfriend"—that could make Lin a possible co-conspirator to homicide.

Further, the notion that Scarpa had learned the whereabouts of the rented panel truck used in the Eighty-Second Street shootout—which Favo himself had uncovered—must have sent a chill through Favo. In his book, Lin DeVecchio effectively blames Favo for "start[ing]" the Colombo war by "stirring up Billy Cutolo."[4] In fact the Feds had attributed the attack outside Scarpa's house on November 18, 1991, to "Wild Bill." Now, with Mazza's revelations, the opposite could be said: If the Girlfriend had tipped off Scarpa that "the Orena faction" had plotted to kill him, that revelation might have prompted his killing spree.

Finally, Mazza's assertion that Scarpa had learned about Imbriale's cooperation had surely come from DeVecchio—because Favo had overheard DeVecchio telling "34" as much over the "Hello" phone in C-10. That was evidence in and of itself that Lin DeVecchio was the Girlfriend. At that point, Favo and his fellow agents could no longer look away from the growing Scarpa-DeVecchio scandal.

"Getting SSA DeVecchio in Trouble"

On Sunday, January 17, 1994, the day before the Martin Luther King holiday, Favo, Tomlinson, and Leadbetter went to DeVecchio's boss, ASAC Donald North. What happened next was recounted by Favo in a sworn statement made to OPR Supervisory Special Agents Robert J. O'Brien and Timothy T. Arney. Because that statement, in Favo's own words, provides so many details on the events that occurred after he and the other agents blew the whistle, we're reproducing sections of it here.

> FAVO: For a long time I have had a concern that SSA DeVecchio may have divulged information to his former source Gregory Scarpa Sr. . . . .
>
> We were about to begin one of several trials with respect to the "Colombo LCN Family War" and were concerned about information from the Confidential Witnesses (CWs) indicating that Scarpa, Sr., had a law enforcement source, specifically in the FBI New York Office.
>
> ASAC North met with us in the New York field office. We were not interested in getting SSA DeVecchio in trouble, we only wanted to see if he could be transferred to another squad and replaced by another supervisor so we would be able to continue our investigations and prosecutions in the "Colombo LCN Family War" matters, without a concern that he might . . . disclose information regarding certain of our cases.[5]

According to Favo, North told him that he would "switch" DeVecchio with another supervisor in the C-6 squad—presumably to remove Lin from the loop. But later Favo said North told him that the agent swap wouldn't happen, "because it would disrupt both C-10 and C-6 and it made no sense to disrupt both squads." Favo said another proposal was made a few days later to have DeVecchio trade places with Chris Mattiace, the former C-10 supervisor, who was then working out of the New Rochelle office.

In order to bring Mattiace up to speed, Favo prepared a detailed seven-page 302 memo recounting a number of incidents during the war when information developed in C-10 somehow found its way to Scarpa. Among his revelations:

> Over the length of the war I began to withhold information concerning Gregory Scarpa or what could not be leaked to the media because I believed SSA DeVecchio was leaking information to both Scarpa Sr. and Jerry Capeci.[6]

In that 302, Favo also revealed that DeVecchio had asked him to use the FBI's Fast Track system for linking telephone numbers to addresses. After running down two area code 516 (Long Island) numbers, which Favo said Lin told him were tied to the safe houses of Jo Jo and Chuckie Russo, Favo wrote that he personally checked the locations—one of which turned out to be a pay phone at a Waldbaum's supermarket. When he questioned his boss about it, DeVecchio told him that "the numbers were for one of Scarpa's loan shark victims."[7]

As it turned out, after Favo filed that 302, North *didn't* transfer DeVecchio. The previous fall, during a meeting at the EDNY, Lin DeVecchio had threatened to have Favo's "ass" if he triggered an OPR investigation.[8] Now, ten days after Favo first went to North, DeVecchio called him into his office. Clearly word had gotten back to him that his number two was the primary source of the accusations. In his sworn statement, Favo revealed what happened next:

> SSA DeVecchio . . . asked me who had been saying things about him. I told SSA DeVecchio that I could not discuss the matter with him. SSA

DeVecchio told me to get out of his office. 15 minutes or so later, SSA DeVecchio called me back into his office and told me that SSA Thomas Fuentes of the Organized crime section, criminal Investigative Division, FBIHQ, was going to come up to New York and clear him.

I believe SSA DeVecchio had spoken to ASAC North and learned that SSA Fuentes was going to be in charge of the OPR inquiry. SSA DeVecchio asked me who was in charge of handling a CW by the name of Billy Meli. Meli is a very important CW in our prosecutions and had identified Scarpa's source as an FBI agent. I told DeVecchio that Meli is being handled by SSA Leadbetter. . . . I told SSA DeVecchio that I was not going to answer his questions about what Meli had said or about this matter.[9]

The disclosures by Meli were troubling. A longtime member of Scarpa's Wimpy Boys crew, Meli confirmed for Leadbetter the allegation that Scarpa had received one of the 1987 DEA arrest lists and the fact that Cosmo Catanzano, a crew member on that list, might cooperate with authorities. That was the revelation that had caused Scarpa to order Meli and others to dig Cosmo's grave in anticipation of his murder.[10]

Continuing in his sworn statement, Chris Favo then described DeVecchio's reaction to the charges.

SSA DeVecchio reiterated that he would be cleared and then would return to the squad. SSA DeVecchio was angry about being accused of releasing information. DeVecchio told me that despite what had happened, he would deal with me professionally.[11]

According to Favo, though, that never happened. Worse, as Favo saw it, North had already decided to back DeVecchio, and Lin's response to the accusations was that cooperating witnesses like Mazza and Meli were "liars."[12]

Favo then found out that SSA Fuentes and SSA Jack Barrett, tasked to run the OPR, "were now, or had been in DeVecchio's chain of command, were close friends of North's [and] could not be viewed as independent."[13] At the time, Fuentes was supervisor of the Organized Crime Section of the Criminal Investigative Division at Bureau Headquarters in Washington.[14] In Chris Favo's mind, the foxes had been assigned to investigate the chicken coop. He was so worried, he wrote, that he went to AUSA Valerie Caproni and warned that "SSA Fuentes monitors New York's OC program and . . . DeVecchio indicated Fuentes would clear him."

According to Favo, word quickly spread through the squad that it was he and the other agents who had informed on DeVecchio:

> We felt our request for confidentiality had not been taken seriously. On one occasion . . . ASAC North came out to Howard Leadbetter and me in the squad room and in front of other agents asked whether we had the 302s ready. When we asked what 302s he meant, ASAC North indicated they were the 302s from the CWs concerning Scarpa. I believe it is possible that ███████ and ███████ may have heard ASAC North make the comment to us. It was unprofessional for ASAC North to ask that question in the squad room.[15]

Then, wrote Favo, the OPR investigation seemed to be abruptly terminated:

> Mattiace did not want to transfer to New York City from New Rochelle. Later I heard that De Vecchio had been cleared of wrongdoing and would not be transferred. . . .
>
> ASAC North told me that SSAs Fuentes and Barrett had conducted an inquiry and found that SSA De Vecchio could not have given the "DEA list" information to Scarpa, Sr. ASAC North told me that the inquiry had been terminated.[16]

According to Favo, Lin made that clear to the other squad members at an open meeting.

> Three days later DeVecchio called a squad meeting attended by everyone except Andjich who was at a neutral site meeting. DeVecchio said he had been cleared but the case could be reopened later. DeVecchio declared his innocence and was critical of anyone who believed a CW over him.
>
> DeVecchio added that the whole situation was handled incorrectly by the agents who went to the EDNY and in the future anyone with a problem should bring it to him. It was speculated that SSA DeVecchio may decide to retire and that would solve problem with SSA DeVecchio's presence as supervisor of C-10.[17]

Favo then wrote, "Some of us on C-10 were still in a rather untenable position since we felt uncomfortable about not being able to discuss certain elements of our investigation of Scarpa's crew with SSA DeVecchio."[18]

Caproni's solution, according to Favo, was for them to pass on any new information to the DEA and let Drug Enforcement agents conduct the war investigation from there on. But Favo wrote, "We had worked very hard to put these cases together and preferred that the FBI handle its problems properly rather than rely on the DEA to solve our problems."[19]

"Understand the position that Favo, Leadbetter, Tomlinson, and Andjich were in," says defense lawyer Flora Edwards.[20] "They had taken a shot at the king and missed. Lin was the most powerful organized crime agent in New York. He had a direct pipeline to the Director and the DC officials, like Agent Fuentes. Favo and the others were effectively accusing him of a possible murder conspiracy for which he might not just lose his job but get indicted, and now they realized that they weren't being taken seriously by Donald North."

So Favo, whose wife was pregnant, put in an application for six weeks' annual leave to begin on March 16, two months after he'd first gone to North.[21] But at that point, when an official whose name was redacted from Favo's statement heard that he'd put in for the leave, it was suggested that Favo meet with another official he "trusted."[22]

After a three-hour discussion, this person, whose name was also redacted, relayed Favo's allegations to Bill Gavin, then the deputy assistant director in charge (ADIC) of the FBI's New York Office.[23]

Apparently sensing that he would now be taken seriously by the FBI leadership, Favo then recommended that OPR interviews be conducted with a dozen agents in the NYO; four assistant U.S. attorneys including Caproni, Stamboulidis, Andrew Weissmann, and Ellen Corcella; and half a dozen cooperating witnesses: Carmine Sessa, Larry Mazza, Joseph Ambrosino, Jimmy Del Masto, Billy Meli, and Mario Parlagreco, all members of Scarpa's Wimpy Boys crew who had not only committed dozens of crimes with "34" but had also been a party to the special attention he seemed to get from his law enforcement source.[24]

Further emboldened at that point, Favo even recommended that the OPR investigators talk to the three EDNY judges who had presided over various Scarpa-related cases, including I. Leo Glasser, who brokered Scarpa's deal in the credit card case; Magistrate John L. Caden, who'd arraigned Scarpa after the gun-toss bust; and Judge Jack B. Weinstein.[25]

In his affidavit, Favo argued, "The sentencing of [Scarpa] was lighter than expected, and it is possible that SSA DeVecchio might have contacted the judges prior to sentencing."[26] Favo used a kind of formal "FBI-speak" in that affidavit, but in a diary he kept that became part of the OPR record, he revealed more of the distress he was feeling.

Chris Favo's Diary

The entries below track the trajectory of Favo's emotions, beginning with his hope that coming forward would produce some results, and ending with the sense that he and the other agents had made a huge strategic mistake in challenging DeVecchio:

> **January 21** *North commends us for taking action. North says everything will be confidential. North supports us.*
>
> **January 26** *Lin calls me into office . . . throws me out. Says he will be cleared. "That's fine, I don't care." I call North.* <u>*North says he believes Lin.*</u> *I complain that investigation is not confidential. . . . Lin has been telling people he will be cleared & return. North says there is nothing we can do about that. North says we can still call him if there is any new evidence but we will have to live with the problems.*
>
> **January 31** *In full view of squad, Don North approached me & Howard and told us to write the 302s on the OPR matter and turn them in to him. (There is no longer any doubt who will be held responsible for Lin's problems.)*
>
> **February 4** *Lin holds squad meeting . . . denies any wrongdoing. But critical of anyone who believes CW over him . . . I was reminded that when Lin was declaring his innocence he said that anyone that did not believe him could go F— themselves.*[27]

But Favo and the other agents had already gone on the record with their accusations, and the Office of Professional Responsibility was duty-bound to investigate. That put Valerie Caproni, who was supervising the war prosecutions, in a difficult position, since the leaks Lin DeVecchio appeared to have made to "34" could seriously damage her cases.

Caproni Asks for a Delay in the OPR

In February 1994, Caproni was preparing to go to trial against Anthony "Chuckie" Russo and a series of codefendants in a major war prosecution before Judge Charles P. Sifton.

"So what Valerie did," says defense lawyer Alan Futerfas, "was to push the Justice Department to delay the OPR. But worse than that, when Judge Sifton later demanded that the prosecutors turn over all documents relating to the DeVecchio-Scarpa investigation, she failed to turn over a key 302 involving a confession by Scarpa Sr.'s underling Larry Mazza."[28]

It was the "Girlfriend 302," in which Larry Mazza had confessed that there were so many potential leaks to Greg Scarpa.

"Understand the significance of this," says Ellen Resnick, Futerfas's partner. "The production of that 302 to defense attorneys at a critical time would have been devastating." So where was it? According to a later sworn affirmation by Caproni, it remained in the drawer of her desk.[29] In a subsequent pleading to Judge Sifton, Futerfas noted:

> The undisclosed "Girlfriend 302" was created on February 7th, 1994 and given to AUSA Valerie Caproni on February 23rd, 1994 . . . the "Girlfriend 302" is a bombshell providing potent corroborating evidence of an SSA's misdeeds. Prosecutors receiving this document had to know that it was an extraordinary piece of paper, one which, if disclosed, would open the flood gates resulting in agents and others being subpoenaed, demands for additional discovery and probably requests for continuances or mistrials by trial counsel. The fact that this document was received by the USAO just seven (7) days after this Court's direct order, and not disclosed to the Court is not explained.[30]

But Caproni, who ran the criminal division in the Eastern District at the time, went even further. As the FBI geared up to conduct its OPR investigation of DeVecchio, she called one of the two initial investigating agents and asked him to delay the investigation.

"Caproni . . . contacted SSA FUENTES and requested that no interviews of the LCN CWs occur until after the conclusion of the first trial, which was expected to last approximately six weeks."[31]

"In other words," says defense attorney Edwards, "further corroboration by the Colombo turncoats of the Scarpa-DeVecchio 'marriage' could result in an acquittal."[32]

Caproni couldn't have made her request for a slowdown in DeVecchio's OPR because she thought DeVecchio was innocent. Four days after that January 27 phone call to Fuentes, the OPR special agent interviewed her again. In a five-page 302, Caproni revealed that she'd known as far back as 1987 that Scarpa Sr. was an FBI informant. She admitted that information she obtained from DeVecchio on Scarpa's crew was "of little prosecutive value" and that DeVecchio had threatened "to get" Chris Favo if an OPR was opened on him.[33]

But following a discussion with Ralph A. Regalbuto, the unit chief of the OPR Inspection Division in Washington, Caproni was advised that "further investigation of this matter would be held in abeyance as requested."[34]

In a twenty-two-page memo, Alan Futerfas effectively accused the U.S. attorney's office of obstructing justice and deceiving not only the defense but the judge.[35]

Meanwhile, Chris Favo, DeVecchio's first accuser, was beginning to regret coming forward. In a diary entry from late April 1994, he recounts a visit to William Doran, Donald North's boss in the New York Office:

April 22 *He told me that he refused to move Lin from the squad pending the completion of the investigation. . . . He said that he would not bury Lin somewhere. We argued about whether the OPR had been closed. . . . He emphasized the importance of following the chain of command. I told him I went to* ▮▮▮▮▮▮ *for advice [and] not to open an OPR. . . . I told him I believe it was a mistake that would follow us for our careers and that we would never be trusted.*

By now, though, the genie was out of the bottle. The OPR investigation would go on for another twenty-eight months. But two years after Favo met with Doran, there was a signal that the younger special agent's prediction had been correct. Rather than being celebrated for their honesty in reporting their suspicions, DeVecchio's accusers—Favo, Leadbetter, Tomlinson, and Andjich—were seen by many in the FBI's New York Office as instigators who had kicked over a hornet's nest.

The Smoking Gun

The best evidence of that is a memo I uncovered that was sent by Doran's boss James Kallstrom, the assistant director in charge of the New York Office, to FBI Director Louis Freeh, himself a former special agent in the NYO.

The memo was drafted by James Roth, the principal legal officer (PLO) of the NYO, and sent to Freeh under Kallstrom's aegis. Although Lin's name was misspelled, the intent of the memo was clear:

"NY requests that whatever investigation is to be conducted as a result of this letter be conducted expeditiously," wrote Roth on behalf of Kallstrom.

"The failure of the DOJ . . . to administratively resolve this matter continues to have a serious negative impact on the government's prosecutions of various LCN figures in the EDNY and casts a cloud over the NYO."[36]

That was it: the smoking-gun memo confirming the FBI's fear that the DeVecchio-Scarpa scandal could scuttle the many Colombo war prosecutions. Now, when it came to the OPR investigation of Lin DeVecchio, Kallstrom was effectively urging Washington to end it and end it soon.

Despite the sworn testimony of six cooperating Colombo family witnesses, including Scarpa's own protégé Larry Mazza, despite the charges brought by agents Favo, Leadbetter, Tomlinson, and Andjich that DeVecchio had crossed the line and repeatedly supplied intelligence to a vicious killer, the FBI eventually closed the OPR. But not before Lin DeVecchio, who refused to take a polygraph, took the Fifth Amendment and received something that agents I interviewed for this book said was virtually *unheard of* in the Bureau: a grant of immunity.

"If you're investigating an agent for alleged misconduct," says former agent Dan Vogel, "he or she has a lot of incentives to cooperate. As in the case of DeVecchio, they could be looking at criminal charges. So there's no incentive for management to let them off the hook with a grant of immunity. Otherwise, why would they ever be motivated to tell the truth?"[37]

Later in this book, we'll examine the decision by the Justice Department's Public Integrity Section to terminate the OPR inquiry—but suffice it to say that, despite an investigation that produced nearly one thousand pages of sworn statements from FBI agents, prosecutors, judges, and cooperating witnesses, the Justice Department concluded that "prosecution of SSA DeVecchio in this matter is not warranted."[38]

At least in the short run, Lin DeVecchio had scored a victory.

Chapter 34

THE DYING DECLARATION

Given the kind of violent life that Greg Scarpa Sr. had led, it's no surprise that, in the end, he would take a page from Dylan Thomas and not go gentle into that good night. After his sentencing, Scarpa was transferred to the Federal Medical Center in Rochester, Minnesota. There he lay in a hospital bed in a prison ward, where Linda Schiro visited him daily. Despite the reports of AIDS-related dementia at his sentencing hearing and the fact that he was now down to a birdlike weight of 116 pounds, he reportedly remained lucid to the end.[1] He also seemed to embrace a new level of sentimentality.

Linda Schiro told me that, in contrast to his reputation as a cold-blooded killer, Greg always showed a human side at home. "One time my daughter's baby was sick," she said, "and Greg just sat on the couch and cried. He was crying because the baby was going to the hospital."[2] Little Linda told an interviewer that, after the purported attempt on his life outside the house on Eighty-Second Street—when she and her son were allegedly caught in the line of fire—her father came home and "just broke down and cried like a baby."[3]

Now on April 7, 1994, with less than two months to live, Scarpa sent his lawyer Stephen Kartagener a card. On the cover it had a sketch of two bear cubs under an umbrella during a downpour. The caption read, "Thanks for being such a good friend . . . even on my bad days." Inside he'd written "Good Luck," signing it simply "Greg."

Greeting card sent by Greg Scarpa to his attorney, April 7, 1994

Because of his deteriorating condition, however, there was a concern among defense lawyers that the real truth about the third Colombo war might die with Scarpa. After all, many attorneys representing war defendants were arguing that the conflict had been fomented by the man the FBI knew as Top Echelon Criminal Informant NY 3461-C-TE.

Not only was that the argument enunciated by Vic Orena, who was now doing life in a federal prison, it was also the position taken by Carmine Persico's son Alphonse "Allie Boy" Persico, for whom the war was ostensibly fought. The Feds' theory had been that Scarpa had spilled all that blood out of loyalty to Allie Boy, who was due to be paroled in 1993 and thus was expected to assume control of the family.

But on May 13 of that year, the younger Persico was indicted on racketeering charges that also included the pastry shop murders of John Minerva and Michael Imbergamo. Indicted along with him and the Russo brothers were a number of Scarpa's crew members, including Robert "Bobby Zam" Zambardi, Larry Mazza, and Jimmy Del Masto.[4]

Their trial was due to start on June 28, 1994. So on May 24 attorney Barry Levin, who represented Allie Boy, asked EDNY judge Charles Sifton to allow the ailing Scarpa to be deposed by videotape.[5] An FBI memo describing Levin's motion noted his opinion that "Scarpa [would] not survive until the trial." The next day, Sifton granted the motion. After the interview, Scarpa signed a sworn affidavit—a statement that represents his last recorded words. Most of the statement is reproduced in the following pages.

In the affidavit, Scarpa not only exonerates Allie Boy Persico of any involvement in inciting the war on behalf of the so-called Persico faction but provides new insights into how the Killing Machine continued to affect dozens of Colombo family members even to the end—seeming to blame the start of the war entirely on his surrogate, Carmine Sessa.

1. On May 20, 1994 I was interviewed by Margaret D. Clemons, an investigator representing the offices of Barry Levin, an attorney representing Alphonse Persico. I requested this interview through my wife, Linda Schiro. This interview took place in my hospital room where I am currently incarcerated at FMC Rochester, Rochester, Minnesota.

2. During this one hour interview, I told Ms. Clemons the following:

3. Carmine Sessa respected me and looked to me as the "Boss" of the family. Sessa knew me to be the most powerful family member at the onset of the war.

4. In fact, I was the most powerful entity in the Colombo Family and an authoritative figure who bowed down to no one.

5. I was not aware of the attempt on Vic Orena's life. I first learned of the attempt on Orena's life when Carmine Sessa told me about it. Sessa came to me two weeks after the attempt to request my assistance.

6. Carmine Sessa never once mentioned Allie Persico to me. Allie Persico was of no concern to anybody. Allie Persico is a friend who was not going to and who had no intentions of taking over the leadership of the Colombo Family. . . . Allie was never earmarked to take on any position in the family at all.

7. There was never any plan for family members to engage in a shooting war at all. At Joe Saps' wake, the rebels were given two weeks to come back into the fold and if they didn't, they would be killed. This was an empty threat and there were no plans to kill anyone.

8. In November, 1991, members of the Orena faction shot at me while I was in a car with my daughter and two year old grandchild. I was

so upset over this that my only intention was to retaliate for what had happened to me and my family. I had no instructions to retaliate from anyone, especially Allie Persico who is a "nobody" and who is completely insignificant within the family regardless of his relationship to his father, Carmine Persico. I did not need anybody's permission to act. By the end of November, 1991, nobody could have stopped me from retaliating.

9. The war began at this point in time and plans were made to kill Orena faction members. Prior to November, 1991, there were no meetings or agreements between anyone to engage in a war. This war began with Lawrence Mazza, James Del Masto and myself in the forefront. I wanted to finish them all for what they had done to me and my family.

10. Carmine Sessa's duty as Consigliere was to get involved. Sessa was happy and eager to do so.

11. After the attempt on my life in November, 1991, I never, nor did anyone else to my knowledge, communicate with, speak with or have anything to do with Allie Persico.

12. Nobody financed the war. Everybody did their own thing. I never gave the Persico's [sic] any money and nobody ever gave me one cent.

13. . . . . The Fusaro killing was entirely unplanned. . . . I shot Fusaro and hit him with the first shot. It was just good luck.

14. In all of the meetings that I attended during the war with Persico faction members, Allie Persico's name was never mentioned by anyone. There was no reason to mention Allie because he was totally uninvolved and unimportant. Allie has no power to give orders, permission, approval or anything else. . . .

I am giving this sworn and truthful statement in the event of my demise so that the court will have the benefit of my testimony in the event a deposition is not held in time.[6]

In the statement, Scarpa let Allie Boy Persico off the hook for his alleged participation in the war—albeit by dismissing him as a toothless heir to the throne. But he also told the truth, for the first time, about his own position in the Colombos, describing himself as the "Boss" and "the most powerful family member" when the war commenced.

The only part of the statement that seemed entirely disingenuous was his claim that he'd been unaware of the initial move on Vic Orena by Sessa in June 1991. Given Scarpa's position of power at the time, his ability to control and manipulate Sessa, and his antipathy for Orena—the one family leader who truly stood in his way—it's simply not believable that Scarpa didn't engineer that drive-by on Long Island, particularly since it was predicated on Sessa's false belief that he was about to be murdered by Orena.

On June 8, 1994, the day after he put his hand to that sworn affidavit, Gregory Scarpa Sr. finally died. Nine days later, an FBI 209 report was sent to DC, stating that the war had been waged largely by "the Persico faction." The 209 admitted nonetheless that "all of his life, COLOMBO LCN Family member GREG SCARPA Sr.—deceased, hated the PERSICO's [sic], although he was frequently under their control. . . . As an example of this hatred, Scarpa had once supported the 'GALLO GANG.' "[7]

But the airtels, memos, and 209s we've produced in this book demonstrate that this statement was untrue—and that Scarpa had conspired against the Gallo brothers just as he did against Carmine Persico, the Gallos' nemesis. That misrepresentation of the family's history calls into question the final statement in that 209: that the FBI's trusted source, "34," was really *lying* when he exonerated Allie Boy Persico. Citing an unnamed source, the 209 alleged that Scarpa Sr. had signed that affidavit only under duress:

SCARPA, SR. would never have voluntarily given the affidavit he gave to the defense lawyers of ALPHONSE PERSICO aka "LITTLE ALLIE BOY", wherein SCARPA, SR. claimed that it was SCARPA, SR. alone who started and ran the recent "COLOMBO War" and that A. PERSICO is innocent and had nothing to do with it. The source has been told that the reason SCARPA, SR. submitted this affidavit, to aid in PERSICO's trial defense, is that [unknown subjects] in PERSICO's "crew" threatened to murder SCARPA's wife if SCARPA did not submit the affidavit.[8]

That may have been the position the government took during Allie Boy's trial later that summer, but the jury didn't buy it. Scarpa's final statement was ruled admissible under the "dying declaration" exception to the hearsay rule, and on August 8 Persico walked out of court a free man.

Although thirty-five other Colombo war defendants had previously been convicted, Allie Boy Persico became the first to be acquitted as a result of the mounting evidence exposing the FBI's secret relationship with Greg Scarpa Sr.[9] Each new trial seemed to undermine the government's theory that the war was the result of a struggle for control of the family between Vic Orena and the Persicos. To use the metaphor Judge Weinstein uttered years later, the Colombo war prosecutions were starting to "unravel."

A New Take on the Eighty-Second Street Shootout

Defense lawyers like Gus Newman, who were working to get a new trial for Vic Orena, even went so far as to argue that the alleged attack on Greg Scarpa and Little Linda Schiro on November 18, 1991, was a creation of Scarpa himself. Citing the sworn testimony in a series of war cases, Newman argued in a 1996 memorandum of law that, "despite Scarpa's ominous predictions to the FBI of a growing conflict, no shooting occurred for five months after Sessa's attempt to kill Victor J. Orena in June, 1991."[10]

The fact that the peace was kept for months after Vic Orena went to the Commission actually reinforced the Commission's value in avoiding bloodshed. A mob war was always bad for business, and profit was the motivating factor among the family bosses who sat on the Five Families' ruling body. But Greg Scarpa, the FBI's in-house Mafioso, decided to do an end run around the Commission and its rules.

On November 4, 1991, in his debriefing to Lin DeVecchio, Scarpa predicted that he and Carmine Sessa "would be the ORENA'S [*sic*] side pick to be hit."[11] And sure enough, two weeks later, he was seemingly proven right when the shootout took place outside of his house, allegedly at the hands of masked Orena gunmen.

Curiously, despite the fact that their faces were hidden, DeVecchio immediately identified the assailants as "members of the ORENA faction."

Quoting Senior in his 209 that same day, Lin then predicted that "this would start the shooting war between the two factions."[12]

At three thirty that afternoon, DeVecchio sent Chris Favo to the house on Eighty-Second Street.[13] Favo interviewed Scarpa but later admitted that he didn't prepare a 302 documenting the meeting, as was customary, because Scarpa was an FBI informant.[14] Favo also interviewed Little Linda Schiro, another purported victim of the attack, but no report on that conversation was prepared either. As attorney Gus Newman noted, "while Scarpa's daughter was obviously an important witness to the events that allegedly occurred, the government has never called her to testify at any of the several 'Colombo War' trials in which the purported November 18th shooting was introduced."[15]

Newman also alleged that "the physical investigation of the crime scene was plagued with irregularities." Though Favo himself took photographs of the Mercedes Little Linda was driving,[16] he testified later that the bullet holes were all grouped in a narrow section of the fender.[17] At the crime scene on November 18, the NYPD collected latent fingerprints on the van that had allegedly blocked Greg Sr.'s escape route.[18] But the prints failed to match any of the alleged suspects, including Cutolo crew members "Chickie" DeMartino and Frank Ianacci, who had reportedly been seen earlier that day getting into a similar-looking van.[19]

Meanwhile, none of the investigators from the NYPD or the FBI took Scarpa's prints. In his later testimony, Favo said that at the time there had been no reason to suspect Scarpa.[20]

The pictures taken by law enforcement investigators were lost sometime before the spring of 1995,[21] and shell casings found at the scene by the NYPD, which might have been used to identify the guns used by the shooters, mysteriously *disappeared* from police custody.[22]

The Shooting Triggers the War

Immediately after that shooting, in meetings with various crew members— including Larry Mazza, Carmine Sessa, and Joseph Ambrosino—Greg Scarpa used the incident to justify retaliation against "the Orena faction."[23] Scarpa and Little Linda were the only witnesses to the incident; the identifications of DeMartino and Ianacci, a.k.a. "Frankie Notch," came later, secondhand, through Carmine Sessa, who claimed that one of his associates saw the pair switching vehicles in front of a club five blocks away.[24]

As Scarpa's surrogate during the war, Sessa helped to sell the shootout story to other family members, later testifying, "Everybody was mad that they broke the truce and they came after us and it was time for us to retaliate."[25] From that point on, according to Sessa, Scarpa decided to attack the "Orena faction."[26]

Given "34's" capacity for treachery, the disappearance of forensic evidence, and the fact that Scarpa and his daughter seemed to be the sole witnesses willing to discuss the "attack," Newman's theory—that the shootout was a kind of "Reichstag fire"[27] fabricated to justify the shooting war—carries considerable weight.

"Would Gregory Scarpa Sr. have created such an event, with guns firing around his daughter and grandson?" asks Andrew Orena. "If he controlled the situation, he would have. If the so-called members of Billy Cutolo's crew were really his own guys, and they fired in a controlled pattern so as not to hit Greg or his family, it's absolutely within the realm of possibility when you consider that so far this war was going nowhere. My father [Vic Orena] was entirely playing defense. The Commission was keeping the peace, and Greg needed something big and loud to set things off."[28]

Funeral in an Empty Church

A week after Scarpa's death, Jerry Capeci, who FBI agents suggested benefited over the years from a close relationship with DeVecchio, wasn't particularly kind to Lin's Top Echelon source. "At the end Greg Scarpa went to his grave unrespected," Capeci wrote in his "Gang Land" column.[29]

Noting that Scarpa had been "a made man for four decades," Capeci nonetheless commented that "not a single confederate" came to pay his respects at Scarpa's funeral, which was held at St. Bernadette's Roman Catholic Church in Bensonhurst. According to Capeci, the funeral procession consisted of only a hearse and four cars, a sparse congregation limited to Scarpa's immediate family and a few neighbors.

Scarpa Sr. was laid to rest in what Capeci described as a "polished golden oak coffin." He quoted the priest, Father Eugene Cole, as reminding the attendees that "none of us live as his own master and none of us dies as his own master." Humbling words over the coffin of the man who had ruled so mercilessly over the streets of Bensonhurst.

"34" Worth More Than a Thousand Special Agents

On the other hand, at least one agent loyal to Lin DeVecchio seemed to regard "34" as something of a mythic hero. In DeVecchio's memoir he quotes Special Agent Pat Marshal, who worked on the Mafia Commission case.

> Those who accused Lin DeVecchio of being used by Greg Scarpa are people who have no understanding of what Greg Scarpa did for us at the risk of his own life. They lack this understanding either because they are ignorant, arrogant, blind, evil, or all of the above, and that includes some very FNGs in way over their heads way too soon. A thousand of them aren't worth a hair on the head of "34," TE Greg Scarpa.[30]

"Think about that statement for a minute," says James Whalen, a retired agent from the New York Office, "and you get some sense of the skewed priorities that existed within the Organized Crime Section of the NYO during this period. Here is a veteran agent insisting that a Mafia killer who took more than fifty lives is worth more than a thousand young agents. What does that tell you?"[31]

Chapter 35

BURNING A GOOD COP

After Allie Boy Persico's acquittal in August, the next big setback for Valerie Caproni and the Eastern District Feds prosecuting the war cases came in December, when a jury found Wild Bill Cutolo and six other Colombo wiseguys not guilty of murder and racketeering charges. "It's my best Christmas ever," Cutolo said as he left the court a free man.[1]

On October 24, as the trial was under way, veteran *Daily News* investigative reporter Greg B. Smith broke the story of the FBI's OPR internal affairs investigation of Lin DeVecchio. Under the headline "G-Man, Fed Atty Eyed in Mob Leaks," Smith reported that the probe included not just DeVecchio but a possible assistant U.S. attorney in the EDNY who might have passed on sensitive information.[2] The piece quoted the Cutolo trial judge, Eugene Nickerson, who seemed to support full disclosure:

"It is best the truth come out,"[3] he said, admitting that the allegations were "relevant to the question at the end   whether I should dismiss the case." Smith also quoted defense attorney Alan Futerfas, who (with partner Ellen Resnick) had first discovered the Scarpa-DeVecchio relationship: "Scarpa was knowingly used by the government to further its attempt to create fratricidal warfare," Futerfas said. It was the first public disclosure of the theory Futerfas and Resnick would later argue in multiple war cases: that "34" was acting not just as a source for the Bureau but as an agent provocateur who took advantage of FBI intelligence to wreak havoc within the crime family.[4]

Later, *New Yorker* writer Fredric Dannen characterized that defense as the "'comrades in arms' theory of the war."[5]

On October 30, in a bylined story shared with Jerry Capeci, Smith reported that "DeVecchio is under criminal investigation for allegedly leaking secrets to Scarpa. The probe threatens to unravel at least five convictions and one ongoing trial."[6]

In a column on the day of Cutolo's acquittal Jerry Capeci wrote that after more than a year in jail "Wild Bill is probably planning a wild Christmas party today."[7]

While that piece seemed at least somewhat sympathetic to Cutolo's point of view, for most of the year Capeci had been merciless in covering another scandal out of 26 Federal Plaza that seemed designed by the Feds to explain the leaks now threatening so many war prosecutions. A year before Cutolo's acquittal, Detective Joe Simone, who with his partner had been responsible for a third of the collars during the conflict, was shocked to learn that he was the target of FBI charges that he'd sold his badge to the Colombos.

"Detective Stung by Feds"

On December 8, 1993, Simone, who had hurt his back in the line of duty, was due to retire with a "three quarters" tax-free pension—the holy grail for cops and firefighters in the City of New York.* But early that morning, a line of police and FBI vehicles pulled up outside the modest house in Staten Island where he'd lived for thirteen years with his wife, Eileen, a nurse, and their five children. Within hours, Simone was under arrest for bribery, accused by agents from his own NYPD-FBI task force of leaking intel to Colombo wiseguys.

The next day, rather than celebrating at a retirement party, Simone saw his name smeared across tabloids.[8] "Detective Stung by Feds" read the ban-

---

* Equal to 75 percent of his salary at the time of retirement.

ner headline over the *Daily News* piece by Capeci and Tom Robbins—a reporter who would later play a key role in demolishing DeVecchio's murder prosecution.

Former Detective Joe Simone, 2004

"Detective Joseph Simone, who worked on the NYPD-FBI Organized Crime Task Force for seven years, was charged with selling information to the Orena faction of the warring Colombo family for two years, earning at least $2,000," Capeci and Robbins reported in the article that ran December 9, 1993.[9] Overnight, Joseph Simone went from a hero in his Staten Island community to a tabloid disgrace. "The roof caved in on my life," Simone told me. "I never saw it coming."[10]

But precisely how Simone became the object of the FBI investigation, and the way it was conducted, raises serious questions about whether Simone was set up to take the fall for Lin DeVecchio—particularly since the government's principal source for the accusation was Salvatore "Big Sal" Miciotta,[11] a notorious Colombo soldier who admitted to his involvement in four murders and was later thrown out of WITSEC, the witness protection program.

For years, Simone had been active with his sons in Little League and the football program at Tottenville High School on Staten Island. Occasionally he visited the home of the school's coach, Phil Ciadella, whose uncle Alfonso "Chips" DeCostanza was a Colombo capo.

"We had locked him up for guns during the war," remembers Joe. "He used to inform for us. I'd go over there once in a while 'cause Phil's mother cooked old-style Italian.[12] So one day I go to Phil's mother's house and who's there but Big Sal and Bobo Malpeso, two Colombo capos." As noted earlier, Malpeso's son James had been shot by the "Persico faction" during the war.

Simone told me he was "shocked" to see the two captains. "I didn't expect them to be there," he said. "I just went there to pick up plays."

In any case, Simone says that the three-hundred-fifty-pound Miciotta and Malpeso started talking to him as if they thought he might be willing to sell them information. "Bobo tried to pass me a piece of paper, but I didn't touch it," recalls Simone. "I couldn't tell you to this day if it was a shopping list or an envelope." Simone, who'd lived by street rules since his days as a kid in Gravesend, Brooklyn, knew a setup when he saw one.

"I told 'em, 'You guys are probably wired. I don't want any part of you.'" At that point, according to Simone, Malpeso stripped down to his pants to show he wasn't wearing a recording device. But as Joe left, he confronted Phil Ciadella. "I told him, 'You got some fuckin' pair of balls puttin' me in a situation like this,'" Simone remembers. "Not long after that, I informed Favo and DeVecchio of what had happened."

Simone believes it was after his meeting with Favo that the Feds decided to set him up formally. In July 1993 he was called back to the same house by Coach Ciadella. As court records show, in the interim Miciotta had agreed to inform for the Bureau. Two agents later claimed that Big Sal approached *them,* but there was suspiciously no paperwork on file indicating that he'd made the offer.[13]

Further, Miciotta alleged that, during their first meeting, the "paper" Bobo Malpeso offered Simone contained $1,500 in bribe money. Big Sal insisted that Simone took it, but the Feds needed corroboration, so a second meeting was arranged.

This time, Miciotta was carrying a tape recorder. A transcript of his conversation with Chips DeCostanza before Simone arrived suggests that Miciotta didn't believe he could corrupt the veteran cop.[14] As the tape begins, Miciotta wonders aloud to DeCostanza whether he might get "help" from Simone because he'd gotten "pinched again."

> **Miciotta:** I need a little information. I wanna find out what the fuck they're gonna do with this case here. . . . You know, I'd do the right thing. I'll take care of him.
> **Decostanza:** He don't want nothin'.
> **Miciotta:** I'm glad to give him a couple o' dollars.
> **Deconstanza:** You don't have to give him nothin'.

Moments later, in a reference to the flowers Wild Bill Cutolo had sent to Simone's mother, Big Sal says:

Miciotta: Billy's the guy who burned him out, he sent him flowers. . . .
In other words, he reached out for the guy; the guy didn't respond.

It was an acknowledgment by Miciotta that Joe wasn't a man who could be bought. Then, for unknown reasons, just before Simone arrived, Miciotta shut off the tape recorder.

During the meeting, according to Simone, Miciotta confessed that his son was "on the lam down in Florida." The younger Miciotta was wanted by the NYPD's Sixth Precinct for attacking a young aspiring priest, but it was his father who had broken the seminarian's arm.

That revelation prompted Simone to make an immediate report to Chris Favo about the meeting. "As soon as I saw Favo again," remembers Simone, "I told him about the son. 'I got it from the horse's mouth,' I said. He was down in Florida. I told him that we ought to notify the Precinct Detective's Squad where he is."[15]

After briefing Favo, Simone thought nothing further of it. It was his job to connect with mob guys and get information, and he'd reported to Favo, his immediate FBI supervisor, about both encounters. Simone continued with his task force work, and as the summer and fall of 1993 passed, he prepared to retire.

Facing Sixty Counts

Then, in the course of filing a claim for a disability pension, Simone obtained copies of his Daily Activity Reports (DARs)—a day-by-day, hour-by-hour record of his movements during his tenure at the task force. As a result, he happened to have those reports with him on the morning of his arrest, when other records in his desk were seized by Bureau investigators. By the end of the day on December 8 he'd been handcuffed and charged with taking a bribe from Miciotta. With the tape off, it came down to the word of a decorated veteran cop versus that of a violent mobster with an interest in cooperating with the Feds. But Simone lost.

Despite the fact that he agreed to talk to NYPD detectives and FBI agents for three hours after his arrest without a lawyer present, and despite the fact that he offered to take a polygraph—which the Feds declined—Detective Joe Simone was indicted. He was so forthcoming that what he told the agents filled twelve and a half pages of an FBI 302.[16] But not a word in that lengthy memo incriminated him.

During the debriefing, Simone patently denied passing any intel to Mafiosi. He dutifully noted that he had kept both Chris Favo and Lieutenant William Shannon, his NYPD supervisor, in the loop regarding his meetings with Phil Ciadella.

"Initially they had sixty counts against me," says Simone. "Everybody was trying to dump what went bad in the Colombo wars on me—like wires . . . giving up CIs. . . . Everything. They ended up coming down to four counts: two attempted alleged bribery and two attempted alleged conspiracies."

In the *Daily News,* however, Capeci and Robbins treated him so harshly that it was as though he'd already been convicted. The sub-headline on their aforementioned "Detective Stung" story read "Sold Information to Colombos: FBI."[17]

"The FBI learned of Simone's turncoat role last May," they reported, "from a Colombo soldier who agreed to wear a wire and later taped Simone and DeCostanza in several incriminating conversations."[18]

That piece never mentioned the fact that the tape was shut off during that meeting, or that there was no record of the alleged bribe encounter. Capeci and Robbins included no qualifiers. The word "alleged" was never used. The article noted that "DeCostanza (whose cooperation the Feds sought) won a dismissal of weapons charges arising from an arrest during the height of the Colombo war." But there wasn't even a suggestion that DeCostanza's plea might have represented a payoff from the FBI for setting up the veteran detective. The story noted that Simone had now been suspended from the NYPD and released on a $50,000 personal-recognizance bond.

Two days later, Capeci and Robbins weighed in with a story about Big Sal Miciotta, under a sixty-point headline reading "Mob Biggie Aids FBI Sting."[19] The piece, which repeated the story that Miciotta had been wired, noted that he had been "hustled into federal protection" for his role in the arrest of "the gang's top-secret mole in FBI headquarters—a New York City police detective."

By April, however, new evidence emerged that should have produced a retraction from Capeci and Robbins. The FBI admitted that Miciotta had switched off his tape recorder just before his meeting with Simone, so there was no record of the alleged bribe the *Daily News* team had reported as fact.

Undeterred, Capeci filed a story under the headline "Short FBI Tape May Aid 'Rogue Cop' Defense."[20]

"Ever since he was charged with selling his badge to the mob," wrote Capeci, "Detective Joseph Simone has waged a fierce and desperate battle for his reputation, his job, his pension and his freedom. . . . And thanks to a screw-up in the FBI plan to trap the suspected rogue cop, the double agent defense may work for him."

The piece never mentioned Simone's heretofore unblemished nineteen-year career, or the fact that it was his word versus that of Big Sal Miciotta, a violent Colombo killer who had mercilessly brutalized a young priest.[21]

Miciotta was later dropped by the Feds from witness protection after he lied on the witness stand in the murder-racketeering trial of six other Colombo members. Meanwhile, as ham-handed as the Feds had been in their attempt to set up Simone on the bribery charge, they were even more inept in trying to frame him.

Eight Agents Tail Detective Simone

At trial, in the same Brooklyn courthouse where Vic Orena had been convicted, the government presented evidence alleging that Detective Joe Simone had used his desk phone at 26 Federal Plaza to signal Colombo members (Scarpa style), typing the code 6-6-6 into a beeper. They also alleged that a female FBI agent on a pay phone outside a Staten Island deli had overheard him attempting to contact a known mob associate.

On the day of his arrest, the FBI had emptied Simone's desk. As far as federal prosecutors knew, the detective had no records to support his defense. "But what they didn't count on," says Simone, "was that I had my DARs. . . . Every time they had me at work tipping off one of these made guys," he says, "the DARs proved that either my tour of duty was over or I was on vacation."

When I first interviewed Simone, in 2004, he showed me the pink DARs that convinced a federal jury of the FBI frame-up.

"One time they actually used my office phone to beep a wiseguy, claiming I was trying to tip him off with the 666, and it turned out that I was in Wildwood, New Jersey, at the time with my family. No way was I gonna drive all the way back to Federal Plaza, three and a half hours, dial some sixes, and then go back down to Wildwood."

At trial, FBI Special Agent Lynn Smith testified under oath that, on September 23, 1993, she was part of an eight-person FBI surveillance team following Simone. She alleged that they tracked him to the deli-superette on the corner of Arthur Kill Road and Elverton Avenue, and that she overheard him talking on a phone "located outside [the] door of the superette." Asked by Simone's defense lawyer John Patton if there was one phone or two, she replied, "One on the left and one on the right, on each side of the door."[22]

But Simone's attorney established that only *one phone* was located on a side wall of that deli—not a pair of phones by the front door, as Smith alleged. "We had the deli owner," says Simone, "who was prepared to testify that there had never been two phones where this agent said she'd been."

"Understand the significance of this," says Angela Clemente, the forensic investigator whose lawsuit uncovered the newly released Scarpa files. "The FBI is so intent on nailing this poor cop that they put eight agents on him. A female agent testifies under oath to a phone that doesn't exist so they can make it look like Joe is calling to tip off wiseguys. The truth is he used to stop at that deli before coming home to call his wife and ask if she wanted him to bring home cold cuts for dinner. But the Bureau goes to all this trouble to make it look like he's caught up in some major leak to the Colombos."[23]

In another instance, Patton showed the jury a series of documents supplied by the FBI that purported to prove that Simone had taken that $1,500 bribe. But the lawyer, a veteran of defending cops, lined up the staple marks on the copies to demonstrate that one of the incriminating pages had been replaced by the Feds *after* Joe's arrest.[24]

Favo's Role in the Simone Investigation

One of Simone's chief accusers at trial was his immediate superior in C-10, Special Agent Chris Favo. What the jury didn't realize, at the time, was that for almost two years leading up to Simone's arrest, Favo had suspected *his* immediate supervisor, Lin DeVecchio, as the source of the Colombo war leaks. But he'd kept quiet about his suspicions until January 1994, a month *after* Simone's arrest, when he came forward with agents Leadbetter and Tomlinson.

As noted, in the months that followed, Favo poured out his concerns about the alleged tainted Scarpa-DeVecchio relationship in a series of FBI 302s.[25] But none of that kept him from taking the stand against Joe Simone.

"At the start of trial, I was worried," recalls Simone. "Not because I was guilty, but because of the way the jury was made up. There were these twelve Nordic, blue-eyed, blond-haired people," he said. "There wasn't an Italian American among them except for an alternate. No blacks. No Hispanics. None of the people you think of as New Yorkers. And I'm sittin' there scared shitless. I see these people starin' at me—especially the foreman. He just stared me down during the whole trial."

The real turn in the proceedings came during a lunch break, when Simone's brother John was reading—ironically—the *Daily News*. "There had been a huge DEA bust," remembers Joe. "And my brother calls me over with the paper and says, 'Do you know any of these guys?' And I looked at it and it said that Lindley DeVecchio was in charge of this *DEA* task force. I'm thinking, that can't be right. He's Mr. Organized Crime. So I go up to John Patton and say, 'This doesn't make sense—DeVecchio's supposed to be the top guy in the country on wiseguys. Why would he be working drugs?'"

Neither Patton nor his client had any idea that by then, under FBI suspicion, DeVecchio had been moved over to the DEA position. The OPR investigation had commenced, but except for some rumors Simone had heard, no one outside the Bureau or the Justice Department knew that DeVecchio was a target of an FBI internal affairs probe.

"So right after lunch, when Favo gets on the stand," says Simone, "John Patton decides to play a hunch and he takes a shot. 'Is it true,' he asks, 'that your supervisor DeVecchio is under investigation for corruption?' Suddenly, you can hear a pin drop in the courtroom and Favo says, 'I'm not allowed to disclose that at this time.'"

"That was it," says Simone. "Confirmation that something was wrong. John turned around and gave me the Groucho eyebrows. That's how we discovered that Lin DeVecchio was the bad guy and I had been set up to take the heat off him."

But the Feds, who by then were well aware of DeVecchio's alleged leaks to Scarpa, didn't make it any easier on Simone's lawyer. "We tried several times to get the phone records," Patton recalled. "LUDS—records from Joe's phone that we could compare against his DARs. And each time, mysteriously, for those particular weeks, the phone people told us they were missing."[26]

"Sal Miciotta was the personification of evil," says Patton. "The guy had no moral center. And it was simply his word against Joe's, without a shred of probative corroborating evidence. The fact that they even got an *indictment* was outrageous. These prosecutors ruined the life of a great cop, just to cover for a dirty agent."

And yet, in the end, after hearing all the evidence, the jury acquitted Joe Simone on all counts. "I cried like a baby," he says, "and the foreman, who I was scared of, stood up and yelled out, *'Not guilty!'*"

Double Jeopardy

The *New York Times* covered the verdict in a prominent two-column story: "Detective Is Found Not Guilty of Selling Secrets to the Mafia."[27] *Newsday* did the same: "Cop Not Guilty of Fed Rap."[28] Simone's hometown paper, the *Staten Island Advance,* gave him a banner headline: "Detective Acquitted of Mob Charges."[29] Later, they followed up with a piece headlined "Cop Puts His Life Back Together. Simone: 'It Feels Good to Be Free.'"[30]

But Jerry Capeci was absent from the *Daily News* coverage of the acquittal. That job was left to Greg B. Smith. In a short one-column piece headlined "Juries Show Little Respect for 'Big Sal,'" Smith reported, "A Brooklyn federal jury took just two hours to declare Detective Joseph Simone innocent."

Even that vindication was buried in the third paragraph of a story that focused on the extraordinary efforts by the Feds to protect the murderer and priest-beater Salvatore Miciotta. Still, Smith quoted a juror who told him that "no one believed the Feds' witnesses, including Miciotta, who claimed Simone had fed him secrets."

Jerry Capeci's "Gang Land" column two weeks later was headlined "Cop Still Treading Hot Water."[31]

"He was acquitted of federal charges that he sold his badge to mobsters during the bloody Colombo war," wrote Capeci, "but it may not yet be all over for Detective Joe Simone. . . . The Feds can't simply call a 'do over' in Simone's case. But they can—and are—pushing city cops to pick up the ball they dropped and prosecute Simone on departmental charges that would cost the 19-year veteran his pension. Despite the acquittal charges, Gang Land sources say FBI agent Chris Favo and assistant U.S. Attorneys Stanley Okula and Karen Popp firmly believe Simone was guilty as charged." Quoting an unnamed cop, Capeci blamed the acquittal on "just a bad jury."

Once again, the reading public was in the dark. Because of the secretive nature of the OPR process, no one outside of the FBI and Justice Department knew that one of the charges DeVecchio would face was Chris Favo's accusation that his boss had regularly leaked confidential FBI information to none other than Jerry Capeci. The only hint of Simone's point of view in that "Gang Land" piece was a quote from his lawyer, John Patton: "'We're not afraid of a G.O. 15,' Patton said, in a reference to the regulation that forces cops to answer all questions or be fired."

Sure enough, the NYPD's internal affairs division went ahead and filed charges. "They essentially mirrored the federal indictment," said Patton, who was confident of an acquittal, especially after several former FBI colleagues of Simone agreed to testify on his behalf. But the NYPD "indictment" included a charge that Simone had "wrongfully failed and neglected to report to this Department a bribe offer"—a reference to the piece of paper Joe had refused to touch, which Miciotta had described as an envelope full of cash. It didn't seem to matter that there was no independent proof that the paper Miciotta had tried to hand Simone was "a bribe."

Again, the proceedings would hinge on the word of a decorated detective—who the hearing examiner admitted had been "handpicked" for the elite Colombo task force—versus the allegations of Big Sal, one of the very suspects he had investigated.

Now, in the NYPD hearing, Chris Favo was determined not to get caught off guard. When asked if his immediate supervisor, DeVecchio, was under investigation for leaking information, Favo said that he had been "directed not to answer."[32]

This time, the hearing officer—who tried the case without a jury—came down with what Patton described as "a horrendous decision." Despite the fact that it was part of Simone's job description to meet with mobsters and elicit information for the OCID Task Force, Deputy NYPD Commissioner Rae Downes Koshetz decided that the paper offered to Joe *had* been a bribe and that he should have reported it to his police department superiors, even though he had told both Chris Favo and DeVecchio about the encounter.

Further, Koshetz seemed to conclude that Simone's "guilt" was also directly related to his association with Phil Ciadella, the high school football coach, whose uncle was in the mob.

Joe had testified fondly that he enjoyed going over to Phil's house because Ciadella's elderly mother and father "would treat [him] like their own son." He described them as "seventy-, eighty-year-old people that I had respect for." Despite the fact that neither of those pensioners had a criminal record, Commissioner Koshetz righteously declared:

> Members of this Department are forbidden to associate with known criminals. Even if Ciadella was not on a data base, his connection to the mob was too close for comfort. Moreover, the Respondent's claim that associating with such people is part and parcel of living and raising a family in certain parts of Staten Island, is unavailing; if a New York City police officer can not conduct his personal life without associating with mobsters or their close relatives, he is expected to move elsewhere.

"This astonishing decision, in which Detective Simone was found guilty and stripped of his pension, suggested one of two things," said Patton. "Either the hearing officer was incredibly naïve with respect to the fact that Joe was working in an OC squad and expected to mix with wiseguys as part of his job, or she was doing the bidding of the Feds."

One hint of an answer to that question came when William J. Bratton, who was police commissioner at the time of Simone's guilty verdict, put off signing the final papers that would have stripped Joe of his pension. Bratton, who later served as LAPD chief, eventually retired from the NYPD and was replaced by Howard Safir, then FDNY commissioner. The appointment was made by then Mayor Rudolph Giuliani.[33]

No Mercy from a Veteran Fed

Safir had spent thirty-five years with the federal government. He had been assistant DEA director before becoming chief of the U.S. Marshals' WIT-SEC Program—a unit with intimate ties to the Southern and Eastern Districts that monitored many of the turncoat mobsters that the FBI's New York Office sought to protect.

"The day Howard Safir became police commissioner after Bratton left," says Joe, "that morning at nine something, he signed the papers saying that I was through."

Ironically, Rae Downes Koshetz, the hearing examiner who seemed so clueless about the way an OCID cop like Simone got intelligence from the mob, ended up serving as co-counsel along with legendary defense lawyer Eddie Hayes in representing ex-detective Stephen Caracappa, one of the so-called Mafia Cops.[34]

As a measure of the injustice in the Simone case, because Caracappa and ex-detective Lou Eppolito were charged and convicted *after* their NYPD retirements, they were allowed to collect their tax-free disability pensions even though they are serving life terms.[35] But Simone, who was acquitted of federal charges, was arrested just hours *before* his pension would have vested, allowing the department to take it from him.

"How outrageous can you get?" says Patton. "Joe was set up. They should have given him a chance to get out and take care of his five kids. To honor nineteen years of great service."

The blow to his family and his reputation sent Simone into a spiral. "First there was severe depression; then I wound up becoming an alcoholic," he says. Simone was bitter. "At one point during the trial, Favo had this smirk on his face," he remembers. "And I went up to him and I said, 'You little shit. You didn't cheat *me* out of my pension. You cheated my wife and my kids. And I will never forgive you for that.'"

Today, Simone, the veteran cop who helped lock up a third of the wiseguys during the Colombo war, resorts to working odd jobs to pay the bills. His wife works full-time as a nurse. Having gone through rehab, he now attends seven AA meetings a week as he tries to piece his life together, enjoy his grandchildren, and forget.

Not surprisingly, Lin DeVecchio weighs in on Simone's case in his book. In a long section, he relates a conversation he says he had with Dave Stone, whom he describes as a "well respected supervisor" in the FBI's NYO.[36]

"No way Joe Simone is corrupt," DeVecchio writes, quoting Stone. "No way Joe is a dirty cop." Lin then replies, "Favo says he's got a good case." Then, after Stone's assurance that Simone was one of his best detectives, Lin adds, "Favo said he's got him on tape with Big Sal Miciotta"—an allegation that was proven entirely untrue at Simone's trial.

A few paragraphs later in the book, DeVecchio describes an exchange he says he had with Stone about Simone's impending arrest, writing that he gave Stone permission to make the collar.

"I'll take him in my car. No cuffs," he quotes Stone as saying. "Favo worked with Joe on my squad for a year," Dave added. "Joe Simone helped teach him a lot. They should . . . let him surrender himself." Lin then writes that he told Stone, "It's in the Eastern District's hands. The best I can do is let you arrest him."

Earlier in the book, seemingly sympathetic to Simone, DeVecchio writes, "Detective Joseph Simone, a twenty-year veteran and a father of six [sic], was the first fellow law enforcement officer that Chris Favo ever officially accused of corruption—even before me." But on the morning of Simone's arrest, and in the months that followed, there's no record of Lin DeVecchio doing a thing to intervene on Simone's behalf.

"I want to know where Lin was when my life was being destroyed," Joe told me in an interview.[37] "He just sat there and let me twist in the wind. He even writes in his book that Favo said he had a tape of me and Miciotta. But there was no tape. It's outrageous."

More outrageous was *the timing* of Simone's arrest. If DeVecchio, who was the squad supervisor at the time, had waited another twenty-four hours, Simone would have retired, and under NYPD rules he'd have his pension today. Now, nearly ten years after "the roof caved in," he still doesn't have his retirement benefits from the department.

"Of all the many injustices exposed in the scandal over Gregory Scarpa Sr. and Lin DeVecchio," says Angela Clemente, "what the Feds did to Joe Simone—one of their own—is among the worst."[38]

Chapter 36

GASPIPE'S CONFESSION

By the spring of 1994 the Feds were in damage-control mode, seeking to protect their war prosecutions from the growing taint of the Scarpa-DeVecchio scandal. At that point they'd offered two explanations for the leaks: first that Detective Joe Simone had passed on intel to the Colombos, and second, as alleged during that meeting with Valerie Caproni in the fall of 1993, that the intelligence had come to Scarpa via his good friend Anthony Casso.[1] But despite the NYPD's punitive move on Simone's pension, he was entirely vindicated in federal court, and by April, Casso was about to shatter the second theory—that he had shared his "crystal ball" of intelligence received from the Mafia Cops with Greg Scarpa.[2]

Within days of being seized at his New Jersey hideout in January, Casso was taken from the Metropolitan Correctional Center (MCC) to the U.S. attorney's office in Brooklyn. Ostensibly, the meeting was to discuss whether he should provide handwriting samples as ordered by Judge Eugene Nickerson. But when he got into a room with FBI agent Richard Rudolph from the Lucchese squad, Gaspipe dropped a bomb.[3]

"If you guys make me a good offer . . . I'll work with you," he said, knowing that AUSA Charlie Rose's office was a few doors away. Rose* was the senior Eastern District prosecutor who had been assigned to Casso's case, along with Assistant U.S. Attorney Greg O'Connell.[4]

At that point, Casso was well aware that his former crime partner Greg Scarpa had earned a generous plea deal after offering to cooperate and renounce his ties to LCN. And Casso, like Scarpa, was known for his Machiavellian playbook.

As Phil Carlo put it in *Gaspipe,* "For Charlie Rose this was truly a monumental occasion. Anthony Gaspipe Casso turning was a milestone in the annals of crime history." In February, a deal was structured in which Casso would serve six and a half years after pleading guilty to a seventy-two-count indictment. Considering the fact that Casso, who had been made in 1974 at the age of thirty-two,[5] would take responsibility for fifteen murders and reportedly admit to another twenty-one, it was a plea bargain worthy of Sammy Gravano's.[6]

At that moment in late February, however, it was far from a done deal. The plea was in a preliminary stage that the Feds call a "proffer." It wouldn't be official until it was reduced to writing and all parties, including the court, had agreed to the terms. In the meantime, according to Casso, his then lawyer, who represented a number of other Mafiosi, withdrew from representing him. As Carlo explained it, this attorney didn't want "to get a reputation as [one] who facilitated such cooperation."[7]

With other wiseguys, that might be bad for business.

So Casso was assigned a new lawyer, Matthew Brief. In his memoir, Casso alleges that Brief told federal prosecutors he didn't think the proffer protected his client enough. But according to Casso, Brief, who is now deceased, never informed *him* of that position at the time.[8]

On March 1, 1994, Anthony Casso pled guilty to the full seventy-two counts, expecting to get the short sentence in exchange for sharing everything he knew with the Feds. Immediately after his appearance before EDNY Magistrate Steven M. Gold, Casso was whisked by agent Rudolph to LaGuardia Airport, where they boarded a private plane bound for Texas. At

---

* Not to be confused with the PBS talk show host and CBS News coanchor of the same name.

that point in the FBI's war against the Mafia, Casso, a Lucchese acting boss, was the most notorious CW the Feds had turned since Gravano. Befitting his star status, he was assigned to the "Valachi Suite" at La Tuna, a minimum-security federal prison twelve miles north of El Paso.[9] In years past, the suite, a multiroom accommodation complete with a kitchen, had housed Mafia turncoats "Fat Vinnie" Teresa and Jimmy "the Weasel" Fratianno.[10]

When Casso started to talk, his debriefings were handled by Rudolph and James Brennan, the same special agent from the Lucchese squad who had been called to that meeting with Scarpa and DeVecchio in the fall of 1993, when "34" reportedly identified Gaspipe as his source for law enforcement intelligence.

Over the weeks that followed, Casso unleashed so many Mafia secrets that they filled 504 pages of FBI 302s. William Oldham, a former NYPD detective who later worked the Mafia Cops case as an investigator for the EDNY, described them in his 2006 book, *The Brotherhoods: The True Story of Two Cops Who Murdered for the Mafia*.[11]

Casso during his *60 Minutes* interview

"I spent the next two days and nights reading and rereading Casso's 302s," Oldham writes in the book, coauthored with Guy Lawson. "Casso was forthcoming in an unusually detailed way. [He] clearly didn't want to get into trouble for holding anything back. To the contrary. He was meticulously forthcoming."[12]

But in his interview with me and several follow-up letters, Casso insists that one crucial admission he made to Rudolph and Brennan never showed up in those 302s. He went into even more detail in Phil Carlo's original manuscript, which I obtained during the research for this book:

One of the first things Casso began to talk about . . . was corrupt police and FBI agents he had dealt with over the years. As part of the debriefing process, the agents were taking notes to memorialize exactly what Casso said. It is mandated that notes are written down on what is referred to as a 302 form. The "302s" would become viable legal documents that could be, and more than likely would be, used in a court of law.

Gaspipe then identified what he described as two "crooked agents" who had passed information to him. The first was reportedly a special agent from the Gambino squad. Because he is not the focus of this book, I've omitted that agent's name from the section of Carlo's original manuscript excerpted below.

According to what Casso told Phil Carlo, about halfway through his account, after he'd named this first agent as the source of "vitally important" information, Special Agent Richard Rudolph reacted loudly and negatively:

> Agent Rudolph "literally jumped up," according to Casso, from the table and shouted that he didn't want to hear anything more about ███. He threw his pen down on the table and refused to take notes. Agent Rudolph leaned over, pointed his finger in Casso's face and warned him not to mention ███ or any other corrupt agents, not only to them, but to any assistant U.S. attorneys, i.e. Charlie Rose and Greg O'Connell. Both Charlie Rose and O'Connell were slated to arrive the next day to begin the task of making Casso a viable government witness. Writing up the 302s was the first step in that process and it wasn't going well at all. Casso was shocked. He expected the agents to be happy; he expected them to be pleased that he was exposing crooked FBI agents. Just the opposite was true.[13]

"When Agent Richard Rudolph was contacted for this book," Carlo noted, "he did not return phone calls."[14] As this book neared completion I was able to reach Special Agent Brennan, and his reaction to Casso's allegation is reflected later in this chapter.[15]

Meanwhile, I uncovered some independent evidence that corroborates Casso's allegation that he paid a special agent on the Gambino squad for information. It's in the form of an FBI 302 memo dated January 17, 1992, memorializing the debriefing of Lucchese underboss "Little Al" D'Arco. In it, D'Arco described a payment of four thousand dollars a month made by Casso via Lucchese capo Salvatore Avellino, who controlled the family garbage-industry interests on Long Island.

> Source advised every month AVELLINO would deduct a $4,000.00 expense for a Federal Agent who was supplying confidential information

to AVELLINO. . . . AVELLINO informed source that this Federal Agent was on the Gambino squad and he (AVELLINO) was very nervous when meeting him. . . . Source advised he was sure it was a federal agent, meaning Federal Bureau of Investigation Agent, that AVELLINO was paying off, and in turn, receiving confidential information. AVELLINO was quizzed on a number of occasions and advised that this money should be going to a Federal Agent and not a cop.[16]

D'Arco's confession is significant because when Burt Kaplan, Casso's liaison with the Mafia Cops, became a cooperating witness, he told the Feds that Eppolito and Caracappa were on the payroll for four thousand dollars a month.[17] Further, as evidenced by his testimony against Vic Orena, D'Arco was a CW whose credibility the Feds swore by. So, if nothing else, his confirmation that Casso had ordered a monthly payment in that same amount to an FBI agent on the Gambino squad supports Gaspipe's first allegation to agents Rudolph and Brennan at La Tuna about a "crooked Fed."

According to Carlo's account, Rudolph explained to Casso that he and this Gambino squad agent "had been friends for over twenty years and that agent ██████ had integrity and honesty and was above reproach." So, as Carlo writes, realizing that "the wind was already blowing against him," Casso didn't mention that agent's name again.

But Gaspipe wasn't finished. Undaunted, he then offered the name of "another crooked agent." This is what Carlo wrote in his original manuscript, quoting Casso:

> Let's talk about him. His name is Lindley DeVecchio. He worked with Greg Scarpa for many years. He supplied LCN with a lot of information.[18]

At that point, according to Carlo, Rudolph said:

> "Don't you get it? I don't want to hear about any crooked agents here. We aren't here to talk about crooked agents. We're here to talk about what you know about the Mafia—got it?"
>
> Casso suddenly felt like he was standing naked in a cold room, his skin reddened by the frigid air. As he looked at Agent Rudolph, he saw enmity, anger, foreboding in his face. "I thought you wanted to know the truth about all the criminal things I was involved with," Casso said.

"Yes, I do," the agent said. "But I'm not interested in hearing your bullshit about crooked agents, Casso. If you're here to pull my chain, I'm going to end this right here, right now, and you can go fuck yourself. You got that?"

By now, realizing that these FBI agents didn't want to hear anything about other "crooked Feds," Gaspipe, according to Carlo, revealed that he "had two NYPD detectives killing people" for him.

"You interested in that?" Casso asked.

"Getting warm," Rudolph reportedly replied.[19]

Insisting That Lin Was a "Crooked Fed"

In my interview with Casso, he underscored Carlo's account regarding the two allegedly "crooked Feds."

"I told [Rudolph and Brennan] the[se other agents] were crooked," he said, "and they didn't want to hear it. When I brought this up in Texas they threw the yellow pad on the table with the pen. They refused even to write down what I was saying."[20]

Beyond accusing Rudolph and Brennan of refusing to document his allegations, Casso went even further in Carlo's book. Shortly after Gaspipe's initial debriefing, Carlo writes, Special Agent Chris Favo came to the Valachi Suite to interview him.

> Agent Rudolph made sure he sat between Casso and Agent Favo and he constantly gave Casso the hairy eyeball, making sure that Casso said nothing about DeVecchio's misdeeds. When Agent Favo left, Rudolph told Casso that no one would listen to Favo.[21]

Casso also confirmed that account to me: "Chris Favo, when he came to see me, the agents sat right there . . . in between us. Even when the prosecutors came, they made sure they were right between us."[22]

Former EDNY investigator William Oldham, who has read the entire 504 pages of Casso 302s, told me he is certain that "Casso told the truth the first time." But he recalled that there was no mention of Gaspipe's allegations about DeVecchio or the Gambino squad agent in those 302s.[23]

"In the 302s," Oldham says, "Casso does not mention, to my recollection, anything other than the crystal ball of information [he got from the Mafia Cops]. He didn't say a thing about federal law enforcement."

I tried to get Special Agent Rudolph's version of events. But after my repeated attempts to reach him, he never got back to me. However, retired SA James Brennan had this to say: "During the Casso debriefings, Casso did not relate to us at any time that he dealt with and received law enforcement intel from federal agents."[24]

Casso's credibility was later challenged, and the Feds ultimately reneged on his plea deal. Gaspipe insists that they broke the deal because he was too honest with them about their star cooperating witness, Sammy Gravano.

As Carlo writes, "When Anthony Casso, in the course of being debriefed by federal agents, talked about dealing drugs with Gravano, talked about murders by Gravano other than the ones Gravano said he committed, the agents didn't want to hear it. No one in the federal government was interested."[25]

The official reason the Feds broke the deal was their allegation that Casso committed crimes while in prison, including assaulting an inmate and bribing prison guards with cash, auto tires, and tickets to Broadway shows to supply him with liquor, wine, and steaks.[26] The assistant U.S. attorney who alleged that Casso had violated his plea agreement was none other than George Stamboulidis, who had prosecuted Vic Orena and helped convict him on the testimony of Sammy the Bull and Al D'Arco.

Now, instead of the initial six-and-a-half-year proffer, Casso was given 13 life sentences plus 455 years. After spilling his guts to the Feds in 504 pages of 302s—in which Oldham, the former EDNY investigator, had insisted he'd been initially honest—Gaspipe was now locked away in the Supermax prison and was never called to testify for the government at any subsequent trial. In the manuscript for his book Carlo writes that Casso was a victim of his own candor. The consequences of his challenging Sammy the Bull were clear:

If the defense attorneys could prove that Gravano had perjured himself, there would surely be a wave of appeals and an influx of complaints, creating a nightmare for the Justice Department and an embarrassment of monumental proportions.[27]

John Gotti wasn't the only Mafia boss who could have earned a new trial if juries had believed Casso. Vic Orena might also have merited judicial relief. But the Feds insisted it was Casso's "lack of credibility" that rendered him ineffective as a witness. Carlo quotes AUSA Greg O'Connell as stating, "Using Casso as a witness would have been like putting Adolf Hitler on the witness stand."[28]

But O'Connell never got to hear about the "crooked Feds" from whom Gaspipe Casso insists he received information. After Eastern District prosecutors broke their deal with Casso, Oldham told me, "He tried to mold his story to whoever he was talking to." But the former EDNY investigator insists that, in Casso's initial debriefings, he "never found anything that wasn't true."[29]

Blaming the Mafia Cops

While Casso insists that he gave up Eppolito and Caracappa as his NYPD sources only *after* FBI agents Rudolph and Brennan refused to hear any talk of "crooked agents," Lin DeVecchio seized on the Mafia Cops in his book to explain the leaks. In furnishing the evidence that prompted DeVecchio's OPR investigation, Chris Favo and agents Tomlinson and Andjich had speculated that their boss may have leaked information to Jerry Capeci.[30] Now, in his book, crediting Capeci with breaking the Mafia Cops story, DeVecchio writes:

> No earlier than March 1994, two months after Favo reported me to North, Gaspipe gave up the Mafia Cops to his debriefers at the Valachi Suite in El Paso. When Jerry Capeci broke the Mafia Cops story, did any of my accusers stop to consider that in view of the close relationship between the Lucchese Family and the Colombo Family, Scarpa's law enforcement information, if he truly got any, could have come down the pipeline from Gaspipe? Gaspipe was getting extremely singular information from the Mafia Cops.[31]

Later in his book, DeVecchio recounts that fall 1993 meeting in Valerie Caproni's office where Greg Scarpa reportedly claimed he'd received his tips from Gaspipe.

"Jim Brennan told me," writes Lin, that "during Gaspipe's debriefing in the Valachi Suite in El Paso, Gaspipe denied that he gave information to Scarpa, but that doesn't change what Scarpa said."[32]

Thus Lin DeVecchio's principal explanation for the massive leaks of FBI intelligence to Scarpa seems to be that "34" received the intel from Casso via the two NYPD detectives. The question is, how likely is it that the depth and breadth of intelligence—particularly the intel supplied during the third Colombo war from 1991 to 1993—could have come from Eppolito, who retired in 1990, and Caracappa, who went out on disability in 1992?

Prior to Lin's indictment in 2006, Fred Dannen wrote the most definitive magazine piece on Scarpa and DeVecchio for the *New Yorker*.[33] It was based on multiple interviews Dannen conducted with the key Feds involved, including DeVecchio himself. After he read *We're Going to Win This Thing*, I asked Fred for his reaction to DeVecchio's theory about the source of the leaks. He focused first on the implication that Scarpa had obtained the 1987 DEA arrest lists and the name of Cosmo Catanzano from Casso.

> DeVecchio denies tipping off Scarpa Sr. (and consequently Junior) about the DEA case. And he denies endangering the life of Cosmo Catanzano. He instead blames Gaspipe Casso for supplying that information, which Gaspipe supposedly had learned from the Mafia Cops. This borders on the ridiculous. It does not account for the piece of paper that Junior showed his associates, listing ten people targeted for arrest in the DEA case—a list, Junior said, supplied by "a friend" of his father's, whom Junior described as "an agent."[34]

Defense attorney Flora Edwards goes further. "Virtually all of the information that was leaked to Scarpa Sr. over the years had to do with *federal* law enforcement activities," she says. "Not only was this pair of NYPD detectives not privy to much of that, but Scarpa and Casso were in the most jeopardy from *the Feds*, not the NYPD. So if they were going to protect themselves and stay out of jail, and they were able to corrupt *anyone* in law enforcement, their first choice would have been the kind of 'crooked Feds' that Gaspipe describes in his book."[35]

Considering all the evidence uncovered in this investigation, it's now clear that whatever "crystal ball" of intelligence Eppolito and Caracappa may have provided to Anthony Casso, it was a *secondary* source compared to what he could have gotten from Gregory Scarpa Sr., who was a trusted Top Echelon FBI informant.

Exposing the Agent Provocateur

By November 1994, the work done by defense attorneys Alan Futerfas and Ellen Resnick in peeling back the layers on the Scarpa-DeVecchio relationship was taking a serious toll on the war prosecutions. Selwyn Raab reported in the *New York Times* that Lin DeVecchio was being investigated by the Bureau "to determine if he leaked information to Mr. Scarpa about mob rivals and pending arrests."[36]

Raab quoted DeVecchio's lawyer Douglas Grover as calling the allegations "ridiculous and pure nonsense" but also took note—for the first time in the media—of the "assertions by defense lawyers that the F.B.I. used Mr. Scarpa as an agent provocateur to provoke a war among factions in the Colombo family and thereby provide evidence for indictments." Raab quoted Grover as saying that DeVecchio was "angry and annoyed . . . because he knows he is going to be completely cleared." But he also reported that, on November 10, defense attorney Alan Futerfas had asked Judge Charles P. Sifton for a hearing to determine if "34's" informant files should be released.

In his pleadings, Futerfas asserted what was now the emerging defense theory about the third Colombo war: that the government had "turned a blind eye to Scarpa's activities" in a plan "to create and further a divisive conflict which would enable the FBI to make, it hoped, dozens of arrests and convictions."

By the following spring, the stage was set for Futerfas to make that argument in front of a jury in the trial of Vic Orena Jr., his brother John, and five other defendants indicted on murder conspiracy and related racketeering charges.[37] But before the trial even began, Valerie Caproni, who was supervising the war prosecutions, and Ellen Corcella, the lead prosecutor in the Orena brothers' case, were forced to make stunning admissions about the nature of the intelligence that may have gone to Scarpa Sr. from celebrated Supervisory Special Agent Lin DeVecchio.

Chapter 37

INSANE MAD-DOG KILLER

By April 12, 1995, a month before the Orena brothers' trial, Valerie Caproni, the EDNY criminal division chief who had been so outspoken about the FBI's handling of the DEA indictment leak in 1987, issued a sworn affirmation in which she made some surprising admissions. As far back as January 27, 1994—ten days after Favo and the other agents first approached ASAC Donald North—Caproni had successfully lobbied Supervisory Special Agents Thomas Fuentes and Jack Barrett, who were first assigned to the DeVecchio OPR, to delay their interviews of CWs. The agreement was that they would hold off for at least six weeks, pending the war prosecutions.[1] Given the impact that the disclosures in the OPR might have had on juries, Caproni not only asked Barrett and Fuentes to delay their investigation but insisted that AUSAs be present when any cooperating witnesses, like Larry Mazza, were interviewed.[2]

"There's little doubt," says defense attorney Ellen Resnick, "that tactic was designed to contain the potential damage to the government that the CW's statements might inflict at trial."[3]

Now, in her sworn affirmation—in a move that might be interpreted as an effort to deflect criticism that she had acted to slow the OPR investigation—Caproni stated that as early as March 1994 Fuentes and Barrett were no longer working on the investigation.[4] Since SSA Robert O'Brien from DC then took over the OPR,[5] Caproni said, "From that point on, the pace of the investigation was essentially dictated by the schedule of . . . O'Brien and not by trial schedules of CWs or AUSAs."

Having issued those disclaimers, Caproni nonetheless went on to state, under penalty of perjury, that "there is some reason to believe" the following leaks occurred:

A. In 1987, DeVecchio told Scarpa that the DEA planned to arrest Gregory Scarpa, Jr. and his crew. This information was conveyed in advance of the arrests and led to Scarpa, Jr., becoming a fugitive. Further, Scarpa correctly knew that law enforcement believed that Cosmo Catanzano was a "weak link," who might cooperate with authorities if arrested;

B. On or about February 27, 1992, DeVecchio told Scarpa that Carmine Imbriale was cooperating with law enforcement;

C. During the Colombo Family war, DeVecchio provided Scarpa with information on at least one member of the Orena faction who had a hit team that was looking for members of the Persico faction;

D. Following the arrest of Joseph Ambrosino, DeVecchio informed Scarpa that although there were arrest warrants outstanding for Lawrence Mazza and James Del Masto (two of Scarpa's closest associates), if they stayed away from their normal "hangouts," they could avoid being arrested (as supervisor of C-10, DeVecchio could control who was assigned to find the fugitives Mazza and Del Masto and how extensive that agent's efforts would be);

E. In or around January 1992, DeVecchio told Scarpa that it was believed that Orena was staying at his girlfriend's house, the location of which (as then known by law enforcement) was also conveyed;

F. In or around January 1992, DeVecchio told Scarpa the address of the house in which Salvatore Miciotta, an Orena faction captain, was residing; and

G. In early 1992, DeVecchio provided Scarpa subscriber information for telephone numbers of two of Scarpa's loan shark customers.

Additionally, in the mid to late 1980's Scarpa had information that his social club was subject to court ordered electronic surveillance and that he would soon be arrested on charges involving dealing with fraudulent credit cards. It is believed that the source of that information was also DeVecchio.[6]

Later in that sworn affirmation, Caproni made the extraordinary admission that "DeVecchio may have personally wished for the Persico side of the war to be victorious."[7] Here was the chief criminal prosecutor in the Eastern District effectively embracing Chris Favo's view of DeVecchio's "We're going to win this thing!" cry: "Mr. Organized Crime" was a cheerleader for one of the Mafia factions in the bloody conflict that left at least a dozen dead.

Finally, in her affirmation Caproni wrote, "Because OPR conducted a criminal investigation, Agent DeVecchio was not compelled to submit to an interview. Last fall, however, he was asked to appear voluntarily [but] ultimately DeVecchio declined."[8]

Although the OPR investigators couldn't prevent DeVecchio from taking the Fifth, his reputation as the preeminent organized crime agent in the New York Office was at stake. Also, as Judge Jack B. Weinstein later noted, DeVecchio faced "serious criminal charges and certainly civil and administrative charges" as a result of the allegations surrounding his relationship with Scarpa.[9] "So, concluding that Lin might have to testify in future war trials," says Flora Edwards, "the Justice Department made the extraordinary decision to grant him immunity."[10]

To make that happen, according to section 13-6.2 of the FBI's *Manual of Administrative Operations and Procedures,* the OPR Inspection Division had to determine whether the "the allegations, if true, would have potential" for DeVecchio's criminal prosecution. Once that determination was made, Lin was allowed to sign a Form FD-645, captioned "Warning and Assurance to Employee Required to Provide Information."[11] After he had signed it, any potentially incriminating statement he made would be inadmissible in any future criminal prosecution, state or federal. That

effective grant of immunity ended up having enormous consequences
down the line. As we'll see, the FD-645, which DeVecchio acknowledged
signing,[12] effectively prevented the DOJ from prosecuting him based on
anything he said relating to the OPR charges—and it almost derailed the
Brooklyn DA's murder case against him even before the start of the trial
in 2007.

DeVecchio's Version of Events

On May 5, 1995, DeVecchio made his "compelled statement" to Supervisory Special Agent O'Brien. Throughout the twenty-eight-page statement,
DeVecchio professed his innocence of the OPR allegations. It's notable,
however, that he made several admissions that bore on his credibility.

First, he stated that before reopening Scarpa in 1980, he conducted a
"review" that determined that Scarpa "had been opened as an informant
early in the 1960s." He even identified Scarpa's previous FBI contacting
agents, giving their names (though they were redacted).

If Lin had read "34's" file dating back to the 1960s it's difficult to understand why he would continue to deny that Scarpa was a captain. As noted
previously, as early as June 18, 1962, an airtel sent to J. Edgar Hoover on a
debriefing of Scarpa identified him as "a Caporegima [*sic*] in the JOSEPH
PROFACI family"[13] (see Appendix D). But in his memoir, Lin states
emphatically that "34" was "never a capo."

> He later confided in me that he would never agree to be a capo because it
> would draw too much attention to himself. He remained a soldier.[14]

How could DeVecchio have reached that conclusion when even the OPR
documents identify "34" as "COLOMBO LCN CAPO GREGORY
SCARPA SR."[15] But Scarpa's status in the family was only one of the assertions in DeVecchio's compelled statement that raised questions. After
describing his unique one-on-one relationship with the Top Echelon informant, DeVecchio went on to discuss how he met Scarpa at least once a
month, and on some occasions "a few times per week."

They met in various locations in New York City and on "one or two occasions" in New Jersey. He admitted to multiple phone contacts with Greg via the "Hello" phone, but he stated to SSA O'Brien that Scarpa "never made any emergency calls to" him.[16]

That assertion conflicts with the statement that AUSA George Stamboulidis made to O'Brien and SSA Kevin Donovan on September 9, 1994, when he described the 1992 incident in which NYPD detectives saw Scarpa tossing a gun from his car and said Scarpa was so worried about a possible arrest that he contacted DeVecchio "in a panic."[17]

Continuing in his compelled statement and asserting that the code name he and Scarpa used for each other was "Dello," Lin then wrote, "Scarpa Sr. never told me that he referred to me as the 'Girlfriend.' "[18]

DeVecchio then stated emphatically that Linda Schiro "was never in a position close enough to have overheard anything we discussed." But that allegation was contradicted by multiple cooperating witnesses, including Carmine Sessa, Larry Mazza, and Billy Meli, who told OPR investigators how Scarpa "would talk about all kinds of criminal efforts including murders, right in Schiro's presence"—most notably the Joe Brewster murder the night it happened.[19]

Later in the statement, DeVecchio admitted that he "did make an official contact with Judge I. Leo Glasser" on Scarpa's behalf in the 1986 credit card case and that "the contact was endorsed by the FBI and AUSA Norman Bloch, who approached Judge Glasser on behalf of Scarpa Sr." That intervention resulted in Scarpa's getting a sentence of probation.[20]

But in that instance DeVecchio's sworn statement conflicted with his testimony under oath during Michael Sessa's war trial of November 1992, when he told defense attorney Gavin Scotti that he had never intervened to help an informant get "back on the street" in return for helping the FBI.[21]

On the next page of his compelled statement, Lin seemed either disingenuous or downright clueless about Scarpa's drug-dealing activities. "I had no idea that Scarpa Sr. or Scarpa Jr. were involved in drug distribution," he said. "It was my understanding that the Colombo Family had a disdain for drugs."[22]

"You have to ask," says Flora Edwards, "how DeVecchio's own CI, Scarpa Sr., is grossing seventy thousand dollars a week selling marijuana and cocaine in a Staten Island drug ring and Lin somehow misses that. It's just not believable that DeVecchio was that incompetent, especially when you consider that he was running two FBI organized crime squads."[23]

Indeed, former AUSA John Kroger, who prosecuted Greg Scarpa Jr., among others, theorizes in his own book that DeVecchio may have fallen prey to what he calls "moral capture." Kroger writes that agents like DeVecchio who run informants like Scarpa "spend so much time living in the underworld with crooks and crooked informants, they come to adopt [their] perspective." He concludes, "It is possible that happened to DeVecchio as well. But only he knows for sure."[24]

In the next several pages of his statement, DeVecchio proceeded to deny, point by point, each of the disclosures made by Valerie Caproni three weeks earlier in her sworn affidavit regarding his possible leaks to Scarpa. He then blamed the revelations of intelligence on "sources in law enforcement, in police departments and prosecutor's offices."

Then, in a stunning suggestion that the leaks to Scarpa had come from Detective Joe Simone, he wrote, "The Colombo Family war investigations resulted in charging a New York police officer with providing information."[25] At that point—early May 1995—DeVecchio surely knew that Simone had been entirely vindicated by a federal jury more than six months earlier. But even though he feigned sympathy for Simone in his 2011 book, in this 1995 compelled statement he was clearly hinting that Simone was the source of the leaks.

On the next page, DeVecchio made an interesting admission that pointed to the inaccuracies in many of his Scarpa 209s. He wrote, "I knew Larry Lampesi [sic] was a Colombo Family member but he was not very active. I do not believe that Lampesi [sic] was a prime player in our investigations."

Interestingly, just two years into his tenure as Scarpa's contacting agent, DeVecchio filed the following 209 with Washington on a debriefing he'd had with Scarpa on October 18, 1982:

Source advised that "Nick Black" Grancio has become more active in the Colombo family illegal activities, particularly with Dominick Montemarano, and was in on the hit of John Aratico who was shot in front of his house on 21st Avenue Brooklyn New York in April, 1982. The source noted *that Aratico* was *the stepson of the late Colombo member Larry Lam-pasi.**26

Apart from the fact that Scarpa was blaming Nicholas Grancio for a murder he claimed was committed with "Donnie Shacks" Montemarano, DeVecchio's reference to "the late" Larry Lampasi came ten years *before* he was shot to death in front of his house by Scarpa, Mazza, and Del Masto. "When you read that," said Andrew Orena, "you come back to that same old question. Did Lin know that Scarpa Sr. was lying to him through his teeth? If he did, did he care?"27

"An Unusual Twist"

Three days after DeVecchio submitted his sworn OPR statement, the trial of seven Colombo members, including Vic Orena Jr. and his brother John, began in EDNY federal court before Judge Edward R. Korman. In advance of the trial, Korman, who later served as chief judge of the Eastern District,28 ordered the Feds to provide the defense with details of the possible leaks from DeVecchio to "34," since they clearly amounted to "Brady material." The result was a two-page letter from lead prosecutor Ellen Corcella to Gerald Shargel, Alan Futerfas, and the five other attorneys representing the battery of defendants.

As Selwyn Raab reported in the *Times,* "In an unusual twist that could damage the government's campaign against the Colombo crime family, Federal prosecutors in Brooklyn said yesterday that an F.B.I. agent had for years disclosed confidential information to a high-ranking member of that Mafia group. . . . In effect, the prosecutors indicated that while Mr. Scarpa was a mole for the Federal Bureau of Investigation inside the Mafia, he was also getting potentially valuable information from Mr. DeVecchio."29

Corcella's letter echoed the earlier sworn affidavit of Valerie Caproni. Curiously, it was originally dated May 2, three days *before* Lin's statement, but when the letter reached the defense lawyers, the typed date had been

---

* Emphasis added.

scratched out and the date of the trial's commencement, May 8, was written in by hand. Because the letter represents such an extraordinary series of admissions by the government, we're reproducing it here in its entirety:

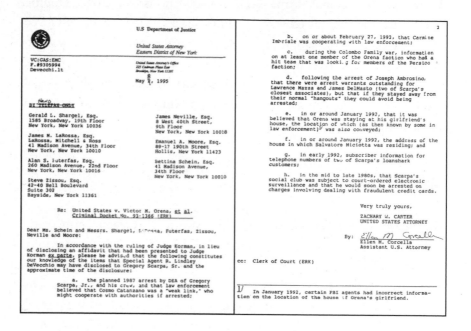

At an earlier hearing, Judge Korman had shaken his head in disapproval of DeVecchio's alleged conduct, declaring that Scarpa's control agent "had certainly crossed the line by a fairly wide mark."[30] Now, in a May 10 story on Corcella's letter, Douglas Grover, Lin's attorney, told the *Daily News*, "It's a disgrace that the government has allowed these allegations to fester for so long without resolving them."[31]

In his opening statement at the Orena brothers' trial, Gerry Shargel, who represented Vic Jr., called Scarpa "an insane mad dog killer" who used the Colombo war as an excuse for settling private scores with his enemies.[32] Referring to the gang war as a "sham," Shargel told the jury that Scarpa "shaped the FBI's investigation by deciding what information to feed to DeVecchio."[33] Calling DeVecchio a "rogue agent," Shargel argued that "the idea that this was a war with two sides is nonsense. This war was sparked and fomented, believe it or not, by a special agent of the FBI."[34]

Clearly the defense's strategy was to put Lin DeVecchio on trial—and, if Ellen Corcella's opening statement was any indication, it was working.

Corcella actually hinted that DeVecchio might someday face criminal charges. "Don't get distracted," she told jurors. "We are not here to try an FBI agent.[35] . . . You are not here to determine if Agent DeVecchio was incompetent or guilty of venality or if Scarpa compromised DeVecchio. He'll get his day in court."[36]

The next day, it was Orena defense lawyer Alan Futerfas's turn. Futerfas reminded the jury of Scarpa's extraordinary run as a TE informant. "He's committed oodles of crimes and . . . was he told [by the Bureau], 'We don't want you. We don't want to mess with the likes of you'? No. The silence, ladies and gentlemen, was deafening."[37]

After nearly two months of trial, given the first opportunity to expose jurors to the full truth behind the Scarpa-DeVecchio relationship, which he termed "a Faustian pact," Futerfas argued that DeVecchio *must* have known that his star source was committing crimes.

"This is a Machiavellian scenario but it's a true scenario. . . . This isn't fiction," he said in his summation. "DeVecchio is a thirty-year agent for the FBI. He taught informant development. . . . He's been around the block. This is a seasoned agent. He knew just what he was doing. He knows what happens when you let Scarpa loose, when you give him information about people you want him to kill. Favo knew what would happen. Because when DeVecchio told Scarpa that Imbriale was an informant Favo went and said, 'You can't do that. Scarpa will kill him.' And is it a mere coincidence . . . that the man, Scarpa, who had this corrupt relationship with DeVecchio, is the same man who's the most prolific killer and provocateur in this so-called conflict?"[38]

The best that Ellen Corcella could offer in response was to plead with the jury not to turn the proceedings "into the trial of the FBI and Lin DeVecchio rather than a trial about the defendants." She warned them not to think that with "a verdict of guilty everyone will forget DeVecchio's misdeed. This is not so, ladies and gentlemen. Do not let them lay Lin DeVecchio at the United States Attorneys' Office feet, because I will not accept that."[39]

Then, clearly sensing that the jury had bought the defense's arguments about the alleged "unholy alliance" between the SSA and his source, Corcella told jurors that their verdict was "not in any way going to cover up Lin DeVecchio's actions. You are not going to let the FBI escape embarrassment. . . . Regardless of what your verdict says, there are legal ways to deal with the problem of Lin DeVecchio."[40]

"That's when we had a sense that we'd won it," Shargel told me in an interview.[41] "Ellen Corcella had actually become a member of the defense team. That's how shocked the jury was at the evidence of this unbelievable misconduct by DeVecchio."

"Black Eye for the FBI"

That was the boldfaced page-one headline in *Newsday* the day after the jury came in on July 1. "7 Acquitted in Mob Case," ran the subhead. "Brooklyn Jury Says Federal Agent Fueled Mob Feud." The story on the inside ran under the banner headline "FBI Guilty." Reporters Joseph A. Gambardello and Patricia Hurtado noted that this was "the fourth defeat for Brooklyn federal prosecutors in a Colombo family case and the second in which Colombo captain Gregory Scarpa's ghost dealt the fatal blow."[42]

Juror No. 186 told the reporters that "the defendants were a group of guys trying to keep themselves alive" while "Scarpa was running free doing what he wanted to do," including murder. "It was him [Scarpa] who made it seem like a war," said Juror 238. "It was a bit scary," she said. "That the FBI was feeding information to anyone so deadly," Juror 180 chimed in.[43]

A *Daily News* piece by Greg B. Smith the same day listed the war trials scorecard. Of the seventy-five initial indictments, sixteen Colombo defendants had been acquitted and forty convicted, "including five who've demanded new trials."[44] Smith also reported that, with the clearing of his sons, Vic Orena Sr. was now going to petition the Feds for a new trial as well. In a *New York Post* piece, Al Guarte quoted Gerry Shargel as saying that "the jurors were all just absolutely shocked by the testimony about the relationship between DeVecchio and Scarpa."[45]

That trial was as close as Lin DeVecchio would ever come to a guilty verdict. But now the stakes were enormous for the Feds. Quoted in a *New York Times* piece the next day, James Kallstrom, the ADIC of the FBI's New York Office, cautioned that "no conclusions should be drawn concerning the allegations against Mr. DeVecchio until the internal inquiry is completed." He noted that DeVecchio had not been suspended or demoted and that his salary of $105,000 a year had not been cut.[46]

James Kallstrom, former ADIC, FBI, New York Office

But as we've pointed out, the OPR would drag on for another nine months before Kallstrom sent the memo to FBI Director Louis Freeh warning him that if the probe continued it would "have a serious negative impact on the government's prosecutions of various LCN figures in the EDNY and cast a cloud over the NYO."[47]

As former EDNY AUSA John Kroger admitted in his book, "The Scarpa Senior–DeVecchio scandal derailed the government's assault on the Colombo Family."[48]

And what about Ellen Corcella's promise to the jury that Lin would see his day in court? If he was going to be prosecuted, the senior AUSA who had to make that happen was Corcella's boss, Valerie Caproni. The question was, would Caproni press for a no-holds-barred investigation of DeVecchio, or would she circle the wagons in an effort to contain the potential damage to her war prosecutions?

On July 17, 1995, two weeks after charges against the Orena brothers were dismissed, Caproni was contacted by phone and asked to answer questions submitted by the Public Integrity Section (PIS) of the Justice Department "concerning allegations against . . . SSA R. Lindley DeVecchio."[49]

One of the questions submitted to Caproni by a PIS attorney was "DO YOU HAVE INFORMATION ABOUT SSA DEVECCHIO THAT YOU INTEND TO USE TO INDICT OR PROSECUTE HIM?"[50]

Keep in mind that as recently as April 12, three months earlier, Caproni had disclosed eight probable leaks from DeVecchio to Scarpa. During the Orena brothers' trial, Corcella had promised the jury that Lin would "get his day in court."[51] Yet now Caproni passed the ball back to Justice, telling the Public Integrity Section that "any prosecution of SSA DeVecchio was now up to the PIS, DOJ."[52]

Meanwhile, throughout the summer of 1995, as DeVecchio's OPR investigation continued, Valerie Caproni did her best to minimize the impact the probe might have on those ongoing war prosecutions. She sent a letter dated July 24, 1995, to Ralph Regalbuto Jr., a supervisory special agent in the Office of Professional Responsibility in Washington, which she termed "the first installment of mark-ups of 302s prepared during the OPR."

> In this group, I am sending back my 302s, as well as a memorandum that is based largely on certain conversations I had with various agents, and the 302 of George Stamboulidis. Andrew Weissmann's 302 should be marked up shortly, and I hope to have the 302s of the cooperating witnesses available by the end of the week.[53]

That package from Caproni contained multiple pages of 302s memorializing her OPR debriefings and those of AUSAs George Stamboulidis and Andrew Weissmann. Virtually every page contained Caproni's handwritten comments. Many were heavily redacted.

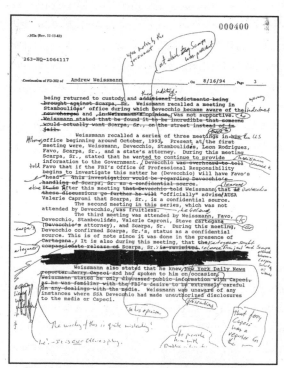

FBI 302 of Assistant U.S. Attorney Andrew Weissmann, with handwritten notes by Valerie Caproni, head of the EDNY Criminal Division

"Valerie Caproni had succeeded in getting the OPR delayed and getting assistant U.S. attorneys to sit in with the cooperating witnesses to contain whatever damage they might do to the war prosecutions," says Flora Edwards. "I don't know how you can look upon her editing of the 302s in any other way than as a further effort to interfere. The FBI agents who interviewed Caproni,

Weissmann, and Stamboulidis were supervisors in the Bureau. Experienced investigators. They wrote the 302s based on what they had been told and now here was Caproni coming in and seemingly trying to rewrite them."[54]

In the page reproduced opposite, from Weissmann's August 16, 1994, debriefing, Caproni crossed out Weissmann's comment that he found it "incredible that someone [i.e., DeVecchio] would actually want Scarpa Sr. on the Street instead of jail."

Now, by early September 1996, with the Feds' grant of immunity ensuring that DeVecchio would never be convicted for the alleged crimes that had prompted the OPR investigation, the writing was on the wall. Despite the shocking revelations of misconduct uncovered during the thirty-one-month-long investigation, and the admissions two separate federal prosecutors had made regarding DeVecchio's alleged leaks, the chief of the Justice Department's Public Integrity Section, Criminal Division, informed Lin's attorney Douglas Grover, "We have determined that prosecution of SSA DeVecchio in this matter is not warranted."[55]

The OPR was closed. No indictment, no prosecution. And Lin DeVecchio retired from the FBI with a full pension.

Chapter 38

ORGANIZED CRIME
AND TERRORISM

The Feds wasted no time in rebounding from their loss in the trial of the Orena brothers. Six days after the "Black Eye for the FBI" headline appeared on the front page of *Newsday,* the *New York Times* ran a piece headed "New Indictment for Reputed Colombo Crime Family Captain."[1] As if to distance itself from charges that the Bureau had been sleeping with the enemy for more than three decades in its relationship with Greg Scarpa Sr., this story heralded a new indictment for his son Greg Jr., whom the *Times* described as having a life that "reads like a script from a gangster soap opera."

Greg Jr., then forty-three, was already serving a twenty-year sentence for racketeering stemming from the 1987 DEA case. Now the EDNY was charging that since 1980, the younger Scarpa had led a thirteen-member crew that had committed a series of felonies, including fifteen murders.[2]

Virtually every crime in the indictment was for a mob-related activity allegedly committed by Greg Jr. on behalf of his father during the period when Senior was being "controlled" by Lin DeVecchio. At least two of the crew members named in the indictment, Kevin Granato and Robert Zambardi, had been part of Senior's Wimpy Boys crew. Bobby Zam was also part of Carmine Sessa's would-be hit team that made the first move on Vic Orena Sr. at the start of the war that Greg Sr. fomented.

And, as if to visit the sins of the father upon the son, two of the war murders—those of Gaetano Amato and Vincent Fusaro—were included in the indictment even though they were executed solely by Greg Sr. while his son was *in prison*.[3]

The al-Qaeda Sting

Considering that his father committed many of the crimes for which Greg Jr. was being charged, the indictment indicated a double standard for the Justice Department. But the younger Scarpa also gave the FBI a tremendous opportunity. As fate would have it, in the spring of 1996, while housed on the ninth-floor tier of the Metropolitan Correctional Center (MCC), the federal jail in Lower Manhattan, he was placed in a cell in between two world-class Islamic terrorists.

On one side was Ramzi Ahmed Yousef, the al-Qaeda bomb maker, who I

proved in my book *1000 Years for Revenge*[4] was not only responsible for the 1993 World Trade Center bombing but also was the architect of the "planes as missiles" plot executed on September 11, 2001, by his uncle

**Ramzi Ahmed Yousef, Greg Scarpa Jr.,
Abdul Hakim Murad**

Khalid Sheikh Mohammed (KSM).* On the other side of Greg Jr.'s cell was Yousef's lifelong friend Abdul Hakim Murad, a pilot trained in four U.S. flight schools, who was to be the lead pilot in the original configuration of what was called "the planes operation," as Yousef had conceived it in Manila in the fall of 1994.[5] Finally, in a nearby cell was Eyad Ismoil, Yousef's codefendant in an upcoming trial for the Twin Towers bombing.

---

* New evidence corroborating that conclusion is contained in the Afterword.

Murad had first met Yousef in the early 1980s at a mosque in the Kuwaiti city of Fahaheel on the Persian Gulf, where they both grew up.[6] By 1991 Murad had attended the Emirates Flying School in Dubai, where he got his single-engine private pilot's license.

On November 19, 1991, as the Colombo war was just beginning to heat up, Murad flew to Washington. Over the next eight months he attended four separate U.S. flight schools: Alpha Tango in San Antonio, Texas;[7] the Richmor Aviation Flight School in Schenectady, New York; Coastal Aviation in New Bern, North Carolina, where he got his multiengine license on June 6, 1992; and the California Aeronautical Institute in Red Bluff, California.[8]

When he passed through Manhattan in 1992, Murad performed a visual inspection of the World Trade Center.[9] Later, he would boast to a Philippine interrogator that *he* had initially chosen the Twin Towers as a target for Yousef.[10] After a fire in their Manila bomb factory in early January 1995, Murad was captured and interrogated by Colonel Rodolfo B. Mendoza of the Philippine National Police.

Right after the fire, Yousef and KSM fled to Islamabad, Pakistan. Yousef was eventually captured and rendered back to New York, but FBI agents arrived at the arrest site late. KSM, who hung around long enough to give an interview to a reporter using his real name, then escaped.[11] By 1996, Yousef and Murad—also rendered back to New York—were on trial in what the Feds called the "Manila Air bombing case."[12] It involved a fiendish plot by Yousef to smuggle a series of improvised explosive devices (IEDs) on board a dozen U.S. airliners leaving Asia for America.[13]

Two months before his capture, Yousef had performed what he called "a wet test" with a nitroglycerine-based device linked to a Casio watch timer. After Yousef planted it aboard the first leg of Philippine Airlines Flight 434 on December 11, 1994, the IED blew a hole in the fuselage of the 747, barely missing the jumbo jet's fuel tank. Before the full plot was aborted by his capture, Yousef planned to hide similar devices on up to twelve airliners, with a potential death toll in the thousands.

By the early summer of 1996, the Feds were prepping to try Yousef for this Casio-nitro bomb plot, which the terrorist had dubbed "Bojinka," a name reportedly derived from the Serbo-Croatian for "explosion" or "loud bang."[14]

After escaping from the custody of the Philippine National Police in early 1995, a fourth co-conspirator, Wali Khan Amin Shah, had also been captured and rendered back to the United States. He would stand trial with Yousef and Murad, with jury selection set to begin in late May 1996.[15] The fourth member of the Manila cell, Khalid Sheikh Mohammed, was still at large, living secretly in Doha, Qatar, plotting to execute his nephew Yousef's separate airliner hijacking plot.

Now, as the trial approached in late winter of 1996, federal prosecutors were obliged under Brady rules to disclose the sum of their case to the defense. So Yousef, who was representing himself pro se, was well aware that Murad's confession to Colonel Mendoza in the Philippines would almost ensure a conviction.[16]

"Yousef believed that Scarpa, being allegedly in the Mafia, was a person who was anti-government," says Larry Silverman, Greg Jr.'s lawyer at the time.[17] "And since Yousef's whole philosophy was anti–U.S. government, they seemed to develop a relationship."

At some point in March, Yousef broke a bed strut away from the wall of his cell, creating a hole, and started passing tiny rolled-up notes, which he called "kites," through Greg Jr. to Murad, who had similarly broken a hole in the wall adjacent to Junior's cell.[18] Scarpa Jr. hoped that spying on Yousef for the Feds might earn him a fraction of the support from the FBI that his father had enjoyed, if not a reduction in charges or, at minimum, some "downward release time" under Rule 5K1.1 of the Federal Rules of Criminal Procedure.[19]

As soon as Greg Jr. passed word to the FBI through Silverman that he was getting notes from al-Qaeda's chief bomb maker, the Bureau sprang into action. The Feds took him so seriously that they gave him a tiny camera to photograph the kites and even supplied an FBI agent, posing as a paralegal named "Susan Schwartz," to retrieve the film.[20]

The initiative began a month before James Kallstrom sent the memo to Louis Freeh urging that the DOJ reach a conclusion in DeVecchio's OPR. Kallstrom later sought to explain the memo, denying that he had been pushing for an early termination of the DeVecchio investigation.

"What I was saying," Kallstrom told an interviewer, "was 'Look, the investigation has been going on for years. Let's get it looked at.' It had nothing to do with a whitewash of the investigation."[21] But a new document, uncovered in this investigation, raises questions about Kallstrom's insistence that the FBI wasn't trying to contain the damage to the war cases that would arise from the Scarpa-DeVecchio scandal. On the very same day the memo went out to Louis Freeh, another communiqué was sent to the FBI director that showed up in DeVecchio's OPR file.

Although the memo is heavily redacted, it's clear that Kallstrom (the ADIC) was worried that what he called "the DelVecchio [sic]/Scarpa Sr. relationship" might have a negative impact on the prosecution of Greg Jr. and other adjudicated war cases, such as Vic Orena Sr.'s. Further, in his concern that the continued OPR investigation was "unfair to SSA DelVecchio [sic]," Kallstrom appears to demonstrate a bias in favor of Lin. For the first time, this memo documents that the New York Office of the FBI had been "pressing for a resolution" of the DeVecchio OPR "for over a year."[22]

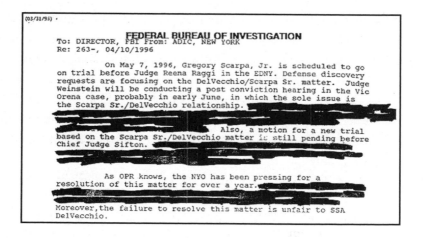

The memo, to Director Louis Freeh, was dated just weeks after Junior started the Yousef sting. So now, while one arm of the Justice Department—the Eastern District in Brooklyn, led by Valerie Caproni—was working to convict Greg Jr. on additional charges, the Organized Crime and Terrorism Unit in the Southern District (Manhattan) was using him as an informant to gather intelligence on a world-class terrorist.

It was in that context that Greg Scarpa Jr., like his father before him, became a mole for the FBI.

"How to Blow Up Airplanes"

By mid-May 1996, Ramzi Yousef started passing notes threatening to have his "people" put a bomb on a plane to get "a mistrial."* One kite was entitled "How to Smuggle Explosives into an Airplane."[23] The Bureau considered Yousef's threats so alarming that FBI agents met with Larry Silverman and his client at least once a week to debrief Scarpa Sr. Their interviews were memorialized in a series of FBI 302 memos.

In April 2004, while writing *Cover Up,* my second book on al-Qaeda terrorism prior to 9/11, I received dozens of these 302s and many of Yousef's kites from Angela Clemente, the forensic investigator whose Freedom of Information lawsuit led to the release of the Greg Scarpa Sr. files. Angela had been looking into Scarpa Jr.'s case pro bono in the winter of 2004 when he passed the documents to her during a visit to ADX Florence, the Supermax prison in Colorado, where he was incarcerated.

When I reviewed the documents—which included details of Yousef's various Manila plots that had not yet surfaced in the mainstream press by the spring of 1996—it was clear to me that Greg Jr. had opened up a significant pipeline to al-Qaeda's most deadly bomb maker. Consider the following excerpts from a 302 dated March 5, 1996:

> YOUSEF told SCARPA I'll teach you how to blow up airplanes and how to make bombs and then you can get the information to your people (meaning Scarpa's people on the outside). YOUSEF told SCARPA I can show you how to get a bomb on an airplane through a metal detector. YOUSEF told SCARPA he would teach him how to make timing devices. . . . YOUSEF told SCARPA that during the trial they had a plan to blow up a plane and hurt a judge or an attorney so a mistrial will be declared.[24]

In that same 302, FBI agents uncovered evidence of an al-Qaeda cell loyal to Yousef that was then active in New York City.

---

* A number of the FBI 302s documenting Scarpa's sting of Yousef can be downloaded from http://www.peterlance.com/PLfbi.htm.

According to SCARPA, YOUSEF has indicated that he has four people here. SCARPA described these four terrorists already here in the United States. SCARPA advised YOUSEF has not indicated who these four individuals are or if he is in contact with these four people or how he contacts them. SCARPA does not know if YOUSEF receives or sends any messages from contacts overseas.

That revelation about the "four terrorists" should have caused shock waves in the FBI's New York Office, because after the 1995 conviction of Blind Sheikh Omar Abdel Rahman and nine other terrorists linked to the plot to blow up the bridges and tunnels into Manhattan—the so-called Day of Terror plot—the conventional wisdom was that the FBI had eliminated the Islamic terror threat to New York City.[25]

By late May 1996, Greg Jr. had also uncovered Yousef's threats to kill federal judge Kevin Duffy, who was about to preside at the Bojinka trial, and Mike Garcia, the AUSA who would be co-prosecutor along with AUSA Dietrich Snell.[26] The Feds took those threats so seriously that they got protection for both targets.

By April, the quality of the Yousef–to–Scarpa Jr. intel was so good that the FBI decided to take the initiative to a new level, setting up Roma Corp., a phony mob front company, allowing the government to monitor Yousef's calls.

Ostensibly located in the historic Flatiron Building, Roma Corp. was an ingenious sting. "The idea was to create a fictitious company that was supposedly a Mafia-run organization," says Silverman. "Yousef would make calls to that organization. They would then patch through his telephone calls to parties outside of the United States, and the FBI would be able to listen in to those calls, record them, and, of course, make use of the information."[27]

Greg Jr. gave Yousef the Roma office number and conned him into believing that the operation was run by Mafiosi, when in fact FBI agents were manning the phones. Yousef was allowed to make calls to Roma Corp. from the pay phone on the ninth floor of the MCC. The Feds then forwarded the calls through to his "people"[28] in New York and abroad.[29] Thanks to the FBI, Greg Jr. even supplied Yousef with a fax number at Roma. Opposite is a copy of the note Junior passed to Yousef announcing the setup of the patch-

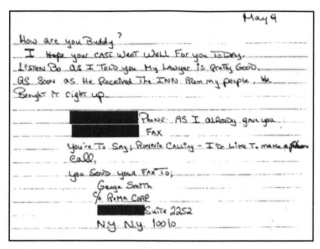

through. When the terrorist called the number, he was to identify himself as "Ronnie."

"It's difficult to describe what a bonanza of intelligence this was for the Bureau," says a former agent now retired from the NYO. "This was raw data, coming directly from bin Laden's chief bomb maker, who we would later learn played a key role in designing the 9/11 plot."[30] The Roma Corp. patch-through would soon hand the New York–based FBI agents a second chance to nab Khalid Sheikh Mohammed, Yousef's uncle, as he hid out in Qatar.[31]

Once the Feds identified KSM's presence there, the FBI's elite Hostage Rescue Team was dispatched to Doha, the capital, for the takedown, but were told to cool their heels in a hotel while the Qataris "put the handcuffs on" KSM. Then, a day later, when the agents finally went to a safe house where KSM had been hiding, he had already fled to the Czech Republic, using the alias Mustafa al Nasir.[32]

The "Scarpa Materials"

Despite the loss of KSM in Doha, as the Bojinka trial got under way in the Southern District of New York against Yousef and two of his co-conspirators, Greg Scarpa Jr. continued feeding Bureau agents a constant stream of intelligence. Among the many revelations contained in the FBI 302s was a plot disclosed by Yousef in which Osama bin Laden, whom he code-named "Bojinga," would arrange the hijacking of a series of U.S. airliners in order to free the Blind Sheikh, Yousef, and his Manila cohorts.[33]

That intelligence alone was considered so important that it turned up in the infamous Presidential Daily Briefing (PDB) delivered to George W. Bush in Crawford, Texas, five weeks before the 9/11 attacks.[34]

The trove of intel contained in the dozens of FBI 302 memos memorializing Scarpa Jr.'s initiative from March 1996 through February 1997 was virtually self-authenticating. For example, in May 1996, Greg Jr. obtained this schematic of Yousef's Casio-nitro IED from the Philippine Airlines bombing plot and passed it to the FBI.

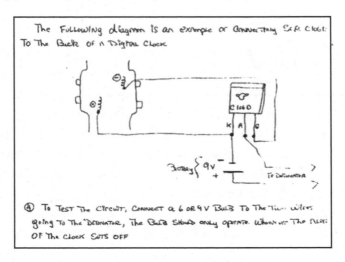

The drawing contained a detail that only the bomb maker could have known about at that time: the C106D semiconductor that Yousef had soldered into each of his "bomb triggers." During testimony in the Bojinka trial, the Feds would later describe that as Yousef's unique "signature." But that information wasn't disclosed by the Feds publicly until August

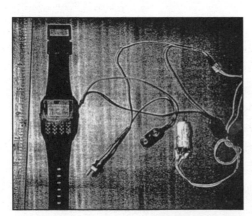

26, 1996, three months *after* Junior passed it to the FBI.[35] Apart from Ramzi Yousef, there was simply no way that Greg Jr. could have come into possession of that singular intelligence.

Any doubt as to the authenticity of the evidence can be dispelled by comparing the schematic to the photograph at left. It was taken from the FBI lab report on items seized in a search of Room 603 at the Doña Josefa apartments in Manila—Yousef's bomb factory. The systems are virtually identical.[36]

Discrediting Scarpa Jr.

In his 1998 trial, Greg Scarpa Jr.'s defense would be that the RICO violations he was charged with were the result of crimes that had effectively been sanctioned by Lin DeVecchio.

"At some point, personnel in the EDNY came to understand the significance of Scarpa Junior's testimony," says defense attorney Flora Edwards, who later used Greg's admissions about his father and DeVecchio in her efforts to secure a new trial for Vic Orena Sr. "Greg Junior had to be discredited. Because once he became credible about Ramzi Yousef, then he'd be credible about what he was going to say in my hearing too."[37]

There's no doubt that key officials tied to the prosecution of the war cases had direct knowledge of Greg Jr.'s intelligence initiative with Yousef. The 302 on the next page, from March 7, 1996, shows that Junior and his lawyer, Larry Silverman, discussed the sting with not only AUSAs Valerie Caproni and Ellen Corcella, and SA Howard Leadbetter II from the C-10 squad, but also Dietrich Snell, the Southern District AUSA who was about to prosecute Yousef in the Bojinka case with Mike Garcia.[38]

Also present was Senior AUSA Patrick Fitzgerald, who was co-head of the SDNY's Organized Crime and Terrorism Unit and thus straddled both the OC and counterterrorism aspects of the Scarpa Jr.–Yousef initiative.

The reams of detailed intel Greg Scarpa Jr. extracted from the bomb maker over eleven months were not only genuine, they were unique to Yousef, and of such complexity that no Mafia wiseguy with Junior's tenth-grade education could have fabricated them. On the other hand, Yousef had nothing to gain by leaking secrets if he knew that Greg Jr. was working with the Feds. The details he let slip—like the presence of his cell members in New York, the bin Laden plot to hijack planes, and the two death threats—could only have earned him additional criminal charges if the Feds had learned of them and decided to prosecute.

Then, on August 22, 1996, four months after his DeVecchio memo to Louis Freeh, James Kallstrom attended a high-level meeting in

```
                              - 1 -

                  FEDERAL BUREAU OF INVESTIGATION


                                     Date of transcription    3/7/96


          At the request of GREGORY SCARPA, JR., Date of Birth:
    August 3, 1951, he was interviewed at the Office of the United
    States Attorney, Eastern District of New York, Brooklyn, New
    York.  Present at this interview was SCARPA's Attorney, Lawrence
    Silverman, Assistant United States Attorneys (AUSA) DEITRICH
    SNELL and PATRICK FITZGERALD, Southern District of New York and
    EVELYN CORCELLA, and VALERIE CAPRONI, Chief of the Criminal
    Division, Eastern District of New York, and Special Agents PAMELA
    M. McDAID and HOWARD LEADBETTER II (FBI); and RICHARD CORAGGIO
    (INS).

          GREG SCARPA, an inmate currently housed at the
    Metropolitan Correctional Center (MCC), is presently serving a 20
    year sentence for a conviction under the RICO statute and is
    awaiting trial on eleven counts to include Conspiracy to Commit
    Murder, eleven counts of Murder, Racketeering, Extortion and
    Narcotics Violations.  The trial is scheduled for sometime in
    August.

          SCARPA voluntarily provided the following information
    on RAMZI AHMED YOUSEF and EYAD MAHMOUD ISMAIL NAJIM, both
    currently being housed in the MCC awaiting trial.
```

Washington with the FBI director. Another person in the room was Deputy Attorney General Jamie Gorelick, who went on to become one of the ten 9/11 commissioners.[39]

Shortly after that meeting, the Feds began to seek another way to explain the Yousef intel without lending credibility to Junior, a witness whose testimony could impact the fifty-nine remaining war prosecutions.

Since the evidence, now contained in dozens of FBI 302s, couldn't be ignored, the Feds came up with a new story: that it wasn't really *evidence* at all. Yousef and Scarpa had concocted it. That was the explanation given in a federal court ruling denying Ramzi Yousef's appeal of the Bojinka case.

"In late 1996," wrote the court, "the government learned from two sources that Scarpa was, in fact, colluding with Yousef and others to deceive it."[40]

It didn't seem to matter that those FBI 302s had documented death threats the terrorist made to Greg Jr. and his family, or that the wiseguy had risked his life for eleven months to "rat out" Yousef and his "people" in New York. The Feds were now taking the position that, together with Ramzi, Scarpa Jr. had made it all up.

Undermining the "Hoax and Scam" Story

The most detailed explanation of the fabrication story was contained in a June 25, 1999, sworn affirmation by then AUSA Patrick Fitzgerald. Though the affirmation remained under seal for many years, I was able to obtain a copy and published it in my previous book *Triple Cross*.* In the affirmation, Fitzgerald wrote that the government initially confirmed that some of Scarpa Jr.'s revelations "appeared to be accurate."[41]

However, Fitzgerald continued, "By late summer 1996, the government made an investigative decision that it no longer wished to pursue the investigation of Yousef using the 'patch through' telephone." Fitzgerald then went on to declare that he had "since learned information which convinced [him] that Scarpa's effort at 'cooperation' was a scam in collusion with Yousef and others. . . . In the latter part of 1996, Scarpa . . . told the government that an inmate, John Napoli, had even better access to Yousef and his colleagues than Scarpa himself."

Napoli, a former Gambino family associate who had been convicted of money laundering, arrived on the ninth floor of the MCC nearby Scarpa Jr. on December 17, 1996, more than nine months *after* Yousef started slipping kites through the cell wall to Junior. Now the Feds, through Patrick Fitzgerald, were claiming that Greg Jr. had confessed to Napoli that his work informing on Yousef was a fabrication.

That position was accepted by a series of judges. In denying a motion by Yousef's codefendant Eyad Ismoil in the second World Trade Center bombing case, Judge Kevin Duffy used the words "hoax" and "scam" to describe the 302s, which the Feds called "the Scarpa materials."

"It is now clear that Scarpa's claims were actually a hoax concocted by Scarpa and the Defendants,"[42] wrote Duffy, who concluded that "Scarpa's allegations of Yousef's threats were merely part of a ruse without any substance behind them."

In a motion opposing a new trial for Yousef, the government insisted that "Napoli understood that Yousef was aware of and a willing participant in [Scarpa's] fraud on the government."[43]

But Larry Silverman, Greg Jr.'s lawyer at the time, argues that "it couldn't possibly have been a hoax . . . because this information that [Junior] provided came forth in stages. And if at any point in any of the stages, the

---

* The full affirmation can be downloaded from http://www.peterlance.com/Fitzgerald_Affirmation_6.25.99.pdf.

information that he was providing was inaccurate or a hoax, the government would have pulled the plug at that time. They would not have given him a camera to use in an institution, which is a highly unusual event. They would not have provided monies to put in Yousef's account on Scarpa's behalf to give him the credibility. They would not have allowed Scarpa to have Yousef make telephone calls through an FBI source. All of these things . . . occurred in sequence; they all didn't occur on one day. To say that all those things were a hoax really does injustice to what information he provided."[44]

Napoli's Denial

Because the quality of the Yousef-Scarpa intelligence is a crucial issue in determining whether federal prosecutors discredited potentially probative evidence, I sought out John Napoli. In 2006, the former Gambino associate was serving a term at the Big Spring Federal Correctional Institution, a minimum-security prison located between El Paso and Dallas, Texas. On February 11, 2006, I arranged for Napoli to call me while I was in the office of his attorney, Gerald LaBush, in New York City. With Napoli's permission, I recorded the conversation—and what he told me was startling.

Napoli said that while Scarpa Jr. had asked him to testify for him in his upcoming RICO case, and offered to cut him in on the Yousef intel in return—as a means of a currying favor with the Feds—the actual intelligence initiative itself was *completely genuine*.

As a measure of his credibility, Napoli even cited Yousef's Toshiba laptop, which the Feds knew contained cryptic references to Osama bin Laden, whom Yousef had code-named "Bojinga" in his communiqués to Scarpa Jr.

My interview with Napoli, transcribed verbatim here, reads like dialogue from *The Sopranos,* complete with references to "Bojangles" (for "Bojinga") and "Saddam" (for "Osama"). But the content of his account is extremely credible.

> **Lance:** John, when they concluded at Greg's trial that the material was a hoax and a scam, they claim that you and one other witness corroborated that.
> **Napoli:** What happened was this: When I got there [to the MCC], Scarpa approached me. We became kind of friends, and he started

telling me what he was doing about cooperating with Yousef. And he had this great plan that I could testify for him, and in return that he would give me information to bring to the Southern District about Yousef. I said, "What information would that be?" And he said, "Well, they found a computer with Bojangles and they don't know the name. I never gave it to the Feds." And he told me who Bojangles was and it was Saddam bin Laden.

So I called [Assistant U.S. Attorney David] Kelly. I never said anything [to Kelly] about [Greg Jr.] giving false information. I never spoke to Ramzi. I never spoke to Ismoil. I never spoke to none of them. Zero. No conversations. Not one. And they [the Feds] said, after this is all done, that *I* came to them and I said that I was gonna go along with Scarpa's plan. At no point did [Greg Jr.] have a deal with Yousef to give false information. Yousef had no clue what Greg was doin'.

As far as my personal[ly] being there, hearing it, seeing it—anything that Yousef gave Greg *wasn't* a scam. It *wasn't* a hoax. He [Greg Jr.] wasn't trying to do *anything* with Ramzi against the government. He was legitimately trying to help them. He was giving them information.

Indeed, a timeline put together by Napoli's attorney indicates that he met with AUSA David Kelly early in 1997, around the time Scarpa Jr. ended his intelligence initiative with Yousef. Kelly, who was then Fitzgerald's partner as co-head of the Organized Crime and Terrorism Unit, went on to become the U.S. Attorney for the SDNY—the top federal prosecutor in New York City. In 2011, Fitzgerald became the U.S. Attorney for the Northern District of Illinois (Chicago) and later came to national attention as special prosecutor in the Valerie Plame CIA leak investigation.[45]

During my research for *Triple Cross,* I sent a series of questions to Fitzgerald relating to his 1999 affirmation, but through his spokesman in Chicago he declined to respond. Then, beginning in October 2007, after *Triple Cross* was published in hardcover, Fitzgerald sent the first of four letters to my publisher, HarperCollins, totaling thirty-two pages, in which he claimed that I had defamed him in the book.*

He not only demanded that we cease publication of the hardcover edi-

---

* All of which can be downloaded, along with HarperCollins's response, from http://www.peterlance.com/Fitzgerald_Libel_Claim_Letters_HCP_Response.pdf.

tion, but also that we kill the planned trade paperback edition.[46] Harper-Collins denied Fitzgerald's claim, but we undertook a twenty-month review of my research during which *Triple Cross* was entirely re-vetted.

Declaring the book "an important work of investigative journalism," HarperCollins published the trade paperback in June 2009. The new edition included twenty-six additional pages, in which most of Fitzgerald's allegations were published verbatim. His detailed assertions with respect to the 1999 sealed affirmation and John Napoli's disclosures are contained in that edition and reproduced in the endnotes of this book.[47]

The Significance of the "Hoax and Scam" Allegation

For Larry Silverman, Greg Jr.'s lawyer at the time, the suppression of "the Scarpa materials" represented a massive counterterrorism setback. "I believe that if the Feds had played this out correctly," says Silverman, "they would have had [an] Italian Mafia mole being accepted as somebody who these terrorists could rely on. By doing that the FBI would have been in a position to have identified and even followed members of the Yousef cell."[48]

"There's little doubt that if the FBI had fully utilized this intelligence that was coming out of Ramzi Yousef through Scarpa Jr., they could have connected major dots on al-Qaeda's strength in the summer of 1996," says Lieutenant Colonel Anthony Shaffer, the Bronze Star winner who started investigating al-Qaeda for the U.S. Special Operations Command in late 1999. "As we found, Yousef and the Blind Sheikh's cell in New York were directly connected to bin Laden and the al-Qaeda leadership."[49]

The decision by federal prosecutors and senior FBI officials to write off "the Scarpa materials" would have far-reaching counterterrorism ramifications in the years to come. As the clocked ticked down on Yousef's "planes as missiles" plot, it would now be carried out by his uncle Khalid Sheikh Mohammed, who had twice eluded the FBI—first in Islamabad, Pakistan, in February 2005, and a year later in Doha, Qatar.

Chapter 39

JUNIOR'S SECOND STING

On May 20, 1996, while Greg Scarpa Jr. was still at work betraying Ramzi Yousef for the FBI, Lin DeVecchio took the stand in a hearing before Judge Jack B. Weinstein to determine whether Vic Orena Sr. should get a new trial.

"On advice of counsel . . . I cannot answer your questions because of my Fifth Amendment privilege," DeVecchio said.[1]

But Orena's lawyer Gerry Shargel kept questioning him. "Did there ever come a time when you met a man named Gregory Scarpa?" he asked.

"My answer is the same as the previous one," said the supervisory special agent.

After two more questions, Judge Weinstein stepped in, asking DeVecchio if his answers would be the same for the rest of the examination. When he replied, "Yes, Your Honor," Shargel tried to press on, but Weinstein halted the questioning.

"I don't want to make a circus of this," he said. "Nothing is to be gained by your asking him . . . one hundred questions or so forcing him publicly to reiterate his constitutional privilege."[2] So Shargel asked the judge to "draw the adverse inference from DeVecchio's taking the Fifth Amendment that he did leak information and that it affected the outcome of Orena's trial."[3]

A few days later, Weinstein ordered the Feds to release more than one hundred pages of FBI 209s and other files detailing the FBI's secret relationship with "34."[4] And by November, Weinstein made it clear that he would grant Shargel's "adverse inference" motion if DeVecchio didn't step out from behind the Fifth Amendment.

By December, the Justice Department announced that it would consider granting Lin immunity *a second time*.[5] In late January 1997, under growing pressure, DeVecchio's attorney Doug Grover promised, "If he gets immunity, he'll tell the truth."[6]

"How many times have you heard that a former FBI agent took the Fifth Amendment?" asks Larry Silverman. "The government was forced to grant him immunity—otherwise he wouldn't testify."[7]

A month later, Judge Charles P. Sifton, who was then chief judge in the EDNY,[8] threw out the murder convictions of Anthony and Jo Jo Russo and Joseph Monteleone for the pastry shop murders of John Minerva and Michael Imbergamo.[9] Noting that the Feds had failed to disclose Greg Scarpa Sr.'s pattern of blaming others in his FBI reports for murders he himself had committed, Judge Sifton strongly criticized the relationship between "34" and his handler, Lin DeVecchio, calling it

> a highly reprehensible trading of information between a law enforcement official and a criminal. . . . Scarpa emerges as sinister and violent and at the same time manipulative and deceptive with everyone including DeVecchio. DeVecchio emerges as arrogant, stupid or easily manipulated but, at the same time, caught up in the complex and difficult task of trying to make the best use of Scarpa's information to bring the war to a close.[10]

Now, on February 28, 1997, after finally getting immunity a second time— and after his lawyer promised he'd tell the truth—Lin DeVecchio took the stand and Gerry Shargel finally got a chance to question him about his alleged "unholy alliance" with Greg Scarpa Sr. Asked if he was Scarpa's "law enforcement source," DeVecchio snapped, "That's nonsense. That's absolutely incorrect."[11] Then, insisting that William Doran, his boss in the

FBI's New York Office, "was well aware the informant committed acts of violence," Lin seemed to get amnesia.

In response to more than fifty questions from Shargel, he responded, "I don't recall," or words to that effect.[12]

"Lin had promised to tell the truth if he got immunity a second time," says Andrew Orena, "and now he was dodging Gerry Shargel's pointed questions. Most of us watching this in the courtroom were amazed."[13] Among the spectators were a number of FBI agents, two federal judges, and Allie Boy Persico, whose release was due in part to Greg Scarpa Sr.'s dying declaration.[14]

On March 10, Judge Weinstein issued a 101-page "judgment, memorandum and order" denying Vic Orena's petition for a new trial. In the opinion Weinstein acknowledged that:

> Scarpa was well-paid by the F.B.I. for his information. What is possible, but not self evident, is that DeVecchio also "paid" Scarpa by passing along information, creating a two-way street for communication that was dangerous and un-authorized. Did DeVecchio do this? Was he so captivated by Scarpa as to have reversed their roles? Defendants emphatically answer "yes" to both questions.[15]

But as to Orena's allegations that key exculpatory "Brady material" was withheld from the defense at the time of Vic Orena's trial—evidence of the allegedly corrupt relationship between Scarpa and his control agent— Weinstein reached this conclusion:

> There was . . . no "suppression" of evidence of this naked fact of informer status. The court concludes that defendants knew, or should have known, that Scarpa was likely to have been an informant. There is no "suppression" where defendant or his attorney "either knew, or should have known, of the essential facts permitting him to take advantage of [that] evidence."[16]

"It's an absolutely astonishing conclusion," says Flora Edwards. "Judge Weinstein decided that defendants like Vic Orena Sr. were somehow supposed to have known about this ultra-secret Top Echelon informant relationship that was known to only a handful of people in the FBI."[17]

Weinstein then crystallized the defense's principal theory for the appeal and rejected it:

> Even accepting these assumptions, and acknowledging the Scarpa-DeVecchio connection's troubling coziness, does not warrant the further inferences that Scarpa had a license to kill bestowed upon him by DeVecchio, that he committed the Ocera murder, that he initiated and fueled a faux Colombo War to consolidate his power, and that he did all this with DeVecchio's authorization and assistance. Even if all the information defendants have presented in their "record" were found to be subject to *Brady*—and it is not . . . the sum of it would still be insufficient to support so fantastic a theory.[18]

Just eighteen days after Charles P. Sifton, chief judge of the Eastern District, had considered the same suppression of evidence of the Scarpa-DeVecchio scandal sufficient grounds to throw out the murder convictions of the Russos and Monteleone, Jack Weinstein interpreted it from the government's point of view—and denied Vic Orena a new trial.

Four Decades in the Supermax

Eighteen months later, in September 1998, Greg Scarpa Jr. came to trial. He arrived hoping that, after he'd risked his life ratting out al-Qaeda terrorists, the Feds might grant him a portion of the consideration they'd shown his father for more than three decades.[19] But Judge Reena Raggi, a former EDNY prosecutor who presided at his trial, was unsympathetic. After allowing less than an hour of testimony from Greg Jr. about the Yousef initiative, Raggi accepted the government's argument that Scarpa's undercover work for the Bureau was insignificant and more likely "part of a scam."[20]

Reena Raggi was no stranger to the Scarpa family. In fact, twelve years earlier as an AUSA in the Eastern District, she signed the indictment of Junior's father in the Secret Service's credit card case—the very case in which Lin DeVecchio had intervened with Judge I. Leo Glasser to urge leniency for Scarpa Sr.[21]

Testifying under a grant of immunity, Lin took the stand at Junior's trial and denied any wrongdoing in his dealings with Greg Jr.'s father.[22]

Although the younger Scarpa was acquitted at trial of five murders, the jury was persuaded that he was guilty of loan sharking, bookmaking, and tax fraud. During the trial, Greg Jr. renounced his life in the Mafia, doing exactly what Judge Weinstein had asked his father to do at the time of his sentencing. "I'm washing my hands of everything," he testified. "I don't want to do nothing with nothing. I don't want to know nobody."

He argued that he'd been in prison during the 1990s war and hadn't received a penny from his old man since 1989.[23] Greg Jr. also tried in vain to call John Napoli as a witness, to help the jury understand what he risked in ratting out Ramzi Yousef.[24]

But Judge Raggi seemed unmoved by Junior's undercover work for the FBI. Accepting the government's "scam" theory, she threw the book at him, sentencing him to forty years in the same prison that housed Yousef and Murad: the Supermax in Florence, Colorado.

"The double standard shown to my brother, considering what he did with those terrorists, was beyond belief," Greg's younger brother Frank told me in an interview. "If you look at the record of what our father did and how Greg Jr. in every instance was executing his orders, the fact that he tried to help his country against Yousef and the others and got forty years in return shows you how the Feds just wanted to bury the DeVecchio scandal with my brother. They were much more concerned with saving those war cases than getting to the truth."[25]

Greg Jr. wasn't heard from again publicly until January 2004, when Flora Edwards managed to convince Judge Weinstein to grant Vic Orena Sr. a second hearing for a new trial.[26] Testifying via video link from ADX Florence, Greg Jr. reiterated what he'd sworn to in affidavits in 1999 and 2002.

Junior, who kept the books for his father, testified that DeVecchio was paid more than $100,000 over the years in return for his inside help, rewarded with vacations to places like Aspen, and treated to call girls in a Staten Island hotel.[27] He testified that he'd watched FBI surveillance videos of the Wimpy Boys club, which were provided to his father by DeVecchio. He swore that Lin had acted as "a lookout" on one of the bank robberies by the Bypass crew.[28] He insisted that his father had killed Tommy Ocera. And he reaffirmed that his brother Joey had planted the bag of guns under

Vic Orena Sr.'s girlfriend's deck while his father and DeVecchio waited in nearby cars.[29]

In a filing prior to trial, Assistant U.S. Attorney Patricia Notopoulos wrote that Junior's allegations "suggest[ed] recent fabrication."[30]

After the hearing on January 7, 2004, Judge Weinstein seemed to agree. In keeping with his refusal to show any mercy to the elder Orena, he issued a brief decision declaring that "the court finds this witness [Gregory Scarpa Jr.] to be not credible."[31]

Weinstein, who had presided over Vic Sr.'s trial—in which the conviction rested in part on the highly questionable testimony of low-level Colombo wannabes Michael Maffatore and Harry Bonfiglio—did not accept the notion that Greg Jr. might be speaking the truth. Despite the astonishing evidence the younger Scarpa had produced from the Ramzi Yousef sting—most of which was self-authenticating—Weinstein simply did not believe Junior's testimony about his father's dealings with DeVecchio.

Informing on a Homegrown Terrorist

The Murrah Federal Building after the 1995 bombing

Then, a year later, an extraordinary event occurred inside the Supermax that once again underscored the younger Scarpa's credibility. Confined to a seven-by-twelve-foot cell in the prison known as the "Alcatraz of the Rockies,"[32] Greg Jr. was locked down in solitary. At some point in 2005 he found himself in a hardened cell adjacent to that of Terry Nichols, the disgruntled army veteran convicted with Timothy McVeigh of planting the bomb on April 19, 1995, that killed 168 people at the Federal Building in Oklahoma City.

Communicating with Nichols via the pipes connected to the back-to-back sinks in their cells,[33] Greg Jr. learned chilling details about a cache of nitro-methane-based high explosives that the FBI had somehow missed during a search of Nichols's former home in Herington, Kansas.

Nichols told Scarpa Jr. that these explosives lay buried in a crawl space beneath the house and the convicted bomber was fearful that unknown persons might find them and use them on the upcoming tenth anniversary of the Murrah Building blast in April.[34] According to Nichols, the binary explosives were buried with an ammunition can under a pile of rocks beneath the house, which the Bureau had supposedly searched following his arrest ten years earlier. He then pinpointed for Greg Jr. the precise location and gave a detailed description of the Kinestik explosives, which could be detonated with blasting caps.

Terry Nichols and his former home in Herington, Kansas

In *Triple Cross* I detailed how the word from Nichols to Scarpa Jr. was passed to forensic investigator Angela Clemente and how the FBI initially refused to take action. At that point Valerie Caproni had risen to become the Bureau's general counsel—the top lawyer at the Hoover Building in Washington. A polygraph specialist was eventually sent to the Supermax and reportedly concluded that Scarpa Jr. had failed a lie detector test.[35] After learning details of the "test" that suggested that it hadn't been properly administered, I contacted John Solomon, who was then chief of the Associated Press's Washington bureau. Following the intervention of two members of Congress, Representative Dana Rohrabacher, a California Republican, and Representative William Delahunt, a Massachusetts Democrat, the FBI reluctantly conducted a search of Nichols's old house.

The result: In precisely the same part of the crawl space in boxes described precisely by Greg Scarpa Jr., the special agents found the Kinestiks.

Two days after the search Solomon reported:

WASHINGTON (AP) The FBI is facing the possibility it made an embarrassing oversight in the Oklahoma City bombing case a decade ago after new information led agents to explosive materials hidden in Terry

Nichols' former home, which they had searched several times before. FBI officials said the material was found Thursday night and Friday in a crawl space of the house in Herington, Kan. They believe agents failed to check that space during the numerous searches of the property during the original investigation of Nichols and Timothy McVeigh. "The information so far indicates the items have been there since prior to the Oklahoma City bombing," Agent Gary Johnson said in a telephone interview from Oklahoma City.[36]

In a follow-up story on April 14, 2005, the AP's Mark Sherman reported, "While the FBI found no evidence supporting the idea that an attack is in the works for Tuesday's 10th anniversary [of the Oklahoma City bombing], the information that explosives had been hidden in Nichols' former home in Herington, Kansas, turned out to be true."[37]

In that story, Sherman confirmed that "the tip came from imprisoned mobster Gregory Scarpa Jr., 53, a law enforcement source said this week."

"Clearly the FBI—particularly Valerie Caproni, the general counsel—had every interest in discrediting Gregory Scarpa Jr.," said Clemente, who first supplied me with Scarpa Jr.'s trove of intel from Yousef back in 2004. "Caproni was privy to Scarpa's intel about Yousef. She thought he would be buried forever and they would throw away the key and now, here he was in March of 2005 tipping the FBI to another major embarrassment connected to a massive act of terror."[38]

It was the second time Greg Scarpa Jr. had given compelling and credible intelligence to the government in an effort to interdict possible acts of terror—a development that obviously supported his credibility. I had told much of his story in my 2004 book *Cover Up*. Now, in the fall of 2005, after Angela Clemente provided Congressman Delahunt with additional intelligence on the Scarpa-DeVecchio relationship, Delahunt's office contacted the Brooklyn DA.

The Other Top Echelon Scandal

Delahunt made the referral because he knew only too well about problems related to a potentially compromised FBI agent. In the mid-1970s, when he was serving as the district attorney of Norfolk County, near Boston, Delahunt's own office had been stonewalled in an almost identical pattern to the Scarpa-DeVecchio case. At the center of that case was James "Whitey" Bulger, the bloodthirsty head of the notorious Winter Hill Gang, who had evaded arrest for years due to his own status as a Top Echelon informant for the FBI.

In Bulger's case the contacting agent was John Connolly, a twenty-two-year Bureau veteran. But the outcome of that Boston case was decidedly different from what transpired with Lin DeVecchio. In 2008, Connolly was convicted of second-degree murder for passing intelligence to Bulger and his associate Stephen "the Rifleman" Flemmi. The leaks had led to the 1982 murder in Miami of a potential witness against Bulger and Flemmi.[39]

The forty-year sentence Connolly received was the final blow to the once-celebrated agent, who had been sentenced to ten years in federal prison in 2002 after being convicted on racketeering counts connected to his handling of Bulger. Released on June 28, 2011, Connolly was transferred to a Massachusetts state prison to serve out the remainder of his sentence.[40]

During the Miami trial the parallels to the Scarpa-DeVecchio case became clear. First, a federal judge, who had been a prosecutor at the time Connolly ran Bulger, testified that Connolly had been a star agent whose work had served to "decimate" the Mafia in New England.[41] "John Connolly . . . had a certain flair that attracted a confidence and trust with underworld figures," said Judge Edward F. Harrington, the former Boston U.S. attorney from 1977 to 1981, who was the defense's first witness at the trial.[42]

Former FBI SSA John Connolly

Like Lin DeVecchio, Connolly had been a highly decorated Bureau comer. He'd received commendations from every FBI director from J. Edgar Hoover to William Sessions. He'd lectured on informant development at Quantico and was even nominated to become Boston's police commissioner.[43] But at his 2008 murder trial, prosecutors charged that John B. Callahan, a World Jai-Alai executive, was murdered on orders from Bulger and Flemmi after Connolly had told them the FBI was investigating Callahan's ties to the Winter Hill Gang.

John Martorano was later identified as the hit man who shot Callahan and left his bullet-riddled body in the trunk of a car at Miami International Airport.[44] Martorano became a cooperating witness and testified for the government along with Connolly's former FBI supervisor John Morris, who had previously admitted that he had accepted $7,000 in bribes from Bulger and Flemmi.

FBI surveillance photo of Flemmi (*left*) and Bulger (*right*)

Federal prosecutors told jurors that Connolly knew he was "signing the death warrant" for Callahan when he passed the sensitive FBI information to Bulger and Flemmi.[45]

Congressman Delahunt had actually gone to grammar school with Martorano, and one night in 1976 he ran into him at a restaurant as the killer met with Bulger and Flemmi, who were about to shake down the restaurant owner for $175,000. After opening an investigation into that possible extortion, in his capacity as Norfolk County DA, Delahunt turned the case over to the FBI. But the Winter Hill pair went unpunished.[46] Delahunt didn't fully understand why until the Connolly-Bulger scandal became public.

In 2004, after his election to Congress and appointment to the House Judiciary Committee, Delahunt started investigating the issue of FBI agents who might have become compromised in relations with their informants.[47] On February 7, 2005, Delahunt's staff sent a prosecution referral to the office of Charles J. Hynes, the district attorney of Kings County (Brooklyn), whose office had been blindsided by the Feds during the third Colombo war. According to Hynes, that initial referral raised questions about Lin DeVecchio's interaction with Greg Scarpa Sr. around the time of the Nicholas Grancio homicide in January 1992.[48]

Meeting at the Brooklyn DA's Office

In 2004, I had told much of the Scarpa-DeVecchio story in my book *Cover Up.*[49] A year after its publication and after the Delahunt referral, I met with Kings County Assistant DA Noel Downey, Bureau Chief in the Rackets Division, and George Terra, the investigator who had arrested Carmine Imbriale in 1992.

Both of them expressed an interest in my findings on Greg Scarpa Sr. It was Terra's arrest of Imbriale that had prompted Lin DeVecchio in the C-10 squad to contact Scarpa and warn him—using the "Hello" line, according to Chris Favo.[50]

As I sat in the DA's conference room across a table from Terra and Downey, they told me that they'd already started looking into the allegations that DeVecchio may have facilitated Scarpa's murder spree.

After the meeting, I returned to California and went back to work on *Triple Cross,* which focused on al-Qaeda master spy Ali Mohamed. Then, early on the morning of January 4, 2006, I was awakened by a call from Bo Dietl, the well-known former NYPD detective, who had read both *1000 Years for Revenge* and *Cover Up.*

"Peter, you better get up," he said. "WNBC just broke the story that the Brooklyn DA has a grand jury examining DeVecchio."

I went to my computer and accessed the story, first reported by Jonathan Dienst:

"The Brooklyn District Attorney's Office has opened a criminal investigation into a former FBI agent who may have leaked information to the mob," the piece began. Citing the Mafia Cops scandal, but describing the DeVecchio matter as "unrelated" to that case, the WNBC piece ended by quoting several unnamed "former federal officials" who "expressed doubts that the investigation would go anywhere."[51]

But three months later, with Noel Downey at his side, DA Hynes announced the indictment of DeVecchio on four counts of murder conspiracy in the deaths of Mary Bari, Joseph "Joe Brewster" DeDomenico, Larry Lampasi, and Patrick Porco. Also charged were Craig Sobel and John Sinagra, described as "Colombo triggermen."[52]

Porco was an eighteen-year-old friend of Joey Scarpa's who was shot to death over Memorial Day weekend in 1990. Seven months earlier on Halloween night he'd witnessed the murder of seventeen-year-old Dominick Masseria, who was killed on the steps of Our Lady of Guadalupe Church in Brooklyn after an altercation with Joey, who was Greg Sr.'s son by Linda Schiro.[53] The alleged shooter in that killing was Craig Sobel.

According to a statement from the DA on the day the indictment was announced, "in May of 1990 Porco was questioned by detectives at the 62nd Precinct about Masseria's murder. DeVecchio contacted Greg Scarpa to tell him that Porco, 18, had been speaking to authorities about Joseph Scarpa's involvement in the Masseria shooting. Sinagra is charged with carrying out a Scarpa-ordered hit on Porco, to prevent him from speaking about Masseria."[54]

After attributing the origin of the investigation to the referral from Congressman Delahunt, Hynes described the underlying charges against Lin DeVecchio as "the most stunning example of official corruption that I have ever seen."

One Million Dollars' Bail

Ten years earlier, the thirty-two-month OPR investigation into DeVecchio's activities had ended with no charges filed. He'd retired to Sarasota, Florida, where he'd led a quiet life, working as a private investigator and

Lin DeVecchio (*left*) surrendering on the night before his arraignment and (*right, in the background*) surrounded by former FBI agents following his release on $1 million bail the next day

serving on the board of his homeowners' association.[55] Now, at the age of sixty-five, DeVecchio was facing four counts of homicide, each one carrying a possible sentence of twenty-five years to life. During the press conference, Hynes had even accused DeVecchio of receiving $66,000 in "payoffs" from Scarpa.[56]

Allowed to fly up to New York to surrender the night before—thus avoiding one "perp walk" before the press—DeVecchio nonetheless spent the night handcuffed to a metal chair and locked in a room adjacent to the DA's detective squad.[57]

The next day he was arraigned and released on $1 million bail. But even though he walked out of the courthouse a free man, he couldn't avoid the de facto "perp walk" that followed, with a pack of reporters and camera crews chasing him. As he moved down Jay Street outside the courthouse, DeVecchio was surrounded by a phalanx of nearly fifty retired FBI agents— five of whom had come up with the $1 million bail money.[58] Dressed in dark suits, white shirts, and red-and-blue ties, they pushed the media mob back as they protected the onetime star agent, who now faced a fate similar to John Connolly's.

The sight of a cadre of former FBI agents swatting aside reporters on a public street created such a stir that Senator Charles Grassley (R-IA) mentioned it during Senate Judiciary Committee hearings on May 2. "After the [arraignment]," Grassley said, "the agents surrounded DeVecchio 'in a human blanket' as he left the courtroom so that he could not be questioned by reporters. One agent wrote, '[I]t might even be said that a few reporters received a few body checks out on the sidewalk' and that he 'was never prouder to be an FBI agent.' "[59]

Noting that DeVecchio was innocent until proven guilty, Grassley nonetheless told the Judiciary Committee members that he was "concerned about the public perception created by such aggressive and broad support of DeVecchio by current and former FBI personnel."

"It could leave the impression," he said, "that the FBI as an institution is circling the wagons to defend itself as well as DeVecchio against the charges."[60]

In an earlier "Gang Land" column, filed after word of the grand jury investigation surfaced, Jerry Capeci predicted that the DeVecchio murder case would have "stunning implications for both law enforcement and some convicted gangsters."[61] And within hours of DeVecchio's arraignment the indictment of "Mr. Organized Crime" created a tabloid sensation.

"Mob Fed's Filthy Lucre—FBI Agent Cashed in As Mafia Slay Mole: DA." That was the page-one headline in the *New York Post* over the story by veteran crime reporter Murray Weiss, who wrote that Lin's alleged motives were "greed and adulation from his bosses."[62] Quoting unnamed sources, the New York *Daily News* reported that "DeVecchio could face charges in as many as three other gangland murders, two of them on Long Island,"[63] a reference to the Minerva-Imbergamo killings.

The Friends of Lin

But a series of former Feds, many of whom would have much to lose if DeVecchio was convicted, rallied to his side. In a move virtually unprecedented in the face of pending charges, James Kallstrom, the retired assistant director in charge of the New York Office, issued a statement on the case to the *Daily News*.

Then working as a senior counterterrorism adviser to New York Governor George Pataki, Kallstrom actually declared DeVecchio *innocent.* "Lin DeVecchio is not guilty and did not partake in what he's charged with," Kallstrom told the paper. "It's as simple as that."[64]

Kallstrom also agreed to serve on the advisory board of the Friends of Lin DeVecchio Trust, a website and fund-raising arm for the ex-agent's defense.[65] Another board member was former FBI undercover agent Joseph Pistone, a.k.a. "Donnie Brasco," who later offered to testify at the trial of John Connolly.

A *Boston Globe* story during that trial described Pistone as Connolly's "longtime friend."[66] Now, with respect to Lin DeVecchio, Pistone told reporter Alan Feuer of the *New York Times,* "We've all worked with Lin since the early 1970s. We're all veteran street guys. If anyone could smell something bad, it would be us. And with Lin, we never smelled bad."[67]

Another staunch defender of DeVecchio, and Friends of Lin advisory board member, was James M. Kossler, the former chief coordinator of organized crime squads in the New York Office, to whom Lin had once reported.[68]

In his book, DeVecchio quotes Kossler as declaring, "This prosecution of Lin DeVecchio is the most outrageous abuse of prosecutorial authority that I have seen in my career."[69] Kossler, whom Lin describes as "the master strategist of our championship season," was a key player in the Mafia Commission case; he too stood to lose if DeVecchio's conviction led to new appeals from any imprisoned survivors of that landmark case.

As an early measure of his disdain for Special Agent Chris Favo, who brought the initial allegations against DeVecchio, Kossler was quoted by Fred Dannen in his 1996 *New Yorker* piece this way: "The trouble with Chris Favo is that Chris Favo has a very high opinion of himself. He works sixteen hours a day, seven days a week, and you lose all objectivity when that happens. You see things you can't relate to or understand. This whole thing was a travesty, and Lin's reputation has been destroyed. Why wasn't Favo stopped? If I'd been there, I would have cut his nuts off."[70]

One of the principals of the Friends of Lin, who later penned a series of updates on DeVecchio's trial, was Chris Mattiace, who ran the Colombo Squad before Lin took it over. Mattiace was the former SSA who downplayed Greg Scarpa's multimillion-dollar-a-year Staten Island drug operation by declaring in DeVecchio's book that "Greg Scarpa himself was not big enough for our interests at the time, much less his son and the Dead End Kids."[71]

Within months of the indictment, the Friends of Lin DeVecchio had raised $80,000 for Lin's defense.[72] But in a precursor of what was to come, less than two weeks after DeVecchio's arraignment, his attorney Douglas Grover, himself a former federal prosecutor, filed pleadings seeking to transfer the case to federal court, arguing that the former supervisory special agent was "immune from prosecution."[73]

"It's important to get some perspective," says defense attorney Ellen Resnick, "on just how devastating DeVecchio's conviction could have been, not just to the Colombo war cases, but to the Mafia Commission case on which Rudy Giuliani had based his political career."[74]

Lin DeVecchio had been the contacting agent for Greg Scarpa Sr., the informant who had provided most of the probable cause for the Title III wiretap warrants in that case.[75] Now, a battery of current and former Feds were lining up to make sure their man Lin didn't go down without a fight.

Chapter 40

THE COVER UP VIRUS

The year 2007 started out badly for DeVecchio's defense. Judge Frederic Block denied DeVecchio's motion to remove his murder case from Brooklyn to the friendlier turf of federal court. Douglas Grover had made two arguments for the removal: first, that everything Lin had done with respect to "34" had been under "the express authority" conferred on him "by virtue of his position as Supervisory Special agent of the FBI investigative organized crime squads," and, second, that the "evidentiary basis for this prosecution" included his OPR-compelled statement and his testimony in the 1997 Orena hearing, for which he was granted immunity.[1] Neither of those immunized statements contained substantive details on any of the four murders in the DA's indictment.[2] Grover nonetheless argued that DeVecchio was effectively insulated from prosecution.

But Judge Block rejected the "express authority" argument, noting that Lin was "simply being charged with outright murders that have nothing to do with his federal duties." He cited the landmark 1932 Supreme Court case *Colorado v. Symes,*[3] which held that, "while homicide that is excusable or justifiable may be committed by an officer in the proper discharge of his duty, murder or other criminal killings may not."[4] So the case went back to state court.

It was the Brooklyn DA's case to lose—and, over the next ten months, the office took a series of actions that virtually guaranteed that the case would be dismissed.

The first hint of trouble actually came in an unrelated case on March 16, 2006, two weeks before the DeVecchio indictment was announced. That was the day *New York Times* reporter Michael Brick filed a story suggesting that Michael Vecchione, Charles Hynes's lead prosecutor for Lin's trial, may have suppressed evidence in the case of Jabber Collins, a former drug addict turned jailhouse lawyer who was serving a thirty-three-year term for the murder of a rabbi—a case Vecchione had prosecuted in 1995.[5]

In 2001, *Newsday* had reported that Vecchione had traveled to Puerto Rico, ostensibly to subpoena a witness in Collins's case, and had taken with him Stacey Frascogna, a DA's assistant, with whom Vecchione later had an affair.[6]

A red-faced Hynes was subsequently forced to drop the murder charges against Collins, who had already served fifteen years. The dismissal came just one day before potentially embarrassing testimony by Vecchione and Frascogna about alleged misconduct in the case.[7]

The next sign of trouble in the DeVecchio prosecution came in early February 2007, when the *New York Post* reported that Greg Scarpa Jr., who had spent months cooling his heels in the Metropolitan Correctional Center after Hynes's office transferred him from the Supermax, might not be called to testify against Lin.[8] In an interview with me later that year, former NYPD detective Tommy Dades, who had worked with Vecchione to develop the Mafia Cops case, said that "Greg Jr. was getting impatient" with the assistant DAs in Hynes's office, who would leave him alone for "a month at a time" in the federal jail without a visit.[9] Dades said the problem began when Noel Downey, who had been the lead prosecutor on *People v. Lin DeVecchio*, left the office to take a job in private practice—another setback for the DA's team.[10]

"When Noel was there," Dades told me, "we would take Greg out once a week from the MCC. Let him breathe, visit with relatives at the DA's office. . . . For years, this guy has been living in a seven-by-twelve-foot cell. He was one of our primary witnesses and we needed him to be happy. But when Noel left and [Assistant DAs] Kevin [Williamson] and Monique [Ferrell] took over the case, they'd leave him there for weeks on end."[11]

Dades, who had been chief investigator on the DeVecchio case, had his own problems. On March 15, the *New York Post* reported that the ex-detective was facing manslaughter charges after an altercation outside his house on December 19, 2006, that left one man dead.[12] In defense of Dades, Vecchione reportedly appeared before a Staten Island grand jury looking into the scuffle, in which one James Coletta, who had tried to intervene, fell to the ground with cracked ribs and later died of internal injuries.[13] Dades was later cleared of the manslaughter charges,[14] but in mid-May 2007 he abruptly resigned from the DA's staff.[15]

The Alleged Affair with a Mob Witness

Meanwhile, Hynes's office was plagued by other staff problems related to the DeVecchio prosecution. A month earlier, Maria Biagini, a fifteen-year veteran of the office who had been assigned to John Napoli—the witness the DA had moved to a jail cell at Fort Dix, New Jersey, to help buttress Greg Jr.'s testimony—was forced to resign amid allegations that she had fallen in love with the former Gambino associate and actually concocted a scheme to bear his child.[16]

Napoli was important to the DA's case because he had vouched for Greg Jr.'s credibility in his 1996–1997 sting of Ramzi Yousef. But Larry Celona of the *New York Post,* who broke the story, reported that "in one letter [Biagini] suggested a bizarre scheme to get [the witness] released to a fertility doctor, who would collect sperm that could be used to impregnate her."[17] According to Celona, Biagini "allegedly loosened her prisoner's strings and allowed him to contact his family and take money from relatives. He used the cash to throw dinner parties, attended by his family and the investigator—all in violation of DA policies, the sources said."

A day later, the *New York Sun* reported that "the FBI [was] now leading an investigation into [Biagini's] actions, which could result in criminal charges."[18]

The next setback for the Brooklyn DA came in mid-March, when Judge Gustin Reichbach, who was presiding over the DeVecchio case,[19] ordered the prosecution team to submit sworn statements that they had not read either DeVecchio's May 1995 compelled statement or his February 1997 testimony in the Vic Orena hearing, when he'd answered, "I don't recall," in response to Gerry Shargel's questions.[20]

Judge Gustin Reichbach

In both instances, Lin had been granted immunity, and in canvassing the DAs this way, Reichbach was acquiescing to the defense's invocation of *Kastigar v. U.S.,* another landmark decision by the U.S. Supreme Court.[21] The Kastigar holding established that if a criminal defendant has previously been granted immunity, a prosecutor has to build a "firewall" between the defendant's prior testimony and any new investigation of criminal charges leading to an indictment. The ruling later became known colloquially as the "Oliver North defense" after it was used by Lieutenant Colonel North during the Iran-Contra scandal.[22]

North, whose attorney had arranged immunity for him during the nationally televised Iran-Contra hearings, was thus protected from conviction in the case built by Special Prosecutor Lawrence Walsh, whose memoir of that 1980s scandal was called *Firewall.*[23]

Now, Hynes's chief prosecutors on the case, Monique Ferrell and Kevin Richardson, had to affirm under oath that they had read neither DeVecchio's compelled statement nor his 1997 testimony as they prepared the prosecution's case.[24]

Problems with Sinagra and Sobel

But before the DA's office even got to a Kastigar hearing in August, Kings County prosecutors experienced two massive setbacks in the parallel cases relating to the Patrick Porco homicide. John Sinagra, a.k.a. "Johnny Loads," accused in the Porco slaying, had pled not guilty on the day of DeVecchio's arraignment.[25] He was scheduled to go to trial before Lin, in June 2007.

But in early May, a twelve-year-old file came to light that threatened the

case. Under New York law, which forces prosecutors to act with "due diligence" in filing murder charges, Sinagra's lawyer argued that an informant
had come forward years earlier who had named Sinagra as a suspect, and the
DA hadn't acted on that information quickly enough.[26]

In response to that allegation, former NYPD detective Tommy Dades
had to file a sworn affidavit. Back in 1995, Dades had investigated the
murder of Joey Scarpa, Greg Sr.'s son by Linda Schiro, who was killed by
rival drug dealers. In the affidavit, Dades stated that while debriefing John
Novoa, an associate of the younger Scarpa, Novoa had effectively fingered
Joey for the Porco hit.

"Novoa did not mention defendant Sinagra to me," Dades testified under
oath.[27] It was not until he was investigating the DeVecchio case in 1995,
Dades stated, that he learned of Sinagra's possible link to Porco's death.

But on April 20, 2007, at a Sinagra pretrial hearing, the DA's office suddenly came forward with a document they said had been "discovered" the
night before. It indicated that an informant *did,* in fact, name Sinagra as a
suspect during a debriefing in 1995.[28] The question was, why hadn't Hynes's
office come forward with it earlier?

At another hearing in mid-May, an angry Judge Reichbach said that he
was "incredulous" and "flabbergasted" that the Kings County DA's office
"could have information on a mob-related shooting and it just disappears
into the ether."[29]

The very next day, under the headline "DeVecchio Cop 'Tryst'
Bombshell," Sinagra's lawyer Joseph Giametta charged that investigator
Dades, already under fire on the due diligence issue, "had a relationship with Little Linda Schiro in the summer of 2005." Judge Reichbach
quickly sustained a DA's objection to that allegation, and the *New York
Post* reported that Little Linda denied the charge. In fact, she insisted
that she would take the witness stand to say so under oath.[30] But at that
point, with the multiple staff and evidence problems that had surfaced
since the first of the year, Charles Hynes's office seemed to be back on
its heels.

By late May, a flurry of finger-pointing had begun. Assistant DA Kevin
Richardson blamed the misplaced document in the Sinagra case on the
NYPD, alleging that the Porco murder investigation had been closed by
the police department back in 1995 "for statistical purposes"[31]—in other

words, to get an unsolved homicide off the books. Judge Reichbach called the closure "not only inexplicable but inexcusable."[32]

On June 3, the lawyer for Craig Sobel, who had been charged in the Dominick Masseria slaying, pursued the Sinagra defense, arguing that the police had information linking Sobel to the church-steps hit ten years earlier but had failed to act.[33]

A few days later, the DA sheepishly offered to let Sinagra cop a plea to a reduced prison sentence of two to six years—but the defendant passed, feeling confident of his chances at a dismissal.[34] Finally, on June 12, Judge Reichbach declared that "negligence [was] not good cause" for the delay in charging Sinagra and threw out the cold-case murder charges, freeing him after fifteen months behind bars.[35] Underscoring the setback for Hynes's office, already plagued by serious personnel issues, the headline in the *New York Post* said it all: "Slay Rap KO'd in 'Mob Fed' Shocker. Judge Blasts 'Too Late' Cops and Brooklyn DA."

It would take another full year, but on June 13, 2008, Craig Sobel was finally found not guilty in the shooting of Dominick Masseria. Calling it "the last of the DeVecchio debacle," Sobel's lawyer Bruce Barket commented on all three of the cases in the Brooklyn DA's March 2006 indictment: "They were all flawed and this one was the weakest," he said.[36]

By June 2007, with Hynes's office on the ropes, Greg Scarpa Jr. was shaping up as the DA's best hope to bolster the testimony of central witness Linda Schiro in the upcoming main event: Lin DeVecchio's prosecution, which was now set for early fall. In a "Gang Land" column published in the *New York Sun*, Jerry Capeci reported that "prosecutors plan to use . . . Scarpa Jr., to back up their key prosecution witness . . . Linda Schiro— regarding two mob rubouts the son was involved in before he was incarcerated in 1988."

Predicting that Greg Jr. would come clean on his alleged involvement in the murders of Mary Bari and Joe Brewster, Capeci wrote that "prosecutors have decided that [Junior's] intimate knowledge of his father's dealings with Mr. DeVecchio far outweighs the heavy baggage that he will carry with him to the witness stand."[37]

The Feds Move a Terrorist

As if the Kings County DA's office wasn't facing enough problems, the judicial scales seemed to tip even further against it when the U.S. Department of Justice made two moves that seemed to benefit DeVecchio's defense.

In March 2007, I discovered that Abdul Hakim Murad, sentenced to life for the 1995 Bojinka plot to smuggle bombs onto U.S. airliners, was moved by the Bureau of Prisons (a division of Justice) to a jail cell in Lower Manhattan next to Greg Scarpa Jr., who was awaiting his chance to testify against DeVecchio. Family members and lawyers close to the case feared that the move may have endangered Junior, since he'd helped the FBI get so much evidence on Murad and Ramzi Yousef in his mid-1990s sting.

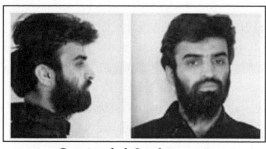

**Convicted al-Qaeda terrorist
Abdul Hakim Murad**

At the Brooklyn DA's request, Greg Jr. was flown to the MCC on December 6, 2006. Then, four months later, for unexplained reasons, the Bureau of Prisons inmate locator showed Murad also in residence there.[38] What would be the possible motive for the Federal government to move a convicted terrorist like Abdul Hakim Murad out of the security of the Supermax and put him in close proximity to Greg Scarpa Jr., the very informant who had "ratted" him out in 1996 during the Yousef sting? Could it be to intimidate Scarpa Jr. prior to his testimony at the DeVecchio trial? Since the trial was cut short before Greg Jr. could get on the stand, we may never know.

But around the time I made the discovery about Murad's trip to the MCC, I uncovered an even more surprising fact suggesting that forces within the Department of Justice were working against the DA's prosecution.

The Feds Pay Part of DeVecchio's Defense

On March 5, 2007, I intercepted a fund-raising e-mail from Chris Matti-ace, who had run the C-10 Colombo Squad and who was now working as a principal behind the Friends of Lin DeVecchio Trust. Mattiace had sent the e-mail soliciting contributions for Lin's legal defense to the Society of For-mer Special Agents of the FBI. In it, he called the DA's case "an unfounded and . . . politically motivated prosecution."

"Any one of us could be in the same position Lin faces now," wrote Mattiace. "There but for the grace of God go any one of us."[39]

"The subtext of that message seemed to be, 'If Lin goes down, more of us might go down,'" said retired agent James Whalen, who worked in the New York Office.[40] In the e-mail* Mattiace revealed that at that point, roughly a year after Lin's indictment, $80,000 had been raised for his defense but that legal fees had "already exceeded $450,000 with the trial still looming."

Then Mattiace made a surprising admission: "The Justice Department has already paid and agreed to continue to pay a portion of the fees and costs, but that is nowhere near enough to pay the total cost of defense." Considering that with respect to the four homicide charges, Judge Block had effectively ruled that Lin was not acting in the course and furtherance of his duties, getting the U.S. taxpayer to foot the bill for any part of his defense seemed unusual, if not illegal.

I forwarded copies of the e-mail to the *New York Times* and both of the major New York tabloids: the *New York Post* and the *Daily News*. Bill Sherman, a Pulitzer Prize–winning reporter for the *News,* was the only one to pick up on my discovery.[41]

In a May 6, 2007, piece he quoted then FBI spokesman John Miller, who confirmed that the Justice Department was paying *some* of the legal fees for DeVecchio's defense.[42] Meanwhile, Senator Charles Grassley (R-IA) began an investigation for the Senate Judiciary Committee. When asked about the payments by the committee, the Justice Department cited two

---

* It can be downloaded in its entirety from http://www.peterlance.com/Chris_Mattiace_email_SOFSAFBI_3_1_07.pdf.

sections of the Code of Federal Regulations[43] that provide for the payment of legal fees for accused government employees whose actions on the job fall within the "scope" of their employment.[44]

But in approving such fees the U.S. attorney general must determine that the legal representation paid for is "in the interest of the United States." At that time in 2007 the Bush administration AG was Alberto Gonzales, who later resigned under fire after a tenure marred by allegations he committed perjury,[45] mishandled top-secret documents,[46] violated the Patriot Act in approving a series of national security letters,[47] and fired eight U.S. attorneys for political reasons.[48]

When pressed by Senator Grassley, who submitted a series of questions relating to the DeVecchio case to FBI Director Robert S. Mueller III, Brian A. Benczkowski, the principal deputy assistant attorney general, responded in a letter to committee chairman Patrick Leahy by stating that "the FBI submitted to DOJ a statement containing its findings as to whether DeVecchio was acting within the scope of his employment and whether such representation would be in the best interests of the United States." Then, without elaborating on the details of that finding or describing AG Gonzales's motivation in approving the legal fee payment, Benczkowski asserted the attorney-client and attorney–work product privileges.[49]

"So we have a conflict," says Flora Edwards, "between the finding of a federal judge, Frederic Block, who declares that Lin was *not* acting within the scope of his duties with regard to the four murders in the indictment, and the FBI, which seems to suggest that *he was,* and the U.S. attorney general finds, based on that conclusion, that it's in the interests of the country to help pay his legal bills. However, we can't know the details of the payment or the Bureau's reasoning because Justice claims that's protected under attorney-client privilege. But one has to ask, who's the client? Lin isn't a government employee in 2006. He's being represented by private counsel. So how does the privilege attach?"[50]

The Mafia Cops Conflict

On the same day that Lin DeVecchio pleaded not guilty to the murder conspiracy charges in Brooklyn Supreme Court, an important conference call relating to the Mafia Cops case took place a few blocks away in the office of the U.S. attorney for the Eastern District. The sensational trial of ex-detectives Lou Eppolito and Stephen Caracappa had begun March 13 amid banner headlines.[51]

An AP story reporting on the start of the trial noted that the two men

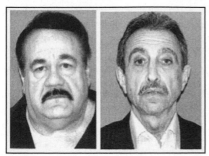

were "charged with racketeering, conspiracy and other charges for allegedly going on the payroll of Lucchese family underboss Anthony 'Gaspipe' Casso." But the man who should have been the star witness for the Feds—Casso himself—was denied an opportunity to testify for the government. So now, at one fifteen P.M., just before Lin DeVecchio walked into Brooklyn

Arrest photos of Lou Eppolito (*left*) and Stephen Caracappa (*right*)

Supreme Court for his arraignment, a conference call began between Casso, who was serving multiple life terms at the Supermax prison in Colorado, and lawyers for Eppolito and Caracappa, who were also present.[52]

The call had been prompted in part by a letter that Casso had sent to U.S. Attorney Roslynn Mauskopf in July 2005, three months after the ex-detectives had been arrested in Las Vegas. In that letter Casso wrote that "from day one and for 3½ years to follow, my FBI handlers have, at times, ordered me to be misleading." He was talking about the source of his law enforcement "crystal ball," which the Feds had attributed exclusively to the Mafia Cops.

Now, in that conference call, which Casso hoped would prompt the Eppolito-Caracappa defense to call him as a witness, he reiterated what he told FBI agents Rudolph and Brennan at La Tuna in 1994: that "most of the information" he got from law enforcement sources "came from an FBI agent." Without identifying Rudolph by name, he also stated what he'd told author Phil Carlo and later told me: that during his La Tuna debriefing, "the case agent," who was debriefing him, blew "his top" and told him not to mention the FBI agent's name.[53]

After that conference call, the defense decided not to put Casso on the witness stand, so the jury in the Mafia Cops case never heard a thing about any "crooked" FBI agent or agents who may have supplied intel to Gaspipe. A week later Eppolito and Caracappa were convicted.[54]

Earlier that year, when WNBC broke the story of the grand jury probe of Lin DeVecchio, reporter Jonathan Dienst insisted it was "unrelated" to the Mafia Cops case.[55] But in the media storm that engulfed Eppolito and Caracappa, it soon became clear that there *was* a connection and it now threatened to impact the DeVecchio prosecution.

In New York, as in few other places, real-life events are sometimes impacted by the very books and movies that chronicle them, and the Mafia Cops case was no exception. As noted, the investigation into the two detectives had originated in the office of the Brooklyn DA. In fact, a year before DA Hynes called the DeVecchio case "the most stunning example of official corruption that [he had] ever seen,"[56] he stood at a press conference next to U.S. Attorney Mauskopf and described that case in almost identical terms. It was "one of the most shocking examples of criminal activity [he'd] ever witnessed," said Hynes.[57]

But the single news story that brought the most attention to the Mafia Cops case was the *60 Minutes* piece by the late Ed Bradley in which Casso described how he'd used the cops to "moonlight" as "hit men."[58] Following the broadcast of that piece in April 2005, the story exploded, spawning no less than three movie deals[59] and four books.[60] The CBS News story featured Dades, who Bradley told viewers "came out of retirement . . . and went to work in the office of the Brooklyn district attorney, digging through old Mafia case files."

After that exposure on *60 Minutes,* Dades was "inundated with offers and pitches to handle his rights," according to the show business daily *Variety.*[61] He reportedly signed with the William Morris Agency and made a deal with a producer at Warner Bros. estimated to be worth between $75,000 and $600,000.[62]

Dades then entered into a separate contract with HarperCollins to write a book with Mike Vecchione and ghost writer David Fisher on the development of the "Cops." That collaboration, ultimately titled *Friends of the Family,* didn't get published until 2009.[63] But the book and Dades's separate movie deal prompted DeVecchio's supporters to attack the Brooklyn DA's "motive(s)" in developing Lin's case.

The Friends of Lin website went so far as to reproduce a July 2005 piece by *Daily News* reporter Hugh Son in which Vecchione was accused of having "talked to Hollywood agents about selling the story of [the] two former cops . . . before their trial has even begun."[64]

The story quoted Hynes's opponent in the upcoming election as calling such discussions "unconscionable."

DA spokesman Jerry Schmetterer shot back that "Vecchione was asked to sign a deal and he said, 'no.' "[65] But that was back in 2005, before the Dades-Vecchione-Fisher book was sold. Then, a year later, John Marzulli filed a story in the *Daily News* headlined "Tell-All Risks Mob Cop Case: Assistant DA's Book May Cut Trial Options."[66] In that piece, Hofstra University law professor Monroe Freedman cited the American Bar Association's code of standards, which he said "forbids prosecutors from entering into any media deal before a case is completely done." But since the Mafia Cops case had been removed to federal court, Hynes's office saw no conflict.[67]

The problem was that, by July 2006, there was a chance that the Eppolito-Caracappa case might well return to the Brooklyn DA. On July 1, Judge Jack B. Weinstein, who had presided over the trial of the two ex-detectives, shocked the New York legal community by tossing out their convictions on the legal grounds that the five-year statute of limitations for RICO conspiracy charges had run out.[68] The *New York Times* piece on that stunning reversal of fortune noted that Weinstein's ruling "threatened to disrupt the careers—and the book deals—of some investigators in the case."

Since there is no statute of limitations on murder, which is a state crime, at that moment, barring a reversal by a federal appeals court, there was the very real prospect that the Mafia Cops case would go back to Brooklyn Supreme Court, where the lead prosecutor was Michael Vecchione, and that raised the possibility that a conflict of interest might force Vecchione to either disgorge his book advance or resign.

The Oliver North Defense

Now, a year later, as he geared up for the biggest trial of his career, Vecchione was under pressure from multiple sides. Not only was he facing those conflict issues, he was also dogged by severe staff and evidence problems. To make matters worse, his opponents Douglas Grover and Mark

Bederow were getting their legal fees underwritten—in part—by the U.S. government.

On the other hand, the prospect of a DeVecchio conviction would have dire consequences, not just for Lin himself, but for the FBI supervisors and DC brass who had supported him for years. It could also negatively impact the long succession of Mafia cases he'd helped to make. This may have been a murder prosecution in Brooklyn Supreme Court, but it had implications for the Justice Department that were farther-reaching than anything the John Connolly–Whitey Bulger scandal in Boston had produced. So as the trial approached, team DeVecchio decided to play some very hard ball.

Andy Kurins was a former Gambino Squad agent working with Thompson Hine, the law firm of Grover and Bederow that represented Lin DeVecchio. Two and a half months after Lin's indictment was announced by the DA, Kurins sent me an e-mail that ended this way:

> I hope that you have not been sucked into this vortex of lies and self serving agendas against Lin and have time to extricate yourself from a pit which will only get deeper and darker.[69]

In a videotaped interview following the press conference the day Lin DeVecchio was indicted, I asked Noel Downey, then the assistant DA heading the case, if my book *Cover Up* had been of any "value" in the DA's investigation. This is how he responded:

> Oh, absolutely, because stage one of any murder investigation is to figure out who's who and what's what and where things occurred, and your book certainly was a wonderful springboard to understand who the parties were and what direction the investigation should go.[70]

It was a statement that he'd be questioned on later, because Thompson Hine had decided to make my reporting on the Scarpa scandal one of the components of their motion for a pretrial dismissal. Their argument was that if the DA's investigators had read *Cover Up*, which contained a few references to DeVecchio's compelled statement and the 1997 Orena hearing, then their official investigation had become "infected with the Kastigar virus . . . contracted through Peter Lance."[71]

In an affidavit filed within weeks of Kurins' e-mail, Douglas Grover wrote that on April 10, 2006, his colleague Mark Bederow met with Noel Downey. According to Grover, "Mr. Bederow observed *Cover Up* by Peter Lance in Mr. Downey's office, standing upright, directly in front of his office's window."[72]

Grover argued that "*Cover Up* utilized the substance of SSA DeVecchio's immunized testimony as a basis for its conclusions."[73]

A year later, I was served with a subpoena from Thompson Hine.[74] Under threat of fine and imprisonment for contempt if I refused to comply, the subpoena "command[ed]" me to turn over "any and all correspondence and documents," including "meeting notes, email messages, facsimile transmissions . . . digital recordings, computerized data compilations or notes" relating to my September 2005 meeting in the DA's office with Noel Downey and George Terra.

At a pretrial hearing on April 20, arguing that I should be called as a witness at the Kastigar hearing, Grover noted the "long history of . . . investigative journalism . . . into this case. It could be—this is a critical part of what led to this prosecution."[75] He concluded that if "the District Attorney's Office was in any way affected directly or indirectly by the immunized testimony," it "may lead to this prosecution never taking place at all."[76] The legal theory seemed to be that regardless of whether DeVecchio was guilty or innocent, he was *immune* from the charges filed.

In that earlier pleading, Grover alleged that my work had provided the DA with a "roadmap" on which to base its investigation and that "the road [Lance] traveled was littered with landmines of immunized testimony."[77] What were those land mines that had supposedly "tainted" the prosecution? In a related pleading he cited my reference in *Cover Up* to a series of alleged presents given to DeVecchio by Greg Scarpa Sr.:

> In defiance of FBI rules, which require two agents to run an informant (to help prevent just such corruption), "Del," as Scarpa called him, ran the Colombo captain by himself. The two men met two or three times a week, with DeVecchio often visiting Scarpa at home. At length they grew so close that they even vacationed together. When Cabbage Patch Kids dolls were scarcer than bags of heroin, Scarpa reportedly furnished one to DeVecchio for his daughter. Plying his control agent with fine wine and pasta, he made

sure that Greg Jr. had the champagne on ice when he paid for call girls to entertain the supervisory special agent at a Staten Island hotel.[78]

Claiming that the wine-and-pasta detail had come from his compelled statement, DeVecchio's lawyer cited my reference in *Cover Up* to a *Pittsburgh Post-Gazette* story that had mentioned the gift.[79]

But in the ninety-six pages of *Cover Up* devoted to the Scarpa-DeVecchio scandal, the so-called immunized testimony was referenced only a handful of times and always from court pleadings or open-source news stories.

Only one of the four murders in the DA's indictment was even mentioned in my book, and in a single paragraph:

On May 22, 1992, Scarpa Sr. killed rival soldier Larry Lampasi with a shotgun; another Orena loyalist was wounded. When Special Agent Chris Favo reported both attacks to DeVecchio, he laughed, slapped his desk with his open hand, and exclaimed "We're going to *win* this thing."[80]

As noted, that very line turned up in the finale for the HBO mob series *The Sopranos;* DeVecchio even used it for the title of his book.[81]

"Ninety-nine percent of *Cover Up* has nothing to do with DeVecchio's immunized state or hearing testimony," says Flora Edwards. "Years after many of these murders were committed, to claim that but for an investigative reporter's enterprise work, DeVecchio would not have been indicted, or that the Brooklyn DA, with a grand jury, didn't have sufficient independent means of building the case . . . is patently ridiculous."[82]

In late July 2007, lawyers retained by HarperCollins on my behalf filed a motion to quash the subpoena from Thompson Hine and a second subpoena I'd received from the DA. The motion cited the New York shield law, which protects reporters from having to give up sources or material uncovered in the course of an investigation.*

---

* The memorandum of law supporting the motion can be accessed via my website at
http://www.peterlance.com/Memo_of_Law_Re_PL's_%20Motion_to_Quash_%20
Subpoenas.pdf, and my own sworn affidavit can be found at http://www.peterlance
.com/Affidavit_of_PL_Re_%20Motion_to_Quash_%20Subpoenas.pdf.

On August 9, I appeared at the Kastigar hearing. While I came prepared to face jail for contempt rather than give up a single confidential source, my lawyers reached an agreement with Judge Reichbach for me to testify on a limited basis without having to betray a source or turn over a single document. The Kastigar hearing proved to be a precursor to what would soon happen at trial.

Warm-Up to the Main Event

In addition to me and forensic investigator Angela Clemente, reporter Jerry Capeci had been subpoenaed to testify at the hearing. On August 2, an article in the *Daily News,* where Capeci's "Gang Land" column had run for many years, reported that he would fight the subpoena, in which the DeVecchio defense team was seeking "conversations between Capeci and Scarpa's girlfriend Linda Schiro."

In court pleadings, Capeci reportedly stated that he'd promised Schiro in 1996 to keep conversations about her life with Greg Sr. "strictly confidential."[83] Ultimately Capeci was never compelled to appear, because Judge Reichbach granted his request to quash the subpoena.[84]

When Noel Downey took the stand at the hearing on August 8, he admitted that he'd read parts of *Cover Up.* But he denied ever reading DeVecchio's compelled statement or his immunized court testimony.[85]

Four days later, I testified that Lin's immunized statements were never discussed during my 2005 meeting with Downey and Terra. I characterized the meeting as "part of my effort as a reporter to learn as much as I could about what may or may not have been the status of [the DeVecchio] investigation for purposes of journalism."[86] On cross-examination, Mark Bederow asked me if I'd ever discussed with Downey any of the four murders in the indictment and I confirmed that I hadn't.[87]

After listening to the testimony of another nine witnesses, including Angela Clemente and Tommy Dades, Judge Reichbach decided to reserve judgment on the Kastigar issue until after the trial. But the hearing proved to be a major success for Thompson Hine, because it ended up costing the DA its second and third "seats"—the two assistant DAs who were scheduled to try the case with lead prosecutor Michael Vecchione.

In the course of the Kastigar proceedings, Monique Ferrell and Kevin Richardson, who had replaced Noel Downey, admitted that in preparing for the hearing they *had* read Lin's controversial 1995 compelled statement and 1987 testimony. So rather than face a possible negative ruling on the Kastigar issue at trial's end, they recused themselves.[88] "In order to protect against any problems down the line," said the DA's spokesman Jerry Schmetterer, "we volunteered to make some changes in the prosecution team."[89]

Turning Down Gaspipe's Offer?

In a sign of how the Mafia Cops case intersected with the DeVecchio prosecution, and how it might have affected Assistant DA Vecchione's attitude toward the case, Anthony Casso told me that he'd sent a letter to the Brooklyn DA's office offering to testify about the intelligence he says he got from Scarpa Sr. via his FBI contacting agent.

"It's difficult to see how that wouldn't have been a huge plus for the DA," says Flora Edwards, "getting corroboration on the leaks from a living family boss. Remember how successfully the Feds had used Al D'Arco, who was an acting Lucchese boss just like Gaspipe."[90] But when I asked Casso what response, if any, he got from Vecchione, he said, "He never answered me."[91] I made several attempts to confirm Casso's allegation with Vecchione, but he never got back to me.

Casso says that if he had been allowed to testify at Lin's trial, he was prepared to tie DeVecchio to other leaks. He told me that beyond the identity of Jimmy Hydell—whose murder he confessed to Ed Bradley—"Greg [Scarpa Sr.] got more information from DeVecchio. He got the locations of other people, where they were living." That revelation corroborated the disclosures Valerie Caproni and Ellen Corcella had made back in 1995 relating to leaks DeVecchio may have made to "34."

"We'll never know," says Andrew Orena, "whether or not Casso would have helped the prosecution of Lin DeVecchio. But you have to wonder whether Mike Vecchione was worried about those charges of a potential conflict with his book deal on the Mafia Cops and he didn't want to muddy the waters by risking bringing the Cops case into the DeVecchio trial."[92]

In the late summer of 2007, as the DA's office scrambled to prepare for what would soon become the biggest murder trial in Brooklyn Supreme Court in years, Judge Reichbach postponed the trial date to October 1 to give Monique Ferrell and Kevin Richardson's replacements time to prepare.

But on October 1, the next major shock occurred in the case. Lin DeVecchio waived his right to a jury trial. Now Gustin Reichbach—who'd been a member of the radical Students for a Democratic Society in the 1960s—would have sole responsibility for determining the former SSA's fate. The judge himself even seemed surprised, admitting from the bench that in 1969 the FBI had kept a file on him in which he'd been referred to as "one of the most dangerous people" in SDS.[93] He went even further, trying to talk the defense out of their decision.[94] But Lin DeVecchio, who appeared at the hearing, told Reichbach he was confident that he would be impartial.

Gaveling down, Judge Reichbach set the new start date for October 15.

PART V

Chapter 41

AGENT OF DEATH

As the trial began, the *New York Post*'s page-one headline read "Agent of Death: FBI 'Rogue' on Trial." The double-truck story inside focused on the DA's opening references to the Mary Bari murder and how Greg Scarpa Sr. had allegedly made light of it with Lin DeVecchio. "Mob Mirth at Moll's Slay" read the banner headline above the piece, which carried the subhead " 'Crooked Fed' & 'Grim Reaper' Joked."[1]

The sidebar column, by veteran *Post* crime reporter Steve Dunleavy, was captioned "Dirt Bag Is Grime of Century." In the column, Dunleavy quoted retired detective Joe Coffey, who once ran the NYPD's Organized Crime Task Force:

"It was no secret in the '80s that DeVecchio was on the take from [Colombo crime-family mobster Gregory] Scarpa," Joe Coffey said. "He was a loudmouth walking around with pinky rings and, even in those days, $2,000 suits. I worked on the same cases as he did, and a lot of us and other feds knew about him, too."[2]

Coffey is something of an NYPD legend. Among other career bench-marks, he led the successful hunt for David Berkowitz, the "Son of Sam" serial killer.[3] In the course of DeVecchio's trial, the defense would produce a memo from Lin, dated September 4, 1984, in which Scarpa reportedly called the celebrated Coffey a "bad cop" with Mafia ties.[4]

That memo was not among the 1,153 Scarpa files released to me by the FBI, and Coffey, who is credited with solving eighty mob murders in his career, called the charge "laughable," insisting that Scarpa's allegations were "completely disproved" after an investigation.[5] In a subsequent interview with me for this book, Coffey called DeVecchio "one of the dirtiest FBI agents [he'd] ever met."[6] Still, Coffey's allegations about DeVecchio, cited in Dunleavy's column, and the defense's attack on him are some indication of how this murder trial turned into a bare-knuckle proceeding from day one.

The trial opened to a courtroom so packed with observers that members of the press were relegated to the empty jury box. Facing the bench on the left side was Team DeVecchio, consisting of the defendant and three law-yers from Thompson Hine: lead counsel Douglas Grover, Mark Bederow, and Ginnine Fried, a young associate who went on to work as assistant chief counsel at the Department of Homeland Security.[7] On the People's side was Racket Bureau chief Mike Vecchione, along with Assistant DAs Laura Neubauer, Jacqueline Linares, and Joe Alexis—the latter three all recent additions to the prosecution team after Monique Ferrell and Kevin Richardson were forced to withdraw over the Kastigar issue.

The rows in the galley not filled with reporters were occupied by more than a dozen former agents from the Friends of Lin DeVecchio, as well as a series of Mafia buffs, Brooklyn Supreme Court watchers, and family members related to victims of the third Colombo war. The expansive blond walls of the modern courtroom were decorated with framed pictures from the Civil Rights era, including a photograph of Paul Robeson, the African American singer who was blacklisted during the McCarthy years for his left-leaning political views. Robeson had graduated from Columbia Law School, which was also the alma mater of the man on the bench, Gustin Reichbach. Throughout the proceedings, while he demonstrated a steel-trap legal mind, Reichbach, who died in 2012 from pancreatic cancer,[8] brought an unmistakable panache to the trial. Each day he came into court dressed flamboyantly, with striped shirts and bright ties under his judge's robes.

Behind him on the wall, next to the words "In God We Trust," was a black plastic frame with the scales of justice lit up in red and blue neon lights.

On trial for crimes that carried four sentences of twenty-five years, the sixty-seven-year-old defendant had aged significantly since the 1980s, when he'd reopened Greg Scarpa. In those days, Lin DeVecchio had had a full head of curly hair and a drooping mustache. Known as a dapper dresser, he wore expensive suits with pocket squares and monogrammed shirts,[9] and occasionally sported a gold bracelet and a wiseguy-style pinky ring.[10] Now he was clean-shaven. His hair had mostly turned to gray and he wore it in a military-style brush cut.

In contrast to the swaggering image he'd projected as a senior organized crime supervisory agent, DeVecchio now maintained the demeanor of an accountant, in conservative suits and understated ties. While he drove a Harley-Davidson back home in Florida, here in Brooklyn, on trial for his life, he came across as a kind of victim.

The "first seat" for the DA was Mike Vecchione. A short, mustached bulldog of a man, he'd been off for some time during the summer after back-to-back prosecutions, so the job of delivering the opening statement fell to Joe Alexis, a big, barrel-chested assistant DA who'd recently been assigned to the case. As he got up to begin, the unspoken question was whether his office could overcome the Kastigar challenge and convict the former supervisory special agent, who had already been twice immunized by the Justice Department. But if he was worried, Alexis didn't show it:

> During trial we will prove beyond a reasonable doubt, that on September twenty-fifth, nineteen eighty-four, Greg Scarpa killed Mary Bari here in Brooklyn, and the defendant helped him do it. That on September seventeenth, nineteen eighty-seven, Greg Scarpa killed Joseph DeDomenico here in Brooklyn, and the defendant helped him do it. That on May twenty-seventh, nineteen-ninety, Greg Scarpa killed Patrick Porco in Brooklyn, and the defendant helped him do it. And on May twenty-second, nineteen ninety-two, Greg Scarpa killed Lorenzo Lampasi here in Brooklyn, and the defendant helped him do it.[11]

Alexis told the court that Scarpa "ran the most bloodthirsty of crews" and that he "lived a double life." He wasn't just an informant, said Alexis, but "a special informant. Because rather than working for the FBI, Scarpa had the defendant, FBI agent Roy Lindley DeVecchio, working for him."[12]

That was the essence of the DA's case: not that Lin had ever pulled the trigger himself but that, by allegedly leaking intel to Scarpa Sr. over the years and keeping him out of prison, DeVecchio had become his enabler—his effective partner in crime.

At the time of trial, not being privy to the 1,153 pages of secret "Scarpa files" from the Bureau—which proved the killer's Machiavellian strategy to ignite the third Colombo war—the DA adopted the Feds' explanation for the conflict: that Vic Orena had moved to "seize . . . control" of the family and that "Greg Scarpa and his men sided with the Persico faction."[13]

Continuing his opening statement, Alexis promised that Larry Mazza would sit on the witness stand to document the war murders in the indictment.[14] Later he signaled that Linda Schiro, "the love of Greg Scarpa's life," would also testify.[15] But he never mentioned the name of the DA's true "star witness," Greg Scarpa Jr., who had been waiting patiently in the MCC for more than ten months to reveal what he knew about his father's relationship with "Dello" or "D," as he'd known DeVecchio. Detective Tommy Dades, who had resigned from the DA's office, told me that after Noel Downey's departure the prosecutor's office had seemed to neglect Junior; now it seemed that, for unknown reasons, they were abandoning him as a witness.

When it was Doug Grover's chance to frame the case for his client, he described Scarpa, DeVecchio's coveted TE source, as an "ugly" and "miserable human being," but an "informant with a fuel that made the engine of all these [Mafia] investigations run."

Citing the landmark Mafia Commission case, Grover reminded the court that those investigations, driven by Scarpa's intel, later turned into "prosecutions and convictions" for the government.[16] Early in his opening, as if sensing that the case would rise and fall on Scarpa's gumar, Grover tried to preempt Linda Schiro's testimony, dismissing it in advance as "a fantasy."[17] For some time, the DA's office had been paying Schiro a fee—not unlike the FBI's multiyear stipend to Greg Sr.—and now Grover used that to attack her credibility.

> What you are going to see on this witness stand [in Schiro], is someone who is so desperate and so financially driven, that . . . she will say any-

thing for the two thousand dollars a month the District Attorney has been giving her for the last two years. . . . She is a person who cannot be trusted.[18]

Moving on to Chris Favo and the allegations against DeVecchio during the OPR, Grover conceded that "perhaps DeVecchio [became] too careless . . . in his dealings with Scarpa." But he insisted that, as a result of that OPR probe, "there were no administrative sanctions, there were no criminal sanctions, and life went on."[19]

Still working to undermine Schiro, Grover noted that "the one thing that came out of the [OPR] investigation in 1994 and 1995 and sticks with every witness today with the exception of Linda . . . no one knew who [Scarpa's] law enforcement source was, no one, not Larry Mazza, not no one."[20]

"As far as the defense was concerned," says attorney Flora Edwards, "if Schiro's credibility could be seriously impeached it would be game over."[21] Indeed, in his opening statement—which ran for forty pages of trial transcript—Douglas Grover devoted more than thirty pages to an attack on Schiro, whom he described as

> the foundation of this case [and] someone who you will see is patently untrustworthy, who has her own agendas, and frankly who is capable of concocting any story. She's not credible. And no human being, Your Honor, Lin DeVecchio or anybody, deserves to be sitting here as a result of the stories that this woman is making up.[22]

The Second String

The trial of Lin DeVecchio, accused by DA Joe Hynes of committing "the most stunning example of official corruption [he'd] ever seen,"[23] was about to commence with its first witness.

But just like the prosecution team itself—the late-term replacements who filled in for Assistant DAs Downey, Ferrell, and Richardson—the lead witness, NYPD detective sergeant Fred Santoro, was a stand-in for Detective

Tommy Dades, the chief investigator on the case, who had abruptly quit five months earlier.[24]

Worse for the DA's office, and proof that the Kastigar sword of Damocles still hung over the proceedings, Grover argued that Santoro's testimony would be "tainted," since he had sat with Dades through part of DeVecchio's 1997 immunized testimony during the Vic Orena hearing.[25]

Noting that this was a nonjury bench trial and that he could "separate" out the Kastigar issues, Judge Reichbach allowed Santoro to be sworn. But for the next several hours Santoro offered little more than a boilerplate primer on the organization of Cosa Nostra—with zero testimony about DeVecchio's alleged connections to any of the murders in the indictment. The closest he got was describing the players in the Colombo family, using an organizational chart prepared by the DA. It was the kind of general testimony Lin DeVecchio himself had given in countless LCN trials, including Vic Orena's.

The next day, when Grover started cross-examining him, Santoro admitted that during the previous day's testimony he had confused the Commission case with the "Windows" case, a separate prosecution of Lucchese family members that involved Gaspipe Casso.[26] Santoro then admitted that this was the first time he had ever testified as "an organized crime expert" and that his familiarity with the DeVecchio case came "from reading the newspaper."[27]

After developing little or no inculpatory evidence from Santoro, the DA then called FBI agents Ray Andjich and Jeffrey Tomlinson, two of Chris Favo's colleagues, whose reports about Lin DeVecchio had, in part, prompted the OPR investigation. The Justice Department was apparently concerned enough about what the two agents might say on the stand that it dispatched two attorneys from Washington, Robert S. Tully and Jay F. Kramer, to "observe" them. Tully and Kramer sat in the jury box just a few feet away from the special agents, who were still on active duty.

As with Favo himself, who was later called as a witness, the two senior DOJ lawyers monitored every word of their testimony.[28] "How can you interpret their presence," says Andrew Orena, who attended the trial, "as anything short of intimidation? They were literally breathing down on these guys."[29]

Under direct examination, Andjich described his three visits to Scarpa's house, the first on the day of the November 18, 1991, shootout and the other two when DeVecchio "parked" Andjich in front of a TV while he spoke to Scarpa in the kitchen. Andjich testified that he believed it was Lin DeVecchio who had "turned up" the volume on the living room TV, preventing him from hearing the conversation later described in the infamous "Kitchen 302."[30] And, just as he'd sworn in his OPR statement, Andjich recalled Scarpa using the words "murder" and "hit" but testified that he "couldn't make out anything more of the conversation."[31]

During the OPR, Andjich had complained that while one of the visits lasted "thirty to forty-five minutes," DeVecchio's 209 memorializing the interview contained "less than half a page of content."[32] But he didn't volunteer any of that now on the stand, nor did the ADA elicit those facts from him—evidence that might have shown that DeVecchio was hiding information about "34" from the agents who worked under him.

Under cross-examination by Mark Bederow, Andjich did admit that he was "shocked" that he hadn't been part of DeVecchio's debriefing of Scarpa.[33] The agent conceded that it may have been Scarpa who had turned on the TV but recalled that it was Lin who "raised the volume."[34]

Under direct examination, Andjich had testified that in 1992, when the FBI was about to arrest Scarpa, he'd been concerned that DeVecchio might warn his source. Now, Judge Reichbach asked Andjich "whether or not that assumption was based on something concrete."

In his sworn OPR statement, Andjich had stated that, besides Favo, Tomlinson, Leadbetter, and possibly SA Maryann Walker-Goldman, he didn't know of any other agents on the C-10 squad who "were worried that SSA DeVecchio was divulging information to Scarpa Sr."[35] But the fact that he'd cited those names back then was significant. It underscored the sense that at least three special agent in the C-10 squad were concerned that DeVecchio may have been leaking intel to his source. Now, as DeVecchio stared at him from a few feet away, Andjich testified that he didn't "have a recollection" of any concrete reason to conclude that DeVecchio might have "tipped off" Scarpa.[36]

When Special Agent Jeff Tomlinson took the stand, he testified that he'd participated in the debriefings of both Carmine Imbriale and "Joey Brains" Ambrosino. Then, about half an hour into his testimony, when Judge Reichbach asked Tomlinson whether his duties included "evaluat[ing] the information provided by informants," Jay Kramer, one of the DOJ lawyers, intervened.

"Our assessment of the [DOJ] authorization for him to testify today in this proceeding," he said, "does not include opinion testimony; rather his substantive knowledge regarding the contents of either report, including whether they are consistent; inconsistent. Not his opinion regarding them."[37]

Even the ADA who conducted the direct examination seemed unable to get Tomlinson to repeat his most damning criticism of DeVecchio: the allegation, which he made in his sworn OPR statement, that Imbriale had told him Scarpa admitted killing Nicholas Grancio, and that Tomlinson was "confident [that that information] was provided to SSA DeVecchio."[38] In fact, neither Scarpa's role in the murder of Nicky Black nor Lin DeVecchio's knowledge of it ever came up while Tomlinson was on the stand.

Finally, after questioning by Judge Reichbach himself, Tomlinson admitted that Carmine Sessa had told him "he believed that Lin DeVecchio was Greg Scarpa's law enforcement source."[39] Tomlinson, a former state police officer, was one of the three agents who'd found DeVecchio's relationship with Greg Scarpa Sr. so problematic that he'd risked his career by complaining about it. But his testimony at DeVecchio's trial ended without the DA ever eliciting the full depth of what "bothered" Tomlinson "about SSA DeVecchio's relationship with Scarpa Sr.," as expressed in his OPR statement.[40]

At this stage of the trial, virtually every round had gone to the defense.

Favo Takes the Stand

Early in his testimony, Chris Favo testified that an official FBI investigation into the Colombo war hadn't been opened until December 9, 1991, three weeks after the shootout on Eighty-Second Street that Scarpa claimed had marked the start of hostilities.[41] At that point, DeVecchio still had enough faith in Favo to make him the case agent on the probe and Favo retained that role until June 1996, when the last of the war cases had been litigated at the trial level. That was less than three months before the OPR was concluded and DeVecchio was allowed to retire with a full pension.

For the next half hour, the direct examination by Senior Assistant DA

Mike Vecchione took Favo through a discussion of various war events, starting with the November 18 shootout and moving forward through February 1992. But curiously, the pit-bull-like prosecutor never touched on the murder of Nicholas Grancio—after which Favo was sued in civil court, along with Lin DeVecchio, for allegedly making Nicky Black vulnerable by pulling away the FBI and NYPD surveillance details. Detective Tommy Dades had told me that the Brooklyn DA had originally planned to add the Grancio hit to its indictment of DeVecchio.[42] Now, in questioning Favo, who learned that Scarpa had been involved in the homicide four days after the rubout,[43] Vecchione inexplicably ignored it.

"It might have been," says Andrew Orena, "that Vecchione didn't want to visit this sensitive subject with Favo, since the civil suit was still pending. But it's not as if he got anything substantial out of Favo. As it turned out, his testimony was incredibly weak."[44]

Later, Vecchione did get Favo to discuss how he'd overheard his boss talking to his informant "34" over the "Hello" line in the squad after Carmine Imbriale's arrest in February 1992, and how DeVecchio had told Scarpa, "I don't know what he's saying about you. Brooklyn District Attorney's Office has him."[45] Favo also admitted that he'd suggested to DeVecchio that he tell Scarpa he'd been overheard in a wiretap threatening Imbriale, so that the Grim Reaper would think twice before killing him.[46]

Favo then confirmed that part of the teletype DeVecchio had sent to DC in order to get Scarpa reopened after he'd been closed on March 31 wasn't "truthful."[47] But he'd used much stronger language in his sworn 1995 statement during DeVecchio's OPR, calling the teletype "false."[48] The best Vecchione got out of Favo was a few more details regarding the infamous "we're going to win this thing" incident: As DeVecchio uttered those words, Favo recalled now, he "slammed his hands on the desk" and was "chuckling. . . . Not laughing out loud," added Favo, "but laughing a little."[49]

Later, in a signal that Favo, a Notre Dame graduate with a law degree from Columbia, might be dialing back on his memory of events relating to his boss's OPR, Vecchione asked him whether he knew the results of the thirty-one-month internal affairs investigation he had prompted.

"I don't," Favo answered with a straight face.[50]

"That had to take the cake," says Andrew Orena. "Here's Favo, whose career in the FBI almost got derailed over that OPR, and he's saying he doesn't remember how it turned out?" After Grover objected, Favo back-pedaled. "I was never informed of the results of the investigation, directly," he said.[51]

Later, on cross-examination, Doug Grover asked Favo: "In the winter and spring of 1992, did the FBI make efforts to prevent murders of various members of the two factions?" Favo answered, "Yes."[52] Once again, however, the murder of Nicky Grancio never came up.

Meanwhile, the presence of DOJ lawyers Tully and Kramer continued to be a factor in the courtroom. They seemed to intimidate even Grover. At one point, while asking Favo whether the C-10 squad dealt with "encryption issues" involving police radios, Grover began by saying, "Without getting into details so I don't upset the guys in the jury box. . . ."[53]

Favo's testimony ended on the third day of the trial, with little or no new evidence emerging to link Lin DeVecchio to the four murders in the indictment. If, in fact, Vecchione had decided to go easy on Favo and bypass the embarrassment of the Nicholas Grancio homicide, he seemed to get little in return from the testimony of Lin's chief FBI accuser. The most explosive testimony of the trial, from Larry Mazza, was still to come—including the moment when Mazza broke down on the stand.

"Mob Killer Becomes a Crybaby"

That was the headline on the *Daily News* story by Scott Shifrel the day after Larry Mazza took the stand and recalled the plans he'd made before becoming Greg Scarpa's murderous protégé.[54] Mazza was about half an hour into his direct examination by Mike Vecchione when he referred to his enrollment at John Jay College at the age of eighteen.

When asked "what was it" that brought him to John Jay, Mazza suddenly burst into tears.[55] The proceedings had to be halted while he was given a tissue and a glass of water, but he continued to weep until Judge Reichbach called a break.

After a five-minute recess, Mazza, who had earlier admitted to participating in the murders of Gaetano Amato, Vincent Fusaro, and Nicky Grancio, pulled himself together enough to describe how his father, an FDNY lieutenant, had inspired him to go to college. By 1993, however, he said he had become the "confidant" and "right hand man" to Greg Scarpa, whom he described as "a vicious, violent animal."[56]

Later, Mazza testified about the events on the night of Halloween 1989, when Joey Scarpa, Greg's son by Linda Schiro, had gotten into an altercation with Dominick Masseria, who was killed on the steps of a Fifteenth Avenue church in Brooklyn. After the killing, Mazza said, Joey and his good friend eighteen-year-old Patrick Porco, who had witnessed the murder, "went on the lam,"[57] shipped off to Scarpa Sr.'s horse farm in Lakewood, New Jersey.

Vecchione then asked Mazza if he recalled a conversation he'd had with Greg on May 27, 1990. Mazza nodded, recalling that it happened over the Memorial Day weekend. Scarpa was "very concerned," he said, that Porco "was a rat and he could hurt Joey." According to Mazza, Scarpa "wanted to kill him." Later, after Porco was shot to death, Mazza said he went to the Scarpa house and found Joey "extremely upset. Distraught." Scarpa told Mazza "they killed [Porco,] and Joey was so reclusive he couldn't even speak." In fact, he "didn't want to leave [his] room."[58]

Ten days after Mazza's testimony, Linda Schiro supplied the details that allegedly linked Porco's murder to Lin DeVecchio—an allegation for which Schiro has never been effectively impeached.

Joey and Patrick "were like brothers," she recalled.[59] After staying on the New Jersey farm for about two and a half weeks, the two returned to Brooklyn. Then, during the Memorial Day weekend, she said, DeVecchio called the house and asked for Scarpa in a tone she described as "serious."

Scarpa took the phone, Schiro recalled, and the conversation lasted "a couple of seconds." He hung up and asked her to drive him to a pay phone. They got in her car and she drove to the phone, which Scarpa, she said, had used before to communicate with DeVecchio.[60] Greg left the car, Schiro said, and went to the phone.

He then made a call that lasted "maybe five minutes," Schiro said. Though she didn't hear the conversation, when Scarpa got back in the car he was "really upset."

"This fuck[ing] kid. I cannot believe that he is going to rat on Joey," he exclaimed, according to Schiro. When she asked what he was talking about, Scarpa reportedly told her, "Patrick. Lin just told me that he is fucking ratting Joey out."[61]

Schiro said she told Scarpa, "Patrick would never do that." But Scarpa replied, "Listen to what I am telling you. He is ratting him out." With that, she said, they drove back to the house. At that point, said Schiro, Scarpa yelled for Joey to come downstairs.[62] Her testimony continued:

Vecchione: Did Joey come out?
Schiro: Oh yeah. Joey came down.
Vecchione: What happened?
Schiro: He came into the dining room and Greg said, "Sit down." At first Joey sat, and then he said, "What is going on?" [Greg] says, "Something has to be done with this Patrick—you know—he is fucking going to rat you out." So, Joey went nuts. He said, "Dad, what are you nuts? You don't know what you are talking about. Patrick would never do that to me." He says, "You're crazy." And he is telling his father that. So Greg says, "Listen to me." And he banged his hand really hard on the table. "Where this came from, Joey, it is high up." But that's when Joey stood up, and he said, "I don't give a fuck. . . . Patrick would never do that, Dad. You and him don't know what the hell you are talking about." And Joey just didn't want to know nothing. He just walked upstairs.
Vecchione: Did he tell him—did Scarpa mention to him—what it is that Porco was going to be ratting on him about?
Schiro: Yes. That murder of Dominick Masseria.[63]

Later on, Schiro testified that Scarpa called her nephew John Sinagra and ordered him to go with Joey and kill Patrick. After furnishing some additional details about the murder, Schiro testified that Joey returned.

Schiro: And he just went upstairs and I followed him up. And he was crying. He was in a fetal position in the hallway upstairs. . . . He just kept saying, "Mom . . . I can't believe Daddy. . . ." He was just in shock, Joey. He kept telling me, "I loved Patrick."[64]

Shortly after the Porco murder, according to Schiro, Lin DeVecchio came to Scarpa's house. Schiro said that she heard their conversation in the kitchen.

Vecchione: What did Scarpa say to DeVecchio and what did DeVecchio say to him?

Schiro: Lin walked in with a serious type of face. And Greg, he said "This kid [Joey] is sick. All he is doing is crying—you know?" And he says . . . [to DeVecchio,] "You told me he was ratting. I killed him and the kid . . . won't come out of his room."
Vecchione: What, if anything, did DeVecchio say?
Schiro: He says, "Well, listen, better he cries now than he goes to jail."[65]

Schiro's Earlier Interviews

About twenty minutes later, Vecchione asked Schiro about a series of books she had collaborated on with several writers, including the former cop turned magazine writer John Connolly and Sandra Harmon, who had cowritten a book about Priscilla Presley.[66] Both Connolly and Harmon had interviewed her and developed book proposals.[67] After talking to Harmon, Schiro said she was approached by Jerry Capeci, who she said was interested in "a book about the mob and Lin."

As noted, in 1997 Capeci had conducted a series of audio interviews with Schiro in partnership with Tom Robbins, his former colleague at the *Daily News,* who went on to write for the *Village Voice.* Capeci had also been cited in DeVecchio's OPR investigation as a possible recipient of some of Lin's alleged leaks. Chris Favo had told FBI agents that his boss had asked him to call Capeci on the day Carmine Sessa was arrested "so he could send a photographer over."[68] Favo had also insisted that "throughout the course of the war, important [FBI] investigative information was disclosed in Jerry Capeci's weekly column."[69]

On January 12, 2006, barely a week after it was announced that a Brooklyn grand jury was investigating DeVecchio, Capeci wrote a column for the *New York Sun* describing Schiro as "a central figure in the investigation."[70] Writer Sandra Harmon later insisted that on that same day— January 12—she sent an e-mail to the Brooklyn DA's office, citing both the Connolly and Capeci-Robbins book proposals along with the book proposal on Schiro she'd written.[71] The implication was that, some twenty-one months before the trial, Vecchione and company were on notice of at least three sets of interviews that Linda Schiro had given to various writers—

interviews the defense could later use to try to impeach her if she'd given any prior statements inconsistent with her testimony before the grand jury or at trial.

As recently as August 2007, Capeci had received a subpoena for his sources and notes relating to DeVecchio for the Kastigar hearing. In fact, according to a *Daily News* report, in fighting the subpoena, Capeci had stated in court pleadings that he'd promised Schiro in 1996 that their interviews would be kept "strictly confidential."[72] So it was no secret to Mike Vecchione that Robbins and Capeci had elicited statements from Schiro a decade before DeVecchio's trial that might conflict with her sworn testimony.

Now, twenty-one months after Capeci first cited Schiro as a "central figure" in his case, Vecchione was questioning Schiro on the stand about the very interviews the columnist had conducted with her in preparing his book proposal with Robbins.[73] In response, Schiro testified that Capeci's book was "supposed to be fiction. A lot of fiction and fact."[74]

The next day, October 30, Doug Grover subjected Schiro to a blistering cross-examination, repeatedly attempting to demonstrate that she had made a number of prior inconsistent statements over the years—particularly to FBI agents—when it came to her knowledge of Scarpa's dealings with Lin DeVecchio. In questioning her about a conversation she had with FBI agent George Gabriel, who interviewed her in December 1994 during DeVecchio's OPR investigation, Grover asked:

> **Grover:** Do you recall that it was during that conversation with Gabriel, that for the first time you said that Greg Scarpa had received information about impending arrests from Lin DeVecchio?
> **Schiro:** Yes.
> **Grover:** And do you recall that, for the first time, you made the statement DeVecchio informed Scarpa of the identification of, and you used the words "potential rats." Is that right?
> **Schiro:** Yes . . .
> **Grover:** And was this the first time you ever said that?
> **Schiro:** To George Gabriel?
> **Grover:** To anybody?
> **Schiro:** Yes. I believe so.[75]

Later, after a recess, Grover homed in on a conversation Schiro had had with Gabriel on May 10, 1995. This was two days after Assistant U.S. Attorney Ellen Corcella had given a letter to defense attorneys disclosing eight potential leaks by DeVecchio to "34" in the course of the war—including the whereabouts of Orena loyalist Sal Miciotta.

> **Grover:** Do you recall telling George Gabriel words to the effect that DeVecchio never provided Scarpa with any information about where Colombo Family members were hiding during the war?
> **Schiro:** I might have. I might have said that.[76]

Grover then refreshed her recollection by showing her Gabriel's 302 memorializing that May 10 debriefing session and Schiro admitted she'd told him that "DeVecchio never provided Scarpa with any information about where family members were hiding during the war."[77]

Vecchione Expresses Confidence in Schiro

During the next recess, I caught Mike Vecchione in the hallway and asked him if he was worried that Grover was successfully impeaching the credibility of his chief witness. Vecchione smiled and looked me straight in the eye.

With great bravado he said, "Peter, the FBI can put whatever it wants into a 302. Back then Linda was scared. Greg had died. She was looking to DeVecchio and the FBI to protect her. She said a lot of things in order to cope. To survive. But I can tell you with certainty, she was telling the truth about Lin in the grand jury and she's telling the truth about him now on the witness stand. I'm not worried in the least."[78]

With that he patted me on the back and went into the courtroom. I was so struck by his tone of certainty that I went into a stall in the men's room, pulled out a small microcassette recorder, and recorded that conversation verbatim while it was fresh in my mind. Within twenty-four hours, Michael Vecchione would eat those words.

Chapter 42

G-MAN STICKS
IT TO DA

On October 30, 2007, the second day of Schiro's testimony, Tom Robbins, the former *Daily News* reporter who had years ago published a flawed account of Scarpa's Mississippi missions, rocked the DeVecchio murder trial with a story in the *Village Voice,* where he now worked. Entitled "Tall Tales of a Mafia Mistress," the story revealed that ten years earlier, he and Jerry Capeci, who had cowritten the Mississippi stories, had interviewed Linda Schiro for a book they planned to write.[1]

As noted, Capeci himself had identified Schiro as a "central figure" in the case as early as January 2006; indeed, after Lin was indicted, Schiro was described in a *New York Times* piece as "the key witness" in the case against DeVecchio.[2] Given the early warning that Schiro would be playing such an important role, it strains belief to think that Capeci and Robbins wouldn't have sought to examine the audiotapes of their interviews with her long before trial—especially since Capeci's notes had been subpoenaed months earlier by the defense for the Kastigar hearing.

But according to Capeci, his former partner Robbins, whom he called a "dogged investigative newsman," didn't search for the recordings until the first day of trial, just two weeks before Schiro's testimony.[3] Now, in his *Voice* piece, Robbins wrote, "The story she told us then is dramatically different from the one she has now sworn to as the truth."

The very next day, Robbins showed up in court with a lawyer and waived his privilege under Section 79 H of the New York Civil Rights Law, which permits reporters to keep their interviews and notes confidential.[4]

Jerry Capeci, Tom Robbins, Mike Vecchione

But before he'd even listened to the tapes, and apparently based solely on Robbins's description of their contents in the *Voice* article, a red-faced Mike Vecchione made an astonishing announcement to the court: "I think that if after listening to these tapes we cannot go forward or should not go forward . . . because of what's on these tapes, then we're prepared to do what would be necessary, and that would be to dismiss this case if that is the situation."[5]

"When I heard about that admission," says defense attorney Flora Edwards, "I almost fell over. Here was the chief prosecutor on the biggest murder case in recent Kings County memory. They had put years into the preparation. They'd been at trial for two weeks—and without even hearing what was on those tapes Vecchione was prepared to fold the tent and go home. He didn't say to the judge, 'We want to weigh our options.' He didn't allow himself any wiggle room to finish his case-in-chief and maybe call Greg Scarpa Jr. to bolster Linda. He just painted himself into a corner. . . . It was absolutely unbelievable."[6]

"Keep in mind," says Andrew Orena, "this was a bench trial before a really smart judge—not a jury. Judge Reichbach had already stated that he was in a position to separate out the Kastigar issues. Why couldn't the DA have waited for a full damage assessment?"[7]

But within hours, after Vecchione had listened to the tapes, the case was finished.[8]

"Ex-F.B.I. Agent's Murder Trial Fizzles, as Does Chief Witness," read the headline in the *New York Times*.[8] The *New York Post* declared, "DeVecchio Off Hook,"[9] followed by "Moll Rat Is a Tape Worm,"[10] a pair of stories written by Alex Ginsberg who, just two weeks earlier, had filed a piece about Lin under the headline " 'Crooked Fed' & 'Grim Reaper' Joked."

The banner headline across the double-truck story in the *Daily News* was "Tapes Show Mob Moll Made It Up."[11] In the *New York Sun,* Jerry Capeci was ebullient. His "Gang Land" column was headlined: "G-Man Wins. Tapes Foil Mob Moll."[12] The next day, a page-one follow-up story by Ginsberg in the *Post* showed a smiling DeVecchio and his wife toasting with champagne at Sparks Steak House—the site of Paul Castellano's murder—under the headline "Up Yours: G-Man Sticks It to DA with Toast at Mob-Slay Site."[13]

Suddenly, in the eyes of the New York media, Lin DeVecchio was the victim and Linda Schiro the perpetrator. Back in 1997, when they interviewed her, Capeci and Robbins had promised Schiro they would keep their interviews secret. But DeVecchio was facing twenty-five years to life on each of the four murder counts, so Robbins justified his last-minute production of the tapes this way:

"Tell me what else I could have done? If you sit silent, then someone could go to jail for life. I chose not to live with that."[14]

On the other hand, the Schiro tapes didn't clear DeVecchio of all the charges in the DA's indictment—not by a long shot. They never addressed his possible role in the Mary Bari murder. And they actually *implicated* him in the murder of Patrick Porco, Joey Scarpa's teenage friend. There's little doubt that they definitively cleared him in the May 1992 murder of Lorenzo "Larry" Lampasi. But that was one murder out of four. And as we'll see, a new analysis of the tape transcripts compared to the trial transcript raises serious questions about why the DA precipitously dismissed his entire case.

The Two Transcripts Compared

When the case against Lin DeVecchio collapsed on November 1, no verbatim transcript of Schiro's trial testimony was available to allow for an independent comparison of her interviews with Capeci and Robbins from 1997. The trial transcript was almost immediately sealed. But I later managed to secure a copy, and what I found when measuring Schiro's 1997 statements against her sworn testimony in 2007 was eye-opening.

Of particular concern was the suggestion, published widely in the media, that the tapes exonerated DeVecchio in the murder of Joseph "Joe Brewster" DeDomenico.[15] Jerry Capeci's "Gang Land" column was one of many venues reporting that on the tapes, Schiro had "specifically excluded [DeVecchio] from participating in the murder of mobster Joseph (Joe Brewster) DeDomenico."[16] But a careful comparison of the tape transcript against Schiro's trial transcript suggests otherwise.

On October 29, 2007, under questioning by prosecutor Michael Vecchione, Schiro testified that DeVecchio had made two trips to meet with Scarpa sometime before March 1986. Both meetings, Schiro insisted, took place in the kitchen of their house with the SSA and his informant sitting in a "breakfast nook," their usual meeting place, as Schiro stood a few feet away. The direct examination went like this:

> **Vecchione:** What did Greg say to DeVecchio in your presence?
> **Schiro:** He just told Lin that he doesn't understand what is going on with Joe Brewster. He doesn't come around anymore. He is doing burglaries with an alarm guy that Greg did work with. . . . And he was becoming this born-again Christian. Drugs, drinking.
> **Vecchione:** What if anything did he say to DeVecchio about that stuff?
> **Schiro:** To see what you could find out about him.
> **Vecchione:** And what, if anything did DeVecchio say at that point?
> **Schiro:** That he would take care of it.[17]

Schiro then recounted what happened a week or two later, when DeVecchio returned.

> **Vecchione:** What if anything did DeVecchio say and what did Scarpa say?
> **Schiro:** He said he was right about what he was saying about Joe Brewster.
> **Vecchione:** Who is doing the talking now?
> **Schiro:** Lin was doing the talking to Greg.

Vecchione: And what did Lin say to Scarpa?

Schiro: After he said he was right about him drinking, doing drugs, and the burglaries, he says, you know we got to take care of this guy before he starts talking.

Vecchione: Let the record reflect, the witness has used her right hand to make a motion with her fingers and her thumb, moving them together.[18]

Eighteen months later, Joe Brewster was murdered. Linda testified that the job was done by Greg Scarpa Jr., Mario Parlagreco, and William Meli, another member of Greg Sr.'s Wimpy Boys crew.[19]

Later, after becoming a government witness, Meli told FBI agents that "it was incredible the way Scarpa Sr. trusted Schiro." The FBI 302 memo on Meli's debriefing went on to say that Scarpa "would talk about all kinds of criminal efforts including murders, right in Schiro's presence." Meli even recalled Scarpa "talking about the murder of Joseph DeDomenico, aka Joseph Brewster, in front of Schiro after they had killed DeDomenico that same evening."[20]

Now, consider what Schiro reportedly told Robbins and Capeci during their interview in 1997. In his initial *Voice* piece on October 30, 2007, Robbins writes, "That interview took place on March 1, the day after agent DeVecchio had himself been forced to take the witness stand in Brooklyn federal court, where he was grilled by attorneys for a pair of Colombo crime family members seeking to have their convictions overturned."[21]

He's referring to the cross-examination by attorney Gerald Shargel, in which DeVecchio answered, "I don't recall," or words to that effect, more than fifty times and denied that he had ever intervened with prosecutors to keep a confidential informant like Scarpa on the street.[22] Robbins cited that testimony in his *Voice* story, noting:

> Brewster's name had been raised by one of the defense attorneys, who asked DeVecchio if he'd ever given Scarpa information about him. DeVecchio angrily denied it. Having heard that exchange, we asked Schiro whether Lin DeVecchio had had anything to do with the death of Joe Brewster. She seemed briefly confused by the question. "No," she said. "He never met Joe Brewster."

The following is a portion of the transcript of that interview, published after the release of the tapes in the New York *Daily News,* Robbins and Capeci's former newspaper:

> **Schiro:** Greg had him killed. Greg didn't kill him. It was Billy and Mario. . . . I remember Joe came over one day on Avenue J and he was kind of drooling, he was starting to use coke; 'cause he was going out with this girl from Manhattan and he had refused Greg something. And Greg told Gregory, Billy, Mario in fact they told him they had to go someplace, they got all dressed up. Joe Brewster, and they killed him.[23]

Forty-two lines later in that *Daily News* transcript there is this exchange between Robbins and Schiro:

> **Robbins:** Lin had nothing to do with Joe Brewster?
> **Schiro:** No. Lin never met Joe Brewster.[24]

In an interview with the *Daily News* published November 1, 2007, Robbins had this to say about Schiro's account of the Brewster killing:

> Schiro said in our interviews that as far as she knew DeVecchio had nothing to do with the 1987 murder of a long time Scarpa pal, a Colombo soldier named Joe DeDomenico who went by the nickname of Joe Brewster.[25]

After the dismissal of the DeVecchio case, former New York supreme court judge Leslie Crocker Snyder was appointed as a special district attorney to determine whether Linda Schiro had committed perjury.[26]

On October 22, 2008, Crocker Snyder issued a report declining to prosecute Schiro. One of the exhibits to the report included twelve pages of heavily redacted typewritten notes from Robbins, which appear to be a verbatim transcript of the interview portions he released to the Brooklyn DA along with the tapes.

As revealed on page twelve of those notes, reproduced on the next page, when Robbins asked Schiro, "Lin had nothing to do with Joe Brewster?" it was during a point in the interview when Schiro was reviewing family pictures with Robbins. The sequence began with Schiro referring to an entirely different murder that took place in Florida.

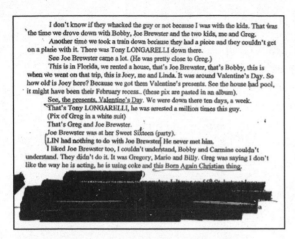

I don't know if they whacked the guy or not because I was with the kids. That was the time we drove down with Bobby, Joe Brewster and the two kids, me and Greg.
Another time we took a train down because they had a piece and they couldn't get on a plane with it. There was Tony LONGARELLI down there.
See Joe Brewster came a lot. (He was pretty close to Greg.)
This is in Florida, we rented a house, that's Joe Brewster, that's Bobby, this is when we went on that trip, this is Joey, me and Linda. It was around Valentine's Day. So how old is Joey here? Because we got them Valentine's presents. See the house had pool, it might have been their February recess.. (these pix are pasted in an album).
See, the presents, Valentine's Day. We were down there ten days, a week.
That's Tony LONGARELLI, he was arrested a million times this guy.
(Pix of Greg in a white suit)
That's Greg and Joe Brewster.
Joe Brewster was at her Sweet Sixteen (party).
LIN had nothing to do with Joe Brewster He never met him.
I liked Joe Brewster too, I couldn't understand, Bobby and Carmine couldn't understand. They didn't do it. It was Gregory, Mario and Billy. Greg was saying I don't like the way he is acting, he is using coke and this Born Again Christian thing.

In that transcript, Robbins asks, "Lin had nothing to do with Joe Brewster?" She responds, "He never met him." But unlike the transcript republished in the *Daily News,* the complete transcript turned over to the DA's office does *not* include the word "No" preceding Linda's answer.

The *Daily News* transcript also lacks the reference to "pix . . . pasted in an album." In fact, Schiro's response about whether Lin DeVecchio had anything "to do" with Brewster comes several minutes *after* her earlier discussion of Brewster's murder (as reflected by the transcript) and that response follows the sequence in which she's showing Robbins the pictures from the Florida trip.

In saying "He never met him," Schiro may well have been speaking literally—that Lin DeVecchio had never made Joe Brewster's *acquaintance.* But whether DeVecchio "met" DeDomenico is immaterial to the question of whether he twice visited Scarpa's house and conspired with Scarpa to kill him, as Schiro testified to under oath.

Nonetheless, in the telling of the story after the case's dismissal, Robbins insisted that the tapes definitively cleared DeVecchio in both the Lampasi and Brewster homicides. Here is an excerpt of an interview he gave Bob Garfield for OntheMedia.org on November 2, 2007:

> Three of the four murders that she was putting in Lin DeVecchio's mouth, she'd never even mentioned to us his involvement. In two of them, when I went back and dug out an old cardboard box and looked at the transcripts I'd made back then and listened to the tapes, I was astonished to see that she had explicitly told us—when we'd asked her whether or not he'd had any involvement with two of the murders, she said, absolutely not. One of the quotes was, "Lin didn't do that. I know it for a fact."[27]

The murder he refers to in that last statement is the rubout of Larry Lampasi, for which Schiro did explicitly clear DeVecchio. But that was the *only* one of the four murders in the DeVecchio indictment where she exonerated the former SSA on those tapes. When it came to Robbins's own transcript of his interview with Schiro on the Brewster murder—the same transcript he submitted to the Brooklyn DA—Schiro did *not* rule out Lin's connection to the hit.

"At the time of the case's dismissal," says Andrew Orena, "these tapes from Robbins and Capeci were portrayed in the media—particularly the *Daily News*—as the ultimate smoking gun that proved Lin DeVecchio's innocence and made Linda a liar. But if you look at them now in the cold light of day, when it comes to Joe Brewster, Linda's words on those tapes don't go against her words on the stand. The tapes don't mention Lin one way or another in the Bari murder and they do put him into Porco's hit. So, out of the four murders, the only one that Linda clears Lin on is Lampasi. But that's not the impression you got from Vecchione or the media after he dismissed the case."[28]

The Deal with the Devil

After the case fell apart, there were a host of postmortems in the media. DA Joe Hynes was quoted in the *Daily News* as saying that "he never would have brought charges against Lindley DeVecchio if he knew about the tapes."[29] In relation to Linda Schiro, Vecchione told Michael Brick of the *New York Times,* "We knew what her problems were, and it was important for us to corroborate everything she gave us. And we believed we had."[30]

Both comments suggested that the Kings County prosecutor's office was blindsided by the tapes. But as we've pointed out, Vecchione actually *questioned* Schiro on the stand about her interviews with Capeci for the book. At that time there was no mention of Capeci *recording* the interviews, but given that the DA's office knew Schiro had opened up to him, one wonders why they didn't press to find out if her conversation with the columnist had been taped.

The two reporters were quick to tell the *Post* that nobody from Hynes's office had asked them about the recordings. "At no time did the DA's office ever call me," said Capeci. Robbins chimed in: "If someone had asked me to give them [Hynes's prosecutors] a reality check I would have done that."[31]

But how believable is the claim made in Capeci's "Gang Land" column that Robbins hadn't decided to "look for cassette tape recordings" until just weeks before the dismissal—especially in light of the twenty-one-month notice Capeci had that Schiro would be the DA's star witness?

Remember that, as far back as 1994, Capeci had been identified by multiple agents in the FBI's C-10 squad as a recipient of DeVecchio's alleged leaks. When the Feds decided to frame Detective Joe Simone for the leaks, Robbins and Capeci were merciless in their coverage. Capeci even went so far as to attribute Simone's federal court vindication to a "bad jury."[32] Further, after the DeVecchio case collapsed, Capeci was quoted in the *Daily News* as saying, "It seems pretty obvious that this case was built on a house of cards."[33]

"I certainly wouldn't call the nine hundred pages in Lin's OPR suggesting he'd leaked intelligence to Scarpa a 'house of cards,'" says former FBI agent James Whalen. "With reporters as sharp as Capeci and Robbins who cover the mob, you have to wonder, what took them so long? If they knew how important Linda Schiro was and they could see from the indictment that the DA was charging Lin on Brewster and Lampasi, why wait till the last minute to step forward?"[34]

The only major New York journalist to offer a minority report on the dismissal was *Daily News* columnist Michael Daly, who wrote about how Dominick Masseria's murder on the church steps had devastated his family. The seventeen-year-old Masseria's only "crime" was getting involved in an egg-throwing fight with Joey Scarpa and his friends that Halloween night in 1989. The youngest of five children, who hoped to attend college, Masseria had started out the night, according to Daly, watching cartoons and babysitting his two-year-old niece.[35] "He was not in any way involved in the bad stuff," his sister Dorothy Garucchio told Daly. "He was an innocent bystander."

But his brush with Joey Scarpa, whose complaint to his father had resulted in that 1992 Bay Ridge gun battle, proved fatal. It was another murder in the roster of victims who had crossed paths with the Grim Reaper. In his column, Daly noted that "the FBI is to blame for allowing Scarpa to strut about as a homicidal role model." And in acquiescing to the DA's desire to dismiss the charges, Judge Reichbach agreed, using his decision and order ending the case to issue a scathing indictment of the Bureau and its decades-long relationship with Scarpa. The complete decision is reproduced in Appendix H, but a portion is cited here. Keep in mind that the late Judge Reichbach reached his conclusions without the benefit of viewing the 1,153 pages of Scarpa-related FBI files uncovered for this book:

> Friedrich Nietzsche sagely observed at the end of the nineteenth century "that he who fights with monsters might take care lest he thereby become a monster . . . and if you gaze for long into an abyss, the abyss gazes also into you. . . ."
>
> What is undeniable was that, in the face of the obvious menace posed by organized crime, the FBI was willing, despite its own formal regulations to the contrary, to make their own deal with the devil. They gave Scarpa virtual criminal immunity for close to fifteen years in return for the information, true and false, he willingly supplied. Indeed, this Court is forced to conclude that Scarpa's own acknowledgment of criminal activity to the FBI could only be explained by his belief that the agency would protect him from the consequences of his own criminality, which the record suggests is what they did.
>
> Not only did the FBI shield Scarpa from prosecution for his own crimes, they also actively recruited him to participate in crimes under their direction. That a thug like Scarpa would be employed by the federal government to beat witnesses and threaten them at gunpoint to obtain information regarding the deaths of civil rights workers in the south in the early 1960s is a shocking demonstration of the government's unacceptable willingness to employ criminality to fight crime.[36]

Lin DeVecchio was ecstatic after the case was closed, but he was also bitter. "I will never forgive the Brooklyn DA for irresponsibly pursuing this case," he told the *New York Post* after celebrating his victory at the site of Paul Castellano's rubout.[37]

But in the months after the trial ended, he started to spin what happened as if to suggest that the Brooklyn DA never even had enough evidence for an indictment. Here is what he told former Guardian Angels leader Curtis Sliwa in a radio interview:

The indictment. . . . It was obtained by the Brooklyn DA's office who were either incredibly stupid or incredibly arrogant, thinking that there was a case there— They had been given information, long before the indictment, that exonerated me in every crime because cooperating witnesses had already come in and testified in Federal Court about all these crimes.[38]

But that was patently untrue. The cooperating witnesses who testified in the war trials never exonerated Lin DeVecchio per se; nor was there evidence before the trial that cleared DeVecchio, except for Schiro's single account regarding Larry Lampasi. Still, Lin DeVecchio went further in his characterization of her testimony:

And the only witness that came in against me was Linda Schiro, who had absolutely fabricated the entire thing. . . . And we had ample proof that everything she said was completely fabricated. And I couldn't have been happier when Robbins and Capeci came in with their tapes showing that she not only was a liar but that she had made all this up. . . . She completely exonerated me in the criminal acts for which I was charged.

DeVecchio's interview with Sliwa was also revealing for the way Lin characterized his OPR investigation and its aftermath:

Sometime before I closed [Scarpa] there was an agent assigned to me who felt that I was giving him too much information. . . . And without any proof of any kind, those suspicions were reported and I was put under what's called an Office of Professional Responsibility (OPR) investigation for allegedly leaking information to an organized crime informant. This went on for two and a half years and the investigation, I was exonerated. They found no harm, no foul. . . . Literally no proof that I had ever done that.

As we've seen, however, the DeVecchio OPR generated more than nine hundred pages of FBI 302 memos, trial transcripts, and other communiqués from the Bureau and Department of Justice, including a great deal of troubling content that was far from exculpatory. In the end, DOJ's Public

Integrity Section declared that prosecution of Lin wasn't "warranted. " But that conclusion came sixteen months after they'd granted him immunity, making his indictment and trial problematic if not impossible.

The Unanswered Questions

The only significant legal postmortem on the case was conducted by Leslie Crocker Snyder, who was commissioned to determine whether Linda Schiro had, in fact, committed perjury. In issuing her twenty-eight-page report, with more than two hundred pages of documentary appendices, Crocker Snyder concluded that Schiro had *not* perjured herself. And, in an addendum to her report, she raised a series of compelling, unanswered questions.[39]

1. Did DeVecchio pass information to Scarpa Sr. regularly, setting aside the four murders charged in the indictment? Witnesses, and possibly records, appear to exist which would be probative of this issue.

2. Is there probative evidence that the FBI—or at least DeVecchio—knew that Scarpa Sr. was ordering, and committing, numerous murders and, nevertheless, allowed him to continue his status as a Top Echelon FBI informant?

3. Was there an effort by the FBI to protect Scarpa and DeVecchio in order to protect/insulate/preserve numerous mob prosecutions and some convictions relating to the Colombo crime family?

4. Was Detective Joseph Simone, of the New York Police Department, a scapegoat for the misconduct of others, as a number of people who came forward have suggested?

5. Were the FBI agents who reported their suspicions regarding DeVecchio shunned and ostracized? And did they later modify their positions regarding DeVecchio?

6. Why was DeVecchio allowed to retire with a full pension, despite the Government's acknowledgment that he leaked information to a murderous informant, and why was he granted immunity after he invoked his Fifth Amendment privilege in post-conviction proceedings related to convictions in the Colombo War?

7. Have any of the witnesses, potential witnesses, or people who cooperated in the DeVecchio investigation and/or prosecution been harassed by various agencies because of their cooperation, as many of these individuals now claim?

After spending more than five years investigating Greg Scarpa Sr.'s relationship with Lin DeVecchio, I come away with those identical questions, but I have a few more to add.

8. Why did the Brooklyn DA devote such an enormous amount of public resources to the indictment and prosecution of Lin DeVecchio—and then so precipitously drop the charges in the face of what we can now clearly say was *equivocal evidence* contradicting their lead witness, Linda Schiro?

9. Why did the U.S. Justice Department approve the payment of untold thousands in legal fees for Lin DeVecchio's defense when a federal judge, Frederic Block, had determined before his trial that the crimes alleged in the indictment had "nothing to do with his federal duties"?

10. Why did the Bureau of Prisons, a division of the Justice Department, move Abdul Hakim Murad out of the Supermax and put him into a cell in close proximity to Greg Scarpa Jr. at the Metropolitan Correctional Center (MCC)? What possible justification could there be for moving a convicted al-Qaeda terrorist across the country, only to put him in a cell near the very CI who had informed on him?

11. Indeed, why did the district attorney go to the trouble of holding Greg Jr. in the MCC for ten months if they didn't intend to hear his testimony in open court?

12. Why didn't the Brooklyn DA take Anthony "Gaspipe" Casso up on his offer to testify as a prosecution witness at Lin DeVecchio's trial? As indicated by his interview for this book, his testimony would have included his allegation that he killed Jimmy Hydell, one of the Mafia Cops' principal murder victims, after getting the intel on him from Lin DeVecchio via Greg Scarpa Sr.

13. Why hasn't the NYPD granted Detective Joseph Simone, a decorated officer who with his partner was responsible for a third of the arrests in the Colombo war, a new hearing to reevaluate the decision to take his pension away—especially in consideration of his vindication by a jury in federal court?

14. In light of the newly disclosed 1,153 pages of FBI files on Gregory Scarpa Sr. and the evidence presented in this book linking Scarpa to the murder of Tommy Ocera, will federal judge Jack B. Weinstein reconsider Vic Orena's motion for a new trial? And is Judge Weinstein prepared to reconsider the credibility of Greg Scarpa Jr. in light of the evidence produced in this book about the legitimacy of his two intelligence initiatives aimed at thwarting acts of terror, against Ramzi Yousef in 1996–1997 and Terry Nichols in 2005?

15. Given the evidence we've produced that John Napoli was not a witness to any fabrication of the "Scarpa material," which was documented in dozens of FBI 302s, will the Justice Department reconsider its decision to renege on a promise to grant Greg Scarpa Jr. a reduction in sentence or at least admit to the fact that he provided "substantial" assistance to the FBI in 1996–1997 and 2005?[40]

Out of the Supermax

I had always intended to end this book at this point. But as I was completing the final chapters, I made a surprising discovery: After spending twenty-three years in federal prison, the last fourteen of which he served in a seven-by-twelve-foot cell at ADX Florence—the Supermax prison where Yousef, Murad, and Nichols are housed—Greg Scarpa Jr. was moved to a maximum-security prison in the Midwest.

Back in 2004, I got some insight into just how impregnable the Supermax was when I sought to interview Greg Jr. there. At first my request was turned down by Warden Robert Hood, who claimed that my interview of Junior "could pose a risk to the internal security" of the Supermax and "to the safety of staff, inmates and members of the public."[41] He later rejected my appeal on the grounds that such an interview would "disrupt the good order and security of the institution."[42]

Just how a journalist with a reporter's notebook, a pen, and a tiny digital recorder might disrupt the order of a hardened federal prison was a puzzle to me, but that was how Warden Hood saw it.

Scarpa Jr.

Then, in late March 2012, as I was writing the final chapters of this book, I noticed on the Bureau of Prisons Inmate Locator website that Greg Scarpa Jr. was now in residence at a less restrictive facility. So I reached out to him through his younger brother Frank, a former sulky driver who had grown up on Greg Sr.'s horse farm in New Jersey. Frank put me in touch with Greg Jr.—and soon I began a series of interviews with him.

Though author Sandra Harmon had purported to tell Junior's story in her 2009 book *Mafia Son*,[43] Greg Jr. told me that her book was an inaccurate and "sensationalized" account.[44] Now, for the first time, we have a hint of what it was like to grow up under the Killing Machine.

Scripture tells us that "the sins of the father shall not be visited upon the son." So I approached Greg Jr. without judgment. He's the one living person who arguably knew his father best. A Mafia captain himself, he committed many crimes on his father's orders, but later twice risked his life to provide the FBI with intelligence on a pair of world-class terrorists.

In the hundreds of pages of FBI airtels, memos, and 209s documenting DeVecchio's debriefings of Greg Scarpa Sr., nothing comes close to hearing the story as Greg Jr. tells it. And while there isn't sufficient time or space in this book to tell it all, Junior's account suggests that we've only begun to uncover the full truth.

Chapter 43

THE SON ALSO RISES

The first thing I wanted to confirm with Greg Jr. was whether he stood by the various statements he'd previously made under oath—including the testimony he gave at his own trial in October 1998, his multiple sworn affidavits or affirmations, and the allegations he had made on January 7, 2004, when he appeared via video from the Supermax at the hearing for Vic Orena.[1]

In those statements, sworn to under penalty of perjury, Junior had alleged that Lin DeVecchio not only passed key intelligence to his father, but that he'd been on Greg Sr.'s payroll and that he'd actually appeared on the scene of at least one bank robbery committed by the Scarpa Bypass crew. Greg Jr. had also claimed that DeVecchio was present with his father when his half brother Joey allegedly planted the bag of guns under the deck of Vic Orena's girlfriend's house in an effort to frame Little Vic for the Tommy Ocera murder.

When I pressed him on those claims, Junior confirmed them without hesitation. "Right. Everything I said was right [i.e., correct] in those words."[2]

"So you stand by what you said and you have no reason to change your mind?"

His reply was immediate. "Right, right, right."

I was particularly interested in whether he would confirm his earlier sworn statements that his father was involved in the murder of Tommy Ocera and that the framing of Vic Orena had been done as a "trophy" for Lin DeVecchio.

"Yeah, yeah, yeah," he said emphatically, with the confidence of a street guy who had spent half of his adult life doing crimes and the other half behind bars.

"What about your allegation that Lin DeVecchio was on your father's payroll?" I asked him, reminding him that DeVecchio had reopened his father in June 1980 after Senior had been closed for five years. "In the book Lin says he met him in June 1980 and then a couple of weeks later he recruited him," I said, wanting Junior to clear up a discrepancy in the 209s. "But one of the 209s said it took six months,[3] and in one of your sworn statements you said it took Senior a long time to agree to work with him. You were out [of prison] during that period. So for how long did Lin woo your father?"

That's when Junior made his first stunning revelation to me: the allegation that his father had been associating with DeVecchio from at least the mid-1970s—years before reopening him. "In the seventies he was together with him," said Greg. "Seventy-five, seventy-six, seventy-seven they were friends. They were goin' out to restaurants. My father told me everything he did and who he was goin' with, just in case somethin' happened, so I would know, you understand?"[4]

I asked him if he had a precise memory of when DeVecchio first started connecting with his father. Was there an event he could fix in his mind?

"It had to be seventy-five, seventy-six," he said. "Without a doubt, because there was something [between them] that had to do with me getting straightened out"—a reference to Junior's induction into the Colombo family. I asked him when he'd gotten made and he said, "I was twenty-five." Junior was born in 1952, so that would have been some time in 1977.

I asked him where they'd had the ceremony and he said, "Queens Terrace." That was the same location where Joseph Colombo had celebrated his son's wedding back in 1967. At that time, "34" had even given his FBI contacting agent, Anthony Villano, the details in a 209.[5] So it made sense that Greg Sr., who was very close to Colombo, would use that location as the site where his eldest son and namesake would "get his button."

But the implication that Lin DeVecchio had been auditioned by Greg Sr. for years before he agreed to return to his Top Echelon role was staggering. If Junior was correct, this suggested that DeVecchio had lied to the FBI brass in his 209, as well as to Anderson Cooper when he described the 1980 reopening during his *60 Minutes* interview. But that wasn't the most damning aspect of what Junior told me.

Junior also fixed the mid-1970s as the time when his father started offering *payoffs* to DeVecchio.

In his sworn affidavit of July 30, 2002, Greg Jr. had alleged that "DeVecchio's cut of the proceeds came out of my father's numbers racket. Over the years DeVecchio received over $100,000 from my father, including an all-expense trip to Aspen, Colorado, in the 1980s."[6]

I asked him about that now. "So he was paying him as early at the mid-seventies?"

"Oh yeah, yeah. See, I used to take care of the books—the rackets, the numbers. We'd put our expenses down. It would depend on the numbers—whatever we'd do—and he'd say, 'Deduct eight hundred, deduct twelve hundred [dollars].' So I'd put down 'miscellaneous' and that was for him [DeVecchio]. I tried to explain that to them [the prosecutors] and they said, 'He's lyin', 'cause he [Senior] didn't start 'til the nineteen eighties.' "[7]

I asked him how the money would be delivered.

"It was paid in different ways," he said. "He [Senior] would wrap it in a rubber band. He wouldn't hand it to him. It was paid in envelopes. There was no set pattern. There were times when he would meet him in New Jersey. We'd be on our way back from the farm, into Brooklyn, and this guy [Lin] would be on a side road, off the Garden State."

In his May 1995 compelled statement, when he swore under oath that he opened Greg Sr. in 1980, Lin admitted to meeting Senior in New Jersey "on one or two occasions" but insisted that it was on official business and only *after* the 1980 reopening. Further, he has categorically denied ever taking bribes from "34." But Junior stressed that some of the alleged payoffs happened in New Jersey, and sometimes the exchanges, he said, were two-way.

"When we'd go home and he [Scarpa] had to see him for information or to give him cash [DeVecchio] would be on the side road. And we'd stop and my father'd get out of the car. I'd be sitting there and he'd go in the car with him. They'd do what they had to do. And he'd come back. And a couple of times he would come back with notes. He would show me the notes."

At this point, Junior dropped another bomb, insisting that one of the "notes" his father received from DeVecchio included the name of one of the four victims in the Brooklyn DA's indictment.

"There was Joe Brewster's name on a note one time," he said, "and that's when it all started, with Joe. That's the conversation with Joe. You understand? It wasn't like DeVecchio was callin' any shots or nothin' like that. He was just giving that information, and the brains of what had to be done was from Senior."[8]

But during our interviews Junior emphasized time and again how his father had felt protected and insulated by DeVecchio—recounting how Senior acted with incredible bravado even when making calls to him while he was doing time in hardened facilities like Leavenworth.

"These were conversations in general," he said. "There was no hiding. No 'Don't talk now.' First of all, Senior—this guy really, really believed he had a license to kill, Peter, because he used to tell me when I was on the phone in Leavenworth—he would actually tell me when guys got whacked."

The "Big Bang"

Whether or not Lin DeVecchio was "callin' any shots" with Greg Scarpa Sr., or directed him in any way, it's clear from what Junior told me that DeVecchio was capable of trying to manipulate his father to achieve a goal. Until now, the evidence I'd examined from the 302s of cooperating witnesses, trial transcripts, and DeVecchio's many 209s on Scarpa had convinced me that Senior incited the third war for control of the family. While I'm still confident of that, one thing I hadn't managed to determine conclusively, before talking with Junior, was what role, if any, the Bureau may have played in provoking the conflict. Greg Jr. added some new insight on that issue as well.

He told me a story that suggests that two years *before* Carmine Sessa and his surveillance team rolled up on Vic Orena in June 1991, the FBI had planted a false rumor with Greg Sr. in an effort to provoke a fight between him and the Orena faction.

"There was an incident when I was in Lewisburg," Junior said, meaning the federal prison. It involved an alleged threat to him.

"I spoke to my father about it," said Greg, "and he told me that Lin told him that this [threat] had come from Ralph Scopo and the other side—the Orena faction."

After word of the threat was communicated to Senior, Greg Jr. got stabbed by another inmate at Lewisburg. That sent Senior into a tailspin. Junior insisted to me that the incident that led to the stabbing had nothing to do with any interfamily rivalry. Still, he said, his father "went crazy" after "the FBI" told him that the stabbing had been ordered by Scopo, the elder capo who was convicted during the Mafia Commission case.

Junior was certain that Scopo had nothing to do with it. In fact, he insisted to me that Scopo had treated him like a son in prison. "He'd been really nice to me," Greg Jr. said. "But to start the war . . . they [the FBI] were feeding my father information."

After the stabbing, Junior said, his father came to see him on a surprise visit. "I say, 'Dad. Listen to me. I don't know what's going on out there. But I'm telling you that [the stabbing] had nothin' to do with those [Orena] guys.' But he says, 'It came from Ralphie Scopo.' And I says, 'Dad. You're wrong.' And he says, 'Don't argue with me, Greg. They [the FBI] told me. They've got it down. They know what they're doin'.' He was convinced whatever that guy [DeVecchio] told him was concrete."

To make the situation worse, Junior said his father kept insisting, based on what he'd been told by the Bureau, that Ralph Scopo had put the word out that he (Senior) "might be a rat." According to Junior his father told him, "This is what you got to do. You got to go tell Ralphie that if anything happens to your father outside, then you've got *him* in there. And I'm gonna do the same thing out here. I'm gonna go to all those guys and tell them, if anything happens to my son, I'm gonna kill yous all out here."

So I asked Greg Jr., point-blank, "Are you saying that the Feds were putting false information into your father's mind and making him paranoid?"

"That's exactly what they were doing," said Junior. "They were workin' on him. As smart as my father was, he trusted them. So it got to the point where he was ready to retire, but they wanted a *big bang*! Do you understand? They wanted a big fuckin' bang. And that's how they're celebratin' it now." As Greg Jr. described it to me, that "big bang" the Feds wanted was the third Colombo war.

The Lookout

Another allegation Greg Jr. had previously sworn to under oath was that Lin DeVecchio was "present during a bank robbery at which Junior was present."[9] In his interviews with me, he said that DeVecchio was on the scene of "a couple" of heists, but one in particular he remembered was the botched burglary at the Dime Savings Bank in 1980 that had led to the death of Dominick "Donnie" Somma.

"It was the one where the cleaning guy showed up," said Greg. I asked him where DeVecchio was and he said, "He was on the street prowlin' around. He was lookin' after me. That's what my father had him there for. For me. My father wasn't there. I was there and he wanted to make sure—as much damage as he did to me over the years, Senior was lookin' out when he had to look out."[10]

In light of that, I asked Greg Jr. how he felt about his father.

"My feelings aren't good," he said. "I always thought he was giving me one hundred percent in sincerity, loyalty, and love—which is what I was giving him—and then I find out that it wasn't the case. And it wasn't the case really with anybody. That was just him. He just maneuvered everybody. Including the FBI. Including my mom. Including Linda. He played the fuckin' chess game with everybody. My brothers, my sister. Forget about it. This guy was just out for himself. I mean, don't get me wrong, he made everybody around him happy, but it was all to make him succeed in what he was lookin' to do."

I asked him what he thought it was that drove his father. Was it money? Was it power? "It was all that," he said. "It was money. It was power. And it was to stay out of prison. He couldn't do jail time."[11]

In that single sentence, Greg Scarpa Jr. provided the Rosetta Stone to the complex mystery that was his father. A brilliant, brutal, manipulative strategist who used the FBI and the people around him, including his Mafia family and his blood family, to get what he wanted: the fortune he amassed from drug dealing, hijackings, stock fraud, high-end bank heists, and scores of other violent crimes; the power he derived by operating at the upper echelons of the Colombos; the intel he received from his handlers to eliminate his enemies and rise higher and higher in the borgata; and ultimately the freedom that "time out of jail" bought him. It was the freedom to murder and racketeer—an effective license to kill conferred, or at least allowed to stand, by the FBI.

Greg Scarpa Sr. had used his eldest son to further his personal ends—literally demanding that Junior kill his "second son," Joe Brewster, so that Senior could continue walking the knife's edge between Mafia über-capo and "rat." Still, Junior was his father's son, and as bitter as he may be over how his father used him, in our interviews he expressed a lingering admiration for his old man.

"Don't get me wrong," he said. "This man ruined my life and the lives of my brothers and sisters, and he put a mark on my name that I'll have to live with forever. He was the Grim Reaper, but he was still my father. Would I follow him again? Never. Would I break the law for him? Absolutely not. Do I pray each day for the people he killed and the bodies he had buried? You bet. He got to renounce this life at his sentencing, and I renounced it a long time ago. I carry around a huge amount of remorse. But Senior wasn't just a capo. He operated for years at the boss level of the family. He knew things and saw things that few made guys ever did, and he played the FBI for everything he could get. In his book, DeVecchio said he admired him, and I have to say to a small degree I go along with this. I admire him the way you might stand back and look at a tornado or a hurricane—some really powerful force of nature. Do you want it in your life? No. Do you feel bad for the bodies it leaves behind? Damn right. But hating my father would be like hating an earthquake or a tidal wave. When you see something like that coming, you just have to get out of its way."

A Chance to Make It Right

For several years, an attorney for Gregory Scarpa Jr. has been litigating a 2255 motion in Eastern District federal court so that new evidence can be presented that accurately reflects the service Junior rendered in his stings of Ramzi Yousef and Terry Nichols, two terrorists responsible for the collective loss of thousands of lives. Between the 1993 World Trade Center bombing, the 1995 Oklahoma City bombing, and the "planes as missiles" plot spawned by Yousef in 1995 and executed by his uncle Khalid Sheikh Mohammed on 9/11, thousands of innocents died—countless more victims than have ever been killed by any figure in the history of American organized crime.

Even though Judge Jack B. Weinstein, who showed clemency to Greg Sr. in 1993, found Greg Jr. "not credible" in the 2004 hearing for Vic Orena, Judge Edward Korman, the former chief judge of the EDNY, is now considering Junior's case.[12] It was Korman who presided over the trial that acquitted Vic Orena Jr. and John Orena in 1995 after Assistant U.S. Attorney Ellen Corcella was forced to turn over the letter disclosing eight potential leaks that may have come to Senior from Lin DeVecchio.[13]

The fact that Korman saw enough merit in Greg Jr.'s petition to continue the case suggests a willingness at least to hear the evidence.

I asked Greg Jr. what he would do with his freedom if he is granted that hearing and succeeds in getting released after twenty-four years behind bars.

"All I can tell you is that if I have a chance to get out and live on the outside for the first time in all these years, I will do everything I can to set the record straight on what my father did. I can't bring back the lives he took or the people he ordered to be whacked, but I can try and make the name Gregory Scarpa stand for something other than 'killer' and 'made guy.' After all this time inside, one of the things I learned is that it's how you finish that counts, not how you start out."[14]

AFTERWORD

Philip L. Graham, the former publisher of the *Washington Post,* is credited with describing daily deadline journalism as "the first rough draft of history."[1] If that's the case, investigative journalism gives us the second draft. Unlike beat reporters, who are subject to the tyranny of the ticking clock, an investigative reporter has the luxury of digging into a story in depth over time. As the layers get peeled away, one lead begets another, and eventually, if the reporter is tenacious, a broader understanding of the truth will emerge. That's just what I found when my initial focus on the FBI's counterterrorism performance led me to Ramzi Yousef, and in turn that probe, through Greg Scarpa Jr., led me to the questionable relationship between his father and Lin DeVecchio.

In 2003, when I began the reporting for my second HarperCollins book, *Cover Up,* I wasn't setting out to tell a Mafia story. But when I came upon the treasure trove of FBI 302s documenting Greg Jr.'s eleven-month sting of Yousef, I couldn't look away. Now the detailed pursuit of that organized crime story has put the terrorism story into sharper focus, and I'm happy to report that the central allegation in my first book on Yousef—denied for years by the Justice Department and the 9/11 Commission—has been confirmed by the Feds.

In *1000 Years for Revenge,* I offered prima facie evidence from the Philippine National Police of a direct connection between Yousef's bombing of the World Trade Center in 1993 and the "planes as missiles" plot realized on September 11, 2001—a plot that Yousef designed and set into motion in Manila in the fall of 1994.

It was ultimately carried out by his uncle Khalid Sheikh Mohammed (KSM), the al-Qaeda terrorist identified by the FBI in 2002 as 9/11's "mastermind."[2] In *1000 Years for Revenge,* I reported that as early as 1995 federal prosecutors in the office of the U.S. Attorney for the Southern District of New York (SDNY) became aware of the link between Yousef and KSM, who had been operating out of the Philippines in a cell that also included Abdul Hakim Murad, a commercial pilot trained in four U.S. flight schools who had been the intended lead pilot in the first configuration of "the planes operation."[3] But for years prominent DOJ officials and the 9/11 Commission staff refused to accept that the two attacks on the Twin Towers were executed by the same terrorists, or that they were directly funded by Osama bin Laden and al-Qaeda.

Staff Statement No. 15 from the 9/11 Commission, published in August 2004, stated that "whether [Ramzi Yousef] became a member of al Qaeda remains a matter of debate," calling him "part of a loose network of extremist Sunni Islamists."[4]

In a 2005 interview, Patrick Fitzgerald, the former head of the Organized Crime and Terrorism Unit in the SDNY, said, "People assume that the World Trade Center bombing was an al Qaeda operation. . . . I've never assumed that. . . . What I would say is, we learned that the World Trade Center bombing and the Day of Terror plots were part of a jihad network. I wouldn't necessarily conclude that that was al Qaeda."[5] But in 2010, positive confirmation that the two attacks were linked came when the SDNY unsealed the fourteenth superseding indictment against Yousef for the 1993 bombing. That indictment included his uncle KSM, who was now charged for the 9/11 attacks.

A *New York Times* piece dated April 10, 2010, confirmed that this latest indictment affirmatively linked the Trade Center bombing to the attacks of September 11, 2001.[6] "It runs 80 pages," the story said, "with almost half devoted to a list of 2,976 [9/11] victims."[7] All fourteen indictments can be accessed via the *Times* website.[8] The cover pages on the two key indictments (shown on the next page) share the same docket number: 93 Cr. 180 (KTD). The last three letters are the initials of Kevin T. Duffy, the federal judge who has presided over the case from the first World Trade Center bombing trial in 1994.

The decision by federal prosecutors to include KSM in the ongoing

**The original WTC indictment, March 31, 1993, and the fourteenth
superseding indictment, April 2010**

series of terrorism cases spawned by the 1993 Twin Towers bombing is proof
positive that the plots and cell members were inextricably bound. They were
not, as the 9/11 Commission staff characterized them, "part of a loose network." Further, the fact that the two attacks on the WTC were part of
an ongoing conspiracy, funded by bin Laden and al-Qaeda, underscores
the case I made in my third book on terrorism, *Triple Cross,* that various
officials in the FBI and the SDNY who had knowledge of the Yousef-KSM
Manila connection in 1995 were negligent in failing to connect the dots
years before Khalid Sheikh Mohammed sent American Airlines Flight 11
crashing into the North Tower of the World Trade Center.

New Proof the FBI Could Have Stopped the
1993 Bombing

Another central allegation in *1000 Years for Revenge* was that the FBI had
sufficient warning to have prevented the 1993 bombing by Ramzi Yousef,
which claimed six lives and left a thousand people injured. In that book
I chronicled a series of events leading up to Yousef's planting of a 1,500-

pound urea-nitrate fuel-oil device on the B-2 level beneath the North Tower around noon on February 26, 1993.

The first evidence came three and a half years earlier, in July 1989, when FBI agents followed a group of "MEs"—a Bureau term for "Middle Eastern men"—from the al-Farooq mosque on Atlantic Avenue in Brooklyn to the Calverton shooting range at the end of Long Island.[9] Firing a series of weapons, including AK-47s and handguns, the group included Mahmoud Abouhalima, a.k.a. "the Red," a six-foot-two-inch Egyptian cabdriver; Mohammed Salameh, a diminutive Palestinian; Nidal Ayyad, a Kuwaiti who had graduated from Rutgers University; and El Sayyid Nosair, a janitor from Port Said, Egypt, who worked in the basement of the civil courthouse in Manhattan.[10]

FBI Calverton surveillance photo
(*Abouhalima is third from left*)

Each of those terrorists-in-training was instructed by Ali Abdel Saoud Mohamed, the central figure in *Triple Cross*.[11] The details of Mohamed's extraordinary terror spree can be found at http://www.peterlance.com/wordpress/?p=1703.

A former Egyptian army commando from the very unit that killed Egyptian President Anwar Sadat in 1981,[12] Mohamed succeeded in infiltrating the CIA briefly in Hamburg in 1984, slipped past a watch list to enter the United States a year later, enlisted in the U.S. Army, and got posted to the JFK Special Warfare Center at Fort Bragg, where elite Green Beret officers train. From there, he traveled on weekends to New York City to school the Calverton shooters in paramilitary techniques.[13]

Ali Mohamed was so trusted by Osama bin Laden that he was dispatched to move the Saudi billionaire's entire entourage from Afghanistan to Khartoum in 1991, set up al-Qaeda's training camps in the Sudan, and train bin Laden's personal bodyguards. He was also one of the principal planners in the simultaneous truck bomb attacks on the U.S. embassies in Kenya and Tanzania in 1998 that killed 223 and injured thousands.[14]

As a further testament to his skills, Abouhalima, Salameh, and Ayyad, three of his Calverton trainees, were later convicted in the World Trade Center

Abouhalima, Salameh, Nosair, Ayyad, Hampton-El

bombing plot, while Clement Hampton-El, a U.S.-born Black Muslim, was convicted with Nosair in the 1993 "Day of Terror" plot to blow up the bridges and tunnels into Manhattan, along with the United Nations building and the skyscraper that houses the FBI's New York Office.[15]

One of the lead FBI investigators on that Calverton surveillance was NYPD detective Tommy Corrigan, who later went on to work directly with Squad I-49, the "bin Laden Squad," in the Bureau's NYO. For unknown reasons, the surveillance of those MEs was suspended. But the FBI got its next chance to interdict the WTC bombing plot a year later with the arrival in New York of Sheikh Omar Abdel Rahman, the so-called Blind Sheikh. Rahman, the spiritual emir of al-Qaeda, had somehow managed to get a CIA-approved visa, slip past a watch list, and land at John F. Kennedy International Airport in July 1990.[16]

Within months, the Sheikh began to quarrel openly with Mustafa Shalabi, a tall, strapping Egyptian émigré who ran the Alkifah Center at the al-Farooq mosque.[17] The Alkifah was the principal U.S. office for the Makhtab al-Khidamat (MAK), a worldwide center of storefronts where millions of dollars in cash was collected to support the Afghan war against the Soviets.[18] In November 1989, after the MAK's founder was killed by a car bomb, Osama bin Laden and Dr. Ayman al-Zawahiri merged their new terror network with the MAK. So by early 1990, al-Qaeda had what amounted to a New York clubhouse at Shalabi's Alkifah Center. And soon Sheikh Omar began to covet the funds still pouring into the center on Atlantic Avenue.[19]

The First Blood Spilled by al-Qaeda in the United States

By the fall of 1990, El Sayyid Nosair had joined the al-Gamma'a Islamiyah (IG), the Blind Sheikh's ultra violent group, and he was itching to make his bones for the jihad. He set his sights on Rabbi Meir Kahane, founder of the ultra nationalist Jewish Defense League, who advocated the removal of all Arabs from Israel.[20] On the night of November 5, 1990, as Kahane left the podium of the Morgan D Room at the East Side Marriott hotel, Nosair lunged forward and fired the same .357 Magnum that had been photographed by the FBI at Calverton sixteen months before. Struck in the neck by one shot, the rabbi was blown to the floor.

Meir Kahane after the shooting

Outside the hotel, Nosair was wounded in a shootout. A pair of ambulances rushed him and the rabbi to Bellevue Hospital. Nosair survived, but Kahane died.

After the killing, Abouhalima and Salameh, who were to have been Nosair's getaway drivers, regrouped at his home in Cliffside Park, New Jersey. But they were soon taken into custody after the house was raided. Detectives and FBI agents seized forty-seven boxes of evidence proving an international bombing conspiracy, with the World Trade Center as a target.[21] Among the files seized were maps of the Twin Towers. A passage inside Nosair's notebook called for the "destruction of the enemies of Allah . . . by . . . exploding . . . their civilized pillars . . . and *their high world buildings.*"*[22]

The presence of these documents, not to mention Abouhalima and Salameh, clearly pointed toward a conspiracy in the Kahane murder. Yet the very next day, the NYPD's chief of detectives, Joseph Borelli, concluded that the killing was a "lone gunman" shooting. More astonishing, though the raid on Nosair's house was led by the FBI, which had the Calverton surveillance photos of Abouhalima, Salameh, and Nosair (firing the very gun used on Kahane), the Red and Salameh were released within hours and never charged in the crime.[23] Years after the 9/11 attacks, the House-Senate

---

* Emphasis added.

Joint Inquiry revealed that Osama bin Laden himself had helped pay for Nosair's defense.[24]

The next significant warning of al-Qaeda's ongoing involvement with the Calverton cell came in February 1992, with the murder of Mustafa Shalabi.

Death of a "Bad Muslim"

Even though it was Shalabi himself who sponsored Sheikh Omar's entry into the United States, he balked when the blind cleric demanded half of the Alkifah's million dollars in annual income.[25] By the late summer of 1990, in speeches in area mosques, the Sheikh began denouncing Shalabi as a "bad Muslim."[26] Rahman even suggested that his fellow Egyptian was embezzling the Alkifah's funds. On February 26, the eve of the Gulf War, Shalabi hurriedly packed for a flight to Cairo, where his family was waiting. He never made it to the airport.

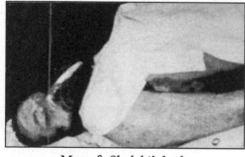

Mustafa Shalabi's body

A few days later, a neighbor of Shalabi's noticed that the door to his Sea Gate, Brooklyn, apartment was open. Shalabi was sprawled on the floor.[27] "He was knifed, shot and beaten with a baseball bat," said former Joint Terrorism Task Force (JTTF) investigator Tommy Corrigan. "This wasn't some . . . genteel thing. He was made an example of."[28]

Detectives from the NYPD's Sixty-First Precinct took control of the crime scene. In the course of their investigation, they discovered that more than $100,000 in Alkifah cash was missing from the apartment.[29] Abouhalima came in and identified the body, falsely claiming that he was the victim's brother. Neither the Red nor the Blind Sheikh was ever charged.[30]

The murder remained an open cold case in the files of the Sixty-First Precinct until the end of June 2010, when I uncovered evidence from the JTTF that not only solved the Shalabi murder but identified a second gunman in the Meir Kahane assassination. I also discovered a recording of a phone conversation made by a top FBI undercover operative. It contained an admission by a senior JTTF agent that the Bureau could have prevented the 1993 Trade Center blast.

The Shocking New Evidence

In January 2010, during interviews for a *Playboy* magazine article,[31] I learned new details on the Shalabi killing that had never been publicly disclosed. That led the NYPD to reopen the case. The subject of my piece, "The Spy Who Came in for the Heat," was Emad Salem, a remarkable former Egyptian Army major who became a naturalized U.S. citizen and succeeded in infiltrating the cell around the Blind Sheikh responsible for both the WTC bombing and the Day of Terror plot.*

Salem was so skillful as an undercover operative that within weeks of contacting the cell members, he became Sheikh Omar's personal bodyguard.

Emad Salem and Sheikh Omar Abdel Rahman

Then, after months undercover, Salem was effectively forced out of the cell by the newly appointed head of the JTTF, who insisted that he wear a wire— changing Salem's initial deal with the FBI. That left the cell around the Blind Sheikh without a bomb maker, so they called in Ramzi Yousef. In the fall of 1992, working directly with Abouhalima, Salameh, and Ayyad, Yousef then built the 1,500-pound device, which he delivered to the Trade Center in a Ryder rental truck.[32]

While I was researching the *Playboy* piece, Salem provided me with an audiotape he'd made of a phone conversation with his FBI control agent, John Anticev, after the bombing. In the recording Salem can be heard say-

---

* http://www.peterlance.com/wordpress/?p=629.

ing, "If we was continuing what we were doing, the bomb would never go off." At that point Anticev says, "Absolutely. But don't repeat that."

That recording is the first concrete admission by a JTTF agent that the FBI could have stopped the World Trade Center bombing.[33]

At that point, in March 1993, even though he'd been vastly unappreciated by the management in the Bureau's New York Office, Salem volunteered to go back undercover, this time wired up. As the government's linchpin witness in the "Day of Terror" case, he spent more than thirty days on the stand. But his testimony led directly to the conviction of Sheikh Omar and nine others in 1995.[34]

Solving the Shalabi Cold-Case Murder

In the fall of 2009, after spending years in the Witness Protection Program, Salem contacted me and asked to meet in New York City. I was giving a lecture at New York University and Salem arranged to meet me afterward. We ended up talking for hours, and in the days ahead he gave me a series of lengthy interviews.

During one session, Salem happened to comment that in the midst of an undercover conversation in the early 1990s, Hampton-El, the U.S. Black Muslim convicted in the "Day of Terror" plot, had told him that a .22 pistol was used to kill Shalabi. That detail had never been made public by the NYPD detectives, who interviewed a series of witnesses in 1991 but couldn't produce enough evidence for charges to be filed.

After some research, I learned that in 1993 the Feds had reopened the Shalabi case and leaked information that led to a series of articles in the *New York Times*. Those stories identified Hampton-El, Abouhalima, and Salameh as possible suspects.[35] The U.S. attorney's office for the SDNY even subpoenaed witnesses to a Shalabi grand jury, but for reasons unknown, the Feds dropped the case in 1994; it stayed cold until the winter of 2010.[36]

In mid-February of that year, I contacted the Brooklyn South homicide squad, which commenced a new investigation of the Shalabi murder.[37] The lead investigator was James Moss, a veteran detective. He visited Salem in the state where he'd been living for years under an assumed identity. After finding him highly credible, Moss began searching for the forensic evidence from the bloody Shalabi crime scene.

By late May, Moss discovered that this key evidence, once stored in the NYPD property clerk's office, had been signed out by an investigator for the Joint Terrorism Task Force back in October 1993. I later learned through a source that the investigator who removed the evidence was none other than the late Detective Tommy Corrigan—the same JTTF investigator who had been present during the 1989 Calverton surveillance of Salameh and Hampton-El.[38]

The Feds Produce a Series of Stunning Confessions

In June, after Detective Moss hit a brick wall, I sent the first in a series of detailed e-mails to the Intelligence Division of the NYPD, asking them to contact the Bureau so that the forensic evidence seized by Corrigan might be returned. On June 30, 2010, apparently in response, the Feds produced a series of FBI 302 memos dating from 2004 to 2006. They shed extraordinary new light on the Shalabi and Kahane murders. Among the revelations in the more than twenty pages of FBI 302s was evidence that:

- Shalabi was shot and stabbed by three al-Qaeda terrorists who were indicted in the original 1993 WTC bombing, including Nidal Ayyad and Mohammed Salameh.[39]
- The third alleged killer, a twenty-five-year-old Jordanian cabdriver named Bilal Alkaisi, was not only identified as the leader of the Shalabi hit team but was also fingered as the second gunman in the Kahane murder—a fact corroborated by his former attorney.[40]
- In 1994, after Alkaisi was initially indicted by the SDNY in the World Trade Center bombing,[41] he was allowed to make a plea deal and was released after serving only eighteen months on a minor immigration charge.[42]

Perhaps most significant, these 302s, together with another FBI memo from a 1996 debriefing of an al-Qaeda turncoat, prove a *direct* link between

Osama bin Laden and the Kahane murder.[43] The chilling details are contained in my *Playboy* piece on Salem and another article I wrote for *Tablet* magazine entitled "First Blood."[44]*

In a series of confessions given to JTTF investigators and an SDNY prosecutor, Kuwaiti immigrant Nidal Ayyad, who helped supply the chemicals for the 1993 World Trade Center bomb, described how he had been the wheelman of a three-man Shalabi hit team including Salameh and Alkaisi.

Salameh, Ayyad, Alkaisi

In one 302, Ayyad described how the trio gained entry to Shalabi's home in the gated Sea Gate community as he was preparing to flee back to Egypt. Using a silenced .22 provided by Alkaisi, Salameh shot Shalabi twice in the head, but the big Egyptian got up and chased the smaller Palestinian after the gun jammed. At that point, Alkaisi pulled out a knife and started stabbing Shalabi, whereupon Salameh put a new magazine in the gun and fired four more shots, finishing the job. The three fled the bloody crime scene, leaving Shalabi with thirty puncture wounds from Alkaisi's blade.[45]

The murder took place precisely two years to the day before the WTC blast executed by Ramzi Yousef.

The Lost Opportunity to Connect the Dots

When it comes to the Shalabi murder—as with other aspects of this counterterrorism investigation—the question again is, what did the FBI know about the crime and when did they know it? They thought the homicide important enough to subpoena witnesses before a grand jury and remove key forensic evidence from the NYPD property clerk's office in 1993. Yet for unknown reasons, the Feds shut the investigation down the following year

---

* http://www.peterlance.com/wordpress/?p=106.

and didn't effectively reopen it again for another decade, when they began to question Nosair and Ayyad.

Since Mustafa Shalabi was killed in Brooklyn and homicide is a state crime, I contacted Assistant District Attorney Mike Vecchione in the Kings County DA's office and informed him of the evidence unearthed in those FBI 302s that implicated Ayyad, Salameh, and Alkaisi in the murder. After a brief e-mail exchange in January 2011, Vecchione referred me to his office's homicide bureau.

When I didn't get a response, I contacted Jerry Schmetterer, the DA's media liaison, and explained the trajectory of my investigation, which began with the revelation about the .22 from Emad Salem. I told him that Detective James Moss, from Brooklyn South Homicide, had reinvestigated the bloody slaying and asked whether the DA's office would take steps to locate Bilal Alkaisi, named by both El Nosair and Ayyad as the lead killer. I even offered to furnish the district attorney with copies of the 302s.[46] The day after I sent him that e-mail, Schmetterer got back to me with this reply: "Peter, We have read the materials and I have discussed this with our Chief of the Homicide Bureau and we will not be commenting."[47]

Why Should We Care?

How is all this related to the FBI's relationship with a Mafia killer that spanned more than three decades? Why should we be concerned today, in 2013, whether the Bureau failed to stop the first attack on the World Trade Center twenty years ago? Certainly there is value to correcting the historical record when it comes to the FBI's performance in countering terrorism and suppressing organized crime. But the real value comes in considering George Santayana's prediction that "those who cannot remember the past are condemned to repeat it."[48]

The killing of Osama bin Laden during a raid by the Navy's Seal Team Six on May 2, 2011, represented a significant advance in the "war on terror" and a true victory for the Obama administration. But prior to bin Laden's death, how many opportunities had the New York Feds blown in their inability to slow his deadly juggernaut?

As for why any of that matters now, consider that as late as early 2013, there was continuing violent unrest throughout the Middle East over demands to release Sheikh Omar Abdel Rahman, the spiritual leader of al-Qaeda, whom Patrick Fitzgerald and Andrew McCarthy convicted in 1995 thanks to Emad Salem.[49]

The Blind Sheikh is the linchpin connecting much of the contemporary violence in the Arab world to the FBI's decades-long terrorism investigations. But for years, U.S. intelligence analysts have failed to appreciate his key role in the hierarchy of al-Qaeda.

Beginning in 1996, the FBI received the first of three warnings that bin Laden would attempt to hijack a plane to free the Sheikh.[50] When al-Qaeda took credit for the embassy bombings in 1998, the Sheikh's release was one of their demands.[51] Weeks before the attack on U.S.S. *Cole* in October 2000, al-Zawahiri and bin Laden appeared in a video fatwa, demanding that the Sheikh be set free.[52] Rahman was cited in that infamous Presidential Daily Briefing (PDB) to George Bush in August 2001,[53] and just days before the 9/11 attacks the Taliban government in Kabul offered to swap a group of U.S. missionaries for the Blind Sheikh. As recently as April 22, 2005, in entering a plea, Zacarias Moussaoui, the so-called twentieth hijacker in the 9/11 plot, declared that his goal in seizing a plane to fly into the White House was to free the Blind Sheikh.[54]

Meanwhile, the blind cleric himself, in federal prison since 1993, has demonstrated extraordinary staying power. In mid-December 2006, while in custody at the U.S. Medical Center in Springfield, Missouri, the sixty-eight-year-old Rahman was diagnosed with a tumor on his liver and rushed to an area hospital after spitting up blood.[55] It was believed at the time that he was near death and the FBI issued a bulletin warning that the Sheikh's last will and testament, distributed by al-Qaeda in 1998, had exhorted his followers to "extract the most violent revenge" after he died.[56]

Then, exhibiting the kind of Rasputin-like resilience demonstrated by Greg Scarpa Sr., Rahman not only pulled through, but began to thrive. He was eventually moved to the Federal Medical Center at Butner, North Carolina, where his continuing influence on world events became clear in the summer of 2012.

Impacting the Egyptian Election

In June 2012, just before the new elections in Cairo, Emad Salem learned through Egyptian sources that the Sheikh, then seventy-four, had managed to issue a fatwa from prison endorsing the presidency of Mohammed Morsi, the Muslim Brotherhood candidate for president.[57] Soon, followers of the Blind Sheikh started rallying in Tahrir Square, demanding his release.[58] The day after Morsi's narrow victory, Salem discovered that Sheikh Omar, who is supposed to get a single, fifteen-minute "humanitarian" call to his family each month, was able to make a second call congratulating the president-elect.[59]

Within days of his election, Morsi returned the favor by declaring, at a huge rally in Tahrir Square in front of Abdel Rahman's family, that he would press for the freedom of Sheikh Omar and other Egyptian terrorists convicted in the United States.[60]

After Morsi's call for the Sheikh's release, the issue became a cause célèbre for the political right in the United States. "U.S. State Dept. Considers Release of Blind Sheikh to Egypt" was the headline on the late conservative Andrew Breitbart's website in September. Two days later, the *New York Post* ran a headline referencing President Barack Obama: "O Eyes 'Blind Sheik' Release: GOPers Blast Idea to Appease Egypt."[61]

In response, then Secretary of State Hillary Clinton made it clear that the Sheikh had been rightfully convicted,[62] and she emphatically denied that the United States had plans to extradite him.[63] But there's little doubt that the September 11, 2012, attack on the U.S. consulate in Benghazi, Libya, which killed the U.S. ambassador and three other diplomats, was tied to growing violence related to Abdel Rahman. By September 13, CNN was reporting that one group thought to be responsible was called "the Imprisoned Omar Abdul Rahman Brigades."[64]

"What happened in New York two decades ago," says Emad Salem, "is still causing blood to be spilled in the Mideast and threatening U.S. security. The Sheikh is the prince of jihad and even from inside a prison cell he wields tremendous power."[65]

Rahman's deadly influence as a rallying point for jihadists was reinforced on October 28, 2012, when bin Laden's successor, Ayman al-Zawahiri, issued a two-hour video calling on Muslims worldwide to kidnap westerners and "spare [no] efforts" to free Sheikh Omar.[66]

Such developments leave no doubt that the threat to world security posed by Omar Abdel Rahman, the leader of the terror cell spawned in New York in 1989, continues to resonate. But what lessons can be learned from that going forward? A case in point that takes us back to the organized crime story involves a mailbox and check-cashing store in Jersey City, first detailed in *Triple Cross*.

Sphinx Trading

As far back as 1991, FBI agents were onto a storefront called Sphinx Trading on Kennedy Boulevard, located in the same building as the Blind Sheikh's al-Salam mosque.

Within weeks of Rabbi Meir Kahane's murder, the Feds knew that El Sayyid Nosair kept a mailbox at the store. Three years later, Patrick Fitzgerald and Andrew McCarthy put the store's co-incorporator, Waleed Abdu al-Noor, on a list of 172 unindicted co-conspirators that included bin Laden, Ali Mohamed, and Mustafa Shalabi.[67] But by 1997 the top investigative goal in the FBI's New York Office was "getting" Gambino family boss John Gotti.[68] So the Bureau's priorities were misplaced. At that time the NYO was conducting virtual round-the-clock surveillance of Gotti's Ravenite Social Club—the same location where prosecutors claimed Vic Orena had met with the "Dapper Don."

As noted in a *Huffington Post* article I wrote, if the Feds had devoted just a portion of the surveillance resources that they'd dedicated to the Ravenite to Sphinx, they could have been in the middle of the 9/11 plot months before Black Tuesday.[69]*

Why? Because in July 2001, Khalid al-Midhar and Salem al-Hazmi, two of the 9/11 "muscle hijackers," got their fake IDs delivered to them in

---

* See http://www.huffingtonpost.com/peter-lance/al-qaeda-and-the-mob-how-_b_34336.html.

**Sphinx Trading, located on Kennedy Boulevard
below the al-Salam mosque**

a mailbox at Sphinx. The man who supplied them was Mohammed El-Attriss, Sphinx's co-incorporator with Waleed Abdu al-Noor.[70] How difficult would it have been for the Feds to connect those dots? But in their obsession with defeating the "Mafia enemy," FBI officials allocated massive resources against Cosa Nostra at a time when the al-Qaeda threat to New York was metastasizing.

How Safe Are We from the Terror Threat?

The Boston Marathon bombings, nearly twelve years after 9/11, gave Americans shocking cause to ask how safe they should feel with the FBI guarding their homeland. How many of the 508 terror prosecutions since 9/11 represented viable threats? In April 2012 the *New York Times* reported: "Of the 22 most frightening plans for attacks since 9/11 on American soil, 14 were developed in [FBI] sting operations"—that is, with help from undercover agents.[71] In his 2013 book *The Terror Factory: Inside the FBI's Manufactured War on Terrorism,* Trevor Aaronson wrote that, of those 508 defendants, he "could count on one hand" the number of genuinely dangerous terrorists prosecuted by the government.[72] One exception was another FBI failure: the May 2010 Times Square bombing plot.[73] After the device fizzled, the NYPD brought terrorist Faizal Shazhad to ground in fifty-three hours.[74] But the FBI's Joint Terrorism Task Force (JTTF) had actually had Shazhad on their radar as early as 2004.[75] He'd trained at a Pakistani terrorist camp, returning just three months before parking a WMD in the theater district undetected by the FBI. Then, after the Boston bombings, it emerged that the Bureau had vetted and cleared Tamerlan Tsarnaev in 2011 after a request from Russian authorities.[76] Two stunning counterterrorism failures that may point to the Bureau's lack of capability in the language of terror.

In May 2012, Senator Daniel Akaka (D-HI), the chairman of a Homeland Security subcommittee, held his seventh hearing on what he termed "a national security crisis": the lack of foreign language skills at the intelligence agencies.[77] Six months later, I wrote the FBI to ask how many agents and management they had who were fluent in Arabic, Urdu, and Farsi. They replied: "The FBI has over 100 Special Agents who speak Arabic, Farsi, and/ or Urdu [and] over 340 full and part time linguists who speak, or provide services, in Arabic, Farsi, and/or Urdu."[78] To put that number in context: By 2009 the FBI had roughly 5,000 SAs working counterterrorism.[79] That barely 2 percent are fluent in the language of the "enemy" is some measure of the FBI's preparedness to stop the next domestic terror threat.

Now that the leadership of New York's Five Families has been decimated, the question is, has the Bureau learned its lesson? If the events of January 20, 2011, are any indication, the answer is no.

The "Epic FBI Bust"

That was a line in the subtitle of a story filed on the website of NBC's New York flagship station announcing the "FBI's biggest Mafia bust." On January 20, 2011, in a massive sweep across three states,[80] 127 men were arrested and charged with more than eight hundred mob-related crimes.[81]

Attorney General Eric Holder announcing the mass Mafia arrests

Attorney General Eric Holder called it "one of the largest single-day operations against the Mafia in the FBI's history, both in terms of the number of defendants arrested and charged and the scope of the criminal activity that is alleged." He went on to say that the massive bust "sends the message that our fight against traditional organized crime is strong, and our commitment is unwavering."[82]

But beyond the headlines and the colorful news footage of multiple "perp walks," an examination of the indictments tells a somewhat different story. Of the 127 arrested, only thirty were made members. Some of those charged were geriatric mobsters, ages eighty-three, seventy-six, seventy-four, seventy-three, and sixty-nine. Many of the indictments were for petty infractions, including bookmaking, loan sharking, gambling, and possession of contraband cigarettes. One of those indicted was charged in a homicide that took place during a home invasion in 1992;[83] one double murder involved a dispute over a spilled drink at a bar in Queens.[84]

Yet the cost of this new investigation was enormous. The authorities acknowledged that informants had recorded *thousands* of conversations by suspected mobsters.[85] Seemingly to justify the expense and counter the notion that the Mafia had been degraded, Janice Fedarcyk, assistant director in charge of the FBI's New York Office, noted that "arresting and convicting the hierarchies of the five families several times over has not eradicated the problem."[86] So much for the 1986 prediction by former SDNY U.S. Attorney Rudy Giuliani that the Mafia Commission case would "crush" Cosa Nostra.[87]

But Bruce Barket, who had defended Craig Sobel during the Lin DeVecchio prosecution, disagreed with Fedarcyk, telling Reuters that the Cosa Nostra menace was long ago replaced by a new threat, from Albanian and Russian gangsters. "Privately, law enforcement officials will tell you there isn't anybody left" in the old-school Italian mob, he said.[88]

The question, from a security standpoint, is whether those mass arrests in 2011 amounted to a final attempt by the FBI to maintain its relevance as a mob-busting force at a time when the al-Qaeda threat continues to loom. If that was the strategy, then one of the highest-profile Mafia prosecutions in years proved that the Justice Department still suffers from the same pathology that infected the Colombo war prosecutions.

The Trial of "Tommy Shots"

In May 2012, Thomas "Tommy Shots" Gioeli, the accused acting boss of the Colombo family, was acquitted of six homicides by a federal jury, largely because they didn't believe the testimony of the cooperating witnesses the Feds used to prosecute him.[89] It was a kind of replay of the Orena brothers' acquittal in 1995.

Gioeli had been one of the shooters who had stalked Joseph Peraino and his son Joe Jr. in the 1982 incident that caused the death of former nun Veronica Zuraw. A onetime Orena loyalist who switched to the Scarpa faction during the war, Gioeli was also charged with the murder of Wild Bill Cutolo, who disappeared in May 1999 after he'd been promoted to

underboss.[90] In October 2008, the FBI started searching a field in East Farmingdale, Long Island.[91] The body they unearthed, wrapped in a tarp, was identified as Cutolo's.[92]

Gioeli had also been charged in the 1992 Colombo war pastry shop murders of John Minerva and Michael Imbergamo.[93] Since virtually all the evidence against him for the Cutolo and Long Island hits

Thomas "Tommy Shots" Gioeli

was based on the word of other mobsters, Gioeli walked on the murder charges, though he was convicted of racketeering and murder conspiracy.[94] Described in the *Times* as "a blow to prosecutors," the limited victory against Tommy Shots was some indication of how far the DOJ can go today in prosecuting cases that hinge largely on the hearsay of other wiseguys.

"There's also a question about how Justice should be devoting its resources," says Lieutenant Colonel Anthony Shaffer, whom I interviewed in September 2012 after the Benghazi attack. "It's patently clear that al-Qaeda remains a lethal threat. Consider the massive resources the FBI spent in those mass mob arrests and how those resources might be better directed in the years ahead. My main concern with the Bureau and the other intelligence agencies is whether they've learned from their mistakes and they're committed to true reform, or will they continue to defend old ground?"[95]

A COINTELPRO vs. the Mafia

From the mid-1950s to the early 1970s, the FBI ran an illegal domestic spying operation dubbed the Counter Intelligence Program, or COINTEL-PRO.[96] The secret initiative, in which J. Edgar Hoover initially authorized special agents to spy on a series of leftist groups, including the Communist Party and the Socialist Workers Party as well as white hate groups like the Ku Klux Klan, later grew into a domestic intelligence-gathering operation whose targets included the Black Panther Party and a number of antiwar groups during the Vietnam War.[97]

When it came to what Hoover termed "Black Nationalist" groups like the Panthers and the Nation of Islam, the Director stated in a memo that "the purpose of this new counterintelligence endeavor is to expose, disrupt, misdirect, discredit, or otherwise neutralize" their activities "to counter their propensity for violence and civil disorder." Included in the groups Hoover described as "subversive" were the NAACP and the Southern Christian Leadership Conference (SCLC), headed at the time by the Reverend Martin Luther King Jr.[98]

The program was reportedly closed down by Hoover in April 1971[99] but only after a burglary of an FBI field office, in which files were stolen, which threatened its exposure.[100] Then, after the Watergate scandal in the early 1970s, a U.S. Senate select committee headed by Democrat Frank Church of Idaho held extensive hearings that probed COINTELPRO and the illegal domestic spying operations conducted by the CIA, first exposed by investigative reporter Seymour Hersh in the *New York Times*.[101]

A fifteen-month investigation by the Church Committee found that FBI headquarters alone had developed more than 500,000 domestic intelligence files on Americans and domestic groups.[102] As a direct result of the committee's investigation, the Justice Department adopted the first set of "Attorney General Guidelines," to which Lin DeVecchio and other special agents would become subject.[103]

Initially established under Attorney General Edward Levi on April 6, 1976,[104] the guidelines, which regulated the FBI's use of confidential informants, were further refined by Benjamin Civiletti in December 1980,[105] setting forth strict rules on when the Bureau might sanction the "ordinary" criminal activity of informants.[106] As noted, violent crimes like murder by CIs were never authorized.

A report in September 2005 by the Justice Department's inspector general, which reviewed the AG's Guidelines from their inception, concluded that "the partnership between the FBI and DOJ, in making key operational and oversight decisions, has promoted adherence to the Attorney General's Guidelines and allowed the Department to exercise critical judgments regarding sensitive FBI investigative activities, particularly with respect to its use of confidential informants and undercover operations."[107]

But our analysis of the once-secret files on Gregory Scarpa Sr. (NY 3461-C-TE) demonstrates that, at least until his arrest on September 1, 1992, and for the three decades before that, the FBI conducted what amounted to a COINTELPRO against the Mafia, employing as its central asset a sociopathic killer who acted with utter disregard for human life and the rule of law.

In November 1974, after releasing a DOJ report on COINTELPRO, then Attorney General William B. Saxbe disclosed that, in addition to the Bureau's spying on leftists and so-called hate groups, a more secretive category of COINTELPRO targets dubbed "special operations" had never been made public.[108] We don't know if "special operations" was Hoover's cover name for his secret war against Cosa Nostra, but the memo to the Bureau's assistant director in January 1966, authorizing Greg Scarpa Sr. to make a second mission to Mississippi for what was termed "a special in the Jackson office,"[109] raises the question of whether "34" was part of that undisclosed category of the Bureau's illegal counter intelligence program.

The three words on the banner that emblazons the FBI's seal are "Fidelity," "Bravery," and "Integrity." There's little doubt that over the decades thousands of special agents have exemplified those first two qualities. It's time now for the Bureau to reclaim its right to the third. It's time that the pathology that infected the FBI during its three-decade relationship with Greg Scarpa Sr. is excised and his son shown some mercy. An

important first step in that direction would be to grant Greg Jr. a hearing in open court, where all of the evidence of his help to the Bureau can be vetted. The next step would be to offer clemency to Vic Orena, who has paid his price for racketeering after more than eleven years behind bars and, at the age of seventy-eight, deserves to see the light of day.

ACKNOWLEDGMENTS

Deal with the Devil was six years in the making. I first proposed the book in the winter of 2007 to Jane Friedman, who was then the president and CEO of HarperCollins, and as we say in the media business, "she bought it in the room." After I'd written two investigative books critical of the FBI and one that audited the 9/11 Commission, Jane was intrigued by this story of a senior Bureau supervisory special agent who had been indicted for murder as a result of his clandestine relationship with a Mafia killer.

From that point on, the trajectory of the book took many twists and turns, which accounts for the years it's taken to come to press. First, there was the aborted DeVecchio trial, after which the transcript was immediately sealed. Then came the first of thirty-two pages of letters from Chicago U.S. Attorney Patrick Fitzgerald threatening to sue me and HarperCollins for libel if we didn't cease publication of the hardcover edition of *Triple Cross,* which was critical of his performance as head of the SDNY's Organized Crime and Terrorism Unit.

Given who the threat was coming from and out of an abundance of caution, we undertook a re-vetting of the entire book, which took twenty months. The trade paperback edition was published in June 2009 to critical acclaim and support by media watchers on the left and the right, and Fitzgerald never made good on his threats. But the reexamination of every fact in a book that ran 604 pages in hardcover was a daunting task, and that caused me to put this book on the back burner for many months.

In 2008 I was able to get a copy of the DeVecchio trial transcript. I then obtained more than ten thousand pages of court pleadings in a number of the Colombo war cases and got a copy of the file from the DeVecchio OPR investigation, which ran to almost a thousand pages. I spent much of 2009, after the publication of *Triple Cross* in paperback, trying to get into the Supermax prison in Florence, Colorado, to interview Greg Scarpa Jr. and Anthony Casso, but I was repeatedly stymied by the Bureau of Prisons, which is a wing of the Justice Department.

Finally, in the fall of 2011 I was able to interview "Gaspipe," and I conducted a number of interviews with Greg Jr. in 2012 after he was moved from ADX Florence to a prison in the Midwest with less restrictive conditions. Over the years I conducted extensive interviews with the Orena brothers and a number of FBI agents, some on active duty who asked not to be identified and some retired. I did many interviews with defense lawyers who had gone to battle with the Feds during the seventy-five Colombo war prosecutions, but I was anxious to know more about the Bureau's secret dealings with the Grim Reaper, so I approached Angela Clemente, who had filed a federal lawsuit pursuant to the Freedom of Information Act to get what eventually amounted to the 1,153 pages in airtel memos, teletypes, and 209s.

I'd first encountered Angela in 2004 when I was finishing *Cover Up,* my book on the 9/11 Commission. She was able to get me dozens of FBI 302s documenting Scarpa Jr.'s Yousef sting, many of which can be accessed at my website, http://www.peterlance.com/wordpress/?p=682.

With no formal training, this single mother from New Jersey who describes herself as a "forensic investigator" is one of the best researchers of organized crime–related material I've ever encountered. After I was able to get the first five hundred pages released via her FOIA suit, there were no more pages forthcoming from the website that allows access to federal court case pleadings. So it wasn't until the fall of 2011 that I received the remaining 653 pages directly from the Bureau with the help of a Washington, DC, federal judge.

It was important for me to get Lin DeVecchio's perspective in all of this. I had been scheduled to talk with him on the day of his indictment, March 30, 2006, but after he left the Brooklyn Supreme Court surrounded by that phalanx of former FBI agents, that didn't happen. I wrote to his lawyer Douglas Grover requesting an interview and never heard back from him, so I decided to wait for Lin's book to come out to get his side of the story. *We're Going to Win This Thing,* which had been scheduled for publication in December 2009, didn't come out until February 2011, so that was another cause for my delay in delivering *Deal with the Devil.*

Now it is done—twice the size of the book that I had contracted for, and much more of an audit of the FBI's organized crime history than I ever envisioned. I had set out to write a simple "true crime" book on the DeVecchio trial and I've finished with a book that I trust will change much of the conventional wisdom about the FBI's multidecade war with what Lin calls "the Mafia enemy."

As it goes to press this book runs more than 210,000 words. It contains more than 2,000 endnote annotations, twenty pages of documentary appendices, and almost 130 illustrations. Getting a book of this magnitude published requires an editor and a production team of immense dedication. Fortunately for me, the man directing that effort is Cal Morgan.

This is my fourth book with Cal. We started together in the trenches with *1000 Years for Revenge* when he was the top executive for ReganBooks, Judith Regan's extraordinarily successful imprint for HarperCollins. Along the way Cal saw *Cover Up* and *Triple Cross* through to publication. He took great care during the re-vetting process of the latter to ensure that the trade paperback, which ran twenty-six additional pages, was a cut above the hardcover edition.

Because of his talent and tenacity he has now advanced within the company to the point where he is editorial director of Harper Perennial, oversees Harper Design, and was named publisher of his own imprint, It Books. To have a publishing executive with Cal's immense skill as the editor of a book like *Deal with the Devil* is a gift for which I'm deeply appreciative.

There is another man of letters deserving of great thanks in my investigation of the Scarpa-DeVecchio story, and that's Fredric Dannen, who published the seminal piece on their alleged "unholy alliance" in the *New Yorker* on December 16, 1996. Even to this day "The G-Man and the Hit Man" remains the gold standard when it comes to reporting on this story, and Fred was incredibly generous to me during my research phase, giving me access to hundreds of pages from his extraordinary Scarpa-DeVecchio files.

I want to thank my daughter Mallory Lance, who graduated from Barnard College at Columbia University in 2011. That summer, when I faced the challenge of organizing more than twenty thousand pages of disparate files into a coherent series of three-ring binders, she flew to Santa Barbara, where I work, and spent weeks with me putting together a system that allowed me to access any given FBI 209 or 302 in a matter of seconds. If Mallory had not devoted the time she did to helping me, this book would not have come together as it has. I am extremely proud of her, as I am of her brother Christopher and her sister Alison.

I'd also like to thank Cal Morgan's two assistants, Brittany Hamblin and Kathleen Baumer, who have shown tireless dedication—Brittany particularly during the publication of the trade paperback of *Triple Cross,* and Kathleen now on this book.

I owe a great debt of gratitude to Beth Silfin, the vice president and deputy general counsel for HarperCollins, who has shown great courage and determination over many years in supporting me with these books that have been highly critical of the FBI.

When it comes to the latest reporting I've been able to do on Sheikh Omar Abdel Rahman, whose position as the spiritual emir of al-Qaeda continues to wreak havoc worldwide, I have to thank the amazing Emad Salem. After I had written about his role in convicting the Blind Sheikh in both *1000 Years for Revenge* and *Triple Cross,* he reached out to me after years in the WITSEC program. When we finally met in New York and I visited him in the state where he lives with his family under an assumed name, I was struck by the fact that he is a man of deep Islamic conviction who is also one of the most tolerant people I've ever encountered. Emad has a great love for America, his newfound country, and would be a tremendous asset to the FBI if they hired him formally to advise on the radical jihadist mind-set.

He's done a number of lectures for agents at Quantico in the past, but the Bureau has vastly underutilized this patriot and natural born undercover operative. Emad risked his life multiple times to enter what he called the "nest of vipers" surrounding Omar Abdel Rahman back in New York in the early 1990s, and he is willing to put his life on the line again if it means protecting this country. If the violence in the Middle East linked to the Blind Sheikh continues, the top executives in the Bureau should be speed-dialing him. I'm proud to say that Emad and I have become close friends and I am in his debt.

Further, a particular thank-you goes to Detective James Moss of

Brooklyn South Homicide, who is now retired. "Jimmy," as he calls himself, is a larger-than-life personification of all that we hope an NYPD murder cop will be: clever, resourceful, undaunted by bureaucracy, and dedicated to bringing those who take human life to justice. Without his belief in Emad Salem and his willingness to work with an investigative reporter, the bloody twenty-year-old Shalabi murder would have stayed a cold case.

I owe another debt to Don Katich, Director of News Operations for the *Santa Barbara News-Press,* the local paper here in my adopted hometown, who has supervised three separate investigative series I've written on local corruption. Don and City Editor Scott Steepleton are two of the gutsiest editors I've ever worked with, and they represent the best in local journalism at a time when newspapers are an endangered species.

In the course of reporting one of those series, relating to an allegedly corrupt police officer, I had the benefit of working with James Blanco, one of the foremost handwriting experts in the nation. He was entirely unselfish in offering months of his time in the pursuit of the truth and I have rarely worked with a more consummate professional.

Finally, I'd like to thank Darryl Genis, a tenacious lawyer in Santa Barbara who not only "had my back" for many months in 2011 as I investigated the Santa Barbara Police Department, but also helped me get one of the most important interviews for the book. I'll always be grateful for his sharp legal mind and fearlessness as a litigator.

Peter Lance
Santa Barbara, California
April 23, 2013
www.peterlance.com

Appendix A:
The Principal Figures

Joseph Profaci

Joseph Colombo

Carmine Persico

Joseph Gallo

Greg Scarpa Sr., 1976

Greg Scarpa Sr., 1992

Lin DeVecchio, 1980s

Lin DeVecchio, 2006

Larry Mazza, 2006

Linda Schiro, 1990

Linda Schiro, 2007

Little Linda, 2007

Appendix B:
The Marriage Certificate of
Gregory Scarpa and Lili Dajani

The 1975 marriage license of Gregory Scarpa and Lili Dajani;
her new address in the apartment Scarpa owned on Sutton Place
in Manhattan was typed at the top

Appendix C:
Gregory Scarpa Sr.'s Arrest Record

No.	Date	Charge	Disposition
1	September 1, 1950	Possession of a firearm	Case dismissed
2	December 5, 1950	Possession of a firearm	Case dismissed
3	October 7, 1959	Incitement of a breach of peace	Acquitted
4	March 7, 1960	Theft of an interstate shipment	Case dismissed April 3, 1961
5	April 28, 1960	Possession of stolen goods	Case dismissed March 28, 1963
6	January 7, 1961	Consorting with thieves & criminals	Unknown
7	January 20, 1962	Bookmaking	Unknown
8	September 18, 1962	Possession of Policy Slips	Unknown
9	September 25, 1964	Vagrancy	Unknown
10	November 3, 1965	Pilfering coins from a pay phone	Dismissed
11	January 31, 1968	Second-degree assault	Case dismissed
12	February 23, 1968	Second-degree assault	Unknown
13	October 8, 1969	Attempted grand larceny; hijacking 870 cases of J&B	Case dismissed

No.	Date	Charge	Disposition
14	November 4, 1971	Possession of stolen mail, $450,000 in securities	Case dismissed
15	June 7, 1974	Interstate transport and sale, $4 million in IBM stock certificates	Case dismissed
16	March 11, 1976	Gambling	Unknown
17	May 9, 1978	Attempted bribery of police officers	Guilty plea, served 30 days
18	November 5, 1985	Purchase of counterfeit credit cards	Plea bargain, $10,000 fine, five-year suspended sentence
19	August 31, 1992	Possession of a firearm	House arrest
20	August 1992	Homicide (three counts)	Guilty plea
	December 1993		Sentenced to 10 years, $200,000 fine
	June 8, 1994		Dies in prison of AIDS

Appendix D:
June 18, 1962, Airtel to J. Edgar Hoover Debriefing Gregory Scarpa Sr.

UNITED STATES GOVERNMENT

Memorandum

TO : DIRECTOR, FBI   DATE: 6/18/62

FROM : SAC, NEW YORK
CONF. INFT.

SUBJECT:
TOP ECHELON CRIMINAL
INFORMANT PROGRAM

Re NY airtels to Director, 6/6/62 and ᵋ '7/62.

This informant is not paid on a regular scale, but is paid on a COD basis.

The informant has been paid [   ] on SAC authority in compliance with Section 108J2, Manual of Instructions, and [   ] on the authority of Assistant Director, C. A. EVANS, based on information provided through 6/6/62, in connection with the below captioned case.

It is requested that the Bureau authorize payment of [   ] to the informant at this time.

The informant states that he is a Caporegima in the JOSEPH PROFACI family. The informant has at the present time 10 men under his control and has been a member of this organization since 1951. [   ] that informant is at least a button in the PROFACI family). It is to be noted that the informant has indicated that he will press for advancement within this group if the Bureau desires that he advance.

EX-102

3 - Bureau
1 - New York

MRF: vmc
(4)

REC

JUN 19 1962

b2 -2

The informant has provided information
on a continous basis concerning the feud between
the PROFACI - GALLO groups, which has been of great
value. He has described in detail the organizational
setup of a family within the overall criminal
organization (set forth below). In addition, the
informant is in the process of identifying by name
and/or photograph a large number of additional
members of the PROFACI family. He is also in
the process of attempting to identify the members of
the other 4 New York families down through the rank
of Caporegima.

It should be noted that none of this
information is currently available to the NYO from
an admitted member of the criminal organization.

At the present time the informant manages
a numbers operation in Brooklyn for CHARLES LO CICERO,
Consuleri of the PROFACI family. The informant
currently is required to make payments of $150 per
week to LO CICERO from this numbers operation. He
stated that as a result of the GALLO - PROFACI feud
and as a result of stepped up local police action
against gamblers, the numbers business has fallen off
badly.

Informant advised he must always maintain
the reputation of being a "money man" and that to
indicate to anyone that he is in need of money could
seriously injure his reputation within the organization.
He stated that he cannot ask for money from the
organization because of his status and reputation
and at this time is anticipating an assessment to pay
the cost incurred by the family in the GALLO - PROFACI
feud. Informant stated that he is in extremely bad
shape financially to the extent that he has
pawned his ring and watch and his wife's wedding
ring. Informant also indicated that he does

- 2 -

b2 -2

not desire to participate in any local burglaries
or commit any other crimes because of his relationship with the agents and the remote possibility
that he would be caught, which would at least
temporarily end his usefulness to the Bureau. He
stated that he must obtain money from some source
to maintain his reputation and status in the
organization. He advised he is currently indebted
in the amount of $3,000 and that if he were in a
position to pay off these debts he feels that his
income from his organization activities would be
sufficient to cover his operating expenses and
maintain his position within the organization.

At the time the informant was originally
contacted by agents he was in the process of attempting
to bring his activities in the organization to a minimum.
He stated that he had ceased all activities relating
to the organization except those which were absolutely
necessary. The informant related that he could not
resign from the organization, but that by withdrawing
from all except essential activities he could more
or less retire.

During the period of this informant's
development by NYO agents, the informant has reactivated
his status in the organization in an attempt to be in a
position where he could obtain information of greater
value to the Bureau. This reactivation process has
necessitated that the informant spend more time with
other members of the PROFACI group at considerable
expense to himself. The informant stated that he
feels he is now attaining the position where he will
be able to furnish information on a continuous basis
and will continue to do so as long as the Bureau is
desirous of his assistance.

The informant has repeatedly stated that the
FBI is the only police agency, local, State or Federal,
in which he has any confidence. He has stated that in

- 3 -

b2 -2

the event he is suspected by any members of the
organization of furnishing information, it would
automatically mean his death with no chance to
explain or defend his actions. He stated that his
life is dependent entirely upon the manner in which
the contacts are made and the manner in which
information provided by him is handled to protect
his identity.

The following is a brief description.
of the information furnished by the informant
thus far concerning the criminal organization.

The informant is considered to be
emotionally stable and reliable and to this date
has furnished no information known to be false.

THE CRIMINAL COMMISSION, ET AL
ANTI-RACKETEERING
NY 92-2300

Informant stated that the movement had its
origin in Sicily years ago where a majority of the people
were oppressed by the feudal lords and was organized at
that time on a "Robin Hood" basis or the idea of stealing
from the rich to give to the poor. He stated, however,
that as time went on and as is typical under dictatorship
or power organization those who were in power becamee
hungry for power and money and that the movement changed
from stealing from the rich to give to the poor to
stealing from the rich to give to the bosses.

Informant stated that this organization or
group has continued from that time to the present and
has been known at different periods of time as "The Black
Hand", "Mafia", or "Comarada". He stated that the name
Comarada originated with the Neopolitan branch of the
organization, but that actually the terms are all synonymous
and refer only to the one organization. He stated that
the name Black Hand originated with the Sicilian group
and the title was derived from the symbol of the
organization which was a black hand print. He stated
that at the time this name was used if a family found on
their front door an imprint of a hand in black, It

- 4 -

b2 -2

indicated to the family that some member had violated
a rule or rules of the organization and was slated
for death. He stated that no explanations were
allowed and that this sign was an arbitrary one
and that if the sign was utilized someone within
the family always met a violet death. He pointed
out that this sign could be utilized by any member
of the organization at his descretion.

Informant stated that at the present
time there is no name for the overall organization
and that the organization is now made up of numerous
groups which are known as "families" and which operate
throughout the entire world with the exception of
Communist dominated areas. He stated that the organization
had at least one family which was active in Cuba, but with
the rise of CASTRO that family ceased its operations, that
most of the family departed from Cuba, and that to his
knowledge there is no organization family in Cuba as
far as the organization is concerned.

Informant stated that each family throughout
the world is made up generally in the same way and carries
the same titles and positions. He stated that the order
which is followed from top to bottom is as follows:

1-   The Boss or Representanda (PH), who is the
head of the family and is automatically as the head of the
family a member of the overall governing body of the
organization which is known as "The Commission".

2-   The Underboss who is the person who will
act for the Boss in his absence and who is the number 2
man in power in the family.

3-   The Consuleri or Counselor who acts as a
neutral counsel for anyone in the family who needs his
advice or services in settling disputes and is available
to represent members of the families who have been accused
of violations of rules. He pointed out that the Counselor
is normally the person who mediates disputes between
families and is supposed to remain neutral at all times.

4-   Caporegima or Captain is a person who has
a group of members of the organization under him who follow
his directions and orders. The Captain relays orders
from the Boss to the individual

- 5 -

b2 -2

members and is directly responsible for their
activities and actions. Informant pointed out that
the number of members assigned to any Captain may
vary greatly and that there is no set number of
Captains in any family. He advised that all
Captains hold an equal rank regardless of the
number of individuals assigned to them.

     5- Acting Captain who is a person
appointed by the Captain with the approval of the
Boss and who acts for the Captain in his absence
and assists in the controlling of the members in
general.

     6- Good fellows also known as button
men or soldiers. These terms are synonymous and
indicate that the persons are members of the
organization who have not attained any rank or
position of authority.

     Informant advised that the procedure
for making new members in the organization is as follows:

     A member of a family becomes acquainted
or his acquainted with a person whom he feels has
the general qualifications and who would be acceptable
for membership in the organization. The member will
then closely associate with this person and will
attempt to control and direct his activities and
generally observe all his actions for a period of time,
usually at least 6 months to a year and often times
longer. If he is still satisfied that this person
has the qualifications and would be acceptable for
membership, he then meets with his Captain and proposes
that this person be accepted for membership in the
organization. If the Captain agrees with the member,
the member must furnish to the Captain the name, address,
names of members of the family and as much additional
background information as possible concerning the proposed

- 6 -

b2 -2

member. The Captain will then present the name of
the one who has been proposed at a meeting at
which all of the Captains, the Boss, Underboss
and Counselor are present. If the proposed new
member is acceptable to these people they will
then order that a thorough background investigation
be conducted, which will include investigations
of all relatives. During this investigation it
will be determined if the person was ever a
Government witness, furnished information to the
police and verified any arrests for himself as well
as his relatives. If the results of this investigation
are considered satisfactory, the proposed member
will then probably be accepted for membership at some
later date. During the period that the proposed
new member is being directed toward membership
and while he is waiting to be brought into membership,
he is led to believe that before being admitted as
a member it will be necessary to kill someone. The
informant stated that prior to about 10 years ago
it was necessary for a proposed new member to participate
in the execution of a member before being accepted
into the organization. He stated that during that time
the number of members remained relatively constant
and pointed out that the proposed member did not
necessarily have to kill anyone himself, but had
to participate in it to some extent. He stated that
during the past 10 years this rule has actually been
abandoned, but that each proposed new member is still
led to believe that he must participate in an execution
prior to becoming a member. The informant stated
that members can be taken into the organization only
during certain periods of time when the Bosses are
authorized by the Commission to accept new members.
He stated that the last new members were accepted into
the organization in about 1957, and that since that time
the Commission has not authorized the making of any
new members.

Informant stated that after the investigation
of a proposed member has been completed and if new members
are being accepted, the proposed member will be
summoned to a meeting place which may be in a home,
apartment, hotel or restaurant, and that present there

- 8 -

b2 -2

will be the Boss, the Underboss, the Counselor, all
of the Captains, and the sponsor of new member who
proposed him. The proposed member and his sponsor
unless he is a Captain will then be called into the
meeting room where the proposed member will be
questioned by the Boss. He will be asked if he
knows why he is there and the general answer is
"Yes I have been told (by my sponsor) that someone
has to be killed". The Boss will then ask him
if he feels he is capable of killing a person and
the usual response is "Yes" and the indication also
given that all the sponsor or Boss has to do is
name the person to be killed. He is also usually
asked if he believes that his sponsor is a good fellow
and if he will accept and follow out any orders given
him by his sponsor or anyone else in authority.
If the proposed member has answered the questions in
the affirmative and proper manner, the sponsor and
the sponsor's Captain then stand beside him in front
of the group and at that time the Boss asked him if
he is right-handed or left-handed and indicates he
is to extend the right hand if right-handed and the
left hand if left-handed. The Boss will then take
a pin and prick the end of the trigger finger until
blood is drawn. He then passes into the proposed
member's hand a piece of paper, generally tissue
paper, and sets fire to it. The proposed member will
then move the burning piece of paper from one hand to
the other and at the same time repeats in Italian
the following oath:

        "With this oath I swear that if I ever
violate the oath I may burn as this paper".

        This action ends the ritual of initiation
and the proposed member is then considered to be a
member in good standing of the organization.

- 8) -

b2 -2

Informant stated that one of their requirements is that the father of the proposed member must be of Italian descent, however, the mother may be of any other nationality and the member may marry a person of any other nationality.

The informant stated that if a member of any family moves from one location to another, he is given a letter of introduction from his Boss to the Boss in the area to which he is moving. This letter entitles the member to be accepted into membership in the family covering the area to which he moves. The only other way one member can meet other members of the organization with whom he is not previously acquainted is to be introduced by a third member who is acquainted with both and knows that both are members of the organization. He stated that when introducing one member to another the person making the introduction must use the phrase a "friend of ours." For example, JOE meet JOHN, who is a "friend of ours." He stated that any other terminology such as a friend of mine or anything else would indicate that the person being introduced is not a member of the organization. He stated that it is a violation of rules for one member to attempt to introduce himself to another member even though he may know that the other is a member of the organization.

The informant stated that all of the executions within the organization are authorized by the Boss of the family and that the persons who perform the executions are assigned to the job by the Boss.

The informant stated that all Bosses or heads of the families are automatically members of "The Commission", and that if a problem arises

- 9 -

b2 -2

which requires action by "The Commission", a group
of Bosses or heads of family are appointed to serve
as the Commission to solve that particular problem.
He stated that the number serving on any one
Commission will vary with the seriousness of the
problem and its effect on the overall operation
of the organization. He pointed out that any actions
or rulings which result from a meeting of the
Commission are binding on all families even though
the boss of one family did not serve as a member
of the Commission.

With regard to the JOSEPH PROFACI
family, he hadvised that JOSEPH PROFACI is the Boss,
JOSEPH MAGLIOCCO is the Underboss and that CHARLES
LO CICERO is the Acting Counselor of the family.
He stated that in addition there are 8 Captains
in the family consisting of SALVATORE MUSSACHIO,
AMBROSE MAGLIOCCO,⬛⬛⬛⬛⬛ (PH), SAM
BADALAMENTE, HARRY FONTANA, SIMONE (LNU) (PH), JOHN
ODDO, and GREGORY SCARPA. All of the above are   b6 -2
known to the NYO except⬛⬛⬛⬛⬛and SIMONE.   b7C -2
In addition to this the informant has to date
provided the identities of 25 persons in varying
positions who he knows to be members of the organization
and has stated that there are 5 families within the
New York area which are controlled by the following
persons:

    1-   JOSEPH PROFACI

    2-   CARLO GAMBINO

    3-   JOE BONNANO

    4-   VITO GENOVESE

    5-   THOMAS LUCHESE

The informant stated that punishment for
violation of the rules of the organization was a
reprimand by the Boss or death depending on the seriousness
of the violation. According to the informant violation
of the following rules is punishable by death; furnishing
information to any law enforcement agency, having an
affair with another member's wife (the wife will also
be killed), a married member having an affair with another.

- 10 -

b2 -2

member's sister or daughter, stealing from another
member, anyone striking member knowing him to be a
member, and being involved in the sale of narcotics.
He stated that a reprimand is usually the result
of arguments between members or some other minor
activity not enumerated above.

A comparison of the information furnished
by this informant with information received from
other informants indicates that the informant is
furnishing accurate information. A portion of the
information received to date from the informant has
been previously received from other informants.
However, this informant is the only informant in the
NYO who has been able to supply all the information
set forth. This informant also was able to furnish
more details and to supply names, which are not
available from other sources.

The full potential of this informant is yet
to be realized, however, it is felt that if the requested
payment is authorized it will solidify the informant's
faith in the Bureau and provide the necessary incentive
for the informant to fully reactivate himself in the
organization so that he will be in an even better
position to be of assistance to the Bureau.

It is recommended that the Bureau approve
[   ] to be paid to the informant for information
furnished; and for additional information which he
is to furnish in the immediate future as well as an   b2
incentive for the informant [   ]

It is recommended that payments be made
in installments of [   ] initially and an additional
[   ] following additional interviews with the
informant. This method of payment is recommended
so that there will be no doubt in the informant's
mind that he is to be paid only as information is
received.

- 11 -

Appendix E:
The "Girlfriend 302"

FD-302 (Rev. 3-10-82)

- 1 -

FEDERAL BUREAU OF INVESTIGATION

Date of transcription   2/7/94

       LAWRENCE MAZZA was interviewed by properly identified
Special Agents of the Federal Bureau of Investigation. MAZZA then
provided the following information, as well as information not
included here:

       SCARPA SR. told MAZZA that he received information from a
source in law enforcement, and a source from the ORENA faction. One
of the sources that supplied information on a regular basis was
referred to as "THE GIRLFRIEND". The source would call him at home,
as well as beep him, and was always referred to by SCARPA SR. as the
"GIRLFRIEND". SCARPA SR.'s wife, LINDA, also referred to the source
as "THE GIRLFRIEND" when giving messages to SCARPA SR. regarding phone
calls. On occasions when the source beeped SCARPA SR., he would stop
whatever he was doing in order to return the call. When in his own
home, SCARPA SR. always returned the calls to the "GIRLFRIEND" using
the telephone in the basement, which was registered to MARYANN TURSI.
SCARPA Sr. also received messages regularly to call "THE GIRLFRIEND"
at the "store", which referred to the source's place of business.

       The information that SCARPA SR. received through his
source(s) included, but was not limited to, the address of VICTOR
ORENA's girlfriend's home in Queens, New York, including descriptive
information that it was a white, two family home with aluminum siding.
Shortly after SCARPA SR. is shot at, he learns that the panel truck
used in the murder attempt was rented from Queens, New York. JOSEPH
RUSSO's, an associate of WILLIAM CUOTOLO, address on 74th Street near
12th or 13th Avenue, as well as SALVATORE MICIATTA and JOSEPH SCOPO's
addresses. He also received information regarding the scheduled drug
arrest of GREGORY SCARPA JR. and his crew, and the scheduled Credit
Card arrest of SCARPA SR.. He received a copy of the Complaint issued
against himself, and was told that his problems with the Law might
disappear if he stayed out of trouble.

       On one occasion, MAZZA was in SCARPA SR.'s house when he
received a telephone call from "THE GIRLFRIEND" on the basement
telephone. After the call, he told MAZZA that the "GIRLFRIEND" said
that the members of the ORENA faction were very close to killing him.

Investigation on 1/7/94-2/7/94 at Undisclosed   File #   281A-NY-214955

   Maryann C. Walker
by Christopher M. Favo   Date dictated   2/7/94

This document contains neither recom—   · ·

Appendix F:
302 from Scarpa Jr.'s Sting of Ramzi Yousef

SCARPA advised that YOUSEF began slipping papers to
him, 1/2 sheet of paper rolled up with writing on them.
According to SCARPA, YOUSEF writes in sentences. SCARPA advised
that when YOUSEF slips him these papers he writes on the paper
that he wants them back. SCARPA advised he has only kept the
notes for a matter of minutes, approximately 10 minutes, just
long enough to write some things down. SCARPA advised he may get
one note a day or one every couple of days. According to SCARPA,
the number of notes varies according to the circumstances at the
mcc. SCARPA advised YOUSEF does not give his notes back to him,
but expects SCARPA to return YOUSEF's notes quickly. SCARPA
believes YOUSEF throws the notes in the toilet.

SCARPA advised these notes, referred to as "kites" are
passed from inmate to inmate, in newspapers, or through holes in
the walls of the cells.

SCARPA advised that there is a guard permanently
assigned to both ISMAIL and YOUSEF and sometimes they check the
newspaper before its given to ISMAIL or YOUSEF and sometimes they
do not.

According to SCARPA, YOUSEF told him, "if you're
interested, I'll teach you things nobody knows."

YOUSEF told SCARPA I'll teach you how to blow up
airplanes, and how to make bombs and then you can get the
information to your people (meaning SCARPA's people on the
outside). YOUSEF told SCARPA I can show you how to get a bomb on
an airplane through a metal detector. YOUSEF told SCARPA he
would teach him how to make timing devices.

According to SCARPA, YOUSEF wants to hurt the United
States Government and wants to teach SCARPA how. SCARPA advised
YOUSEF has not asked for any specific help. SCARPA advised that
YOUSEF wants to blow things up, but he does not say why.

YOUSEF told SCARPA that during the trial they had a
plan to blow up a plane to show that they are serious and then
make their demands, or kidnap and hurt a judge or an attorney so
a mistrial will be declared. SCARPA advised that blowing up an
airplane during the trial seems easy to YOUSEF. YOUSEF never
mentioned a specific airline as a target.

According to SCARPA, YOUSEF believes that SCARPA is in
touch with people on the outside. YOUSEF told SCARPA if things
get going we may be able to hook up, if you're serious my people
and your people can meet. SCARPA believes YOUSEF needs help

Appendix G:
Ramzi Yousef's "Kite" from the
Scarpa Jr.–Yousef Sting

How To Smuggle Explosives INTo an Airplane   Sual 5/19

1. When Talking about Smuggling Explosives into an airplane, It is meant By That Explosive Substances which are going To Be placed INTo an airplane Later, To Be Used For Blowing up The airplanes. Therefore The quantity OF Explosive Substances which we'll Be Talking about, is The quantity needed To Blow up an airplane, which is equivalent To 300 gm of TNT. For 747–400 airplanes, aT 30,000 Feet altitude. For Substances which are more powerful Than TNT, The quantity needed Would Be Less Than 300 gm. depending ON it's power compared To TNT.

2. ALL metalic Substances, or Substances which contains metals, cannot Be used or smuggled INTo The airplane Because They are easily detected By X-Ray machines and Metal Detectors, Therefore, ALL Azioeas and Mercury Compounds Explosive Substances Should NOT Be used.

3. ALL Explosive Substances of A Density higher Than 2 Kg/L Should NOT Be used due To The possibility of Detecting Them by X-Ray Machines.
The Following Explosive Substances Have a Density Less Than 2 gm can Easily Be Smuggled. 1. TeTrazene (Guanyl NitroSonminoguannylTeTrazene)
2. Acetone Peroxide
3. R.D.X.
4. HMTD (Hexamethylenetriperoxioediamine)
5. DDNP (DiaXediNitrophenol)
6. HMX (cyclotetramethylenetetra(anitramine)

ALL Liquid Explosives CAN Be used
1. When an Explosive Substance is smuggled into AN Airplane, Then it can Be assembled easily inside The airplane
2. A Detonator can Be hito in a Heel of a Shoe
3. The wiring and 9V Battery CAN Be Hidden INside a shaving machine or a Toy.
The above Explosive Substances which are in powder Form can also Be smuggled in AN Airplane easily By Hiding Them in The Holes in The Heal of a Shoe, or By putting Them in Medicine Capsules.

Appendix H:
Judge Reichbach's Decision and Order
Dismissing the DeVecchio Case

SUPREME COURT OF THE STATE OF NEW YORK
COUNTY OF KINGS: PART 27

---x

THE PEOPLE OF THE STATE OF NEW YORK,   :   <u>DECISION and ORDER</u>

     -against-   :   Ind. No 6825/05

R. LINDLEY DEVECCHIO,   :   November 1, 2007
         Defendant   :

---x

     Friedrich Nietzsche sagely observed at the end of the 19th Century "that he who fights with monsters might take care lest he thereby become a monster...and if you gaze for long into an abyss, the abyss gazes also into you..." I will not comment much on the specific evidence in this case in light of the fact that the record is not yet complete. I do, however, feel obliged to make some observations based on the evidence revealed to date. These observations based on the testimony and exhibits introduced so far in this case, particularly by the defendant's own colleagues, is directed not so much to defendant's individual actions but to the institutional question raised by the evidence.

     I was particularly struck by the testimony of Carmine Sessa, former Consigliere of the Colombo family and multiple murderer, and who testified that when he and his fellow mobsters were discussing the possibility that Greg Scarpa was an FBI informant, they ultimately discounted the idea, reasoning that it was impossible for Scarpa to be an FBI informant: that it would be antinomic for the FBI, charged with fighting crime, to employ as an informer a murderer as vicious and prolific as Greg Scarpa. Apparently, and sadly, organized crime attributed to the FBI a greater sense of probity than the FBI in fact possessed.

     It is certainly true that through the years, Greg Scarpa provided valuable and, in some instances, unique information on the workings and structure of the organized crime families in New York and the Columbo family in particular. Interestingly, and perhaps inexplicably, Scarpa provided information not only on others, but also on his own son, Greg Scarpa Jr., and, indeed, on himself as well. Scarpa readily admitted to his own involvement in loan-sharking, gambling and bank burglaries. He informed on rivals and those closest to him, including members of his own crew. And in keeping with his treacherous nature, he also provided information to the FBI that was purposely deceptive and untrue in an attempt to point the finger of accusation away from his own misdeeds and on to that of gang rivals. He provided information on the murder of Joe "Brewster" DeDomenico and the attempt to kill Joe "Waverly" Cacase without indicating that he himself was involved in both. Similarly, he blamed on others the murder of Nicky "Black" Grancio that he had committed. On the limited evidentiary record provided to the Court, it is impossible to determine how much of Scarpa's information was accurate and valuable and how much was not.

What is undeniable was that in the face of the obvious menace posed by organized crime, the FBI was willing, despite its own formal regulations to the contrary, to make their own deal with the devil. They gave Scarpa virtual criminal immunity for close to 15 years in return for the information, true and false, he willingly supplied. Indeed, this Court is forced to conclude that Scarpa's own acknowledgement of criminal activity to the FBI could only be explained by his belief that the agency would protect him from the consequences of his own criminality, which the record suggests is what they did.

Not only did the FBI shield Scarpa from prosecution for his own crimes, they also actively recruited him to participate in crimes under their direction. That a thug like Scarpa would be employed by the federal government to beat witnesses and threaten them at gunpoint to obtain information regarding the deaths of civil rights workers in the south in the early 1960s is a shocking demonstration of the government's unacceptable willingness to employ criminality to fight crime. It is redolent of the current mindset of some in the government who argue that the practice of terror and torture can be freely employed against those the government claims are terrorists themselves: that it is permissible to make men scream in the name of national security. These are shortcuts that devalue legitimate police work, their yield is insignificant and the cost to the fundamental values they debase is enormous.

This court is not unaware of the delicate balancing act required in the waltz that must be danced between informant and handler. A relationship of trust must be established, but the handler must not lose sight of with whom he is dealing. As Detective Sergeant Fred Santoro so colorfully but accurately put it, informants were "the scum of the earth, that one had to assume they lied, that they were not to be trusted, they gave false information and false leads and that it was necessary to confirm what they tell you."

2

The Court would be remiss if it did not single out for praise Special Agents Favo, Tomlinson and Andjich. In the face of what must have been enormous institutional pressure to turn a blind eye when they grew increasingly concerned that the defendant had lost the necessary perspective and had grown too close to his informant, they stepped forward, risking the opprobrium of their colleagues. There was no evidence presented at this trial, save the now discredited testimony of Linda Schiro, that the defendant committed any of the acts charged in the indictment. On the other hand, credible evidence was presented that indicated that the defendant was so eager to maintain Scarpa as an informant that he was willing to bend the rules, including sending misinformation to headquarters in order to re-open him as an informant.

However, the inappropriate relationship with Scarpa and the FBI's maintenance of him as an informant cannot be attributed solely to this defendant. Any sentient being reading Scarpa's informant file could divine that Scarpa was involved in illegal and violent acts. While lying about his involvement in murders, Scarpa freely acknowledged a host of other criminal activities including, as noted, loan-sharking. It is a belief bordering on thaumaturgy to think that a loan-shark operation could be conducted without violence; both threatened and actual. Under all the circumstances it would have been impossible for the FBI not to appreciate that Scarpa was involved in violence. And if the Bureau was not aware of it, it would suggest a level of incompetence that this Court is not prepared to attribute to this vital law enforcement agency. At best, the FBI engaged in a policy of self-deception, not wanting to know the true facts about this informant-murderer whom they chose to employ. There was testimony at this trial that informant files were to be reviewed at the highest levels of the Agency at least once a month. Even the most cursory review would have revealed the extent of Scarpa's criminality, which, as the Court has observed, it appears obvious the Bureau was not interested in knowing.

A top echelon informant, that is, a made member of organized crime who is willing to provide valuable intelligence, presents a difficult challenge to those who are sworn to fight crime. It is the inescapable aporia of law enforcement that they must sometimes turn a blind eye to criminality in order to prevent or combat greater criminality. It is a difficult balancing act but one, this Court is forced to conclude, the

3

Bureau failed miserably to accomplish in their dealings with Greg Scarpa. I have great respect for the decision of the District Attorney's office to dismiss this prosecution in the face of the contradictions between the testimony here at trial of their chief witness with statements she's made previously on the matters in issue. Even more, the Court must pay tribute to Tom Robbins of the Village Voice, who came forward at considerable professional risk to reveal Schiro's perfidy. Whatever improprieties the defendant may have committed to protect and keep his informant operational, that is far different than joining Scarpa in his criminal undertakings. It was only the discredited testimony of Linda Schiro that tied the defendant to any of the crimes charged in the indictment. The Court agrees with the District Attorney's conclusion that this was insufficient to establish the defendant's guilt on the crimes charged. Indictment dismissed, bail exonerated, defendant discharged.

This constitutes the Decision and Order of the Court.

NOTES

EPIGRAPHS

1. FBI wiretap transcript, Wimpy Boys social club, tape 42, April 7, 1986; tape 52, April 18, 1986.
2. *People v. R. Lindley DeVecchio,* testimony of Larry Mazza, October 18, 2007; Alex Ginsberg, "Hit Man for Mob Lost Count of Corpses," *New York Post,* October 19, 2007.
3. R. Lindley DeVecchio and Charles Brandt, *We're Going to Win This Thing: The Shocking Frame-up of a Mafia Crime Buster* (New York: Berkley, 2011), 218.
4. Ibid., 119.
5. *U.S. v. Victor M. Orena et al.,* testimony of Special Agent Chris Favo, transcript, 5209–10.
6. Kings County District Attorney, press release, March 30, 2006; transcript of press conference in which DA Hynes repeated that allegation; Michael Brick, "Ex-FBI Agent's Murder Trial Fizzles, as Does Chief Witness," *New York Times,* November 1, 2007.
7. Alex Ginsberg, "Up Yours: G-Man Sticks It to DA with Toast at Mob-Slay Site," *New York Post,* November 2, 2007.
8. Gustin Reichbach, decision and order of dismissal, *People v. R. Lindley DeVecchio,* November 1, 2007, http://online.wsj.com/public/resources/documents/reichbach.pdf.

INTRODUCTION

1. Selwyn Raab, "The Mobster Was a Mole for the FBI: Tangled Life of a Mafia Figure Who Died of AIDS Is Exposed," *New York Times,* November 20, 1994.
2. Brad Hamilton, "My Life as a Colombo Hit Man," *New York Post,* March 4, 2012.
3. Letter from Edward A. McDonald, attorney in charge, U.S. Department of Justice Organized Crime Strike Force, EDNY, to Hon. I. Leo Glasser, July 22, 1986.
4. Memo: Debriefing of Robert "Rabbit" Stasio, May 16, 1996.
5. John Kroger, *Convictions* (New York: Farrar, Straus & Giroux, 2008), 133; *U.S. v. Gregory Scarpa Jr.,* Second Circuit Court of Appeals, 897 F2d 63, February 23, 1990.
6. Memo from special agent in charge, FBI New York Office, to director, FBI, January 20, 1966.

7. Memo from special agent in charge, FBI New York Office, to director, FBI, November 21, 1961.

8. Anthony Villano with Gerald Astor, *Brick Agent: Inside the Mafia for the FBI* (New York: Quadrangle, 1977), 97.

9. Richard Stratton, "The Grim Reaper's Girlfriend," *Penthouse,* August 1, 1996.

10. *U.S. v. Victor Orena,* testimony of Joseph Ambrosino, transcript, 975–76.

11. Joseph Gambardello and Patricia Hurtado, "Black Eye for the FBI: 7 Acquitted in Mob Case," *Newsday,* July 1, 1995.

12. Alex Ginsberg, "'95 Words May Save 'Mob' Fed," *New York Post,* February 12, 2007.

13. Brad Hamilton, "Mafia Daughter Says Dad Was Grim Reaper," *New York Post,* May 27, 2012.

14. *Gregory Scarpa v. Victory Memorial Hospital,* deposition transcript, March 1, 1988, 5–7.

15. *Gregory Scarpa Jr. v. U.S.,* 2255, petition, sworn affidavit of Connie Scarpa, May 15, 2002.

16. Author's interview with Linda Schiro, November 3, 2007. N.B. Throughout the book, Scarpa Sr.'s relationship with Linda Schiro is described as "common law." While strictly speaking, that legal definition does not exist in the state of New York, it is included because Scarpa Sr. repeatedly referred to Ms. Schiro as his "wife" and she referred to him as her "husband."

17. "Hadassah Events Fete Miss Israel," Long Beach *Press Telegram,* August 1, 1960.

18. Gregory Scarpa and Lili Dajani, marriage certificate, state of Nevada, February 2, 1975. See Appendix B.

19. Jerry Capeci, "Ex-FBI Agent Is Probed in Murder of a Doctor," *New York Sun,* April 27, 2006.

20. *People v. R. Lindley DeVecchio,* October 19, 2007, transcript, 714–40.

21. Jerry Capeci, "10-Yr Prison Term for Mob Turncoat," New York *Daily News,* August 10, 1998.

22. Greg B. Smith and Jerry Capeci, "Mob, Mole & Murder," New York *Daily News,* October 31, 1994.

23. Jerry Capeci, "No Tipping the Capo to Legendary Mobster," New York *Daily News,* June 14, 1994.

24. Alex Ginsberg, "Hit Man Lost Count on Corpses," *New York Post,* October 19, 2007.

25. *People v. R. Lindley DeVecchio,* testimony of Larry Mazza, October 18, 2007, transcript, 714.

26. Author's interview with Little Linda Schiro, December 3, 2011.

27. Hamilton, "Mafia Daughter Says."

28. Ibid.

29. Lee A. Daniels, "Brooklyn Slaying Tied to Mob Feud," *New York Times,* December 8, 1991.

30. George James, "Killing in Brooklyn Social Club Is Linked to Mob Power Struggle," *New York Times,* December 6, 1991.

31. Author's interview with Larry Mazza, January 8, 2013.

32. Lee A. Daniels, "Brooklyn Slaying May Be 6th in Mob Families' 2-Month Feud," *New York Times,* January 8, 1992.

33. Special Agent Howard Leadbetter II, FBI 302 memo on confession of William Meli, January 21, 1994, 1–2; Jerry Capeci, "Mob's Man Saved by the Cell," New York *Daily News,* June 14, 1995.

34. Raab, "The Mobster Was a Mole for the FBI."

35. Capeci, "No Tipping the Capo to Legendary Mobster."
36. Joseph Randazzo, a twenty-one-year-old associate of Scarpa's son Joey, died after being struck by one of sixteen bullets fired in the exchange by Ronald "Messy Marvin" Moran. The former crack dealer, who became a government witness, pleaded guilty to the Randazzo murder in 1997. In Brooklyn federal court in December 1997, Moran testified about the Scarpa gun battle. "I had no bullets left in the gun," he said. "I was trying to . . . run in the house and he [Scarpa] was just waving his gun around, shooting it." Helen Peterson, "Feds Have New Canary," New York *Daily News,* December 21, 1997.
37. Hamilton, "Mafia Daughter Says."
38. Bob Drury, "Mafia Mole," *Playboy,* January 1997.
39. Ibid.
40. Memo from special agent in charge, FBI New York Office, to director, FBI, June 18, 1962, 2.
41. R. Lindley DeVecchio, FBI 209 memo for Top Echelon (TE) informant designated "NY3461," January 24, 1992.
42. Memo from special agent in charge, FBI New York Office, to director, FBI. Subject: Gregory Scarpa Top Echelon Criminal Informant Program, New York Division, November 3, 1970, 4.
43. Memo from special agent in charge, FBI New York Office, to director, FBI. Subject: Gregory Scarpa Top Echelon Criminal Informant Program, New York Division, September 2, 1971.
44. Memo from special agent in charge, FBI New York Office, to director, FBI. Subject: Gregory Scarpa Top Echelon Criminal Informant Program, New York Division, June 29, 1971; memo from special agent in charge, FBI New York Office, to director, FBI. Subject: Gregory Scarpa Top Echelon Criminal Informant Program, New York Division, September 2, 1971.
45. Memo from special agent in charge, FBI New York Office, to director, FBI. Subject: Gregory Scarpa Top Echelon Criminal Informant Program New York Division, July 25, 1972.
46. Addendum: Criminal Investigative Division, April 8, 1987, requesting additional authority for payment to Scarpa Sr. It describes broadly the "services" the informant provided in three major investigations identified as "Shooting Star," "Gambino Family," and "Starquest."
47. Robert M. Stutman and Richard Esposito, *Dead on Delivery: Inside the Drug Wars, Straight from the Street* (New York: Warner Books, 1992), 17–19.
48. One of the Colombos who lured Farace to his death was Joseph Scalfani, one of the few members of Greg's crew he trusted to give blood during his 1986 transfusion. *Gregory Scarpa v. Victory Memorial Hospital and Dr. Angelito L. Sebollena,* transcript of deposition of Gregory Scarpa, August 12, 1991, 27; *Scarpa v. Victory Memorial et al.* transcript, May 11, 1992, 16.
49. FBI teletype from director, FBI, to FBI New York Office, September 25, 1991.
50. Villano, *Brick Agent,* 105.
51. "Jewelry Recovered by FBI for Church," Associated Press, in the *Lubbock Avalanche-Journal,* January 22, 1973.
52. *The People v. R. Lindley DeVecchio,* October 29, 2007, transcript, 1544–1552; Tom Robbins and Jerry Capeci, "FBI Used Wiseguy to Crack KKK Man," New York *Daily News,* June 21, 1994; author's interviews with Judge W. O. Chet Dillard, October 10, 2011, and June 11, 2004.

53. W. O. Chet Dillard, *Clear Burning: Civil Rights, Civil Wrongs* (Jackson, MS: Persimmon Press, 1992); memo to assistant director, FBI, from ███████, January 21, 1966.

54. *People v. R. Lindley DeVecchio,* testimony of Linda Schiro, October 29, 2007, transcript, 1553; author's interview with Linda Schiro, November 3, 2007.

55. Rudy Johnson, "13 Indicted on Stock Theft and Counterfeit Counts," *New York Times,* June 8, 1974.

56. Memo from Newark to Bureau (1) Headquarters, December 19, 1977; letter from Edward A. McDonald, attorney in charge, U.S. Department of Justice Organized Crime Strike Force, EDNY, to Hon. I. Leo Glasser, July 22, 1986.

57. FBI 302 memo, interview with Judge I. Leo Glasser, conducted by Supervisory Special Agents Timothy B. Kilund and Kevin P. Donovan, August 16, 1994.

58. Special Agent Chris Favo, sworn affidavit, April 4, 1994.

59. Al Guarte, "FBI Big Shots Knew Mob Rat Killed His Rivals," *New York Post,* March 1, 1977.

60. Kings County District Attorney Indictment No. 6825/2005, unsealed March 30, 2006.

61. Ginsberg, "Hit Man for Mob Lost Count of Corpses."

62. Hamilton, "Mafia Daughter Says."

63. Linda Schiro interview, November 3, 2007.

64. *People v. R. Lindley DeVecchio,* testimony of Larry Mazza, October 19, 2007.

65. Hamilton, "My Life as a Colombo Hit Man."

66. A list of seventeen homicides committed by Greg Scarpa Sr., or executed at his direction, compiled in the course of my investigation from court files, FBI 302s and 209s, and a series of appellate court decisions, can be found in Chapter 20. Scarpa pled guilty to three murders during the 1991–1993 war, but the evidence suggests that he directly participated in three more, bringing the death toll to twenty-three. See Chapter 27, "The Hit on Nicky Black," and Chapter 28, "Closing and Reopening '34,'" concerning John Minerva and Michael Imbergamo. This investigation also makes a compelling case that Scarpa was involved in the murders of Thomas Ocera in 1989 and Jack Leale, the man identified by the Feds as Ocera's killer, murdered on November 4, 1991. Lin DeVecchio stated in his 2011 memoir that Scarpa had killed one of the drug dealers who had threatened his son in the December 29, 1992, shootout that also resulted in the death of Patrick Porco, a friend of Scarpa's son Joey. That would bring the total number of murder victims killed by Greg Scarpa Sr. directly or on his orders from 1980 to 1992 to twenty-six—all during the twelve-year period when former supervisory special agent Lin DeVecchio was Scarpa's contacting or "control" agent.

67. Gustin Reichbach, decision and order of dismissal, *People v. R. Lindley DeVecchio,* November 1, 2007. See Appendix H.

68. *U.S. v. Michael Sessa,* transcript of proceedings before Judge Jack B. Weinstein, September 24, 2001.

69. Author's interview with Ellen Resnick, February 21, 2012.

CHAPTER 1: THE KISS OF DEATH

1. Emanuel Perlmutter, "Valachi Queried by Senate Panel," *New York Times,* September 27, 1963.

2. Peter Maas, *The Valachi Papers* (New York: G. P. Putnam's Sons, 1968), 36–38.

3. Valachi was also known as "Charles Chambano," "Joseph Siano," and "Anthony Sorge." http://en.wikipedia.org/wiki/Joseph_Valachi.

4. Maas, *The Valachi Papers*, 272–73.

5. Emanual Perlmutter, "Valachi Accuses Mafia Leader at Senate Inquiry," *New York Times*, September 28, 1963.

6. In *The Godfather: Part II* (1974), the character of Frank "Frankie Five Angels" Pentangeli appears for the first time as the successor to Corleone family underboss Peter Clemenza. Biography for Frankie Pentangeli (character), http://www.imdb.com/character/ch0000819/bio.

7. "U.S. Now Asks Ban on Valachi's Book. Sues After Protests to Bar Memoirs It Had Cleared," *New York Times*, May 10, 1966; Maas, *The Valachi Papers*, 54.

8. Fred Graham, "Valachi Allowed to Print Memoirs," *New York Times*, December 28, 1965.

9. Roger Greenspun, "The Screen: 'Valachi Papers' Arrives; Work Covers 30 Years of Criminal History; Bronson in Lead Role of Mafia Informant," *New York Times*, November 4, 1972.

10. Maas, *The Valachi Papers*, 38.

11. Perlmutter, "Valachi Accuses Mafia Leader."

12. In *Five Families*, his history of the American underworld, former *New York Times* organized crime reporter Selwyn Raab writes, "Valachi was presented through television at hearings before Senator McClellan's investigations committee as the nation's first reliable witness on the inner workings of the Mafia." Selwyn Raab, *Five Families: The Rise, Decline, and Resurgence of America's Most Powerful Mafia Empires* (New York: St. Martin's Press, 2005). See also: "Their Thing," *Time*, August 16, 1963; "The Valachi Hippodrome," editorial, *New York Times*, October 3, 1963.

13. Robert F. Kennedy, "Robert F. Kennedy Defines the Menace," *New York Times Magazine*, October 13, 1963.

14. Maas, *The Valachi Papers*, 59.

15. Sanford J. Unger, *FBI: An Uncensored Look Behind the Walls* (Boston: Atlantic Monthly Press, 1975), 392.

16. Ibid.

17. Ralph Ranalli, *Deadly Alliance: The FBI's Secret Partnership with the Mob* (New York: HarperTorch, 2001).

18. The primary proponent of this theory is author Anthony Summers, who presented hearsay evidence, from a series of questionable sources, that Hoover was seen on two occasions in 1958 and 1959 cross-dressing at the Plaza Hotel in New York and that he'd maintained a sexual relationship for years with his chief aide, Clyde Tolson. Anthony Summers, *Official and Confidential: The Secret Life of J. Edgar Hoover* (New York: Putnam, 1993). But in his book *The Bureau*, author Ronald Kessler devotes multiple pages to debunking Summers's cross-dressing allegations and conceding, with respect to Tolson, that "the fact that Hoover spent most of his leisure time with a man and that they took adoring photos of each other leaves open the question of whether Hoover was a closet homosexual who was either unaware of his orientation or suppressed it." Ronald Kessler, *The Bureau: The Secret History of the FBI* (New York: St. Martin's Press, 2002), 107–12.

19. Carl Sifakis, *The Mafia Encyclopedia* (New York: Checkmark Books, 2005), 20.

20. Neil J. Welch and David W. Marston, *Inside Hoover's FBI: Top Field Chief Reports* (New York: Doubleday, 1984).

21. Ranalli, *Deadly Alliance,* 47.
22. Claire Sterling, *Octopus: How the Long Reach of the Sicilian Mafia Controls the Global Narcotics Trade* (New York: Simon & Schuster, 1990), 56.
23. Ibid., 82–89.
24. Ibid., 81.
25. Alfred W. McCoy, *The Politics of Heroin in Southeast Asia* (New York: Harper & Row, 1972). "Luciano's Plan," as Sterling called it, was executed and resulted in $1.6 billion in illegal narcotics brought into the United States between 1975 and 1984.
26. The trial lasted seventeen months at a cost of several million dollars. Seventeen of the original thirty-two accused Mafiosi indicted were convicted. The lead assistant U.S. attorney presiding over the case was Louis Freeh, a former FBI agent who would go on to become FBI director in 1993. Shana Alexander, *The Pizza Connection: Lawyers, Money, Drugs, Mafia* (New York: Weidenfield & Nicolson, 1988); Ralph Blumenthal, *Last Days of the Sicilians: At War with the Mafia: The FBI Assault on the Pizza Connection* (New York: Times Books, 1988).
27. Thomas Repetto, *American Mafia: A History of Its Rise to Power* (New York: Henry Holt & Co., 2004); "Apalachin Meeting," Wikipedia, http://en.wikipedia.org/wiki/Apalachin_Meeting.
28. Sterling, *Octopus,* 82–96.
29. "Apalachin Meeting," Wikipedia, http://en.wikipedia.org/wiki/Apalachin_Meeting.
30. Selwyn Raab, "Joe Bonanno Dies; Mafia Leader, 97, Who Built Empire," *New York Times,* May 12, 2002.
31. Ranalli, *Deadly Alliance,* 49.
32. Anthony Villano with Gerald Astor, *Brick Agent: Inside the Mafia for the FBI* (New York: Quadrangle, 1977), 44.
33. Ranalli, *Deadly Alliance,* 70.
34. Raab, *Five Families,* 136.
35. Ibid., 50.
36. William E. Roemer, *Man Against the Mob: The Inside Story of How the FBI Cracked the Chicago Mob by the Agent Who Led the Attack* (New York: Ballantine, 1989), 69.
37. On Celano's Custom Tailors at 620 North Michigan in Chicago: Roemer, *Man Against the Mob.* On the members of Congress: Kessler, *The Bureau,* 103.
38. "Investigations: Bobby's High Life," *Time,* November 8, 1963.
39. Thomas Repetto, *Bringing Down the Mob: The War Against the American Mafia* (New York: Holt, 2007), 90.
40. Unger, *FBI,* 397.
41. Ibid.
42. House Committee on Government Reform, *Everything Secret Degenerates: The FBI's Use of Murderers as Informants, 3rd Report,* HR Rep. No. 108-414 at 454 (2004).
43. Ranalli, *Deadly Alliance,* 58.
44. The primary agent, an alternate, and their supervisor. *U.S. v. Victor M. Orena et al.,* testimony of Special Agent Howard Leadbetter II, May 18, 1995, 1313.
45. Ronald J. Ostrow and Robert L. Jackson, "Agents Could Face Charges in Presser Inquiry," *Los Angeles Times,* August 22, 1985.
46. Nicholas Pileggi, *Casino: Love and Honor in Las Vegas* (New York: Simon & Schuster, 1995).
47. Jane Ann Morrison, "'Lefty' Rosenthal Was an FBI Snitch," *Las Vegas Review Journal,* October 30, 2008.

48. *Plain Dealer* staff, "Car Bomb Kills Danny Greene," *Plain Dealer,* October 7, 1977.
49. Dick Lehr and Gerard O'Neill, *Black Mass: The True Story of an Unholy Alliance Between the FBI and the Irish Mob* (New York: HarperPaperbacks, 2001).
50. "FBI Helped Bulger Evade Detection, Ex-Cop Says," *CBS News,* June 24, 2011, http://www.cbsnews.com/stories/2011/06/24/earlyshow/main20073987.shtml.
51. Memo from special agent in charge, FBI New York Office, to director, FBI. Subject: Gregory Scarpa Top Echelon Criminal Informant Program, New York Division, November 21, 1961.

CHAPTER 2: A TRUE MACHIAVELLI
1. Ronald Kessler, *The Bureau: The Secret History of the FBI* (New York: St. Martin's Press, 2002), 106.
2. Curt Gentry, *J. Edgar Hoover: The Man and the Secrets* (New York: W. W. Norton, 1991), 533.
3. John A. Goldsmith, "Valachi Says Gang Menaces Society," United Press International, October 3, 1963.
4. Selwyn Raab, *Five Families: The Rise, Decline, and Resurgence of America's Most Powerful Mafia Empires* (New York: St. Martin's Press, 2005), 135–38.
5. National Geographic Channel, *Inside the Mafia: What Mafia?,* May 26, 2009, http://www.youtube.com/watch?v=NhXRa0g_has&feature=related.
6. Ibid.
7. Thomas L. Jones, "The Dying of the Light: The Joseph Valachi Story," TruTV.com, http://www.trutv.com/library/crime/gangsters_outlaws/mob_bosses/valachi//index_1.html.
8. Raab, *Five Families,* 137.
9. Peter Maas, *The Valachi Papers* (New York: G. P. Putnam's Sons, 1968), 123–28.
10. Ibid., 43.
11. Raab, *Five Families,* 137.
12. Memo by liaison, December 4, 1967. Subject: Gregory Scarpa, FBI #584217A.
13. On April 3, 1961. See Appendix C, a list of Scarpa Sr.'s twenty arrests.
14. Memo, June 27, 1966 memorandum from special agent in charge, FBI New York Office, to director, FBI. Subject: Gregory Scarpa. Top Echelon Criminal Informant Program, New York Division, July 6, 1967.
15. One of the most famous scenes in *The Godfather* (novel and film) was inspired by an incident during the war in which Profaci gunmen killed Gallo loyalist Joseph "Joe Jelly" Gioiello and tossed his clothing, filled with fish, in front of a restaurant frequented by the Gallo brothers. The message, immortalized by Mario Puzo, was that he "sleeps with the fishes." Raab, *Five Families,* 194.
16. Memo from special agent in charge, FBI New York Office, to director, FBI. Subject: Gregory Scarpa. Top Echelon Criminal Informant Program, New York Division, March 28, 1963.
17. Letter from special agent in charge, FBI New York Office, to director, FBI. June 27, 1966. This letter was written during a period when Scarpa's initial contacting agents had been transferred and he was withdrawing his cooperation.
18. Ibid.
19. Memo from special agent in charge, FBI New York Office, July 6, 1967.
20. Letter from special agent in charge, FBI New York Office, June 27, 1966.
21. Memo by liaison, December 4, 1967.

22. Memo from special agent in charge, FBI New York Office, to director, FBI. Subject: Gregory Scarpa. Top Echelon Criminal Informant Program, New York Division, November 21, 1961.

23. Addendum: Criminal Investigative Division, April 8, 1987, memorializing an April 3, 1987, teletype requesting payment for "captioned source" for supplying "extremely singular information which led to 17 Title III intercepts and 50 reauthorizations forming the basis for the prosecution of the Colombo family." *U.S. v. Carmine Persico,* No. 84 Cr.809 (JFK), opinion of Judge John F. Keenan denying motions to dismiss, http://www.ipsn.org/court_cases/us_v_persico_1986-09-25.htm.

24. Lou Diamond, in an interview with Fredric Dannen, "The G-Man and the Hit Man," *New Yorker,* December 16, 1996.

25. Memo, FBI New York Office, October 3, 1966.

26. Letter from special agent in charge, FBI New York Office, June 27, 1966.

27. Memo from J. H. Gale, assistant director, FBI, to Cartha DeLoach, deputy director, FBI, August 4, 1967.

28. Memo from special agent in charge, FBI New York Office, to director, FBI. Subject: Gregory Scarpa Top Echelon Criminal Informant Program, New York Division, June 18, 1962, 11 pages.

29. R. Lindley DeVecchio and Charles Brandt, *We're Going to Win This Thing: The Shocking Frame-up of a Mafia Crime Fighter* (New York: Berkley, 2011), 108: "Although never a capo, Scarpa had his own very special status. He later confided in me that he would never agree to be a capo because it would draw too much attention to himself. He remained a soldier under capo Anthony 'Scappi' Scarpati, although their relationship was a mere formality. Scarpa always did his own thing."

30. The title of Fredric Dannen's seminal piece on the Scarpa-DeVecchio scandal in the *New Yorker,* December 16, 1996.

31. *U.S. v. Michael Sessa,* testimony of R. Lindley DeVecchio, November 2, 1992.

CHAPTER 3: HITTING THE BOSS

1. Memo from director, FBI, to New York ████████ authorizing payment of $3,000 to ████████ informant, June 26, 1962.

2. Memo from special agent in charge, FBI New York Office, to director, FBI, June 6, 1963.

3. Emmanuel Perlmutter, "Valachi Accuses Mafia Leader at Senate Inquiry," *New York Times,* September 28, 1963.

4. Author's interview with DEA Special Agent Michael Levine (ret.), October 8, 2011.

5. Michael T. Kaufman, "Profacis' Roots Deep in Brooklyn," *New York Times,* August 18, 1964.

6. Ibid.

7. Joseph A. Gambardello, "Colombo Family Has Bloody Past," *Newsday,* December 17, 1991.

8. Memo from special agent in charge, FBI New York Office, to director, FBI. Subject: Gregory Scarpa. Top Echelon Criminal Informant Program, New York Division, June 25, 1962.

9. Selwyn Raab, "Even to the 5 Families, the Fighting Colombos Have Been Black Sheep," *New York Times,* December 10, 1991.

10. Kaufman, "Profacis' Roots Deep in Brooklyn."

11. Selwyn Raab, *Five Families: The Rise, Decline, and Resurgence of America's Most Powerful Mafia Empires* (New York: St. Martin's Press, 2005), 322–23.

12. Burton B. Turkus and Sid Feder, *Murder, Inc.: The Story of the Syndicate Killing Machine* (New York: Tenacity Media Books, 2012), 20. See link to the Foreword of a new edition of the book published in 2012: http://peterlance.com/wordpress/?p=450.

13. Meyer Berger, "Anastasia Slain in a Hotel Here; Led Murder, Inc." *New York Times,* October 26, 1957.

14. Raab, *Five Families,* 328.

15. Tom Folsom, *The Mad Ones: Crazy Joe Gallo and the Revolution at the Edge of the Underworld* (New York: Weinstein Books, 2008), 35.

16. David J. Krajicek, "Frankie Abbatemarco Is the Opening Casualty in the Profaci Family Civil War," New York *Daily News,* September 19, 2010.

17. Nicholas Gage, "Key Mafia Figure Tells of 'Wars' and Gallo-Colombo Peace Talks," *New York Times,* July 7, 1975.

18. Memo from special agent in charge, FBI New York Office, to director, FBI. Subject: Gregory Scarpa. Top Echelon Criminal Informant Program, New York Division, March 20, 1962, 7.

19. Nicholas Gage, "Grudge Against Gallo Date to 'War' with Profaci," *New York Times,* April 8, 1972.

20. Memo from special agent in charge, FBI New York Office, to director, FBI. Subject: Gregory Scarpa. Top Echelon Criminal Informant Program, New York Division, March 20, 1962, 6–8.

21. Gage, "Grudge Against Gallo."

22. Ibid.

23. FBI letterhead memo (LHM) re: Gregory Scarpa, May 1, 1962, 2.

24. Author's interview with Alan Futerfas, May 24, 2004.

25. Gambardello, "Colombo Family Has Bloody Past."

CHAPTER 4: THE SPECIAL GOES SOUTH

1. Author's interview with Fredric Dannen, October 2, 2011.

2. *U.S. v. Cecil Ray Price et al.,* Criminal Action Number 5291, U.S. Court for the Southern District of Mississippi, October 7, 1968.

3. Jerry Mitchell, "Experts: Autopsy Reveals Beating," *Jackson Clarion-Ledger,* June 4, 2000.

4. Peter Lance, *Cover Up: What the Government Is Still Hiding About the War on Terror* (New York: ReganBooks, 2004), 14.

5. Andrew Jacobs, "The Southern Town Struggles with a Violent Legacy," *New York Times,* May 29, 2004.

6. Author's interviews with Judge W. O. Chet Dillard, October 10, 2011, and June 11, 2004.

7. *People v. R. Lindley DeVecchio,* October 29, 2007, transcript, 1544–52.

8. Tom Robbins and Jerry Capeci, "FBI Used Wiseguy to Crack KKK Man," New York *Daily News,* June 21, 1994.

9. Dillard interview, October 10, 2011.

10. Dillard interview, June 11, 2004.

11. Fredric Dannen, interview with confidential source, October 1996.

12. Mitchell, "Experts: Autopsy Reveals Beating."

13. Author's interview with Linda Schiro, November 3, 2007.

14. Jennifer S. Lee, "Samuel Bowers, 82, Klan Leader Convicted in Fatal Bombing, Dies," *New York Times,* November 6, 2006.

15. Fredric Dannen, "The G-Man and the Hit Man," *New Yorker,* December 16, 1996; Taylor Branch, *At Canaan's Edge: America in the King Years, 1965–68* (New York: Simon & Schuster, 2007), 411.

16. Dillard interview, October 10, 2011.

17. Memo to assistant director from ███████████, January 21, 1966. Although no airtel in the recently disclosed material documents Scarpa's 1964 assignment, that memo, memorializing Scarpa's recruiting for the Vernon Dahmer case, uses the term "special."

18. Ibid.

19. W. O. Chet Dillard, *Clear Burning: Civil Rights, Civil Wrongs* (Jackson, MS: Persimmon Press, 1992). In an interview with the author on October 9, 2011, Judge Dillard said that in recent years he had identified an eyewitness to the kidnapping—a man whose father had run a welding shop adjacent to the alley behind Byrd's store. Though only a boy at the time of the abduction, the witness confirmed the details for Dillard.

20. Dillard interview, October 10, 2011.

21. Dillard interview, July 11, 2004.

22. Dannen, "The G-Man and the Hit Man."

23. FBI 302 memo, interrogation of Lawrence Byrd, February 2, 1966.

24. Signed confession of Lawrence Byrd, Hattiesburg, Mississippi, March 2, 1996. Ruth A. Olenski, reporter.

25. Ibid., testimony of Linda Schiro, 2007, transcript, 1552.

26. Lee, "Samuel Bowers, 82."

27. Robert D. McFadden, "First Murder Charge in '64 Civil Rights Killings of 3," *New York Times,* January 7, 2005.

28. Shaila Dewan, "Former Klansman Guilty of Manslaughter in 1964 Deaths," *New York Times,* June 22, 2005.

29. Ariel Hart, "41 Years Later, Ex-Klansman Gets 60 Years in Civil Rights Deaths," *New York Times,* June 24, 2005.

30. "Sarah Wallace Killer Says Civil Rights Violated," WABC-TV, February 4, 2009.

31. A series of hearings into intelligence abuses by the CIA and FBI was conducted by Senator Frank Church (D-ID) and Congressman Otis D. Pike (D-NY), who chaired separate Select Committees on Intelligence. The multiple reports of the Church Committee, which held hearings from 1975 to 1976, can be accessed at http://en.wikipedia.org/wiki/Church_Committee. The House of Representatives voted not to release Pike's report without presidential approval, but it was published by the *Village Voice* after NPR reporter Daniel Schorr leaked a copy to the weekly. http://blogs.villagevoice.com/runninscared/2010/07/the_village_voi_3.php.

32. Author's interview with DEA Special Agent Michael Levine (ret.), October 8, 2011.

33. Anthony Villano with Gerald Astor, *Brick Agent: Inside the Mafia for the FBI* (New York: Quadrangle, 1977), 93.

34. Sandra Harmon, *Mafia Son: The Scarpa Mob Family, the FBI, and a Story of Betrayal* (New York: St. Martin's Press, 2009), 60–64. A self-professed "Love Coach, Life Coach, Love Trainer" (http://www.sandraharmon.com), Harmon is the coauthor of the Priscilla Presley tell-all *Elvis & Me* (New York: Putnam, 1985).

35. Richard Esposito, "Former Fave FBI Stool Pigeon Indicted," ABC News, March 30, 2006, http://abcnews.go.com/US/story?id=1786440&page=2.

36. Jerry Capeci, "Ex-FBI Agent Probed in Mob Hits," *New York Sun,* January 12, 2006.

37. Tom Robbins, "Mobster on a Mission," *Village Voice,* January 10, 2006.

38. Testimony of Marty Light before the President's Commission on Organized Crime, Washington, DC, January 29, 1986.

39. *U.S. v. Victor Orena,* November 19, 1992, 976.

CHAPTER 5: SINATRA, CAPOTE, AND THE ANIMAL

1. Memo from special agent in charge, FBI New York Office, to director, FBI, June 6, 1963.

2. Memo from special agent in charge, FBI New York Office, to director, FBI, September 21, 1964.

3. Memo from special agent in charge, FBI New York Office, to director, FBI, November 3, 1965.

4. Amount is closer to $120,794.97 according to the website U.S. Inflation Calculator, http://www.usinflationcalculator.com/.

5. Memo from special agent in charge, FBI New York Office, to director, FBI, August 16, 1966.

6. Memo from special agent in charge, FBI New York Office, to director, FBI, July 29, 1967.

7. Memo from special agent in charge, FBI New York Office, August 16, 1966.

8. Memo from special agent in charge, FBI New York Office, July 29, 1967.

9. Author's interview with FBI Special Agent Dan Vogel (ret.), October 14, 2011.

10. Memo from J. H. Gale, assistant director, to Cartha DeLoach, deputy director, August 4, 1967.

11. Memo from special agent in charge, FBI New York Office, to director, FBI, July 29, 1967.

12. *People v. R. Lindley DeVecchio,* testimony of Linda Schiro, October 29, 2007, transcript, 1554.

13. Anthony Villano with Gerald Astor, *Brick Agent: Inside the Mafia for the FBI* (New York: Quadrangle, 1977), 9.

14. Ibid.

15. Memo from special agent in charge, FBI New York Office, to director, FBI, August 25, 1967.

16. Ibid.

17. Author's interview with DEA Special Agent Michael Levine (ret.), October 8, 2011.

18. Villano, *Brick Agent,* 93–94.

19. Villano died in 1978, but in researching his 1996 piece for the *New Yorker,* Fredric Dannen interviewed his coauthor, Gerald Astor. He confirmed that the two Mafiosi were based on Scarpa. "We did that to give him more cover," Astor told Dannen. Fredric Dannen, interviews with Gerald Astor, September 30 and October 1, 1996.

20. Villano, *Brick Agent,* 90–94. Villano doesn't mention the Dahmer case by name. In fact, he implies that Scarpa's work was in connection with FBI efforts to solve the murder of civil rights leader Medgar Evers — a possible third Mississippi mission for the TE informant. But the facts as related in *Brick Agent* suggest that the expenses were owed in relation to the Lawrence Byrd interrogation.

21. Memo from Gale to DeLoach, August 4, 1967.

22. Amount is closer to $3,969.33 according to U.S. Inflation Calculator, http://www.usinflationcalculator.com/.

23. Memo from special agent in charge, FBI New York Office, to director, FBI, January 23, 1968.

24. Memo from special agent in charge, FBI New York Office, to director, FBI, January 18, 1968.

25. Levine interview, October 8, 2011.

26. Vogel interview, October 14, 2011.

27. Burton B. Turkus and Sid Feder, *Murder, Inc.: The Story of the Syndicate Killing Machine* (New York: Tenacity Media Books, 2012), 359–60.

28. House Committee on Government Reform, *Everything Secret Degenerates: The FBI's Use of Murderers as Informants, 3rd Report*, HR Rep. No. 108-414 at 454 (2004), 62.

29. FBI teletype from special agent in charge, FBI New York Office, to director, FBI, February 15, 1968.

30. FBI teletype from special agent in charge, FBI New York Office, to director, FBI Boston Office, February 16, 1968.

31. Deborah Davis, *The Party of the Century: The Fabulous Story of Truman Capote and His Black and White Ball* (New York: Wiley, 2006).

32. Charlotte Curtis, "Capote's Black and White Ball: 'The Most Exquisite of Spectator Sports,'" *New York Times,* November 29, 1966.

33. Ibid.

34. The initial name was "American-Italian Anti-Defamation Council." Colombo later changed it to the "Italian-American Civil Rights League." Peter Maas, *The Valachi Papers* (New York: G. P. Putnam's Sons, 1968), 12; memo from special agent in charge, FBI New York Office, to director, FBI. Subject: Gregory Scarpa. Top Echelon Criminal Informant Program, New York Division, April 11, 1966.

35. Fred Ferretti, "Italian-American League's Power Spreads," *New York Times,* April 4, 1971.

36. Craig Whitney, "Italians Picket F.B.I. Office Here," *New York Times,* May 2, 1970.

37. Fred Ferretti, "TV's 'F.B.I.' to Drop 'Mafia' and 'Cosa Nostra' from Its Scripts," *New York Times,* March 24, 1971.

38. Nicholas Gage, "A Few Family Murders, but That's Show Biz," *New York Times,* March 19, 1972.

39. Nicholas Pileggi, "The Making of 'The Godfather'—Sort of a Home Movie," *New York Times,* August 15, 1971.

40. Morris Kaplan, "Kahane and Colombo Join Forces to Fight U.S. Harassment," *New York Times,* May 14, 1971.

41. Pileggi, "The Making of 'The Godfather.'"

42. William E. Farrell, "Colombo Shot, Gunman Slain at Columbus Circle Rally Site," *New York Times,* June 29, 1971.

43. Fred Ferretti, "Suspect in Shooting of Colombo Linked to Gambino Family," *New York Times,* July 20, 1971.

44. Arnold H. Lubasch, "11 Indicted by U.S. as the Leadership of a Crime Family," *New York Times,* October 25, 1984.

CHAPTER 6: AGENT PROVOCATEUR

1. One definition given by Webster's is similar: "a person employed to encourage people to break the law so that they can be arrested," http://www.learnersdictionary.com/search/agent%20provocateur.

2. FBI teletype on reopening of Gregory Scarpa, FBI NY #534217A, July 1, 1980.

3. Conclusion of Judge Gustin Reichbach, decision and order of dismissal, *People v. R. Lindley DeVecchio,* November, 1, 2007, http://online.wsj.com/public/resources/documents/reichbach.pdf. See Appendix H.

4. FBI teletype from director, FBI, to FBI New York Office, September 25, 1991.

5. Anthony Villano with Gerald Astor, *Brick Agent: Inside the Mafia for the FBI* (New York: Quadrangle, 1977), 105.

6. That figure was determined by breaking down the $158,400 in total payments made to Scarpa Sr. from September 1962 to September 25, 1991, the date of a teletype to the director from the New York SAC. Based on the 149 months of "34's" first term as a TECI, from September 1962 through May 1975, and the 134 months of his second term, from July 1980 through September 1991, and adjusting the average of fees paid annually to 2013 dollars via www.usinflationcalculator.com, the totals were $526,355.32 for the first term (1962–1975) and $155,114.49 for the second term (1980–1991).

Further, in his memoir, Scarpa Sr.'s third contacting agent, Anthony Villano, estimated that "34" had earned $52,000 in insurance rewards brokered by Villano for various hijackings that Scarpa Sr. told the FBI about during an unspecified eighteen-month period. Reckoning that period as commencing in January 1968, the date of the Olympic Airways heist, after which Scarpa Sr. informed Villano of the most hijackings, that $52,000 figure adjusted to 2013 dollars represented $337,035.25. Adding it to the adjusted totals for Scarpa Sr.'s two terms as a Top Echelon Criminal Informant, the combined figure in payments from the FBI and insurance rewards represented $1,007,668.50 in 2013 dollars.

7. Description of the Colombo family drawn from Selwyn Raab, *Five Families: The Rise, Decline, and Resurgence of America's Most Powerful Mafia Empires* (New York: St. Martin's Press, 2005), 326.

8. Memo from J. H. Gale, assistant director, to Cartha DeLoach, deputy director, July 9, 1970.

9. Memo from special agent in charge, FBI New York Office, to director, FBI. Subject: Gregory Scarpa. Top Echelon Criminal Informant Program, New York Division, November 3, 1970, 4.

10. Memo from special agent in charge, FBI New York Office, to director, FBI. Subject: Gregory Scarpa. Top Echelon Criminal Informant Program, New York Division, November 24, 1967, 7.

11. Memo from special agent in charge, FBI New York Office, to director, FBI. Subject: Gregory Scarpa. Top Echelon Criminal Informant Program, New York Division, November 5, 1969, 1; memo from special agent in charge, FBI New York Office, to director, FBI. Subject: Gregory Scarpa. Top Echelon Criminal Informant Program, New York Division, November 9, 1970, 4–6.

12. Memo from special agent in charge, FBI New York Office, to director, FBI. Subject: Gregory Scarpa. Top Echelon Criminal Informant Program, New York Division, July 2, 1970.

13. FBI memo, November 9, 1970.

14. Memo from special agent in charge, FBI New York Office, to director, FBI. Subject: Gregory Scarpa. Top Echelon Criminal Informant Program, New York Division, June 16, 1971.

15. Memo from special agent in charge, FBI New York Office, to director, FBI. Subject: Gregory Scarpa. Top Echelon Criminal Informant Program, New York Division, June 29, 1971.

16. Memo from special agent in charge, FBI New York Office, to director, FBI. Subject: Gregory Scarpa. Top Echelon Criminal Informant Program, New York Division, September 2, 1971.

17. Raab, *Five Families,* 324.
18. Fredric Dannen, interview with Louis Diamond, October 16, 1966.
19. Raab, *Five Families,* 194.
20. Author's interview with Mario Puzo, April 12, 1999.
21. Larry McShane, "Matty the Horse's Ride Could End in Prison," Associated Press, March 4, 2007.
22. Eric Pace, "Joe Gallo Is Shot to Death in Little Italy Restaurant," *New York Times,* April 8, 1972.
23. Nicholas Gage, "Two Are Hunted in Gallo Murder," *New York Times,* April 14, 1972.
24. Nicholas Gage, "Story of Joe Gallo's Murder: 5 in Colombo Gang Implicated," *New York Times,* May 3, 1972.
25. Memo from special agent in charge, FBI New York Office, to director, FBI. Subject: Gregory Scarpa. Top Echelon Criminal Informant Program, New York Division, July 25, 1972.
26. Indictment, *U.S. v. Gregory Scarpa, Gennaro Ciprio et al.,* 72 CR997. 72 CR866, July 18, 1972. Fourteen-page indictment.
27. Nicholas Gage. "Slain Brooklyn Man Described as Colombo Family Associate," *New York Times,* April 11, 1972.
28. Order to Transfer, July 18, 1972. Ciprio, a senior Colombo family associate, was standing a few feet away from the boss, Joseph Colombo, when he was shot. Five months after the indictment was handed down, Ciprio was murdered. The shooting occurred just four days after the rubout of Colombo's archrival, Crazy Joe Gallo, in Little Italy. It's unclear what impact Ciprio's death may have had on the stolen-securities case.
29. U.S. District Court, Eastern District of New York, order of dismissal, April 6, 1973.
30. Gage, "Slain Brooklyn Man."
31. Special Agents David M. Parker and Robert J. O'Brien, FBI 302 memo re: Carmine Sessa, April 18, 1994, 2.
32. Author's interview with Flora Edwards, November 3, 2011.

CHAPTER 7: GOD, THE MOB, AND THE FBI

1. Nicholas Gage, "Key Mafia Figure Tells of 'War' and Gallo-Colombo Peace Talks," *New York Times,* July 7, 1975.
2. Memo from special agent in charge, FBI New York Office, to director, FBI. Subject: Gregory Scarpa. Top Echelon Criminal Informant Program, New York Division, July 25, 1972.
3. "Smiling New Yorker Refuses Answers on Mail Theft Ring," Associated Press, July 21, 1971.
4. Testimony of Gregory Scarpa before the Permanent Subcommittee on Investigations of the Senate Government Operations Committee, OC and Stolen Securities, 1971, 633–35; 616; David Scheim, *Contract on America: The Mafia Murder of President John F. Kennedy* (New York: Shapolsky Publishers, 1971), 345.
5. Memo from special agent in charge, FBI New York Office, to director, FBI. Subject: Gregory Scarpa. Top Echelon Criminal Informant Program, New York Division, September 2, 1971, referencing a Scarpa debriefing on June 29, 1971, 2.
6. Memo from special agent in charge, FBI New York Office, to director, FBI, August 21, 1968.

7. Memo from special agent in charge, FBI New York Office, to director, FBI, November 24, 1967, 3.

8. Ibid., 4.

9. Ibid., 8.

10. Memo from special agent in charge, FBI New York Office, to director, FBI, December 20, 1968, 2–3.

11. Memo from special agent in charge, FBI New York Office, to director, FBI, May 5, 1969, 2–3.

12. Memo from special agent in charge, FBI New York Office, to director, FBI, May 5, 1970, 3.

13. Memo from special agent in charge, FBI New York Office, to director, FBI, November 9, 1970, 1–2.

14. Author's interview with Ellen Resnick, February 21, 2012.

15. Anthony Villano with Gerald Astor, *Brick Agent: Inside the Mafia for the FBI* (New York: Quadrangle, 1977), 105–106.

16. Author's interview with FBI Special Agent Dan Vogel (ret.), October 14, 2011.

17. Affidavit of Gregory Scarpa Jr. sworn before a notary at the ADX Florence prison, July 30, 2002.

18. *U.S. v. Victor Orena,* decision of Judge Jack B. Weinstein, habeas hearing, January 16, 2004.

19. The first terrorist was Ramzi Yousef, the convicted mastermind of the 1993 World Trade Center bombing and the 1995 Bojinka plot to blow up U.S. airliners over the Pacific. As chronicled in Chapter 38, Greg Scarpa Jr. obtained reams of intelligence from Yousef in an FBI-directed sting between 1996 and 1997, when they were in adjacent cells in the Metropolitan Correctional Center, the federal jail in Lower Manhattan. A series of FBI 302 memos documenting that investigation can be downloaded from http://www.peterlance.com/PLfbi.htm. The second terrorist was Terry Nichols, convicted with Timothy McVeigh of the Oklahoma City bombing. As detailed in Chapter 39, that story was documented by Associated Press reporters Jim Solomon and Mark Sherman in 2005: John Solomon, "Explosives Found in Former Home of Terry Nichols," Associated Press, April 2, 2005; Mark Sherman, "FBI Waited to Check Out Tip on Nichols," Associated Press, April 14, 2005.

20. Keith Wheeler and Sandy Smith, "Murph the Surf and His Jewel Studded Jinx," *Life,* April 21, 1967.

21. "Murph the Surf Held in a Miami Burglary," *New York Times,* January 3, 1965.

22. Memo from special agent in charge, FBI New York Office, to director, FBI, March 13, 1968, 2–3.

23. Starting in 1980, Yablonsky ran the FBI's Las Vegas Office. Michael Newton, *Mr. Mob: The Life and Crimes of Moe Dalitz* (Jefferson, NC: McFarland, 2009), 262–63.

24. Memo from special agent in charge, FBI New York Office, to director, FBI, May 3, 1968, 2.

25. *U.S. v. Gregory Scarpa et al.,* U.S. District Court, Northern District of Illinois Indictment, Case No. 72 CR866, July 18, 1972. The indictment charged Scarpa, Gerry Ciprio, and nine others in the theft of a series of municipal bonds, including five bonds with a face value of $5,000 from Cleveland, Ohio, and another five $5,000 bonds from Columbus, totaling $50,000. The case dovetails with the May 1970 airtel in which Greg Scarpa Sr., according to Anthony Villano, helped the Feds recover a cache of bonds worth an estimated $550,000—among them municipal bonds from

Cleveland and Columbus in the same $5,000 denominations as those listed in the Chicago indictment. Memo from New York SAC to the director, FBI, May 5, 1970.

26. Archives of the Brooklyn Public Library, "Regina Pacis and the Case of the Missing Crowns," Brooklynology.org, August 5, 2009. The $100,000 cost would equal $868,758.49 in 2013 dollars according to http://www.usinflationcalculator.com.

27. "Religion: Thieves in the Shrine," *Time,* June 9, 1952.

28. Brooklyn Public Library, "Regina Pacis."

29. "Religion: Thieves in the Shrine."

30. "Hush-Hush Relationship between Mob and Church," *Philadelphia Inquirer,* August 10, 1999.

31. Memo from special agent in charge, FBI New York Office, to director, FBI, August 31, 1962, 10.

32. Villano, *Brick Agent,* 111–14.

33. Memo from special agent in charge, FBI New York Office, to acting director, FBI, April 5, 1973, 1–3.

34. "Jewelry Recovered by FBI for Church," Associated Press, in *Lubbock Avalanche-Journal,* January 22, 1973.

35. Memo from special agent in charge, FBI New York Office, April 5, 1973.

36. Author's interview with James Whalen, May 19, 2011.

CHAPTER 8: THIRTY DAYS IN FORTY-TWO YEARS

1. Selwyn Raab, "The Mobster Was a Mole for the FBI: Tangled Life of a Mafia Figure Who Died of AIDS Is Exposed," *New York Times,* November 20, 1994.

2. Letter from Edward A. McDonald, attorney in charge, U.S. Department of Justice, Organized Crime Strike Force, EDNY, to Hon. I. Leo Glasser, July 22, 1986.

3. Ibid.

4. Ibid.

5. Ibid.

6. Ibid.

7. Letter from Edward A. McDonald, attorney in charge, U.S. Department of Justice, Organized Crime Strike Force, EDNY, to Louis E. Diamond, Gregory Scarpa Sr.'s attorney, setting forth terms of plea agreement, July 18, 1986.

8. U.S. District Court judgment and probation/commitment order, February 6, 1987; satisfaction of judgment, filed February 5, 1992; Greg Smith and Jerry Capeci, "Mob, Mole & Murder," New York *Daily News,* October 31, 1994.

9. Raab, "The Mobster Was a Mole."

10. *U.S. v. Michael Sessa,* testimony of Supervisory Special Agent R. Lindley DeVecchio, transcript, 119.

11. R. Lindley DeVecchio and Charles Brandt, *We're Going to Win This Thing: The Shocking Frame-up of a Mafia Crime Buster* (New York: Berkley, 2011), 116.

12. Nicholas Gage, "Slain Brooklyn Man Described as Columbo 'Family' Associate," *New York Times,* April 11, 1972.

13. Memo from special agent in charge, FBI New York Office, to director, FBI, May 5, 1970, 3.

14. Order to transfer, July 18, 1972; Nicholas Gage, "Slain Brooklyn Man."

15. U.S. District Court, Eastern District of New York, order of dismissal, April 6, 1973.

16. Memo (airtel) from special agent in charge, FBI Newark Office, to assistant director, FBI, April 10, 1973.

17. Memo (airtel) from special agent in charge, FBI Newark Office, to assistant director, FBI, April 30, 1973.
18. Author's interview with James Whalen, May 19, 2011.
19. Memo (airtel) from special agent in charge, FBI Newark Office, to director, FBI, October 9, 1973.
20. Ibid.
21. Teletype from FBI Newark Office to director, FBI, June 6, 1974.
22. Cover of special-delivery package addressed to director, FBI, time-stamped March 13, 1976.
23. Memo from special agent in charge, FBI Newark Office, to Brooklyn Strike Force, December 6, 1976.
24. Memo from special agent in charge, FBI Newark Office, to director, FBI, March 30, 1977.
25. Memo from special agent in charge, FBI Newark Office, to director, FBI, September 9, 1977, 2.
26. Memo from FBI Newark Office to Bureau (1) Headquarters, December 19, 1977.
27. Letter from McDonald to Glasser.
28. Author's interview with Flora Edwards, October 13, 2011.
29. Memo from special agent in charge, FBI New York Office, to director, FBI, January 20, 1966.
30. Ibid.
31. Ibid.
32. Author's interview with confidential FBI source, October 14, 2011.
33. "6 Charged with Hijacking 870 Cases of Scotch Here," *New York Times,* October 10, 1969.
34. *People of the State of New York v. Gregory Scarpa Sr. et al.,* indictment, October 8, 1969.
35. Letter from McDonald to Glasser.
36. Memo from special agent in charge, FBI Newark Office, to director, February 24, 1969.
37. Author's interview with former special agent in FBI New York Office, November 22, 2011.
38. Michael T. Kaufman, "Profaci's Roots Deep in Brooklyn," *New York Times,* August 18, 1964.
39. Memo from special agent in charge, FBI New York Office, to director, FBI, March 20, 1962, 9.
40. Memo from special agent in charge, FBI New York Office, to director, June 18, 1962, 2.
41. Memo from special agent in charge, FBI New York Office, to director, FBI, April 3, 1962, 2.
42. Kaufman, "Profaci's Roots."
43. Christopher Hoffman, "Whitey," *New Haven Independent,* August 31, 2009, http://www.newhavenindependent.org/archives/2009/08/whitey.php.
44. Memo from special agent in charge, FBI New York Office, to director, FBI, May 1, 1964, 2.
45. Ibid.
46. Kaufman, "Profaci's Roots."
47. Memo from special agent in charge, FBI New York Office, to director, FBI, July 9, 1962.

48. Memo from special agent in charge, FBI New York Office, to director, FBI, January 20, 1964.

49. Memo from special agent in charge, FBI New York Office, to director, FBI, November 7, 1963, 3.

50. Memo from special agent in charge, FBI New York Office, to director, FBI, November 6, 1964.

51. Michael T. Kaufman, "Mafia Elder Slain in Brooklyn Sipping Drink at Soda Fountain," *New York Times,* April 20, 1968.

52. Memo from special agent in charge, FBI New York Office, to director, FBI, August 12, 1965, 2.

53. Memo from special agent in charge, FBI New York Office, to director, FBI, September 2, 1965.

54. Ibid.

55. Memo from special agent in charge, FBI New York Office, to director, FBI, September 13, 1966.

56. In some source material Richard LoCicero is referred to as the Sidge's "nephew" or "grand-nephew." See testimony of Michael Gallinaro, an investigator for the McClellan subcommittee, at the 1971 hearing cited later in this book: Permanent Subcommittee on Investigations of the Senate Government Operations Committee, OC and Stolen Securities, June 8–10 and 16, 1971, 633–35; 616. However, in a later airtel, boss Joseph Colombo himself identified Richard as LoCicero's "grandson." Memo from special agent in charge, FBI New York Office, to director, FBI, May 3, 1968, 5–6.

57. Emmanuel Perlmutter, "'Star Witness' in Big Robbery Slain in Brooklyn," *New York Times,* April 6, 1967.

58. Memo from special agent in charge, FBI New York Office, to director, FBI, July 29, 1967.

59. Ibid.

60. Ibid.

61. Perlmutter, "'Star Witness' in Big Robbery."

62. Gallinaro testimony, 1971.

63. Perlmutter, "'Star Witness' in Big Robbery."

64. Ibid.

65. Ibid.

66. Memo from special agent in charge, FBI New York Office, July 29, 1967.

67. Kaufman, "Mafia Elder Slain."

68. Ibid.

69. Nancy Katz, Greg B. Smith, and William Sherman, "Probing Mob Links to G-Man," New York *Daily News,* January 5, 2006.

70. Kaufman, "Mafia Elder Slain."

71. Memo from special agent in charge, FBI New York Office, to director, FBI, April 1, 1964, 2.

72. Kaufman, "Mafia Elder Slain."

CHAPTER 9: THE OCTOPUS

1. Claire Sterling, *Octopus: How the Long Reach of the Sicilian Mafia Controls the Global Narcotics Trade* (New York: Touchstone, 1990), 13, quoting *Encyclopaedia Britannica.*

2. Memo from special agent in charge, FBI New York Office, to director, FBI, January 20, 1966, 2.

3. Paid Notice in the *New York Times:* Deaths: Obituary of Elliott Golden, July 29, 2008.

4. Memo from special agent in charge, FBI New York Office, to director, FBI, August 25, 1967, 4.

5. Memo from special agent in charge, FBI New York Office, to director, FBI, May 3, 1968, 5–6.

6. Ibid.

7. Ibid.

8. "The FBI's Compliance with the Attorney General Investigative Guidelines," Inspector General's Report, September 2005, 18.

9. Memo from special agent in charge, FBI New York Office, to director, FBI, March 1, 1974, 6.

10. Memo from special agent in charge, FBI New York Office, to director, FBI, May 18, 1974, 1.

11. FBI letterhead memo (LHM), March 1, 1975, 3.

12. Memo from special agent in charge, FBI New York Office, to director, FBI, May 5, 1975, 1.

13. Letter from Edward A. McDonald, attorney in charge, Organized Crime Strike Force, EDNY, to Hon. I. Leo Glasser, July 22, 1986.

14. Fredric Dannen, "The G-Man and the Hit Man," *New Yorker,* December 16, 1996.

15. R. Lindley DeVecchio and Charles Brandt, *We're Going to Win This Thing: The Shocking Frame-up of a Mafia Crime Buster* (New York: Berkley, 2011), 64.

16. Ibid., 107.

17. Dannen, "The G-Man and the Hit Man."

18. DeVecchio and Brandt, *We're Going to Win This Thing,* 108.

19. Ibid., 114.

20. Addendum: Criminal Investigative Division, April 8, 1987, requesting additional authority for payment to Gregory Scarpa Sr. It describes broadly the "services" the informant provided in three major investigations, identified as "Shooting Star," "Gambino Family," and "Starquest."

21. District Attorney Charles Hynes at the press conference announcing the indictment of Lin DeVecchio, March 20, 2006.

22. Jerry Capeci, "I Spy," New York *Daily News,* October 19, 1998.

CHAPTER 10: GUNS AND RABBIS

1. R. Lindley DeVecchio and Charles Brandt, *We're Going to Win This Thing: The Shocking Frame-up of a Mafia Crime Buster* (New York: Berkley, 2011), 109–10.

2. Jenner & Block employs 450 attorneys and has offices in Chicago, Washington, New York, and Los Angeles, http://jenner.com/people/JayDeVecchio.

3. DeVecchio and Brandt, *We're Going to Win This Thing,* 21.

4. Ibid., 35.

5. Ibid., "costume," 118; "gold chains," 68.

6. Ibid., 69.

7. Ibid., 107.

8. *U.S. v. Orena,* transcript of direct examination of R. Lindley DeVecchio by Gerald Shargel, February 28, 1997, 166–67.

9. Interview with R. Lindley DeVecchio, "The Grim Reaper: Greg Scarpa," *Monsters,* Biography Channel, airdate September 4, 2012.

10. *U.S. v. Orena* transcript, 67.

11. Memo from special agent in charge, FBI New York Office, to director, FBI. Subject:

Gregory Scarpa. Top Echelon Criminal Informant Program, New York Division, November 21, 1961.

12. DeVecchio and Brandt, *We're Going to Win This Thing,* 54–55.

13. Ibid., 32.

14. Author's interview with John Patton, April 29, 2004.

15. Anderson Cooper, "The FBI's Lin DeVecchio and 'the Grim Reaper,'" *60 Minutes,* CBS, airdate May 18, 2011.

16. DeVecchio and Brandt, *We're Going to Win This Thing,* 109.

17. FBI teletype memo from FBI New York Office to director, FBI, July 1, 1980.

18. *U.S. v. Gregory Scarpa Jr.,* testimony of R. Lindley DeVecchio, October 14, 1998, transcript, 3384–85.

19. R. Lindley DeVecchio, FBI 209 memos for Top Echelon (TE) informant designated "NY3461," December 2, 1980, to August 27, 1993.

20. Bob Drury, "Mafia Mole," *Playboy,* January 1997.

21. Scott Shifrel, "Mob Hit Man Testifies, Weeps at Lindley DeVecchio Trial," New York *Daily News,* October 19, 2007.

22. DeVecchio and Brandt, *We're Going to Win This Thing,* 73.

23. Accessing Bureau pay scales from that period, a former FBI agent consulted for this book estimated that the base salary for a GS-13—DeVecchio's estimated General Schedule (GS) pay scale after ten years of service—would have been roughly $27,756, with a 25 percent voluntary overtime increase, for a total of $34,695. Certain agents in New York were awarded cost-of-living increases over the years, so it's impossible to calculate DeVecchio's 1976 salary precisely, but the retired agent called it a "fair estimate."

24. *U.S. v. Orena* transcript, 165.

25. Alan Feuer, "For Ex-F.B.I. Agent Accused in Murders, a Case of What Might Have Been," *New York Times,* April 15, 2006.

26. *U.S. v. Orena* transcript, 164.

27. Ibid., 161.

28. Al Guarte, "FBI Big Shots Knew Mob Rat Killed His Rivals," *New York Post,* March 1, 1977.

29. 18 U.S. Code section 924, http://codes.lp.findlaw.com/uscode/18/I/44/924; 18 U.S. Code section 922, http://www.law.cornell.edu/uscode/18/922.html.

30. DeVecchio and Brandt, *We're Going to Win This Thing,* 74.

31. *U.S. v. Orena* transcript, 165.

32. DeVecchio and Brandt, *We're Going to Win This Thing,* 114; FBI teletype memo from FBI New York Office to director, FBI, March 8, 1985.

33. William Sherman, "You Pay G-Man's Legal Bills," New York *Daily News,* March 6, 2007.

34. According to an aide to Senator Chuck Grassley (R-IA) investigating the payments, the Justice Department cited two sections of the Code of Federal Regulations, 28 C.F.R. 50.15(a) and 50.16, that provide for the payment of legal fees for accused government employees if their actions on the job fall within the "scope" of their employment *and* the U.S. attorney general determines that the legal representation paid for is "in the interest of the United States," http://cfr.vlex.com/vid/representation-private-counsel-expense-19679481.

35. Author's interview with Gerald Shargel, November 9, 2011.

CHAPTER 11: THE ROYAL MARRIAGE

1. FBI, *Manual of Investigative and Operational Guidelines,* section 137-4, "Operation of Informant," (6): "An alternate Agent must be assigned at the time the informant is opened. The alternate Agent must handle some contacts with the informant and must meet or observe the informant by the second contact after conversion. . . . Any deviation from this requirement must be approved personally by the special agent in charge and documented in a memorandum in the informant's file."

2. Author's interview with Special Agent James Whalen (ret.), May 19, 2011.

3. U.S. Department of Justice, Office of the Inspector General, "The Federal Bureau of Investigation's Compliance with Attorney General's Investigative Rules," September 2005, www.justice.gov/oig/special/0509/chapter3.htm.

4. Memo to special agent in charge from Supervisory Special Agent R. Lindley DeVecchio (C-10), January 24, 1992, 5.

5. R. Lindley DeVecchio and Charles Brandt, *We're Going to Win This Thing: The Shocking Frame-up of a Mafia Crime Buster* (New York: Berkley, 2011), 70.

6. Jack B. Weinstein, judgment, memorandum, and order, *U.S. v. Victor J. Orena and Pasquale Amato,* March 10, 1997, 33.

7. DeVecchio and Brandt, *We're Going to Win This Thing,* 144.

8. Interview with Whalen, March 16, 2011.

9. DeVecchio and Brandt, *We're Going to Win This Thing,* 114.

10. Memo from FBI New York Office to director, FBI, November 10, 1980, citing an August 26, 1980, meeting reported that "Source furnished a complete up-to-date structural breakdown, placing all the members under the appropriate capos," 3.

11. Ibid., 2–4.

12. DeVecchio and Brandt, *We're Going to Win This Thing,* 13.

13. Ralph Ranalli, *Deadly Alliance: The FBI's Secret Partnership with the Mob* (New York: HarperTorch, 2001), 70.

14. Memo re: debriefing of Robert "Rabbit" Stasio, May 16, 1996.

15. Special Agents Jeffrey W. Tomlinson and Howard Leadbetter II, FBI 302 memo re: Carmine Sessa, May 29, 1993.

16. Special Agents Jeffrey W. Tomlinson and Howard Leadbetter II, FBI 302 memo re: Carmine Sessa, April 27, 1993.

17. John Connolly, "Who Handled Who?" *New York,* December 2, 1996.

18. Jerry Capeci, "No Tipping the Capo to Legendary Mobster," New York *Daily News,* June 14, 1994.

19. DeVecchio and Brandt, *We're Going to Win This Thing,* 123.

20. U.S. Department of Justice, "The Federal Bureau of Investigation's Compliance," 6–7; *1982 Final Report of the Senate Select Committee to Study Undercover Activities,* at 523 (Civiletti Informant Guidelines, section F.2).

21. R. Lindley DeVecchio, FBI 209 memo for Top Echelon (TE) informant designated "NY3461," December 2, 1980.

22. Gregory Scarpa and Lili Dajani, marriage certificate, State of Nevada, February 2, 1975. See Appendix B.

23. "Hadassah Sets Teas," Long Beach *Press-Telegram,* August 12, 1960.

24. "Miss Israel of 1960 on East Honeymoon," Long Beach *Press-Telegram,* March 26, 1961.

25. "IBC Beauty in Romance: Miss Israel Elopes, Weds in Las Vegas," Long Beach *Press-Telegram,* March 25, 1961.

26. "Miss Israel Gets a Congratulatory Call After the Show," Long Beach *Press-Telegram,* August 12, 1960.
27. Ibid.
28. Jerry Capeci, "Ex-Agent Is Probed in Murder of a Doctor," *New York Sun,* April 27, 2006.
29. Jerry Capeci, "Search for Lili Dajani," *New York Sun,* February 11, 2007.
30. Jerry Capeci, "Prosecutors: Murder Is FBI Man's 'Bad,'" *New York Sun,* September 6, 2007.
31. Ibid.
32. Ibid.
33. Alice McQuillan, "Judge: 5th Mob Hit Can't Be Linked to DeVecchio," WNBC-TV, October 10, 2007: "A fifth mob hit can't be linked to a retired FBI agent about to go on trial for allegedly helping the mafia commit four other slayings, according to a ruling Wednesday. However Brooklyn prosecutors did win their bid to raise allegations that retired agent R. Lindley DeVecchio accepted money and gifts from the mob for feeding confidential law enforcement information to the late Gregory Scarpa Sr., a powerful Colombo family capo who was also a government informant. Brooklyn supreme court justice Gustin Reichbach called the fifth murder 'highly prejudicial,' suggesting that prosecutors already had ample allegations of homicide."
34. FBI letterhead memo (LHM), March 1, 1981, 1–4.
35. Transcript of press conference unsealing indictment in *People v. R. Lindley DeVecchio,* March 30, 2006.
36. Anderson Cooper, Andy Court, and Anya Bourg, "The FBI's Lin DeVecchio and 'the Grim Reaper,'" *60 Minutes,* CBS News, May 18, 2011.
37. Anthony Villano with Gerald Astor, *Brick Agent: Inside the Mafia for the FBI* (New York: Quadrangle, 1977), 68.
38. Jerry Capeci, "Echoes of Mob War Reverberate 15 Years Later," New York *Daily News,* July 20, 2006.
39. DeVecchio and Brandt, *We're Going to Win This Thing,* 219.
40. Special Agents Jeffrey W. Tomlinson and Howard Leadbetter II, FBI 302 memo re: Carmine Sessa, May 10, 1993.
41. Tomlinson and Leadbetter II, FBI 302 memo, April 27, 1993.
42. Special Agents Jeffrey W. Tomlinson and Howard Leadbetter II, FBI 302 memo re: Carmine Sessa, May 6, 1993.
43. John Kroger, *Convictions* (New York: Farrar, Straus & Giroux, 2008), 135.
44. Ibid.
45. Tomlinson and Leadbetter II, FBI 302 memo, May 6, 1993.
46. Ibid.
47. Interview with Little Linda Schiro, "I Married a Mobster," *Investigation,* episode 6, Discovery Channel, airdate December 3, 2011.
48. Brad Hamilton, "Daddy's a Death Machine," *New York Post,* May 27, 2012.
49. DeVecchio and Brandt, *We're Going to Win This Thing,* 123.
50. Hamilton, "Daddy's a Death Machine."
51. "Attorney General's Guidelines on FBI Use of Informants and Confidential Sources," part F (promulgated 1980; superseded 1996).
52. "Attorney General's Guidelines Regarding the Use of Confidential Informants," part C(l)(b)(i) (promulgated 2002).
53. Kroger, *Convictions,* 135.

CHAPTER 12: GOING TO HELL FOR THIS

1. "Alphonse Persico, 61, Is Dead; Leader of Colombo Crime Family," *New York Times,* September 13, 1989.
2. *People v. R. Lindley DeVecchio,* testimony of Detective Tommy Dades, NYPD (ret.), August 15, 2007, transcript of Kastigar hearing, 622.
3. Jennifer Fermino and Todd Venezia, "Romance and Rubout of Mafia Kingpin's Moll Doll," *New York Post,* February 26, 2006, reproduced on the website: theChicago Syndicate.com, http://www.thechicagosyndicate.com/2006/02/romance-and-rubout -of-mafia-kingpins.html.
4. Jerry Capeci, "Former Mob-Busting Agent to Be Charged with Murder in Mafia Hits," *New York Sun,* March 9, 2006.
5. John Kroger, *Convictions* (New York: Farrar, Straus & Giroux, 2008), 130.
6. Leonard Buder, "Colombo Figure Given 25 Years on '80 Charge," *New York Times,* December 19, 1987.
7. "Alphonse Persico, 61, Is Dead."
8. Fermino and Venezia, "Romance and Rubout."
9. *People v. R. Lindley DeVecchio,* testimony of Carmine Sessa, October 25, 2007, transcript, 1359.
10. Ibid., 1342.
11. Ibid., 1454.
12. *People v. R. Lindley DeVecchio,* testimony of Larry Mazza, October 18, 2007, transcript, 753.
13. *People v. R. Lindley DeVecchio,* Sessa testimony, 1360–61.
14. Ibid., 1455–56.
15. Ibid., 1426.
16. *People v. R. Lindley DeVecchio,* testimony of Linda Schiro, October 29, 2007, transcript, 1601–2.
17. Ibid.
18. *People v. R. Lindley DeVecchio,* Sessa testimony, 1362.
19. Ibid., 1365–66.
20. *People v. R. Lindley DeVecchio,* Schiro testimony, 1608. In the *New York Post,* veteran crime reporter Murray Weiss quoted a grand jury witness who reportedly testified that, in commenting to Scarpa on the placement of Bari's body, DeVecchio had told him, "You got some pair of balls." Murray Weiss, " 'Mob' Fed's Filthy Lucre—FBI Agent Cashed in as Mafia Slay Mole: DA," *New York Post,* March 30, 2006.
21. Michael Brick, "Ex-F.B.I. Agent's Murder Trial Fizzles, as Does Chief Witness," *New York Times,* November 1, 2007.
22. Tom Robbins, "Tall Tales of a Mafia Mistress," *Village Voice,* October 30, 2007; Jerry Capeci, "G-Man Wins: Tapes Foil Mob Moll," *New York Sun,* November 1, 2007; Scott Shifrel, "Ex–News Reporters Step Forward with Crucial Recordings," *New York Daily News,* November 1, 2007
23. "The Schiro Tapes," *Village Voice,* November 1, 2007.
24. Author's interview with Linda Schiro, November 3, 2007.
25. Judge Leslie Crocker Snyder (ret.), "Report of the Special District Attorney in the Matter of the Investigation of Linda Schiro," October 22, 2008, 18–28.
26. *People v. R. Lindley DeVecchio,* Mazza testimony, 713.
27. Ibid., 757.
28. Ibid., 759.

29. Brad Hamilton, "Moll's 'G-Man' Torment: I Gave Up a Lot to Come Forward. I've Been Victimized," *New York Post,* November 4, 2007.

30. *People v. R. Lindley DeVecchio,* Dades testimony, 636–37.

31. John Marzulli, "Prober's Life: Zero to Hero," New York *Daily News,* March 12, 2005.

32. Jerry Capeci, "Mob Scion May Bolster Turncoat Case," *New York Sun,* June 28, 2007.

33. *People v. R. Lindley DeVecchio,* Dades testimony, 595–602.

34. Alex Ginsberg, "We're Going to Hell for This," *New York Post,* August 16, 2007.

35. *People v. R. Lindley DeVecchio,* Dades testimony.

36. Ibid., 622.

37. Fermino and Venezia, "Romance and Rubout."

38. Buder, "Colombo Figure Given 25 Years."

39. "Alphonse Persico, 61, Is Dead."

40. R. Lindley DeVecchio and Charles Brandt, *We're Going to Win This Thing: The Shocking Frame-up of a Mafia Crime Buster* (New York: Berkley, 2011), 5.

41. Kroger, *Convictions,* 135–36.

42. Todd S. Purdum, "Puzzle of Gangland-Style Killings Eludes Brooklyn Police," *New York Times,* October 10, 1987.

CHAPTER 13: LOVE COLLISION

1. Brad Hamilton, "My Life as a Colombo Hit Man," *New York Post,* March 4, 2012.

2. Carmine Persico was a member of an early 1950s gang called the South Brooklyn Boys, which was an outgrowth of a violent World War II–era gang known as the Garfield Boys. "Boy 16, Arraigned as Gang Slayer; Father of Victim Accuses Police," *New York Times,* May 14, 1950.

    Salvatore Gravano was a member of the Rampers, an early 1960s gang that roamed the streets of Bensonhurst, Brooklyn. Peter Maas, *Underboss: Sammy the Bull Gravano's Story of Life in the Mafia* (New York: HarperCollins, 1997), 13.

    While Persico and Gravano came from working-class families (Carmine's father was a legal stenographer, Sammy's father a housepainter who owned his own home), they both gravitated to criminal activity in their midteens. By Mazza's account he didn't commit his first felony until he was in his early twenties.

3. Author's interview with Larry Mazza, January 8, 2013.

4. *People v. R. Lindley DeVecchio,* testimony of Larry Mazza, October 18, 2007, transcript, 715–48.

5. Author's interview with Little Linda Schiro, November 3, 2007.

6. *People v. R. Lindley DeVecchio,* testimony of Linda Schiro, October 29, 2007, transcript, 1536–38.

7. Ibid.

8. Ibid., 1539.

9. Ibid., 1543.

10. John J. Goldman, "Gotti Accuser Sentenced to Five Years in Plea Deal: Mafia: Salvatore Gravano Is Rewarded for Testifying Against the Notorious Gambino Family Boss and Other Organized Crime Figures," *Los Angeles Times,* September 27, 1994.

11. *Gregory Scarpa v. Victory Memorial Hospital et al.,* deposition transcript, March 1, 1988, 6–7.

12. *People v. R. Lindley DeVecchio,* Schiro testimony, 1157–58.

13. Schiro interview.

14. Hamilton, "My Life as a Colombo Hit Man."

15. Ibid.

16. *People v. R. Lindley DeVecchio,* Mazza testimony, 747.

17. Ibid., 745.

18. Hamilton, "My Life as a Colombo Hit Man."

19. *People v. R. Lindley DeVecchio,* Mazza testimony, 745.

20. Hamilton, "My Life as a Colombo Hit Man."

21. *People v. R. Lindley DeVecchio,* Mazza testimony, 721–22.

22. Hamilton, "My Life as a Colombo Hit Man."

23. John Kroger, *Convictions* (New York: Farrar, Straus & Giroux, 2008), 132–33.

24. *People v. R. Lindley DeVecchio,* Mazza testimony, 739–40.

25. Schiro interview.

26. *People v. R. Lindley DeVecchio,* Schiro testimony, 1553.

27. Nicholas Gage, "Organized Crime Reaps Huge Profits from Dealing in Pornographic Films," *New York Times,* October 12, 1975.

28. Attorney General's Commission on Pornography, "The Meese Report," final report, July 1986, 1168, http://www.porn-report.com/404-organized-crime-and -pornography.htm.

29. Peter Maas, *The Valachi Papers* (New York: G. P. Putnam's Sons, 1968), 95–99.

30. Selwyn Raab, *Five Families: The Rise, Decline, and Resurgence of America's Most Powerful Mafia Empires* (New York: St. Martin's Press, 2005), 26–30.

31. Edna Buchanan, "Lucky Luciano: Criminal Mastermind," *Time,* December 7, 1998.

32. "Anthony Peraino," Wikipedia, http://en.wikipedia.org/wiki/Anthony_Peraino.

33. Gage, "Organized Crime Reaps Huge Profits."

34. Commission on Pornography, "The Meese Report," 1145.

35. Ibid.

36. Ibid., 1179.

37. "8 in 'Deep Throat' Case Receive Prison Sentence," *New York Times,* May 1, 1977.

38. Schiro interview.

39. Bruce Weber, "Joel J. Tyler, Judge Who Pronounced 'Deep Throat' Obscene, Dies at 90," *New York Times,* January 15, 2012.

40. Mitchell Maddux and Jeremy Olshan, "Mobster Admits Nun Slay, Fears He'll Rot in Hell!," *New York Post,* May 13, 2011.

41. R. Lindley DeVecchio, FBI 209 memo for Top Echelon (TE) informant designated "NY3461," September 17, 1982.

42. William Bastone, "The Wiseguy and the Nun," *Village Voice,* February 9, 1999.

43. *U.S. v. Victor M. Orena et al.,* testimony of Chris Favo, May 17, 1995, transcript, 5218.

CHAPTER 14: TWENTY GRAND A WEEK

1. Memo from FBI New York Office to director, FBI, December 11, 1981, section 2 of four, 2–3.

2. Ibid., 6.

3. Ibid., section 3 of four, 4.

4. Memo from FBI New York Office to director, FBI, September 17, 1982, section 1 of four, 2–3.

5. Ibid., section 2 of four, 2.

6. Ralph Blumenthal, "28 Are Ordered Arrested in USA Mafia Inquiry," *New York Times,* October 2, 1984.

7. Selwyn Raab, *Five Families: The Rise, Decline, and Resurgence of America's Most Powerful Mafia Empires* (New York: St. Martin's Press, 2005), 345.

8. Gene Mustain and Jerry Capeci, *Mob Star: The Story of John Gotti* (New York: Franklin Watts, 1988), 190–91.

9. *U.S. v. William Cutolo et al.,* October 1994, transcript, 3418–19.

10. Ibid., 3498.

11. Ibid., 3528–29.

12. Special Agents Jeffrey W. Tomlinson and Howard Leadbetter II, FBI 302 memo re: Larry Mazza, April 28, 1994.

13. Robert D. McFadden, "8 Charged with Mafia Drug Plot Including Murders and Extortion," *New York Times,* November 13, 1987; John Kroger, *Convictions* (New York: Farrar, Straus & Giroux, 2008), 133.

14. Ibid.

15. Ibid.

16. *U.S. v. Gregory Scarpa Jr.,* Second Circuit Court of Appeals 897 F2d 63, February 23, 1990.

17. Robert M. Stutman and Richard Esposito, *Dead on Delivery: Inside the Drug Wars, Straight from the Street* (New York: Warner Books, 1992), 251–52.

18. *U.S. v. Victor M. Orena,* testimony of FBI agent Howard Leadbetter II, April 1994, transcript, 1667–69.

19. *People v. R. Lindley DeVecchio,* testimony of Carmine Sessa, October 25, 2007, transcript, 1373–74.

20. Special Agent Howard Leadbetter II, FBI 302 memo re: William Meli, January 21, 1994.

21. Special Agent Howard Leadbetter II, FBI 302 memo, April 6, 1994.

22. *Pasquale Amato and Victor Orena v. U.S.,* hearing before Hon. Jack B. Weinstein, January 7, 2004, transcript, 41.

23. Supervisory Special Agents Timothy T. Arney and Robert J. O'Brien, FBI 302 memo re: Mario Parlagreco debriefing, May 12, 1994.

24. Ibid.

25. Agents John L. Barrett and Thomas V. Fuentes, FBI 302 memo re: Valerie Caproni, February 1, 1994.

26. Ibid.

27. Jan M. Von Bergen, "TV Show Aids in Arrest of Fugitive at Motel," *Philadelphia Inquirer,* August 20, 1988.

28. Ibid.; Tomlinson and Leadbetter II, 302 memo, April 28, 1994.

29. FBI 302 memo re: Valerie Caproni, January 26, 1994.

30. Ibid.

31. R. Lindley DeVecchio, sworn statement in OPR investigation, May 5, 1995.

32. Greg Smith and Jerry Capeci, "Mob, Mole & Murder," New York *Daily News,* October 31, 1994.

33. Sworn affirmation of Valerie Caproni in OPR investigation, April 12, 1995.

34. *Pasquale Amato and Victor Orena v. U.S.,* hearing before Hon. Jack B. Weinstein, January 7, 2004, testimony of Gregory Scarpa Jr., transcript, 40.

35. Arney and O'Brien, FBI 302 memo re: Parlagreco debriefing, May 12, 1994.

36. Kroger, *Convictions,* 147.

37. Ibid.

38. Ibid.

39. R. Lindley DeVecchio and Charles Brandt, *We're Going to Win This Thing: The Shocking Frame-up of a Mafia Crime Buster* (New York: Berkley, 2011), 168.

40. Special Agent Michael Tabman, sworn affidavit, August 16, 1994.

41. Ibid., 4.
42. DeVecchio, OPR sworn statement.
43. Author's interview with FBI Special Agent Dan Vogel (ret.), October 14, 2011.
44. Tabman sworn affidavit, 3.
45. DeVecchio, OPR sworn statement.
46. Ibid.
47. Marlene Malamy, "In the Matter of and Placement of Eavesdropping Devices to Overhear and Record Certain Communications within a Social Club Located at 7506 13th Avenue, Brooklyn, New York," July 11, 1986.
48. *U.S. v. Gregory Scarpa Jr.,* Valerie Caproni, sealed affidavit, April 29, 1988.
49. *U.S. v. Gregory Scarpa Jr.,* testimony of R. Lindley DeVecchio, October 14, 1998, transcript, 3386–87.
50. Ibid., 3360.
51. DeVecchio and Brandt, *We're Going to Win This Thing,* 162–63.
52. Ibid.
53. R. Lindley DeVecchio, FBI 209 memo for Top Echelon (TE) informant designated "NY3461," September 17, 1982.
54. Arney and O'Brien, FBI 302 memo re: Parlagreco debriefing, May 12, 1994.

CHAPTER 15: ENTER THE SECRET SERVICE
1. Memo from director, FBI, to FBI New York Office, March 15, 1985.
2. Memo from FBI New York Office to director, FBI, March 2, 1985, 2.
3. FBI memo, March 8, 1985.
4. FBI memo, March 2, 1985.
5. Ibid.
6. Ibid.
7. While in most of the Scarpa Sr. 209 informant memos from 1980 to 1992 the author's name was redacted, Lin DeVecchio made it clear in his book that he had written them. R. Lindley DeVecchio and Charles Brandt, *We're Going to Win This Thing: The Shocking Frame-up of a Mafia Crime Buster* (New York: Berkley, 2011), 7, 67–71, 106, 113, 115, 117. And since he was the only contacting agent authorized to interact with Scarpa during this twelve-year time frame—except for a brief period during Senior's final year as a TECI—DeVecchio was the only agent who could have supplied the details from "34" in those confidential informant memos.
8. The amount is $32,094.01 according to http://www.usinflationcalculator.com.
9. Memo from director, FBI, to FBI New York Office, March 15, 1985.
10. Letter from Edward A. McDonald, attorney in charge, Organized Crime Strike Force, EDNY, to Judge I. Leo Glasser, July 22, 1986.
11. Memo from FBI New York Office to director, FBI, November 18, 1985.
12. Memo from director, FBI, to FBI New York Office, December 18, 1985.
13. Memo from FBI New York Office to director, FBI, January 2, 1986.
14. Ibid.
15. Ibid.
16. Memo from director, FBI, to FBI New York Office, January 15, 1985.
17. Author's interview with Special Agent James Whalen (ret.), May 19, 2011.
18. *U.S. v. Michael Sessa,* direct examination of Supervisory Special Agent R. Lindley DeVecchio, November 2, 1992, transcript, 118–19.
19. R. Lindley DeVecchio, sworn statement in OPR investigation, May 5, 1995, 6.

20. Ibid., 8.

21. Bios of Norman Bloch and Douglas Grover, website of Thompson Hine, http://www .thompsonhine.com/lawyer/NormanBloch/; http://www.thompsonhine.com/lawyer/ DouglasGrover/.

22. *U.S. v. Gregory Scarpa Sr.,* indictment no. CR 86-00351, 1986.

23. Memo from S. L. Pomerantz, chief, Investigative Support Section, FBI, to Paul E. Coffey, deputy chief, Organized Crime and Racketeering Section, Department of Justice, April 22, 1986.

24. Author's interview with FBI Special Agent Dan Vogel (ret.), October 14, 2011.

25. Memo from Paul E. Coffey, deputy chief, Organized Crime and Racketeering Section, Department of Justice, to S. L. Pomerantz, chief, Investigative Support Section, FBI, April 29, 1986.

26. Memo from FBI New York Office to director, FBI, March 18, 1986.

27. Linda Schiro, sworn affidavit, August 11, 1998, 2.

28. *Pasquale Amato and Victor Orena v. U.S.,* hearing before Hon. Jack B. Weinstein, January 7, 2004, testimony of Gregory Scarpa Jr., transcript, 35.

29. *U.S. v. Gregory Scarpa Jr.,* October 13, 1988, transcript, 3095.

30. Supervisory Special Agents Timothy B. Kilund and Kevin P. Donovan, FBI 302 memo, interview with Judge I. Leo Glasser, August 16, 1994.

31. Letter from Edward A. McDonald and Norman Bloch to Louis E. Diamond, attorney for Gregory Scarpa Sr., June 18, 1986.

32. Judgment and Probation Commitment Order, Gregory Scarpa Sr., February 6, 1987.

33. *U.S. v. Michael Sessa,* transcript, 118–19.

34. *U.S. v. Orena,* transcript of direct examination of R. Lindley DeVecchio by Gerald Shargel, February 28, 1997, 155.

35. Memo from director, FBI, to FBI New York Office, January 15, 1985.

36. Including Scarpa's probable involvement in the murders of Tommy Ocera in 1989 and Jack Leale (one of Ocera's purported killers) in 1991, the war dead included Hank Smurra, Gaetano Amato, Sam Nastasi, Matteo Speranza, Vincent Fusaro, Nicholas Grancio, John Minerva, Michael Imbergamo, Larry Lampasi, Vincent Giangiobbe, Steven Mancusi, and Joseph Scopo.

CHAPTER 16: DEATH OF A SECOND SON

1. *People v. R. Lindley DeVecchio,* testimony of Linda Schiro, October 29, 2007, transcript, 1613.

2. *People v. R. Lindley DeVecchio,* testimony of Carmine Sessa, October 25, 2007, transcript, 1344.

3. Special Agents David M. Parker and Robert J. O'Brien, FBI 302 memo re: Carmine Sessa, April 18, 1994, 2.

4. Rudy Johnson, "13 Indicted on Stock Theft and Counterfeit Counts," *New York Times,* June 8, 1974.

5. Memo from FBI Newark Office to Bureau (1) Headquarters, December 19, 1977; letter from Edward A. McDonald, attorney in charge, U.S. Department of Justice, Organized Crime Strike Force, EDNY, to Hon. I. Leo Glasser, July 22, 1986.

6. Transcript of Linda Schiro's 1997 interview with Tom Robbins and Jerry Capeci, New York *Daily News,* November 2, 2007.

7. Philip Carlo, *Gaspipe: Confessions of a Mob Boss* (New York: William Morrow, 2008), 78–80.

8. In the book, Carlo identifies Villano as "Anthony Vescone."

9. Author's interview with confidential source, July 31, 2008.

10. Carlo, *Gaspipe,* 81.

11. Selwyn Raab, *Five Families: The Rise, Decline, and Resurgence of America's Most Powerful Mafia Empires* (New York: St. Martin's Press, 2005), 515.

12. John J. Goldman, "Gotti Accuser Sentenced to Five Years in Plea Deal: Mafia: Salvatore Gravano Is Rewarded for Testifying Against the Notorious Gambino Family Boss and Other Organized Crime Figures," *Los Angeles Times,* September 27, 1994.

13. Author's interview with Anthony Casso, September 23, 2011.

14. *People v. R. Lindley DeVecchio,* Schiro testimony, 1613.

15. Special Agents Jeffrey W. Tomlinson and Howard Leadbetter II, FBI 302 memo re: Carmine Sessa, May 29, 1993.

16. *People v. R. Lindley DeVecchio,* Sessa testimony, 1354–55.

17. Tomlinson and Leadbetter II, FBI 302 memo re: Carmine Sessa, May 11, 1993.

18. R. Lindley DeVecchio, FBI 209 memo for Top Echelon (TE) informant designated "NY3461," December 11, 1981, 5.

19. R. Lindley DeVecchio, FBI 209 memo for Top Echelon (TE) informant designated "NY3461," November 16, 1983, 5.

20. Carlo, *Gaspipe,* 70–71.

21. Author's interview with Flora Edwards, November 3, 2011.

22. R. Lindley DeVecchio, FBI 209 memo for Top Echelon (TE) informant designated "NY3461," February 28, 1984.

23. R. Lindley DeVecchio and Charles Brandt, *We're Going to Win This Thing: The Shocking Frame-up of a Mafia Crime Buster* (New York: Berkley, 2011), 108.

24. "Boy, 16, Arraigned as Gang Slayer; Father of Victim Accuses Police," *New York Times,* May 14, 1950.

25. Ibid.

26. Author's interview with Vic and John Orena, February 8, 2007.

27. FBI teletype from FBI New York Office ██████████ to director, FBI, February 19, 1983.

28. Ibid.

29. Author's interview with Andrew Orena, January 13, 2012.

30. DeVecchio and Brandt, *We're Going to Win This Thing,* photo section.

31. Ibid., 168.

32. *The People v. R. Lindley DeVecchio,* opening statement of Assistant District Attorney Joseph Alexis, October 15, 2007, transcript, 9–10; DeVecchio and Brandt, *We're Going to Win This Thing,* 162–66.

33. R. Lindley DeVecchio, FBI 209 memo for Top Echelon (TE) informant designated "NY3461," June 8, 1988, 2.

34. Scott Shifrel, "Mob Hit Man Testifies, Weeps at Lindley DeVecchio Trial," New York *Daily News,* October 19, 2007.

35. DeVecchio and Brandt, *We're Going to Win This Thing,* 164.

36. Author's interview with Flora Edwards, January 13, 2012.

37. DeVecchio and Brandt, *We're Going to Win This Thing,* 167.

CHAPTER 17: THE CASE OF CASES

1. Arnold H. Lubasch, "Judge Sentences 8 Mafia Leaders to Prison Terms," *New York Times,* January 14, 1987.

2. Ed Magnuson, "Hitting the Mafia," *Time,* September 29, 1986.

3. Richard Stengel, "The Passionate Prosecutor," *Time,* February 10, 1986.

4. FBI teletype, February 19, 1983, 2–4.

5. Ibid.

6. Magnuson, "Hitting the Mafia."

7. Stengel, "The Passionate Prosecutor."

8. R. Lindley DeVecchio and Charles Brandt, *We're Going to Win This Thing: The Shocking Frame-up of a Mafia Crime Buster* (New York: Berkley, 2011), 13.

9. Ibid., 143.

10. Ibid., 156.

11. John Sullivan, "Crime Bosses Considered Hit on Giuliani," *New York Times,* October 25, 2007.

12. Michael Brick, "'80s Plot to Hit Giuliani? Mob Experts Doubt It," *New York Times,* October 26, 2007.

13. Sullivan, "Crime Bosses Considered Hit."

14. Brick, "'80s Plot."

15. Brick later cited McCarthy in the piece for the proposition that "if any prosecutor could prompt the Mafia to make an exception, it was Mr. Giuliani," and Jerry Capeci reportedly told Brick that he was "pretty sure . . . Carmine Persico wanted to kill Rudy Giuliani."

16. Author's interview with Flora Edwards, November 3, 2011.

17. Todd S. Purdum, "Reputed Mob Figure Fatally Shot in Brooklyn Club," *New York Times,* January 16, 1987.

18. Robert D. McFadden, "Black Man Dies After Beating in Queens," *New York Times*, December 21, 1986.

19. Ronald Smothers, "Hynes Is Elected to Be Prosecutor in Queens Attack," *New York Times,* January 14, 1987.

20. Nick Ravo, "12 Defendants in Attacks Case: A Diverse Group," *New York Times,* February 11, 1987.

21. Memo by liaison, subject: Gregory Scarpa FBI #584217A, December 4, 1967.

22. Memo, June 27, 1966; memo from special agent in charge, FBI New York Office, to director, FBI. Subject: Gregory Scarpa. Top Echelon Criminal Informant Program, New York Division, July 6, 1967.

23. Memo from special agent in charge, FBI New York Office, to director, FBI. Subject: Gregory Scarpa. Top Echelon Criminal Informant Program, New York Division, November 21, 1961.

24. Memo from special agent in charge, FBI New York Office, to director, FBI, May 18, 1974, 1.

25. "The City: Ex-City Aide Held in $250,000 Theft," *New York Times,* February 11, 1981.

26. Ralph Blumenthal, "Auditors Assail Navy Yard Park in New Report," *New York Times,* April 16, 1982.

27. "Contractor Admits Navy Yard Fraud," *New York Times,* October 4, 1983.

28. Alan Feuer, "Lawsuit on F.B.I. Informant Seeks a Mobster's Link to Kennedy's Assassination," *New York Times,* July 22, 2008.

29. Angela Clemente, "Sal Scarpa and Matty Ianiello Homicides," http://sites.google .com/site/scarpaclementefiles/sal-scarpa-and-matty-ianiello-homicides.

30. FBI 302s documenting the sting of Ramzi Yousef by Gregory Scarpa Jr. at the Metropolitan Correctional Center from March 1996 to February 1997. See a selection of 302s and other intelligence at http://www.peterlance.com/PLfbi.htm.

31. Murray Weiss, "'Mob' Fed's Filthy Lucre—FBI Agent Cashed in as Mafia Slay

Mole: DA," *New York Post,* March 30, 2006; Nancie L. Katz, "The Probe of G-Man Pays Off Big," New York *Daily News,* April 2, 2006.

32. Feuer, "Lawsuit on F.B.I. Informant."

33. Judge Leslie Crocker Snyder (ret.), "Report of the Special District Attorney in the Matter of the Investigation of Linda Schiro," October 22, 2008, 18.

34. Clemente, "Sal Scarpa and Matty Ianiello Homicides."

35. Tommy Dades and Mike Vecchione, *Friends of the Family: The Inside Story of the Mafia Cops Case* (New York: William Morrow, 2009), 86.

36. Todd S. Purdum, "Puzzle of Gangland-Style Killings Eludes Brooklyn Police," *New York Times,* October 10, 1987.

37. "Another Man Is Slain in Mob Style Killing," *New York Times,* October 9, 1987.

38. Philip Carlo, *Gaspipe: Confessions of a Mob Boss* (New York: William Morrow, 2008), 68.

39. EDNY press release on Mafia Cops indictment, March 10, 2005.

40. Clemente, "Sal Scarpa and Matty Ianiello Homicides."

41. *U.S. v. Victor J. Orena,* testimony of Joseph Ambrosino, transcript, 807–9.

42. Supervisory Special Agents R. Patrick Welch and Robert J. O'Brien, FBI 302 memo re: debriefing of Joseph Ambrosino, May 24, 1994.

43. Anthony Casso, letter to the author, December 22, 2011.

44. Ibid.

45. Brad Hamilton, "Daddy's a Death Machine," *New York Post,* May 27, 2012.

46. Andris Kurins and Joseph F. O'Brien, *Boss of Bosses: The Fall of the Godfather: The FBI and Paul Castellano* (New York: Simon & Schuster, 1991), 11.

47. Arnold Lubasch, "Shot by Shot, an Ex-Aide to Gotti Describes the Killing of Castellano," *New York Times,* March 4, 1992.

48. Kurins and O'Brien, *Boss of Bosses.*

49. Carlo, *Gaspipe,* 141.

50. R. Lindley DeVecchio, FBI 209 memo for Top Echelon (TE) informant designated "NY3461," December 17, 1985.

51. Carlo, *Gaspipe,* 145.

52. Ibid.

53. Selwyn Raab, "Defector Says Bomb that Killed Underboss Was Meant for Gotti," *New York Times,* January 24, 1995.

54. Peter Maas, *Underboss: Sammy the Bull Gravano's Story of Life in the Mafia* (New York: HarperCollins, 1997), 208.

CHAPTER 18: I SHOT HIM A COUPLE OF TIMES

1. Philip Carlo, *Gaspipe: Confessions of a Mob Boss* (New York: William Morrow, 2008), 150.

2. Supervisory Special Agent J. Bruce Mouw and Special Agents George Gabriel and Carmine F. Russo, FBI 302 memo re: Salvatore Gravano, November 25, 1991.

3. Tommy Dades and Mike Vecchione, *Friends of the Family: The Inside Story of the Mafia Cops Case* (New York: William Morrow, 2009), 11.

4. Ibid.

5. Ed Bradley, "Ex Mob Boss Points a Finger," *60 Minutes,* CBS News, April 11, 2005; CBS News press release, "Ex-Mafia Boss Anthony Casso Describes Murders," April 7, 2005, http://www.cbspressexpress.com/cbs-news/releases/view?id=9450.

6. Dades and Vecchione, *Friends of the Family,* 62.

7. Denis Hamill, "Finally Justice for Victims of Mafia Cops Louis Eppolito and Stephen Caracappa," New York *Daily News,* March 4, 2009.

8. Carlo, *Gaspipe,* 114.

9. John Marzulli, "2 Cops Who Killed for Mafia: Feds Say Retired Detective Pals Are Linked to at Least 8 Murders," New York *Daily News,* March 9, 2005.

10. Press release, "Kings County District Attorney Charles J. Hynes Announces Murder Indictment Against Retired FBI Agent and Two Mob Hit Men in Multiple Murder Cases," March 30, 2006.

11. "Mafia Cops Louis Eppolito and Stephen Caracappa Sentenced to Life in Prison," New York *Daily News,* March 6, 2006.

12. Benjamin Weiser, "Convictions Reinstated in Mob Case," *New York Times,* May 11, 2010; "Appeals Court Upholds NY Mafia Cops Conviction," Associated Press, July 23, 2010.

13. Dades and Vecchione, *Friends of the Family,* 191.

14. Author's interview with Andrew Orena, February 8, 2008.

15. Dades and Vecchione, *Friends of the Family,* 3.

16. Ibid., 26.

17. Author's interview with Anthony Casso, September 23, 2011.

18. Supervisory Special Agents Timothy B. Kilund and Kevin P. Donovan, FBI 302 memo re: interview with Judge I. Leo Glasser, August 16, 1994.

19. Jerry Capeci, "Fading Mobster Hits on Pal's Alibi," New York *Daily News,* May 31, 1994.

20. *Gregory Scarpa v. Victory Memorial Hospital and Dr. Angelito L. Sebollena,* transcript of the deposition of Gregory Scarpa, March 1, 1988, 24.

21. Ibid., 28.

22. *Gregory Scarpa v. Victory Memorial Hospital and Dr. Angelito L. Sebollena,* transcript of the deposition of Linda Schiro, July 14, 1988, 10.

23. *Scarpa v. Victory Memorial Hospital,* Scarpa transcript, March 1, 1988, 8.

24. Ibid., 13.

25. U.S. Individual Income Tax Returns (Form 1040s) for Gregory Scarpa, 436 Holton Avenue, Staten Island, NY, 1984–85.

26. *Scarpa v. Victory Memorial Hospital,* Scarpa transcript, March 1, 1988, 14.

27. Memo from special agent in charge, FBI New York Office, to director, FBI, July 9, 1962.

28. *Scarpa v. Victory Memorial Hospital,* Schiro transcript, July 14, 1988, 17–26.

29. Ibid., 34.

30. Ibid., 36.

31. Ibid., 52.

32. *Gregory Scarpa v. Victory Memorial Hospital and Dr. Angelito L. Sebollena,* transcript of the deposition of Gregory Scarpa, August 12, 1991, 52.

33. Ibid., 61.

34. Ibid., 64.

35. *Scarpa v. Victory Memorial Hospital,* Scarpa transcript, August 12, 1991, 7.

36. Ibid., 8.

37. Mary Tabor, "Settlement in Lawsuit on H.I.V.-Tainted Blood," *New York Times,* August 30, 1992.

38. *Scarpa v. Victory Memorial Hospital,* Scarpa transcript, August 12, 1991, 14.

39. J. B. Alimonti, T. B. Ball, and J. K. R. Fowke, "Mechanisms of CD4+ T Lymphocyte

Cell Death in Human Immunodeficiency Virus Infection and AIDS," *Journal of General Virology* 84, no. 7 (April 22, 2003), 1649–61. Abstract: http://vir.sgmjournals .org/content/84/7/1649.abstract.

40. *Scarpa v. Victory Memorial Hospital,* Scarpa transcript, August 12, 1991, 20.

CHAPTER 19: MURDER ON THE OVERPASS

1. Michael Marriott, "The Perplexing Killing of a Drug Agent," *New York Times,* March 2, 1989; Mary Engels and David J. Krajicek, "Feds Hunt Killer of Drug Agent," New York *Daily News,* March 2, 1989.

2. Robert M. Stutman and Richard Esposito, *Dead on Delivery: Inside the Drug Wars, Straight from the Street* (New York: Warner Books, 1992), 4.

3. Profile of Everett E. Hatcher, "DEA Agents Killed in the Line of Duty," http://www .justice.gov/dea/agency/10bios.htm.

4. Eric Pooley, "Death of a Hood: The Bloody End of Big Bad Gus," *New York,* January 29, 1990.

5. Eric Pooley, "A Federal Case," *New York,* March 27, 1989.

6. Stutman and Esposito, *Dead on Delivery,* 3–5.

7. Ibid.

8. Author's interview with DEA Special Agent Michael Levine (ret.), November 30, 2011.

9. Stutman and Esposito, *Dead on Delivery,* 11–12.

10. Ibid., 13–14.

11. Ibid., 263.

12. Author's interview with Frank Scarpa, September 13, 2012.

13. Pooley, "A Federal Case."

14. "6 Charged with Hijacking 870 Cases of Scotch Here," *New York Times,* October 10, 1969.

15. *U.S. v. Gregory Scarpa Jr.,* October 13, 1988, transcript, 3087. Greg Scarpa Jr. names himself, his father, Anthony Cappucio, and Sam Weiss, but leaves out Frank Farace and Robert Stasio—another Colombo associate. Stasio was indicted in 1978 for allegedly seeking to sell stolen IRS refund checks. He pled guilty, and his alleged co-conspirator Anthony J. Costanzo was found guilty. *U.S. v. Anthony J. Costanzo,* U.S. Court of Appeals, Third Circuit 625F.2d 465, http://openjurist.org/625/f2d/465/ united-states-v-j-costanzo.

16. Special Agents Jeffrey W. Tomlinson and Howard Leadbetter II, FBI 302 memo re: Carmine Sessa, May 29, 1993.

17. Supervisory Special Agents Kevin P. Donovan and Robert J. O'Brien, FBI 302 memo re: debriefing of William Meli, May 26, 1994.

18. Pooley, "A Federal Case."

19. Engels and Krajicek, "Feds Hunt Killer of Drug Agent."

20. David J. Krajicek, "Mob Man Scarpa: Gus Not 'Family,'" New York *Daily News,* March 5, 1989.

21. Stutman and Esposito, *Dead on Delivery,* 257.

22. David J. Krajicek, *Gotti and Me: A Crime Reporter's Close Encounters with the New York Mafia* (New York: News Ink Books, 2012), 417–548.

23. Krajicek, "Mob Man Scarpa."

24. R. Lindley DeVecchio, FBI 209 memo for Top Echelon (TE) informant designated "NY3461," March 13, 1989.

25. Stutman and Esposito, *Dead on Delivery*, 251.
26. Ibid., 253.
27. *People v. R. Lindley DeVecchio,* testimony of Chris Favo, October 17, 2007, 532.

CHAPTER 20: A CONNECTION BY BLOOD

1. Robert M. Stutman and Richard Esposito, *Dead on Delivery: Inside the Drug Wars, Straight from the Street* (New York: Warner Books, 1992), 257.
2. Ibid., 264.
3. "6 Charged with Hijacking 870 Cases of Scotch Here," *New York Times,* October 10, 1969.
4. David J. Krajicek, "Mob Man Scarpa: Gus Not 'Family,' " New York *Daily News,* March 5, 1989.
5. Stutman and Esposito, *Dead on Delivery*, 265.
6. Ibid.
7. Joseph P. Fried, "In Plea Bargain, Two Admit Guilt in Mob Figure's '89 Murder," *New York Times,* September 18, 1997.
8. Alan Feuer, "Mob Leader Is Guilty of Ordering 3 Murders," *New York Times,* April 6, 2001; Alan Feuer, "Old-Style Mob Trial for a Murder Case in Brooklyn," *New York Times,* March 7, 2001.
9. Stutman and Esposito, *Dead on Delivery*, 266.
10. *Gregory Scarpa v. Victory Memorial Hospital and Dr. Angelito L. Sebollena,* transcripts of the depositions of Gregory Scarpa, August 12, 1991, 27, and May 11, 1992, 16.
11. Jonathan Dienst and Shimon Prokupecz, "Mob Members with Ties to 1989 DEA Killing Arrested on Drug Charges," WNBC New York, August 11, 2011.
12. *U.S. v. Victor M. Orena,* testimony of Joseph Ambrosino, November 30, 1992, 806, 881, 887–88, 903.
13. *People v. R. Lindley DeVecchio,* testimony of Carmine Sessa, October 25, 2007, transcript, 1490–91.
14. Supervisory Special Agents R. Patrick Welch and Robert J. O'Brien, FBI 302 memo re: Joey Ambrosino, May 24, 1994.
15. Anthony Casso, letter to the author, December 22, 2011.
16. Author's interview with Little Linda Schiro, December 4, 2011.
17. Krajicek, "Mob Man Scarpa."
18. R. Lindley DeVecchio, FBI 209 memo for Top Echelon (TE) informant designated "NY3461," January 20, 1990.
19. Author's interview with DEA Special Agent Michael Levine (ret.), October 8, 2011.
20. *U.S. v. Larry Sessa*, defendant Gregory Scarpa Jr., defendant-appellant, No. 1363, Docket 96-1631, United States Court of Appeals, Second Circuit. Argued January 14, 1997, decided September 9, 1997. 125 F.3d 68. http://openjurist.org/125/f3d/68/united-states-v-sessa.
21. Todd S. Purdum, "Reputed Mob Figure Fatally Shot in Brooklyn Club," *New York Times,* January 16, 1987.
22. Todd S. Purdum, "Puzzle of Gangland-Style Killings Eludes Brooklyn Police," *New York Times,* October 10, 1987.
23. R. Lindley DeVecchio, FBI 209 memo for Top Echelon (TE) informant designated "NY3461," March 28, 1989, 5.
24. Robert D. McFadden, "8 Charged with Mafia Drug Plot Including Murders and Extortion," *New York Times,* November 13, 1987. The *Times* piece, which reports that the group charged was "led by Gregory Scarpa Jr.," goes on to state that "a

complaint by United States Attorney Andrew J. Maloney accused the defendants of 'a pattern of racketeering' in which 'each committed at least two acts.' Among the crimes cited were the murders of Peter Crupi, found shot in Brooklyn Aug. 2, 1985, and of Albert Nacha, found shot on Staten Island Dec. 10, 1985, and beatings and other violence over the last three years."

25. "The Federal Bureau of Investigation's Compliance with Attorney General's Investigative Rules," U.S. Department of Justice, Office of the Inspector General, September 2005, 6–7; *1982 Final Report of the Senate Select Committee to Study Undercover Activities,* at 523 (Civiletti Informant Guidelines section F.2).

26. R. Lindley DeVecchio and Charles Brandt, *We're Going to Win This Thing: The Shocking Frame-up of a Mafia Crime Buster* (New York: Berkley, 2011), 123.

27. *People v. R. Lindley DeVecchio,* Sessa testimony, 1410.

CHAPTER 21: RUMBLINGS OF WAR

1. Supervisory Special Agents Timothy B. Kilund and Kevin P. Donovan, FBI 302 memo re: interview with Judge I. Leo Glasser, August 16, 1994.

2. Jack B. Weinstein, judgment, memorandum, and order, *Victor J. Orena v. United States,* March 1, 1997, 29.

3. Ibid., 30.

4. Ibid., 34.

5. *U.S. v. Victor J. Orena et al.,* superseding indictment, 1992, paragraph 22.

6. Arnold H. Lubasch, "Acting Crime Boss Is Convicted of Murder and Racketeering," *New York Times,* December 22, 1992. This piece was typical, reporting that "although Mr. Persico selected Mr. Orena as acting boss in 1989, they soon began feuding and Mr. Persico was said to want his son, Alphonse, to take over as boss next year."

7. Jerry Capeci, "Colombos Set to Play Family Feud," New York *Daily News,* September 3, 1991.

8. Special Agent Chris Favo, FBI 302 memo, February 6, 1994, 2. "Over the length of the war I began to withhold information concerning Gregory Scarpa or what could not be leaked to the media because I believe SSA DeVecchio was leaking information to both Scarpa and Jerry Capece [*sic*]."

9. Weinstein, judgment, memorandum, and order, March 1, 1997, 24.

10. Gregory Scarpa Jr., sworn affidavit, U.S Penitentiary, Florence, CO, July 30, 2002, 3–4.

11. Weinstein, judgment, memorandum, and order, March 1, 1997, 99.

12. Jack B. Weinstein, memorandum and order, *Orena v. United States,* January 15, 2004.

13. Jack B. Weinstein, judgment, memorandum, and order, *Victor J. Orena v. United States,* March 10, 1997, 9. "To date, the United States Attorney's Office, with the critical assistance of the F.B.I. and the New York City Police Department, has prosecuted seventy-five Colombo Family members. Forty of those prosecuted were Persicos, and the rest Orenas. These figures do not include New York State's prosecutions of Colombo Family members."

14. *United States v. Michael Sessa,* transcript of criminal motion before the Honorable Jack B. Weinstein, September 24, 2001, 20.

15. Author's interview with former attorney for Vic Orena, January 3, 2012.

16. Ibid.

17. Dennis Hevesi, "7 Found Not Guilty in Plot Tied to a Mob Family Feud," *New York Times,* July 1, 1995.

18. Joseph Gambardello and Patricia Hurtado, "Brooklyn Jury Acquits 7 Accused in Mob War: Jurors Blame FBI Agent for Fueling Feud Through Former Islander,"

Staten Island Advance, July 1, 1995; Greg B. Smith, "7 Cleared in B'Klyn Mob Case: Jurors Fault FBI," New York *Daily News,* July 1, 1995; Al Guarte, "Wiseguys Acquitted in Colombo Murders," *New York Post,* July 1, 1995.

19. Author's interview with Andrew Orena, Victor M. Orena, and John Orena, February 7–10, 2007.
20. "Lincoln Hall Building Begun," *New York Times,* December 12, 1951.
21. Selwyn Raab, *Five Families: The Rise, Decline, and Resurgence of America's Most Powerful Mafia Empires* (New York: St. Martin's Press, 2005), 333.
22. R. Lindley DeVecchio and Charles Brandt, *We're Going to Win This Thing: The Shocking Frame-up of a Mafia Crime Buster* (New York: Berkley, 2011), 198.
23. R. Lindley DeVecchio, FBI 209 memo for Top Echelon (TE) informant designated "NY3461," June 1988.
24. Selwyn Raab, "Mafia-Aided Scheme Evades Millions in Gas Taxes," *New York Times,* February 6, 1989.
25. Roy Rowan, "The 50 Biggest Mafia Bosses," *Fortune,* November 10, 1986.
26. *United States v. Victor Orena,* CR-92-351, testimony of Kenneth A. Geller, December 8, 1992, transcript, 1756.
27. Ibid., 1851.
28. Ibid., 1885.
29. Ibid.; *United States v. Victor Orena,* opening statement of Assistant U.S. Attorney Andrew Weissmann, November 19, 1992, 34.
30. *United States v. Victor Orena,* cross-examination of Kenneth A. Geller, November 19, 1992, transcript, 2040.
31. Orena brothers interview.
32. Special Agents Jeffrey W. Tomlinson and Howard Leadbetter II, FBI 302 memo re: Carmine Sessa, May 18, 1993.
33. *U.S. v. Victor J. Orena,* testimony of Joseph Ambrosino, November 30, 1992, transcript, 876–80.
34. Memo from special agent in charge, FBI Newark Office, to assistant director, FBI, August 8, 1967.
35. Memo from special agent in charge, FBI Newark Office, to assistant director, FBI, March 10, 1970.
36. Memo from special agent in charge, FBI New York Office, to director, FBI. Subject: Gregory Scarpa. Top Echelon Criminal Informant Program, New York Division, September 2, 1971.
37. Memo from special agent in charge, FBI New York Office, to director, FBI. Subject: Gregory Scarpa. Top Echelon Criminal Informant Program, New York Division, July 25, 1972.
38. Addendum: Criminal Investigative Division, April 8, 1987, memorializing an April 3, 1987, teletype requesting payment for "captioned source," for supplying "extremely singular information which led to 17 Title III intercepts and 50 reauthorizations forming the basis for the prosecution of the Colombo family"; *U.S. v. Carmine Persico,* No. 84 Cr.809 (JFK), opinion of Judge John F. Keenan denying motions to dismiss, http://www.ipsn.org/court_cases/us_v_persico_1986-09-25.htm.
39. FBI 209 memo, June 17, 1994.
40. Author's interview with Flora Edwards, November 3, 2011.
41. Arnold H. Lubasch, "Persico, His Son and 6 Others Get Long Terms as Colombo Gangsters," *New York Times,* November 18, 1986.

42. Arnold H. Lubasch, "Judge Sentences 8 Mafia Leaders to Prison Terms," *New York Times,* January 14, 1987.

43. R. Lindley DeVecchio, FBI 209 memo for Top Echelon (TE) informant designated "NY3461," December 15, 1986.

44. *U.S. v. Victor J. Orena et al.,* superseding indictment, 1992, paragraph 10.

45. R. Lindley DeVecchio, FBI 209 memo, February 10, 1987.

46. "Alphonse Persico, 61, Is Dead: Leader of Colombo Crime Family," *New York Times,* September 13, 1989.

47. Leonard Buder, "Colombo Figure Given 25 Years on '80 Charge," *New York Times,* December 19, 1987.

48. R. Lindley DeVecchio, FBI 209 memo, July 17, 1987.

49. R. Lindley DeVecchio, FBI 209 memo, December 3, 1987.

50. R. Lindley DeVecchio, FBI 209 memo, April 8, 1988.

51. Raab, *Five Families,* 333.

52. Author's interview with Andrew Orena, September 21, 2011.

53. Raab, *Five Families.*

54. DeVecchio and Brandt, *We're Going to Win This Thing,* 198.

CHAPTER 22: DEATH BY WIRE

1. *U.S. v. Victor J. Orena,* testimony of Joseph Ambrosino, November 30, 1992, transcript, 856.

2. *U.S. v. Victor J. Orena,* testimony of Diane Montesano, December 2, 1992, transcript, 1167–69; 1246.

3. Ibid., 1190.

4. Ibid., 1244.

5. *U.S. v. Victor J. Orena,* opening statement of Assistant U.S. Attorney Andrew Weissmann, November 19, 1992, transcript, 37.

6. *U.S. v. Victor J. Orena,* testimony of Harry Bonfiglio, transcript, 349.

7. *U.S. v. Victor J. Orena,* Montesano testimony.

8. Ibid.

9. Special Agents Jeffrey W. Tomlinson and Howard Leadbetter II, FBI 302 memo re: Carmine Sessa, May 29, 1993.

10. Selwyn Raab, "Mafia Reported to Be Seeking New Trash Sites," *New York Times,* November 11, 1989.

11. *U.S. v. Victor J. Orena,* Montesano testimony, 1238.

12. Ibid., 1216.

13. Ibid., 1219–20.

14. Ibid., 1223.

15. Ibid., 1229.

16. Ibid.

17. Mary B. W. Tabor, "Man Accused as Colombo Chief Is Held in Slaying of Ex-Member," *New York Times,* April 2, 1992.

18. *U.S. v. Victor J. Orena,* Weissmann opening statement, 47.

19. *U.S. v. Victor J. Orena,* transcript, 2248.

20. Joseph Gambardello and Patricia Hurtado, "FBI Guilty: Jury Finds Feds Fueled a Mob War," *Newsday,* July 1, 1995.

21. Gregory Scarpa Jr., sworn affidavit, U.S. penitentiary, Florence, Colorado, July 30, 2002.

22. *U.S. v. Victor J. Orena,* testimony of Special Agent Joseph Fanning, December 10, 1992, transcript, 2555–57, 2567.

23. Ibid., 2567, and Government Exhibit 1100, 2449–50.

24. *U.S. v. Victor J. Orena,* Weissmann opening statement, 38.

25. *U.S. v. Victor J. Orena,* testimony of Michael Maffatore, transcript, 230.

26. *U.S. v. Victor J. Orena,* Bonfiglio testimony, 470.

27. *U.S. v. Victor J. Orena,* ruling of Jack B. Weinstein, transcript, 822–23.

28. *U.S. v. Victor J. Orena,* Maffatore testimony, 212–13.

29. Ibid., 267.

30. *U.S. v. Victor J. Orena,* Bonfiglio testimony, 391.

31. Andrew Orena insists that this location on Central Avenue was never the site of an Orena social club—that, in fact, it was the location of a Pontiac dealership he ran at the time. "It was a very high-end shopping area," he said in an interview. "Ask yourself first whether my father who is the acting boss would be talking to a soldier about anything like a murder and whether he'd be doing it so openly and publicly and within earshot of bottom-feeders like Maffatore and Bonfiglio. It just never happened." Author's interview with Andrew Orena, January 13, 2012.

32. *U.S. v. Victor J. Orena,* Maffatore testimony, 151.

33. *U.S. v. Victor J. Orena,* Bonfiglio testimony, 334.

34. *U.S. v. Victor J. Orena,* Maffatore testimony, 154.

35. Ibid., 157.

CHAPTER 23: BRAINS, BUTCHER, AND BULL

1. *U.S. v. Victor J. Orena,* testimony of Michael Maffatore, transcript, 297.

2. *U.S. v. Victor J. Orena,* testimony of Harry Bonfiglio, transcript, 345.

3. Ibid., 343.

4. R. Lindley DeVecchio, FBI 209 memo for Top Echelon (TE) informant designated "NY3461," November 4, 1991.

5. *U.S. v. Victor J. Orena,* Maffatore testimony, 302.

6. *U.S. v. Victor J. Orena,* Bonfiglio testimony, 353.

7. *U.S. v. Victor J. Orena,* testimony of Joseph Ambrosino, transcript, 856.

8. Ibid., 826–48; Special Agents Jeffrey W. Tomlinson and Howard Leadbetter II, FBI 302 memo re: Carmine Sessa, April 28, 1993.

9. Author's interview with Flora Edwards, November 3, 2011.

10. *U.S. v. Pasquale Amato,* cross-examination of Diane Montesano, transcript, 1297.

11. Laurie Goodstein, "Gotti Convicted of 13 Crimes, May Face Life in Jail," *Washington Post,* April 3, 1992.

12. Robert D. McFadden, "For Gotti Prosecutors, Hard Work and Breaks Pay Off in Conviction," *New York Times,* April 3, 1992.

13. Jack B. Weinstein, judgment, memorandum, and order, *U.S. v. Victor J. Orena and Pasquale Amato,* March 10, 1997, 13.

14. Philip Carlo, *The Butcher: Anatomy of a Mafia Psychopath* (New York: William Morrow, 2009), 203, 251–53, 274.

15. Ibid., 293.

16. Ibid., 274.

17. Weinstein, judgment, memorandum, and order, March 10, 1997, 95–96.

18. Author's interview with Andrew Orena, January 6, 2012.

19. Greg B. Smith, "Feds' Superstar Turncoat Gets Tiny Prison Sentence," *New York Daily News,* October 24, 2002.

20. John J. Goldman, "Gotti Accuser Sentenced to Five Years in Plea Deal: Mafia: Salvatore Gravano Is Rewarded for Testifying Against the Notorious Gambino Family Boss and Other Organized Crime Figures," *Los Angeles Times,* September 27, 1994.

21. Selwyn Raab, "Singing for Your Sentence: How Will It Pay Off? Ex-Crime Underboss May Find Out Today What He Gets for Turning U.S. Witness," *New York Times,* September 26, 1994.

22. Ibid.

23. Philip Carlo, *Gaspipe: Confessions of a Mob Boss* (New York: William Morrow, 2008), 284–85.

24. Selwyn Raab, *Five Families: The Rise, Decline, and Resurgence of America's Most Powerful Mafia Empires* (New York: St. Martin's Press, 2005), 519.

25. Alan Feuer, "New Charges in Ecstasy Case Are Filed Against Gravano," *New York Times,* December 15, 2000.

26. Carlo, *Gaspipe,* 292.

27. Anthony Casso, letter to the author, October 4, 2011.

28. Weinstein, judgment, memorandum, and order, March 10, 1997, 99.

29. *U.S. v. Victor J. Orena,* rebuttal, John Gleeson, 3023.

30. Ibid.

31. Gregory Scarpa Jr., sworn affidavit, U.S. penitentiary, Florence, CO, July 30, 2002.

32. *Pasquale Amato and Victor Orena v. U.S.,* transcript of hearing before the Honorable Jack B. Weinstein, January 7, 2004, 47–48.

33. Gregory Scarpa Jr. affidavit.

34. John Marzulli, "Mobster's Retrial Nixed," New York *Daily News,* January 16, 2004.

35. Weinstein, judgment, memorandum, and order, March 10, 1997.

36. *Orena v. U.S.,* U.S. District Court for the Eastern District of New York, memorandum and order of Jack B. Weinstein, January 15, 2004, http://ny.findacase.com/research/wfrmDocViewer.aspx/xq/fac.20040115_0000018.ENY.htm/qx.

37. Ibid.

38. Helen Peterson, "Fed's Set to Tattle," New York *Daily News,* February 23, 1997.

39. Judge Jack B. Weinstein during a hearing in the case of *U.S. v. Michael Sessa,* CR-92-351, September 24, 2001, 20.

40. Author's interview with Flora Edwards, April 27, 2004.

41. Author's interview with Alan Futerfas, May 24, 2004.

CHAPTER 24: COUP D'ÉTAT

1. Victor Ehrenberg, *From Solon to Socrates: Greek History and Civilization During the 6th and 5th Centuries B.C.* (London & New York: Routledge, 2001), 46.

2. Jonathan Law and Elizabeth A. Martin, eds., *Oxford Dictionary of Law* (Oxford: Oxford University Press, 2009).

3. 18 United States Code Section 1111, http://www.law.cornell.edu/uscode/usc_sec_18_00001111----000-.html.

4. New York Penal Code, sections 125.27 (Murder in the First Degree) and 125.25 (Murder in the Second Degree), http://ypdcrime.com/penal.law/article125.htm.

5. Ibid., section 125.13.

6. Ibid.

7. *People v. R. Lindley DeVecchio,* Supreme Court of New York, Kings County. Indictment No. 6825/2005, unsealed March 30, 2006.

8. Twenty-six if he also set up the murder of his nephew Gus Farace.

9. R. Lindley DeVecchio and Charles Brandt, *We're Going to Win This Thing: The Shocking Frame-up of a Mafia Crime Buster* (New York: Berkley, 2011), 218.

10. "William Cutolo," Wikipedia, http://en.wikipedia.org/wiki/William_Cutolo.

11. Special Agents Jeffrey W. Tomlinson and Howard Leadbetter II, FBI 302 memo re: Carmine Sessa, June 1, 1993.

12. Kevin Flynn, "Union Inquiry Looks at Charity's Tie to Reputed Mobster," *New York Times,* December 12, 1998.

13. Author's interview with Victor M. Orena, February 7–10, 2007.

14. DeVecchio and Brandt, *We're Going to Win This Thing,* 152.

15. Ibid.

16. R. Lindley DeVecchio, FBI teletype, June 8, 1988, 3.

17. *People v. R. Lindley DeVecchio,* testimony of Carmine Sessa, October 25, 2007, transcript, 1359.

18. Tomlinson and Leadbetter II, FBI 302 memo re: Carmine Sessa, May 10, 1993.

19. *People v. R. Lindley DeVecchio,* Sessa testimony, 1342.

20. Tomlinson and Leadbetter II, FBI 302 memo re: Carmine Sessa, April 27, 1993.

21. Dave Goldiner, "A Mobster's Trail of Bodies," New York *Daily News,* September 29, 2000.

22. *U.S. v. Victor J. Orena,* testimony of Joseph Ambrosino, 826–48; Tomlinson and Leadbetter II, FBI 302 memo re: Carmine Sessa, April 28, 1993.

23. Tomlinson and Leadbetter II, 302 memo, April 28, 1993.

24. R. Lindley DeVecchio, FBI 209 memo for Top Echelon (TE) informant designated "NY3461," August 4, 1988.

25. Special Agents Lucian J. Gandolfo and Jeffrey Tomlinson, FBI 302 memo re: Carmine Sessa, September 28, 1993.

26. Author's interview with Vic Orena Jr., February 7, 2007.

27. "Ninety-weight" is the English translation of the Mafia slang term for a "big shot," i.e., *pezza novante,* http://www.urbandictionary.com/define.php?term=pezzonovante.

28. Tomlinson and Leadbetter II, FBI 302 memo re: Carmine Sessa, May 16, 1993; Arnold H. Lubasch, "Prosecutors Tell of Colombo Family Murder Plot," *New York Times,* September 1, 1991.

29. R. Lindley DeVecchio, FBI 209 memo, June 13, 1989.

30. DeVecchio, teletype, June 8, 1988, 3.

31. *People v. R. Lindley DeVecchio,* Sessa testimony, 1372.

32. Tomlinson and Leadbetter II, FBI 302 memo re: Carmine Sessa, May 28, 1993.

33. Author's interview with Flora Edwards, January 13, 2012.

34. John Kroger, *Convictions* (New York, Farrar, Straus & Giroux, 2008), 135.

35. Supervisory Special Agents Kevin Donovan and Robert J. O'Brien, FBI 302 memo re: Carmine Sessa, September 1, 1994, 3.

36. Ibid.

37. Author's interview with Andrew Orena, January 13, 2012.

38. DeVecchio, 209 memo, August 1, 1989.

39. DeVecchio, 209 memo, November 16, 1989.

40. DeVecchio, 209 memo, December 26, 1989.

41. FBI wiretap transcript, Wimpy Boys social club, tape 42, April 7, 1986, and tape 52, April 18, 1986.

42. Author's interview with John Orena, February 7, 2008.

43. DeVecchio, 209 memo, June 12, 1990.

44. Frederick B. Lacey, "Opinion of the Independent Administrator," August 20, 1990, http://irbcases.wrlc.org/bitstream/handle/38989/c01m37qvx/gwu_ibt_irb_case_00106_ia.pdf?sequence=1.
45. FBI addendum, Criminal Investigative Division, September 16, 1991.
46. Andrew Orena interview, January 13, 2012.
47. *People v. R. Lindley DeVecchio,* Sessa testimony, 1390.
48. Ibid., 1385.
49. Ibid., 1392–93.
50. R. Lindley DeVecchio, teletype from FBI New York Office to director, FBI, March 8, 1989, 5.
51. Ibid., 6.
52. Edwards interview, January 13, 2012.
53. Tomlinson and Leadbetter II, FBI 302 memo re: Carmine Sessa, April 7–May 10, 1993.
54. DeVecchio, 209 memo, June 5, 1991.
55. *U.S. v. Victor J. Orena,* Ambrosino testimony, 886.
56. Tomlinson and Leadbetter II, FBI 302 memo re: Carmine Sessa, April 7–May 10, 1993.
57. *U.S. v. Victor J. Orena,* Ambrosino testimony, 849.
58. Ibid., 885.
59. Tomlinson and Leadbetter II, FBI 302 memo re: Carmine Sessa, May 13, 1993.
60. *People v. R. Lindley DeVecchio,* Sessa testimony, 1397; Tomlinson and Leadbetter II, 302 memo, May 16, 1993: "SESSA and the others realized they had to kill ORENA before ORENA killed SESSA."

CHAPTER 25: PEARL HARBOR

1. *U.S. v. Victor Orena,* testimony of Joseph Ambrosino, transcript, 886–87.
2. *People v. R. Lindley DeVecchio,* testimony of Carmine Sessa, October 25, 2007, transcript, 1401.
3. *U.S. v. Victor Orena,* Ambrosino testimony.
4. Ibid., 888.
5. *U.S. v. Victor Orena,* opening statement of Assistant U.S. Attorney Andrew Weissmann, November 19, 1992, transcript, 43.
6. Special Agents Jeffrey W. Tomlinson and Howard Leadbetter II, FBI 302 memo re: Carmine Sessa, April 7–May 10, 1993, 2.
7. Greg B. Smith, "Family Wants Retrial for 'Different Man,'" New York *Daily News,* September 21, 2003.
8. Tomlinson and Leadbetter II, FBI 302 memo re: Carmine Sessa, April 7–May 10, 1993, 2.
9. Author's interview with Victor M. Orena, February 8, 2007.
10. *People v. R. Lindley DeVecchio,* Sessa testimony, 1399.
11. Author's interview with John Orena, February 7–8, 2007.
12. Tomlinson and Leadbetter II, FBI 302 memo re: Carmine Sessa, April 7–May 10, 1993, 3.
13. Ibid.
14. Ibid., 2–3.
15. Tomlinson and Leadbetter II, FBI 302 memo re: Carmine Sessa, May 13, 1993.
16. *U.S. v. Victor J. Orena,* Weissmann opening statement, transcript, 43.

17. Victor M. Orena interview.
18. John Orena interview, February 7–8, 2007.
19. *U.S. v. Victor Orena,* Ambrosino testimony, 896–97.
20. R. Lindley DeVecchio, FBI 209 memo for Top Echelon (TE) informant designated "NY3461," August 1991, 3.
21. R. Lindley DeVecchio, 209 memo, July 8–August 13, 1991.
22. *People v. R. Lindley DeVecchio,* testimony of Larry Mazza, October 18, 2007, transcript, 792.
23. Ibid., 782–83.
24. John Orena interview.
25. Curtis Sliwa, interview with R. Lindley DeVecchio, WNYM Radio, May 10, 2011.
26. Tomlinson and Leadbetter II, FBI 302 memo re: Carmine Sessa, May 17, 1993.
27. Selwyn Raab, *Five Families: The Rise, Decline, and Resurgence of America's Most Powerful Mafia Empires* (New York: St. Martin's Press, 2005), 335.
28. Author's interview with Andrew Orena, January 13, 2012.
29. DeVecchio, 209 memo, October 9, 1991.
30. Ibid.
31. "FBI: Gotti Missed Date with Draft Board," Associated Press, March 28, 2004.
32. DeVecchio, 209 memo, October 9, 1991.
33. DeVecchio, 209 memo, November 4, 1991.
34. Ibid.
35. Interview with Victor M. Orena. In 1996, after being cleared in a 1995 racketeering trial, Victor M. Orena was serving four years for loan sharking. He was offered a chance to get out of prison by the Feds if he pleaded guilty to new charges that he tampered with a jury and conspired to murder Leale. (Helen Peterson, "Five-State Ban's Part of Plea Deal," New York *Daily News,* March 17, 1996.) "My brother was looking at many more years behind bars or a chance at freedom," says Andrew Orena. "So he took the plea. But the Feds made it clear that if he hadn't admitted to something in relation to Jack Leale they'd have thrown away the key. That's how important it was for them to blame that murder on the Orenas."
36. *People v. R. Lindley DeVecchio,* testimony of Linda Schiro, October 29, 2007, transcript, 1662–63.
37. Linda Schiro interview, *I Married a Mobster,* Investigation Discovery Channel, airdate December 3, 2011.
38. Special Agents Jeffrey W. Tomlinson and Howard Leadbetter II, FBI 302 memo re: Larry Mazza, April 28, 1994, 6.
39. Tomlinson and Leadbetter II, FBI 302 memo re: Carmine Sessa, May 17, 1993, 1–2.
40. Special Agent Chris Favo, FBI 302 memo, November 16, 1995. Supervisory Special Agents R. Patrick Welch and Richard L. Lambert, 5.
41. Special Agents Maryann Walker-Goldman and Christopher Favo, FBI 302 memo re: Larry Mazza, February 7, 1994. While Mazza also stated, per that 302, that Scarpa received information from a "source from the ORENA faction," most of that FBI debriefing, including details that federal prosecutors later suggested DeVecchio had leaked, came from the source Mazza identified as the "Girlfriend." That particular 302 memo became infamous as "the Girlfriend 302" when defense lawyers argued that it had been withheld by Assistant U.S. Attorney Valerie Caproni. For more on other leaks see: Letter from Assistant U.S. Attorney Ellen Corcella to defense counsel in *U.S. v. Victor M. Orena et al.,* May 8, 1995, listing eight possible

disclosures of FBI intelligence by SSA DeVecchio to Gregory Scarpa Sr. See Chapter 37, page 410.

42. DeVecchio, FBI 209 memo, November 18, 1991.
43. Schiro, *I Married a Mobster.*

CHAPTER 26: GO OUT AND KILL SOMEBODY
1. *U.S. v. Victor Orena,* testimony of Joseph Ambrosino, transcript, 910–12.
2. Ibid.
3. Special Agents Jeffrey W. Tomlinson and Howard Leadbetter II, FBI 302 memo re: Carmine Sessa, May 17, 1993.
4. Ibid.
5. George James, "Killing in Brooklyn Social Club Is Linked to Mob Power Struggle," *New York Times,* December 6, 1991.
6. Anne Murray and Karen Phillips, "Wrong Man Killed in Mob War: Cops," *New York Post,* December 4, 1991.
7. Tomlinson and Leadbetter, 302 memo, May 17, 1993.
8. *U.S. v. Victor Orena,* Ambrosino testimony, 902.
9. R. Lindley DeVecchio, FBI 209 memo for Top Echelon (TE) informant designated "NY3461," November 25, 1991.
10. *People v. R. Lindley DeVecchio,* testimony of Carmine Sessa, October 25, 2007, transcript, 1426.
11. Richard Stratton, "The Grim Reaper's Girlfriend," *Penthouse,* August 1, 1996.
12. Ibid.
13. *U.S. v. Victor Orena,* Ambrosino testimony, 908.
14. Jerry Capeci, "I Spy," New York *Daily News,* October 19, 1998.
15. *U.S. v. Victor Orena,* Ambrosino testimony.
16. Jack B. Weinstein, judgment, memorandum, and order, *U.S. v. Victor J. Orena and Pasquale Amato,* March 10, 1997, 30–31.
17. Author's interview with former attorney for Gregory Scarpa, January 10, 2012.
18. Tomlinson and Leadbetter II, FBI 302 memo re: Carmine Sessa, January 26, 1994, 1.
19. Supervisory Special Agents Kevin P. Donovan and Robert J. O'Brien, FBI 302 memo re: Carmine Sessa, September 14, 1994.
20. Special Agents David M. Parker and Robert J. O'Brien, FBI 302 memo re: Carmine Sessa, April 18, 1994, 6.
21. Ibid., 3.
22. *U.S. v. Theodore Persico,* testimony of Carmine Sessa, transcript, 2239–40.
23. Parker and O'Brien, FBI 302 memo re: Carmine Sessa, May 31, 1994, 2.
24. Author's interview with Flora Edwards.
25. James, "Killing in Brooklyn Social Club."
26. Murray and Phillips, "Wrong Man Killed."
27. Ibid.
28. Ibid.
29. James, "Killing in Brooklyn Social Club."
30. DeVecchio, 209 memo, December 5, 1991.
31. Brad Hamilton, "My Life as a Colombo Hit Man," *New York Post,* March 4, 2012.
32. *U.S. v. Theodore Persico,* testimony of Larry Mazza, transcript, 3711.
33. Hamilton, "My Life as a Colombo Hit Man."

34. Gregory Scarpa Sr., sworn affidavit, June 7, 1994; *People v. R. Lindley DeVecchio*, testimony of Larry Mazza, October 18, 2007, 698.

35. Lee A. Daniels, "Brooklyn Slaying Tied to Mob Feud," *New York Times*, December 8, 1991.

36. Ibid.

37. Robert McFadden, "Brooklyn's Mob War Interrupted with a Quiet Day in Court," *New York Times*, December 17, 1991.

38. Selwyn Raab, "Even to the 5 Families, the Fighting Colombos Have Been Black Sheep," *New York Times*, December 10, 1991.

39. Ibid.

40. *People v. R. Lindley DeVecchio*, Sessa testimony, 1426.

41. Author's interview with Andrew Orena, January 23, 2012.

42. *U.S. v. Gregory Scarpa Sr.*, transcript of sentencing before Judge Jack B. Weinstein, December 15, 1993, 6; *People v. R. Lindley DeVecchio*, Mazza testimony, 698. The three homicide charges to which Greg Scarpa Sr. pled guilty are those of Vincent Fusaro, Nicholas Grancio, and Larry Lampasi. Larry Mazza pled guilty to the murder of Gaetano Amato and implicated Scarpa in that crime as well. Scarpa is also linked to the March 1992 murders of John Minerva and Michael Imbergamo, which "34" attributed to Jo Jo and Chuckie Russo.

43. Joseph A. Gambardello, "Colombo Family Has Bloody Past," *Newsday*, December 17, 1991; Greg B. Smith, "Innocent Victim's Dad Rages," New York *Daily News*, September 4, 1995.

44. George James, "Killing Is Tied to Mafia War in Brooklyn," *New York Times*, December 9, 1991.

45. Ibid.

46. Patricia Hurtado, "3 Convicted in Mob-War Shootings," *Newsday*, August 22, 1995.

47. Jerry Capeci, "A Father's Calm Gives Way at Trial of His Son's Killer," New York *Daily News*, August 2, 1995.

48. Edward Doherty, "The Twilight of the Gangster," *Liberty*, October 24, 1931, http://www.libertymagazine.com/crime_doherty.htm.

49. R. Lindley DeVecchio and Charles Brandt, *We're Going to Win This Thing: The Shocking Frame-up of a Mafia Crime Buster* (New York: Berkley, 2011), 213.

50. Ibid., 310. In a conversation with his wife that DeVecchio describes, he writes, "There was no need to kill me anymore, just frame me a little better than Favo and Caproni had done."

51. Ibid., 213.

52. Supervisory Special Agent R. Lindley DeVecchio and Special Agents Raymond Andjich and Jeffrey W. Tomlinson, FBI 302 memo, debriefing of Gregory Scarpa Sr., December 10, 1991.

53. Special Agent Chris Favo and Supervisory Special Agents R. Patrick Welch and Richard L. Lambert, FBI 302 memo, November 16, 1995, 5; Chris Favo, sworn affidavit, July 7, 1995, 2.

54. DeVecchio, 209 memo, December 11, 1991.

55. *People v. R. Lindley DeVecchio*, Mazza testimony, 699.

56. Selwyn Raab, *Five Families: The Rise, Decline, and Resurgence of America's Most Powerful Mafia Empires* (New York: St. Martin's Press, 2005), 338.

57. DeVecchio, 209 memo, December 19, 1991.

58. DeVecchio, 209 memo, December 30, 1991.

CHAPTER 27: THE HIT ON NICKY BLACK

1. Selwyn Raab, "Even to the 5 Families, the Fighting Colombos Have Been Black Sheep," *New York Times,* December 10, 1991.
2. Robert McFadden, "Brooklyn's Mob War Interrupted with a Quiet Day in Court," *New York Times,* December 17, 1991.
3. Jack B. Weinstein, judgment, memorandum, and order, *U.S. v. Victor J. Orena and Pasquale Amato,* March 10, 1997, 7.
4. Author's interview with Detective Joseph Simone, NYPD (ret.), April 30, 2004.
5. Amanita Duga, "Police Tie 2 Islanders to Organized Crime Family," *Staten Island Advance,* December 17, 1991.
6. R. Lindley DeVecchio, FBI 209 memo for Top Echelon (TE) informant designated "NY3461," January 7, 1992.
7. Simone interview, April 30, 2004.
8. "4 Cops Catch 36-Time Rapist and 3 Communities Breathe a Sigh of Relief," *Kings Courier,* October 5, 1981.
9. Glenn Chapman, "Cops Arrest Leader of Alleged Drug Ring," *Staten Island Advance,* January 30, 1985.
10. Lee A. Daniels, "Brooklyn Slaying May Be 6th in Mob Families' 2-Month Feud," *New York Times,* January 8, 1992.
11. Simone interview.
12. Ibid.
13. Author's interview with Larry Mazza, January 8, 2013.
14. Brad Hamilton, "My Life as a Colombo Hit Man," *New York Post,* March 4, 2012.
15. *People v. R. Lindley DeVecchio,* testimony of Larry Mazza, October 18, 2007, 710–12.
16. Ibid.
17. Mazza interview.
18. Hamilton, "My Life as a Colombo Hit Man."
19. Author's interview with Flora Edwards, April 27, 2004.
20. *U.S. v. Pasquale Amato and Victor Orena,* hearing before Hon. Jack B. Weinstein, testimony of Stephen Dresch, January 7, 2004, transcript, 127–28.
21. *People v. R. Lindley DeVecchio,* Mazza testimony, 114.
22. Ibid., 113.
23. Senior U.S. District Judge Frederic Block, memorandum and order, *Maria Grancio v. R. Lindley DeVecchio, Christopher Favo and the United States of America,* July 24, 2008.
24. Ibid., 23.
25. Ibid., 8, citing DeVecchio affidavit at paragraph 3.
26. Ibid., citing Favo affidavit at paragraph 17.
27. Ibid., section 26.
28. Author's interview with Flora Edwards, January 13, 2012.
29. DeVecchio, 209 memo, January 7, 1992.
30. Special Agent Chris Favo, February 6, 1994, 2, "Over the length of the war I began to withhold information concerning Gregory Scarpa or what could not be leaked to the media because I believe SSA DeVecchio was leaking information to both Scarpa and Jerry Capece [*sic*]."
31. Author's interview with Andrew Orena, January 23, 2012.
32. *U.S. v. William Cutolo et al.,* October 1994, transcript, 1286.
33. Author's interview with Flora Edwards, April 26, 2004.
34. Larry Mazza affidavit, paragraph 8.

35. Ibid., paragraph 9.

36. Ibid., Judge Block, 25.

37. Ibid., 22.

38. DeVecchio, 209 memo, January 8, 1992.

39. *U.S. v. William Cutolo et al.,* October 1994, transcript, 660–61.

40. Mazza interview.

41. R. Lindley DeVecchio and Charles Brandt, *We're Going to Win This Thing: The Shocking Frame-up of a Mafia Crime Buster* (New York: Berkley, 2011), 218.

42. *U.S. v. William Cutolo et al.,* 5035.

43. *U.S. v. Joseph Simone,* transcript of cross-examination of Special Agent Lynn Smith, 665–69.

CHAPTER 28: CLOSING AND REOPENING "34"

1. *U.S. v. William Cutolo et al.,* October 1994, transcript, 4271.

2. Ibid., 5034–35.

3. R. Lindley DeVecchio, FBI 209 memo for Top Echelon (TE) informant designated "NY3461," January 24, 1992.

4. Author's interview with FBI Special Agent Dan Vogel (ret.), February 8, 2012.

5. *Victor J. Orena and Pasquale Amato v. U.S. 2255,* hearing before Judge Jack B. Weinstein, testimony of Special Agent Chris Favo, May 20, 1996, transcript, 11–12.

6. DeVecchio, 209 memo, January 24, 1992.

7. *U.S. v. William Cutolo et al.,* testimony of Sal Miciotta, transcript, 2420.

8. R. Lindley DeVecchio, FBI 209 memo for Top Echelon (TE) informant designated "NY3461," January 29, 1992.

9. DeVecchio, 209 memo, January 24, 1992.

10. *U.S. v. Theodore Persico et al.,* Larry Mazza testimony, transcript, 3728–29.

11. "Suspect Mob Capo, 51, Shot in Brooklyn," *New York Times,* January 27, 1992.

12. Erika Martinez, "Mob Eyed in Cop Slay—Colombo Big Was Widow's Ex-Lover," *New York Post,* August 26, 2002.

13. *U.S. v. Theodore Persico,* Larry Mazza testimony, transcript, 3781–82.

14. *U.S. v. Victor M. Orena et al.,* testimony of Carmine Sessa, May 1995, transcript, 2301–2.

15. *U.S. v. Victor M. Orena et al.,* Special Agent Chris Favo testimony, transcript, 5161–84; Special Agent Chris Favo, FBI 302 memo, February 6, 1994, 3.

16. Ibid.

17. *U.S. v. Victor M. Orena et al.,* transcript, 5184.

18. Ibid., 5242.

19. R. Lindley DeVecchio and Charles Brandt, *We're Going to Win This Thing: The Shocking Frame-up of a Mafia Crime Buster* (New York: Berkley, 2011), 221.

20. *U.S. v. Victor M. Orena et al.,* transcript, 5152.

21. DeVecchio, 209 memo, February 25, 1992.

22. *Victor J. Orena and Pasquale Amato v. U.S.,* hearing, March 3, 1997, transcript, 360–72.

23. Memorandum from special agent in charge, Organized Crime, to special agent in charge II, subject: NY: ▆▆▆▆▆▆▆, February 27, 1992.

24. Memo from special agent in charge Donald North, Organized Crime, to special agent in charge II (copying Supervisory Special Agent R. Lindley DeVecchio), February 27, 1992.

25. Matthew Chayes, "People Still Nervous at Scene of Massapequa Killings," *Newsday*, June 4, 2008.

26. DeVecchio, 209 memo, March 31, 1992.

27. Mitchell Maddux and Jeremy Olshan, "Mobster Admits Nun Slay, Fears He'll Rot in Hell!," *New York Post*, May 13, 2011.

28. Special Agents Jeffrey W. Tomlinson and Howard Leadbetter II, FBI 302 memo re: Carmine Sessa, June 1, 1993.

29. *Pasquale Amato and Victor Orena v. U.S.*, hearing before Hon. Jack B. Weinstein, testimony of Gregory Scarpa Jr., January 7, 2004, transcript, 57–58.

30. Ibid.

31. In granting the new trial, the U.S. district court found: "Most significantly for purposes of this appeal, the 209s also revealed that, in discussions with the FBI, Scarpa had lied about or misrepresented his own involvement in several murders, which he either attributed to the 'Persico faction' without identifying himself as the member of the faction responsible for the murders or falsely attributed to someone else." The Second Circuit citing the district court's decision per Judge Charles P. Sifton, *U.S. v. Russo, Russo and Monteleone*, 257 F.3d 210, paragraph 18, http://law .justia.com/cases/federal/appellate-courts/F3/257/210/625356/#fn2.

32. *U.S. v. Orena*, 145 F.3d 551, 1998, http://174.123.24.242/leagle/xmlResult.asp x?page=6&xmldoc=1998696145F3d551_1629.xml&docbase=CSLWAR2-1986- 2006&SizeDisp=7.

33. John Marzulli, "Colombo Crime Family Hit Man 'Frankie Blue Eyes' Sparaco Lied and Killed While FBI Informant," New York *Daily News*, September 20, 2011.

34. Press release, U.S. attorney for the Eastern District of New York, "Colombo Organized Crime Family Acting Boss, Underboss, and Ten Other Members and Associates Indicted," June 4, 2008, http://www.justice.gov/usao/nye/pr/2008/ 2008jun04.html.

35. Tom Hays, "Thomas Gioeli, Reputed NYC Mob Boss, Cleared of Killing Officer," Associated Press, May 9, 2012.

36. DeVecchio, 209 memo, December 30, 1991.

37. *Pasquale Amato and Victor Orena v. U.S.*, hearing before Hon. Jack B. Weinstein, January 7, 2004, transcript, 56.

38. DeVecchio and Brandt, *We're Going to Win This Thing*, 223.

39. Joseph Gambardello and Patricia Hurtado, "FBI Guilty: Jury Finds Feds Fueled a Mob War," *Newsday*, July 1, 1995.

40. Author's interview with Andrew Orena, February 8, 2012.

41. Mary B. Tabor, "Man Accused as Colombo Chief Is Held in Slaying of Ex-Member," *New York Times*, April 2, 1992.

42. *U.S. v. Victor J. Orena*, testimony of Special Agent Joseph Fanning, December 10, 1992, transcript, 2467–564.

43. FBI teletype RETEL from FBI New York Office to director, FBI, March 3, 1992.

44. FBI teletype from director, FBI, to FBI New York Office, April 2, 1992.

45. FBI teletype from FBI New York Office (R. Lindley DeVecchio) to director, FBI, April 2, 1992.

46. FBI teletype from director, FBI, to FBI New York Office, April 7, 1992.

47. Author's interview with Flora Edwards, January 13, 2012.

48. *Victor J. Orena and Pasquale Amato v. U.S. 2255*, hearing before Judge Jack B. Weinstein, testimony of Special Agent Donald North, May 21, 1996, transcript, 371, 374.

49. Ibid., 376.
50. FBI teletype from director, FBI, to FBI New York Office, April 7, 1992.
51. Special Agent Chris Favo, sworn statement, July 7, 1995, 3.
52. FBI teletype from FBI New York Office (R. Lindley DeVecchio) to director, FBI, April 22, 1992.
53. *Victor J. Orena and Pasquale Amato v. U.S. 2255,* North testimony, 383.
54. Douglas Martin, "Donald V. North, 62, Leader in F.B.I.'s Fights Against Mafia, Is Dead," *New York Times,* January 29, 2005.
55. DeVecchio and Brandt, *We're Going to Win This Thing,* 226.

CHAPTER 29: WHO'S GOING TO WIN THIS THING?
1. Linda Stasi, "Show's Finale Fires 'Blanks,'" *New York Post,* June 11, 2007.
2. Nicholas Pileggi, "Mobsters at the Wheel," *New York,* March 12, 1979.
3. Special Agents Jeffrey W. Tomlinson and Howard Leadbetter II, FBI 302 memo re: Carmine Sessa, May 29, 1993.
4. *U.S. v. William Cutolo et al.,* testimony of Carmine Sessa, transcript, 795.
5. *U.S. v. Victor M. Orena et al.,* testimony of Carmine Sessa, transcript, 2308–9.
6. Tomlinson and Leadbetter II, 302 memo, May 29, 1993.
7. Ibid.
8. Tom Robbins, "Tall Tales of a Mafia Mistress," *Village Voice,* October 30, 2007.
9. *U.S. v. Theodore Persico,* testimony of Larry Mazza, transcript, 3788–89.
10. Tomlinson and Leadbetter II, 302 memo, May 29, 1993.
11. *U.S. v. Theodore Persico,* Mazza testimony, 3792–93.
12. Ibid. Pileggi wrote that "on December 13, 1973 Lampasi was shot during the Gallo-Colombo war by a couple of ski-masked hit men who had barged into a Bath Beach, Brooklyn hairstyling salon and opened fire."
13. Tomlinson and Leadbetter II, 302 memo, May 29, 1993.
14. Author's interview with Larry Mazza, January 8, 2013.
15. Author's interview with Andrew Orena, January 13, 2012.
16. Dennis Hevesi, "7 Found Not Guilty in Plot Tied to a Mob Family Feud," *New York Times,* July 1, 1995.
17. Special Agent Chris Favo, FBI 302 memo, February 6, 1994, 5.
18. *U.S. v. Victor M. Orena et al.,* testimony of Chris Favo, transcript, 5209–10.
19. *U.S. v. Theodore Persico,* testimony of Joseph Ambrosino, transcript, 1115–18.
20. *U.S. v. Victor M. Orena,* testimony of R. Lindley DeVecchio, transcript, 93.
21. *U.S. v. Victor J. Orena,* testimony of Joseph Ambrosino, transcript, 923–24.
22. Ibid., 972.
23. *U.S. v. Theodore Persico,* Mazza testimony, 3845.
24. R. Lindley DeVecchio, FBI 209 memo for Top Echelon (TE) informant designated "NY3461," November 17, 1992.
25. *U.S. v. Victor M. Orena et al.,* Favo testimony, 5213.
26. Special Agents Jeffrey W. Tomlinson and Chris Favo, FBI 302 memo re: Joseph Ambrosino, April 25, 1994, 5.
27. *U.S. v. Victor M. Orena et al.,* Favo testimony, 5181–83.
28. Ibid., 5152–53, 5181.
29. Ibid., 5214–15.
30. Ibid., 5273.
31. Ibid., 5182.

32. Letter from Assistant U.S. Attorney Ellen Corcella to defense counsel, *U.S. v. Victor M. Orena et al.*, May 8, 1995, listing eight possible disclosures of FBI intelligence by Supervisory Special Agent R. Lindley DeVecchio to Gregory Scarpa. See Chapter 37, page 410.

33. Special Agents Maryann Walker-Goldman and Chris Favo, FBI 302 memo, debriefing of Larry Mazza, February 7, 1994.

34. Special Agent Raymond Andjich, sworn statement, April 7, 1994, 2.

35. Ibid., 3.

36. *U.S. v. Victor M. Orena et al.*, Favo testimony, 5216–17.

37. Special Agent Howard Leadbetter II, sworn statement, April 6, 1994, 3–4.

38. *U.S. v. Victor M. Orena et al.*, Favo testimony, 5217.

39. *U.S. v. Victor M. Orena et al.*, testimony of Howard Leadbetter II, transcript, 1291, 1328.

40. *U.S. v. Victor M. Orena et al.*, Favo testimony, 5218.

41. *Washington Square Post No. 1212 v. City of New York*, 808 F. Supp. 264 (1992), http://www.leagle.com/xmlResult.aspx?xmldoc=19921072808FSupp264_11045 .xml&docbase=CSLWAR2-1986-2006.

42. *U.S. v. Victor M. Orena et al.*, Favo testimony, 5187–89.

43. Statement of Assistant U.S. Attorney George Stamboulidis and Supervisory Special Agents Kevin P. Donovan and Robert J. O'Brien, FBI 302 memo, September 9, 1994, 3.

44. *U.S. v. Victor M. Orena et al.*, Favo testimony, 5189, 5219–20.

45. Author's interview with Flora Edwards, January 13, 2012.

46. *U.S. v. Victor M. Orena et al.*, Favo testimony, 5185.

CHAPTER 30: SCARPA'S WAR

1. R. Lindley DeVecchio, FBI 209 memo for Top Echelon (TE) informant designated "NY3461," July 9, 1992.

2. R. Lindley DeVecchio, FBI 209 memo for Top Echelon (TE) informant designated "NY3461," July 13, 1992.

3. Special Agent Chris Favo, FBI 302 memo, November 15, 1995, 3.

4. Letter from Assistant U.S. Attorney Ellen Corcella to defense counsel, *U.S. v. Victor M. Orena et al.*, May 8, 1995, listing eight possible disclosures of FBI intelligence by Supervisory Special Agent R. Lindley DeVecchio to Gregory Scarpa. See Chapter 37, page 410; *U.S. v. Victor M. Orena et al.*, transcript, 5171–75.

5. R. Lindley DeVecchio and Charles Brandt, *We're Going to Win This Thing: The Shocking Frame-up of a Mafia Crime Buster* (New York: Berkley, 2011), 239–40.

6. Author's interview with Andrew Orena, January 13, 2012.

7. Patricia Hurtado, "Assassination Plot; Doc and Aide Are Charged," *Newsday,* July 31, 1992.

8. Jerry Capeci and Tom Robbins, "Mafia Big Shot Battling AIDS: He Was Infected During '86 Operation," New York *Daily News,* August 17, 1992.

9. Patricia Hurtado, "Civil Suit Juror Cries at Scarpa's AIDS Tale," *Newsday,* August 20, 1992.

10. Patricia Hurtado, "Alleged Capo's Dr. Testifies," *Newsday,* August 22, 1992.

11. Mary B. W. Tabor, "Settlement in Lawsuit on H.I.V.-Tainted Blood," *New York Times,* August 30, 1992.

12. Patricia Hurtado, "Amicable End to AIDS Suit; Hospital Settles with Scarpa," *Newsday,* August 29, 1992.
13. Selwyn Raab, "The Mobster Was a Mole for the F.B.I.," *New York Times,* November 20, 1994.
14. Frederic Dannen, "The G-Man and the Hit Man," *New Yorker,* December 16, 1996.
15. Supervisory Special Agents Robert J. O'Brien and R. Patrick Welch, FBI 302 memo, statement of Assistant U.S. Attorney Andrew Weissmann, August 16, 1994, 2.
16. Supervisory Special Agents Kevin P. Donovan and Robert J. O'Brien, FBI 302 memo re: statement of Assistant U.S. Attorney George Stamboulidis, September 9, 1994.
17. Dannen, "The G-Man and the Hit Man."
18. Fredric Dannen, interview with Joseph Benfante, October 4, 1996.
19. Jonathan Rabinovitz, "2 Men Slain in Brooklyn Said to Have Ties to Mob," *New York Times,* October 19, 1992.
20. Ibid., Stamboulidis FBI 302 memo, 4.
21. Ibid., 1.
22. *Victor J. Orena and Pasquale Amato v. U.S. 2255,* hearing before Judge Jack B. Weinstein, testimony of Special Agent Chris Favo, May 20, 1996, transcript, 32–33.
23. Ibid., 59.
24. *U.S. v. Victor M. Orena,* transcript of direct examination of R. Lindley DeVecchio by Gerald Shargel, February 28, 1997, 174–202.
25. Author's interview with Gerald Shargel, November 9, 2011.
26. Interview with Linda Schiro, *I Married a Mobster,* episode 6, Investigation Discovery Channel, airdate December 3, 2011.
27. Helen Peterson, "Feds Have New Canary," New York *Daily News,* December 21, 1997.
28. Ibid.
29. Dannen, "The G-Man and the Hit Man"; Brad Hamilton, "My Life as a Colombo Hit Man," *New York Post,* March 4, 2012.
30. Memo to FBI director from assistant director in charge, New York, April 10, 1996, regarding the ongoing DeVecchio OPR investigation: "NY requests that whatever investigation is to be conducted as a result of this letter be conducted expeditiously. . . . The failure of the DOJ . . . to administratively resolve this matter continues to have a serious negative impact on the government's prosecutions of various LCN figures in the EDNY and casts a cloud over the NYO."
31. Mazza confirmed that number as recently as March 2012, telling Brad Hamilton of the *New York Post* that he participated in twenty-five murder plots from the time he met Greg Scarpa Sr. in 1979—"four of them slayings where he delivered the kill shot." Hamilton, "My Life as a Colombo Hit Man." That homicide count (twenty-five) beginning in 1979 is just shy of the number of murders directly linked to Greg Scarpa Sr. in this investigation during the period 1980 to 1992, when Lin DeVecchio was Scarpa's contacting agent.

CHAPTER 31: A GRAIN OF SAND ON JONES BEACH

1. Jack B. Weinstein, judgment, memorandum, and order, *U.S. v. Victor J. Orena and Pasquale Amato,* March 10, 1997, 9.
2. Ibid.
3. Judge Jack B. Weinstein during a hearing in the case of *U.S. v. Michael Sessa,* CR-92-351, September 24, 2001, 20.
4. DeVecchio's conversation on the "Hello" phone to Scarpa following Imbriale's arrest

was proof positive of that. Special Agent Chris Favo, FBI 302 memo, February 6, 1994, 3.

5. Sworn statement of Special Agent Howard Leadbetter II, April 6, 1994, 4.
6. *Brady v. Maryland,* 373 U.S. 83 (1963).
7. Robert Hochmann, "*Brady v. Maryland* and the Search for Truth in Criminal Trials," *University of Chicago Law Review* 63, no. 4 (Fall 1996).
8. Author's interview with Ellen Resnick, February 21, 2012.
9. Author's interview with Flora Edwards, January 13, 2012.
10. *U.S. v. Michael Sessa,* order of Judge Allyne R. Ross, January 25, 2011, 3.
11. *U.S. v. Orena,* transcript of direct examination of R. Lindley DeVecchio by Gerald Shargel, February 28, 1997, 155.
12. William Sherman, "Mob Retrials Loom," New York *Daily News,* January 9, 2006.
13. *Victor J. Orena and Pasquale Amato v. U.S. 2255,* hearing before Judge Jack B. Weinstein, testimony of Special Agent Chris Favo, May 20, 1996, transcript, 55–66.
14. Supervisory Special Agents Kevin P. Donovan and Robert J. O'Brien, FBI 302 memo re: statement of George Stamboulidis, September 9, 1994, 2.
15. Ibid. 3.
16. *U.S. v. Michael Sessa,* 2.
17. U.S. District Court judgment and probation/commitment order, February 6, 1987; satisfaction of judgment, filed February 5, 1992; Greg Smith and Jerry Capeci, "Mob, Mole & Murder," New York *Daily News,* October 31, 1994.
18. Edwards interview, January 13, 2012.
19. Gustave H. Newman, "Victor J. Orena's Memo of Law in Support of His Motions to Dismiss the Indictment or for a New Trial Pursuant to Rule 33 of the Federal Rules of Criminal Procedure and 28 USC Section 2255," January 16, 1996, 123.
20. Ibid., 123–24.
21. Ibid., 124–25.
22. *U.S. v. Victor J. Orena,* summation of Gustave H. Newman, transcript, 3122.
23. Gregory Scarpa Jr., sworn affidavit, U.S. penitentiary, Florence, CO, July 30, 2002.
24. Author's interview with Gustave Newman, October 4, 2011.
25. *U.S. v. Victor J. Orena,* rebuttal, John Gleeson, 3217; Weinstein, judgment, memorandum, and order, March 10, 1997, 21–22.
26. Judgment and probation commitment order, Gregory Scarpa Sr., February 6, 1987.
27. Letter from Assistant U.S. Attorney Ellen Corcella to defense counsel, *U.S. v. Victor M. Orena et al.,* May 8, 1995, listing eight possible disclosures of FBI intelligence by Supervisory Special Agent R. Lindley DeVecchio to Gregory Scarpa. See Chapter 37, page 410.
28. *U.S. v. Victor J. Orena,* Gleeson rebuttal, 3204.
29. Ibid., 3023.
30. Ibid., 3204.
31. *U.S. v. Victor J. Orena,* summation by George Stamboulidis, 3021.
32. Ibid., 3024.
33. For example, there's an exception to the Rule Against Hearsay for the statements of co-conspirators [Rule 801 (d)(2)(E) Federal Rules of Evidence]. Much of the testimony against Orena by Michael Maffatore and Harry Bonfiglio, particularly with respect to that alleged walk-and-talk between Vic Orena and Jack Leale, amounted to hearsay. Orena's lawyer Gus Newman argued that once the war had commenced in June 1991, Vic Orena could hardly be seen as being a co-conspirator with members of the Persico faction—particularly witnesses like Joe Ambrosino,

who testified against him. However, seeming to ignore that a schism had taken place in the family, Judge Weinstein ruled that "the ongoing Colombo conspiracy was continuing and that these conversations were in aid and during the continuance of the conspiracy" (*U.S. v. Victor J. Orena*, ruling of Judge Jack B. Weinstein, transcript, 822–23). He also held that other hearsay statements could come in because they were "offered as evidence of a material fact . . . more probative on the point than other evidence which can be gotten through reasonable efforts" (*U.S. v. Victor J. Orena*, ruling of Judge Jack B. Weinstein, transcript, 1286–87). Rule 807 [formerly Rule 803(24)] provides for exceptions in certain circumstances: "(a) In General. Under the following circumstances, a hearsay statement is not excluded by the rule against hearsay even if the statement is not specifically covered by a hearsay exception in Rule 803 or 804: (1) the statement has equivalent circumstantial guarantees of trustworthiness; (2) it is offered as evidence of a material fact; (3) it is more probative on the point for which it is offered than any other evidence that the proponent can obtain through reasonable efforts; and (4) admitting it will best serve the purposes of these rules and the interests of justice. (b) Notice. The statement is admissible only if, before the trial or hearing, the proponent gives an adverse party reasonable notice of the intent to offer the statement and its particulars, including the declarant's name and address, so that the party has a fair opportunity to meet it."

34. When evidence surfaced that Reiter had been killed by Tommy "Karate" Pitera and that Mark Reiter, Greg's father, had hired white supremacist Jack Stancell to kill Billy Bright under the mistaken assumption he was responsible for his son's death. See Chapter 23, pages 233–234.
35. Weinstein, judgment, memorandum, and order, March 10, 1997, 5.
36. Ibid., 95–98.
37. *U.S. v. Victor J. Orena*, summation by George Stamboulidis, 2978.
38. *U.S. v. Victor J. Orena*, Gleeson rebuttal, 3213.
39. Ibid., 3223.
40. Edwards interview, January 13, 2012.

CHAPTER 32: EXPECTING TO GO HOME
1. Selwyn Raab, "Prosecutors Shift Attack Against the Mafia," *New York Times*, January 23, 1993.
2. Philip Carlo, *Gaspipe: Confessions of a Mob Boss* (New York: William Morrow, 2008), 246–47.
3. Author's interview with Anthony Casso, September 23, 2011.
4. Carlo, *Gaspipe*, 253.
5. Ibid., 254.
6. Assistant U.S. Attorney George Stamboulidis, sworn affidavit, January 27, 1995, 7.
7. "Reputed Mobster Sent to Hospital by Judge," *New York Times*, February 23, 1993.
8. *U.S. v. Victor M. Orena et al.*, transcript, 1294.
9. Special Agent Chris Favo, FBI 302 memo, February 6, 1994, 7.
10. Ibid.
11. Ibid., 1.
12. Ibid.
13. Special Agent Jeffrey Tomlinson, sworn affidavit, April 7, 1994, 5.
14. Ibid., 7.
15. Ibid., 5.
16. Ibid.

17. Ibid., 6–7.
18. Ibid., 8.
19. Ibid., 9.
20. "Mobster with AIDS Gets Special Sentence," *New York Times,* April 25, 1993.
21. R. Lindley DeVecchio, FBI 209 memo for Top Echelon (TE) informant designated "NY3461," August 27, 1993.
22. Special Agents John L. Barrett and Thomas Fuentes, FBI 302 memo re: Valerie Caproni, January 26, 1994, 2.
23. FBI official biography of Valerie Caproni, http://web.archive.org/web/20080813135548/http://www.fbi.gov/libref/executives/caproni.htm.
24. Barrett and Fuentes, 302 memo, January 26, 1994, 4.
25. R. Lindley DeVecchio and Charles Brandt, *We're Going to Win This Thing: The Shocking Frame-up of a Mafia Crime Buster* (New York: Berkley, 2011), 253–54.
26. Ibid.
27. Barrett and Fuentes, 302 memo, January 26, 1994, 4.
28. DeVecchio and Brandt, *We're Going to Win This Thing,* 289.
29. Ibid., 290.
30. Supervisory Special Agents Timothy T. Arney and Robert J. O'Brien, FBI 302 memo re: Valerie Caproni, September 14, 1994, 5–6.
31. Philip Carlo, *Gaspipe: Confessions of a Mob Boss,* original draft manuscript, 311–14. In the final published edition of *Gaspipe,* DeVecchio and a second alleged "crooked agent" on the Gambino Squad were combined into a single composite character, agent "Doug McCane." The full details are revealed in Chapter 36.
32. E-mail to author from FBI Special Agent James Brennan (ret.), January 19, 2013.
33. Arney and O'Brien, 302 memo, September 14, 1994, 6.
34. George James, "Man Tied to Crime Family Is Shot to Death in Queens," *New York Times,* October 22, 1993.
35. Selwyn Raab, "Ex-F.B.I. Official Is Pressured to Testify on Ties to Mobster," *New York Times,* January 26, 1997.
36. Al Guarte, "Wiseguys Acquitted in Colombo Murders," *New York Post,* July 1, 1995.
37. *U.S. v. Victor Mr. Orena,* testimony of R. Lindley DeVecchio, November 19, 2002, transcript, 88–94.
38. Jonathan Rabinovitz, "2 Men Slain in Brooklyn Said to Have Ties to Mob," *New York Times,* October 19, 1992.
39. Arnold H. Lubasch, "Peace Efforts by Mobsters Recounted," *New York Times,* November 14, 1992.
40. R. Lindley DeVecchio, FBI 209 memo for Top Echelon (TE) informant designated "NY3461," November 4, 1991, on the murder of Jack Leale, attributed by Gregory Scarpa Sr. to the "Persico faction."
41. *U.S. v. Gregory Scarpa,* hearing before Judge Jack B. Weinstein, December 15, 1993, first transcript, 3–4.
42. Ibid., 6.
43. Ibid., 7–8.
44. Ibid., 9.
45. Ibid., 10.
45. Ibid., 10–11.
47. Ibid., 11.
48. Ibid., 13.

49. *People v. R. Lindley DeVecchio,* testimony of Larry Mazza, October 18, 2007, transcript, 714.

50. *People v. R. Lindley DeVecchio,* testimony of Carmine Sessa, October 25, 2007, transcript, 1426.

51. *U.S. v. Gregory Scarpa,* hearing before Judge Jack B. Weinstein, December 15, 1993, second transcript, 2.

52. *U.S. v. Gregory Scarpa,* hearing before Judge Jack B. Weinstein, December 15, 1993, third transcript, 6.

53. Ibid., 7.

54. Author's interview with Flora Edwards, November 3, 2011.

CHAPTER 33: THE OPR

1. Letter from Assistant U.S. Attorney Ellen Corcella to defense counsel, *U.S. v. Victor M. Orena et al.,* May 8, 1995, admitting to eight possible disclosures of FBI intelligence by Supervisory Special Agent R. Lindley DeVecchio to Gregory Scarpa. The precise language used by Corcella in referring to the eight leaks was: "Special Agent R. Lindley DeVecchio *may* have disclosed [them] to Gregory Scarpa Sr." (emphasis added). See Chapter 37, page 410.

2. Special Agents Maryann Walker-Goldman and Christopher Favo, FBI 302 memo, Larry Mazza, February 7, 1994.

3. Special Agents Maryann Walker-Goldman and Christopher Favo, FBI 302 memo, Larry Mazza, February 11, 1994. Note that while the interview with Mazza took place sometime between January 7 and February 11, it was dictated and dated February 11.

4. R. Lindley DeVecchio and Charles Brandt, *We're Going to Win This Thing: The Shocking Frame-up of a Mafia Crime Buster* (New York: Berkley, 2011), 227.

5. Christopher Favo, sworn affidavit, April 4, 1994, 2–3.

6. Special Agent Christopher Favo, FBI 302 memo, February 6, 1994, 1.

7. Ibid., 4.

8. Supervisory Special Agents Kevin P. Donovan and Robert J. O'Brien, FBI 302 memo, statement of Assistant U.S. Attorney George Stamboulidis, September 9, 1994, 4.

9. Favo affidavit, 4.

10. Special Agent Howard Leadbetter II, FBI 302 memo, William Meli, January 21, 1994.

11. Favo affidavit, 4.

12. Ibid., 5.

13. Ibid.

14. A bio of Thomas Fuentes can be found at http://www.silobreaker.com/biography-for-thomas-fuentes-5_2259328017513840640_4. By 2010, Fuentes had become a regular contributor to CNN, http://www.cnn.com/video/?/video/bestoftv/2010/08/11/ac.terror.baby.cnn#/video/bestoftv/2010/08/11/ac.terror.baby.cnn.

15. Favo affidavit, 6.

16. Ibid., 7.

17. Ibid.

18. Ibid., 8.

19. Ibid.

20. Author's interview with Flora Edwards, January 13, 2012.

21. Favo affidavit, 8.

22. Ibid., 9.

23. Ibid.

24. Ibid., 9–11.
25. Ibid., 12.
26. Ibid.
27. Chris Favo, appointment diary, OPR investigation of R. Lindley DeVecchio, Bates-stamped pages 000316–000329.
28. Author's interview with Alan Futerfas, May 24, 2004.
29. *U.S. v. Anthony Russo et al.*, 92 CR351 (S9) (CPS), affirmation of Valerie Caproni, May 28, 1996.
30. *U.S. v. Anthony Russo*, 92 CR 351 (S-9) (CPS), memorandum of law by Alan Futerfas,19–20.
31. FBI memo from Mr. Reutter to L. A. Potts. Subject: Unauthorized Dissemination of Information to Colombo LCN Capo Gregory Scarpa Sr., New York Division, OPR Matter, March 21, 1994, 2.
32. Author's interview with Flora Edwards, November 3, 2011.
33. Special Agents Thomas Fuentes and John L. Barrett, FBI 302 memo, phone call with Valerie Caproni, February 1, 1994.
34. Reutter-Potts memo, March 21, 1994.
35. *U.S. v. Anthony Russo,* Futerfas memo, 1–22.
36. Memo from assistant director in charge, FBI New York Office, to director, FBI, April 10, 1996.
37. Author's interview with FBI Special Agent Dan Vogel (ret.), October 14, 2011.
38. Letter from Lee J. Radek, chief, Public Integrity Section, Criminal Division, Department of Justice, to Douglas E. Grover, attorney for Lin DeVecchio, September 4, 1996.

CHAPTER 34: THE DYING DECLARATION

1. Jerry Capeci, "Fading Mobster Hits on Pal's Alibi," New York *Daily News,* May 31, 1994.
2. Author's interview with Linda Schiro, November 3, 2007.
3. Interview with Little Linda Schiro, *I Married a Mobster,* episode 6, Investigation Discovery Channel, airdate December 3, 2011.
4. *U.S. v. Victor J. Orena et al.,* option of the U.S. Second Circuit Court of Appeals, decided June 3, 1998.
5. Memo from Chris Favo to special agent in charge, FBI Division II, May 25, 1994.
6. Sworn affidavit of Greg Scarpa Sr., Rochester, MN, June 7, 1994.
7. FBI 209 memo on Top Echelon (TE) informant designated "NY3461," June 17, 1994.
8. Ibid.
9. Joseph Friend, "Mob Figure Acquitted in Murder and Racketeering Case," *New York Times,* August 9, 1994.
10. Gustave H. Newman, "Victor J. Orena's Memo of Law in Support of His Motions to Dismiss the Indictment or for a New Trial Pursuant to Rule 33 of the Federal Rules of Criminal Procedure and 28 USC Section 2255," January 16, 1996, 83.
11. DeVecchio, 209 memo, November 4, 1991.
12. DeVecchio, 209 memo, November 18, 1991.
13. *U.S. v. Victor M. Orena et al.,* testimony of Chris Favo, transcript, 5252.
14. Ibid., 5253–54; *U.S. v. William Cutolo et al.,* October 1994, transcript, 4952–53.
15. Newman, "Victor J. Orena's Memo."
16. *U.S. v. William Cutolo,* 2756, 4959; *U.S. v. Victor M. Orena,* 5248–50.

17. *U.S. v. Victor M. Orena,* 5250.
18. Ibid., 5255–56.
19. Ibid.
20. Ibid., 5256.
21. Ibid., 5248–49.
22. Ibid., 5257–59.
23. *U.S. v. Theodore Persico,* 3692–96; *U.S. v. Victor J. Orena,* transcript, 896–97; *U.S. v. Victor M. Orena,* 2208–9.
24. Ibid., 2212–14.
25. Ibid., 2209.
26. Ibid., 2211.
27. "Reichstag fire," Wikipedia, http://en.wikipedia.org/wiki/Reichstag_fire: "The fire was used as evidence by the Nazis that Communists were beginning a plot against the German government. Van der Lubbe and four Communist leaders were subsequently arrested. Adolf Hitler, who was sworn in as Chancellor of Germany four weeks before, on 30 January, urged President Paul von Hindenburg to pass an emergency decree to counter the 'ruthless confrontation of the Communist Party of Germany.' With civil liberties suspended, the government instituted mass arrests of Communists, including all of the Communist parliamentary delegates. With them gone and their seats empty, the Nazis went from being a plurality party to the majority; subsequent elections confirmed this position and thus allowed Hitler to consolidate his power."
28. Author's interview with Andrew Orena, January 13, 2012.
29. Jerry Capeci, "No Tipping the Capo to Legendary Mobster," New York *Daily News,* June 14, 1994.
30. R. Lindley DeVecchio and Charles Brandt, *We're Going to Win This Thing: The Shocking Frame-up of a Mafia Crime Buster* (New York: Berkley, 2011), 129.
31. Author's interview with James Whalen, May 19, 2011.

CHAPTER 35: BURNING A GOOD COP

1. Greg B. Smith, "Mob Pigeons Wouldn't Fly," New York *Daily News,* December 21, 1994.
2. Greg B. Smith, "G-Man, Fed Atty Eyed in Mob Leaks," New York *Daily News,* October 24, 1994.
3. Ibid.
4. Ibid.
5. Fredric Dannen, "The G-Man and the Hit Man," *New Yorker,* December 16, 1996.
6. Greg B. Smith and Jerry Capeci, "Mob, Mole & Murder," New York *Daily News,* October 30, 1994.
7. Jerry Capeci, "Colombo Capo Gets a Big Present," New York *Daily News,* December 21, 1994.
8. Jerry Capeci and Tom Robbins, "Detective Stung by Feds: Sold Information to Colombos: FBI," New York *Daily News,* December 9, 1993.
9. Ibid.
10. Author's interview with NYPD detective Joseph Simone (ret.), April 27, 2004.
11. Jerry Capeci, "Mob Canary Hears Birds Singing, Picked Wrong Foe for Prison Fight," New York *Daily News,* January 20, 1997.
12. Simone interview, April 27, 2004.
13. *U.S. v. Joseph Simone,* testimony of Christopher Favo, October 18, 1994.

14. Transcript of taped conversation between Salvatore Miciotta and Alfonso "Chips" DeCostanza, 194C-NY-240371, July 14, 1993.
15. Simone interview, April 27, 2004.
16. Special Agent Patrick McConnell, FBI 302 memo re: Detective Joseph Simone, December 8, 1993.
17. Capeci and Robbins, "Detective Stung by Feds."
18. Ibid.
19. Jerry Capeci and Tom Robbins, "Mob Biggie Aids FBI Sting," New York *Daily News,* December 11, 1993.
20. Jerry Capeci, "Short FBI Tape May Aid 'Rogue Cop' Defense," New York *Daily News,* April 13, 1994.
21. Greg Smith, "DA Gilds Case for Pet Canary," New York *Daily News,* October 21, 1994.
22. *U.S. v. Joseph Simone,* cross-examination of Special Agent Lynn Smith, transcript, 665–69.
23. Author's interview with Angela Clemente, April 11, 2004.
24. Author's interview with John Patton, April 29, 2004.
25. FBI 302 memos, interview with Christopher Favo, June 1–2, 1994; November 16, 1995; December 8, 1995.
26. Patton interview.
27. Joseph P. Fried, "Detective Is Found Not Guilty of Selling Secrets to the Mafia," *New York Times,* October 21, 1994.
28. Pete Bowles, "Cop Not Guilty of Fed Rap," *Newsday,* October 21, 1994.
29. Ann Marie Calzolari, "Detective Acquitted of Mob Charges," *Staten Island Advance,* October 22, 1994.
30. Angela Mosconi, "Cop Puts His Life Back Together," *Staten Island Advance,* November 6, 1994.
31. Jerry Capeci, "Cop Still Treading Hot Water," New York *Daily News,* November 8, 1994.
32. Fogel Draft, "In the Matter of the Charges and Specifications—against—Detective Joseph Simone," Tax Registry No. 87061, Medical Division, before Rae Downes Koshetz, Deputy Commissioner—Trials.
33. "Howard Safir," Wikipedia, http://en.wikipedia.org/wiki/Howard_Safir.
34. John Marzulli, "Caracappa Lawyer AWOL; Mistrial Bid Is Shot Down," New York *Daily News,* April 1, 2006.
35. Sewell Chan, "2 Ex-Detectives Get Life Terms in Mob Killings," *New York Times,* March 6, 2009.
36. R. Lindley DeVecchio and Charles Brandt, *We're Going to Win This Thing: The Shocking Frame-up of a Mafia Crime Buster* (New York: Berkley, 2011), 192–95.
37. Author's interview with NYPD detective Joseph Simone (ret.), February 22, 2012.
38. Clemente interview.

CHAPTER 36: GASPIPE'S CONFESSION

1. Special Agents John L. Barrett and Thomas Fuentes, FBI 302 memo re: Valerie Caproni, January 26, 1994, 2; R. Lindley DeVecchio and Charles Brandt, *We're Going to Win This Thing: The Shocking Frame-up of a Mafia Crime Buster* (New York: Berkley, 2011), 253–54.
2. Philip Carlo, *Gaspipe: Confessions of a Mob Boss,* original draft manuscript, 311–14.

3. Philip Carlo, *Gaspipe: Confessions of a Mob Boss* (New York: William Morrow, 2008), 264–67.

4. Ibid.

5. Ibid., 85–86.

6. Helen Peterson, "Wiseguy Won't Get Fed Aid on Sentence," New York *Daily News,* July 1, 1998.

7. Carlo, *Gaspipe* (Morrow edition), 266.

8. Ibid., 267.

9. "FCI La Tuna," Federal Bureau of Prisons, http://www.bop.gov/locations/institutions/lat/index.jsp.

10. Carl Sifakis, *The Mafia Encyclopedia* (New York: Checkmark Books, 2005), 258.

11. William Oldham, *The Brotherhoods: The True Story of Two Cops Who Murdered for the Mafia* (New York: Scribner, 2006), 290–91.

12. Ibid.

13. Carlo, *Gaspipe* (draft manuscript), 311–12.

14. Ibid.

15. E-mail to author from FBI Special Agent James Brennan (ret.), January 19, 2013.

16. Special Agents Stephen A. Grimaldi and Donald W. McCormick, FBI 302 memo re: debriefing of Al D'Arco, January 17, 1992.

17. Tommy Dades and Mike Vecchione, *Friends of the Family: The Inside Story of the Mafia Cops Case* (New York: William Morrow, 2009), 178.

18. Ibid., 313.

19. Ibid.

20. Author's interview with Anthony Casso, September 23, 2011.

21. Carlo, *Gaspipe* (draft manuscript), 319.

22. Casso interview.

23. Author's interview with William Oldham, June 10, 2011.

24. Brennan e-mail to author, January 19, 2013.

25. Carlo, *Gaspipe* (draft manuscript), 323.

26. Selwyn Raab, "Plea Deal Rescinded, Informer May Face Life," *New York Times,* July 1, 1998.

27. Carlo, *Gaspipe* (draft manuscript), 329.

28. Ibid.

29. Oldham interview, August 21, 2011.

30. Special Agent Chris Favo, FBI 302 memo, February 6, 1994, 7; sworn statement of Special Agent Jeffrey Tomlinson, April 6, 1994, 4; sworn statement of Special Agent Raymond Andjich, April 6, 1994, 3–4.

31. DeVecchio and Brandt, *We're Going to Win This Thing,* 251.

32. Ibid., 289.

33. Fredric Dannen, "The G-Man and the Hit Man," *New Yorker,* December 16, 1996.

34. Author's interview with Fredric Dannen, October 2, 2011.

35. Author's interview with Flora Edwards, January 13, 2012.

36. Selwyn Raab, "The Mobster Was a Mole for the FBI: Tangled Life of a Mafia Figure Who Died of AIDS Is Exposed," *New York Times,* November 20, 1994.

37. Selwyn Raab, "7 Suspects Say F.B.I. Helped Incite Mob Violence," *New York Times,* May 10, 1995.

CHAPTER 37: INSANE MAD-DOG KILLER

1. FBI memo from Mr. Reutter to L. A. Potts. Subject: Unauthorized Dissemination of Information to Colombo LCN Capo Gregory Scarpa Sr., New York Division, OPR Matter, March 21, 1994.
2. Sworn affidavit of Valerie Caproni, April 12, 1995, 3; Reutter-Potts memo.
3. Author's interview with Ellen Resnick, February 21, 2012.
4. Caproni affidavit, 4.
5. Ibid.
6. Ibid., 7–9.
7. Ibid., 9.
8. Ibid., 6–7.
9. *Victor J. Orena and Pasquale Amato v. U.S. 2255,* hearing before Judge Jack B. Weinstein, statement by the court, May 20, 1996, transcript, 6.
10. Author's interview with Flora Edwards, January 13, 2012.
11. Section 13-6.2, *FBI Manual of Administrative Operations and Procedures,* http://vault .fbi.gov/maop/maop-part-02-of-07/view.
12. R. Lindley DeVecchio, sworn compelled statement to Supervisory Special Agent Robert J. O'Brien, May 5, 1995, 1–2.
13. Memorandum from special agent in charge, FBI New York Office, to director, FBI. Subject: Gregory Scarpa. Top Echelon (TE) Criminal Informant Program, New York Division, June 18, 1962, 1.
14. R. Lindley DeVecchio and Charles Brandt, *We're Going to Win This Thing: The Shocking Frame-up of a Mafia Crime Buster* (New York: Berkley, 2011), 108.
15. Reutter-Potts memo.
16. DeVecchio, compelled statement, 4.
17. Supervisory Special Agents Kevin P. Donovan and Robert J. O'Brien, FBI 302 memo, statement of Assistant U.S. Attorney George Stamboulidis, September 9, 1994, 3.
18. DeVecchio, compelled statement, 4.
19. Supervisory Special Agents Kevin P. Donovan and Robert J. O'Brien, FBI 302 memo, William Meli, June 13, 1994, 6.
20. DeVecchio, compelled statement, 8.
21. *U.S. v. Michael Sessa,* testimony of R. Lindley DeVecchio, November 2, 1992, transcript, 118–19.
22. DeVecchio, compelled statement, 9.
23. Edwards interview, January 13, 2012.
24. John Kroger, *Convictions* (New York: Farrar, Straus & Giroux, 2008), 148.
25. DeVecchio, compelled statement, 17.
26. R. Lindley DeVecchio, FBI 209 memo for Top Echelon (TE) informant designated "NY3461," October 18, 1982.
27. Author's interview with Andrew Orena, January 6, 2012.
28. Edward Robert Korman, *Biographical Directory of Federal Judges,* http://www.fjc.gov/ servlet/nGetInfo?jid=1309&cid=999&ctype=na&instate=na.
29. Selwyn Raab, "Prosecutors Say F.B.I. Agent Passed Information to a Colombo Mob Figure," *New York Times,* May 9, 1995.
30. Greg B. Smith and Jerry Capeci, "FBI Big Tipped Off Mob: Prosecutor Speaks at Trial," New York *Daily News,* May 10, 1995.
31. Ibid.
32. Richard Pyle, "Mob Prosecutor Concedes FBI Leak," *Staten Island Advance,* May 10, 1995.

33. Ibid.
34. Selwyn Raab, "7 Suspects Say F.B.I. Helped Incite Mob Violence," *New York Times,* May 10, 1995.
35. Pyle, "Mob Prosecutor Concedes."
36. Raab, "7 Suspects Say F.B.I. Helped."
37. Greg B. Smith, "Mobster Had Deal with FBI," New York *Daily News,* May 11, 1995.
38. *U.S. v. Victor M. Orena et al.,* transcript, 5761–62.
39. Ibid., 5960–64.
40. Ibid., 5964.
41. Author's interview with Gerald Shargel, November 9, 2011.
42. Joseph Gambardello and Patricia Hurtado, "Black Eye for the FBI: 7 Acquitted in Mob Case," *Newsday,* July 1, 1995.
43. Ibid.
44. Greg B. Smith, "7 Cleared in B'klyn Mob Case," New York *Daily News,* July 1, 1995.
45. Al Guarte, "Wiseguys Acquitted in Colombo Murders," *New York Post,* July 1, 1995.
46. Selwyn Raab, "The Thin Line Between Mole and Manager," *New York Times,* July 2, 1995.
47. Memo from assistant director in charge, FBI New York Office, to director, FBI, April 10, 1996.
48. Kroger, *Convictions,* 149.
49. Supervisory Special Agent R. Patrick Welch and Inspector David V. Ries, FBI 302 memo, Valerie Caproni, July 17, 1995, 1.
50. Ibid., 3.
51. Pyle, "Mob Prosecutor Concedes."
52. Welch and Ries, 302 memo, July 17, 1995, 3.
53. Assistant U.S. Attorney Valerie Caproni, FBI Eastern District of New York, letter to Supervisory Special Agent Ralph Regalbuto Jr., FBI Office of Professional Responsibility, July 24, 1995.
54. Edwards interview, January 13, 2012.
55. Letter from Lee. J. Radek to Douglas Grover, September 8, 1996.

CHAPTER 38: ORGANIZED CRIME AND TERRORISM

1. David M. Herszenhorn, "New Indictment for Reputed Colombo Crime Family Captain," *New York Times,* July 7, 1995.
2. Ibid.
3. Ibid.
4. The thirty-two-page illustrated timeline created for *1000 Years for Revenge* documents how both attacks on the Twin Towers, masterminded by Ramzi Yousef, were bankrolled by al-Qaeda. Available at www.peterlance.com/1000_Years_Timeline.pdf.
5. Author's interview with Colonel Rodolfo B. Mendoza, Philippine National Police, March 19, 2002.
6. Ibid.
7. Transcript of interrogation of Abdul Hakim Murad, Colonel Rodolfo B. Mendoza, Philippine National Police, January 20, 1995.
8. FBI 302 memo, interrogation of Abdul Hakim Murad, April 12–13, 1995.
9. Ibid.
10. Mendoza interview.
11. The account of Yousef's arrest and KSM's subsequent interview and escape was first revealed in a story by Christopher John Farley ("The Man Who Wasn't There," *Time,*

February 20, 1995) and later detailed in a piece by Terry McDermott and other reporters for the *Los Angeles Times* in December 2002. Terry McDermott, Josh Meyer, and Patrick J. McDonnell, "The Plots and Designs of Al Qaeda's Engineer: Khalid Shaikh Mohammed, the Man Believed to Be Behind 9/11, Hides in Plain Sight—and Narrowly Escapes Capture in Pakistan," *Los Angeles Times,* December 22, 2002.

12. "The Long Arm of the Law: FBI International Presence Key to Bringing Terrorists to Justice," FBI.gov, February 6, 2004, http://www.fbi.gov/news/stories/2004/february/law020604.

13. *U.S. v. Ramzi Ahmed Yousef et al.,* indictment, S1293CR.180 (KTD).

14. For years, terrorism analysts, reporters, and historians have described "Bojinka" as a Serbo-Croatian word used variously to mean "explosion," "big noise," or "loud bang," an allegation that a number of ethnic Serbs have since challenged. Terry McDermott, "The Plot: How Terrorists Hatched a Simple Plan to Use Planes as Bombs," *Los Angeles Times,* September 1, 2002; Mitch Frank, "Four Dots American Intelligence Failed to Connect," *Time,* April 26, 2004 (Bojinka = "explosion"); Steve Fainaru, "Clues Pointed to Changing Terrorist Tactics," *Washington Post,* May 18, 2002 (Bojinka = "loud bang"); David Horowitz, "Why Bush Is Innocent and the Democrats Are Guilty," FrontPageMagazine.com, May 20, 2002 (Bojinka = "big bang"). The Croation word "bočnica" translates as "boom": http://www.eudict.com/?lang=croeng&word=boènica.

15. *U.S. v. Ramzi Ahmed Yousef et al.,* S1293CR.180 (KTD), May 29, 1996.

16. PNP transcript, interrogation of Abdul Hakim Murad, January 7, 1995, government's exhibit 760-T, *U.S. v. Ramzi Yousef et al.*

17. Author's interview with Larry Silverman, June 12, 2006.

18. FBI 302 memo, Gregory Scarpa Jr. and Ramzi Yousef intelligence, March 5, 1996, 3.

19. Letter from Jeremy Orden, attorney for Gregory Scarpa Jr., to Judge Reena Raggi, April 29, 1999, *U.S. v. Gregory Scarpa Jr.,* 94 Cr. 1119 (S-5).

20. Author's interview with Larry Silverman, April 13, 2004.

21. Interview with James Kallstrom for documentary *Conspiracy?,* History Channel, 2005.

22. Assistant Director in Charge James Kallstrom, FBI New York Office, memo to director, FBI, April 10, 1996.

23. http://www.peterlance.com/howto.htm.

24. FBI 302 memo, interview with Greg Scarpa Jr. re: Ramzi Yousef intelligence, May 5, 1996.

25. That position was ratified by then National Security Adviser Condoleezza Rice in her April 8, 2004, testimony before the 9/11 Commission, when she testified that until the attacks of September 11, any warnings of a threat to the United States, specifically New York City, were "historic" and devoid of "actionable intelligence." See Rice testimony at http://www.cnn.com/2004/ALLPOLITICS/04/08/rice.transcript/.

26. FBI 302 memo, Yousef handwritten notes, March 27–28, 1996; FBI 302 memo, September 7, 1996; Angela Clemente & Associates, "The Scarpa Intelligence on the Terrorist Threat: An Evaluative Report," February 20, 2005.

27. Silverman interview, April 13, 2004.

28. FBI 302 memo, March 5, 1996, 4.

29. Roma Corp. "kite," May 9, 1996. Reproduced as an appendix in Peter Lance, *Cover Up: What the Government Is Still Hiding About the War on Terror* (New York: Regan Books, 2004), 301.

30. Author's interview with confidential FBI source, February 10, 2006.

31. Bill Gertz, *Breakdown: How America's Intelligence Failures Led to September 11* (New York: Regnery, 2002); McDermott, "The Plot."

32. Brian Ross, "Al Qaeda Ally? Member of Qatari Royal Family Helped Senior Al Qaeda Official Get Away," ABC News, February 7, 2003.

33. FBI 302 memo, September 9, 1996, http://www.peterlance.com/302/9996.htm.

34. Entitled "Bin Laden Determined to Strike in U.S.," the PDB cited a 1998 report from an undisclosed intelligence service that "Bin Laden wanted to hijack a U.S. aircraft to gain the release of 'Blind Shaykh,' 'Umar Abd al-Rahman,' and other US-held extremists." "Bin Ladin Determined to Strike in U.S.," Wikipedia, http://en.wikipedia.org/wiki/Bin_Ladin_Determined_To_Strike_in_US.

35. *U.S. v. Ramzi Ahmed Yousef et al.,* S1293CR.180 (KTD), August 26, 1996.

36. The Feds were so desperate to keep that picture secret that in September 2002, when Associated Press reporter Jim Gomez express-couriered a copy of the lab report to John Solomon, the AP's deputy bureau chief in Washington, the U.S. Customs Service, acting on a tip from the FBI, took the almost unprecedented step of seizing the package from a FedEx facility in the Midwest. "The interception was improper and clandestine," complained AP president and CEO Louis D. Boccardi at the time. "A.P. Protests Government Seizure of Package Sent from One Reporter to Another," Associated Press, May 13, 2003. Only when Senator Chuck Grassley (R-IA) pushed for an FBI OPR investigation to be opened on the seizure did the Bureau withdraw its objection and apologize. The incident pointed out just how much the Feds wanted to keep secret any evidence that might prove the validity of the Yousef-Scarpa intelligence initiative. Pete Yost, "FBI Unit Probes Intercepted Package Case," *Washington Post,* April 23, 2003.

37. Author's interview with Flora Edwards, April 27, 2004.

38. http://www.peterlance.com/302/41196.htm.

39. Michael Arena and Silvia Adcock, "Probers Kept in the Dark," *Newsday,* August 24, 1996.

40. Jerry Capeci, "Mobster Gets 40-Year Term," New York *Daily News,* May 9, 1999.

41. *U.S. v. Ramzi Yousef and Eyad Ismoil,* affirmation of Patrick Fitzgerald, June 25, 1999, http://peterlance.com/Fitzgerald_Affirmation_6.25.99.pdf.

42. Denial of Recusal Motion, Judge Kevin Duffy, *U.S. v. Ramzi Ahmed Yousef and Eyad Ismoil,* S1293CR.180 (KTD).

43. *John Napoli v. U.S.,* "Petitioner's Supplement and Reply to Government's Memorandum in Opposition to Section 2255 Petition and Request for Evidentiary Hearing," Neil M. Shuster, August 2003, citing *U.S. v. Yousef,* 327 F. 3rd, 166–170 [C.A.2 (N.Y. 2003)]. Gov. App. 581–82, Napoli Ex F.

44. Silverman interview, June 12, 2006.

45. David Schaper, "Fitzgerald Leads Way on Plame Case," National Public Radio, July 28, 2005.

46. http://www.peterlance.com/Fitzgerald_Libel_Claim_Letters_HCP_Response.pdf.

47. Patrick Fitzgerald's Allegations and Peter Lance's reply:

The Allegations Regarding My Dealings with Gregory Scarpa

Triple Cross alleged that "I filed a false affidavit with a federal judge to conceal the purported 'fact' that the fatal crash of TWA 800 was really a terrorist attack to which I had been tipped in advance by an organized crime figure, and that I otherwise conspired with the National Transportation Safety Board, the 9/11 Commission and numerous others to hide the truth." (Fitzgerald letter at p. 2.)

Regarding that claim, you contend that "the Book never accuses you of the misconduct that you allege" (Jackson letter at p. 2). You then parsed statements in the book that contain the phrase "if Napoli's account is accurate . . ." and ". . . in my opinion" to state that "Lance sets forth certain allegations and states that if those allegations were true, then in his opinion, certain federal agencies and employees were engaged in wrongdoing. Lance is clearly permitted, as a matter of law, to set forth underlying statements of fact and then give his opinion based on those disclosed facts" (Jackson letter at p. 2).

I will not belabor the fantastically paranoid nature of Lance's theory that the victims of TWA 800 died as a result of a terrorist attack, but that a massive conspiracy—involving the leadership of the FBI, multiple federal prosecutors in different districts, the National Transportation Safety Board, the 9/11 Commission and others, aided and abetted by the press (save the heroic Lance)—falsely portrayed the deaths as the result of an accidental crash. I will focus on that part of the allegation which specifically defames me.

The facts appear to be that one organized crime inmate, Greg Scarpa, claimed to the government in 1996 that another incarcerated organized crime member, John Napoli, had direct access to information about the terrorist plans of terrorist Ramzi Yousef (p. 559-565).* The government, through me, later represented in a June 1999 affidavit that the information Scarpa provided was a scam because, among other things, Scarpa provided the information to Napoli for Napoli to furnish to the government as if Napoli had obtained it himself. (*Id.*) The government further contended that Scarpa sought to influence Napoli to testify—falsely—at an upcoming trial that Scarpa's father had carried out the murders that Scarpa himself was charged with.[†] (*Id.*)

In preparation for the book, Lance apparently spoke with Napoli who corroborated that, contrary to what Scarpa told the government, Napoli did not, in fact, have any access to Yousef. Lance specifically quotes Napoli as stating that "I never spoke to Ramzi. I never spoke to Ismoil. I never spoke to none of them. Zero. No conversations. Not one" (p. 312). Napoli also corroborated that Scarpa "had this great plan that I could testify for him and in return that he would give me information to bring to the Southern District." (*Id.*) Thus, if Napoli's account is accurate, Scarpa both obstructed justice—at the very least by providing false information to the government indicating that Napoli had received information directly from Yousef when he knew he did not—and committed the crime of offering something of value to a witness to influence testimony at a federal criminal trial. (See generally Title 18, United States Code. Section 201(b)(3).) Yet in Lance's unique style of "investigative journalism," faced with proof that Scarpa obstructed

---

* I note that my discussion here is limited to facts (or purported facts) I know to have appeared in the public record or to be discussed in *Triple Cross.*

† I also note that there were recent published accounts—which I do not know either to be true or false—that Scarpa was expected to testify at the recently concluded criminal trial of former FBI supervisor Lin DeVecchio that Scarpa in fact committed various murders for which he had previously been charged and which he denied under oath in prior testimony. If that were so, that would be additional reason not to believe Scarpa's account. However, the DeVecchio case was dismissed during trial without Scarpa testifying.

justice, Lance instead concludes that two federal prosecutors committed obstruction of justice:

> If Napoli's account is accurate, it appears that two senior federal prosecutors, Fitzgerald and Kelly, went along with a government story that characterized the Yousef-Scarpa Jr. intelligence as fraudulent . . . *the creation of the "hoax" and "scam" story by the Feds could, in my opinion, amount to a serious obstruction of justice.* (p. 313) (emphasis added).

In short, Lance takes a witness who exposes Scarpa as a fraud and treats him as corroboration of Scarpa. It is of no moment that Lance claims that Mr. Napoli adds to his account his claimed belief that the information coming from Yousef was genuine, as Napoli admits he never spoke to Yousef at all. Nor does it matter that Napoli denies saying to Mr. Kelly that the information was fraudulent—Napoli's own statements prove that Scarpa was fraudulently claiming that Napoli had access to Yousef. Nor is it significant that the information passed by Scarpa and Yousef to the government contained information about bomb formulas and drawings of explosives and timers. Mr. Lance conveniently overlooks the facts clear from the trial record (and other public record) that the government already had such information in its possession—something Yousef no doubt knew when he reviewed the discovery material and passed the information through Scarpa. Lance no doubt also knew this when he "pored" over the 40,000 pages of transcripts which he represented included the transcripts of Yousef's trial.

In any event, if my recollection of the public record is accurate, Scarpa later testified at his own trial in 1998, but was convicted of racketeering by the jury that heard his testimony. At sentencing, Judge Reena Raggi (then on the district court in the Eastern District of New York) rejected the truthfulness of Scarpa's trial testimony. Still later, Scarpa testified at a hearing in 2004 before Judge Jack B. Weinstein who has been quoted stating: "The court finds this witness [Scarpa] to be not credible." For good measure, I understand that a third federal judge, Judge Kevin Duffy of the Southern District of New York, found Scarpa's efforts at cooperation to have been fraudulent.

Author's Response to Fitzgerald's Claims

If there has ever been a "non-denial denial" by a public official, Fitzgerald's response to my Napoli revelation is a case in point. First of all, he attempts to undermine Napoli's claims that he never told the Feds the Yousef-Scarpa intel was a fabrication by impeaching his own witness's credibility. Keep in mind that, as per his June 1999 affirmation, Fitzgerald contended that Napoli was a key source for the "hoax" story and now he contends Napoli is not to be believed.

Second, he alleges that per "the trial record (and other public record)" the government "already had such information in its possession—something Yousef no doubt knew when he reviewed the discovery material and passed the information through Scarpa." But that doesn't explain how Greg Scarpa Jr., a wiseguy with a tenth-grade education, came into possession of bomb formulas and schematics that didn't surface at the Bojinka trial until *weeks* after he presented the intelligence to the Feds. It doesn't explain how Greg Jr. revealed details that could only have come from Ramzi Yousef and ignores the fact that Yousef, then on trial for capital crimes, had absolutely no motive for scamming the prosecutors. What would the fabrication of evidence gain him? Nothing. Most important, if the government already had the intelligence in its possession, as Fitzgerald contends, why, for eleven months, was the FBI so taken with it? Why did agents dutifully record the intel in dozens of 302 memos? If the "kites" had no value, why did the FBI first give Scarpa Jr. a camera to photograph them and later set up the elaborate Roma Corp. sting? Fitzgerald, in his letter threatening HarperCollins with a libel suit, doesn't answer any of those questions.

Third, it's not surprising that multiple federal judges believed the "hoax" and "scam" story proffered by Patrick Fitzgerald over Greg Scarpa Jr., a made member of the Mafia. But what is truly astonishing is the fact that Fitzgerald's primary source for the fabrication story was *also* a mob wiseguy—John Napoli—and that Napoli was so utterly credible in his insistence to me that he never accused Greg Jr. of scamming the Feds.

48. Silverman interview, April 13, 2004.
49. Author's interview with Lieutenant Colonel Anthony Shaffer, U.S. Army, November 28, 2005. An excerpt from the author's book *Triple Cross,* detailing Col. Shaffer's participation in Operation Able Danger can be accessed at http://peterlance.com/wordpress/?p=227.

CHAPTER 39: JUNIOR'S SECOND STING

1. *Victor J. Orena and Pasquale Amato v. U.S. 2255,* hearing before Judge Jack B. Weinstein, testimony of R. Lindley DeVecchio, May 20, 1996, transcript, 4.
2. Ibid., 5.
3. Selwyn Raab, "F.B.I. Agent Won't Testify at Mafia Figure's Hearing," *New York Times,* May 18, 1996.
4. Tom Robbins and Jerry Capeci, "Judge Frees Canary's Files," New York *Daily News,* May 25, 1996.
5. Al Guarte, "Former FBI Agent to Bare His Links with Mafia Killer," *New York Post,* January 12, 1997.
6. Selwyn Raab, "Ex-F.B.I. Official Is Pressured to Testify on Ties to Mobster," *New York Times,* January 26, 1997.
7. Author's interview with Larry Silverman, April 14, 2004.
8. James Barron, "Courthouse Gallery Honors Judge's Passion for Art," *New York Times,* September 29, 2010. "Judge Sifton, who died last year at age 74[,] . . . was the chief judge in Brooklyn from 1995 to 2000 and after he assumed senior status when he turned 65 in March 2000."
9. Helen Peterson, "Three Mob War Convictions Tossed," New York *Daily News,* February 20, 1997.
10. Lynette Holloway, "Conviction of 3 in Mob Overturned in Slayings," *New York Times,* February 20, 1997.
11. *U.S. v. Orena,* transcript of direct examination of R. Lindley DeVecchio by Gerald Shargel, February 28, 1997.
12. Al Guarte, "FBI Big Shots Knew Mob Rat Killed His Rivals: 'Mole,'" *New York Post,* March 1, 1997.
13. Author's interview with Andrew Orena, January 13, 2012.
14. Helen Peterson, "Didn't Leak to Mob, Retired G-Man Sez," New York *Daily News,* March 1, 1997.
15. *U.S. v. Victor J. Orena and Pasquale Amato,* Jack B. Weinstein, judgment, memorandum, and order, March 10, 1997, 33.

16. Ibid., 55.

17. Author's interview with Flora Edwards, January 13, 2012.

18. Weinstein, judgment, memorandum, and order, 72–73.

19. Jerry Capeci, "My Father Did It," New York *Daily News,* September 28, 1998.

20. Jerry Capeci, "Mobster Gets 40-Year Term," New York *Daily News,* May 9, 1999.

21. Indictment CR No. 86-00351, United States of American against Gregory Scarpa Jr., Grand Jury Charges for violation of 18, U.S. Code Sections 1029 (b)(2), 1029 (a) (1), (b)(1), 1029 (a)(3), (b)(1) and 1029 (e)(1), (2), (5). Signed by Reena Raggi, United States Attorney, Eastern District of New York, 1986.

22. Jerry Capeci, "I Spy," New York *Daily News,* October 19, 1998.

23. *U.S. v. Gregory Scarpa Jr.,* docket number 99-1312, decision of the U.S. Court of Appeals for the Second Circuit.

24. Ibid.

25. Author's interview with Frank Scarpa, February 15, 2012.

26. *Pasquale Amato and Victor Orena v. U.S.,* hearing before Judge Jack B. Weinstein, testimony of Gregory Scarpa Jr., January 7, 2004.

27. Ibid., 32, 55.

28. Ibid., 33.

29. Ibid., 56.

30. Greg B. Smith, "Family Wants Retrial for 'Different' Man," New York *Daily News,* September 21, 2003.

31. John Marzulli, "Mobster's Retrial Nixed," New York *Daily News,* January 16, 2004.

32. Edna Fernandes, "Supermax Prison, the Alcatraz of the Rockies," London *Sunday Times,* May 4, 2006.

33. Author's interview with Gregory Scarpa Jr., March 28, 2012.

34. Stephen P. Dresch, "Report of Explosive Cache Secreted by Terry Lynn Nichols," March 23, 2005; author's interview with Angela Clemente, April 8, 2005.

35. Mark Sherman, "FBI Waited to Check Out Tip on Nichols," Associated Press, April 14, 2005.

36. John Solomon, "Explosives Found in Former Home of Terry Nichols," Associated Press, April 2, 2005.

37. Sherman, "FBI Waited to Check Out Tip."

38. Clemente interview.

39. Shelly Murphy, "Miami Jury Convicts Connolly," *Boston Globe,* November 7, 2008.

40. William LaForm, "Former Lynnfielder Connolly Ends Federal Sentence Next Week," *Lynnfield–North Reading Patch,* June 24, 2011.

41. Shelly Murphy, "Judge Testifies Connolly Helped Decimate the Mafia," *Boston Globe,* October 14, 2008.

42. Ibid.

43. Dan Kennedy, "O Brother, Where Art Thou? Making Sense of Bill Bulger's Testimony and the Media Frenzy It Inspired," *Boston Phoenix,* June 27, 2003.

44. "John B. Callahan," profile, *Boston Globe,* September 17, 2008, http://www.boston.com/news/specials/whitey/articles/profile_of_john_callahan/.

45. Shelly Murphy, "Sides Make Case to Connolly Jurors," *Boston Globe,* November 4, 2008.

46. Shelly Murphy, "Cases Disappear as FBI Looks Away," *Boston Globe,* July 22, 1998.

47. Statement of Charles J. Hynes, press conference announcing indictments of DeVecchio, Sobel, and Sinagra, March 30, 2006.

48. Ibid.

49. Peter Lance, *Cover Up: What the Government Is Still Hiding About the War on Terror* (New York: ReganBooks, 2004), 1–128.

50. Special Agent Chris Favo, FBI 302 memo, February 6, 1994, 3.

51. Jonathan Dienst, "Brooklyn DA Opens Mob Leak Investigation," WNBC.com, January 4, 2006.

52. Press release, "King's County District Attorney Charles J. Hynes Announces Murder Indictment Against Retired FBI Agent and Two Mob Hit Men in Multiple Murder Cases," March 30, 2006.

53. Ibid.

54. Ibid.; *People v. R. Lindley DeVecchio and John Sinagra,* indictment no. 6825/2005, unsealed March 30, 2006.

55. Carole E. Lee, "Who Is R. Lindley DeVecchio?" *Sarasota Herald-Tribune,* January 21, 2007.

56. "Kings County District Attorney" press release, March 30, 2006.

57. R. Lindley DeVecchio and Charles Brandt, *We're Going to Win This Thing: The Shocking Frame-up of a Mafia Crime Buster* (New York: Berkley, 2011), 9–17.

58. William Rashbaum, "F.B.I. Colleagues Help Ex-Agent Post Bail," *New York Times,* March 31, 2006.

59. Senator Charles Grassley (R-IA), statement before the U.S. Senate Judiciary Committee, FBI Oversight Hearing, May 2, 2006.

60. Ibid.

61. Jerry Capeci, "Former Mob-Busting FBI Agent to Be Charged with Murder in Mafia Hits," *New York Sun,* March 9, 2006.

62. Murray Weiss, " 'Mob' Fed's Filthy Lucre—FBI Agent Cashed in as Mafia Slay Mole: DA," *New York Post,* March 30, 2006.

63. Nanci L. Katz, "G-Man Denies Errands for Mob," New York *Daily News,* March 31, 2006.

64. Angela Mosconi, "Boss: Ex-Agent No Thug," New York *Daily News,* April 16, 2006.

65. A PDF of the Friends of Lin DeVecchio website can be accessed at http://peterlance .com/Friends_of_Lin_Bail_Hearing_3_1_07.pdf.

66. Shelly Murphy, " 'Donnie Brasco' Refuses to Testify in Connolly Trial," *Boston Globe,* October 15, 2008. When the trial judge denied Pistone's demand that photographers not be allowed to take pictures of his testimony, he withdrew his offer. As *Globe* reporter Murphy wrote, "His photo is all over the Internet, most recently on a blog promoting his alleged efforts to solve the 1990 theft of $300 million worth of artwork from Boston's Isabella Stewart Gardner Museum. But today, Joseph D. Pistone refused to take the witness stand at the state murder trial of his longtime friend, former FBI Agent John J. Connolly Jr., because the judge rejected his request for an order prohibiting the media from filming or photographing him as he testified." Pistone's undoctored photo was also published in the photo section of DeVecchio's book *We're Going to Win This Thing* (photo section, p. 4).

67. Alan Feuer, "In Role Reversal, Ex-F.B.I. Agents Align Themselves with Defendant," *New York Times,* September 11, 2006.

68. "Court Battle to Revoke Bail of Reputed Mob Boss Continues," Associated Press, May 3, 1986, https://www.ncjrs.gov/App/publications/Abstract.aspx?id=166510.

69. DeVecchio and Brandt, *We're Going to Win This Thing,* 16.

70. Fredric Dannen, "The G-Man and the Hit Man," *New Yorker,* December 16, 1996.

71. DeVecchio and Brandt, *We're Going to Win This Thing,* 168.
72. Lee, "Who Is R. Lindley DeVecchio?"
73. Michael Brick, "Agent Accused in Mob Murders Seeks Immunity," *New York Times,* April 11, 2006.
74. Author's interview with Ellen Resnick, February 21, 2012.
75. Addendum: Criminal Investigative Division, April 8, 1987, requesting additional authority for payment to Gregory Scarpa Sr. It describes broadly the "services" the informant provided in three major investigations identified as "Shooting Star," "Gambino Family," and "Starquest."

CHAPTER 40: THE COVER UP VIRUS
1. *People v. R. Lindley DeVecchio,* case no. 06-CR-235 (FB), memorandum and order of Frederic Block, January 9, 2007, 5, http://www.peterlance.com/Grancio_Block_DeVecchio_decision-1_9_07.pdf.
2. Ibid., 7.
3. *Colorado v. Symes,* 286 U.S. 510 (1932).
4. Block, memorandum and order, January 9, 2007, 21.
5. Michael Brick, "From Jail Cell, a Convict Challenges a Prosecutor," *New York Times,* March 16, 2006.
6. Ibid.
7. A. G. Sulzberger, "Facing Misconduct Claims, Brooklyn Prosecutor Agrees to Free Man Held 15 Years," *New York Times,* June 8, 2010; Len Levitt, "Mike Mad, Joe Worse," *New York Confidential,* June 7, 2010; Tom Robbins, "Jabbar Collins to Go Free on 1994 Murder Rap as Judge Scores Brooklyn DA," *Village Voice,* June 8, 2010.
8. Alex Ginsberg, "Canary Set to Peck at DeVecchio," *New York Post,* February 2, 2007.
9. Author's interview with Tommy Dades, November 12, 2007.
10. Jerry Capeci, "In FBI Murder Trial, Some Missteps and One Big Relief," *New York Sun,* March 22, 2007.
11. Dades interview.
12. "Dades Facing Murder Charges," *New York Post,* March 15, 2007.
13. Ibid.
14. Capeci, "In FBI Murder Trial, Some Missteps."
15. Heidi Singer and Alex Ginsberg, "Mob-Busting Prober Quits Brooklyn DA," *New York Post,* May 25, 2007.
16. Larry Celona, "DA Boots Prober-Turned-Mob-Sweetie," *New York Post,* February 19, 2007.
17. Ibid.
18. Bradley Hope, "DA's Office Gets a Warning over Office's Ethics Procedures," *New York Sun,* February 20, 2007.
19. "Former 'Radical' Judge Presides over Former FBI Agent's Trial," Associated Press, October 2, 2007.
20. Capeci, "In FBI Murder Trial, Some Missteps."
21. *Kastigar v. U.S.,* 406 U.S. 441 (1972).
22. *Oliver North v. Lawrence E. Walsh,* "Independent Counsel," 881 F2d 1088, U.S. Court of Appeals, July 25, 1989; Gerald S. Greenberg, ed., *Historical Encyclopedia of U.S. Independent Counsel Investigations* (Westport, CT: Greenwood Press, 2000).
23. Lawrence E. Walsh, *Firewall: The Iran-Contra Conspiracy and Cover-Up* (New York: W. W. Norton, 1997).

24. Capeci, "In FBI Murder Trial, Some Missteps."
25. William Rashbaum, "F.B.I. Colleagues Help Ex-Agent Post Bail," *New York Times,* March 31, 2006.
26. Alex Ginsberg, "Mob-Hit Case Is in Peril," *New York Post,* May 7, 2007.
27. Sworn affidavit of Detective Tommy Dades (ret.), February 26, 2007.
28. Ginsberg, "Mob-Hit Case Is in Peril."
29. Michael Brick, "Long Hidden, Stories Clash over Killing Tied to the Mob," *New York Times,* May 17, 2007.
30. Austin Fenner and Alex Ginsberg, "DeVecchio Cop Tryst Bombshell," *New York Post,* May 18, 2007.
31. Michael Brick, "At Murder Trial, Prosecutors Doubt Police and Each Other," *New York Times,* May 30, 2007.
32. Alex Ginsberg, "Mob-Case Judge Gives DA a Whack," *New York Post,* May 30, 2007.
33. Charles Sweeney, "Two Mob-Related Murder Cases on Rocks," *Brooklyn Daily Eagle,* June 4, 2007.
34. Alex Ginsberg, "'Mob-Fed' Defendant Passes on Plea," *New York Post,* June 8, 2007.
35. Alex Ginsberg, "Slay Rap KO'd in 'Mob-Fed' Shocker: Judge Blasts 'Too Late' Cops and Brooklyn DA," *New York Post,* June 12, 2007.
36. Scott Shifrel, "Beats Slay Rap in 'Last of DeVecchio Debacle,'" New York *Daily News,* June 13, 2008.
37. Jerry Capeci, "Mob Scion May Bolster Turncoat Case," *New York Sun,* June 28, 2007.
38. Download from http://www.peterlance.com/Peter_Lance/GREG_JR_MURAD .html.
39. Christopher Mattiace, e-mail to Society of Former Special Agents of the FBI, March 1, 2007.
40. Author's interview with FBI Special Agent James Whalen (ret.), March 1, 2007.
41. Download from http://www.peterlance.com/Peter_Lance/DeVecchios_legal_fees .html.
42. William Sherman, "You Pay G-Man's Legal Bills," New York *Daily News,* March 6, 2007.
43. 28 C.F.R. 50.15(a) and 50.16.
44. Letter and answers to questions posed to FBI Director Robert S. Mueller III, to Senator Patrick J. Leahy, chairman, U.S. Senate Judiciary Committee, from Brian A. Benczkowski, principal deputy assistant attorney general, January 25, 2008, 72.
45. Letter dated July 21, 2010, from Ronald Welch, assistant attorney general, to John Conyers Jr., chairman, Committee on the Judiciary, Office of the Inspector General and the Office of Professional Responsibility for the Department of Justice; "An Investigation into the Removal of the U.S. Attorney in 2006," unclassified report on the President's Surveillance Program, July 10, 2009, prepared by the Office of the Inspector General of the Department of Defense, Department of Transportation, CIA, National Security Agency, and Office of the Director of National Intelligence.
46. Nina Totenberg, "Report: Ex-AG Gonzales Mishandled Classified Info," National Public Radio, September 2, 2008.
47. "A Review of the Federal Bureau of Investigation's Use of National Security Letters," U.S. Department of Justice, Office of the Inspector General, retrieved April 12, 2007, http://en.wikipedia.org/wiki/Alberto_Gonzales - cite_ref-usdoj_42-0.
48. "Bush Ally Gonzales Resigns Post," BBC.com, August 27, 2007; "Republican Support for Attorney General Erodes," MSNBC.com, March 25, 2007.

49. Ibid.
50. Author's interview with Flora Edwards, January 13, 2012.
51. "Trial Starts for 'Mafia Cops' Accused of Murder," Associated Press, March 13, 2006; "Prosecutor: Cops Went on Decades-Long Crime Spree at Bidding of Mobsters," Associated Press, published on MSNBC.com, http://www.msnbc.msn .com/id/10958649/ns/us_news-crime_and_courts/t/trial-starts-mafia-cops-accused -murder/#.T3Im2I60dJ8.
52. Transcript of conference call among Anthony Casso, Lou Eppolito, Stephen Caracappa, Bettina Schein, and Rae Downes Koshetz, March 30, 2006.
53. Ibid., 14.
54. "NYPD 'Mafia Cops' Convicted of Murders," Associated Press, April 7, 2006.
55. Jonathan Dienst, "Brooklyn DA Opens Mob Leak Investigation," WNBC.com, January 4, 2006.
56. Rashbaum, "F.B.I. Colleagues Help Ex-Agent Post Bail."
57. John Marzulli, "2 Cops Who Killed for Mafia: Feds Say Retired Detective Pals Are Linked to at Least 8 Murders," New York *Daily News,* March 9, 2005.
58. Ed Bradley, "Ex-Mob Boss Points a Finger," *60 Minutes,* CBS News, April 11, 2005.
59. Michael Fleming, "Wolf, NBC Universal calling 'Cops,' " *Variety,* April 17, 2007.
60. William Oldham, *The Brotherhoods: The True Story of Two Cops Who Murdered for the Mafia* (New York: Scribner, 2006); Greg B. Smith, *Mob Cops: The Shocking Rise and Fall of New York's "Mafia Cops"* (New York: Berkley, 2006); Jimmy Breslin, *The Good Rat: A True Story* (New York: Ecco, 2008); Tommy Dades and Mike Vecchione with David Fisher, *Friends of the Family: The Inside Story of the Mafia Cops Case* (New York: William Morrow, 2009).
61. Michael Fleming, "Col Corners Corrupt Cops," *Variety,* April 21, 2005.
62. Ibid.
63. Dades, Vecchione, and Fisher, *Friends of the Family.*
64. Friends of Lin DeVecchio website, March 1, 2007. Download from http://peterlance .com/Friends_of_Lin_Motives_3_1_07.pdf.
65. Ibid.
66. John Marzulli, "Tell-All Risks Mob Cop Case: Assistant DA's Book May Cut Trial Options," New York *Daily News,* July 11, 2006.
67. Ibid.
68. Alan Feuer, "Judge Acquits 2 Ex-Detectives in Mob Killings," *New York Times,* July 1, 2006.
69. E-mail to author from Andy Kurins, June 14, 2006.
70. Author's interview with Noel Downey, March 30, 2006.
71. Grover memorandum, January 29, 2007, 38.
72. *People of the State of New York v. R. Lindley DeVecchio,* affidavit in opposition to remand, Douglas Grover, June 23, 2006.
73. Ibid., 16.
74. *People v. R. Lindley DeVecchio,* subpoena duces tecum served on Peter Lance June 23, 2007, dated June 12, 2007, by Mark A. Bederow, Thompson Hine, LLP, attorney for the defendant. Download from http://peterlance.com/Kastigar_DeVecchio%27s_ subpoena_of_PL.pdf.
75. *People v. R. Lindley DeVecchio,* pretrial hearing, statement of Douglas Grover, April 20, 2007, 21.
76. Ibid., 25–26, 21.
77. *People v. R. Lindley DeVecchio,* memorandum of law, Douglas Grover, January 29, 2007.

78. Peter Lance, *Cover Up: What the Government Is Still Hiding About the War on Terror* (New York: ReganBooks, 2004), 84.
79. Bill Moushey, "Switching Sides," *Post-Gazette,* December 1, 1998.
80. Lance, *Cover Up,* 87, citing Fredric Dannen, "The G-Man and the Hit Man," *New Yorker,* December 16, 1996.
81. Linda Stasi, "Show's Finale Fires 'Blanks,'" *New York Post,* June 11, 2007: "With his wife and the giggling tykes looking on, Phil [Leotardo] gets out, looks back and is then shot at point-blank range by Tony's guy. . . . Ironically, when Harris gets word of the hit, he sputters, 'We're gonna win this one,' quoting a real-life alleged dirty fed, Lindley DeVecchio."
82. Author's interview with Flora Edwards, November 3, 2011.
83. "Ex-Newser Fights FBI-Mole Case Subpoena," New York *Daily News,* August 2, 2007.
84. Charles Sweeney, "Author/Reporter, Former Prosecutor, Testify in Hearing on Ex-FBI Agent's Murder Indictment," *Brooklyn Daily Eagle,* August 13, 2007.
85. *People v. R. Lindley DeVecchio,* Kastigar hearing, testimony of Noel Downey, August 8, 2007, 75–78.
86. *People v. R. Lindley DeVecchio,* Kastigar hearing, testimony of Peter Lance, August 12, 2007, 270.
87. Ibid., 304.
88. Jerry Capeci, "Gaffe Benches G-Man Prosecutors," *New York Sun,* September 6, 2007.
89. Ibid.
90. Edwards interview, November 3, 2011.
91. Author's interview with Anthony Casso, September 23, 2011.
92. Author's interview with Andrew Orena, January 13, 2012.
93. Alice McQuillan, "Prosecution: Retired FBI Agent Involved with Murder, Robbery, Prostitution," WNBC.com, October 1, 2007.
94. "Former 'Radical' Judge Presides over Former FBI Agent's Trial."

CHAPTER 41: AGENT OF DEATH

1. Alex Ginsburg, "Mob Mirth at Moll's Slay," *New York Post,* October 16, 2007.
2. Steve Dunleavy, "Dirt Bag Is Grime of Century," *New York Post,* October 16, 2007.
3. Lester Holt, "Son of Sam 35 Years Later," *NBC Nightly News,* http://video.msnbc.msn.com/nightly-news/43956634#43956634.
4. Scott Shifrel, "Celebrated Cop Laughs Off Memo Alleging Mafia Ties," New York *Daily News,* October 27, 2007.
5. Ibid.
6. Author's interview with NYPD detective Joe Coffey (ret.), February 13, 2010.
7. Michael Brick, "On Trial, Ex-FBI Agent Faces Years of Scrutiny over Mob Killings," *New York Times,* October 16, 2007; Ginnine Fried LinkedIn profile, http://www.linkedin.com/pub/ginnine-fried/3/b64/83a.
8. Jim Dwyer, "Gustin Reichbach, Judge with a Radical History, Dies at 65," *New York Times,* July 17, 2012.
9. Fredric Dannen, "The G-Man and the Hit Man," *New Yorker,* December 16, 1996.
10. R. Lindley DeVecchio and Charles Brandt, *We're Going to Win This Thing: The Shocking Frame-up of a Mafia Crime Buster* (New York: Berkley, 2011), 68.
11. *People v. R. Lindley DeVecchio,* October 15, 2007, transcript, 4–5.
12. Ibid., 5.
13. Ibid., 15–16.
14. Ibid., 19.

15. Ibid., 24.

16. Ibid., 31.

17. Ibid., 35.

18. Ibid., 36–37.

19. Ibid., 38–39.

20. Ibid., 40.

21. Author's interview with Flora Edwards, January 13, 2012.

22. *People v. R. Lindley DeVecchio,* October 15, 2007, 69.

23. Press release, Kings County district attorney, March 30, 2006, transcript of press conference in which DA Hynes repeated that allegation; Michael Brick, "Ex-FBI Agent's Murder Trial Fizzles, as Does Chief Witness," *New York Times,* November 1, 2007.

24. Heidi Singer and Alex Ginsberg, "Mob-Busting Prober Quits Brooklyn DA," *New York Post,* May 25, 2007.

25. *People v. R. Lindley DeVecchio,* October 15, 2007, 70.

26. Ibid., 188.

27. Ibid., 190.

28. Ibid., 422.

29. Author's interview with Andrew Orena, January 13, 2012.

30. Ibid., 275.

31. Ibid., 277.

32. Special Agent Raymond Andjich, sworn statement, April 7, 1994, 3.

33. *People v. R. Lindley DeVecchio,* October 15, 2007, 297.

34. Ibid., 307.

35. Andjich, sworn statement, 6.

36. *People v. R. Lindley DeVecchio,* October 15, 2007, 333.

37. Ibid., 370.

38. Special Agent Jeffrey W. Tomlinson, sworn affidavit, April 7, 1994, 8–9.

39. *People v. R. Lindley DeVecchio,* October 15, 2007, 412–13.

40. Tomlinson, sworn affidavit, April 7, 1994, 8.

41. *People v. R. Lindley DeVecchio,* October 15, 2007, 433.

42. Author's interview with Tommy Dades, November 12, 2007.

43. *U.S. v. William Cutolo et al.,* testimony of Detective Pat Maggiore, October 1994, transcript, 4271.

44. Andrew Orena interview.

45. *People v. R. Lindley DeVecchio,* October 15, 2007, 473.

46. Ibid., 480.

47. Ibid., 502.

48. Chris Favo, sworn statement, July 7, 1995, 3.

49. *People v. R. Lindley DeVecchio,* October 15, 2007, 505.

50. Ibid., 525.

51. Ibid.

52. Ibid., 588.

53. Ibid., 611.

54. Scott Shifrel, "Mob Killer Becomes a Crybaby: Weepy Testimony of His Lost Life and Murderous Boss," New York *Daily News,* October 19, 2007.

55. *People v. R. Lindley DeVecchio,* October 15, 2007, 716.

56. Ibid., 714.

57. Ibid., 774.

58. Ibid., 777.
59. Ibid., 1646.
60. Ibid., 1648.
61. Ibid., 1650.
62. Ibid.
63. Ibid., 1651.
64. Ibid., 1655.
65. Ibid., 1658.
66. Priscilla Beaulieu Presley and Sandra Harmon, *Elvis and Me* (New York: Penguin, 1986).
67. *People v. R. Lindley DeVecchio,* October 15, 2007, 1709–14.
68. Special Agent Chris Favo, FBI 302 memo, February 6, 1994, 7.
69. Ibid.
70. Jerry Capeci, "Ex-FBI Agent Probed in Mob Hits," *New York Sun,* January 12, 2006.
71. Matt Nestel and Alex Ginsberg, "DA Played 'Dumb D-Dum Dumb,'" *New York Post,* November 3, 2007.
72. "Ex-Newser Fights FBI-Mole Case Subpoena," New York *Daily News,* August 2, 2007.
73. *People v. R. Lindley DeVecchio,* October 15, 2007, 1716–17.
74. Ibid.
75. Ibid., 1820–22.
76. Ibid., 1847.
77. Ibid., 1848.
78. Author's interview with Mike Vecchione, October 30, 2007.

CHAPTER 42: G-MAN STICKS IT TO DA
1. Tom Robbins, "Tall Tales of a Mafia Mistress," *Village Voice,* October 30, 2007.
2. William Rashbaum, "F.B.I. Colleagues Help Ex-Agent Post Bail," *New York Times,* March 31, 2006.
3. Jerry Capeci, "G-Man Wins: Tapes Foil Mob Moll," *New York Sun,* November 1, 2007.
4. *People v. R. Lindley DeVecchio,* October 15, 2007, transcript, 2001–2002.
5. Ibid., 2007.
6. Author's interview with Flora Edwards, January 13, 2012.
7. Author's interview with Andrew Orena, January 13, 2012.
8. Michael Brick, "Ex-F.B.I. Agent's Murder Trial Fizzles, as Does Chief Witness," *New York Times,* November 1, 2007.
9. Alex Ginsberg, "DeVecchio Off Hook," *New York Post,* October 31, 2007.
10. Alex Ginsberg, "Moll Rat Is a Tape Worm," *New York Post,* November 2, 2007.
11. Scott Shifrel, William Sherman, and Helen Kennedy, "Tapes Show Mob Moll Made It Up," New York *Daily News,* November 1, 2007.
12. Capeci, "G-Man Wins."
13. Alex Ginsberg, "Up Yours: G-Man Sticks It to DA with Toast at Mob-Slay Site," *New York Post,* November 2, 2007.
14. Scott Shifrel, "Ex-News Reporters Step Forward with Crucial Recordings," New York *Daily News,* November 1, 2007.
15. Alex Ginsberg, "Moll Tape a Real Killer," *New York Post,* November 1, 2007: "Sources familiar with the tapes said Schiro specifically says DeVecchio had nothing to do with the 1987 murder of Scarpa protégé-gone-bad Joseph 'Joe Brewster' DeDomenico"; Shifrel, Sherman, and Kennedy, "Tapes Show Mob Moll Made It Up": "Testimony of Linda Schiro implicated Lindley DeVecchio in four mob hits.

But a 1997 taped interview she gave to reporters Jerry Capeci and Tom Robbins contradicted her claims in three cases, [including] the 1987 murder of Colombo soldier Joe DeDomenico."

16. Capeci, "G-Man Wins."

17. *People v. R. Lindley DeVecchio,* testimony of Linda Schiro, October 29, 2007, transcript, 1615.

18. Ibid., 1617.

19. Ibid., 1630.

20. Supervisory Special Agents Kevin P. Donovan and Robert J. O'Brien, FBI 302 memo, William Meli, June 13, 1994, 6.

21. Robbins, "Tall Tales."

22. Al Guarte, "FBI Big Shots Knew Mob Rat Killed His Rivals," *New York Post,* March 1, 1977; *U.S. v. Michael Sessa,* testimony of R. Lindley DeVecchio, November 2, 1992, transcript, 118–19.

23. "Transcript from Linda Schiro's Conversations with Reporters," New York *Daily News,* November 2, 2007, http://www.nydailynews.com/news/crime/transcript-linda-schiro-conversations-reporters-article-1.256537.

24. Ibid.

25. Shifrel, Sherman, and Kennedy, "Tapes Show Moll Made It Up."

26. Scott Shifrel, "Special Prosecutor Appointed to Probe Linda Schiro Perjury Charge," New York *Daily News,* November 8, 2007.

27. Bob Garfield, "The Fed, the Mobster, the Mistress and the Reporter," OntheMedia .org, November 2, 2007, http://www.onthemedia.org/2007/nov/02/the-fed-the -mobster-the-mistress-and-the-reporter/transcript/.

28. Andrew Orena interview, January 13, 2012.

29. Frank Lombardi and Tracy O'Connor, "Hynes Is Having Second Thoughts on Botched Case," New York *Daily News,* November 2, 2007.

30. Michael Brick, "How the Murder Case Against a Former F.B.I. Supervisor Collapsed," *New York Times,* November 2, 2007.

31. Matt Nestel and Alex Ginsberg, "DA Played 'Dumb D-Dum Dumb,'" *New York Post,* November 3, 2007.

32. Jerry Capeci, "Cop Still Treading Hot Water," New York *Daily News,* November 8, 1994.

33. Scott Shifrel, "Ex-News Reporters Step Forward with Crucial Recordings," New York *Daily News,* November 1, 2007.

34. Author's interview with James Whalen, May 19, 2011.

35. Michael Daly, "For a Victim's Family It's the Cruelest Halloween Trick," New York *Daily News,* November 1, 2007.

36. Gustin Reichbach, decision and order of dismissal, *People v. R. Lindley DeVecchio,* November 1, 2007, http://online.wsj.com/public/resources/documents/reichbach.pdf. See Appendix H.

37. Ginsberg, "Up Yours."

38. Curtis Sliwa, interview with R. Lindley DeVecchio, *Curtis Sliwa in the Morning,* Radio AM 970 (Hasbrouck Heights, NJ), May 10, 2011.

39. Judge Leslie Crocker Snyder (ret.), "Report of the Special District Attorney in the Matter of the Investigation of Linda Schiro," October 22, 2008.

40. Ibid.

41. Warden Robert A. Hood, letter to the author, July 6, 2004.

42. Warden Robert A. Hood, letter to the author, August 10, 2004.

43. Sandra Harmon, *Mafia Son: The Scarpa Mob Family, the FBI, and a Story of Betrayal* (New York: St. Martin's Press, 2009).

44. Author's interview with Gregory Scarpa Jr., April 9, 2012.

CHAPTER 43: THE SON ALSO RISES

1. *U.S. v. Gregory Scarpa Jr.,* trial testimony, October 13, 1988; *U.S. v. Gregory Scarpa Jr.,* sealed affirmation, April 29, 1999; sworn affidavit, March 1, 2002; affidavit in support of the petitioner's motion for the appointment of counsel, May 9, 2002; affidavit of Gregory Scarpa Jr. sworn before a notary at the ADX Florence prison, July 30, 2002; *Pasquale Amato and Victor Orena v. U.S.,* hearing before Judge Jack B. Weinstein, testimony of Gregory Scarpa Jr., January 7, 2004.

2. Author's interview with Gregory Scarpa Jr., March 28, 2012.

3. R. Lindley DeVecchio, FBI 209 memo for Top Echelon (TE) informant designated "NY3461," July 1, 1980, 2–3: "SOURCE WAS CLOSED BY COMMUNICATION DATED MAY 5, 1975. IT IS NOTED THAT APPROXIMATELY SIX MONTHS HAVE BEEN REQUIRED TO DISCREETLY RE-CONTACT THE SOURCE AND TO PURSUADE [*sic*] HIM TO RESUME FURNISHING INFORMATION WHICH IS OF EXTREMELY HIGH QUALITY AND UNOBTAINABLE FROM ANY OTHER CURRENT NYO SOURCE."

4. Author's interview with Gregory Scarpa Jr., April 3, 2012.

5. Memorandum from special agent in charge, FBI New York Office, to director, FBI. Subject: Gregory Scarpa. Top Echelon (TE) Criminal Informant Program, New York Division, November 24, 1967, 7.

6. Sworn affidavit of Gregory Scarpa Jr., March 1, 2002, 2.

7. Author's interview with Gregory Scarpa Jr., April 6, 2012.

8. Ibid.

9. Scarpa affidavit, March 1, 2002.

10. Scarpa interview, April 3, 2012.

11. Author's interview of Gregory Scarpa Jr., April 9, 2012.

12. "Edward R. Korman," Wikipedia, http://en.wikipedia.org/wiki/Edward_R._Korman.

13. Letter from Assistant U.S. Attorney Ellen Corcella to defense counsel, *U.S. v. Victor M. Orena et al.,* May 8, 1995, admitting to eight possible disclosures of FBI intelligence by Supervisory Special Agent R. Lindley DeVecchio to Gregory Scarpa. See Chapter 37, p. 410.

14. Author's interview of Gregory Scarpa Jr., June 4, 2012.

AFTERWORD

1. Jack Shafer, "Who Said it First? Journalism Is the 'First Rough Draft of History,'" Slate.com, August 30, 2010.

2. James Risen, "Traces of Terror: The Intelligence Reports; Sept. 11 Suspect May Be Relative of '93 Plot Leader," *New York Times,* June 5, 2002.

3. Peter Lance, *1000 Years for Revenge: International Terrorism and the FBI: The Untold Story* (New York: ReganBooks, 2003), 232–302. The book's thirty-two-page illustrated timeline documents how both attacks on the Twin Towers were bankrolled by al-Qaeda, http://www.peterlance.com/1000_Years_Timeline.pdf.

4. *Final Report of the National Commission on Terrorist Attacks Upon the United States,* Staff Statement 15, "Overview of the Enemy," 5.

5. Patrick Fitzgerald interview, transcript, *Inside 9/11,* Towers Productions Inc./National Geographic Channel, airdate August 22, 2005.

6. Benjamin Weiser, "In Federal Court, a Docket Number for Global Terror," *New York Times,* April 10, 2011.

7. Ibid.

8. "New York Terrorism Indictments," *New York Times,* http://www.nytimes.com/interactive/2011/04/11/nyregion/20110411-indict-docs.html?ref=nyregion.

9. *U.S. v. Omar Abdel Rahman et al.,* S5 93 Cr. 191 (MBM), February 7, 1995.

10. John Kinfer, "Police Say Kahane Suspect Took Anti-Depressant Drugs," *New York Times,* November 9, 1990.

11. Peter Lance, *Triple Cross: How Bin Laden's Master Spy Penetrated the CIA, the Green Berets, and the FBI* (New York: Harper, 2009).

12. Author's interview with FBI Special Agent Jack Cloonan (ret.), for *Triple Cross,* June 1, 2006.

13. *U.S. v. Ali Mohamed,* S(7) 98CR.1023 (LBS) Sealed Complaint, September 1998. Affidavit of Daniel Coleman, FBI Special Agent, bin Laden unit New York Office. The complaint can be downloaded as a pdf from http://www.peterlance.com/Ali_Mohamed_Coleman_affidavit_9_98.pdf.

14. *U.S. v. Ali Mohamed,* S(7) 98 Cr. 1023 (LBS), transcript of plea session, U.S. District Court, Southern District of New York, October 20, 2000.

15. Joseph P. Fried, "Sheik Sentenced to Life in Prison in Bombing Plot," *New York Times,* January 18, 1996.

16. Questions about the Sheikh's U.S. entry surfaced publicly in early 1993 and continued throughout the year following the bombing of the World Trade Center on February 26, 1993, and the Sheikh's surrender to federal agents on July 3, 1993. Chris Hedges, "A Cry of Islamic Fury, Taped in Brooklyn for Cairo," *New York Times,* January 7, 1993; Timothy Carney and Mansoor Ijaz, "Intelligence Failure? Let's Go Back to Sudan," *Washington Post,* June 30, 2002; James C. McKinley Jr., "Islamic Leader on U.S. Terrorist List in Brooklyn," *New York Times,* December 16, 1990; James Risen, "Case of Spy in Anti-Terrorist Mission Points Up CIA's Perils," *Los Angeles Times,* February 11, 1996.

17. Mary B. W. Tabor, "Slaying in Brooklyn Linked to Militants," *New York Times,* April 11, 1993.

18. Steven Emerson, *American Jihad: The Terrorists Living Among Us* (New York: Free Press, 2002), 128–130.

19. "Profile: Al-Kifah Refugee Center," History Commons, http://www.historycommons.org/entity.jsp?entity=al-kifah_refugee_center.

20. "Meir Kahane," Wikipedia, http://en.wikipedia.org/wiki/Meir_Kahane.

21. FBI 302 memo on the contents seized from Nosair's house on November 8, 1990. The 302 was originally dated November 13, 1990.

22. Daniel Benjamin and Steven Simon, *The Age of Sacred Terror* (New York: Random House, 2002), 6.

23. Ralph Blumenthal, "Clues Hinting at Terror Ring Were Ignored," *New York Times,* August 27, 1993.

24. Joint Inquiry Statement of Staff Director Eleanor Hill, October 8, 2002; Greg B. Smith, "Bin Laden Bankrolled Kahane Killer Defense," New York *Daily News,* October 9, 2002.

25. Jailan Halawai, "Jihad Implicated in U.S. Embassy Bombings," *Al Ahram Weekly,* May 27–June 2, 1999.

26. Jim Dwyer, David Kocieniewski, Deidre Murphy, and Peg Tyre, *Two Seconds Under the World* (New York: Crown, 1994), 151.

27. Hedges, "A Cry of Islamic Fury."

28. Interview with Tommy Corrigan, NYPD-JTTF (ret.), for *Triple Cross* documentary, June 13, 2006.

29. Dwyer, Kocieniewski, Murphy, and Tyre, *Two Seconds Under the World.*

30. Tabor, "Slaying in Brooklyn Linked to Militants."

31. Peter Lance, "The Spy Who Came in for the Heat," *Playboy,* September 2010. A PDF of the article can be accessed at http://www.peterlance.com/wordpress/?p=99.

32. *U.S. v. Mohammed A. Salameh, Nidal Ayyad, Mahmoud Abouhalima, also known as Mahmoud Abu Halima, Ahmad Mohammad Ajaj, also known as Khurram Khan, Defendants-Appellants, Ramzi Ahmed Yousef, Bilal Alkaisi, also known as Bilal Elqisi, Abdul Rahman Yasin, also known as Aboud,* Defendants nos. 94-1312 to 94-1315, argued Dec. 18 and 19, 1997–August 04, 1998.

33. It was played during an interview with Salem on Fox News, August 13, 2010, and can be accessed at http://peterlance.com/wordpress/?p=803.

34. Joseph P. Fried, "Sheikh and 9 Followers Guilty of a Conspiracy of Terrorism," *New York Times,* October 2, 1995; Mary B. W. Tabor, "Transcript of Tapes Reveals Sheik Talked of Merits of Bomb Targets," *New York Times,* August 4, 1993.

35. Tabor, "Slaying in Brooklyn Linked to Militants."

36. Mary B. W. Tabor, "Inquiry into Slaying of Sheikh's Confidant Appears Open," *New York Times,* November 23, 1993.

37. Ralph Blumenthal, "Suspect in Blast Believed to Be in Pakistan," *New York Times,* March 18, 1993.

38. Author's interview with confidential FBI source, July 31, 2010.

39. The first two pages of Ayyad's confession can be downloaded from http://www .peterlance.com/FBI_302_Nidal_Ayyad_Shalabi_murder_12_28_05.pdf.

40. FBI 302 debriefing of El Sayyid Nosair, December 20, 2005. It can be accessed at http://www.scribd.com/doc/35687185/FBI-302-El-Sayyid-Nosair-12-20-05.

41. Robert L. Jackson and Gebe Martinez, "Key Suspect Is Charged in N.Y. Bombing," *Los Angeles Times,* March 26, 1993.

42. Tabor, "Inquiry into Slaying of Sheikh's Confidant."

43. FBI 302, debriefing of Jamal al-Fadl, a.k.a. Gamal Ahmed Mohamed Al-Fedel, on November 4 and 5, 1996, dictated November 11, 1996. It can be accessed at http:// www.peterlance.com/FBI_302_11.10.96_Jamal_al-Fadl_Fitzgerald.pdf.

44. Peter Lance, "First Blood: Was Meir Kahane's Murder al-Qaida's Earliest Attack on U.S. Soil?" *Tablet,* September 1, 2010.

45. Detective Michael Hanratty, Detective Thomas Bidell, and Special Agent Frank Pellegrino, FBI 302 memo, debriefing of Nidal Ayyad, February 8, 2006, 3–4.

46. E-mail from author to Jerry Schmetterer, January 31, 2011.

47. E-mail from Jerry Schmetterer to author, February 1, 2011.

48. George Santayana, *The Life of Reason: Reason in Common Sense* (Boston: MIT Press, 2011).

49. Sara Lynch and Oren Dorell, "Deadly Embassy Attacks Were Days in the Making," *USA Today,* September 12, 2012.

50. FBI 302 memo detailing threat from Ramzi Yousef to FBI informant Greg Scarpa Jr., December 30, 1996; Presidential Daily Brief to President Clinton, 1998; Presidential Daily Brief to President Bush, August 6, 2001.

51. "Radical Muslim 'Demands' Have Foundation and History," Agence France Press, August 10, 1998.

52. *U.S. v. Ahmed Abdel Sattar et al.,* April 30, 2002.

53. "Bin Ladin Determined to Strike in US," Presidential Daily Brief, August 6, 2001, http://en.wikipedia.org/wiki/Bin_Ladin_Determined_To_Strike_in_US.

54. Neil A. Lewis, "Moussaoui Tells Court He's Guilty of a Terror Plot," *New York Times,* April 23, 2005.

55. Richard Esposito, "Terror Fears as Blind Sheikh Faces 'Medical Emergency,'" ABC News, December 14, 2006.

56. Ibid.

57. Author's interview with Emad Salem, June 16, 2012.

58. Robert Mackey, "Just Off Tahrir Square, Protesters Demand Release of Blind Sheikh Jailed in U.S.," *New York Times,* June 29, 2012.

59. Salem interview, June 16, 2012.

60. David D. Kirkpatrick, "Egypt's New Leader Takes Oath, Promising to Work for Release of Jailed Terrorist," *New York Times,* June 29, 2012.

61. Josh Margolin and Chuck Barrett, "O Eyes 'Blind Sheik' Release. GOPers Blast Idea to Appease Egypt," *New York Post,* September 20, 2012; Awr Hawkins, "U.S. State Dept. Considers Release Blind Sheikh to Egypt," Breitbart.com, September 18, 2012; Michael B. Mukasey, "Will Obama Free the Blind Sheikh?," *Wall Street Journal,* September 24, 2012; Letter to Eric H. Holder and Hillary Rodham Clinton from Representatives Lamar Smith, Ileana Ros-Lehtinen, Mike Rogers, Howard P. "Buck" McKeon, Peter King, Hal Rogers, Frank Wolf, and Kay Granger, September 19, 2012.

62. "Clinton Says Trial Proceedings for 'Blind Sheikh' Were Correct," *Egypt Independent,* July 2, 2012.

63. "Bachmann-Clinton Showdown over Blind Sheikh," Frontpagemag.com, September 21, 2012.

64. Nic Robertson and Paul Cruickshank, "Pro al-Qaeda Group Seen Behind Deadly Benghazi Attack," CNN.com, September 13, 2012.

65. Salem interview, June 16, 2012.

66. Chelsea J. Carter, "Al Qaeda Leader Calls for Kidnapping of Westerners," CNN.com, October 28, 2012.

67. The list can be downloaded from http://www.peterlance.com/172_unindicted_co-conspirators_Day_of_Terror.pdf.

68. "FBI: Gotti Missed Date with Draft Board," Associated Press, March 28, 2004.

69. Peter Lance, "Al Qaeda and the Mob: How the FBI Blew It on 9/11," *Huffington Post,* November 17, 2006.

70. Robert Hanley and Jonathan Miller, "4 Transcripts Are Released in Case Tied to 9/11 Hijackers," *New York Times,* June 25, 2003.

71. David K. Shipler, "Terrorist Plots, Hatched by the F.B.I." *New York Times,* April 28, 2012.

72. Trever Aaronson, *The Terror Factory: Inside The FBI's Manufactured War on Terrorism* (Brooklyn, New York: Ig publishing, 2013), 15.

73. Al Baker, "Unexploded Car Bomb Left Trove of Evidence," *New York Times,* May 3, 2010.

74. William K. Rashbaum and Al Baker, "Smoking Car to Arrest in 53 Hours," *New York Times,* May 4, 2010.

75. James Barron and Michael S. Schmidt, "From Suburban Father to a Terrorism Suspect," *New York Times,* May 4, 2010.

76. Sarah Titterton "Boston Marathon Bombs: Tamerlan Tsarnaev 'interviewed by FBI in 2011,'" Telegraph.co.uk, April 20, 2013.

77. Senator Daniel K. Akaka (D-HI), statement before the Subcommittee on Oversight of Government Management, Hearing: "A National Security Crisis: Foreign Language Capabilities in the Federal Government," Senate Committee on Homeland Security, May 21, 2012.

78. E-mail exchange between author and Betsy R. Glick, FBI, November 13, 2012.

79. Eric Schmitt, "F.B.I. Agents' Role Is Transformed by Terror Fight," *New York Times,* August 18, 2009.

80. William K. Rashbaum, "Nearly 125 Arrested in Sweeping Mob Roundup," *New York Times,* January 20, 2001.

81. "Indictments Unsealed Against 127 Accused Mobsters in Epic FBI Bust," WNBC, January 20, 2011.

82. Ibid.

83. "Indictments Unsealed."

84. Rashbaum, "Nearly 125 Arrested in Sweeping Mob Roundup."

85. "Indictments Unsealed."

86. Bernd Debusmann Jr., "U.S. Arrests 119 in Biggest Mafia Bust," Reuters, January 20, 2011.

87. Ed Magnuson, "Hitting the Mafia," *Time,* September 29, 1986.

88. Ibid.

89. Tim Stelloh, "Two Are Cleared in '97 Killing of an Officer but Convicted of Plotting Mob Murders," *New York Times,* May 9, 2012.

90. Michael Wilson and William K. Rashbaum, "11 Years After Officer's Slaying, Reputed Mob Figures Are Indicted," *New York Times,* December 18, 2008.

91. Alan Feuer, "Awaiting a Burial, This Time an Actual One," *New York Times,* October 8, 2008.

92. "Body Identified as Missing Mobster's," *New York Times,* October 7, 2008.

93. Department of Justice, "Colombo Organized Crime Family Acting Boss, Underboss, and Ten Other Members and Associates Indicted," press release, June 4, 2008.

94. Tom Hays, "Thomas Gioeli, Reputed NYC Mob Boss, Cleared of Killing Officer," Associated Press, May 9, 2012.

95. Author's interview with Lieutenant Colonel Anthony Shaffer, September 30, 2012.

96. "COINTELPRO: The FBI's Covert Action Programs Against American Citizens," *Final Report of the Select Committee to Study Governmental Operations with Respect to Intelligence Activities,* United States Senate, April 23, 1976, http://www.icdc.com/~paulwolf/cointelpro/churchfinalreportIIIa.htm.

97. Ibid.

98. Ibid.

99. John M. Crewdson, "F.B.I. Reportedly Harassed Radicals After Spy Program," *New York Times,* March 23, 1975.

100. John M. Crewdson, "Saxbe Says Top Officials Knew Something of F.B.I. Drive on Various Groups," *New York Times,* November 19, 1974.

101. Seymour Hersh, "Huge C.I.A. Operation Reported in U.S. Against Antiwar Forces, Other Dissidents in Nixon Years," *New York Times,* December 22, 1974.

102. "The Federal Bureau of Investigation's Compliance with the Attorney General's Investigative Guidelines ███████████," Special Report Office of Inspector General, U.S. Department of Justice, September 2005.

103. "Attorney General's Guidelines on FBI Use of Informants and Confidential Sources" (hereafter "Civiletti Informant Guidelines") can be found at *1982 Final Report of the Senate Select Committee to Study Undercover Activities,* 517–30.

104. The Levi Guidelines can be found at "FBI Statutory Charter: Hearings Before the Senate Committee on the Judiciary, 95th Cong, Part I," 20–26 (1978) (hereafter "1978 Senate Hearings on FBI Statutory Charter Part I") and in "FBI Oversight: Hearings Before the Subcommittee on Civil and Constitutional Rights of the House Judiciary Committee on the Judiciary," 95th Cong., 181–87 (1978).

105. "Civiletti Informant Guidelines," *1982 Final Report of the Senate Select Committee to Study Undercover Activities,* 517–30.

106. 1979–1980 House FBI Charter Bill Hearings 3–15 (Testimony of Benjamin R. Civiletti, Attorney General, and William Webster, FBI Director). The Senate's bill was S. 1612, The Federal Bureau of Investigation Charter Act of 1979, 96th Cong. (1979), reprinted in FBI Charter Act of 1979, S. 1612: Hearings on S. 1612 Before the Senate Committee on the Judiciary, 96th Cong., Part II, 427 (1980). Section 537 of the bill authorized the FBI director to impose fines up to $5,000 on agents who willfully abused "sensitive investigative techniques," which included misuse of informants or intrusive surveillance authorities. Id. at 469.

107. Inspector general's report, "IV Conclusion," September 2005.

108. Crewdson, "FBI Reportedly Harassed."

109. Memo to assistant director, from ██████████████, January 21, 1966.

CREDITS

INDEX

NOTE: Page references in *italics* refer to photos.